D1711238

Secure Messaging with PGP and S/MIME

For quite a long time, computer security was a rather narrow field of study that was populated mainly by theoretical computer scientists, electrical engineers, and applied mathematicians. With the proliferation of open systems in general, and the Internet and the World Wide Web (WWW) in particular, this situation has changed fundamentally. Today, computer and network practitioners are equally interested in computer security, since they require technologies and solutions that can be used to secure applications related to electronic commerce (e-commerce). Against this background, the field of computer security has become very broad and includes many topics of interest. The aim of this series is to publish state-of-the-art, high standard technical books on topics related to computer security. Further information about the series can be found on the WWW by the following URL:

http://www.esecurity.ch/serieseditor.html

Also, if you'd like to contribute to the series and write a book about a topic related to computer security, feel free to contact either the Commissioning Editor or the Series Editor at Artech House.

Recent Titles in the Artech House Computer Security Series

Rolf Oppliger, Series Editor

Information Hiding Techniques for Steganography and Digital Watermarking, Stefan Katzenbeisser and Fabien A. P. Petitcolas
Secure Messaging with PGP and S/MIME, Rolf Oppliger
Security Fundamentals for E-Commerce, Vesna Hassler
Security Technologies for the World Wide Web, Rolf Oppliger

For a complete listing of the *Artech House Computing Library,* turn to the back of this book.

Secure Messaging with PGP and S/MIME

Rolf Oppliger

Artech House
Boston • London
www.artechhouse.com

Library of Congress Cataloging-in-Publication Data
Oppliger, Rolf.
Secure messaging with PGP and S/MIME / Rolf Oppliger.
p. cm. — (Artech House computer security library)
Includes bibliographical references and index.
ISBN 1-58053-161-X (alk. paper)
1. Telecommunication systems—Security measures. 2. PGP (Computer file). 3. Data encryption (Computer science). 4. Electronic mail systems—Security measures. I. Title. II. Series.

TK5102.85 .O67 2000 00-048097
005.8—dc21 CIP

British Library Cataloguing in Publication Data
Oppliger, Rolf
Secure messaging with PGP and S/MIME. — (Artech House computer security library)
1. Telecommunication systems—Security measures
2. Electronic mail systems—Security measures 3. Data encryption (Computer science)
I. Title
005.8

ISBN 1-58053-161-X

Cover design by Igor Valdman

685 Canton Street
Norwood, MA 02062

International Standard Book Number: 1-58053-161-X
Library of Congress Catalog Card Number: 00-048097

10 9 8 7 6 5 4 3 2 1

To my son Marc

Contents

Preface

Electronic mail is one of the most important and widely used network applications today. More commonly called *e-mail*, or *mail* in short, it enables users to send and receive written correspondence over wide area networks, such as the Internet. Many estimates indicate that a big percentage of all correspondence that previously would have gone via physical communication channels, such as postal delivery services, is now being exchanged via e-mail [1]. But in spite of its importance for private communications and business applications, contemporary e-mail systems must still be considered to be insecure. In fact, attackers can read, fake, modify, or even delete e-mail messages as they are stored, processed, and transmitted between computer systems. This is because the entire e-mail system — including its user agents (UAs) and message transfer agents (MTAs) — has not been designed with security in mind.

In the late 1980s and early 1990s, there was a considerable effort to put some strong security features into message handling systems (MHSs) based on the X.400 series of ITU-T recommendations.[1] The resulting security architecture for X.400-based MHSs has been extensively described and discussed in the security literature [2]. Unfortunately, in the real world, security hardly plays a role for the commercial value and success of a standard or product, and this rule of thumb also applies for

[1]The X.400 series of ITU-T recommendations were first published in 1984. In the 1988 revision, however, a comprehensive set of security features were added. These features include support not only for the basic message protection services discussed in Chapter 1, but also for enhanced message protection services, such as confirmation services.

X.400-based MHSs [3]. As of this writing, there is virtually no market for X.400-based MHSs with built-in security features (at least outside military environments). Consequently, this book does not address X.400-based MHSs and their features to provide support for secure messaging. The same is true for the Message Security Protocol (MSP) or P42 that has been specified by the U.S. government for its Defense Messaging System (DMS) [4]. It is essentially irrelevant in commercial applications.

The e-mail systems that are used and widely deployed in the commercial world either depend on standardized and open Internet messaging protocols (e.g., SMTP and ESMTP for message transport, as well as POP3 and IMAP4 for message store access) or use proprietary protocols (e.g., Microsoft Exchange and Lotus Notes).[2] In either case, additional software is used to provide security services at or above the application layer (in the OSI reference or Internet model) in a way that is transparent to the underlying e-mail system(s).[3] This transparency is in fact very important for the commercial value of a secure messaging scheme. A message that is secured above the application layer can be transported by any e-mail system, including Internet messaging systems, Microsoft Exchange, Lotus Notes, or even the DMS and X.400-based MHSs (with or without built-in security features). This transparency is very important for the large-scale deployment of a secure messaging scheme.

In the past, three primary schemes for secure messaging on the Internet have emerged:

- Privacy enhanced mail (PEM) and MIME object security services (MOSS);
- Pretty Good Privacy (PGP);
- Secure MIME (S/MIME).

PEM was an early standardization effort initiated by the Internet Research Task Force (IRTF) Privacy and Security Research Group, and later continued by the

[2]The terms "open" and "proprietary" are often used in the computer literature without giving precise definitions. In this book, we use the term *proprietary* to refer to a computer software product or system, if it is created, developed, and controlled by a single company. This can be achieved by treating various aspects of the design as trade secrets or through explicit legal protection in the form of patents and copyrights. Contrary to that, the details about an *open* system are available for anyone to read and use, ideally without paying royalties.

[3]This is in contrast to network security protocols that operate at the lower layers in the TCP/IP protocol stack, such as the IP security (IPsec) protocol suite or the Secure Sockets Layer (SSL) or Transport Layer Security (TLS) protocols.

Internet Engineering Task Force (IETF) Privacy Enhanced Mail (PEM) Working Group (WG) [5 – 9].[4] Unfortunately, the PEM specification was limited to 7-bit encoded ASCII messages and a three-layer hierarchy of certification authorities (CAs) that constituted the public key infrastructure (PKI) for PEM. Both limitations are far too strict, and MOSS was actually an attempt to overcome the implications thereof [10 – 12]. More specifically, MOSS was designed to additionally handle messages that make use of the Multipurpose Internet Mail Extensions (MIME) and to be more liberal with regard to the PKI requirements. But MOSS has so many implementation options that it is possible, and very likely, for two independent software developers to come up with MOSS implementations that would not interoperate. MOSS can be thought of as a framework rather than a specification, and considerable work in implementation profiling has yet to be done.[5]

While PEM and MOSS failed to become commercially successful and have sunk into oblivion, the secure messaging schemes that are in widespread use (i.e., PGP and S/MIME) copied the good features of their predecessors while attempting to avoid the bad ones. For example, PEM introduced the use of digital envelopes and the base-64 encoding scheme, and all secure messaging schemes that were proposed afterwards retained these features.

Today, PGP and S/MIME are the way to go for secure messaging on the Internet. S/MIME is actually a specification, whereas PGP can be thought of as both a specification and a software package. PGP and S/MIME are very similar in nature. For example, they both use public key cryptography and digital enveloping techniques to sign and encrypt e-mail messages. However, there are (at least) two fundamental differences that lead to a situation in which PGP and S/MIME implementations do not interoperate (these points are further addressed in the book):

- First, PGP and S/MIME use different message formats.
- Second, PGP and S/MIME handle public keys and public key certificates in fundamentally different ways:
  - PGP relies on users to exchange public keys and establish trust in each other.[6] This informal approach to establish a "web of trust" works well for small workgroups, but can become hard to manage for large groups.

[4]Both working groups no longer exist.

[5]This situation has not changed so far.

[6]The public key exchange can occur directly or through PGP key servers.

- Contrary to that, S/MIME relies on public key certificates that are issued by official (or at least "officially looking") and hierarchically organized certification authorities (CAs) and distributed by corresponding directory services.

As of this writing, the use of PGP and S/MIME is being standardized by two IETF WGs within the Security Area of the IETF, namely the IETF Open Specification for Pretty Good Privacy (OpenPGP) WG and the IETF S/MIME Mail Security (SMIME) WG. However, except for the Internet-Drafts and Request for Comments (RFC) documents that have been published by these IETF WGs, there is hardly any literature that addresses secure messaging with PGP and S/MIME. There are some manuals that describe the installation, configuration, and use of PGP and S/MIME plug-ins for several UAs and e-mail clients, but there is barely any literature that goes beyond the mere graphical user interfaces (GUIs) of these software packages, and that also addresses the conceptual and technical approaches followed by PGP and S/MIME. This is also true for PGP, for which several books have been written and published for earlier versions of the software [13 – 17]. With regard to S/MIME, the situation is even worse. There are single chapters in security books that address S/MIME (e.g., Chapter 5 of [18] and Section 12.2 of [19]), but there is little comprehensive treatment of S/MIME in any of these books.

Against this background, I decided to write a book on secure messaging with PGP and S/MIME for Artech House's computer security series. The resulting book, *Secure Messaging with PGP and S/MIME*, attempts to bring together all relevant and important information that is needed to understand and use PGP- and S/MIME-compliant software. As such, the book is aimed to fill the gap between the manuals that describe the GUIs of various software packages and the Internet-Drafts and RFC documents that mainly focus on packet formats and bit encoding schemes of PGP and S/MIME.

Unfortunately (and due to the limited space in a book), we have to make some assumptions. In particular, we have to assume that the reader is familiar with both the fundamentals of TCP/IP networking and the basic concepts of cryptology. Some points are briefly addressed in this book (e.g., the protocols that are used for Internet messaging), but most aspects are assumed to be known by the reader. Refer to [20 – 22] for a comprehensive introduction to TCP/IP networking, or Chapter 2 of [23] for a corresponding summary. Also, refer to [24 – 26] for a comprehensive introduction to cryptology, or Chapter 4 of this book for a corresponding summary.

Secure Messaging with PGP and S/MIME is primarily intended for security managers, network practitioners, professional system and network administrators, product implementors, and end users who want to learn more about the rationale behind and the possibilities of secure messaging with PGP and S/MIME. The book can be used for self-study or to teach classes.

More specifically, *Secure Messaging with PGP and S/MIME* is organized in four parts that can also be read individually:

- Part 1, *Fundamentals*, introduces the fundamentals that are necessary to understand the rest of the book.
- Part 2, *PGP*, addresses the conceptual and technical approaches followed by the developers of the PGP software packages and the IETF OpenPGP WG.
- Part 3, *S/MIME*, addresses the conceptual and technical approaches followed by the developers of S/MIME-compliant software and the IETF SMIME WG.
- Part 4, *Epilogue*, concludes with some final remarks and an outlook on possible developments in the field.

The book also includes a glossary that defines major terms, as well as a list of abbreviations and acronyms. References are included at the end of each chapter. At the end of the book, an "About the Author" page is appended to tell you a little bit about me. Also, there is an index that will help you find particular terms.

While time brings new technologies and outdates current technologies, I have attempted to focus primarily on the conceptual and technical approaches for secure messaging in general, and PGP and S/MIME in particular. The Internet is changing so rapidly that any book is out of date by the time it hits the shelves of the bookstores. By the time you read this book, several of my comments will probably have moved from the future to the present, and from the present to the past, resulting in inevitable anachronisms.

Due to the nature of this book, it is necessary to mention company, product, and service names. It is, however, important to note that the presence or absence of a specific name neither implies any criticism or endorsement, nor does it imply that the corresponding company, product, or service is necessarily the best available. For a more comprehensive products overview, I particularly recommend the *Computer Security Products Buyers Guide* that is compiled and published annually by the Computer Security Institute (CSI) based in San Francisco, California.[7] Note that the new U.S. export controls (mentioned in Chapter 4) will change the landscape on the global marketplace for cryptographic products, including, for example, products

[7] `http://www.gocsi.com`

for secure messaging, considerably. As of this writing, we are right at the beginning of this changing process.

Whenever possible, I add some uniform resource locators (URLs) as footnotes to the text. The URLs point to corresponding information pages provided on the Web. While care has been taken to ensure that the URLs are valid now, due to the dynamic nature of the Web, these URLs as well as their contents may not remain valid forever.

Finally, I would like to take the opportunity to invite you as a reader of this book to let me know your opinion and thoughts. If you have something to correct or add, please let me know. If I haven't expressed myself clearly please let me know, too. I appreciate and sincerely welcome any comment or suggestion, in order to update the book periodically. The best way to reach me is to send an e-mail message (whether cryptographically secured or not) to `rolf.oppliger@esecurity.ch`. You can also visit the URL `http://www.esecurity.ch/Books/secmess.html` to access the latest information regarding this book. Finally, a repository for documents on secure messaging, including, for example, links to relevant RFC documents, can also be found on the homepage of a project on secure mail of eSECURITY Technologies Rolf Oppliger.[8] The homepage is available at `http://www.esecurity.ch/Projects/securemail.html`.

REFERENCES

[1] L. Hughes, *Internet E-Mail: Protocols, Standards, and Implementations*, Artech House, Norwood, MA, 1998.

[2] W. Ford, *Computer Communications Security: Principles, Standard Protocols and Techniques*, Prentice Hall, Upper Saddle River, NJ, 1994.

[3] J. Rhoton, *X.400 and SMTP: Battle of the E-Mail Protocols*, Digital Press, 1997.

[4] C. Dinkel (Ed.), "Secure Data Network System (SDNS) Network, Transport, and Message Security Protocols," U.S. Department of Commerce, NIST Report NISTIR 90-4250, 1990.

[5] J. Linn, "Privacy Enhancement for Internet Electronic Mail: Part I — Message Encryption and Authentication Procedures," Request for Comments 1421, February 1993.

[6] S.T. Kent, "Privacy Enhancement for Internet Electronic Mail: Part II — Certificate-Based Key Management," Request for Comments 1422, February 1993.

[7] D. Balenson, "Privacy Enhancement for Internet Electronic Mail: Part III — Algorithms, Modes, and Identifiers," Request for Comments 1423, February 1993.

[8] eSECURITY Technologies Rolf Oppliger (`http://www.esecurity.ch`) is the name of a company that was founded in 1999 to provide scientific, state of the art, and leading-edge consulting, education, and engineering services related to information technology (IT) security.

[8] B. Kaliski, "Privacy Enhancement for Internet Electronic Mail: Part IV — Key Certification and Related Services," Request for Comments 1424, February 1993.

[9] S.T. Kent, "Internet Privacy Enhanced Mail," *Communications of the ACM*, 36(8), August 1993, pp. 48 – 60.

[10] J. Galvin, and M.S. Feldman, "MIME object security services: Issues in a multi-user environment," *Proceedings of USENIX UNIX Security V Symposium*, June 1995.

[11] J. Galvin, S. Murphy, S. Crocker, and N. Freed, "Security Multiparts for MIME: Multipart/Signed and Multipart/Encrypted," Request for Comments 1847, October 1995.

[12] S. Crocker, N. Freed, J. Galvin, and S. Murphy, "MIME Object Security Services," Request for Comments 1848, October 1995.

[13] P.R. Zimmermann, *The Official PGP User's Guide*, MIT Press, Cambridge, MA, 1995.

[14] P.R. Zimmermann, *PGP Source Code and Internals*, MIT Press, Cambridge, MA, 1995.

[15] S. Garfinkel, *PGP: Pretty Good Privacy*, O'Reilly & Associates, Sebastopol, CA, 1995.

[16] B. Schneier, *E-Mail Security: How to Keep Your Electronic Messages Private*, John Wiley & Sons, New York, NY, 1995.

[17] A. Bacard, *The Computer Privacy Handbook: A Practical Guide to E-Mail Encryption, Data Protection, and PGP Privacy Software*, Peachpit Press, Berkeley, CA, 1995.

[18] J. Feghhi, J. Feghhi, and P. Williams, *Digital Certificates: Applied Internet Security*, Addison-Wesley Longman, Reading, MA, 1999.

[19] W. Stallings, *Cryptography and Network Security: Principles and Practice*, 2nd Edition, Prentice-Hall, Upper Saddle River, NJ, 1998.

[20] D. Comer, *Internetworking with TCP/IP: Principles, Protocols, and Architecture*, 3rd Edition, Prentice-Hall, Upper Saddle River, NJ, 1995.

[21] A.S. Tanenbaum, *Computer Networks*, 3rd Edition, Prentice-Hall, Upper Saddle River, NJ, 1996.

[22] F. Wilder, *A Guide to the TCP/IP Protocol Suite*, 2nd Edition, Artech House, Norwood, MA, 1998.

[23] R. Oppliger, *Internet and Intranet Security*, Artech House, Norwood, MA, 1998.

[24] D. Stinson, *Cryptography Theory and Practice*, CRC Press, Boca Raton, FL, 1995.

[25] B. Schneier, *Applied Cryptography: Protocols, Algorithms, and Source Code in C*, 2nd Edition, John Wiley & Sons, New York, NY, 1996.

[26] A. Menezes, P. van Oorschot, and S. Vanstone, *Handbook of Applied Cryptography*, CRC Press, Boca Raton, FL, 1996.

Trademark Information

Acknowledgments

One of the more pleasurable tasks of being an author is to thank all the people who have contributed to and been involved in the conception, research, writing, and production of a book. Once again, my warmest thanks are due to Kurt Bauknecht from the University of Zürich, Switzerland, for his ongoing interest, encouragement, and support. Also, the book has gained a lot from discussions with and information provided by Dieter Hogrefe, Hansjürg Mey, and Günther Pernul (in alphabetical order). A preliminary draft of this book was read and commented by Michael Gautschi, Christian Graber, Bruno Gschwend, Jean Michel Karr, Erich Rütsche, Paul Schöbi, Jürg Spörndli, and Urs Würgler (again in alphabetical order). My brother, Hans Oppliger, has done a great job in reviewing the entire manuscript and providing me with some valuable comments, suggestions, and pointers for further material. Also, the staff at Artech House was enormously helpful in producing this book, including Taylor Blanquera, Ruth Harris, Julie Lancashire, Patrick Peterson, Tim Pitts, Susanna Taggart, Igor Valdman, Viki Williams, Jon Workman, and Ruth Young. It has been a pleasure to work with all of them. Finally, I want to thank my wife, Isabelle, for her love and support throughout the frequently stressed period in which this book was written and published. Once again, she really has been a great help.

Part I

FUNDAMENTALS

Chapter 1

Introduction

In this chapter, we overview the scope of this book. More specifically, we address Internet messaging in Section 1.1, discuss possible threats and attacks against Internet-based e-mail systems in Section 1.2, and further elaborate on secure messaging in Section 1.3. Finally, we conclude the chapter by giving a brief outline of the book in Section 1.4.

1.1 INTERNET MESSAGING

As mentioned in the Preface, *electronic mail* (*e-mail* or *mail* in short) is one of the most important and widely used network applications on the Internet today. While various e-mail systems have been around for decades, the real growth has occurred only during the last couple of years as part of the explosion of TCP/IP networking in general, and the Internet in particular [1 – 3].

Generally spoken, the term *Internet messaging* refers to the use of e-mail systems that conform to the relevant standards specified by the Internet Engineering Task Force (IETF).[1] These standards address various aspects of a messaging infra-

[1] The Internet standardization process is summarized in many books, including, for example, Section 2.2 of [4]. It is not further addressed in this book.

structure or e-mail system, such as message formats and protocols for the communications between the various components of the e-mail system. We elaborate on some relevant specifications in Chapter 3. In the meantime, we mainly focus on the functional components of a messaging infrastructure or e-mail system.

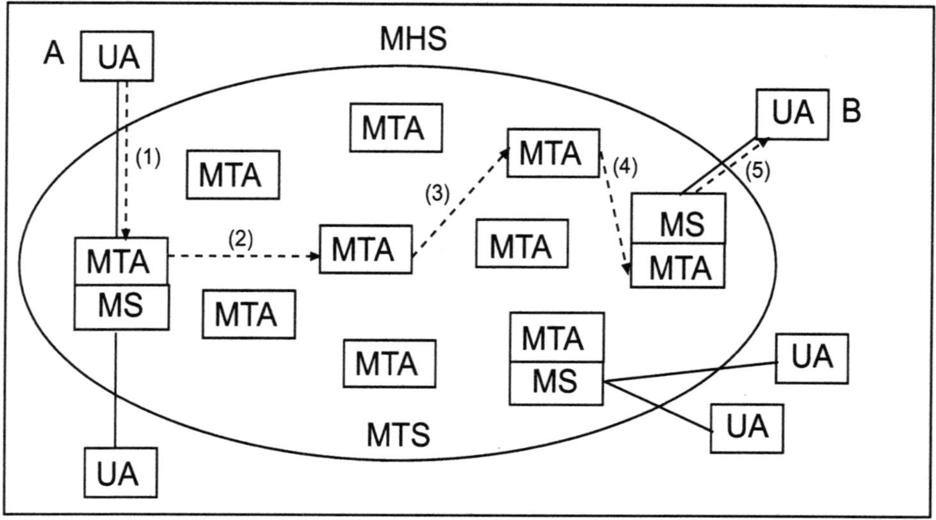

Figure 1.1 A simplified model of an Internet-based message handling system (MHS).

First, let's introduce some basic terms:[2]

- *Messages* (or *e-mail messages*) are data units that originate from and are ultimately received by users.
- A message usually has one originating user (the *originator* of the message) and one or more receiving users (the *recipients* of the message).
- A *user*, in turn, may be a human user or an application program that handles e-mail messages on a human user's behalf.
- In either case, a user is supported by software that is conventionally called *user agent* (UA). The UA, in turn, performs such tasks as preparing, sending,

[2]Note that the use of some of the terms introduced here is controversial, because they originate from the specifications of the X.400 series of ITU-T recommendations, and because they tend to "complexify" things. Alternatively, one could use the term "mail client" to refer to a user agent (UA), "POP3 server" to refer to a mail store (MS), and "SMTP server" to refer to a message transfer agent (MTA). In this book, these terms are used synonymously and interchangeably.

and receiving e-mail messages for its user. It may be a stand-alone software application (sometimes also called a "mailer"), or it may be integrated into another software application, such as a Web browser.[3]

- A *message transfer system* (MTS) basically consists of a collection of *message transfer agents* (MTAs). A message is submitted by a UA at the originating MTA and then forwarded along a path of MTAs to its final MTA. MTAs may be store-and-forward message switches of a given messaging technology, or they may be mail gateways between different technologies.
- Each MTA may contain *message stores* (MSs) to store e-mail messages on their users' behalf.

A simplified model of an Internet-based message handling system (MHS) is shown in Figure 1.1. Note that the term MHS was first introduced in the context of X.400-based MHSs, but is also used for Internet-based MHSs today. The MHS of Figure 1.1 contains an MTS and five UAs (including UAs for A and B). The UAs, in turn, either communicate with the MTAs or with their MSs. The MTAs are fully connected, so each MTA can communicate with every other MTA. Figure 1.1 also illustrates the path of a message delivery from A to B. First, A sends the message to its MTA (step 1). The message is then forwarded multiple times (steps 2 to 4), until it finally arrives at B's MTA, where it is stored in B's MS. Finally, B accesses his MS to retrieve the message (step 5). As further addressed in Chapter 3, the main protocols that are used to transfer messages between MTAs are the Simple Mail Transfer Protocol (SMTP) and the Extended SMTP (ESMTP). In addition, there are several protocols a UA can use to access the MS of its MTA. The most important protocols are the Post Office Protocol version 3 (POP3) and the Internet Message Access Protocol version 4 (IMAP4). This simple model is sufficient to overview and discuss some relevant threats and attacks for Internet-based messaging infrastructures and e-mail systems. These threats and attacks are addressed next.

1.2 THREATS AND ATTACKS

Most e-mail systems have not been designed with security in mind. This is equally true for open and proprietary e-mail systems, and it's particularly true for Internet-

[3]Today, the use of Web-based messaging is getting increasingly popular. In this case, the UA is provided by the Web server while the Web browser is only used to display the messages (the browser's integrated messaging features are not used at all). We'll briefly elaborate on some Web-based secure messaging schemes in Chapter 17.

based e-mail systems.[4] In these systems, it's usually easy to spoof or fake messages, read messages as they are transmitted between MTAs, modify and destroy messages, or generate dummy messages to flood the MS of a recipient's MTA. As further addressed in the remaining part of this section, Internet-based messaging infrastructures and e-mail systems are wide open to passive and active attacks.

1.2.1 Passive Attacks

A *passive attack* threatens the confidentiality of data being transmitted. The situation is illustrated in Figure 1.2. The data transmitted from the originator (on the right side) to the recipient (on the left side) may be observed by the intruder (in the middle).[5] This data may include e-mail messages or passwords transmitted in cleartext from a UA to a corresponding MS (e.g., a password that is required by the user to access his MS). With respect to the intruder's possibilities to interpret the information that the transmitted data encodes, passive wiretapping and traffic analysis attacks must be distinguished:

Figure 1.2 A passive attack threatens the confidentiality of data being transmitted.

- In a *passive wiretapping attack*, the intruder is able to interpret the data and to extract the information accordingly.
- In a *traffic analysis attack*, the intruder is not able to extract the information. Consequently, traffic analysis refers to the inference of information from the observation of external traffic characteristics. For example, if an attacker

[4]Note that there are some proprietary e-mail systems with sophisticated security features. Also note that X.400-based MHSs and the DMS of the U.S. government have some strong security features built-in (as discussed in the Preface). Both systems are not further addressed in this book.

[5]Note that many publications on network security use names, such as "Alice" and "Bob," to refer to the sending and receiving network entities, and other names, such as "Eve," to refer to a possible intruder. This is a convenient way of making things unambiguous with relatively few words, since the pronoun "she" can be used for Alice, and "he" can be used for Bob. However, the advantages and disadvantages of this naming scheme are controversial, and we are not going to use it in this book.

observes that two companies — one financially strong, the other financially weak — begin to trade a large number of messages, he may infer that they are discussing a merger. Other examples occur in military environments. In general, protection against traffic analysis attacks requires more sophisticated techniques than protection against passive wiretapping attacks. For example, the use of encryption techniques generally does not protect against traffic analysis attacks. In this book, we briefly discuss some possible techniques to protect against traffic analysis attacks in Chapter 17.

Note that the feasibility of a passive attack primarily depends on the physical transmission media in use and its physical accessibility for an intruder. For example, mobile communications is by its very nature easy to tap, whereas metallic transmission media at least require some sort of physical access. Lightwave conductors can also be tapped, but this is quite expensive. Also note that the use of concentrating and multiplexing techniques, in general, makes it more difficult to passively attack a communications line. Nevertheless, it is also fair to mention that a passive attacker does not necessarily have to tap a physical communications line. Most local area network interfaces can operate in a so-called "promiscuous mode." In this mode, they are able to capture all frames transmitted on the local network segment they are connected to, rather than just those frames addressed to the machines they are part of. This capability has useful purposes for network analysis, testing, and debugging (e.g., by utilities such as `etherfind` and `tcpdump` in the case of the UNIX and Linux operating systems). Unfortunately, this capability can also be used by attackers to snoop on all traffic on a particular network segment. Several software packages are available for monitoring network traffic, primarily for the purpose of network management (e.g., SnifferPro from Network Associates, Inc.). These software packages are dual-use, meaning they can, for example, be effective at eavesdropping and capturing e-mail messages or passwords as they are transmitted over shared media and communications lines. Fortunately, the use of switching technologies makes it more difficult for an attacker to passively attack and eavesdrop on a network segment, since network traffic is directed only to the intended network interfaces.

1.2.2 Active Attacks

An *active attack* threatens the integrity or availability of data being transmitted. The situation is illustrated in Figure 1.3. In this case, the intruder is able to observe and fully control the data that is passing by. In general, the intruder can modify, extend, delete, or replay data. The intruder can also influence or modify the routing tables of the systems to redirect traffic. Very often, the intruder manipulates the Internet's domain name system (DNS) to place himself between the sender and recipient of a message. In this situation, the intruder acts as a man-in-the-middle. With regard to Internet messaging, a commonly used active attack is to spoof messages on another (or nonexistent) user's behalf. There are several possibilities to achieve this:

- For example, the attacker can reconfigure his UA with the name and e-mail address of the spoofed user. When a message is sent out, the UA automatically generates the spoofed e-mail sender address information in the header section of the message text;
- Similarly, it is often possible to configure and use wrong display names, such as `Administrator <rolf.oppliger@esecurity.ch>`, since many UAs only show the display name if it is available (`Administrator` in this example);[6]
- A more sophisticated possibility is to establish a TCP connection to an SMTP server (usually running at port 25), and to directly launch STMP commands to build the spoofed message from scratch (the corresponding SMTP commands and an exemplary spoofing attack are summarized in Chapter 3).

Figure 1.3 An active attack threatens the integrity or availability of data being transmitted.

In addition to the attacks mentioned above, an active attacker can also flood a recipient and cause a denial-of-service. In short, a denial-of-service (DoS) refers to the prevention of authorized access to resources or the delaying of time-critical operations. Consequently, a DoS attack prevents resources from functioning according to their intended purposes. It may range from a lack of available memory or disk space to a partial shutdown of an entire network segment. Typically, a denial-of-service attack leaves one or more systems incapable of serving their original purposes. For example, in February 2000 some distributed denial-of-service (DDoS) attacks were successfully launched against commercial Internet sites, such

[6]The format for user names is introduced in Chapter 3.

as Yahoo, Amazon, eTrade, eBay, CNN, and ZDNet.[7] In the past, many DoS and DDoS attacks have made use of particular messages to crash the victim's MTA or UA. Furthermore, e-mail bombing is an example of an increasingly popular DoS attack. It may take three forms:

- The first form is to write a script that constantly bombards an e-mail account with messages that contain very long binary attachments;
- The second form is to post something offensive to a Usenet newsgroup with a forged return e-mail address (the address of the victim);
- Finally, the third form is to send an e-mail with a forged originator address and a subscribe request to large listservers that generate in excess of a hundred messages a day.

There are many tools freely available on the Internet that can be used to launch e-mail bombing attacks against victim e-mail accounts. Similar to traffic analysis attacks, protection against DoS and DDoS attacks is generally hard to achieve. This is similar to the physical world: how can you protect your mailbox against somebody filling it up with useless paper and other physical material? Finally, a less serious degradation of service attack is caused by the widespread abuse of using e-mail for mass mailing of unsolicited messages based on address lists collected from various sources. The act of sending "junk" e-mail messages to advertise a product or service is called *spamming*, and is now threatening to thwart legitimate use of e-mail. Again, we briefly address technologies to protect against spam in Chapter 17.

Finally, note that passive and active attacks are used together to effectively intrude an intranet environment. For example, a passive wiretapping attack can be used to grab authentication information transmitted in the clear, whereas this information can later be used to access computer systems or the MSs of particular users' e-mail accounts.

---

[7]There are many tools that can be used to launch DDoS attacks. Examples include Tribe Flood Network (TFN), Trinoo, and "Stacheldraht" (German word for "barbed wire"). Most of these tools are publicly and freely available on the Internet. David Dittrich from the University of Washington has analyzed the tools. The corresponding reports are available at `http://staff.washington.edu/dittrich/misc/tfn.analysis` (for TFN), `http://staff.washington.edu/dittrich/misc/trinoo.analysis` (for Trinoo), and `http://staff.washington.edu/dittrich/misc/stacheldraht.analysis` (for "Stacheldraht").

1.3 SECURE MESSAGING

Having discussed some possible threats and attacks against Internet-based messaging infrastructures and e-mail systems, providing support for "secure messaging" appears relevant. Unfortunately, there are many possibilities to define the term "secure" in the context of "messaging," and there are many possibilities to implement a particular notion of secure messaging. Let us briefly address these two questions — what does "secure messaging" mean and how can "secure messaging" be implemented — before we overview and briefly discuss the secure messaging schemes that have been proposed in the past (the ones mentioned in the Preface).

1.3.1 What Does "Secure Messaging" Mean?

First of all, it is important to properly define the term "secure messaging" and to say what we actually mean by using it. According to the OSI security architecture [5], there are various security services that may be considered for network applications. Among these security services, the following ones seem to be particularly interesting for Internet messaging:

- Data origin authentication service;
- Data confidentiality services:
  - Connectionless confidentiality service;
  - Selected field confidentiality service;
  - Traffic flow confidentiality service;
- Data integrity services:
  - Connectionless integrity service;
  - Selected field connectionless integrity service;
- Nonrepudiation services:
  - Nonrepudiation service with proof of origin;
  - Nonrepudiation service with proof of delivery.

Refer to [5] or Chapter 3 of [4] for a discussion of the above-mentioned communication security services. From a security point of view, many other issues must be considered with care when it comes to a discussion or evaluation of the overall security of an e-mail system. For example, both the application software packages and the underlying operating systems must be properly installed, configured, and administered. It is generally much simpler for an intruder to break the security of a specific operating system or application software package than it is to cryptanalyze encrypted and/or digitally signed data. For example, there is a long history of bugs and corresponding security vulnerabilities and exploits related to the Sendmail SMTP daemon. An attacker will more likely try to exploit some of these vulnerabilities than cryptanalyze data traffic. This should always be kept in mind when discussing and evaluating the overall security of an e-mail system.

Against this background, this book is rather narrow in scope. It only addresses the provision of some of the communication security services mentioned above, but does not address the security of operating systems and application software packages. There are many computer security books revolving around these particular issues. If you are in charge of establishing and operating a secure messaging infrastructure or e-mail system, you may want to look into these additional sources of information, too.

In this book, the term "secure messaging" is used to refer to a messaging scheme that is able to provide at least the following four security services:

- A *data origin authentication service* (or *message origin authentication service*) provides a recipient with assurance that a message came from the claimed originator;
- A *connectionless confidentiality service* protects message contents against disclosure to eavesdroppers between the originator and recipient;
- A *connectionless integrity service* protects message contents against modification between the originator and recipient, including modification by an active attacker;
- Last but not least, a *nonrepudiation service with proof of origin* provides a recipient with strong evidence of the origin of a message and its contents.

In the literature, these four security services are sometimes collectively referred to as *basic message protection services*, because they can be applied to single messages, and because they are, in general, independent from message submission, transfer, and delivery mechanisms. As such, they can be implemented entirely in UA software.

Contrary to that, *enhanced message protection services* do more than simply protect e-mail messages as stand-alone objects. Examples include confirmation services that provide secure notifications back to a message originator that the message was delivered to the intended recipient or, at least, reached some other point on the message delivery path. Enhanced message protection services are not further addressed in this book. Only in Chapter 17, we briefly elaborate on nonrepudiation services with proof of receipt as a means to provide certified or registered mail.

More recently, several companies have started to develop and market e-mail protection technologies and corresponding systems that can be used to enforce policies on the usage and/or secure removal of e-mail messages that are sent and delivered within the system. Typically, these systems allow their users to specify and enforce policy statements, such as expiration dates for messages, password protection schemes, and the disabling of specific operations, such as print, cut and paste, or dump screenshots. Exemplary systems include Interosa[8] from QVtech, Inc.,[9] MailVault from Authentica, Inc.,[10] as well as a system from Disappearing, Inc.[11] Systems like the ones from QVtech, Disappearing, or Authentica have great marketing appeal. From a user's point of view it is interesting to have the possibility to enforce policies on the usage and/or secure removal of e-mail messages. From a security point of view, however, there are at least two points that should be kept in mind and considered with care:

- First, the systems require additional components in the e-mail system, such as dedicated server systems (e.g. for the distribution of cryptographic keys) and additional UA components (e.g., plug-ins) to render the e-mail messages according to user-specified policies;
- Second, the systems only use software to enforce the user-specified policies.

The first point leads to an increase in complexity for the resulting e-mail system (this is bad from a security point of view). More worrisome, however, the second point leads to a situation, in which the overall security of the e-mail system is at least doubtful. Note that the approach being followed and employed by these systems is usage control, and that both the software industry and the providers of digital content have been struggling for years with the problem of developing, implementing, and deploying scalable software-based usage control systems. This problem is hard and many unfortunate initiatives in the past bear witness to this fact. Remember, for example, the cryptanalytical attack against the contents scrambling system (CSS) designed for DVD (digital versatile disc) media that was published in November 1999. Because of the inherent difficulty of software-based usage control and the open future for e-mail systems that employ such technologies, this topic is

[8] `http://www.interosa.com`
[9] `http://www.qvtech.com`
[10] `http://www.authentica.com`
[11] `http://www.disappearing.com`

not further addressed in this book. Instead, we focus on the provision of the basic message protection services mentioned above.

In essence, there are two cryptographic mechanisms that can be used to provide basic message protection services:

- *Digital signature mechanisms* can be used to provide data origin authentication, connectionless integrity, and nonrepudiation with proof of origin services.
- *Data encryption* and *digital envelope mechanisms* can be used to provide connectionless confidentiality service.

Digital signature, data encryption, and digital envelope mechanisms are introduced and further discussed in Chapter 4 when we address cryptographic techniques.

1.3.2 How Can "Secure Messaging" Be Implemented?

Once we know what "secure messaging" means and what security services a secure messaging scheme should provide, it is an interesting exercise to discuss the various possibilities to implement the corresponding security services. At a high level of abstraction, there are two approaches to either "build-in" or "add-on" mechanisms to provide the security services mentioned above in a messaging infrastructure or e-mail system:

- The first approach is to build the security mechanisms into the messaging infrastructure or e-mail system (this approach may be called "built-in security"). In this case, the message formats and messaging protocols must be modified to incorporate the security mechanisms, and to provide the security services accordingly.
- The second approach is to leave the messaging infrastructure or e-mail system as it is, and to only modify the message formats to incorporate the security mechanisms, and to provide the security services accordingly (this approach may be called "add-on security"). In this case, the messaging protocols must not be modified at all.

From a theoretical point of view, built-in security is certainly the right way to go. However, from a practical and more pragmatic point of view, there are several shortcomings and limitations that must be considered with care. First of all, built-in security requires a redesign of all (or most) message formats and messaging protocols (to incorporate the security mechanisms). Furthermore, the redesigned message formats and messaging protocols must be implemented, deployed, and supported by all UAs and all MTAs on a message delivery path. This makes built-in security generally hard to achieve and expensive. Contrary to that, add-on security has advantages, since it does not require large modifications on the messaging infrastructures or e-mail systems. All (or most) modifications can be done entirely in the UAs. This makes add-on security simple and comparably inexpensive to implement and deploy.

As discussed in the Preface, the first approach (built-in security) was followed when strong security features were designed for X.400-based MHSs and the MSP of the DMS. Meanwhile, the general trend is to follow the second approach (add-on security), and to provide security services in a way that is transparent for the underlying messaging infrastructure or e-mail system. More specifically, this approach has also been followed by all major schemes for secure messaging on the Internet. These schemes are addressed next.

1.3.3 Secure Messaging Schemes

In the past, three primary schemes for secure messaging on the Internet have emerged:[12]

- Privacy enhanced mail (PEM) and MIME object security services (MOSS);
- Pretty Good Privacy (PGP);
- Secure MIME (S/MIME).

PEM was an early standardization effort initiated by the IRTF Privacy and Security Research Group and later continued by the Internet Engineering Task Force (IETF) PEM Working Group (WG) [6].[13] In fact, PEM was the first serious effort to provide security services for Internet messaging. The PEM work led to the publication of a four-part protocol specification in February 1993 [7 – 10]. Unfortunately, PEM was never a recognized success in terms of commercial deployment. One of the main reasons for its lack of success was due to the fact that it was limited to 7-bit encoded ASCII messages, and that it was incompatible with the MIME format which was developed around the same time. The other main reason for its lack of commercial success was its strict use of a three-layer hierarchy of certification authorities (CAs) that serves as a public key infrastructure (PKI) for PEM.

After the publication of the original PEM specifications in 1993, the IETF PEM WG continued to work on the development of PEM-like security services for use in

[12]In addition, there are also some Web-based secure messaging schemes, such as HushMail (`http://www.hushmail.com`) and ZipLip (`http://www.ziplip.com`). These schemes are further addressed in Chapter 17.

[13]Both working groups no longer exist.

conjunction with MIME messages. This work was completed in 1995 and resulted in two separate specifications which solve two parts of the MIME incompatibility problem:

- On the one hand, RFC 1847 entitled "Security Multiparts for MIME: Multipart/Signed and Multipart/Encrypted" specifies two additional MIME content types for encrypted and digitally signed messages (`multipart/encrypted` and `multipart/signed`) [11].
- On the other hand, RFC 1848 entitled "MIME Object Security Services" defines a set of procedures and formats for digitally signing and encrypting MIME body parts for use in conjunction with the content types introduced in RFC 1847 [12]. When a digital signature is applied to a MIME object the `multipart/signed` content type is used. When encryption is applied the `multipart/encrypted` content type is used. Contrary to PEM, digital signature and encryption mechanisms can also be used independently (whereas PEM required that encrypted objects are always digitally signed).

Following the terminology introduced in RFC 1848, the entire architecture was named MOSS. It's further described in [13]. In summary, MOSS was an attempt to overcome the limitations and shortcomings of PEM (namely the incompatibility with MIME messages and the far too strict PKI requirements). But MOSS also had so many implementation options that it was possible and very likely for two independent software developers to come up with MOSS implementations that would not interoperate. MOSS can be thought of as a framework rather than a specification, and considerable work in implementation profiling remains to be done.[14]

While PEM and MOSS failed to become commercially successful and have sunk into oblivion, the secure messaging schemes that are in widespread use (i.e., PGP and S/MIME) copied the good features of their predecessors while attempting to avoid the bad ones. For example, PEM introduced the use of digital envelopes and the base-64 encoding scheme, and all secure messaging schemes that were proposed afterwards retained these features.

Today, PGP and S/MIME are the way to go for secure messaging on the Internet. S/MIME is a specification, whereas PGP can be thought of as both a specification and a software package. PGP and S/MIME are very similar in nature. For example, they both use public key cryptography and digital enveloping techniques to digitally sign and cryptographically protect e-mail messages. However, there are (at least)

[14]This has not changed so far.

two fundamental differences that lead to a situation in which PGP and S/MIME implementations do not interoperate:

- First, PGP and S/MIME use different message formats.
- Secondly, PGP and S/MIME handle public keys and public key certificates in fundamentally different ways:
  - PGP relies on users to directly or indirectly exchange public keys and establish trust in each other.[15] This informal approach to establish a "web of trust" works well for small workgroups, but can become hard to manage for large groups.
  - Contrary to that, S/MIME relies on public key certificates that are issued by official (or at least "officially looking") and hierarchically organized CAs and distributed by corresponding directory services.

The first difference between PGP and S/MIME is minor and similar to the differences between various formats for image files, such as GIF and JPEG. They basically do the same things from a user's point of view, but their formats are different. The second difference is more severe with regard to a long-term convergence of PGP and S/MIME. Fortunately (as discussed later in this book), newer versions of PGP additionally support CA-issued public key certificates.

As of this writing, the use of PGP and S/MIME is being standardized by two IETF WGs within the Security Area, namely the IETF Open Specification for Pretty Good Privacy (OpenPGP) WG and the IETF S/MIME Mail Security (SMIME) WG. However, except for the Internet-Drafts and Request for Comments (RFC) documents that have been published by these IETF WGs, there is barely any literature that addresses secure messaging with PGP and S/MIME. There are some manuals that describe the installation, configuration, and use of PGP and S/MIME plug-ins for several UAs and e-mail clients, but there is hardly any literature that goes beyond the graphical user interfaces (GUIs) of these software packages, and that addresses the conceptual and technical approaches followed by PGP and S/MIME. This is also true for PGP, for which several books had been written and published for earlier versions of the software [14 – 18]. With regard to S/MIME, the situation is even worse. There are single chapters in security books that briefly address S/MIME (e.g., Chapter 5 of [19] and Section 12.2 of [20]), but there is little comprehensive treatment of S/MIME in any of these books.

This book, *Secure Messaging with PGP and S/MIME*, is an attempt to change this situation, and to provide a comprehensive book that addresses the major tech-

[15]Indirect public key exchange makes use of directory services and PGP key servers.

nologies that can be used to provide basic message protection services for Internet messaging. As such, the book is aimed to fill the (increasingly large) gap between the manuals that describe the GUIs of various software packages and the Internet-Drafts and RFC documents that mainly focus on packet formats and bit encoding schemes of PGP and S/MIME. In fact, it attempts to bring together all relevant and important information that is needed to fully understand and use PGP- and S/MIME-compliant software.

1.4 OUTLINE OF THE BOOK

The rest of the book is organized as follows:

- In Chapter 2, *Character Sets, Message Formats, and Encoding Schemes*, we overview and briefly discuss the character sets, message formats, and encoding schemes that are used for Internet messaging.
- In Chapter 3, *Internet Messaging*, we elaborate on the message formats and protocols that are used for Internet messaging.
- In Chapter 4, *Cryptographic Techniques*, we introduce the basic cryptographic techniques that are employed by secure messaging schemes, including, for example, PGP and S/MIME.
- In Chapter 5, *ASN.1 and Encoding Rules*, we address the Abstract Syntax Notation One (ASN.1) and some related sets of encoding rules.
- In Chapter 6, *History and Development*, we outline the history and development of PGP.
- In Chapter 7, *Technological Approach*, we overview and discuss the conceptual and technological approach employed by PGP.
- In Chapter 8, *Web of Trust*, we elaborate on public key and certificate management for PGP.
- In Chapter 9, *Standardization and Products*, we briefly overview the standardization of PGP and the products that conform to the emerging standards.
- In Chapter 10, *Conclusions and Outlook*, we conclude the part on PGP and give an outlook about possible developments in the field.
- In Chapter 11, *History and Development*, we outline the history and development of S/MIME.
- In Chapter 12, *Technological Approach*, we overview and discuss the conceptual and technological approach employed by S/MIME.

- In Chapter 13, *Public Key Infrastructure*, we address the public key infrastructure (PKI) requirements for S/MIME.
- In Chapter 14, *Standardization and Products*, we briefly overview the standardization of S/MIME and the products that conform to the emerging standards.
- In Chapter 15, *Conclusions and Outlook*, we conclude the part on S/MIME and give an outlook about possible developments in the field.
- In Chapter 16, *Comparison*, we compare PGP and S/MIME with regard to a number of evaluation criteria.
- In Chapter 17, *Outlook*, we give an outlook about possible developments related to secure messaging on the Internet.

Finally, the appendix also includes a glossary, a list of abbreviations, an "About the Author" page, and an index to find particular terms. Again (as already mentioned in the Preface), more information about secure messaging with PGP and S/MIME is available on this book's homepage[16] and on the homepage of a secure mail project of eSECURITY Technologies Rolf Oppliger.[17]

REFERENCES

[1] B.F. Shimmin, *Effective E-mail Clearly Explained: File Transfer, Security, and Interoperability*, AP Professional, Orlando, FL, 1997.

[2] L. Hughes, *Internet E-Mail: Protocols, Standards, and Implementations*, Artech House, Norwood, MA, 1998.

[3] D. Strom, and M.T. Rose, *Internet Messaging*, Prentice Hall, Upper Saddle River, NJ, 1998.

[4] R. Oppliger, *Internet and Intranet Security*, Artech House, Norwood, MA, 1998.

[5] ISO/IEC 7498-2, Information Processing Systems — Open Systems Interconnection Reference Model — Part 2: Security Architecture, 1989.

[6] S.T. Kent, "Internet Privacy Enhanced Mail," *Communications of the ACM*, 36(8), August 1993, pp. 48 – 60.

[7] J. Linn, "Privacy Enhancement for Internet Electronic Mail: Part I — Message Encryption and Authentication Procedures," Request for Comments 1421, February 1993.

[8] S.T. Kent, "Privacy Enhancement for Internet Electronic Mail: Part II — Certificate-Based Key Management," Request for Comments 1422, February 1993.

[9] D. Balenson, "Privacy Enhancement for Internet Electronic Mail: Part III — Algorithms, Modes, and Identifiers," Request for Comments 1423, February 1993.

[16] `http://www.esecurity.ch/Books/secmess.html`

[17] `http://www.esecurity.ch/Projects/securemail.html`

[10] B. Kaliski, "Privacy Enhancement for Internet Electronic Mail: Part IV — Key Certification and Related Services," Request for Comments 1424, February 1993.

[11] J. Galvin, S. Murphy, S. Crocker, and N. Freed, "Security Multiparts for MIME: Multipart/Signed and Multipart/Encrypted," Request for Comments 1847, October 1995.

[12] S. Crocker, N. Freed, J. Galvin, and S. Murphy, "MIME Object Security Services," Request for Comments 1848, October 1995.

[13] J. Galvin, and M.S. Feldman, "MIME object security services: Issues in a multi-user environment," *Proceedings of USENIX UNIX Security V Symposium*, June 1995.

[14] P.R. Zimmermann, *The Official PGP User's Guide*, MIT Press, Cambridge, MA, 1995.

[15] P.R. Zimmermann, *PGP Source Code and Internals*, MIT Press, Cambridge, MA, 1995.

[16] S. Garfinkel, *PGP: Pretty Good Privacy*, O'Reilly & Associates, Sebastopol, CA, 1995.

[17] B. Schneier, *E-Mail Security: How to Keep Your Electronic Messages Private*, John Wiley & Sons, New York, NY, 1995.

[18] A. Bacard, *The Computer Privacy Handbook: A Practical Guide to E-Mail Encryption, Data Protection, and PGP Privacy Software*, Peachpit Press, Berkeley, CA, 1995.

[19] J. Feghhi, J. Feghhi, and P. Williams, *Digital Certificates: Applied Internet Security*, Addison-Wesley, Reading, MA, 1999.

[20] W. Stallings, *Cryptography and Network Security: Principles and Practice*, 2nd Edition, Prentice-Hall, Upper Saddle River, NJ, 1998.

Chapter 2

Character Sets, Message Formats, and Encoding Schemes

In this chapter, we overview and briefly discuss the character sets, message formats, and encoding schemes that are typically used in network applications, such as Internet messaging. We start with character sets in Section 2.1, continue with message formats in Section 2.2, and finish up with encoding schemes in Section 2.3. Finally, we draw some conclusions in Section 2.4. Note that anybody familiar with character sets, message formats, or encoding schemes can easily skip the corresponding section without losing the context.

2.1 CHARACTER SETS

There are various character sets that are used in network applications, such as Internet messaging. In this section, we overview and put into perspective the ASCII, ISO/IEC 8859, Unicode, as well as ISO/IEC 10646-1 and UTF-8 character sets. There are only a few vendors that use other character sets. For example, IBM has developed and deployed the Extended Binary Coded Decimal Information Code (EBCDIC) as a viable alternative to ASCII. The EBCDIC character set is not expected to be supported in the long-term, and as such it is not addressed in this book. Also, there are character sets used in countries that do not use the roman alphabet (e.g., KOI-8 is used in Russia and JIS X.208 is used in Japan). Again, these character sets are not addressed in this book.

2.1.1 ASCII

The American Standard Code for Information Interchange (ASCII) is a 7-bit character set standardized by the U.S. American National Standards Institute (ANSI) [1]. The set includes $2^7 = 128$ commonly used characters, including uppercase and lowercase alphabetic characters, the decimal digits (0 through 9), many punctuation symbols, and some control codes, such as the carriage return (CR) and the line feed (LF).

Each ASCII character can be represented with 7 bits or two hexadecimal characters, encoded in the range from 0x00 to 0x7F. Consequently, the leftmost and most significant bit in a byte representing an ASCII character is always set to zero. For example, the uppercase letter "A" is represented with the hexadecimal value 0x41, the decimal value 65, or the binary value 01000001.

Table 2.1
ASCII Characters with Hexadecimal Values

	0x00	0x10	0x20	0x30	0x40	0x50	0x60	0x70
+0	NUL	DLE		0	@	P	`	p
+1	SOH	DC1	!	1	A	Q	a	q
+2	STX	DC2	"	2	B	R	b	r
+3	ETX	DC3	#	3	C	S	c	s
+4	EOT	DC4	$	4	D	T	d	t
+5	ENQ	NAK	%	5	E	U	e	u
+6	ACK	SYN	&	6	F	V	f	v
+7	BEL	ETB	'	7	G	W	g	w
+8	BS	CAN	(	8	H	X	h	x
+9	HT	EM	)	9	I	Y	i	y
+A	LF	SUB	*	:	J	Z	j	z
+B	VT	ESC	+	;	K	[	k	{
+C	FF	FS	,	<	L	\	l	|
+D	CR	GS	-	=	M	]	m	}
+E	SO	RS	.	>	N	^	n	~
+F	SI	US	/	?	O	_	o	DEL

Note that the ASCII character set exists in a number of different national variants. For example, Scandinavian countries use a different variant of ASCII from the U.S. one. The different variants of ASCII are created by using all of the eight bits to represent a character (this is similar to the ISO/IEC 8859 character set). Also note that the advantages and disadvantages of a specific character set are minor, but that the advantages of everyone using the same character set are overwhelming. This is especially true for messaging infrastructures and e-mail systems. Consequently, many contemporary e-mail systems make use of the ASCII character set, and we're going to use ASCII characters and corresponding decimal or hexadecimal values at several places throughout this book. The 128 ASCII characters and their hexadecimal values are summarized in Table 2.1.

2.1.2 ISO/IEC 8859

The International Organization for Standardization (ISO) and the International Electrotechnical Committee (IEC) have jointly adapted and slightly generalized the ASCII character set using 8 bits to represent each character. The resulting standard is commonly referred to as ISO/IEC 8859 [2].

Note that 8 bits can be used to represent $2^8 = 256$ different characters. According to ISO/IEC 8859, the first 128 characters are constant and comprise the standard ASCII characters, whereas the second 128 characters vary and may include arbitrary characters. In fact, by having the first 128 characters constant and varying the second 128 characters, one can define an entire family of partly different character sets. The various character sets in the ISO/IEC 8859 standard are distinguished by an appended number. For example, the ISO/IEC 8859-1 character set (also known as Latin alphabet No. 1) is used for the English, French, German, and Italian languages, whereas the ISO/IEC 8859-5 character set is used for Cyrillic languages. The various parts of the ISO/IEC 8859 standard are summarized in Table 2.2.[1]

E-mail software that supports ISO/IEC 8859 can interoperate with ASCII-based systems if it sticks to the first 128 characters, but it can also support the extended characters required by specific languages, such as the "ä," "Ä," "ö," "Ö," "ü," and "Ü" characters of the German language. More and more e-mail systems and gateways are able to properly deal with extended characters.

[1] `http://www.iso.ch/cate/35040.html`

2.1.3 Unicode

Unicode is an international standard developed by the Unicode Consortium.[2] As such, it refers to a generalization of the ASCII and ISO/IEC 8859 character sets, using 16 bits to encode each character [3]. Sixteen bits allow up to $2^{16} = 65,536$ distinct characters. Unicode includes ISO/IEC 8859-1 as the first 256 characters, then both traditional and simplified Chinese ideographs, Japanese and Thai characters, Korean Hangul syllables, and various other glyphs that cover most of the world's major languages.

Table 2.2
The Parts of the ISO/IEC 8859 Standard (as of 1999)

Standard	Title
ISO/IEC 8859-1 (1998)	Information technology – 8-bit single-byte coded graphic character sets – Part 1: Latin alphabet No. 1.
ISO/IEC 8859-2 (1999)	Information technology – 8-bit single-byte coded graphic character sets – Part 2: Latin alphabet No. 2.
ISO/IEC 8859-3 (1999)	Information technology – 8-bit single-byte coded graphic character sets – Part 3: Latin alphabet No. 3.
ISO/IEC 8859-4 (1998)	Information technology – 8-bit single-byte coded graphic character sets – Part 4: Latin alphabet No. 4.
ISO/IEC 8859-5 (1999)	Information technology – 8-bit single-byte coded graphic character sets – Part 5: Latin/Cyrillic alphabet
ISO/IEC 8859-6 (1999)	Information technology – 8-bit single-byte coded graphic character sets – Part 6: Latin/Arabic alphabet.
ISO 8859-7 (1987)	Information processing – 8-bit single-byte coded graphic character sets – Part 7: Latin/Greek alphabet.
ISO/IEC 8859-8 (1999)	Information technology – 8-bit single-byte coded graphic character sets – Part 8: Latin/Hebrew alphabet.
ISO/IEC 8859-9 (1999)	Information technology – 8-bit single-byte coded graphic character sets – Part 9: Latin alphabet No. 5.
ISO/IEC 8859-10 (1998)	Information technology – 8-bit single-byte coded graphic character sets – Part 10: Latin alphabet No. 6.
ISO/IEC 8859-13 (1998)	Information technology – 8-bit single-byte coded graphic character sets – Part 13: Latin alphabet No. 7.
ISO/IEC 8859-14 (1998)	Information technology – 8-bit single-byte coded graphic character sets – Part 14: Latin alphabet No. 8 (Celtic).
ISO/IEC 8859-15 (1999)	Information technology – 8-bit single-byte coded graphic character sets – Part 15: Latin alphabet No. 9.

[2] `http://www.unicode.org`

Unicode is used as a native character set in Microsoft's Windows NT and Windows 2000 operating systems. Also, the Extensible Markup Language (XML) makes use of Unicode. In spite of the fact that only few vendors of Internet messaging products provide support for the Unicode standard today,[3] one may reasonably assume that this situation will change and that we will see more and more products supporting the Unicode standard in the future.

2.1.4 ISO/IEC 10646-1 and UTF-8

ISO/IEC 10646-1 defines a multi-octet character set called the universal character set (UCS) [4]. UCS, in turn, encompasses most of the world's writing systems. Two multi-octet character encoding schemes are defined, a four-octet per character encoding called UCS-4 and a two-octet per character encoding called UCS-2.[4] Unfortunately, the UCS-2 and UCS-4 encoding schemes are hard to use in many applications and application protocols that assume 7-bit or 8-bit characters. Even newer systems able to deal with 16-bit characters cannot process UCS-4 encoded data. This unpleasant situation has led to the development of so-called UCS transformation formats (UTFs), each with different characteristics. UTFs are generally published as amendments to the original ISO/IEC 10646-1 specification.[5]

For the purpose of this book, we are only interested in UTF-8 (since PGP is using UTF-8 and S/MIME is not using UTF at all). It is described in Annex R and published as Amendment 2 of ISO/IEC 10646-1 [4]. As such, it is also part of the Unicode standard [3]. UTF-8 uses 8-bit characters to comprise the ASCII character set. Furthermore, it encodes UCS-2 and UCS-4 characters as a varying number of octets. The number of octets (between 1 and 6) and the value of each depend on the integer value assigned to the character in ISO/IEC 10646-1 (as specified in RFC 2279 [5]).

2.2 MESSAGE FORMATS

In general, an e-mail message and its subparts can either consist of characters in a specific character set, such as ASCII, ISO/IEC 8859, Unicode, or ISO/IEC 10646-1

[3]There are some products for the Macintosh (e.g., PowerMail) that provide support for Unicode.

[4]The same set of characters is defined by the Unicode standard, which further defines additional character properties and other application details of interest to implementors, but does not have the UCS-4 encoding. Up to the present time, changes in Unicode and amendments to ISO/IEC 10646-1 are synchronized, and the relevant standardization committees have committed to maintain this synchronism.

[5]`http://www.iso.ch/cate/35040.html`

and UTF-8, or it can comprise an unformatted stream of binary data. In the first case, it is also possible to include some text formatting information in the message. Against this background, we overview and briefly discuss some message formats that are relevant for Internet messaging in this section.

2.2.1 ASCII Text Format

As of this writing, most e-mail messages still consist of ASCII text. ASCII text, in turn, may comprise the characters summarized in Table 2.1. The ASCII characters are organized into one or more lines, each of which consists of a short sequence of up to 80 or so characters followed by a `<CR><LF>` control code pair.[6] Many (but not all) ASCII text files use the filename extension `.txt`. Note, however, that this is only a recommendation and is not enforced by most systems.

2.2.2 HTML Format

It is getting increasingly popular to send and receive e-mail messages that include Hypertext Markup Language (HTML) tags in addition to normal ASCII text. The resulting HTML messages include text formatting information, such as typeface, font size, or color. Many UAs are able to render HTML messages and to display them in a format that is appropriate. It is possible and very likely that HTML tags will be replaced with corresponding XML tags, once XML is more widely deployed.

2.2.3 Rich Text Format

Similar to HTML (and XML) messages, the rich text format (RTF) can be used to encode ASCII text with additions to specify formatting information. RTF allows sending and receiving e-mail messages that use such information to have a more professional appearance or to include formatting information that is difficult (or impossible) to achieve with ASCII text. There are, however, at least two competing RTF standards:

- The RTF standard used in the Microsoft Office software suite;
- The RTF standard used in the context of MIME as briefly addressed in the following chapter.

[6]Note that the internal representation of ASCII text files on UNIX systems use only an `<LF>` control code as a line terminator, and that most TCP/IP application protocols, such as SMTP, require conversion to and from the standard `<CR><LF>` pair of control codes when these systems are communicating with other systems (even if both systems are using the UNIX operating system).

Furthermore, many UAs do not support RTF at all, and messages composed using RTF may be difficult or impossible to read with them.

Due to the lack of a generally agreed upon and used RTF standard, it is good practice to avoid using RTF in e-mail messages unless the sender specifically knows that the intended recipient(s) support(s) it. Some UAs can keep track of which recipients support RTF and automatically convert RTF messages to simple ASCII text for anyone else. Other UAs can send both simple ASCII and RTF versions of a message, but most currently available UAs still do not know what to do with the RTF version of the message. In this case, it appears as a spurious e-mail attachment.

2.2.4 Binary Data

In the simplest case, an e-mail message (or one of its subparts) simply consists of an unformatted stream of binary data. In this case, each 8-bit sequence of binary data may be represented with two hexadecimal values. For example, the binary 8-bit sequence `10100011` may be represented with `0xA3` (since `1010` refers to `0xA` and `0011` refers to `0x3`). It is up to the application to render, store, or process the data.

2.3 ENCODING SCHEMES

In computer networks and distributed systems, binary or 8-bit data must often be transferred by (intermediate) systems that have been designed to handle only specific characters (e.g., 7-bit ASCII characters). Consequently, the binary or 8-bit data must be encoded into a form that is transferable by these systems. As such, the data is transferred to the recipient where it is decoded to its original form.[7]

There are (at least) three standard encoding schemes that follow this strategy: quoted-printable encoding, as well as the UU and base-64 (or radix-64) encoding schemes. There are also other encoding schemes, such as BINHEX that is mainly used in the Macintosh world. Due to their lack of deployment, however, BINHEX and other encoding schemes are not further addressed in this book.

The following text file `test.txt` is used as a common example to illustrate the effects of the various encoding schemes:

[7] Think of this strategy as the e-mail equivalent of a modem, which performs similar encoding from a digital bitstream into an analog audio signal that passes through a voice-grade telephone line and then back into the original digital bitstream at the other end.

```
The aim of this file is to illustrate the various encoding
schemes that can be used to transform arbitrary data into
printable and transferable character sets (e.g., the UU and
base-64 encoding schemes).
```

2.3.1 Quoted-Printable Encoding

If non-ASCII characters don't occur too frequently in a text to be transferred, a simple quoting mechanism may be used as an encoding scheme. In such a scheme, each character may be represented by a three-character sequence that consists of an equal sign and two hexadecimal values that represent the decimal value (in the range from `0x00` to `0xFF`) of the encoded character. For example, the German characters "ä," "ö," and "ü" are quoted-printable encoded as `=E4`, `=F6`, and `=FC` (referring to the ASCII values in the extended ASCII character set used for the German language). Furthermore, the equal sign (=) itself is represented by the three-character sequence `=3D` (according to Table 2.1, `0x3D` refers to the ASCII value for the equal sign).

The resulting quoted-printable encoding scheme is efficient for messages that are composed of mostly 7-bit ASCII characters, with only few non-ASCII characters. Contrary to that, the scheme is highly inefficient for general binary data or texts that include many 8-bit characters. In these cases, the encoding schemes addressed next should be used instead.

2.3.2 UU Encoding Scheme

The *uuencode/uudecode encoding scheme* (UU encoding scheme) is a standard way of encoding input data streams that consist of arbitrary binary or 8-bit data. In short, the scheme encodes blocks of six bits each into one character represented by eight bits. Consequently, three bytes of input data result in four encoded characters, and the resulting message expansion is one-third.

The characters used in the UU encoding scheme were chosen to be compatible with the largest number of possible e-mail systems and legacy computer systems. The characters used in the UU mapping of the UU encoding scheme are summarized in Table 2.3. They basically include all uppercase alphabetic characters, the decimal digits, and some special characters.

Going back to our exemplary file `test.txt`, the leading three characters (namely "T," "h," and "e") are first represented by their hexadecimal values in the ASCII character set:

Table 2.3
Characters Used in the Standard UU Encoding Scheme (UU Mapping)

	0x00	0x10	0x20	0x30
+0	’	0	@	P
+1	!	1	A	Q
+2	"	2	B	R
+3	#	3	C	S
+4	$	4	D	T
+5	%	5	E	U
+6	&	6	F	V
+7	‘	7	G	W
+8	(	8	H	X
+9	)	9	I	Y
+A	*	:	J	Z
+B	+	;	K	[
+C	,	<	L	\
+D	-	=	M	]
+E	.	>	N	^
+F	/	?	O	_

T ⟶ 0x54
h ⟶ 0x68
e ⟶ 0x65
...

Afterwards, the UU encoding scheme can be used to transfer these values into a given character set. The 8-bit binary representations of the ASCII values are therefore rearranged in groups of six bits each. Each group of six bits then represents a decimal or hexadecimal value. The hexadecimal value, in turn, is used to extract a character from Table 2.3 (using the UU mapping). In summary, the procedure to encode the first three characters can be described as follows:

```
Input data: The
Hex:        5  4     6  8     6  5
8-bit:      01010100 01101000 01100101
6-bit:      010101 000110 100001 100101
Decimal:    21     6      33     37
Hex:        15     6      21     25
Output:     5      &      A      E
```

Consequently, the resulting uuencoded file `test.txt` (e.g., denoted as `test.uue`) starts with the string `5&AE`.

The UU encoding scheme is line-oriented, meaning that a UU encoded message may consist of multiple lines. Each line must indicate its length (the number of data bytes on that particular line) and start with a corresponding uuencoded value. Using the UU mapping, this value is typically set to "M," representing the hexadecimal value `0x2D` or the decimal value `45`, respectively. This basically means that 45 bytes of original data are encoded on that line, resulting in a total of 60 encoded characters. After the encoded count of data bytes follows the encoded form of the corresponding data bytes and a pair of control codes (`<CR><LF>`) that signals the end of the line. Furthermore, the uuencoded file may include `begin` and `end` lines, as well as access control information and the original name of the file. Unfortunately, additional information, such as file creation date and time, size, and ownership, cannot be included in an uuencoded file. For example, our exemplary file `test.txt` is uuencoded as follows (using the UU mapping):

```
begin 666 test.txt
M5&AE(&%I;2!O9B!T:&ES(&9I;&4@:7,@=&\@:6QL=7-T<F%T92!T:&4@=F%R
M:6]U<R!E;F-O9&EN9PT*<V-H96UE<R!T:&%T(&-A;B!B92!U<V5D('1O('1R
M86YS9F]R;2!A<F)I=')A<GD@9&%T82!I;G1O#0IP<FEN=&%B;&4@86YD('1R
M86YF97)A8FQE(&-H87)A8W1E<B!S971S("AE+F<N+"!T:&4@554@86YD#0I"
;87-E+38T(&5N8V]D:6YG('-C:&5M97,I+@T*
`
end
```

Note that the uuencoded file comprises the string `5&AE` after the uuencoded line count (represented by the character "M"). Also note that the final line contains only 27 bytes of original data (encoded count is represented by the character ";" which corresponds to `0x1B` or `27` in decimal notation). The uuencoded message is enclosed in a pair of `begin` and `end` lines. Furthermore, the code `666` refers to the access control information for the file (read and write access for everybody), and `test.txt` refers to its original filename.

Obviously, the UU encoding is reversible and a uuencoded file can easily be decoded. In our example, we start the decoding process by assigning hexadecimal values to the characters in the uuencoded file (after the first character on each line). For the first line, the process starts as follows:

```
5   ⟶  0x15
&   ⟶  0x06
A   ⟶  0x21
E   ⟶  0x25
...
```

The resulting hexadecimal values can be written in binary format:

```
00010101 00000110 00100001 00100101 ...
```

In each group of 8 bits, the top 2 bits can be discarded:

```
010101 000110 100001 100101 ...
```

The resulting bitstream is rearranged into groups of 8 bits each:

```
01010100 01101000 01100101 ...
```

The resulting bytes can be rewritten as hexadecimal values:

```
54 68 65 ...
```

As such, the hexadecimal values can be translated into ASCII characters (according to Table 2.1). The result is as follows:

```
The ...
```

This decodes the first three characters of the original file. In this example, the original file happens to be ASCII text, but any file could have been fed into the encoder program, including, for example, a word processor file (e.g., a `.doc` file), a compressed archive (e.g., a file compressed with the ZIP algorithm), an executable program (e.g., an `.exe` file), or a video or audio file. In either case, the resulting encoded file would have been an ASCII text file suitable for going through even the most restrictive communication channel.

Obviously, the UU mapping of the UU encoding scheme can only be used if all uppercase characters, decimal digits (0 through 9), and several special characters can be transferred (the characters summarized in Table 2.3). If, however, the transfer system is more likely to be able to transfer lowercase characters (instead of decimal digits and special characters), another character set or mapping may be used for the UU encoding scheme. Such an alternative mapping is the XX mapping

Table 2.4
Characters Used in the UU Encoding Scheme (XX Mapping)

	0x00	0x10	0x20	0x30
+0	+	E	U	k
+1	-	F	V	l
+2	=	G	W	m
+3	1	H	X	n
+4	2	I	Y	o
+5	3	J	Z	p
+6	4	K	a	q
+7	5	L	b	r
+8	6	M	c	s
+9	7	N	d	t
+A	8	O	e	u
+B	9	P	f	v
+C	A	Q	g	w
+D	B	R	h	x
+E	C	S	i	y
+F	D	T	j	z

as summarized in Table 2.4. The XX mapping is less common but more likely to go through modern communication channels. In either case, a good UU encoding utility should provide support for both mappings, and it should be able to recognize and decode either mapping automatically (without having the user make decisions).

The procudure to uuencode and uudecode data is essentially the same for both UU and XX mappings (using Table 2.4 instead of Table 2.3). Using the XX mapping, for example, our file `test.txt` is uuencoded as follows:

```
begin 666 test.txt
hJ4VZ643dPG-jNW-o04Zn64NdP4IU0LAUR4wU0K1gRLBoQa3oNG-o04IURa3m
h0KxpQm-ZPaBjN4ZiNko8QqBcNKpZQm-o043o64BVPW-WNG-pQqJY65Fj65Fm
hMKtnNaxmPG-VQa7dR57VQbYUN43oMG-dPbFj1EdkQaZiR43WP4IUMKtY65Fm
hMKtaNL7VMa1Z64BcML7VMrFZQW-nNLFn60VZ9aQi90-o04IUJJIUMKtY1Ed0
PMLBZ9HMo64JiMqxY0Ktb65BX04JhNLAd9Uo8
+
end
```

Note that the character "h" encodes `0x2D` (decimal 45) in the XX mapping. Consequently, the first four lines start with an "h" instead of an "M." Again, the uuencoded message is enclosed in a pair of `begin` and `end` lines, the code `666` refers to the access control information for the file, and `test.txt` refers to the original file name.

As of this writing, most UAs provide support for the UU encoding scheme and both of its mappings (the UU and XX mappings). For UAs that do not provide support for the UU encoding scheme, there are many utility programs publicly and freely available that can be used to uuencode and uudecode files outside the UA. Using separate utility programs, however, is less convenient from the user's point of view.

2.3.3 Base-64 Encoding Scheme

Similar to the UU encoding scheme, the *base-64 encoding scheme* takes input blocks of six bits and produces output blocks of eight bits to represent the corresponding value as a printable and transferable character. The base-64 encoding scheme is sometimes also referred to as *radix-64 encoding scheme.* In fact, the PGP specifications and documentations use this term to refer to the base-64 encoding scheme. In this book, we use the two terms synonymously and interchangeably.

Table 2.5
Characters Used in the Base-64 Encoding Scheme

	0x00	0x10	0x20	0x30
+0	A	Q	g	w
+1	B	R	h	x
+2	C	S	i	y
+3	D	T	j	z
+4	E	U	k	0
+5	F	V	l	1
+6	G	W	m	2
+7	H	X	n	3
+8	I	Y	o	4
+9	J	Z	p	5
+A	K	a	q	6
+B	L	b	r	7
+C	M	c	s	8
+D	N	d	t	9
+E	O	e	u	+
+F	P	f	v	/

The characters used in the base-64 encoding scheme are the uppercase and lowercase alphabetic characters, the decimal digits (0 through 9), as well as the plus (+) and slash (/) characters. In addition, the equal sign (=) is used to pad data. The characters used by the base-64 encoding scheme are summarized in Table 2.5.

The procedure to encode data using the base-64 (or radix-64) encoding scheme is simple and straightforward. In fact, it is similar to the one used for the UU encoding scheme. In short, the 8-bit input blocks are rearranged into groups of six bits each, and each of these groups is then encoded into a character according to Table 2.5.

Using the base-64 encoding scheme, the procedure to encode the first three characters of our exemplary file `test.txt` can be described as follows:

```
Input data: The
Hex:        5   4    6   8    6   5
8-bit:      01010100 01101000 01100101
6-bit:      010101 000110 100001 100101
Decimal:    21     6      33     37
Hex:        15     6      21     25
Output:     V      G      h      l
```

Consequently, the resulting uuencoded file `test.txt` (e.g., denoted as `test.uue`) must start with the string `5&AE`. More specifically, the base-64 encoded file `test.txt` looks as follows:


```
VGhlIGFpbSBvZiB0aGlzIGZpbGUgaXMgdG8gaWxsdXN0cmF0ZSB0aGUgdmFyaW91cyBlb
mNvZGluZw0Kc2NoZW1lcyB0aGF0IGNhbiBiZSB1c2VkIHRvIHRyYW5zZm9ybSBhcmJpdH
JhcnkgZGF0YSBpbnRvDQpwcmludGFibGUgYW5kIHRyYW5mZXJhYmxlIGNoYXJhY3RlciB
zZXRzIChlLmcuLCB0aGUgVVUgYW5kDQpCYXNlLTY0IGVuY29kaW5nIHNjaGVtZXMpLg0K
```


Contrary to the UU encoding scheme, the base-64 encoding scheme is not line-oriented. The input data is encoded in a stream of characters that can be split into lines of arbitrary lengths. Consequently, there is no need to include any line length information in the output data.

The following exemplary base-64 encodings are taken from Section 6.5 of [6] (they may serve as an exercise to get a better understanding of the base-64 encoding scheme):

```
Input data: 0x14fb9c03d97e
Hex:      1    4     f    b     9    c     | 0    3     d    9     7    e
8-bit:    00010100 11111011 10011100  | 00000011 11011001 11111110
6-bit:    000101 001111 101110 011100 | 000000 111101 100111 111110
Decimal:  5      15     46     28     | 0      61     37     62
Output:   F      P      u      c      | A      9      1      +
```

In this example, the hexadecimal input data 0x14fb9c03d97e is base-64 encoded to FPucA91+.

```
Input data: 0x14fb9c03d9
Hex:      1    4     f    b     9    c     | 0    3     d    9
8-bit:    00010100 11111011 10011100  | 00000011 11011001
6-bit:    000101 001111 101110 011100 | 000000 111101 100100
Decimal:  5      15     46     28     | 0      61     36
Output:   F      P      u      c      | A      9      k      =
```

In this example, the hexadecimal input data 0x14fb9c03d9 is base-64 encoded to FPucA9k=. Note that the last block of 6 bits is padded with two zeros (00), and that the resulting output string is padded with an additional equal sign (=).

```
Input data: 0x14fb9c03
Hex:      1    4     f    b     9    c     | 0    3
8-bit:    00010100 11111011 10011100  | 00000011
6-bit:    000101 001111 101110 011100 | 000000 110000
Decimal:  5      15     46     28     | 0      48
Output:   F      P      u      c      | A      w      =      =
```

In this example, the hexadecimal input data 0x14fb9c03 is base-64 encoded to FPucAw==. Note that the last block of 6 bits is padded with four zeros (0000), and that the resulting output string is padded with two additional equal signs (==).

2.4 CONCLUSIONS

In this chapter, we overviewed and briefly discussed the character sets (e.g., ASCII, ISO/IEC 8859, Unicode, as well as ISO/IEC 10646-1 and UTF-8), message formats (e.g., ASCII text format, HTML messages, rich text format, and binary data), and encoding schemes (e.g., quoted-printable, UU and base-64 encoding schemes) that are typically used in network applications, such as Internet messaging. We use this information in subsequent parts of this book.

Today, most e-mail messages (still) consist of ASCII text and binary data (e.g., binary mail attachments). In the second case, an encoding scheme must be used to transfer the message through systems that natively support only 7-bit data. The suitability of either the quoted-printable or the UU and base-64 encoding schemes primarily depends on the statistical nature of the data to transfer:

- If the data consists mainly of ASCII characters with only a few special characters, then the use of the quoted-printable encoding scheme is appropriate;
- If, however, the data consists mainly of arbitrary 8-bit data, then the use of one of the other encoding schemes is appropriate.

In either case, it is convenient for the user to have the encoding and decoding functions be integrated in the UA software (so they are invisible and mostly transparent to the user). In fact, most UAs are able to transparently encode and decode messages on the fly. This ability is expected to be improved in future versions of UA software.

REFERENCES

[1] ANSI X3.4, Coded Character Set — 7-bit American Standard Code for Information Exchange, 1986.

[2] ISO/IEC 8859, Information technology — 8-bit single-byte coded graphic character sets (multipart standard), 1998.

[3] The Unicode Consortium, *The Unicode Standard — Version 2.0*, Addison-Wesley, Reading, MA, 1996.

[4] ISO/IEC 10646-1, Information Technology — Universal Multiple-Octet Coded Character Set (UCS) — Part 1: Architecture and Basic Multilingual Plane, 1993.

[5] F. Yergeau, "UTF-8, a transformation format of ISO 10646," Request for Comments 2279, January 1998.

[6] J. Callas, L. Donnerhacke, H. Finney, and R. Thayer, "OpenPGP Message Format," Request for Comments 2440, November 1998.

Chapter 3

Internet Messaging

In this chapter, we overview and briefly discuss the message format and protocols that are used for Internet messaging. More specifically, we address the message formats in Section 3.1, message transfer protocols in Section 3.2, message store access protocols in Section 3.3, and directory access protocols in Section 3.4. Finally, we draw some conclusions in Section 3.5. Note that this chapter provides only a broad overview and that it is not at all comprehensive. If you want to get into details, you may refer to the referenced RFC documents or the books that have been written about Internet messaging [1 – 3]. Among these books, I particularly recommend [2].

3.1 MESSAGE FORMATS

There are two RFC documents that were written almost 20 years ago and that collectively define the mode of operation of an Internet-based e-mail system:

- On the one hand, RFC 822 (STD 11) specifies the formats and syntactical rules for text-based e-mail messages [4];

- On the other hand, RFC 821 (part of STD 10) specifies the Simple Mail Transfer Protocol (SMTP) that is used to send and receive e-mail messages by UAs and MTAs [5].

In this section, we address the message formats and syntactical rules as specified in RFC 822. The SMTP and related messaging protocols are further addressed in subsequent sections of this chapter.

In short, an RFC 822-compliant e-mail message includes two sections, one that comprises the message headers and one that comprises the message body. Message headers and message body are separated by an empty (or null) line and are addressed next. Afterwards, we focus on the MIME that are used to transport other contents than simple text.

3.1.1 Message Headers

As mentioned above, an RFC 822-compliant e-mail message must include a header section with an arbitrary number of message headers. The message headers, in turn, need not come in a particular order. Only a few message headers are required and most of them are optional.

In general, a UA automatically creates the message headers on the user's behalf. The information required is extracted from the UA configuration file(s) and the special fields that are entered when a new message is created (e.g., the subject field). In most cases, the message headers are not displayed directly but are interpreted and shown only in lists of messages and special areas at the top of displayed messages. Nevertheless, most UAs have special commands to show messages with all their message headers. For example, in Microsoft Outlook Express the File > Properties command can be used to view a message (General panel) and all of its message headers (Details panel). The corresponding screenshots of an exemplary message are shown in Figures 3.1 and 3.2. Note that the Details panel additionally provides a Message Source button that can be pressed to view the entire message, including all message headers and the message body.

In short, a message header consists of one or more lines of ASCII text with a keyword followed by a colon and one or more parameters. The following lines are taken from a test message sent from `rolf.oppliger@freesurf.ch` to `rolf.oppliger@esecurity.ch` (the same message that is illustrated in Figures 3.1 and 3.2). Note that the two accounts belong to different domains (`freesurf.ch` and `esecurity.ch`) and are served by different mail servers:

```
From: rolf.oppliger@freesurf.ch
To: rolf.oppliger@esecurity.ch
Subject: Test message
```

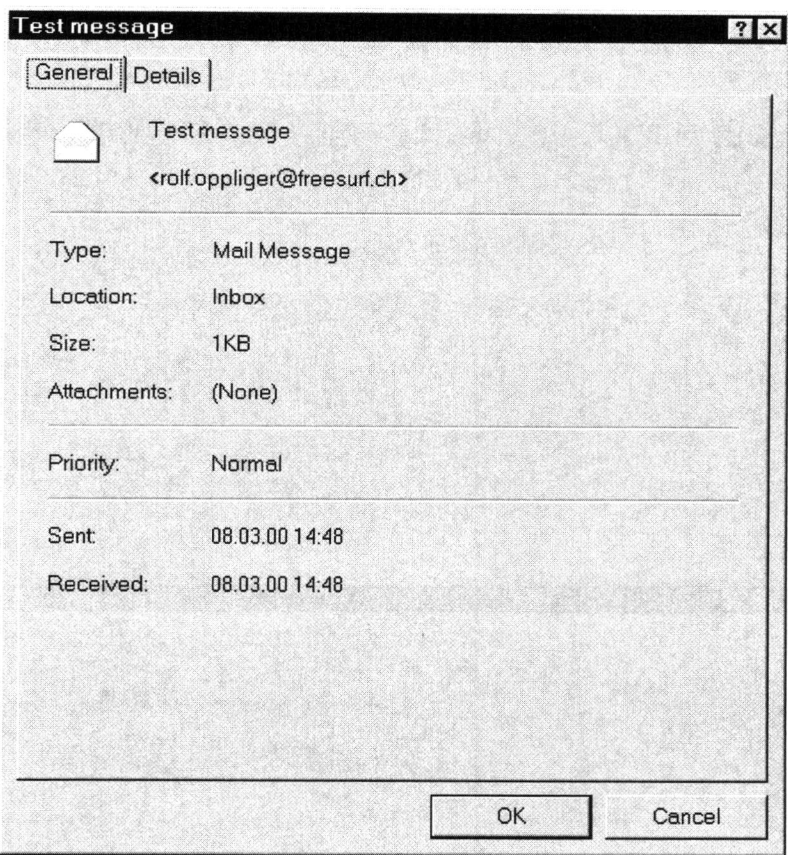

Figure 3.1 General Message Properties panel of Microsoft Outlook Express. © 2000 Microsoft Corporation.

The general format of an e-mail address is `a.b.c@x.y.z`, where `a.b.c` refers to the user name (e.g., `rolf.oppliger`) and `x.y.z` refer to the domain name of the computer system that hosts the SMTP server (e.g., `esecurity.ch`). Note that some parts of the user and domain names may also be empty.

According to RFC 822, an e-mail address may be specified in several ways. If no substrings are delimited by angle brackets (< and >), the entire string is interpreted as an e-mail address. If any substring is delimited by angle brackets, just that substring is interpreted as an e-mail address, and anything else is ignored (it is treated as a comment). Also, any substrings that are delimited by parentheses ((and)) are considered to be comments and are also ignored.

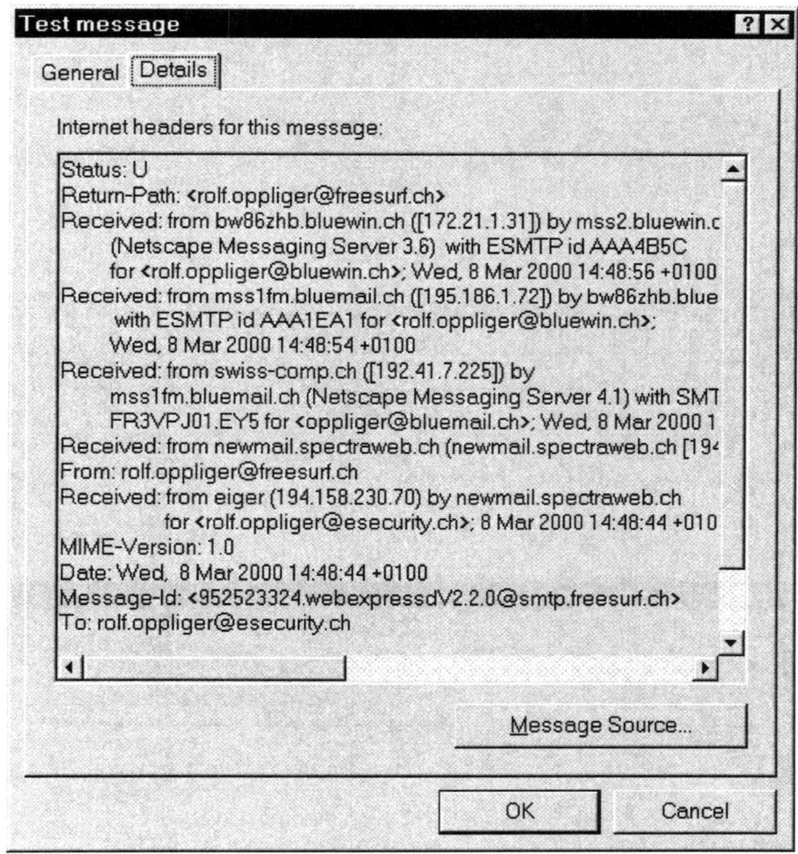

Figure 3.2 Detail Message Properties panel of Microsoft Outlook Express. © 2000 Microsoft Corporation.

Against this background, the following e-mail addresses are all equivalent to `rolf.oppliger@esecurity.ch`:

```
rolf.oppliger@esecurity.ch (Rolf Oppliger)
<rolf.oppliger@esecurity.ch>
Rolf Oppliger <rolf.oppliger@esecurity.ch>
"Rolf Oppliger" <rolf.oppliger@esecurity.ch>
```

In addition to e-mail addresses, there are also several places where timestamps may occur in RFC 822-compliant e-mail messages. Timestamps use a specific format, and this format is illustrated in the following example:

```
Date: Wed, 8 Mar 2000 14:53:03 +0100
```

Obviously, the timestamp includes the day of the week (`Wed` standing for "Wednesday"), the date[1] (`8 Mar 2000` standing for March 8, 2000), the time (`14:53:03`), and the local difference from Greenwich mean time (GMT).[2] The format of the last field is `+/-HHMM`, where `HH` denotes the hours and `MM` the minutes of the time difference. In the exemplary timestamp given above, the local difference from GMT (or UTC) is plus one hour (referring to Western Europe standard time).

The most important message headers specified in RFC 822 are overviewed and briefly discussed next. A few other headers have also been defined, but most of them are rarely (if ever) used, including, for example, the `In-Reply-To`, `References`, `Keywords`, `Comments`, and `Encrypted` message headers. Furthermore, it is possible for many headers to be prefixed with the string `Resent-` in a forwarded copy of a message. For example, a `Resent-From` header would indicate who had forwarded the message, while the `From` header would indicate the originator of the message. Finally, any header keyword not officially defined should be prefixed with `X-`. For example, if Microsoft Outlook Express version 5 was used to compose a message, the following lines could be added to the header section of the resulting message:

```
X-Priority: 3
X-MSMail-Priority: Normal
X-Mailer: Microsoft Outlook Express 5.00.2314.1300
X-MimeOLE: Produced By Microsoft MimeOLE V5.00.2314.1300
```

---

[1] The actual RFC 822 specification defines only two digits for the year, but most current software packages use four digits.

[2] GMT is the same as universal time coordinated (UTC). The different names are due to historical reasons.

In this example, the `X-Priority` and `X-MSMail-Priority` headers refer to the message priority, whereas the `X-Mailer` and `X-MimeOLE` headers refer to the UA software that is used to compose and send out the message. Unfortunately, there is no guarantee that peer UAs will interoperate and interpret `X-`prefixed message headers in exactly the same way, so their use should be minimized or avoided for critical applications. Let's overview and briefly discuss the required and optional message headers next.

Required Message Headers

There are only a few message headers that are required for RFC 822-compliant e-mail messages. These are the `Date`, `From`, and `To` headers (discussed in alphabetical order).[3]

Date: This header specifies the date and time a message was originally composed (and probably sent to the originator's MTA). We elaborated on the timestamp format above, and a corresponding `Date` header may look as follows:

```
Date: Wed, 8 Mar 2000 14:53:03 +0100
```

Unfortunately, UAs behave differently with regard to the timestamps they place in lists of received messages. While some UAs display the timestamp found in the `Date` header of a message, others display the time the message was retrieved from the recipient's MS via POP3 or IMAP4. It is even possible that some UAs show other timestamps, such as the date and time the message was received by the recipient's MTA (extracted from the first `Received` header as explained below). So take care what kind of timestamp your UA actually displays for a given e-mail message. It may or may not be the one the UA extracts from the message's `Date` header.

From: This header is typically inserted by the UA at message creation time and defines who (i.e., what e-mail account) sent out the message. If there is no `Reply-to` or `Return-Path` header, this is also the e-mail address that replies should be sent to. Again, we elaborated on the various formats that are possible to specify e-mail addresses above, and an exemplary `From` header may look as follows:

```
From: rolf.oppliger@freesurf.ch
```

[3]Note that the `To` header is not required for a message that includes either a `Cc` or a `Bcc` header.

If a user can set or change the `From` header, he can also spoof and impersonate other users at will. Consequently, a user should not have control over the `From` header, and his UA should automatically build its content based on the local user e-mail account and domain name. Unfortunately, this is seldom done, and most UAs can be configured by the user to include wrong username and e-mail address information. This should always be kept in mind when discussing the security of an e-mail system.

To: This header specifies the primary recipient(s) of the message. It includes an e-mail address or a list of e-mail addresses (separated by commas). Again, we give an exemplary `To` header:

```
To: rolf.oppliger@esecurity.ch
```

The actual message delivery is determined by protocols, such as SMTP (discussed later in this chapter). In fact, each e-mail address in a list of recipients causes the UA to launch one SMTP command.

Optional Message Headers

According to RFC 822, most message headers are optional. This is particularly true for the `Bcc`, `Cc`, `Message-Id`, `Received`, `Reply-To`, `Return-Path`, `Sender`, and `Subject` headers (again, discussed in alphabetical order).

Bcc: This header is almost identical to the `To` and `Cc` headers, except that no other recipient is aware that the names listed here are also receiving the message (the term "bcc" is an abbreviation of "blind carbon copy"). The `Bcc` header is not sent along with the message to anyone but a `Bcc` recipient. Furthermore, a more sophisticated MTA or UA would allow each `Bcc` recipient to see his e-mail address, but not the addresses of all other `Bcc` recipients.

Cc: This header (the term "cc" is an abbreviation for "carbon copy") is almost identical to the `To` header, except that a UA may not include `Cc` recipients in a "reply to all" function.

Message-Id: This header is automatically generated by a mail server for a message to include a unique identifier (replies and forwards should get different message IDs). The worldwide uniqueness of the message ID is guaranteed by the server that generates it. Typically, the `Message-Id` header is intended for a computer system or UA to read and use, and not for a human being. In fact, UAs often use the `Message-Id` headers to establish a correlation between messages, and to provide more structure than incoming and outgoing messages. As illustrated in Figure 3.2, a `Message-Id` header may look as follows:

```
Message-Id: <952523324.webexpressdV2.2.0@smtp.freesurf.ch>
```

In this example, the `Message-Id` header is generated by a mail server running on host `smtp.freesurf.ch`.

Received: This header is generated automatically by each MTA on the message delivery path. More specifically, a new `Received` header is added in front of the message each time it is received by an MTA. The aim is to document what sites the message went through and the date and time it arrived at each MTA along the message delivery path. The general format of the `Received` header is as follows:

```
Received: [from <domain>]    [by <domain>]
          [via <path>]       [with <protocol>]
          [id <message_id>] [for <addr_spec>]; <timestamp>
```

The optional fields are put in square brackets. Not all optional fields have to be included, but typically the `from` and `by` fields are. The `timestamp` field is the only field that is required. It includes the date and time at which the message was received at the MTA. The `with` field can specify protocol variants, such as Extended SMTP (ESMTP) as explained below, and is the only field that can occur multiple times. For example, the `with` field would actually be a good place to document that an e-mail message has transmitted over a cryptographically secured link (by using, for example, the IPsec protocol suite or SMTP over SSL/TLS). A hypothetical but more complete exemplary chain of `Received` headers may look as follows:

```
Received: from smtpd-extern.it-sec.com
          by mail.esecurity.ch
          with ESMTP
          id AAA6373
          for <rolf.oppliger@esecurity.ch>;
          Wed, 23 Feb 2000 14:51:18 +0100
Received: from smtp-proxy.it-sec.com
          by smtpd-extern.it-sec.com
```

```
           with SMTP
           id OAA22551
           for <rolf.oppliger@esecurity.ch>;
           Wed, 23 Feb 2000 14:51:02 +0100 (MET)
Received:  from smtpd-intern.it-sec.com
           by smtp-proxy.it-sec.com
           with SMTP
           Wed, 23 Feb 2000 14:50:54 +0100
Received:  by smtpd-intern.it-sec.com
           with SMTP
           id <FHD9K7RK>;
           Wed, 23 Feb 2000 14:50:34 +0100
```

This example refers to an e-mail message that was sent from a UA located on the intranet of iT_SEC iT_Security AG (`it-sec.com`) to my personal e-mail account (`rolf.oppliger@esecurity.ch`). More specifically, the message was first sent to an internal SMTP server running at `smtpd-intern.it-sec.com` using SMTP. From there it was sent to an SMTP proxy server running at `smtp-proxy.it-sec.com` using SMTP. Afterwards, the message was sent to the external SMTP server running at `smtpd-extern.it-sec.com` using SMTP. Finally, the message was delivered from this MTA to the recipient's MTA and mail server running at `mail.esecurity.ch`. Note that, in theory, each `Received` header that is put in front of a message should include a timestamp that refers to a later point in time as compared to the timestamp of the next `Received` header. This is true as long as all MTAs on the message delivery path have synchronized clocks. If, however, the clocks are out of synchronization, it may happen that a `Received` header includes a timestamp that refers to an earlier point in time as compared to the timestamp of the next `Received` header.

Reply-To: This header provides the e-mail address that UAs (or MTAs generating diagnostic messages, such as "mail undeliverable") should use to send replies to. If this header is not present, the e-mail address specified in the `From` header is used for replies.

Return-Path: This header is basically the same as the `Reply-To` header, but with the possibility of specifying an optional message delivery path (in addition to the recipient's e-mail address). If this header is present, it specifies the e-mail address and message delivery path that UAs (or MTAs generating diagnostic messages, such as "mail undeliverable") should use to send replies. Obviously, `Reply-To` and `Return-Path` headers should not both occur in a single message. Also, if neither a `Reply-To` nor a `Return-Path` header is present, the e-mail address specified in the `From` header should be used for replies.

Sender: This header can be used to specify the e-mail address of a person sending an e-mail message on behalf of another person (the other person is specified in the `From` header). Most MTAs automatically generate diagnostic messages, such as "mail undeliverable"). If a `Sender` header exists, this is typically the e-mail address used to send such messages to. However, few if any UAs provide any way to make use of this field other than to display it.

Subject: This header can be used to specify a subject or topic for the message. As indicated above, an exemplary `Subject` header may look as follows:

```
Subject: Test message
```

Although it is not defined in RFC 822, it is common practice for UAs to copy the content of the `Subject` header field from the message to which the user is replying into the new `Subject` header, with the string `Re:` put in front of it. Consequently, the automatically generated content of the `Subject` header field in a reply to the above-mentioned message would be `Re: Test message`. Likewise, most UAs prepend the string `Fw:` to the subject of a message that is forwarded to another recipient. Consequently, the automatically generated content of the `Subject` header field in a forwarded message would be `Fw: Test message`.

3.1.2 Message Body

Following the message headers and an empty line, an RFC 822-compliant e-mail message must include a message body. The message body, in turn, may consist of zero or more lines of data. A simple exemplary message body may look as follows:

```
This is a test message that is sent from
sender@esecurity.ch to recipient@esecurity.ch.
```

Also, a message signature may be appended automatically to messages as they are sent out by UAs, but they are not defined in RFC 822. As far as RFC 822 is concerned, a message signature (whether automatically generated or manually appended) is just the last part of the message body. There is nothing that distinguishes the message signature from arbitrary text included in the message body.

Today, message bodies often contain multiple parts containing data of different content type. In this case, it is common to use MIME as explained next.

3.1.3 MIME

The message formats and syntactical rules defined in RFC 822 are appropriate for simple e-mail messages that consist of 7-bit ASCII text. However, an increasingly large number of Internet applications generate streams that consist of binary or arbitrary 8-bit data. Also, there are applications that make use of documents with multiple parts. Consequently, there must be a way to turn such data into character streams that are transferable through various software processes, such as provided by e-mail handlers and MTAs, and that would otherwise be partly interpreted as control codes or otherwise illegal characters. In the previous chapter we have seen that there are some encoding schemes that can be used to address this problem, including, for example, the UU and base-64 (or radix-64) encoding schemes.

Roughly speaking, MIME have been developed and specified to address the problem of transporting binary or arbitrary 8-bit data possibly consisting of multiple parts as 7-bit ASCII text, and to extend the RFC 822 framework accordingly. Since this is a general problem, the resulting MIME specifications are also used and deployed by other network applications. For example, MIME is commonly used by Web servers to specify the content type of requested resources and data files. Also, MIME can be used to encapsulate electronic data interchange (EDI) objects, as further addressed in RFC 1767 [6].

The current version of the MIME specifications was submitted to the Internet standards track and has reached the status of a Draft Standard. As such, it is described in the RFC documents 2045 to 2049 [7 – 11]. The MIME specifications introduce new message headers that can be generated by the sender to instruct the recipient on how to rebuild the original data stream. More specifically, there is a total of six new message headers:

- The `Mime-Version` header indicates the MIME version that is used for the message. The header carries an additional parameter. A MIME message that conforms to the RFC documents mentioned above (RFC documents 2045 to 2049) conforms to MIME version 1 and must have this parameter value set to `1.0`.

- The `Content-Type` header describes the data contained in the message body or one of its parts with sufficient detail that the receiving UA can pick an appropriate application to render or represent the data to the user or otherwise deal with the data in an appropriate way. The `Content-Type` header is heavily used by Web servers to specify the content type of requested resources. The parameters that can be used for this message header are overviewed below.

- The `Content-Transfer-Encoding` header indicates the type of transformation that is used to represent the body of the message in a way that is transferable through the e-mail system. The header has a parameter and possible values for this parameter are `7bit`, `8bit`, `binary`, `quoted-printable`, `base64`, and `x-token` (the last value stands for a nonstandard vendor-specific or application-specific encoding scheme). Obviously, three of these values — `7bit`, `8bit`, and `binary` — indicate that no encoding has actually been used, but provide some further information about the nature of the transported data. The two true encoding schemes are `quoted-printable` and `base64`. We have addressed both of them in the previous chapter.

- The `Content-ID` header is optional and can be used to uniquely identify a MIME entity in multiple contexts.

- The `Content-Description` header is optional and can be used to further describe the body of a MIME entity (e.g., a caption that might be displayed along with an image file).

- The `Content-Disposition` header is optional and can be used to specify what to do with a MIME entity by the receiving UA.

Any or all of these headers may appear in an RFC 822-compliant message header section. An implementation compliant to the MIME specifications must support at least the `MIME-Version`, `Content-Type`, and `Content-Transfer-Encoding` headers. The implementation of the other headers mentioned above, namely `Content-ID`, `Content-Description`, and `Content-Disposition` headers, is optional and left to the developers. Consequently, these headers may be ignored by a receiving MIME-enabled UA.

As mentioned above, the MIME specifications define a number of MIME content types that are used to standardize the representation of multimedia data. In essence, a content type is used to specify the general type of data, whereas an additional subtype may be used to specify a particular format for that content type. Table

Table 3.1
MIME Content Types and Subtypes

Type	Subtype	Description
`text`	`plain`	Unformatted text (e.g., ASCII or ISO-8859).
	`enriched`	MIME enriched text (according to RFC 1896).
`multipart`	`mixed`	The message includes multiple subparts, with no particular relationship between them.
	`alternative`	Similar to `multipart/mixed`, except that the various subparts are different versions of the same message (e.g., one ASCII file and one RTF file with the same contents).
	`parallel`	Similar to `multipart/mixed`, except that all the subparts are intended to be displayed together (e.g., one audio and one video file).
	`digest`	Similar to `multipart/mixed`, except that each subpart is an RFC 822-compliant message of its own.
`message`	`rfc822`	E-mail message that conforms to RFC 822.
	`partial`	Used to allow fragmentation of large messages into a number of parts, which must be reassembled at the destination.
	`external-body`	Pointer to an object that exists elsewhere.
`image`	`gif`	Data in GIF image format.
	`jpeg`	Data in JPEG image format.
`video`	`mpeg`	Data in MPEG video format.
`audio`	`basic`	Data in standard audio format.
`application`	`postscript`	Data in Postscript format.
	`octet-stream`	Binary data consisting of 8-bit bytes.

3.1 summarizes the 7 content types and a total of 15 subtypes that are specified in RFC 2046 [8]. The MIME `multipart` type indicates that the message body contains multiple parts. In this case, the `Content-Type` header includes a parameter, called a boundary, that defines the delimiter string between the body parts of the message. The boundary, in turn, is a string of characters that should not appear elsewhere in the message. Each boundary starts on a new line and consists of two hyphens followed by the delimiter string. The final boundary, which indicates the end of the last part, also has a suffix of two hyphens. Within each part, there may be optional MIME headers.

Because MIME was defined in such a way as to easily incorporate extensions, there is a central registry to locate information about MIME content types.[4] During

[4]`ftp://ftp.isi.edu/in-notes/iana/assignments/media-types/`

the past couple of years, many MIME content types and subtypes have been defined in addition to the ones listed in Table 3.1. Note, however, that MIME is fast evolving, and that the corresponding MIME specifications are moving targets. Due to their richness and dynamics, few vendors have chosen to support all MIME features. Most are using them to do only a slightly cleaner version of what the above-mentioned encoding schemes do. When vendors eventually support all MIME features, Internet messaging will have most of the advanced capabilities of the best proprietary e-mail systems but in a form that is optimized for, and capable of supporting, worldwide interoperation.

Let's briefly look at some examples to get a better feeling for the structure of MIME messages. We start with an exemplary `Test message 1` that illustrates a simple single-part MIME message:

```
From: sender@esecurity.ch
To: recipient@esecurity.ch
Subject: Test message 1
Mime-Version: 1.0
Content-Type: text/plain; charset="us-ascii"

This is a MIME test message that is sent from
sender@esecurity.ch to recipient@esecurity.ch.
```

In addition to the required `From`, `To`, and `Subject` headers, a single-part MIME message should also include a `Mime-Version` and a `Content-Type` header. In short, the `Mime-Version` header specifies the MIME version currently in use (version `1.0` in the exemplary test message given above), whereas the `Content-Type` header specifies the content type of the message. As indicated in Table 3.1, there are many MIME types and subtypes that have been defined so far. In the first exemplary test message, `text/plain; charset="us-ascii"` is used to refer to plain text encoded in the ASCII character set. This is also the default value for the `Content-Type` header if none is specified. Alternatively, `text/plain; charset="ISO-8859-X"` could be used to refer to an extended character set defined in ISO-8859-X (the value of X choosing any character set in the family of ISO/IEC 8859 standards).

As mentioned above, a MIME message can also include multiple parts (MIME entities). The following exemplary `Test message 2` illustrates the format of a multipart message. The message includes a message body and two Postscript files as attachments (`example1.ps` and `example2.ps`):

```
From: sender@esecurity.ch
```

```
To: recipient@esecurity.ch
Subject: Test message 2
Mime-Version: 1.0
Content-Type: multipart/mixed; boundary="<mime-boundary>"

--<mime-boundary>
Content-Type: plain/text; charset="us-ascii"

This is a multipart test message.

--<mime-boundary>
Content-Type: application/postscript; name="example1.ps"
Content-Transfer-Encoding: base64
Content-Disposition: attachment; filename="example1.ps"

...
--<mime-boundary>
Content-Type: application/postscript; name="example2.ps"
Content-Transfer-Encoding: base64
Content-Disposition: attachment; filename="example2.ps"

...
--<mime-boundary>--
```

In this exemplary test message 2, the base-64 encoded Postscript data is indicated with three dots and the `Content-Type` header indicates a MIME multipart document. In fact, there are several MIME multipart content subtypes that can be used for more than one part in a single message (the subtypes are summarized in Table 3.1). In this example, the header line `Content-Type: multipart/mixed; boundary="<mime-boundary>"` indicates that the message body includes a MIME multipart document with no particular relationship between its parts, and that `<mime-boundary>` is used to separate its parts. According to the MIME specifications, `<mime-boundary>` can be an arbitrary delimiter string, such as `=====================_22014995==_`, or any other string that is not likely to appear in the message. In either case, the MIME delimiter string is prefixed with two hyphens and the final delimiter string (the one after the last part of the MIME message) is additionally postfixed with two hyphens.

Since the use of MIME must be signaled with some specific message headers (as discussed above), it is generally not possible to encode a file using a stand-alone MIME encoder, import it into a non-MIME UA, and send it out from there. To send a MIME-encoded message, the encoding software must be integrated into the UA. A MIME-enabled UA, in turn, can recognize an attachment that consists only of plain ASCII text and transmit it in its original form. If only a few characters are outside the ASCII character set, then just those characters can be encoded using the printed-quotable encoding scheme. In the case of arbitrary binary or 8-bit data, however, it is better to encode the entire attachment into ASCII text using either the base-64 or UU encoding scheme. According to the MIME specifications, support for the base-64 encoding scheme is mandatory, whereas support for the UU encoding is optional.

In general, MIME can be extended in several ways for specific purposes. For example, we have already mentioned in the introductory chapter that there are at least two MIME extensions to provide security services: MOSS and S/MIME. Furthermore, PGP can be used in conjunction with MIME and the resulting specifications are sometimes also referred to as PGP/MIME. Contrary to MOSS and S/MIME, however, PGP can also be used with UAs that do not know anything about MIME and PGP/MIME. This is in contrast to MOSS and S/MIME that both require MIME-enabled UAs. PGP and PGP/MIME are addressed in Part II of this book, whereas S/MIME is discussed in Part III.

3.2 MESSAGE TRANSFER PROTOCOLS

There are several application layer protocols involved in the transfer of e-mail messages. In this section, we address the SMTP and ESMTP.

3.2.1 SMTP

SMTP is the Internet standard application protocol for transporting e-mail messages between systems — either UAs or MTAs — that provide support for TCP/IP networking. More specifically, SMTP is used to upload an e-mail message from a UA to an MTA, and to transfer the message from one MTA to another. The final MTA delivers the message to a MS where it may be retrieved by the receiving UA at some later point in time. As mentioned in the beginning of this chapter, the first solid version of SMTP was specified in RFC 821 in 1982 [5], together with RFC 822 that specifies the message formats and syntactical rules [4].

As its name suggests, the basic SMTP (i.e., SMTP without extensions) is a very simple protocol. It requires TCP as its underlying transport layer protocol to ensure a connection-oriented and reliable data delivery service. An SMTP server (or daemon) typically runs at the "well-known" service port 25. Once a TCP connection is established to this port and the server sends a greeting, the entire SMTP session is controlled by the client (either a UA or a peer MTA). The client sends an SMTP command to the server, and the server responds accordingly. Both the SMTP command and response messages are ASCII strings followed by a `<CR><LF>` sequence of control codes. Each SMTP command that is sent from the client to the server consists of a four-letter code (e.g., HELO, DATA, ...) usually followed by another ASCII string that represents an argument. Similarly, each response that is sent from the server back to the client consists of a three-digit numeric response code, followed by optional explanatory text (e.g., a `250 OK` message). The four SMTP response code classes are summarized in Table 3.2. Let's briefly overview and discuss SMTP software and commands next.

Table 3.2
SMTP Response Code Classes

Code	Explanatory text
2xx	Request accepted and processed
3xx	Ready to receive message text
4xx	Some service unavailable, possibly temporarily
5xx	Error, request rejected

SMTP Software

An SMTP server (or daemon) is the software program that implements SMTP on the server side. It is typically called `smtpd`, an acronym standing for SMTP daemon. `Smtpd` software is available for all major platforms, including, for example, UNIX and Windows NT:

- The classic freeware UNIX `smtpd` software package is Sendmail;[5]
- Microsoft does not include an SMTP server with Windows NT, but the Exchange Server includes a kind of SMTP server called Internet Mail Services

[5]Sendmail has a long history with security-related bugs and corresponding patches.

(formerly known as Internet Mail Connector), which is basically a gateway between Exchange Server and SMTP-based e-mail systems.

An SMTP client is the software program that implements SMTP on the client-side. As of this writing, SMTP clients are integrated into most UAs for Internet messaging, such as Netscape Messenger and Microsoft Outlook Express. Most of these UAs also provide support for message store access protocols (e.g., POP3 and IMAP4) and directory protocols (e.g., LDAP) as discussed later in this chapter.

SMTP Commands

As mentioned above, SMTP command and response messages are composed of ASCII characters and terminated with a `<CR><LF>` sequence of control codes. Similar to DNS names (e.g., host or domain names), SMTP command and response messages are not case sensitive. Note, however, that this is not necessarily true for the user part in an e-mail address (e.g., `rolf.oppliger` in `rolf.oppliger@esecurity.ch`). Some network operating systems take this part to identify the MS of the receiving user, and if the network operating system is case sensitive it matters whether the characters are lowercase or uppercase. Consequently, it is important that SMTP implementations preserve the case of the user part in an e-mail address (on the entire message delivery path).

When specifying the general format of SMTP command and response messages, arguments (or special symbols) will be denoted by meta-linguistic variables (or constants), such as `<string>` or `<reverse-path>`. In this case, the angle brackets (`<` and `>`) are used to refer to meta-linguistic variables. Unfortunately, some arguments use angle brackets literally. For example, a reverse-path is always enclosed in angle brackets (i.e., `<rolf.oppliger@esecurity.ch>` is an instance of `<reverse-path>`, and the angle brackets are actually transmitted in the corresponding SMTP command and response messages).

There are several SMTP commands a client can use to interact with a server, but an SMTP transaction typically involves the following three steps:

- First, the transaction starts with a MAIL command that provides sender information;
- Second, a series of one (or more) RCPT command(s) follows to inform the server about the recipient(s) of the message;
- Third, the actual message is provided as part of a DATA command.

We briefly overview the most important commands next. Further information can be obtained from [1 – 3] or the referenced RFC documents.

HELO: This command is used to specify the client's domain name to the server. It must be the first command following the TCP connection establishment to the service port (usually port 25). The syntax of this command is as follows:

```
HELO [<host>.]<domain>
```

Consequently, the sender may optionally specify its host name in addition to its domain name. A more concrete example for this command would be as follows:

```
HELO esecurity.ch
```

In this case, no host name is specified in addition to the domain name `esecurity.ch`.

MAIL: As mentioned above, the first step in the procedure of transmitting an e-mail message is the MAIL command. It is used to specify the sender of the message or a reverse-path (a path by which a message can be sent back to its originator). The syntax of the MAIL command is as follows:

```
MAIL FROM: <reverse-path>
```

More specifically, the <reverse-path> argument specifies who sent the message or how its sender can be reached in terms of a reverse-path. The MAIL command tells the SMTP server that a new mail transaction is starting and that it should therefore reset its state tables and buffers (i.e., the reverse-path, forward-path, and mail data buffers). Finally, the reverse-path buffer should be set to the specified value of the argument. If accepted, the server should return a `250 OK` response message.

RCPT: This command is used to specify one (or several) recipient(s) for an e-mail message. In fact, any number of recipients can be accumulated, one per RCPT command. The general syntax of the RCPT command is as follows:

```
RCPT TO: <forward-path>
```

In this case, the <forward-path> argument specifies a source route to reach the recipient's MS. On receipt of the RCPT command, the server should set its forward-path buffer to the specified value of the argument. If a list of hosts is specified, it is a source route and indicates that the message should be relayed to the next host on that particular list. In fact, the server has the choice to either relay the message or reject it (depending on its configuration settings). If it does relay the message, it must remove its own name from the front of the forward-path and put its name to the front of the reverse-path. For example, host `h1.esecurity.ch` may receive a message with the following two SMTP commands:

```
MAIL FROM: <rolf.oppliger@freesurf.ch>
RCPT TO: <@h1.esecurity.ch,@h2.esecurity.ch:test@h3.esecurity.ch>
```

The SMTP server running on `h1.esecurity.ch` should relay the message with headers changed as follows:

```
MAIL FROM: <@h1.esecurity.ch:rolf.oppliger@freesurf.ch>
RCPT TO: <@h2.esecurity.ch:test@h3.esecurity.ch>
```

This replacement scheme is repeated on each host on the forward-path (message delivery path). Note that this style of relaying is actually a holdover from the days when DNS was not yet put in place and routes had to be specified explicitly by the sender of an e-mail message. Today, it is more likely that the following pair of SMTP commands is used instead:

```
MAIL FROM: <rolf.oppliger@freesurf.ch>
RCPT TO: <test@esecurity.ch>
```

In this case, the SMTP server realizes that the message is not for the local domain and relays it directly to the server of `esecurity.ch`. More specifically, it contacts the registered DNS server for `esecurity.ch` to get the actual IP address of the SMTP server for `esecurity.ch` (resulting in `h3.esecurity.ch` in this example). It establishes a TCP connection to (port 25 of) this IP address and sends the message directly to the server for the local MS of user `test`.

DATA: This command requests the server to prepare to receive the body text of the message.

In Chapter 1 we said that it is possible to establish a TCP connection to an SMTP or mail server (usually running at port 25), and directly use SMTP commands to launch a spoofing attack. In fact, such an attack only uses the three basic

SMTP commands we know so far (the MAIL, RCPT, and DATA commands). The transcript of such an attack is as follows:

```
220 ...
MAIL FROM: administrator@exemplarysite.com
250 OK
RCPT TO: victim@exemplarysite.com
250 OK
DATA
...
Arbitrary text entered by the attacker.
.
250 OK
QUIT
```

First, the attacker establishes a TCP connection to the SMTP server and the server replies with a 220 response code (the additional text is denoted with three dots in the attack transcript). The attacker enters the MAIL command with the spoofed e-mail address or return-path as argument. In the example given above, the fictitious e-mail address `administrator@exemplarysite.com` is put as an argument for the MAIL command. Note that in a real attack scenario this address is likely to be set to the local system or security administrator's e-mail address. The server, in turn, replies with a `250 OK` status code. Next, the attacker enters the RCPT command with the attacked e-mail address or forward-path as argument. In the example given above, the fictitious e-mail address `victim@exemplarysite.com` is put as an argument for the RCPT command. Again, the server replies with a `250 OK` status code. The attacker now launches the DATA command, and the server may reply with a status code and some instructions on how to enter the message body (again, we use three dots to refer to the server's textual response). In either case, the attacker may enter an arbitrary text and finish the message body with a line that contains only a single dot (.). In a realistic attack scenario, this text would contain a request to change a password to a specific value. For example, the text may look as follows:

```
Dear user,

Due to some necessary system update and reconfiguration, we must ask
you to set your password to the temporary value "er45w.jk." As soon
as we have finished work, we'll let you know and you can change your
```

```
password to the old value again. Thanks for your cooperation.

Your system administrator
```

If the attacker spoofed the local system or security administrator's e-mail address in the MAIL command, it is possible and very likely that an innocent user would comply with the request and change his password to a value that is now known to the attacker. Finally, the attacker launches the QUIT command to terminate the SMTP session and TCP connection to the mail server. Afterwards, the SMTP server delivers the message to the e-mail address specified in the RCPT command.

Note that this kind of spoofing attack is simple and efficient, but it is also simple to detect and defeat.

- For example, the SMTP server can be configured in a way that it accepts only local e-mail addresses as arguments to the MAIL command;

- An SMTP proxy server running at the firewall of a corporate intranet can enforce the policy that MAIL commands for outgoing messages cannot comprise external e-mail addresses as arguments;

- Similarly, the same SMTP proxy server can enforce the policy that MAIL commands for incoming messages cannot comprise internal e-mail addresses as arguments;

- Finally and most importantly, the recipient of a spoofed e-mail address can generally detect the attack by having a closer look at the message source and all of its `Received` headers. Remember from our previous discussions that the `Received` headers define a reverse-path to the message originator. It is generally easy to decide whether a reverse-path matches a given sender address.

Note, however, that neither the message nor its headers are authenticated by using standard Internet messaging techniques. So it may be the case that somebody is faking e-mail messages (with all of its headers) that look fine and cannot be detected as being faked. If you want to protect yourself against these kinds of spoofing attacks, you have to enter the field of cryptography and cryptographic protocols. In fact, both technological approaches addressed in this book — PGP and S/MIME — protect against this kind of spoofing attacks.

VRFY: This optional command confirms that a string provided as an argument identifies an existing local e-mail account. If it does, the full name of the user and the fully specified e-mail address are returned. The syntax of the command is `VRFY <string>`, where `<string>` refers to the string argument. There are security concerns related to the VRFY command, and many system or security administrators disable it accordingly.

EXPN: This optional command can be used to expand a mailing list name to a list of subscribed e-mail addresses. The response is typically multiline, each of which contains one e-mail address. The syntax of the command is `EXPN <string>`, where `<string>` refers to a mailing list name. Similar to the VRFY command, there are security concerns related to the EXPN command, and many system or security administrators disable it accordingly.

HELP: This optional command is intended for use by someone accessing an SMTP server interactively (e.g., via Telnet). It typically lists the available SMTP commands with their corresponding syntax.

RSET: This command aborts the current mail transaction. Any processed sender, recipients, and mail data are discarded, and all buffers and state tables are emptied (to return to the state immediately after the HELO command).

NOOP: This command does nothing other than verify that the receiving SMTP server is still alive or keep it from timing out.

QUIT: This command terminates the SMTP session. The server should reply with a 250 response code and close the SMTP session and TCP connection accordingly. A client should not close the connection until it receives the 250 reply.

Other Commands: If a message is delivered to a terminal instead of a MS, the SEND, send or mail (SOML), send and mail (SAML) commands can be used instead of the MAIL command. Also, there is an optional TURN command to specify that the recipient must either send an acceptance reply and then take on the role of the sender, or send a refusal reply and retain the role of the recipient. The TURN command was used to successfully attack SMTP servers in the past. It has therefore been deprecated by the most recent SMTP specifications.

3.2.2 Extended SMTP

Although the message formats and syntactical rules defined in RFC 822 and the SMTP defined in RFC 821 were properly designed and worked well for more than a decade, people wanted to add new and more sophisticated features to Internet messaging. To keep this orderly and to prevent multiple incompatible variants of message transfer protocols from emerging, a mechanism was created to extend the basic SMTP in a controlled way that would ensure backward compatibility. The result is known as ESMTP and has been specified in several RFC documents. The most recent and current version of ESMTP is specified in RFC 1869 [12] and some related documents.

The basic idea of ESMTP is to enhance the basic SMTP handshake between the sender and the recipient to signal support of ESMTP. More specifically, a new extended HELO (EHLO) command is introduced that identifies a sender as supporting ESMTP, and to which the recipient must respond with a list of extensions it supports. Some of the extensions introduce new commands. If either the sender or the recipient does not support ESMTP, they will only use basic SMTP commands. If, however, an ESMTP sender connects to an ESMTP recipient, the sender starts off with the EHLO command, which the recipient recognizes and responds with a multiline answer. The first line of this answer must contain the usual `250 <receiver's domain>` string, whereas the succeeding lines list the ESMTP extensions the recipient actually supports, one per line, such as `250 <extension name>`. All response lines but the final one must follow the 250 with a hyphen instead of a space to indicate that at least one additional response line will follow.

If an ESMTP recipient at `esecurity.ch` understood the SIZE and EXPN extensions, and an ESMTP sender connected to it, the first response line would look as follows:

```
220 esecurity.ch ESMTP Service Ready
```

The ESMTP specification does not require the server to announce its ESMTP support and to send back an `ESMTP Service Ready` message accordingly. In practice, server implementors can put anything they want after the domain name following the 220 status code. In the example given above, the sender knows that the recipient (the SMTP server) supports ESMTP. He sends an EHLO command to the recipient to get a response that looks as follows:

```
250-esecurity.ch
```

```
250-SIZE
250 EXPN
```

Afterwards, the client can start sending SMTP and supported ESMTP commands to the server. Let's overview and briefly discuss some important SMTP extensions next.

Message Size Declaration

The first extension beyond the basic SMTP commands specified in RFC 821 is message size declaration as defined in RFC 1870 [13] (also part of STD 10). The aim of this extension is to guide the server on how much storage may be required for the message to be sent.

When a client connects to an ESMTP server using the EHLO command, the server may announce its support for message size declaration by adding the keyword SIZE to the list of extensions (as illustrated in the example above). With or without a parameter, this indicates that the client may include the SIZE parameter in the MAIL command (and optionally also in the SEND, SOML, and SAML commands). If no parameter is specified, no conclusions can be drawn by the client concerning the maximum message size the server supports. If a parameter of zero is specified, that indicates that no maximum message size is enforced by the server. Otherwise, the parameter should be a numeric value, which is the maximum message size in bytes the server will accept. For example, in the example given above, the server may want to indicate that it will not accept any message larger than 10,000 bytes. In this case, the server's response would look as follows:

```
250-esecurity.ch
250-SIZE 10000
250 EXPN
```

On the other side, a client can specify the actual size of a message (in bytes) with a new parameter in the MAIL command. For example, if `rolf.oppliger@esecurity.ch` wanted to send a message that's 876 bytes long, his ESMTP-enabled UA would send the following MAIL command to the server:

```
MAIL FROM:<rolf.oppliger@esecurity.ch> SIZE=876
```

Command Pipelining

RFC 1854 [14] defines a way to increase throughput by batching multiple SMTP commands into a single TCP connection, if the recipient can handle it. To announce that it can accept batched (or "pipelined") commands, the recipient advertises the keyword PIPELINING in response to the EHLO command. No new commands are defined, nor are any new parameters defined for the MAIL command. If the recipient indicates support for command pipelining, the sender can issue multiple SMTP commands without waiting for any response from the recipient. This is particularly helpful in specifying multiple recipients for a message (using, for example, a series of RCPT commands).

8bit-MIME Transport

The 8bit-MIMEtransport extension as specified in RFC 1652 [15] supports the sending of characters beyond the ASCII character set. The ESMTP keyword for this extension is 8BITMIME (with no additional parameter). A new BODY parameter defined for the MAIL command can be used to indicate whether the message body contains only 7-bit ASCII text (indicated by BODY=7BIT) or can also contain extended 8-bit characters (indicated by BODY=8BITMIME).

Large and Binary MIME Messages

Experimental RFC 1830 [16] defines mechanisms to use an e-mail system to efficiently transfer large quantities of binary data. Unfortunately, the mechanisms are not widely implemented and deployed. More specifically, RFC 1830 defines the following two extensions:

- The CHUNKING extension provides an alternative to the DATA command (called BDAT) and a more efficient way of sending large messages. Before a sender can use the BDAT command and corresponding method of sending message content, he must see the CHUNKING keyword during an ESMTP handshake with the SMTP receiver. Afterwards, he can send one or more BDAT blocks (a BDAT block is a BDAT command followed by data).

- The BINARYMIME extension adds a new parameter (BINARYMIME) to the BODY keyword of the MAIL command, as defined in the 8bit-MIMEtransport extension. An SMTP sender cannot use the BINARYMIME extension unless he sees the BINARYMIME keyword from the corresponding SMTP receiver during the ESMTP handshake.

The CHUNKING extension can be implemented without the BINARYMIME extension and would be useful without it, whereas the BINARYMIME extension works only in conjunction with the CHUNKING extension.

Remote Message Queue Starting

As mentioned previously, the original SMTP command TURN has been deprecated due to some serious security concerns. RFC 1985 [17] defines an extended TURN (ETRN) command that addresses these concerns.

Other SMTP Extensions

In addition to the extensions mentioned above, RFC 1869 [12] (also part of STD 10) defines a way for new extensions to be registered, as well as a way to create proprietary or local extensions. It also provides for an optional parameter to follow the keyword, but none of the initial extensions requires one.

The *delivery status notification* (DSN) mechanism as specified in RFCs 1891 to 1894 [18 – 21] can be used to track the actual delivery status of an e-mail message. DSN is a new feature, and only a few vendors actually support it. To make things worse, DSN must be supported by the sending UA and all MTAs along the message delivery path for it to work correctly. In comparison, for MIME to work, it must be supported only by both the sending and the receiving UAs, but not necessarily by any MTAs inbetween.

More recently, an IETF Message Tracking Protocol (MSGTRK) WG[6] has been established within the IETF Applications Area to "design a diagnostic protocol for a message originator to request information about the submission, transport, and delivery of a message regardless of its delivery status." It is currently not clear to what extent work in this WG differs from the work that is done with regard to DSN.

3.3 MESSAGE STORE ACCESS PROTOCOLS

As of this writing, there are two major protocols that are used to access a MS located at an MTA (namely POP and IMAP). Both protocols are briefly overviewed in this section and fully described in [1 – 3] (examples may be found in [2]).

[6]`http://www.ietf.org/html.charters/msgtrk-charter.html`

3.3.1 POP

The *Post Office Protocol* (POP) is the most commonly used protocol to have a UA retrieve e-mail messages from one or several MSs. In the future, we'll probably see POP being replaced by IMAP, but POP will continue to be supported as a legacy message store access protocol for many years to come. POP has been through quite an evolution:

- The first version of the POP was described in RFC 918 back in 1984;
- The protocol went through major changes, and POP version 2 (POP2) was specified in RFC 937 one year later in 1985;
- Again, the protocol went through major changes, and the current version of POP is version 3 (POP3). As such, it is specified in RFC 1939 (STD 53) [22] and is accompanied by two related RFC documents [23,24].

A POP3 server (or daemon) is the software program that implements the protocol on the server side. It is usually called `pop3d`, an acronym standing for "POP3 daemon." The classic freeware UNIX `pop3d` software package is called Popper. Microsoft does not include a POP3 server with Windows NT, but there is a POP3 frontend in Exchange Server that allows an SMTP/POP3 UA to retrieve messages from an Exchange Server message store. However, at least one `pop3d` software package is commercially available from Microsoft as well. POP3 clients are built into most Internet UAs that are available today, including, for example, Microsoft Outlook Express.

Similar to SMTP, POP3 is a simple client/server protocol implemented over a reliable transport service, such as provided by TCP. The POP3 server typically runs at port 110. It sends a greeting in response to a new TCP connection, then the client (typically a UA) repeats a cycle of sending a command and waiting for the server's response. Each command and response is a short sequence of ASCII characters, followed by a `<CR><LF>` sequence of control codes.

From a security point of view, user authentication is a highly relevant topic. POP3 actually supports three authentication mechanisms:

- The first authentication mechanism involves sending a username (with the USER command) and password (with the PASS command) unencrypted from the client to the server;

- The second authentication mechanism is optional and involves sending a one-way hash value of the user's password and some additional information from the client to the server (APOP command);

- The third authentication mechanism is also optional and separately defined in RFC 1734 (AUTH command) [24]. It involves using one of several cryptographic authentication schemes defined for IMAP, such as S/Key, Kerberos, or GSSAPI.

Password-based authentication is by far the most widely used user authentication mechanism for POP3. However, it is also the most vulnerable due to the fact that the username and password are transmitted in the clear over the network. APOP and AUTH authentication are to protect against simple replay attacks:

- If a POP3 server supports APOP, its greeting includes a timestamp. The basic idea of APOP authentication is for the client to take the timestamp from the greeting, append a shared secret (a string known only to the server and the client), produce an MD5 one-way hash value from the resulting string, and send the username and the hash value back to the server as arguments to the APOP command. The server, in turn, will append the shared secret to the timestamp it sent, produce an MD5 hash value of the resulting string, and compare it with the received hash value from the client's APOP command.

- With AUTH authentication, no change is usually required to the greeting from the POP3 server (that greeting may or may not include a timestamp, depending on whether the POP3 server also supports APOP authentication). The AUTH command itself specifies only the desired cryptographic authentication scheme. Afterwards, the handshake continues according to the selected authentication scheme.

Furthermore, POP3 can also be layered on top of the Secure Sockets Layer (SSL) or Transport Layer Security (TLS) protocol. For the resulting POP3S (POP3 over TLS/SSL) protocol, the relevant IETF body has assigned the well-known port number 995. Using POP3S, the client and server can mutually authenticate each other and transparently encrypt the data traffic between them.

Since the topic of this book is secure messaging, we are not going to delve into the details of the various authentication mechanisms that can be used between the POP3 (or POP3S) client and server. Note, however, that this is a highly relevant topic for all practical purposes.

3.3.2 IMAP

The *Internet Message Access Protocol* (IMAP) is a newer and more advanced alternative to POP3. It is used, for example, by people using the Nokia Communicator to access their message stores over mobile networks. The current version of IMAP is version 4 (IMAP4). It is specified in RFCs 2060 to 2062 [25 – 27]. Again, refer to [2] for a detailed description of IMAP4 commands with examples. Further information about IMAP in general, and IMAP4 in particular, is also available from an organization called "The IMAP Connection" at `http://www.imap.org`.

Like SMTP and POP3, IMAP4 is connection-oriented and assumes a reliable transport service with built-in flow control, so it typically is implemented on top of TCP (using port 143). IMAP4 can be used to do everything that POP3 does. It also supports keeping messages in multiple mailboxes on the central server for access from any number of sites. It allows more sophisticated and selective retrieval of information than does POP3. For example, an obvious advantage for a dial-up user is that not all messages are necessarily downloaded from the MS, but only the message headers. This is particularly useful for low-bandwidth dial-up connections, for example, using SLIP or PPP, or if the MS holds many messages with large attachments. Furthermore, IMAP4 also supports public folders, server-based searching, and various other advanced features not available with POP3. The disadvantage is that IMAP4 also places far more demands on the server and the underlying MS than does POP3.

Due to its advanced features, IMAP will likely replace POP as the primary MS access protocol over the next few years. In the meantime, however, a mail server that supports IMAP4 typically also provides POP3 support as a parallel MS access protocol and mechanism.

More recently, the use of IMAP4 on top of the SSL/TLS protocol has also been specified, and the relevant IETF body has assigned the well-known port number 993 for IMAPS (IMAP over SSL/TLS). Similar to POP3S, using IMAPS, the client and server can mutually authenticate each other and transparently encrypt the data traffic between them. Again, the security of IMAP4 is not further addressed in this book.

3.4 DIRECTORY ACCESS PROTOCOLS

There are various approaches to setting up directory services for the Internet. Simple examples include services provided by protocols, such as Finger, Ph (short for "phone book"), or Whois. More sophisticated examples include directory services that conform to the X.500 series of ITU-T recommendations. Mainly for scalability reasons, a directory service for the Internet should follow a highly distributed approach, and ITU-T X.500 does so.

It is commonly agreed that a UA must provide access to various directory services, and there are several protocols that can be used to provide this access. For example, the *Directory Access Protocol* (DAP) has been specified in conjunction with the X.500 directory services. Unfortunately, DAP has two primary disadvantages:

- First, it requires an OSI protocol stack (or at least an RFC 1006 "short stack" on top of TCP/IP [28]);
- Second, it is a fairly complex protocol and much of its flexibility is not really necessary for typical use.

To address both disadvantages, a simplified version of DAP has been developed at the University of Michigan. In this simplified version, some of the more complex features of DAP have been removed to make it simpler and faster to implement. Also, the requirement for an OSI protocol stack has been removed and replaced with the ability to work with standard Internet transport layer protocols (e.g., UDP and TCP). The resulting protocol has been named *Lightweight Directory Access Protocol* (LDAP) and is specified in RFC 1777 [29]. As such, LDAP is submitted for the Internet standards track and is widely used and deployed on the Internet today. For example, many Web browsers provide support for LDAP.

More recently, the use of LDAP on top of the SSL/TLS protocol has also been specified, and the relevant IETF body has assigned the well-known port number 636 for LDAPS (LDAP over SSL/TLS). Similar to POP3S and IMPAS, LDAPS allows a client and server to mutually authenticate each other and to transparently encrypt the data traffic between them.

3.5 CONCLUSIONS

In this chapter, we overviewed and briefly discussed the message formats and protocols that are used for Internet messaging. With few exceptions, the Internet messaging protocols are widely implemented and deployed today. This is particularly true for SMTP and POP3. With regard to directory services and corresponding directory access protocols, the situation is worse. The DAP and LDAP are not (yet) widely implemented in UA software and support for them is one of the major distinguishing features for otherwise very comparable UA products.

Finally, it is important to note that — due to its own success — Internet messaging is undergoing dramatic and rapid evolution. Existing standards are being revised and new standards are being introduced (possibly replacing the old standards). One example is IMAP4 replacing POP3; another example is ESMTP replacing SMTP. Also, there are several nontrivial extensions that collectively bring Internet messaging near the functionality of more sophisticated proprietary messaging schemes. This is particularly true for the delivery status notification and message tracking mechanisms that are useful for commercial applications. It will be interesting to see in what directions Internet messaging will evolve in the future.

REFERENCES

[1] B.F. Shimmin, *Effective E-mail Clearly Explained: File Transfer, Security, and Interoperability*, AP Professional, 1997.

[2] L. Hughes, *Internet E-Mail: Protocols, Standards, and Implementations*, Artech House, Norwood, MA, 1998.

[3] D. Strom, and M.T. Rose, *Internet Messaging*, Prentice Hall, Upper Saddle River, NJ, 1998.

[4] D.H. Crocker, "Standard for ARPA Internet Text Messages," Request for Comments 822 (STD 11), August 1982.

[5] J.B. Postel, "Simple Mail Transfer Protocol," Request for Comments 821 (part of STD 10), August 1982.

[6] D. Crocker, "MIME Encapsulation of EDI Objects," Request for Comments 1767, March 1995.

[7] N. Freed, and N. Borenstein, "Multipurpose Internet Mail Extensions (MIME) Part One: Format of Internet Message Bodies," Request for Comments 2045, November 1996.

[8] N. Freed, and N. Borenstein, "Multipurpose Internet Mail Extensions (MIME) Part Two: Media Types," Request for Comments 2046, November 1996.

[9] K. Moore, "MIME (Multipurpose Internet Mail Extensions) Part Three: Message Header Extensions for Non-ASCII Text," Request for Comments 2047, November 1996.

[10] N. Freed, J. Klensin, and J. Postel, "Multipurpose Internet Mail Extensions (MIME) Part Four: Registration Procedures," Request for Comments 2048, November 1996.

[11] N. Freed, and N. Borenstein, "Multipurpose Internet Mail Extensions (MIME) Part Five: Conformance Criteria and Examples," Request for Comments 2049, November 1996.

[12] J. Klensin, N. Freed, M. Rose, E. Stefferud, and D. Crocker, "SMTP Service Extensions," Request for Comments 1869 (part of STD 10), November 1995.

[13] J. Klensin, N. Freed, and K. Moore, "SMTP Service Extension for Message Size Declaration," Request for Comments 1870 (part of STD 10), November 1995.

[14] N. Freed, and A. Cargille, "SMTP Service Extension for Command Pipelining," Request for Comments 1854, October 1995.

[15] J. Klensin, N. Freed, M. Rose, E. Stefferud, and D. Crocker, "SMTP Service Extension for 8bit-MIMEtransport," Request for Comments 1652, July 1994.

[16] G. Vaudreuil, "SMTP Service Extensions for Transmission of Large and Binary MIME Messages," Request for Comments 1830, August 1995.

[17] J. De Winter, "SMTP Service Extension for Remote Message Queue Starting," Request for Comments 1985, August 1996.

[18] K. Moore, "SMTP Service Extension for Delivery Status Notifications," Request for Comments 1891, January 1996.

[19] G. Vaudreuil, "The Multipart/Report Content Type for the Reporting of Mail System Administrative Messages," Request for Comments 1892, January 1996.

[20] G. Vaudreuil, "Enhanced Mail System Status Codes," Request for Comments 1893, January 1996.

[21] K. Moore, and G. Vaudreuil, "An Extensible Message Format for Delivery Status Notifications," Request for Comments 1894, January 1996.

[22] J. Myers, and M. Rose, "Post Office Protocol - Version 3," Request for Comments 1939 (STD 53), May 1996.

[23] M. Rose, "Post Office Protocol - Version 3 Extended Service Offerings," Request for Comments 1082, November 1988.

[24] J. Myers, "POP3 AUTHentication command," Request for Comments 1734, December 1994.

[25] M. Crispin, "Internet Message Access Protocol - Version 4rev1," Request for Comments 2060, December 1996.

[26] M. Crispin, "IMAP4 Compatibility with IMAP2bis," Request for Comments 2061, December 1996.

[27] M. Crispin, "Internet Message Access Protocol - Obsolete Syntax," Request for Comments 2062, December 1996.

[28] M.T. Rose, and D.E. Cass, "ISO Transport Service on top of the TCP Version: 3," Request for Comments 1006, May 1987.

[29] W. Yeong, T. Howes, and S. Kille, "Lightweight Directory Access Protocol," Request for Comments 1777, March 1995.

Chapter 4

Cryptographic Techniques

In this chapter, we introduce some basic cryptographic techniques that are used for secure messaging. More specifically, we focus on cryptographic algorithms and protocols in Section 4.1, address message digest algorithms, secret key cryptography, and public key cryptography in Sections 4.2 to 4.4, address digital envelopes in Section 4.5, and elaborate on some techniques to protect private keys and generate pseudorandom bit sequences in Sections 4.6 and 4.7. Finally, we discuss some legal issues that surround the use of cryptography in Section 4.8, and introduce a notation that can be used to describe cryptographic protocols and applications in Section 4.9. Note that this chapter is far too short to give a comprehensive overview about all cryptographic techniques that are relevant for secure messaging. For this purpose, you must read one (or several) of the many books on cryptography that are available today. Among these books, I particularly recommend [1 – 3].

4.1 INTRODUCTION

According to [3], the term *cryptography* refers to the study of mathematical techniques related to various aspects of information security such as confidentiality, data integrity, entity authentication, and data origin authentication. It is commonly agreed that cryptography is a major enabling technology for network security, and that cryptographic algorithms and protocols are the essential building blocks for secure messaging:

- A *cryptographic algorithm* is an algorithm defined by a sequence of steps precisely specifying the actions required to achieve a specific security objective.

- A *cryptographic protocol* is a distributed algorithm defined by a sequence of steps precisely specifying the actions required of two or more entities to achieve a specific security objective.

Cryptographic algorithms and protocols are being studied both in theory and practice. The aim is to design and come up with algorithms and protocols that are both secure and practical. Note, however, that there are at least two basic approaches to discussing the security of cryptographic algorithms and protocols:

- On the one hand, *computational security* measures the computational effort required to break a specific cryptographic algorithm or protocol. An algorithm or protocol is said to be computationally secure if the best method for breaking it requires at least n operations, where n is some specified, usually very large, number. The problem is that no known practical algorithm or protocol can be proven to be secure under this definition. In practice, an algorithm or protocol is called computationally secure if the best known method of breaking it requires an unreasonably large amount of computational resources (e.g., time or memory). Another approach is to provide evidence of computational security by reducing the security of an algorithm or protocol to some well-studied problem that is thought to be difficult. For example, it may be possible to prove that an algorithm or protocol is secure if a given integer cannot be factored or a discrete logarithm cannot be computed. Algorithms and protocols of this type are sometimes called provably secure, but it must be understood that this approach only provides a proof of security relative to the difficulty of solving another problem, not an absolute proof of security.

- On the other hand, *unconditional security* measures the security of a cryptographic algorithm or protocol when there is no bound placed on the amount of computational resources for an adversary. Consequently, an algorithm or protocol is called unconditionally secure if it cannot be broken, even with infinite time and memory at hand.

The computational security of a cryptographic algorithm or protocol can be studied from the point of view of computational complexity, whereas the unconditional security cannot be studied from this point of view (since computational resources are allowed to be infinite). The appropriate framework in which unconditional security must be studied is probability theory and the application thereof in communication or information theory.

Obviously, unconditional security is preferable from a security point of view, since it protects against a potentially very powerful adversary. Unfortunately, unconditional security is hard and expensive to achieve in many cases, and impossible in other cases. For example, theory shows that unconditionally secure encryption systems use very long keys, making them unsuitable for most practical applications. Similarly, there is no such thing as an unconditionally secure public key cryptosystem. The best we can achieve is provable security, in the sense that the problem of breaking the public key cryptosystem is arguably at least as difficult as solving a complex mathematical problem. Consequently, one is satisfied with computational security given some reasonable assumptions about the computational power of a potential adversary. But keep in mind that the security a computationally secure cryptographic algorithm or protocol may provide is, for the most part, based on the perceived difficulty of a mathematical problem, such as the factorization problem or the discrete logarithm problem in the case of public key cryptography. Confidence in the security of such systems may be high because the problems are public and many minds have attempted to attack them. However, the vulnerability remains that a new insight or computing technology may defeat this type of cryptography. There are at least two developments that provide some evidence for this intrinsic vulnerability:

- In 1994, Peter W. Shor from the AT&T Bell Laboratories conceived randomized polynomial-time algorithms for computing discrete logarithms and factoring integers on a quantum computer, a computational device based on quantum mechanical principles [4,5]. Presently it is not known how to actually build a quantum computer, nor if this is even possible.

- In the same year, Len M. Adleman[1] demonstrated the feasibility of using tools from molecular biology to solve an instance of the directed Hamiltonian path problem, which is known to be hard[2] [6]. The problem instance was encoded

[1]Len M. Adleman is a coinventor of the Rivest, Shamir, and Adleman (RSA) cryptosystem.

[2]According to theoretical computer science, the directed Hamiltonian path problem is NP-complete.

in molecules of deoxyribonucleic acid (DNA), and the steps of the computation were performed with standard protocols and enzymes. Adleman notes that while the currently available fastest supercomputers can execute approximately 10^{12} operations per second, it is plausible for DNA computers to execute 10^{20} or even more operations per second. Moreover, a DNA computer would be far more energy-efficient than existing supercomputers. Similar to the quantum computer, it is not clear at present whether it is feasible to actually build a DNA computer with such performance characteristics. Further information on DNA computing can be found in [7].

Should either quantum computers or DNA computers ever become practical, they would have a tremendous impact on cryptography. In fact, most cryptographic algorithms and protocols that are computationally secure today would be rendered worthless.

Cryptographic algorithms and protocols are used to establish secured channels (both in terms of authenticity and integrity, as well as confidentiality). Note the subtle difference between a *secure* channel and a *secured* channel. Certain channels are assumed to be secure, including trusted couriers and personal contacts between communicating parties, whereas other channels may be secured by physical or cryptographic techniques. Physical security may be established through physical means, such as dedicated communication links with corresponding access controls put in place, or the use of *quantum cryptography*. Contrary to conventional cryptography, the security of quantum cryptography does not rely upon any complexity-theoretic or probability-theoretic assumptions, but is based on the Heisenberg uncertainty principle of quantum physics [8]. As such, quantum cryptography is immune to advances in computing power and human cleverness. In the future, quantum cryptography may provide a physical alternative to unconditionally secure cryptographic algorithms and protocols. In the meantime, however, conventional and computationally secure cryptographic algorithms and protocols are much easier to use and deploy. Consequently, we are not going to delve into the details of quantum cryptography in this book.

4.2 MESSAGE DIGEST ALGORITHMS

Mainly because of their efficiency, *one-way hash functions* are of central importance for cryptographic algorithms and protocols. For example, one-way hash functions can be used to compute and verify digests for arbitrary messages. In this context, one-way hash functions are also called *message digest algorithms*, and in this book we use both terms synonymously and interchangeably.

Informally speaking, a one-way function is easy to compute, but hard to invert. More formally speaking, a function $f : X \longrightarrow Y$ is one-way[3] if

- $f(x)$ is easy to compute for all $x \in X$;
- But it is computationally infeasible when given $y \in f(X) = Y$ to find an $x \in X$ such that $f(x) = y$.

This definition is still not precise in a mathematically strong sense, because it does not resolve what the terms "easy" and "computationally infeasible" actually mean. Nevertheless, we want to use this definition in this book. It is important to note that the existence of one-way functions is still an unproven assumption and that, until today, no function has been shown to be one-way in a mathematically pure sense. Obviously, a sufficiently large domain prohibiting an exhaustive search is a necessary but not sufficient condition for a function to be one-way.

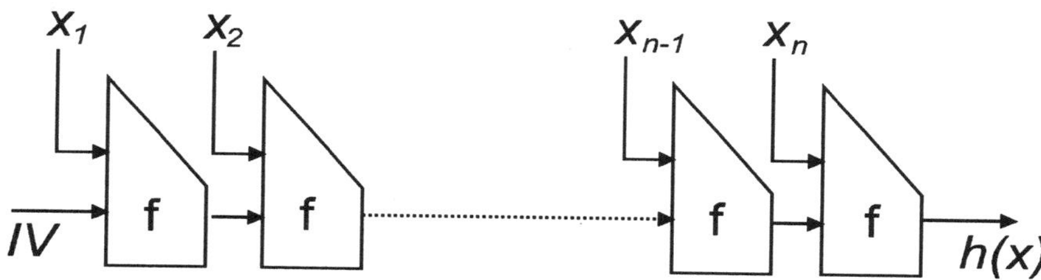

Figure 4.1 An iterative one-way hash function.

In general, it is not required that a one-way function be invertible, and distinct input values may be mapped to the same output value. A one-way function $h : X \longrightarrow Y$ for which $| Y | \ll | X |$ is called a one-way hash function. If, in addition to the conditions for a one-way hash function, it is also computationally infeasible to find distinct input values $x_1, x_2 \in X$ such that $h(x_1) = h(x_2)$, then h is called a collision-resistant one-way hash function. Collision resistance is important, for example, to thwart theft of a digital signature from one message for attachment to another.

Most collision-resistant one-way hash functions in use today are iterative. In short, a one-way hash function is iterative if data is hashed by iterating a basic

[3]An alternative term for "one-way" is "preimage-resistant."

compression function on subsequent blocks of data. The basic idea is illustrated in Figure 4.1. A message x is decomposed into n blocks of data $x_1, \ldots, x_n$. A basic compression function f is then applied to each block and the result of the compression function of the previous block. This continues until the result of the last compression step is interpreted as output $h(x)$. Examples of iterative one-way hash functions include MD2 [9], MD4 [10], MD5 [11], and the secure hash algorithm 1 (SHA-1) [12]. MD2, MD4, and MD5 produce 128-bit hash values, whereas SHA-1 produces 160-bit hash values. RIPEMD is another example of an iterative one-way hash function. It was developed as part of a European research project and is basically a variation of MD4. RIPEMD-160 is a strengthened version of RIPEMD producing another 160-bit hash value [13].

As of this writing, MD5 and SHA-1 are by far the most widely used and deployed one-way hash functions and message digest algorithms. MD5 takes as input a string of arbitrary length and produces as output a 128-bit hash value. In theory, we would need 2^{128} (in the worst case) or 2^{127} (in the average case) trials before finding a collision, and hence a new message that results in the same MD5 hash value. Even if each trial only lasted a nanosecond, this would still require some billions of billions of centuries in computing time. However, recent results in cryptographic research show that it is possible to take advantage of the particularities of the one-way hash function algorithm to speed up the search process. According to Paul van Oorschot and Michael Wiener, you can actually build a machine able to find messages that hash to an arbitrary value [14]. What this means is that cryptanalysis is catching up and that a 128-bit hash value may soon be insufficient. In addition, Hans Dobbertin has shown that MD5 is vulnerable to specific collision search attacks [15]. Taking this into account, SHA-1 and RIPEMD-160 appear to be a cryptographically stronger one-way hash function than MD5. In any case, implementors and users of one-way hash functions and message digest algorithms should be aware of possible cryptanalytic developments regarding any of these functions, and the eventual need to replace them.

4.3 SECRET KEY CRYPTOGRAPHY

Secret key cryptography refers to traditional cryptography. In this kind of cryptography, a secret key is established and shared between communicating peers, and the key is used to encrypt and decrypt messages on either side. Because of its symmetry, secret key cryptography is often referred to as *symmetric cryptography.*

The use of a secret key cryptosystem is overviewed in Figure 4.2. Let's assume that A on the left side wants to send a confidential message to B on the right side. A therefore shares a secret key K with B. This key may be preconfigured manually or distributed by a trusted third party (TTP) or key distribution center (KDC). Note that during its distribution, K must be secured in terms of confidentiality, integrity, and authenticity. This is usually done by having the KDC encrypt K with secret keys that it shares with A and B, respectively. A encrypts a plaintext message P by applying an encryption function E and the key K, and sends the resulting ciphertext $C = E_K(P)$ to B. On the other side, B decrypts C by applying the decryption function D and the key K. B therefore computes $D_K(C) = D_K(E_K(P)) = P$, and recovers the plaintext P accordingly.

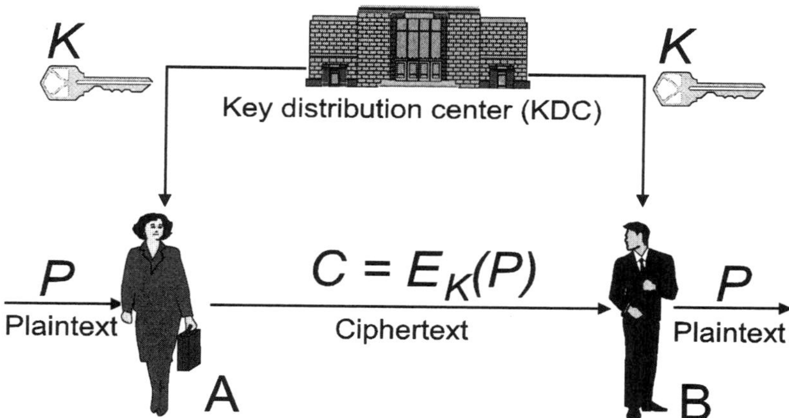

Figure 4.2 A secret key cryptosystem.

Secret key cryptography has been in use for many years in a variety of forms. Two basic categories of secret key cryptosystems are block ciphers and stream ciphers. As their names suggest, block ciphers operate on blocks of data (e.g., 64 bits), whereas stream ciphers usually operate on data one bit or byte at a time. Examples of secret key cryptosystems that are in widespread use (for secure messaging and other applications) are summarized in Table 4.1 and overviewed next. Again, refer to [1 – 3] for a full description of the cryptosystems and corresponding encryption and decryption algorithms.

4.3.1 DES

The Data Encryption Standard (DES) is (still) the most well-known and widely deployed secret key cryptosystem today. It was originally designed by a group

Table 4.1
Secret Key Cryptosystems

Algorithm Name	Main Mode	Effective Key Length
DES	Block cipher	56 bits
Tripe-DES (3DES)	Block cipher	112 or 168 bits
IDEA	Block cipher	128 bits
SAFER	Block cipher	64 or 128 bits
Blowfish	Block cipher	Variable from 1 up to 448 bits
CAST-128	Block cipher	128 bits
RC2, RC5, and RC6	Block cipher	Variable from 1 up to 2048 bits
RC4	Stream cipher	Variable from 1 up to 2048 bits

of researchers at IBM and published as Federal Information Processing Standard (FIPS) 46 in 1977 [16]. As such, it has been used for the encryption of unclassified information by the U.S. National Institute of Standards and Technology (NIST) for almost a quarter of a century.

DES operates as a block cipher with 64-bit blocks, 16 rounds, and a variable key length up to 56 bits. In electronic code book (ECB) mode, DES encrypts data in discrete blocks of 64 bits. To improve its cryptographical strength, DES is often used in cipher block chaining (CBC) mode. In this mode, the encryption of each block depends on the contents of the previous one, preventing an interloper from tampering with the message by rearranging the encrypted blocks. Furthermore, there are two modes that can be used to turn DES into a stream cipher: cipher feedback (CFB) mode and output feedback (OFB) mode.

DES's 56-bit effective key length was sufficiently secure during its first two decades of operation, but it is far too short today.

4.3.2 Triple-DES

One way to improve the cryptographical strength of a secret key cryptosystem with limited key length (e.g., DES), is to apply the algorithm multiple times. Applying the algorithm twice does not improve the situation, due to the existence of a specific cryptanalytical attack (a so-called "meet-in-the-middle" attack). Consequently, at least three applications are necessary for a security improvement, and the three-fold application of DES is called Triple-DES (3DES). It can be used with two or three different keys, and the resulting secret key cryptosystems are usually called two-key 3DES and three-key 3DES. Many contemporary applications use 3DES as a replacement for DES. Note, however, that the use of 3DES is not very efficient (in fact it is approximately three times slower than DES), and that there are many real-time applications that require faster encryption algorithms.

4.3.3 IDEA

The International Data Encryption Algorithm (IDEA) was developed by Xuejia Lai and James Massey in the early 1990s at the ETH Zurich, Switzerland [17]. IDEA is a 64-bit block cipher that uses a 128-bit key. The algorithm is patented and may be licensed from the iT_SEC iT_Security AG.[4]

4.3.4 SAFER

After having developed IDEA, James Massey proposed SAFER K-64 and SAFER K-128. As their names suggest, SAFER K-64 uses a 64-bit key [18], whereas SAFER K-128 uses a proprietary key schedule algorithm that is able to accommodate 128-bit keys. Furthermore, SAFER K-64 uses 6 rounds, whereas SAFER K-128 recommends 10 rounds (12 maximum).

4.3.5 Blowfish

The Blowfish algorithm was developed by Bruce Schneier [19]. It is a DES-like encryption algorithm that can be used as a block cipher with 64-bit blocks, 16 rounds, and variable key lengths up to 448 bits.

4.3.6 CAST-128

The term CAST refers to a design procedure for a family of DES-like encryption algorithms with variable keysize and numbers of rounds. In RFC 2144, a 128-bit CAST encryption algorithm is specified [20]. This algorithm is called CAST-128 and is used and widely deployed for Internet applications (e.g., secure messaging).

4.3.7 RC2, RC4, RC5, and RC6

RC2, RC4, RC5, and RC6 are secret key cryptosystems with variable key lengths that were designed by Ronald L. Rivest for RSA Security, Inc.:

- RC2 is a block cipher (block size is 64 bits), designed as a replacement for DES;

[4] `http://www.it-sec.ch/idea_lic.html`

- RC4 is a stream cipher;
- RC5 is a block cipher that is configurable with regard to word length and number of rounds (in addition to the ley length);
- RC6 is a recent proposal to improve RC5.

The RC2 and RC4 algorithms were originally protected by trade secrets, but were disassembled, reverse-engineered, and anonymously posted to a Usenet newsgroup in 1996 and 1994, respectively.

4.3.8 AES

Most importantly, the U.S. NIST is standardizing an Advanced Encryption Standard (AES) to replace DES in the future. As of this writing, five finalists have been selected among the 15 proposals. The finalists include MARS, RC6, Rijndael, Serpent, and Twofish. Further information about the selection process is available at `http://www.ii.uib.no/~larsr/aes.html` or the official NIST AES Web site.[5] Once the winner is selected, it is possible and very likely that all major security products (including products for secure messaging) will start implementing and incorporating the resulting AES.

4.4 PUBLIC KEY CRYPTOGRAPHY

The idea of using one-way functions, which can only be inverted if a certain secret (a so-called "trapdoor") is known, has led to the invention of *public key cryptography* or *asymmetric cryptography* [21]. Today, public key cryptography is a battlefield for mathematicians and theoretical computer scientists. We are not going to delve into the mathematical foundations of public key cryptography. Instead, we address public key cryptography from a more practical point of view. From this point of view, a public key cryptosystem is simply a cryptosystem in which a user has a pair of mathematically related keys:

- A *public key* that can be published without doing any harm to the system's overall security;
- A *private key* that is assumed to never leave the possession of its owner.

[5]`http://www.nist.gov/aes`

For both the public and the private key, it is computationally infeasible for an outsider to derive one from the other. The use of a public key cryptosystem is overviewed in Figure 4.3. A and B each have a public key pair (k_A, k_A^{-1}) and (k_B, k_B^{-1}). The private keys k_A^{-1} and k_B^{-1} are kept secret, whereas the public keys k_A and k_B are publicly available in certified form (e.g., digitally signed by a certification authority as further addressed below).

If A wants to protect the confidentiality of a plaintext message P, she uses the public key of B, which is k_B, encrypts P with this key, and sends the resulting ciphertext $C = E_{k_B}(P)$ to B (the term $E_{k_B}(P)$ is abbreviated with $E_B(P)$ in Figure 4.3). On the other side, B uses his private key k_B^{-1} to successfully decrypt $P = D_{k_B^{-1}}(C) = D_{k_B^{-1}}(E_{k_B}(P))$ (the terms $D_{k_B^{-1}}(C)$ and $D_{k_B^{-1}}(E_{k_B}(P))$ are abbreviated with $D_B(C)$ and $D_B(E_B(P))$ in Figure 4.3).

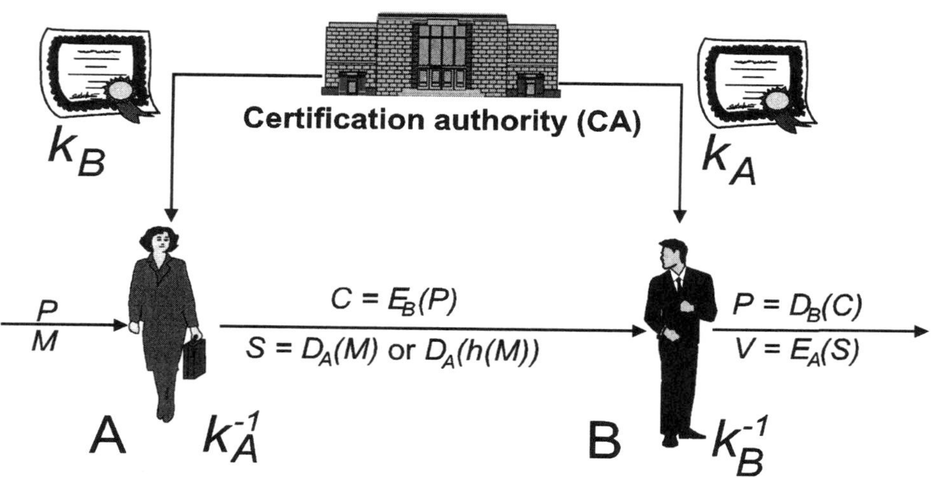

Figure 4.3 A public key cryptosystem.

A public key cryptosystem cannot only be used to protect the confidentiality of a message, but to protect its authenticity and integrity as well. If A wanted to protect the authenticity and integrity of a message M, she would compute a digital signature S for M. Digital signatures provide an electronic analog of handwritten signatures for electronic documents, and — similar to handwritten signatures — digital signatures must not be forgeable, recipients must be able to verify them, and the signers must not be able to repudiate them later. However, a major difference between a handwritten signature and a digital signature is that the digital signature cannot be constant, but must be a function of the entire document on which it appears. If this were not the case, a digital signature, due to its electronic nature, could be copied and attached to arbitrary documents.

Arbitrated digital signature schemes are based on secret key cryptography. In such a scheme, a TTP validates the signature and forwards it on the signer's behalf. True digital signature schemes, however, should come along without TTPs taking an active role. They usually require the use of public key cryptography: signed messages are sent directly from signers to recipients. In essence, a *digital signature scheme* consists of

- A key-generation algorithm that randomly selects a public key pair;
- A signature algorithm that takes as input a message and a private key, and that generates as output a digital signature for the message;
- A signature verification algorithm that takes as input a digital signature and a public key, and that generates as output a message and an information bit according to whether the signature is valid for the message.

A comprehensive overview and discussion of public key-based digital signature schemes are given in [22]. According to the OSI security architecture, a digital signature refers to data appended to, or a cryptographic transformation of, a data unit that allows a recipient of the data unit to prove the source and integrity of the data unit and protect against forgery (e.g., by the recipient). Consequently, there are two classes of digital signatures:

- A *digital signature giving message recovery* refers to the situation in which a cryptographic transformation is applied to a data unit. In this case, the data is automatically recovered if the recipient verifies the signature.
- In contrast, a *digital signature with appendix* refers to the situation in which some cryptographically protected data is appended to the data unit. In fact, the data represents a digital signature and can be decoupled from the data unit that it signs.

In the case of digital signatures with appendix, the bandwidth limitation of public key cryptography is unimportant due to the use of one-way hash functions as auxiliaries. Again referring to Figure 4.3, A can use her private key k_A^{-1} to compute a digital signature $S = D_A(M)$ or $S = D_A(h(M))$ for message M. In the second case, h refers to a collision-resistant one-way hash function that is applied to M prior to generating the digital signature. Anybody who knows the public key of A can verify the digital signature by decrypting it with k_A, and comparing the result with another hash value that is recomputed for the same message with the same one-way hash function.

The use of public key cryptography simplifies the problem of key management considerably. Note that in Figure 4.3, instead of providing A and B with a unique session key that is protected in terms of confidentiality, integrity, and authenticity, the trusted third party (which is now called a "certification authority") has to provide A and B with the public key of the communicating peer. This key is public in nature and must not be protected in terms of confidentiality. Nevertheless, the use of public key cryptography requires an authentication framework that binds public keys to user identities. In fact, a *public key certificate* is a certified proof of such binding vouched for by a TTP or *certification authority* (CA) [23]. According to Webster's dictionary, the term "certificate" refers to a document stating the truth. In the digital world we live in today, the term is mostly used to refer to a collection of information to which a digital signature has been affixed by some authority who is recognized and trusted by some community of certificate users. According to this definition, there exist various types of certificates that potentially serve many purposes. In either case, a certificate is a form of credentials. Examples of credentials used in daily life are driver's licenses, social security cards, or birth certificates. Each of these credentials has some information on it identifying its owner and some authorization stating that someone else has confirmed the information. A public key (or digital) certificate consists of three things:

- A public key;
- Certificate information that refers to the certificate owner's identity, such as his or her name);
- One or more digital signatures.

The aim of the digital signature(s) on the certificate is to state that the certificate information has been attested to by some other person or entity. As such, a digital signature does not attest to the authenticity of the certificate as a whole; it vouches only that the signed identity informatioin is bound to and goes along with the public key.

A digital certificate can be one of a number of different formats. For the purpose of this book, there are two relevant formats:

- PGP certificates as used by PGP (further addressed in Part II of this book);

- X.509 certificates as used by S/MIME[6] (further addressed in Part III of this book).

PGP and X.509 certificates are identified in different ways. More specifically, PGP certificates are identified by user identifiers (IDs) that typically comprise a person's name followed by a bracketed e-mail address, whereas X.509 certificates are identified by X.500 distinguished names (DNs). Another major difference between the two certificate formats is that PGP allows many identities and signatures per certificate, whereas X.509 permits only one identity and one signature per certificate.

As their name suggests, X.509 certificates conform to the ITU-T recommendation X.509. In fact, X.509 specifies both a certificate format and a certificate distribution scheme [24]. It was first published in 1988 as part of the X.500 directory recommendations. The X.509 version 1 (X.509v1) format was extended in 1993 to incorporate two new fields to support directory access control, resulting in the X.509 version 2 (X.509v2) format. Additionally, and as a result of attempting to deploy certificates within the global Internet, X.509v2 was revised to allow for additional extension fields. The resulting X.509 version 3 (X.509v3) specification was officially released in June 1996. Meanwhile, the ITU-T Recommendation X.509 has been approved by the ISO/IEC Joint Technical Committee 1 (JTC1) [25]. The format of an X.509v3 certificate has originally been specified in a notation called Abstract Syntax Notation One (ASN.1). One can apply encoding rules to a certificate specified in ASN.1 format to produce a series of bits and bytes suitable for transmission in computer networks. We address ASN.1 and some of its encoding rules in the following chapter.

According to [26], a *trust model* refers to the set of rules a system or application uses to decide whether a certificate is valid. There are (at least) three different trust models:

- In the *direct trust model*, a user trusts a key that is valid because he knows where it came from (e.g., the user gets the key directly from another user).

- In the *hierarchical trust model*, there are a number of "root" certificates from which trust extends. More specifically, in this model, certificates may certify public keys, or they may certify certificates that certify still other certificates down some chain.

[6]Note that X.509 certificates are used by many other cryptographic security protocols for the Internet, including, for example, SSL/TLS and IPsec.

- The *cumulative trust model* encompasses both the direct and hierarchical trust models, but also adds the notion that trust is in the eye of the beholder and the idea that more information is better. In this model, a certificate might be trusted directly, trusted in some chain going back to a directly trusted root certificate, or trusted by some group of introducers.

Obviously, direct trust is the simplest trust model, and many systems that make use of cryptography depend on it. For example, in Web browsers root CA keys are directly trusted because they are shipped together with the software packages. In PGP (as discussed later), a user who validates keys himself and never sets another certificate to be an introducer is also making use of the direct trust model.

Contrary to that, the trust model employed by ITU-T X.509 is hierarchical in nature [24,25]. In this case, the simplest model one may think of is a certification hierarchy representing a tree with a single root CA. However, more general structures and graphs (including mutually certifying CAs, cross-certificates, and multiple root CAs) are also possible. In X.509 parlance, the term *public key infrastructure* (PKI) refers to an infrastructure that can be used to issue, validate, and revoke public keys and public key certificates. As such, a PKI comprises a set of agreed-upon standards, CAs, structures between multiple CAs, methods to discover and validate certification paths, operational and management protocols, interoperable tools, and supporting legislation. A PKI structure between multiple CAs generally provides one or more certification paths between a subscriber and a certificate-using application. A *certification path* (or *certification chain*) refers to a sequence of one or more connected nodes between the subscriber and a root CA. The root CA, in turn, is a CA that the certificate-using application trusts and has securely imported and stored its public key certificate. S/MIME assumes the existence of CAs that issue and revoke X.509 certificates. The resulting PKI is further addressed in Chapter 13.

Finally, the cumulative trust model is used and has been made popular by PGP, where it is commonly called "web of trust." PGP's web of trust is further addressed in Chapter 8 of this book.

In the following subsections, we overview some public key cryptosystems that are in widespread use today.

4.4.1 RSA

The most widely used public key cryptosystem is RSA, invented by Ronald L. Rivest, Adi Shamir, and Len M. Adleman at MIT in 1977 [27]. The RSA cryptosystem gets its security from the difficulty and intractability of the integer factorization problem. What this means is that it is fairly simple to multiply two large prime numbers, but difficult to compute the prime factors of a large number. One of the nice properties of RSA is that the same algorithm can be used for both message encryption and decryption, as well as digital signature generation and verification. This is not the case for most other public key cryptosystems.

Mathematically spoken, the RSA public key cryptosystem requires two distinct large primes (p and q). Denote $n = pq$ and $\phi(n) = (p-1)(q-1)$, where ϕ refers to the Euler function. Each user chooses a large number $d > 1$ such that $(d, \phi(n)) = 1$ and computes the number e $(1 < e < \phi(n))$ that satisfies the congruence $ed \equiv 1 \pmod{\phi(n)}$. The numbers n and e constitute the public key, whereas the remaining items p, q, $\phi(n)$, and d form the private information. More commonly, d is referred to as the private key. Against this background, message encryption and decryption works as follows:

- To encrypt, one raises the plaintext block P to the power of e and reduces modulo n: $C = P^e \ (\text{mod}\phi(n))$;
- To decrypt, one raises the ciphertext block C to the power of d and reduces modulo n: $P = C^d \ (\text{mod}\phi(n))$.

Digital signature generation and verification uses the same algorithms with different keys (the private key is used to digitally sign a message, whereas the public key is used to verify the signature).

The RSA public key cryptosystem was (and still is) protected by U.S. Patent No. 4,405,829 "Cryptographic communications system and method," issued and granted to MIT on September 20, 1983. The patent will expire on September 20, 2000.[7]

4.4.2 Diffie-Hellman

In 1977, Whitfield Diffie and Martin Hellman proposed a key agreemant protocol that allows participants to agree on a key over an insecure public channel [21]. The protocol gets its security from the difficulty and intractability of the discrete logarithm problem in a finite cyclic group, such as the multiplicative group of a finite field. What this basically means is that, in general, the inverse operation of the exponentiation function is the logarithm function. There are efficient algorithms for computing logarithms in many groups; however, one does not know a polynomial-time algorithm for computing discrete logarithms in cyclic groups. For example, for

[7]By the time you read this book, the RSA patent will already have expired.

a very large prime number p and two smaller numbers y and a, it is computationally intractable to find an x that satisfies the equation $y = a^x \bmod p$.

Mathematically spoken, the Diffie-Hellman key agreemant protocol requires a finite cyclic group G of order $\mid G \mid$ and generator a. In order to agree on a session key, A and B then secretly choose elements x_A and x_B in G. These elements represent A's and B's private keys. A and B compute their public keys $y_A = a^{x_A}$ and $y_B = a^{x_B}$, and exchange these public keys over an insecure public channel. Finally, A and B compute $K_{AB} = y_B^{x_A} = a^{x_B x_A}$ and $K_{BA} = y_A^{x_B} = a^{x_A x_B}$. Note that $K_{AB} = K_{BA}$, so this value can actually be used as a session key to secure communications between A and B.

The Diffie-Hellman key agreemant protocol was protected by U.S. Patent No. 4,200,770 "Cryptographic apparatus and method," issued and granted to Stanford University on April 29, 1980. As such, the patent expired in 1997.

4.4.3 ElGamal

In the early 1980s, Taher ElGamal adapted the Diffie-Hellman key agreement protocol and came up with a public key cryptosystem that can be used for data encryption and digital signatures [28,29]. Contrary to RSA, however, the ElGamal algorithms for data encryption and decryption on the one hand, and digital signature generation and verification on the other hand, are different. This is no serious drawback but is disadvantageous from an implementor's point of view.

Contrary to many other public key cryptosystems, the ElGamal public key cryptosystem is not covered by any patents.

4.4.4 DSS

In the early 1990s, the U.S. NIST published the Digital Signature Standard (DSS) as a viable alternative to RSA signature schemes. The DSS refers to an optimized modification of the ElGamal cryptosystem that can be used only for digital signature generation and verification [30].

4.4.5 ECC

More recently, the use of elliptic curve cryptography (ECC) has attracted a lot of interest. ECC-based public key cryptosystems get their security from the difficulty and intractability of the elliptic curve discrete logarithm problem (that makes use of groups of points on elliptic curves). As illustrated in Table 4.2, a number of different types of cryptography have been defined over elliptic curves. The resulting

ECC-based public key cryptosystems seem to be advantageous with regard to their security properties (meaning that smaller keys are required for a similar level of security). As such, they are particularly useful in situations where small keys are required (e.g., mobile and wireless applications).

Table 4.2
ECC-Based Public Key Cryptosystems

Acronym	Text
ECDH	Elliptic Curve Diffie-Hellman Key Agreement
ECDSA	Elliptic Curve Digital Signature Algorithm
ECES	Elliptic Curve Encryption Scheme
ECMQV	Elliptic Curve MQV Key Agreement
ECNRA	Elliptic Curve Nyberg-Rueppel Signature Scheme with Appendix

Unlike RSA, the general category of ECC is not patented. Individual companies, however, have patented specific efficiency or security algorithms that are related to ECC. Most importantly, the Certicom Corporation[8] holds several patents in this field.

4.5 DIGITAL ENVELOPES

As has become clear, there are advantages and disadvantages related to both secret and public key cryptography. For example, the use of secret key cryptography is efficient but does not scale well beyond a certain number of participants. Furthermore, secret key cryptography does not provide the possibility to digitally sign data. Contrary to that, public key cryptography solves the scalability and digital signature problems, but is highly inefficient in terms of computational resources that are required.

In an attempt to combine the advantages of secret and public key cryptography, a hybrid scheme may be used. In short, a hybrid scheme combines secret and public key cryptography to come up with a scheme that is as efficient and effective as possible. For example, the *digital envelope* is a hybrid scheme that is heavily used in all major secure messaging schemes, including, for example, PEM/MOSS, PGP, and S/MIME. The aim of a digital envelope is similar to a letter envelope: it must protect the confidentiality of a message. As such, the digital envelope provides a

[8] `http://www.certicom.com`

digital analoge for the letter envelope in the physical world (with hopefully better security properties).

When A wants to send a confidential message M to B, he can generate a digital envelope for M and send the envelope to B. On the sender's side the procedure is as follows:

- A retrieves B's public key k_B from a directory service or from his local cache;
- A randomly generates a transaction key K from a secret key cryptosystem;
- A encrypts M with K (the result is $\{M\}K$);
- A encrypts K with k_B (the result is $\{K\}k_B$);
- A concatenates $\{M\}K$ with $\{K\}k_B$, and sends the result to B.

On receipt of $\{M\}K$ and $\{K\}k_B$, B uses his private key k_B^{-1} to decrypt the message. The two-step procedure is as follows:

- B decrypts $\{K\}k_B$ with k_B^{-1} (the result is K);
- B decrypts $\{M\}K$ with K (the result is M).

Obviously, an alternative procedure would be to directly encrypt the message M with B's public key k_B, and to send the result, $\{M\}k_B$, to B. However, the use of a digital envelope as discussed above has at least two advantages compared to this simple scheme:

- First, the use of a digital envelope is more efficient. Remember from our previous discussions that public key cryptography requires much more computational resources than secret key cryptography. Consequently, encrypting a message with a public key requires more computational resources than encrypting a message with a secret key. The longer the message, the more efficient and advantageous is the use of secret key cryptography.

- Second, the use of a digital envelope is more appropriate for messages sent to multiple recipients. If A wanted to send a message M to recipients $B_1, B_2, \ldots, B_n$ $(n > 1)$, he would have to build $\{M\}k_{B_i}$ for each recipient B_i $(i = 1, \ldots, n)$ individually. The resulting message would grow in proportion to the number of recipients. For example, if A wanted to send a 1 MB file to $n = 4$ recipients $(B_1, \ldots, B_4)$, the resulting messages would fill 4 MB of data. Contrary to that, the use of digital envelopes considerably reduces this amount of data. If the public keys of the $n = 4$ recipients are 1,024 bits long each, the digitally enveloped message would fill 1 MB + 4 ∗ 1 KB = 1.004 MB of data. The situation is illustrated in Figure 4.4 (without digital envelopes) and Figure 4.5 (with digital envelopes). Note, however, that in either case it is sufficient to break the security of one single recipient's private key if a message is sent to multiple recipients.

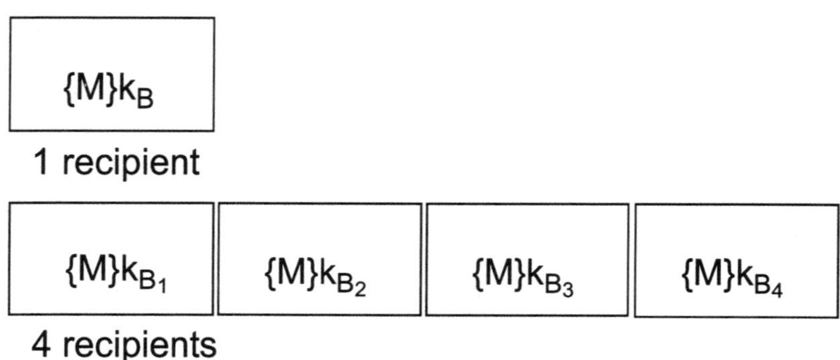

Figure 4.4 An encrypted message for 1 and 4 recipients (without digital envelopes).

Consequently, the use of digital envelopes is almost always advantageous as compared to public key cryptography used for bulk data encryption.

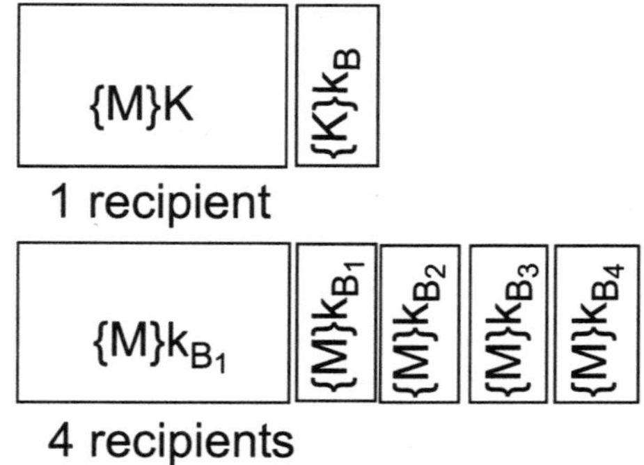

Figure 4.5 An encrypted message for 1 and 4 recipients (with digital envelopes).

4.6 PROTECTION OF PRIVATE KEYS

Any system that makes use of cryptographic techniques has to deal with keys that must be protected against passive and active attacks. This is equally true for session keys that originate from a secret key cryptosystem and private keys that originate from a public key cryptosystem. With regard to secure messaging, the protection of the user's private key is of utmost interest. If a private key is locally stored on a computer system (that runs the corresponding UA), it is vulnerable to access and misuse by unauthorized users. In fact, file permissions alone are not adequate for protecting private keys on most computer systems, though they are part of an overall solution. Private keys protected only by file permissions are vulnerable to intruders and the accidental missetting of permissions.

One obvious solution to the problem of protecting a private key is to store it in a file on a physically removable media, such as a floppy disk. Since drives for floppy disks are typically included with most hardware configurations, the user is not burdened with a significant additional cost. However, if the floppy disk is lost or otherwise not physically well protected, the private key may be compromised, as well.

Encryption is an accepted solution for protecting a private key stored on a removable media. The use of encryption, however, requires access to a cryptographic key that must be protected from disclosure. Consequently, the use of encryption to protect a private key leads to a recursion, and this recursion can only be stopped by making the cryptographic key that is required to encrypt and decrypt the private key derivable from otherwise available information. The recommended advice is to make this information a passphrase selected by the user. A passphrase is different from a password in that no restrictions are usually placed on its length or value. This accomplishes two useful features:

- First, the domain from which the passphrase is chosen is limited only by the input device of the user;
- Second, the user can select an easily remembered value, such as a favorite quotation or other concatenation of easily remembered words.

The cryptographic key that is used to actually encrypt and protect the private key is derived from the user's passphrase (e.g., a one-way hash value). Whenever the private key is needed (e.g., to decrypt an encryption key or to digitally sign a message), the user enters his passphrase, the cryptographic key is derived, the private key is decrypted, and then the private key is available for use. Typically, the file that is used to store the encrypted private key also includes a one-way hash value of the private key. Checking the hash value after decrypting the file contents provides a fast mechanism for determining if the correct passphrase was entered by the user. Without the hash value check, the only mechanism by which the private key's value can be checked would be to use it and see if it works. This may be computationally expensive.

If a user's private key is stored in encrypted form, the user must enter his passphrase to decrypt and locally use his or her private key. From a security point of view, this is the optimal behavior. However, users quickly become irritated if they must send or receive more than a few messages during a session (since they have to reenter their passphrase multiple times). Consequently, some implementations include a feature that allows the passphrases to be kept in memory and users to choose usability over security. For example, an early MOSS implementation developed by Trusted Information Systems (TIS) included a pair of programs, `mosslogin` and `mosslogout`, that allowed a user to enter her passphrase once for the duration of a session she chooses [31]. PGP provides similar options to cache the user passphrase for a certain amount of time.

In summary, the combination of file permissions and passphrase-derived encryption provides effective non-disclosure protection for a user's private key (if the user chooses an appropriate passphrase). Better protection is provided if the file containing the encrypted private key is stored on a removable media, such as a floppy disk. Even better protection is provided if the private key is stored in tamper-resistant hardware tokens, such as a smartcard or PCMCI card. Recent research and development activities also focus on the use of alternative hardware tokens, such as cellular phones, personal assistants (e.g., Palm Pilots), or any other device that implements the Wireless Application Protocol (WAP). There is certainly no single best hardware token to store private keys. Any device the user usually carries around with him is a potentially good hardware token and may serve this purpose (if properly modified). As already mentioned in Chapter 5, the use of PKCS #15 (specifying a cryptographic token information format standard) is particularly useful in this context.

4.7 GENERATION OF PSEUDORANDOM BIT SEQUENCES

Many cryptographic systems use sequences of random (or pseudorandomly generated) bits. For example, if an e-mail message is digitally enveloped, an encryption key (that is sometimes also called "session key") must be randomly selected by the sender of the message. This key is used to encrypt and digitally envelope the message. Also, random or pseudorandom numbers are required to initially generate public key pairs.

Randomness is a statistical property of a sequence of values. In the case of bit values, the requirement is for an adversary to be unable to predict the next bit in a sequence even when all previously generated bits are known. The problem is if it is possible to predict some of the sequence of bits used, it may be possible to reduce the size of the domain from which the key being generated is selected. If the domain is significantly reduced, an exhaustive key search may be feasible.

Locating a source of unpredictable bits presents a unique challenge on most computer systems (because a hardware source of unpredictable bits is usually not available). Consequently, a whole branch of cryptographic research is dedicated to the problem of how to generate random (or pseudorandom) bit sequences using only software. In fact, there are various approaches to address this problem. For example, one software-based approach is to use a cryptographically strong one-way hash function to hash a large amount of information with limited unpredictability available. Such information can, for example, be derived from the current status of the computer system (using corresponding system commands) or the mouse movements and position of keyboard strokes. Since a one-way hash function generates a fixed size quantity, the process is iterated as many times as are necessary to get the required number of bits.

In 1994, an informational RFC was published that addresses the problem of how to randomly or pseudorandomly generate bit sequences [32]. It recommends the use of hardware and shows that the existing hardware on many systems can be used for this purpose. Also, it provides suggestions to ameliorate the problem when a hardware solution is not available.

4.8 LEGAL ISSUES

There are some legal issues to keep in mind when using cryptographic techniques. In particular, there are patent claims, regulations for the import, export, and use of cryptography, as well as legislation for electronic and digital signatures. Some legal issues are briefly mentioned next. You may refer to [33,34] to get more information about the legal implications of using cryptographic techniques.

4.8.1 Patent Claims

Patents applied to computer programs are usually called "software patents." In the U.S. computer industry, software patents are a subject of ongoing controversy.

Some of the earliest and most important software patents granted by the U.S. Patent and Trademark Office were in the field of cryptography. These software patents go back to the late 1960s and early 1970s. Although computer algorithms were widely thought to be unpatentable at that time, cryptography patents were granted because they were written as patents on encryption devices built in hardware. Indeed, most early encryption devices were built in hardware because general-purpose computers simply could not execute the encryption algorithms fast enough in software. For example, IBM obtained several patents in the early 1970s on its Lucifer algorithm, which went on to become the DES [16]. Today, many secret key cryptosystems are also covered by patent claims. For example, DES is patented but royalty-free, whereas IDEA is patented and royalty-free for noncommercial use, but requires a license for commercial use. Later in the 1970s, many pioneers in the field of public key cryptography filed and obtained patents for their work. Consequently, the field of public key cryptography is largely governed by a couple of software patents. Most of them have expired or are about to expire fairly soon.

Outside the United States, the patent situation is quite different. For example, patent law in Europe and Japan differs from U.S. patent law in one very important aspect. In the United States, an inventor has a grace period of one year between the first public disclosure of an invention and the last day on which a patent application can be filed. In Europe and Japan, there is no grace period. Any public disclosure instantly forfeits all patent rights. Because the inventions contained in the original patents related to public key cryptography were publicly disclosed before patent applications were filed, these algorithms were never patentable in Europe and Japan.[9]

Under U.S. patent law, patent infringement is not a criminal offense, and the penalties and damages are the jurisdiction of the civil courts. It is the responsibility of the user of a particular cryptographic algorithm or technique to make sure that correct licenses have been obtained from the corresponding patent holders. If these licenses do not exist, the patent holders can sue the user in court. Therefore, most products that make use of cryptographic algorithms or techniques include the licenses required to use them. This is also true for PGP and S/MIME-compliant software packages.

Finally, it is important to note that the IETF has a special requirement with regard to the use of patented technology in Internet standards track protocols. In fact, prior to approving a protocol specification for the Internet standards track,

[9]As a consequence of the lack of patent claims, public key cryptography has been more widely adapted in European countries and Japan.

a written statement from a patent holder is required that a license will be made available to applicants under reasonable terms and conditions.

4.8.2 Regulations

There are different regulations for the import, export, and use of cryptographic techniques. For example, the United States has been regulating the export of cryptographic systems and technical data regarding them for quite a long time. These regulations have gone far beyond the Wassenaar Arrangement on export controls for conventional arms and dual-use goods and technologies.[10] More specifically, U.S. export controls on commercial encryption products are administered by the Bureau of Export Administration (BXA) in the Department of Commerce (DoC). Regulations governing exports of encryption are found in the Export Administration Regulations (EAR). Consequently, if a U.S. company wants to sell cryptographic systems and technical data overseas, it must have export approval by the BXA according to the EAR.

Unfortunately, the laws that drive the U.S. export controls are not too clear, and their interpretation changes over time. Sometimes vendors get so discouraged that they leave encryption out of their products altogether. Sometimes they generate products that, when sold overseas, have encryption mechanisms seriously weakened or removed. It is usually possible to get export approval for encryption if the key lengths are shortened. So, sometimes vendors intentionally use short keys or cryptosystems with varying key lengths. Probably the most widely deployed example of this kind is browser software (e.g., Netscape Navigator and Microsoft Internet Explorer) that comes in two versions: the U.S. domestic version that uses strong encryption with 128-bit RC4 session keys, and the international version of the same product that uses encryption with only 40-bit RC4 session keys. Due to some recent

[10]The Wassenaar Arrangement is a treaty originally negotiated in July 1996 and signed by 31 countries to restrict the export of dual-use goods and technologies to specific countries considered to be dangerous. The countries that have signed the Wassenaar Arrangement include the former Coordinating Committee for Multilateral Export Controls (COCOM) member and cooperating countries, as well as some new countries such as Russia. The COCOM was an international munitions control organization that also restricted the export of cryptography as a dual-use technology. It was formally dissolved in March 1994. More recently, the Wassenaar Arrangement was updated. The participating countries of the Wassenaar Arrangement are: Argentina, Australia, Austria, Belgium, Bulgaria, Canada, Czech Republic, Denmark, Finland, France, Germany, Greece, Hungary, Ireland, Italy, Japan, Luxembourg, Netherlands, New Zealand, Norway, Poland, Portugal, Republic of Korea, Romania, Russian Federation, Slovak Republic, Spain, Sweden, Switzerland, Turkey, Ukraine, United Kingdom, and the United States. Further information on the Wassenaar Arrangement can be found on the Web by following the URL `http://www.wassenaar.org`.

cryptanalytical attacks and breakthroughs, it seems that a lower bound for a key length that protects against a brute-force attack is 80 bits [35]. This value may serve as a good rule of thumb.

On January 14, 2000, the BXA published a regulation implementing the White House's announcement of a new framework for U.S. export controls on encryption items (the announcement was made on September 16, 1999).[11] The policy is in response to the changing global market, advances in technology, and the need to give U.S. industry better access to these markets, while continuing to provide essential protections for national security. The regulation enlarges the use of license exceptions, implements the changes agreed to at the Wassenaar Arrangement in December 1998, and eliminates the deemed export rule for encryption technology. In addition, new license exception provisions are created for certain types of encryption, such as source code and toolkits. There are some countries exempted from the regulation (i.e., Cuba, Iran, Iraq, Libya, North Korea, Sudan, and Syria). In these countries, some or all technologies and products mentioned in this book will not be available. In all other countries most technologies and products mentioned in this book will be available.

4.8.3 Electronic and Digital Signature Legislation

In the recent past, many countries have enacted or are considering electronic or digital signature legislation in an effort to facilitate electronic commerce (e-commerce) and e-commerce applications. For example, the most well-known comprehensive legislations are the Utah Digital Signature Act and the German Act on Digital Signature ("Signaturgesetz") as Article 3 of the Federal Act on Establishing the General Conditions for Information and Communication Services, also known as Information and Communication Services Act[12] ("Informations- und Kommunikationsdienste-Gesetz").

On December 13, 1999, the European Parliament and the Council of the European Union adopted a directive on a community framework for electronic signatures.[13] The purpose of this directive is to facilitate the use of electronic signatures and to contribute to their legal recognition. More specifically, it establishes a legal framework for electronic signatures and certain certification services in order to ensure the proper functioning of the European market. As such, it does not cover aspects related to the conclusion and validity of contracts or other legal

[11] http://www.bxa.doc.gov/Encryption

[12] http://www.iid.de/rahmen/iukdgebt.html

[13] http://europa.eu.int/comm/internal_market/en/media/sign/

obligations where there are requirements as regards form prescribed by national or (European) Community law nor does it affect rules and limits, contained in national or Community law, governing the use of documents.

Finally, note that electronic and digital signature legislation is a fast-evolving field, and that once this book is printed many countries will have put in place corresponding laws.

4.9 NOTATION

As mentioned before, a cryptographic protocol is a distributed algorithm defined by a sequence of steps precisely specifying the actions required of two or more entities to achieve a specific security objective. The following notation is used in this book to describe cryptographic protocols:

- Capital letters, such as A, B, C, ..., are used to refer to principals, whereas the same letters put in italics are used to refer to the corresponding principal identifiers. Note that many publications on cryptography and cryptographic protocols use names, such as Alice and Bob, to refer to principals. This is a convenient way of making things unambiguous with relatively few words, since the pronoun "she" can be used for Alice, and "he" can be used for Bob. However, the advantages and disadvantages of this naming scheme are controversial, and we are not going to use it in this book.

- K is used to refer to a secret key. A secret key is basically a key of a secret key cryptosystem.

- The pair (k, k^{-1}) is used to refer to a public key pair, whereas k is used to refer to the public key and k^{-1} is used to refer to the corresponding private key.

In either case, key subscripts are used to indicate principals. In general, capital letter subscripts are used for long-term keys, and small letter subscripts are used for short-term keys. For example, K_A is used to refer to A's long-term secret key, whereas k_b is used to refer to B's short-term public key.

- The term $\{M\}K$ is used to refer to a message M that is encrypted with the secret key K. Since the same key K is used for decryption, $\{\{M\}K\}K$ equals M. If K is used to compute and verify a message authentication code (MAC) for message M, then the term $\langle M \rangle K$ is used to refer to $\{h(M)\}K$, with h being a collision-resistant, one-way hash function.

- Similarly, the term $\{M\}k$ is used to refer to a message M that is encrypted with the public key k. The message can only be decrypted with the corresponding private key k^{-1}. If a public key cryptosystem is used to digitally sign messages, the private key is used for signing, and the corresponding public key is used for verifying signatures. Referring to the terminology of the OSI security architecture, the term $\{M\}k^{-1}$ is used to refer to a digital signature giving message recovery, and $\langle M\rangle k^{-1}$ is used to refer to a digital signature with appendix. Note that in the second case, $\langle M\rangle k^{-1}$ in fact abbreviates $M, \{h(M)\}k^{-1}$, with h being again a collision-resistant, one-way hash function.

Finally, the term $X \ll Y \gg$ is used to refer to a public key certificate that has been issued by X for Y's public key. It implies that X has verified Y's identity and certified the binding of Y's long-term public key k_Y with its identity. Contrary to an X.509 certificate, a PGP certificate can be signed multiple times (by different parties). In this case, the term $X, Y \ll Z \gg$ is used to refer to a certificate that has been issued for Z's public key k_Z, and that has been signed by both X and Y. Obviously, this scheme can be iterated an arbitrary number of times.

REFERENCES

[1] D. Stinson, *Cryptography Theory and Practice*, CRC Press, Boca Raton, FL, 1995.

[2] B. Schneier, *Applied Cryptography: Protocols, Algorithms, and Source Code in C*, 2nd Edition, John Wiley & Sons, New York, NY, 1996.

[3] A. Menezes, P. van Oorschot, and S. Vanstone, *Handbook of Applied Cryptography*, CRC Press, Boca Raton, FL, 1996.

[4] P.W. Shor, "Algorithms for Quantum Computation: Discrete Logarithms and Factoring," *Proceedings of IEEE 35th Annual Symposium on Foundations of Computer Science*, 1994, pp. 124 – 134.

[5] P.W. Shor, "Polynomial-Time Algorithms for Prime Factorization and Discrete Logarithms on a Quantumn Computer," *SIAM Journal of Computing*, October 1997, pp. 1484 – 1509.

[6] L.M. Adleman, "Molecular Computation of Solutions to Combinatorial Problems," *Science*, November 1994, pp. 1021 – 1024.

[7] G. Păun, G. Rozenberg, and A. Salomaa, *DNA Computing: New Computing Paradigms*, Springer-Verlag, New York, NY, 1998.

[8] C.H. Bennett, G. Brassard, and A.K. Ekert, "Quantum Cryptography," *Scientific American*, October 1992, pp. 50 – 57.

[9] B. Kaliski, "The MD2 Message-Digest Algorithm," Request for Comments 1319, April 1992.

[10] R.L. Rivest, "The MD4 Message-Digest Algorithm," Request for Comments 1320, April 1992.

[11] R.L. Rivest, and S. Dusse, "The MD5 Message-Digest Algorithm," Request for Comments 1321, April 1992.

[12] U.S. National Institute of Standards and Technology (NIST), "Secure Hash Standard (SHS)," FIPS PUB 180-1, April 1995.

[13] H. Dobbertin, A. Bosselaers, and B. Preneel, "RIPEMD-160: A strengthened version of RIPEMD," *Proceedings of Fast Software Encryption Workshop*, 1996, pp. 71 – 82.

[14] P. van Oorschot, and M. Wiener, "Parallel Collision Search with Applications to Hash Functions and Discrete Logarithms," *Proceedings of ACM Conference on Computer and Communications Security*, November 1994.

[15] H. Dobbertin, "The Status of MD5 After a Recent Attack," *RSA Laboratories' CryptoBytes*, Vol. 2, 1996, No. 2.

[16] U.S. National Institute of Standards and Technology (NIST), "Data Encryption Standard," FIPS PUB 46, January 1977.

[17] X. Lai, *On the Design and Security of Block Ciphers*, Ph.D. Thesis, ETH No. 9752, ETH Zürich, Switzerland, 1992.

[18] J.L. Massey, "SAFER K-64: A Byte-Oriented Block Ciphering Algorithm," *Proceedings of Fast Software Encryption Workshop*, 1994, pp. 1 – 17.

[19] B. Schneier, "Description of a New Variable-Length Key, 64-Bit Block Cipher (Blowfish)," *Proceedings of Fast Software Encryption Workshop*, 1994, pp. 191 – 204.

[20] C. Adams, "The CAST-128 Encryption Algorithm," Request for Comments 2144, May 1997.

[21] W. Diffie, and M.E. Hellman, "New Directions in Cryptography," *IEEE Transactions on Information Theory*, IT-22(6), 1976, pp. 644 – 654.

[22] B. Pfitzmann, *Digital Signature Schemes*, Springer-Verlag, Berlin, Germany, 1996.

[23] J. Feghhi, J. Feghhi, and P. Williams, *Digital Certificates: Applied Internet Security*, Addison-Wesley Longman, Reading, MA, 1999.

[24] ITU-T X.509, *The Directory — Authentication Framework*, November 1987.

[25] ISO/IEC 9594-8, *Information Technology — Open Systems Interconnection — The Directory — Part 8: Authentication Framework*, 1990.

[26] Network Associates, Inc., "PGP and X.509: A Practical Comparison of Trust Models and Validation Mechanisms for E-Business Applications," 1999.

[27] R.L. Rivest, A. Shamir, and L. Adleman, "A Method for Obtaining Digital Signatures and Public-Key Cryptosystems," *Communications of the ACM*, 21(2), February 1978, pp. 120 – 126.

[28] T. ElGamal, *Cryptography and Logarithms Over Finite Fields*, Ph.D. Thesis, Stanford University, 1984.

[29] T. ElGamal, "A Public Key Cryptosystem and a Signature Scheme Based on Discrete Logarithm," *IEEE Transactions on Information Theory*, IT-31(4), 1985, pp. 469 – 472.

[30] U.S. National Institute of Standards and Technology (NIST), *Digital Signature Standard (DSS)*, FIPS PUB 186, May 1994.

[31] J. Galvin, and M.S. Feldman, "MIME object security services: Issues in a multi-user environment," *Proceedings of USENIX UNIX Security V Symposium*, June 1995.

[32] D. Eastlake, S. Crocker, and J. Schiller, "Randomness Recommendations for Security," Request for Comments 1750, December 1994.

[33] L.J. Hoffman, *Building in Big Brother: The Cryptographic Policy Debate*, Springer-Verlag, New York, NY, 1995.

[34] S.A. Baker, and P.R. Hurst, *The Limits of Trust: Cryptography, Governments, and Electronic Commerce*, Kluwer Law International, Cambridge, MA, 1998.

[35] M. Blaze, W. Diffie, R.L. Rivest, B. Schneier, T. Shimomura, E. Thompson, and M. Wiener, "Minimal Key Lengths for Symmetric Ciphers to Provide Adequate Commercial Security," Business Software Alliance, January 1996.

Chapter 5

ASN.1 and Encoding Rules

The aim of computer networks and distributed systems is to have application protocol entities that can exchange messages. These messages must be specified and encoded in a unique way. In this chapter, we address the problem of how to specify and encode them. More specifically, we overview and briefly discuss the Abstract Syntax Notation One (ASN.1) and its related sets of encoding rules in Sections 5.1 and 5.2, address the public key cryptography standards in Section 5.3, and conclude with some final remarks in Section 5.4.

5.1 ASN.1

The Open Systems Interconnection (OSI) reference model is a standardized architecture that governs the interconnection of computer systems from the physical layer up to the application layer.[1] In this model, protocol entities exchange data units according to standardized communication protocols. In order to come up with implementations that conform to standards and are interoperable, communication

[1]A good introduction to the OSI reference model and the rationale behind it is available at `http://www.salford.ac.uk/iti/books/osi/osi.html`.

protocols and their data units must be specified in a unique way. Formal specification languages can be used for this purpose and several of these languages have been proposed in the past.

ASN.1[2] is the formal specification language and notation of choice for the OSI reference model and its communication protocols. It is specified in the multipart standard ISO/IEC 8824 [1 – 5] that has also been approved by the ITU-T in a series of recommendations (ITU-T X.680 to X.683).[3] Using ASN.1, a protocol designer can view and describe the relevant information and its structure at a high level of abstraction and need not be unduly concerned with how it is represented while in transit.

ASN.1 is a very powerful specification language and notation, of which we only use some basic terms in this book. Following is an abbreviated introduction aimed at making the unfamiliar reader sufficiently comfortable to follow this book. Advanced features of ASN.1 can be found in the documents mentioned above.

In short, ASN.1 is a notation for describing (abstract) types and values. In this terminology, a type is just a set of possible values. The main elements of the notation are as follows:

- *Keywords* that are defined in the ASN.1 specifications. Keywords are generally distinguishable by being all uppercase characters (e.g., `INTEGER`).
- *Type-references* that are used to name specific types. The first letter of a type-reference must be an uppercase character, and usually at least some of the remaining characters are lowercase (e.g., `CurrentYear`).
- *Value-references* are used to name specific values of types. The first letter of a value-reference must be a lowercase character, and usually most of the remaining characters are lowercase, too (e.g., `rolf`).
- *Identifiers* are used to name various items in an ASN.1 specification, including, for example, a component of a structured type (as explained below). In this case, the first letter must be a lowercase character (e.g., `dateField`).[4]

[2]Originally, the abbreviation for the Abstract Syntax Notation One was ASN1. However, the abbreviation was often mistyped as ANS1 and then misread as ANSI — the abbreviation for the American National Standards Institute. One solution for this problem was the introduction of the dot (.) into the abbreviation, so we now have "ASN.1" and nobody mistypes it as "ANSI" anymore.

[3]Parts 2, 3, and 4 of ISO/IEC 8824 were introduced in the 1993 revision of the ASN.1 standard.

[4]Note that a value-reference and an identifier can always be differentiated by virtue of the context in which the string occurs.

- *Object identifiers* are used to uniquely identify objects. More specifically, an object identifier is a value, comprising a sequence of integer components, which can be conveniently assigned for some specific purpose and which has the property of being unique within the space of all object identifiers. There is a scheme that allows the registration of arbitrary object identifiers. The scheme works on the basis of a hierarchical structure of distinct value-assigning authorities, with each level of the hierarchy having responsibility for one integer component of the value. Rules for the upper levels of the hierarchy are defined in annexes to the ASN.1 specifications and ISO/IEC 9834-1 [6].
- *Comments* are used to give further information that goes beyond the pure ASN.1 specification. The start of a comment is indicated with two hyphens, whereas the end of the comment is indicated with another two hyphens or the end of the line.

Furthermore, ASN.1 comprises some special items, such as the assignment operator (`::=`), bracketing items for different contexts (e.g., `{`, `}`, `[`, and `]`), and many others.

ASN.1 allows one to define a variety of types, ranging from simple types that are atomic and have no components, such as integers and bit strings, to structured types that have components, such as sets and sequences, as well as complex types defined in terms of others (tagged types and other types). For some types, there are a finite number of possible values, whereas for other types the number of possible values is infinite.

Every ASN.1 type other than `CHOICE` and `ANY` has a tag that consists of a class and a tag number. ASN.1 types are considered the same if and only if their tag numbers are the same. Consequently, the name of an ASN.1 type does not affect its abstract meaning, only the tag does. In general, there are four classes of tags:

1. *Universal tags* denote types whose meaning is the same in all applications.
2. *Application tags* denote types whose meaning is specific to an application, such as e-mail. Consequently, types in two different applications may have the same application-specific tag but different meaning.
3. *Private tags* denote types whose meaning is specific to a given organization.
4. *Context-specific tags* denote types whose meaning is specific to a given structured type. These tags are used to distinguish between component types with the same underlying tag within the context of a given structured types, and component types in two different structured types may have the same tag but different meanings.

Table 5.1
Some ASN.1 Types With Universal Tag Numbers

Type	*Tag number (decimal)*	*Tag number (hexadecimal)*
`INTEGER`	2	02
`BIT STRING`	3	03
`OCTET STRING`	4	04
`NULL`	5	05
`OBJECT IDENTIFIER`	6	06
`SEQUENCE` and `SEQUENCE OF`	16	10
`SET` and `SET OF`	17	11
`PrintableString`	19	13
`T61String`	20	14
`IA5String`	22	16
`UTCTime`	23	17

Some ASN.1 types and their universal tag numbers are standardized (as summarized in Table 5.1). Types with other tags are defined in many places, and are always obtained by explicit or implicit tagging.

ASN.1 types and values are expressed in a flexible notation that looks like a programming language. For example, types and values can be given names with the ASN.1 assignment operator (`::=`) and those names can be used in defining other types and values. The layout of the ASN.1 expressions is not significant, meaning that multiple spaces and line breaks are considered as a single space.

5.1.1 Simple Types

Simple types are atomic and do not consist of components. The following simple types are heavily used in protocol specifications (refer to Table 5.1 for the universal tag numbers of some of these types):

- The simple type `INTEGER` is used to denote arbitrary integer values.
- The simple type `BIT STRING` is used to denote arbitrary strings of bits (consisting of zeroes and ones).
- The simple type `OCTET STRING` is used to denote arbitrary strings of bytes (each byte consisting of 8 bits).
- The simple type `NULL` is used to denote the null value.

- The simple type OBJECT IDENTIFIER is used to denote an object identifier (as mentioned above, an object identifier is represented by a sequence of integer components that collectively identify an object, such as an algorithm or attribute type, in a globally unique way).

- The simple type PrintableString is used to denote arbitrary strings of printable characters.

- The simple type T61String is used to denote arbitrary strings of T.61 characters.

- The simple type IA5String is used to denote arbitrary strings of IA5 (or ASCII) characters.

- The simple type UTCTime is used to denote values representing coordinated universal time or Greenwhich Mean Time (GMT).

Simple types fall into two categories: string types and nonstring types. BIT STRING, OCTET STRING, PrintableString, T61String, IA5String, and UTCTime are string types, whereas INTEGER, NULL, and OBJECT IDENTIFIER are nonstring types.

5.1.2 Structured Types

Structured types consist and are composed of components. These components, in turn, can be of arbitrary type. More specifically, ASN.1 defines the following four structured types (again, refer to Table 5.1 for the corresponding universal tag numbers):

- The structured type SEQUENCE is used to denote ordered collections of one or more types.

- The structured type SEQUENCE OF is used to denote ordered collection of zero or more occurrences of a given type.

- The structured type SET is used to denote unordered collections of one or more types.

- The structured type SET OF is used to denote unordered collections of zero or more occurrences of a given type.

A value for the `SEQUENCE` type is a concatenation of values from the referenced types. A `SEQUENCE` type, in turn, is defined by referencing an ordered list of existing types (some of which may be designated optional as explained below). An illustration of the notation to define a `SEQUENCE` type `NewType` is as follows:

```
NewType ::= SEQUENCE {
  component1    [0]    Component1Type,
  component2    [1]    Component2Type,
  component3    [2]    Component3Type
}
```

In this example, `component1`, `component2`, and `component3` refer to identifiers for the three components of the type `NewType`. Furthermore, the fields `Component1Type`, `Component2Type`, and `Component3Type` are type specifications or type-references. Consequently, a value for the new type `NewType` consists of a collection of three values — one of type `Component1Type`, one of type `Component2Type`, and one of type `Component3Type`. The fields `[0]`, `[1]`, and `[2]` are tags that may be required to ensure that the different components can be distinguished in an encoding. They can be omitted if the encoding would be unambiguous anyway (e.g., if no components were optional). Consequently, a value of the following `SEQUENCE` type `User` would comprise an integer plus two character strings:

```
User ::= SEQUENCE {
  userId        [0]    INTEGER,
  firstname     [1]    IA5String,
  familyname    [2]    IA5String
}
```

Any of the component specifications could be optionally followed by the keyword `OPTIONAL`, or the keyword `DEFAULT` and a value, which would indicate that this component could also be omitted. The following type can be used to illustrate the use of these keywords:

```
User ::= SEQUENCE {
  userId        [0]    INTEGER,
  department    [1]    DepartmentCode DEFAULT production,
  firstname     [2]    IA5String OPTIONAL,
  familyname    [3]    IA5String
}
```

```
DepartmentCode ::= ENUMERATED
  {production (0), finances (1), research (2)}
```

As mentioned above, the type `SEQUENCE OF` is used to denote ordered collection of zero or more occurrences of a given type. Consequently, a value for the type `SEQUENCE OF` is a collection of values, all of the same type. For example, a value of type `SEQUENCE OF INTEGER` refers to an ordered list of integer values. The list size may be limited by inserting a corresponding value between `SEQUENCE` and `OF`.

A `SET` type is essentially the same as a `SEQUENCE` type, except that the order of the components is insignificant and need not be preserved. The notation is the same as for the `SEQUENCE` type (except that the keword `SET` is used to replace the keyword `SEQUENCE`).

5.1.3 Tagged Types

Tagging is useful to distinguish types within an application or component types within a structured type. In general, there are two ways to tag a type:

- Implicitly tagged types are derived from other types by changing the tag of the underlying type. Implicit tagging is denoted by the ASN.1 keyword `IMPLICIT`.
- Explicitly tagged types are derived from other types by adding an outer tag to the underlying type. Implicit tagging is denoted by the ASN.1 keyword `EXPLICIT`.

For the purpose of encoding, an implicitly tagged type is considered the same as the underlying type, except that the tag is different. An explicitly tagged type is considered like a structured type with one component, the underlying type. Implicit tags result in shorter encodings, but explicit tags may be necessary to avoid ambiguity if the tag of the underlying type is indeterminate (e.g., the underlying type is `CHOICE` or `ANY`).

5.1.4 Other Types

Other types in ASN.1 include the `CHOICE` and `ANY` types:

- The type `CHOICE` denotes a union of one or more alternatives;
- The type `ANY` denotes an arbitrary value of an arbitrary type.

A `CHOICE` type is defined by referencing a list of existing types. Each value of the new type is a value of one of the component types. The notation for `CHOICE` is the same as for `SEQUENCE`, with the keyword `CHOICE` replacing `SEQUENCE`, and without any `OPTIONAL` or `DEFAULT` options. For example, a value of the following `User` type is either an integer or a character string:

```
User ::= CHOICE {
  userId    [0]    INTEGER,
  name      [1]    IA5String
}
```

5.2 ENCODING RULES

To be transferable in computer networks, abstract objects (whether specified in a formal language or not) must be represented and encoded as strings of binary data, consisting only of zeros and ones. In general, there are two possibilities to do so:

- A hand-crafted *transfer syntax* is defined and used that specifies how abstract objects are represented and encoded;
- A set of *encoding rules* is defined that collectively specify how abstract objects can be automatically represented and encoded.

A clear advantage of using encoding rules rather than a hand-crafted transfer syntax is that application designers and developers do not need to be familiar with the details of representing and encoding abstract objects. Consequently, they can work on a higher level of abstraction (as compared to their colleagues that use handcrafted transfer syntaxes). This is somehow similar to the situation with contemporary programming languages. Programmers tend to use high-level languages so they do not have to know in detail how data structures are held in memory.

Today, it is commonly agreed that the use of encoding rules is advantageous for network application development. In fact, many application protocols are entirely specified in formal languages (e.g., ASN.1) before or after they are implemented. This trend is likely to continue with the increase in complexity for network application protocols. Note, however, that there are still applications that use handcrafted transfer syntaxes. For example, any application protocol that is ASCII-encoded (e.g., Telnet, SMTP, or HTTP) does not require complicated encoding rules. Similarly, PGP uses specific message and packet formats, as well as a handcrafted transfer syntax (as discussed in Part II of this book).

When the ISO first specified ASN.1, a set of encoding rules was also included in the resulting specification. However, the developers of ASN.1 soon felt that there might be justification for defining different sets of encoding rules. Such encoding rules would not just be different for the sake of being different, but would be designed to meet some functional requirement, such as optimizing compactness of encoding at the expense of computational overhead, or vice versa. It was decided to separate ASN.1 from its encoding rules. At this point in time, the original set of encoding rules was renamed *basic encoding rules* (BER) and specified in ISO ISO/IEC 8825-1 [7]. BER are general-purpose. Consequently, one shortcoming or disadvantage of them is that they permit multiple different representations for some ASN.1 values. Consequently, additional sets of encoding rules were defined. Among these additional sets of encoding rules, the following two are used and widely deployed today:

- First, the *distinguished encoding rules* (DER) as specified in ISO/IEC 8825-3 [8] were designed to reduce options for encoding and thus reduce the computational overhead for decoding [9].
- Second, the *packet encoding rules* (PER) were designed to reduce line overhead. As such, PER provide line efficiency at the cost of processing overhead.

Contrary to BER, DER provide a unique encoding for every ASN.1 value as an octet string. As such, they basically represent a subset of BER.

For the purpose of this book, we only use the DER (since S/MIME is using ASN.1 and DER). Let's briefly look at an example taken from [10] to give you a feeling about the working procedures of DER. Let's assume the serial number of a certificate has an integer value of `127`. According to DER, this element is wire-encoded as `(02 01 7F)`, consisting of the three octets `0x02`, `0x01`, and `0x7F`. In this example, `0x02` is a tag number (representing an integer value), `0x01` indicates a length of one octet, and `0x7F` (representing `127` in decimal notation) refers to the corresponding value.

5.3 PUBLIC KEY CRYPTOGRAPHY STANDARDS

The Public Key Cryptography Standards (PKCS) refer to a suite of specifications that address various aspects related to the implementation of public key cryptography. The PKCS have been defined since 1991 by a consortium of computer vendors, including, for example, Microsoft, Apple, Lotus, and Sun Microsystems, together with RSA Security, Inc. and MIT [11]. Table 5.2 summarizes the PKCS published so far (PKCS #2 and PKCS #4 have been incorporated into PKCS #1 meanwhile).[5]

Table 5.2
PKCS Specifications

PKCS	*Title*
PKCS #1	RSA Cryptography Standard
PKCS #3	Diffie-Hellman Key Agreement Standard
PKCS #5	Password-Based Cryptography Standard
PKCS #6	Extended-Certificate Syntax Standard
PKCS #7	Cryptographic Message Syntax Standard
PKCS #8	Private-Key Information Syntax Standard
PKCS #9	Selected Attribute Types
PKCS #10	Certification Request Syntax Standard
PKCS #11	Cryptographic Token Interface Standard
PKCS #12	Personal Information Exchange Syntax Standard
PKCS #13	Elliptic Curve Cryptography Standard
PKCS #15	Cryptographic Token Information Format Standard

The PKCSs make heavy use of ASN.1 and DER [11]. For the purpose of this book (mainly for the specification of S/MIME) we only need some basic knowledge related to PKCS #1, PKCS #7, and PKCS #10, as well as PKCS #11 and PKCS #15:

- PKCS #1 describes a method for encrypting data using the RSA public key algorithm for digital signatures and digital envelopes. The current version 1.5 of PKCS #1 is also specified in RFC 2313 [12].
- PKCS #7 specifies a cryptographic message syntax and encoding standard for digital signatures and digital envelopes. In addition to S/MIME, PKCS #7 is used in many other security-related standards and applications, including, for example, the secure electronic transaction (SET) specification for secure credit card payments over the Internet. The current version 1.5 of PKCS #7 is also specified in RFC 2315 [13].
- PKCS #10 specifies a message syntax for certification requests. The current version 1.5 of PKCS #10 is also specified in RFC 2314 [14].

[5]The PKCS specifications are publicly and freely available and can be downloaded from `http://www.rsasecurity.com/rsalabs/pkcs/`.

- PKCS #11 specifies an application programming interface (API), called Cryptoki (pronounced crypto-key and short for cryptographic token interface), to devices which hold cryptographic information and perform cryptographic functions. As of this writing, the current version of PKCS #11 is 2.1.

- PKCS #15 specifies a cryptographic token information format standard. As such, it is intended at establishing a standard which ensures that users will be able to use cryptographic tokens to identify themselves to multiple, standards-aware applications, regardless of the application's Cryptoki (or other token interface) provider. As of this writing, the current version of PKCS #15 is 1.1.

To support PKCS #7 and PKCS #10, new MIME `application` subtypes are required. More specifically, the MIME type `application/pkcs7-mime` (or `application/x-pkcs7-mime`, respectively) is used to specify that a MIME entity has been cryptographically protected according to PKCS #7, whereas the MIME type `application/pkcs10` (or `application/x-pkcs10`, respectively) is used to specify that a MIME entity is a certification request message according to PKCS #10. Examples of BER and DER encodings according to the PCKS specifications are provided in [15].

5.4 CONCLUSIONS

In this chapter, we addressed the problem of specifying and encoding (cryptographic and noncryptographic) messages in communication protocols. More specifically, we overviewed and briefly discussed ASN.1 and some related sets of encoding rules as the mechanisms of choice for professional network application designers and developers. Note, however, that some opponents of ASN.1 and related encoding rules argue that the complexity and the size of the resulting ASN.1 parsers are far too big to be used in practice. Consequently, they use alternative encoding schemes. Furthermore, we overviewed and briefly introduced a suite of specifications that address various aspects related to the implementation of public key cryptography. This suite is commonly referred to as PKCS and is widely used in practice.

In Part II of this book, we address PGP that does not make use of any technology addressed in this chapter. PGP still relies on a rather informal specification and a handcrafted transfer syntax. In Part III, however, we elaborate on S/MIME that makes use of all technologies addressed in this chapter. More specifically, S/MIME is based on PKCS #1, PKCS #7, and PKCS #10, and its messages are specified in ASN.1 and encoded according to DER. Furthermore, the use of PKCS #11- and

PKCS #15-compliant tokens (e.g., smartcards and USB tokens) and applications that make use of these tokens is getting increasingly important.

REFERENCES

[1] J. Larmouth, *ASN.1 Complete*, Morgan Kaufmann Publishers, 1999.

[2] ISO/IEC 8824-1, Information Technology — Open Systems Interconnection — Abstract Syntax Notation One (ASN.1) — Part 1: Specification of Basic Notation (also ITU-T recommendation X.680).

[3] ISO/IEC 8824-2, Information Technology — Open Systems Interconnection — Abstract Syntax Notation One (ASN.1) — Part 2: Information Object Specification (also ITU-T recommendation X.681).

[4] ISO/IEC 8824-3, Information Technology — Open Systems Interconnection — Abstract Syntax Notation One (ASN.1) — Part 3: Constraint Specification (also ITU-T recommendation X.682).

[5] ISO/IEC 8824-4, Information Technology — Open Systems Interconnection — Abstract Syntax Notation One (ASN.1) — Part 4: Parameterization of ASN.1 Specifications (also ITU-T recommendation X.683).

[6] ISO/IEC 9834-1, Information Technology — Open Systems Interconnection — Procedures for the Operation of OSI Registration Authorities — Part 1: General Procedures (also ITU-T recommendation X.660).

[7] ISO/IEC 8825-1, Information Technology — Open Systems Interconnection — Specification of ASN.1 Encoding Rules — Part 1: Basic Encoding Rules (BER) (also ITU-T recommendation X.690).

[8] ISO/IEC 8825-3, Information Technology — Open Systems Interconnection — Specification of ASN.1 Encoding Rules — Part 3: Distinguished Canonical Encoding Rules (also ITU-T recommendation X.692).

[9] B.S. Kaliski, "A Layman's Guide to a Subset of ASN.1, BER, and DER," RSA Laboratories Technical Note, November 1993.

[10] J. Feghhi, J. Feghhi, and P. Williams, *Digital Certificates: Applied Internet Security*, Addison-Wesley Longman, Reading, MA, 1999.

[11] B.S. Kaliski, "An Overview of the PKCS Standards," RSA Laboratories Technical Note, November 1993.

[12] B. Kaliski, "PKCS #1: RSA Encryption Version 1.5," Request for Comments 2313, March 1998.

[13] B. Kaliski, "PKCS #7: Cryptographic Message Syntax Version 1.5," Request for Comments 2315, March 1998.

[14] B. Kaliski, "PKCS #10: Certification Request Syntax Version 1.5," Request for Comments 2314, March 1998.

[15] B.S. Kaliski, "Some Examples of the PKCS Standards," RSA Laboratories Technical Note, November 1993.

Part II

PGP

Chapter 6

History and Development

Unlike PEM, MOSS, and S/MIME, the term *Pretty Good Privacy* (PGP) does not only refer to a protocol specification for secure messaging, but also to a software package that is used and widely deployed on the Internet today.[1] The PGP software package was originally developed by Philip R. Zimmermann[2] in the early 1990s [1,2]. At that time, Zimmermann selected some of the best available cryptographic algorithms (i.e., MD5, IDEA, and RSA) as building blocks, integrated them into a platform-independent software package that was based on a small set of easy-to-use commands, and made the resulting software package and its documentation, including the source code written in the C programming language, publicly and freely available on the Internet (at least for citizens from the United States and Canada). In addition, Zimmermann entered into a legal agreement with a company called Viacrypt to provide a fully compatible commercial version of PGP that was reasonably priced.[3] The commercial version of PGP was primarily intended to

[1]The terms "Pretty Good Privacy," "Pretty Good," and "PGP" are registered trademarks of Network Associates, Inc.

[2]Some background information about Philip R. Zimmermann is available on the Web at URL `http://www.nai.com/products/security/phil/phil.asp`.

[3]The company no longer exists and the URL `www.viacrypt.com` leads to the homepage of Network Associates, Inc. (NAI).

satisfy the requirements of users who wanted to have a product with full professional vendor support.

There were at least two legal problems related to the first versions of PGP:

- First, the PGP software used the RSA algorithm for authentication and key distribution. As mentioned in Chapter 4, the RSA algorithm was protected by a U.S. patent (that expired on September 20, 2000);
- Second and more importantly, the U.S. government held that export controls for cryptographic software were violated when the PGP software spread around the world following its publication as freeware.

The first problem was settled with the patent holders of the RSA algorithm by having the PGP software include and make use of a cryptographic subroutine library that was distributed by RSA Security, Inc.[4] More specifically, beginning with version 2.5, the PGP software included and made use of the RSAREF cryptographic subroutine library to perform RSA public key computations. The RSAREF library, in turn, was distributed under a license that allowed noncommercial use within the United States. The commercial use of RSAREF, however, required the payment of a license fee to RSA Security, Inc. Since the commercial version of PGP was sold by Viacrypt, the use of RSAREF in this version was properly licensed.

The second problem was more severe. In fact, it led to a three-year criminal investigation by the U.S. government. Zimmermann was accused of a Federal crime because the software had flowed across national borders. The investigation was carefully followed by both the trade press and the general public as, for example, further described in [3].

After the government dropped the case in early 1996, Zimmermann founded a company called Pretty Good Privacy, Inc.,[5] which was acquired by McAfee Associates in December 1997. At the same time, Network Associates, Inc. (NAI) was formed by a merger of McAfee Associates and Network General. Today, NAI is one of the world's largest independent network security and management software companies with four business units and more than 2,700 employees. Zimmermann, in turn, is employed as a Senior Fellow at NAI (or the PGP Security business unit of NAI, respectively).

In the United States and Canada, the PGP software is publicly and freely available for noncommercial use, but must be licensed for commercial use from NAI:

[4]At that time, RSA Security, Inc. was still named RSA Data Security, Inc.

[5]`http://www.pgp.com`

- The noncommercial version of PGP is distributed by MIT;[6]
- The commercial version of PGP is distributed by NAI and its local resellers.

Outside the United States and Canada, the legal situation is less clear. A couple of years ago, the international PGPi scanning project was initiated and launched.[7] The idea of the project was to export the source code of the PGP software in optical character recognition (OCR) format, and to recompile and rebuild the software entirely outside the United States and Canada. Note that the U.S. Export Administration Regulations (EAR) explicitly state:

> "A printed book or other printed material setting forth encryption source code is not itself subject to the EAR (...)"

Consequently, source code is not subject to the EAR and can be exported from the United States. If the source code is recompiled and rebuilt entirely outside the United States, a fully compatible and interoperable software package is created. The resulting versions of the PGP software (also referred to as PGPi) are publicly and freely available from the International PGP Home Page at `http://www.pgpi.org` (the site is physically located in Norway). Note that the amount of source code is huge. For example, PGP 5.0i was recompiled and rebuilt from source code that was printed in 12 books containing more than 6,000 pages, whereas PGP version 6.5.1 already came along with 40 books containing more than 20,000 pages.

In addition to the PGPi scanning project, NAI used Network Associates International B.V. in the Netherlands to market PGP products outside the United States and Canada. The corresponding Web site is available at `http://www.pgpinternational.com`. More specifically, the PGP products sold by Network Associates International B.V. were recompiled and rebuilt by a Swiss company called cnlab Software AG[8] based on the widely available C source code that was legally exported from the United States (the same source code that is used for the domestic versions of the PGP software). Network Associates International B.V. licensed the PGP software from cnlab AG in order to market it outside the United States and Canada. In order to comply with the EAR, NAI had to make sure that no technical assistance or support was provided from the United States to cnlab Software AG or to any international users of PGP products, and that all

[6] `http://web.mit.edu/network/pgp.html`
[7] `http://www.pgpi.org/pgpi/project/scanning/`
[8] `http://www.cnlab.ch`

support for international users came from non-U.S. nationals, either from employees of Network Associates International B.V., employees of cnlab Software AG, or anybody else.

This situation has changed and the liberalized U.S. export controls have made it possible for NAI and its PGP Security business unit to legally distribute PGP products on a worldwide scale. In fact, on January 20, 2000, PGP Security announced[9] that its software had been successfully exported from the United States for the first time under the new export regulations. At an event launching the new PGP Security business unit of NAI, the software was exported by sending it as a binary e-mail attachment to a recipient in the United Kingdom. This simple act would have been designated a federal crime until January 14, 2000, when new export regulations were adopted by the U.S. Department of Commerce (DoC) to allow use of U.S.-developed cryptographic technology worldwide (refer to Chapter 4 for a brief discussion of the new U.S. export regulations). It will be interesting to see how the new export regulations influence the worldwide distribution of PGP software and products. In either case, NAI still recommends buying the software from its local resellers.

As mentioned above, the first versions of PGP were implemented by Zimmermann. Major parts of later versions of PGP, however, were implemented by an international collaborative effort involving a large number of contributors. In this book, we use the term "PGP" to refer to software developed by NAI (or its PGP Security business unit respectively) or any other software that implements and conforms to the PGP or OpenPGP specifications. There are many versions of PGP in use today:

- PGP 2.6.x was the first version that was widely used and internationally deployed. This version of PGP is specified in the informational RFC 1991 [4]. As such, it requires use of MD5, IDEA, and RSA.

- PGP 5.x was introduced to define new message formats and correct a number of problems in the PGP 2.6.x design. PGP 5.x is also known as PGP 3.

- After the release of PGP 5.x, an IETF OpenPGP WG was formed in the IETF Security Area. The aim of the WG was to use PGP 5.x as a basis and to come up with a new OpenPGP specification. More recently, OpenPGP was specified in RFC 2440 [5] and submitted to the Internet standards track.

[9]The announcement was made during the RSA Data Security Conference that was held on January 16 – 20, 2000, in San José, California (USA).

- Based on PGP 5.x and the OpenPGP specifications, NAI came up with PGP 6.x that introduced some new features that go beyond a tool for secure messaging. Two of these features include PGPnet, which is basically a "bump-in-the-stack" implementation of the IP security (IPsec) protocol suite, and PGPdisk, which allows a user to transparently encrypt and decrypt partitions on local hard disks. These and some additional features of PGP are further discussed in Chapter 9. The focus of this book is the currently available PGP version 6.5.3.[10]

- More recently, NAI publicly released PGP Desktop Security 7.0 in September 2000 for the Windows and Macintosh operating systems. In addition to the functionality of PGP 6.x, PGP Desktop Security 7.0 provides a personal firewall and a personal intrusion detection system. Furthermore, PGP Desktop Security 7.0 fully integrates with X.509-based PKIs and provides a single sign-on (SSO) mechanism for the Windows 2000 operating system. Finally, PGP Desktop Security 7.0 comes with an optional passphrase recovery mechanism.[11] Support for smartcards (primarily for the European market) and USB tokens (primarily for the U.S. market) is announced to become available in PGP 7.1.

In addition, there are several PGP versions that are marked with special characters. For example, we mentioned above that a PGP version number with an appended character "i" (e.g., PGP version 6.0.2i) refers to an international version that is made available as part of the PGPi scanning project, meaning that the software has been recompiled and rebuilt entirely outside the United States and Canada.

Contrary to MOSS and S/MIME, PGP must not be integrated into the UA software. A user can create a message with his favorite word processing program (e.g., a "normal" text editor or Microsoft Word), digitally sign and/or encrypt the file with PGP, optionally encode it for transport with PGP's radix-64 encoding function or any other encoding utility, and finally use a commercial off-the-shelf (COTS) UA of his choice to send the resulting message to the recipient. The point to make (and to remember) is that PGP must not be part of the UA that is finally used to send out the message, and that PGP can reside entirely outside the UA. However, from a user's point of view it is more convenient to have PGP

[10] In August 2000, a bug was found in the additional decryption key (ADK) feature of PGP (refer to CERT Advisory CA-2000-18 "PGP May Encrypt Data With Unauthorized ADKs" at `http://www.cert.org/advisories/CA-2000-18.html` for further information). A corresponding HotFix 1 is available at `http://www.pgp.com/other/advisories/adk.asp`.

[11] The mechanism makes use of five personal questions and answers that are provided by the user during the initialization and configuration process of PGP.

be incorporated into and be part of the UA software. In the simplest case, the user has two buttons, one for signaling the use of digital signatures (to protect the authenticity and integrity of a message) and one for signaling the use of digital envelopes (to protect the confidentiality of a message).

If a UA is MIME-compliant, it may even be possible to combine PGP's functionality with the functionality of MIME. In fact, the approach to combine PGP and MIME is called PGP/MIME and the approach to combine OpenPGP and MIME is called OpenPGP/MIME:

- PGP/MIME is based on the message formats defined in RFC 1991 [4] and further specified in RFC 2015 [6].
- OpenPGP/MIME is based on the message formats defined in RFC 2440 [5] and further specified in a pair of Internet-Drafts[12] that are developed by the participants of the IETF OpenPGP WG. By the time you read this book, these Internet-Drafts will probably have become standard track RFC documents.

Not all UAs implement the PGP/MIME and OpenPGP/MIME specifications. For example, Qualcomm Eudora version 4.3 implements only PGP/MIME, whereas Microsoft Outlook Express version 5 implements neither of the two specifications.

Finally, note that RFC 1991 requires the use of patented cryptographic algorithms (RSA and IDEA), and that it cannot be submitted to the Internet standards track accordingly (it has been published as an informational RFC document). Since RFC 2015 relies on RFC 1991, it cannot be submitted to the Internet standards track either. Consequently, PGP/MIME is not going to become an Internet standard. Contrary to that, it is likely and very possible that OpenPGP/MIME will be submitted to the Internet standards track and that PGP/MIME implementations will be replaced by OpenPGP/MIME implementations in the future.

REFERENCES

[1] P.R. Zimmermann, *The Official PGP User's Guide*, The MIT Press, Cambridge, MA, 1995.

[2] P.R. Zimmermann, *PGP Source Code and Internals*, The MIT Press, Cambridge, MA, 1995.

[3] S. Garfinkel, *PGP: Pretty Good Privacy*, O'Reilly & Associates, Sebastopol, CA, 1995.

[4] D. Atkins, W. Stallings, and P.R. Zimmermann, "PGP Message Exchange Formats," Request for Comments 1991, August 1996.

[12] `draft-ietf-openpgp-mime-*.txt` and `draft-ietf-openpgp-multsig-*.txt`

[5] J. Callas, L. Donnerhacke, H. Finney, and R. Thayer, "OpenPGP Message Format," Request for Comments 2440, November 1998.

[6] M. Elkins, "MIME Security with Pretty Good Privacy (PGP)," Request for Comments 2015, October 1996.

Chapter 7

Technological Approach

After having briefly overviewed the history and development of PGP, we elaborate on its conceptual and technological approach in this chapter. More specifically, we introduce the topic in Section 7.1, address message formats, supported algorithms, and message processing in Sections 7.2 to 7.4. Finally, we focus on the management of cryptographic keys in Section 7.5.

7.1 INTRODUCTION

In short, PGP combines the use of secret and public key cryptography to provide basic message protection services that are relevant for Internet messaging. More specifically, PGP provides data origin authentication and integrity services through the use of digital signatures, and data confidentiality services through the use of digital envelopes (refer to Chapter 4 for an explanation of digital signatures and digital envelopes). Furthermore, PGP is able to compress data (using the ZIP compression algorithm), encode messages for transfer (using the base-64 or radix-64 encoding scheme), and manage public keys in a unique way. Most of these issues are addressed in this chapter. The management of public keys, however, is further discussed in Chapter 8.

Unfortunately, there are some terminological problems in many texts related to PGP (including, for example, some of the original PGP documentation and manuals). We briefly mention two of these problems to make it easier for you to start reading these texts:

- First, the term "Diffie-Hellman" as used in many texts related to PGP is a misnomer. The algorithm to use a modified version of the Diffie-Hellman (DH) key exchange protocol to encrypt data (e.g., a session key) was proposed by Taher ElGamal [1] a couple of years after the original publication of Whitfield Diffie and Martin Hellman [2]. Consequently, it is known as ElGamal encryption scheme, and the expression "DH/DSS" as used, for example, in the user interface of PGP should be replaced with "ElGamal/DSS" or something similar.[1]

- Second, the term "session key" as used in many texts related to PGP is also a misnomer. E-mail is a connectionless application, and there is no session being established between the sender and recipient of an e-mail message (there may only be sessions between pairs of MTAs on the message delivery path). Consequently, the term "session key" should be replaced with "transaction key," "message encryption key," "data encryption key," or something similar. It's basically a one-time key that is used to encrypt and decrypt a single message.

To make it easier to start reading the original PGP documentation and manuals, we sometimes use the above-mentioned and arguably wrong terms in this book.[2] In particular, we use the term "Diffie-Hellman" to refer to ElGamal's encryption scheme, and we use the term "session key" to refer to a message encryption key. There is no need to use different terms to describe the same thing (even if the originally used terms are wrong or misnomers).

Finally, a more serious terminological problem is related to the fact that some of the PGP documentation and manuals use the term "secret key" to refer to a key that is paired with a public key in a public key cryptosystem. Such a "secret key" should be referred to as "private key." The practice of calling the private key of a public key pair "secret key" risks confusion with a secret key from a secret key cryptosystem. In this book, we consistently use the term "private key" to refer to

[1] Note that the ElGamal encryption scheme and the Digital Signature Standard (DSS) are conceptually similar and are based on the same mathematical problem, namely the discrete logarithm problem. While the ElGamal encryption scheme is used to encrypt data, the DSS is used to digitally sign data.

[2] Only in the latest specifications of OpenPGP have the authors started to use the appropriate term for ElGamal's encryption scheme.

the secret key paired with a public key in a public key cryptosystem. So keep in mind when you switch to the original PGP documentation and manuals that the term "secret key" essentially refers to the term "private key" as used in this book.

7.2 MESSAGE FORMATS

We already mentioned in the previous chapter that there are currently two formats for PGP messages:

- The PGP message format as specified in RFC 1991 [3];
- The OpenPGP message format as specified in RFC 2440 [4].

Furthermore, we have seen that PGP and OpenPGP can also be combined with MIME, and that the resulting specifications are referred to as PGP/MIME [5] and OpenPGP/MIME.

For the purpose of this section (which is entitled "message formats"), there is no fundamental difference between PGP and OpenPGP on the one hand, and PGP/MIME and OpenPGP/MIME on the other hand. Consequently, we summarize the message format of PGP together with the message format of OpenPGP, and the message format of PGP/MIME together with the message format of OpenPGP/MIME.

7.2.1 PGP and OpenPGP

The relevant PGP and OpenPGP specifications define the format of a PGP file. A PGP file, in turn, is a file that has been digitally signed and/or digitally enveloped using PGP or OpenPGP. PGP and OpenPGP files use similar formats, so we use the term PGP file to refer to either of them. In the case of e-mail, a PGP file may refer to a message that is sent and received electronically. Note, however, that PGP can also be used to encrypt arbitrary files in a file system or archive.

In short, each PGP file is constructed from a number of records that have traditionally been called "packets." A packet, in turn, is a chunk of data that has a tag specifying its meaning. Consequently, each PGP file consists of a number of packets that collectively define a message, key ring, certificate, or anything else that is relevant for PGP.[3] The PGP packet scheme is recursive, so some of these packets

[3]OpenPGP specifies a packet format that is different from the original PGP packet format. In [4], the former is called "new packet format," whereas the latter is called "old packet format."

may contain other packets. Each packet consists of a variable-length header, followed by the packet body. The first byte of the packet header is called the packet tag. It determines the format of the header and denotes the packet contents. The remainder of the packet header declares the length of the packet. We are not going to replicate the packet format specifications in this book. You may refer to the referenced RFC documents if you are a developer and have to implement either the PGP or OpenPGP packet format.

Before we turn to the general format of PGP files, let's briefly elaborate on a practical problem related to the use of public key cryptography. As we mentioned in Chapter 4, a digitally enveloped message comes along with an encrypted version of the session key that was used to encrypt the message in the first place. The key is encrypted with the recipient's public key. If each user employed a single public key pair, then the recipient would immediately know which key to use to decrypt the session key. However, a PGP user may have multiple public key pairs and there need not be a one-to-one relationship between PGP users and their public keys (this is true for any system that makes use of public key cryptography, not just PGP). How, then, does the recipient of an encrypted message know which of his public keys was used to encrypt the session key? Similarly, how does he know which private key to use to decrypt the session key? In general, there are three different approaches to address this problem:

- First, the recipient could try all private keys he currently holds to decrypt the message.

- Second, the sender could transmit the public key he used to encrypt the message together with the encrypted message. The recipient, in turn, could verify that the transmitted public key is one of his public keys, and proceed accordingly.

- Third, a key identifier (key ID) could be associated with each public key that is unique at least for one user identifier (user ID). In this case, a pair consisting of a user ID and key ID would be sufficient to uniquely identify the appropriate public key. Then only the much shorter key ID would need to be transmitted (as compared to the second approach).

Obviously, the first approach is rather clumsy and inefficient with regard to the computational overhead required on the recipient's side (remember that the use of public key cryptography requires a lot of computational resources). Also, the second approach is inefficient with regard to bandwidth consumption. Note that a public key is typically several hundreds of decimal digits in length, so a transmitted public key occupies and consumes a considerably large amount of bandwidth. Consequently, the third approach seems to provide a more efficient way to address the problem. This approach, however, also raises a management problem, since key IDs must be assigned, stored, and managed so that both sender and recipient can map them to the appropriate public keys.

The elegant solution used by PGP is to assign a key ID to each public key that is, with a very high probability, unique for a given user ID. The key ID, in turn, consists of the least significant 64 bits of the public key it is associated with. That is, the key ID of A's public key k_A refers to the mathematical result of $k_A \pmod{2^{64}}$. This is a sufficient length so that the key ID is unique for all practical purposes, and that the probability of two keys having the same key IDs is negligible. For example, the key ID of my major PGP public key is `8E50 BDB3 0AC2 9A5B` (written in hexadecimal notation). This hexadecimal value refers to the following binary value:

```
1000 1110 0101 0000   1011 1101 1011 0011
0000 1010 1100 0010   1001 1010 0101 1011
```

Furthermore, if key IDs are displayed by PGP, only the lower 32 bits are shown for further brevity. These 32 bits actually refer to the mathematical result of $k_A \pmod{2^{32}}$. Consequently, the key ID of my major PGP public key is shown as `0AC2 9A5B` (again, written in hexadecimal notation). This hexadecimal value refers to the following binary value:

```
0000 1010 1100 0010   1001 1010 0101 1011
```

Sometimes, the 32-bit key ID is called "short key ID," whereas the 64-bit key ID is called "long key ID."

Using the general idea of key IDs, the general format of a PGP file (e.g., a PGP or OpenPGP message) is illustrated in Figure 7.1. Note, however, that the format illustrated in Figure 7.1 is simplified considerably and includes only the most important fields. The PGP file basically consists of three parts: a message part, a signature part, and a session key part. Both the signature and session key parts are optional, and their existence depends on whether digital signatures and digital envelopes are used.

- First, the *message part* is required and includes the following components:

  - A name for the PGP file;

– A timestamp that specifies the time at which the file was created;

– The data of the file (the data to be stored or transmitted);

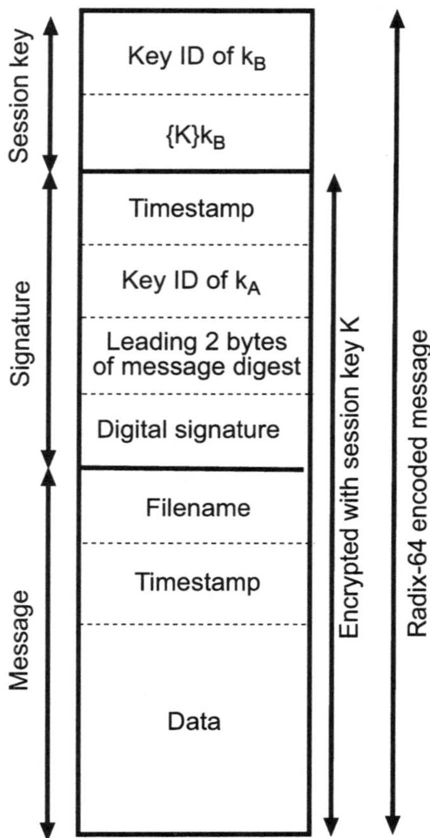

Figure 7.1 The general format of a PGP message (PGP and OpenPGP).

- Second, the *signature part* may include the following components:

  – A timestamp that specifies the time at which the signature was created.

- The key ID[4] of the sender's public key k_A that identifies the public key that should be used to verify the digital signature for the file.

- The leading two bytes of the unencrypted message digest for the file. This binary sequence enables the recipient to determine if the correct public key was used to verify the digital signature.

- The digital signature for the message. It basically consists of the message digest encrypted with the sender's private key k_A^{-1}. The message digest, in turn, is calculated over the signature timestamp concatenated with the data of the PGP file's message part. The inclusion of the signature timestamp in the message digest computation and verification is to protect against replay attacks. Contrary to that, the exclusion of the filename and timestamp of the PGP file's message part is to ensure that detached signatures are exactly the same as attached signatures prefixed to the message (detached signatures are calculated on a separate file that has none of the message part fields, such as filename and timestamp).

- Third, for each recipient B_i $(i = 1, \ldots, n)$ of the message, the *session key part* includes the following components:

  - The encrypted session key $\{K\}k_{B_i}$;

  - The key ID for the recipient's public key k_{B_i} that was used by the sender to encrypt the session key.

For simplicity, Figure 7.1 illustrates a session key part only for one recipient B. As further discussed in Section 4.5, the session key part of a digital envelope must be replicated for each recipient of the message. This is also true for any additional decryption key (ADK) that may be configured by the PGP administrator. In short, a PGP software distribution package can be configured in a way that for each message that is encrypted with PGP, the corresponding session key is additionally encrypted with the ADK. The aim is to provide a simple recovery

[4]For obvious reasons, a key ID is also required for digital signatures. Because a sender may have multiple private keys to encrypt a message digest (and digitally sign the message accordingly), the recipient must know which public key he should use. Consequently, the digital signature component of a PGP message must include the 64-bit key ID of the required public key. When the message is received, the recipient must verify that the key ID is for a public key that is known for that sender and then proceed to verify the signature.

mechanism for the session keys that are used to encrypt messages with PGP. The session keys can only be recovered by someone holding the private key part of the ADK (i.e., the PGP administrator).[5]

It is obvious that a PGP file can be sent in the message body part of an RFC 822-compliant e-mail message. Eventually, the PGP file must be encoded into a character set that is transferable through all major MTAs and MTSs prior to incorporating it into the message body. As discussed later in this chapter, PGP uses the base-64 (also known as radix-64) encoding scheme for this purpose.

A PGP file can be sent and received with commercial off-the-shelf (COTS) UA software that is not aware of cryptography at all. In fact, all cryptographic transformations can be done offline with PGP. Note, however, that from a user's point of view it is more convenient to have PGP be incorporated and be part of the UA software. In this case, the UA typically provides two additional buttons on the graphical user interface (GUI), one for signaling the use of digital signatures (to protect the authenticity and integrity of a message) and one for signaling the use of digital envelopes (to protect the confidentiality of a message). The message, in turn, is digitally signed and/or digitally enveloped according to the buttons the user pushes. Afterwards, there are two possibilities for the UA to transfer the digitally signed and/or digitally enveloped message to the recipient:

- First, the UA can encode the message in a form that is transferable through all major MTAs and MTSs (e.g., uuencode or base-64 encode the message) and attach it to a "normal" RFC 822-compliant e-mail message;
- Second, the UA can make use of MIME to transfer the message.

The first possibility is simple and straightforward. For example, the body part of an encrypted and digitally enveloped PGP message may look as follows:


```
-----BEGIN PGP MESSAGE-----
Version: PGP Personal Privacy 6.5.3

qANQR1DDDQQDAwJQ3AjP29XbWWDJwB1hZRimoQ1QLBAw55tpRRqs9BY27sQabaVA
/UmaQa6RRZXfe5MiNt+Qdm4MZ+R8oxLE8yaCz/WvBxumU5jynb5Lg4YCJoFeiqLJ
rbETqrj4nClQ8VtXmNXyp637UkCvJxViJbPqa1fKffZnLHi/JHelDnDhHCKbmqGJ
h3tkEpNStuw8OozALt0YCdKyY4E0zLRAYX2utSVk66VQAucgibpX308+lAFwqXFr
```


[5] Again, refer to footnote 10 of Chapter 6 for a brief note regarding a bug that was found in PGP's ADK feature in August 2000.

```
rPr4cVIHPDvL+f3tjO8dVjR+pC/i3+WZPATR2//aADKpkX95zTa56TI8u3RDzF7D
iClpnA==
=s4eF
-----END PGP MESSAGE-----
```


Similarly, the body part of a digitally signed PGP message may look as follows:

```
-----BEGIN PGP SIGNED MESSAGE-----
Hash: SHA1

This is a digitally signed test message.

-----BEGIN PGP SIGNATURE-----
Version: PGP Personal Privacy 6.5.3

iQA/AwUBORJRro5QvbMKwppbEQIOcwCgOg6+cbxnZH8gyVD/deWCrbA6desAoKdg
5flmAMSqcKLHV1OQBh5OtpmP
=CN7I
-----END PGP SIGNATURE-----
```

The first possibility (namely to encode the cryptographically protected PGP message into the body part of a "normal" RFC 822-compliant e-mail message) has advantages and disadvantages. The most important advantage is related to the fact that the receiving UA must not support PGP at all. Instead, the recipient can extract the digitally signed and/or digitally enveloped message part and use PGP outside the UA software to verify the signature and/or decrypt the message. Contrary to that, the most important disadvantage is related to the fact that MIME are not supported. The second possibility (namely to combine PGP and OpenPGP) remedies this problem. This possibility is more complex, but also more powerful. The resulting PGP/MIME and OpenPGP/MIME specifications are addressed next.

7.2.2 PGP/MIME and OpenPGP/MIME

The PGP/MIME and OpenPGP/MIME specifications make use of RFC 1847 [6] and RFC 1848 [7] that define two security-related MIME `multipart` subtypes, namely `multipart/encrypted` and `multipart/signed`. These security-related `multipart` subtypes can be used to clearly separate the encryption information and/or digital signature(s) from the corresponding MIME entity (e.g., message body part). Furthermore, the following "protocol" parameters can be used to indicate the use of PGP or OpenPGP:

- The `application/pgp-encrypted` protocol parameter can be used to indicate an encrypted MIME entity;
- The `application/pgp-signature` protocol parameter can be used to indicate a digitally signed MIME entity.

The idea of using the MIME content types `multipart/encrypted` and `multipart/signed` was first used for PGP/MIME [5], and is now being used for OpenPGP/MIME. The resulting message formats for PGP/MIME and OpenPGP/MIME are very similar and overviewed next. More specifically, we focus on PGP/MIME and OpenPGP/MIME encrypted and/or digitally signed messages. Messages for key distribution are conceptually similar (they are also encrypted and/or digitally signed). The major difference is that they are encoded using the MIME content type `application/pgp-keys` (not further addressed in this book).

Encrypted Messages

As mentioned above, PGP/MIME and OpenPGP/MIME encrypted messages are identified with the MIME `multipart/encrypted` content type and a "protocol" parameter set to `application/pgp-encrypted` (note that the value of the protocol parameter must be enclosed in quotes).

The following example illustrates the skeleton of an encrypted test message sent from `sender@esecurity.ch` to `recipient@esecurity.ch` (most message headers are only indicated with three dots):

```
Return-Path:    ...
X-Internal-ID: ...
Received:       ...
Message-Id:     ...
X-Mailer: QUALCOMM Windows Eudora Version 4.3
Date: Thu, 02 Mar 2000 20:53:54 +0100
To: Recipient <recipient@esecurity.ch>
From: Sender <sender@esecurity.ch>
Subject: Encrypted test message
Mime-Version: 1.0
Content-Type: multipart/encrypted;
   boundary="foo";
   protocol="application/pgp-encrypted"
```

```
--foo
Content-Type: application/pgp-encrypted
Version: 1

--foo
Content-Type: application/octet-stream

-----BEGIN PGP MESSAGE-----
Version: PGP Personal Privacy 6.5.3

qANQR1DDDQQDAwKDVmWFpLfZu2DJiVyaEPGkoFLfYv63KKkxhJb77Wgxvpv7c6N4
QYCXsDjSuNr5jC1Gpza5ZA04uGWU4DEbe6jDHuMsrjI/dIv6+qQtf5XQFA8eVrWl
44lRNXuX8KOOCAgew6UPNNEoboImQSHvto3eb1PQONRlPpXBwKsZnrHY/s6niOuz
PeemkplpvOfTA+Ly/ar1
=PDDf
-----END PGP MESSAGE-----

--foo--
```

Note that the message basically consists of two parts (separated with the boundary string `foo`):

- The first part contains some control information for the message. More specifically, it has a `Content-Type` header set to `application/pgp-encrypted` and a `Version` header set to `1`. Since the PGP and OpenPGP packet formats contain all the other information that is required to properly decrypt the message, no other information is provided here.

- The second part contains the encrypted message (e.g., the sentence "`This is an encrypted test message.`" in this example). As such, this part includes a `Content-Type` header set to `application/octet-stream` and the encrypted message. The encrypted message, in turn, includes the PGP version number (e.g., `PGP Personal Privacy 6.5.3` in this example) in use as prepended plaintext.

Finally, note that the `X-Mailer` header indicates the use of the Qualcomm Eudora UA (version 4.3).

Digitally Signed Messages

As mentioned above, PGP/MIME and OpenPGP/MIME digitally signed messages are identified with the MIME **multipart/signed** content type and some additional parameters. More specifically, the "protocol" parameter is set to **application/pgp-signature** (again, this parameter value must be enclosed in quotes), and the "micalg" parameter is set to the message integrity check (MIC) algorithm `pgp-<hash-symbol>`, where `<hash-symbol>` identifies the message digest algorithm that is used in the digital signature scheme (e.g., **md5** for MD5 or **sha1** for SHA-1).

Alternatively, a PGP/MIME or OpenPGP/MIME digitally signed message can also be identified with the MIME **multipart/mixed** content type (with some appropriate parameter settings) if the message contains two or more digital signatures. In this case, each signature is denoted using the content type **application/pgp-signature** inside a **multipart/mixed** entity (as further discussed below).

The following example illustrates the skeleton of a digitally signed test message sent from **sender@esecurity.ch** to **recipient@esecurity.ch** (again, most message headers are only indicated with three dots):

```
Return-Path:   ...
X-Internal-ID: ...
Received:      ...
Message-Id:    ...
X-Mailer: QUALCOMM Windows Eudora Version 4.3
Date: Thu, 02 Mar 2000 21:50:23 +0100
To: Recipient <recipient@esecurity.ch>
From: Sender <sender@esecurity.ch>
Subject: Digitally signed test message
Mime-Version: 1.0
Content-Type: multipart/signed;
   boundary="foo";
   protocol="application/pgp-signature";
   micalg=pgp-sha1

--foo
Mime-Version: 1.0
Content-Type: text/plain; charset="us-ascii"; format=flowed
```

```
This is a digitally signed test message.

--foo
Content-Type: application/pgp-signature

-----BEGIN PGP MESSAGE-----
Version: PGP Personal Privacy 6.5.3

iQA/AwUBOL5xoI5QvbMKwppbEQJTFwCcD3AAKwWF8hzZjILI5fM4SC6u7HsAnRLe
wY5nufbjRU9CijNuMkz0Dcmy
=z5tV
-----END PGP MESSAGE-----

--foo
```

The fact that the message includes a digitally signed message is signaled with the `Content-Type` header and the "protocol" parameter set to "`application/pgp-signature`." The message digest algorithm in use is SHA-1. The message body consists of two parts (again, separated with the boundary string `foo`):

- The first part contains the message text that is digitally signed with some additional MIME message headers. In our example, the message text includes the sentence, `This is a digitally signed test message.`[6]
- The second part contains the digital signature for the first part's message text. The digital signature is signaled with a MIME content type `application/pgp-signature`. Furthermore, the signature block also includes the PGP version in use as prepended plaintext (e.g., `PGP Personal Privacy 6.5.3` in this example).

If the message (included in the first part) is digitally signed multiple times, the second part must include the corresponding signatures. In this case, the second part must include a multipart entity with a `Content-Type` header set to `multipart/mixed` and each part including one signature (denoted using the content type `application/pgp-signature`).

[6]Note that the current OpenPGP/MIME specification suggests that "&" characters are used to indicate the portion of the message over which the signature(s) was (were) calculated.

The following example illustrates the skeleton of a message that includes two signatures:

```
...
Mime-Version: 1.0
Content-Type: multipart/signed;
   boundary="foo1";
   protocol="multipart/mixed";
   micalg="pgp-sha1, pgp-md5"

--foo1
Mime-Version: 1.0
Content-Type: text/plain; charset="us-ascii"

This is a test message that is digitally signed multiple
times.

--foo1
Content-Type: multipart/mixed; boundary="foo2";

--foo2
Content-Type: application/pgp-signature

-----BEGIN PGP SIGNATURE-----
Version: PGP Personal Privacy 6.5.3
Comment: This block contains a SHA-1-based signature

...
-----END PGP SIGNATURE-----

--foo2
Content-Type: application/pgp-signature

-----BEGIN PGP SIGNATURE-----
Version: PGP Personal Privacy 6.5.3
Comment: This block contains an MD5-based signature

...
```

```
-----END PGP SIGNATURE-----

--foo2--

--foo1--
```

If a message includes multiple signatures, the "micalg" parameter of the `Content-Type` header must contain a comma-separated list of hash-symbols that identify the message digest algorithms used to generate the signatures.

Finally, note that it is sometimes desirable to both digitally sign and encrypt a message. In this case, it is possible to first sign a `multipart/signature` body, and then encrypt the result to form a `multipart/encrypted` body.

Table 7.1
Message Digest Algorithm IDs Specified for OpenPGP [4]

ID	Algorithm
1	MD5
2	SHA-1
3	RIPEMD-160
4	Reserved for double-width SHA (experimental)
5	MD2
6	Reserved for TIGER (192 bits)
7	Reserved for 5-pass HAVAL (160 bits)
100 to 110	Private/Experimental algorithm

7.3 SUPPORTED ALGORITHMS

PGP and OpenPGP are based on cryptographic algorithms that have had (and still have) extensive public review. Consequently, one may reasonably expect that the algorithms to be sufficiently secure:

- According to RFC 1991 [3], PGP requires the use of the MD5, IDEA, and RSA algorithms. Today, we know some cryptanalytical weaknesses of the MD5 message digest algorithm, but it's still in widespread use (refer to Chapter 4 for a discussion of these weaknesses). Contrary to that, there are no practically relevant cryptanalytical attacks known that could be launched against the IDEA and RSA algorithms. There are, however, some patent claims for either of the

Table 7.2
Data Encryption Algorithm IDs Specified for OpenPGP [4]

ID	Algorithm	Key length
0	Plaintext or unencrypted data	—
1	IDEA	128 bits
2	3DES	168 bits
3	CAST	128 bits
4	Blowfish	128 bits
5	SAFER-K128	128 bits
6	Reserved for DES/SK	56 bits
7	Reserved for AES	128 bits
8	Reserved for AES	192 bits
9	Reserved for AES	256 bits
100 to 110	Private/Experimental algorithm	—

two algorithms, and these patent claims have made it impossible to submit RFC 1991 for the Internet standards track. As mentioned in Chapter 4, it's a general policy of the IETF not to standardize any specification that mandates the use of patented technology, unless the patent is granted to the general public (which is not the case for the RSA and IDEA algorithms). Since RFC 2015 is based on RFC 1991, PGP/MIME has also not been submitted to the Internet standards track either.

- According to RFC 2440 [4], OpenPGP does not mandate the use of the RSA and IDEA algorithms. Instead, OpenPGP has been intentionally designed to support many cryptographic algorithms. As such, the OpenPGP specification has been submitted to the Internet standards track and the OpenPGP/MIME specification is expected to follow soon.

More specifically, RFC 2440 (specifying OpenPGP) has many constants predefined for various message digest, secret key, public key, and compression algorithms (refer to Section 9 of RFC 2440 for a more comprehensive overview):

- With regard to message digest algorithms, OpenPGP-compliant implementations must implement SHA-1 and should implement MD5. The message digest algorithm IDs specified for OpenPGP are summarized in Table 7.1.

- With regard to data encryption algorithms, OpenPGP-compliant implementations must implement 3DES. Furthermore, they should implement IDEA and

Table 7.3
Public Key Algorithm IDs Specified for OpenPGP [4]

ID	Algorithm
1	RSA (Encrypt or Sign)
2	RSA Encrypt-Only
3	RSA Sign-Only
16	ElGamal (Encrypt-Only)
17	DSA (Digital Signature Standard)
18	Reserved for Elliptic Curve
19	Reserved for ECDSA
20	ElGamal (Encrypt or Sign)
21	Reserved for Diffie-Hellman (X9.42, as defined for IETF-S/MIME)
100 to 110	Private/Experimental algorithm

Table 7.4
Compression Algorithm IDs Specified for OpenPGP [4]

ID	Algorithm
0	Uncompressed
1	ZIP
2	ZLIB
100 to 110	Private/Experimental algorithm

CAST and may also implement other algorithms (e.g., Blowfish, SAFER K-128, and the AES with three different key lengths for future use). The data encryption algorithm IDs specified for OpenPGP are summarized in Table 7.2.

- With regard to public key algorithms, OpenPGP-compliant implementations must implement DSA for signatures, and ElGamal for public key encryption. Furthermore, implementations should implement RSA and may also implement other algorithms. The public key algorithm IDs specified for OpenPGP are summarized in Table 7.3.

- Finally, OpenPGP-compliant implementations should implement the ZIP algorithm [8] and may implement the ZLIB algorithm [9] for message compression and decompression. The compression algorithm IDs specified for OpenPGP are summarized in Table 7.4.

You may refer to Chapter 4 to get some references for the above-mentioned cryptographic algorithms (the references for the compression algorithms are given above and discussed later in this chapter).

7.4 PROCESSING MESSAGES

In this section, we take a closer look at the procedures that are used to digitally sign, compress, encrypt, and/or radix-64 encode e-mail messages according to the PGP and OpenPGP specifications. Note that the order in which the procedures are applied matters (as discussed below). We use the term "sender" to refer to the PGP software that is used on the sending side, and "recipient" to refer to the PGP software that is used on the receiving side.

7.4.1 Digital Signatures

In general, the use of digital signatures requires at least one message digest algorithm and at least one public key algorithm (that can be used to digitally sign and verify messages). Some possible algorithms are summarized in Tables 7.1 and 7.3. Among these algorithms, PGP mandates the use of MD5 and RSA, whereas OpenPGP mandates the use of SHA-1 and DSA.

On the sender's side, the procedure to digitally sign a message (in canonical form) includes three steps that can be summarized as follows:

- First, the sender uses a one-way hash function to generate a message digest;
- Second, the sender encrypts the message digest using one of his private keys (the encrypted message digest represents the digital signature for the message);
- Third, the sender prepends the digital signature to the message.

The resulting message comprises a signature and a message part (refer to Figure 7.1 for a graphical representation). As such, it is transmitted to the recipient(s).

On the recipient's side, the procedure to verify the digital signature prepended to a message includes two steps that can be summarized as follows:

- First, the recipient decrypts the digital signature using the sender's appropriate public key to reveal the message digest. The appropriate key, in turn, is identified by the key ID that is also included in the signature part of the message.

- Second, the recipient generates a new message digest for the received message and compares it to the revealed message digest. If both message digests match, the digital signature is verified and the message is accepted to be authentic.

Note that the recipient must have a way to get the sender's public key in an authentic form (to verify the digital signature). This issue is briefly addressed toward the end of this chapter and fully discussed in the following chapter.

Although digital signatures are usually prepended to the message they sign, this is not always the case. In fact, PGP supports the notion of a detached signature. A detached signature, in turn, may be stored, processed, and transmitted separately from the message it signs. There are several applications for detached signatures. For example, a user may wish to maintain a separate signature log of all messages sent or received. Also, a detached signature of an executable content file may be used to detect subsequent modification (e.g., caused by a computer virus). Finally, detached signatures can be used when more than one party must sign a document, such as a contract. Each contract signer's signature is independent and therefore is applied only to the document. Alternatively, digital signatures would have to be nested, with the second signer signing both the original document and the signature of the first signer (in a situation with two signers).

7.4.2 Data Compression

As a default, PGP compresses a message after prepending a digital signature but before data encryption. There are at least two reasons to generate the digital signature before the message is compressed:

- First, it is preferable to sign an uncompressed message so that one can store only the uncompressed message together with the digital signature for verification and future use. Contrary to that, if one signed a compressed message, it would be necessary to recompress the original message to verify the digital signature (or to additionally store the compressed message).

- Second, there is a more practical problem even if one is willing to dynamically generate a compressed version of the message for verification. The problem is due to the fact that PGP's major compression algorithm (i.e., the ZIP algorithm) is not deterministic, and that various implementations of the algorithm may generate different compressed messages (mainly to achieve different trade-offs in running speed versus compression ratio). The algorithms are interoperable because any version of the algorithm can correctly decompress the output of any other version. Applying the message digest and digital signature after compression, however, would require that all implementations use the same compression algorithm.

Furthermore, it is important to apply compression before encryption, since encrypted data are usually not compressible (at least if the encryption algorithm is cryptographically sound). Also, applying compression before encryption strengthens the security of the encryption, because the compressed message generally has less redundancy than the uncompressed message, and cryptanalysis is made more difficult accordingly.

As mentioned above and summarized in Table 7.4, OpenPGP-compliant implementations should implement the ZIP algorithm [8] and may implement the ZLIB algorithm [9] for data compression. In fact, most PGP implementations make use of a freeware software package called ZIP. ZIP is functionally equivalent to PKZIP, a widely available shareware package developed and distributed by PKWARE, Inc. ZIP and similar algorithms stem from research by Jacob Jiv and Abraham Lempel who, in 1977, described a technique based on a sliding window buffer that holds the most recently processed text. The resulting compression algorithm is generally referred to as LZ77 [10]. Utilities like ZIP, PKZIP, and gzip all use versions of the LZ77 algorithm. The algorithm is described and further explained in many books, including, for example, Appendix 12A of [11]. The descriptions and explanations are not repeated in this book.

7.4.3 Data Encryption

PGP uses two data encryption methods to provide data confidentiality: public key encryption and secret key encryption. A user can decide on a case-to-case basis which method he wants to use.

Public Key Encryption

With public key encryption, a message is encrypted using a secret key encryption algorithm and a session key. More specifically, a new key ("session key") is randomly or pseudorandomly generated for each message. Since it is used only once, the session key is bound to the message and transmitted with it as part of the digital envelope. To protect the session key, it is encrypted with one of the recipient's public keys (this encryption is repeated for each recipient).

On the sender's side, the procedure to send a message using public key encryption includes three steps that can be summarized as follows:

- First, the sender generates a random or pseudorandom number to serve as a session key for the message.
- Second, the message is encrypted using the session key. As mentioned above, various versions of PGP may use different encryption algorithms (refer to Table 7.2 for the algorithms defined for OpenPGP). In either case, data encryption is done in 64-bit cipher feedback (CFB) mode, actually representing a block cipher.
- Third, the session key is encrypted using each recipient's public key[7] and the resulting encrypted session keys are prepended to the encrypted message.

Consequently, the resulting message comprises a session key part (for each recipient) and a message part. Again, refer to Figure 7.1 for a corresponding illustration. As such, it is transmitted to the recipient(s).

On the recipient's side, the procedure to unpack the digital envelope and decrypt the message includes two steps that can be summarized as follows:

- First, the recipient extracts his encrypted session key from the session key part of the message. He then decrypts the encrypted session key with his private key.
- Second, the recipient decrypts the message using the decrypted session key.

Obviously, this procedure must be repeated by every single recipient of the message.

Secret Key Encryption

With secret key encryption, there are two possibilities to encrypt a message (either directly or indirectly):

- First, the message may be encrypted with a secret key derived from a passphrase or another shared secret (direct encryption).
- Second, the message may be encrypted in a two-stage procedure similar to the public key encryption procedure described above. In this case, the randomly or pseudorandomly generated session key is encrypted with a secret key algorithm keyed with a secret key derived from a passphrase or another shared secret (indirect encryption).

[7]Obviously, the session key is also encrypted with each ADK, if ADKs are configured at all.

In either case, both digital signature and data encryption mechanisms can be applied to the same message. First, one (or several) digital signature(s) is (are) generated for the message and prepended to the message. Then, the message plus digital signature is encrypted using a randomly generated session key. Finally, the session key is encrypted using public key encryption and prepended to the encrypted message (to form the digital envelope for the message).

Last but not least, PGP can also be used to encrypt files or folders into self-decrypting archives (SDAs) which may be sent to users who do not have PGP. In essense, an SDA refers to an executable program that includes the decryption procedure to be applied to the file or folder. To start the decryption procedure, the user only has to enter a passphrase. This passphrase must be exchanged out-of-band between the sender and the recipient. The feature to handle SDAs is highly relevant for the large-scale deployment of PGP, but it is not further addressed in this book.

7.4.4 Radix-64 Conversion

When PGP is used, part or all of the resulting message is encrypted:

- If only a digital signature is used, the message digest is encrypted with the sender's private key;
- If data encryption is used, the entire message and its signature(s) are encrypted with the session key.

Consequently, the resulting message comprises or consists of arbitrary 8-bit data. As discussed in Chapter 2, many e-mail systems only permit the transfer of 7-bit data (e.g., ASCII characters). To accommodate this restriction, PGP can convert arbitrary 8-bit data into a set of universally transferable characters. In short, it uses the base-64 (also known as radix-64) encoding scheme to build ASCII armors for messages. An ASCII armor, in turn, consists of the radix-64 encoded message and some additional information. As explained in Chapter 2, the use of the radix-64 encoding scheme expands a message by one-third. Fortunately, the encrypted session key and signature parts of the message are relatively compact, and the message part has been compressed. In fact, the compression should be more than enough to compensate for the message expansion due to the radix-64 conversion.

When PGP encodes data into the ASCII armor format, it puts specific headers around the data, so that PGP can reconstruct the data at some future point in time. In essence, an ASCII armor contains the following items (in concatenated form):

- An ASCII armor headerline (appropriate for the type of data);
- ASCII armor headers;
- A blank line;
- The ASCII-armored data;
- An ASCII armor checksum;
- An ASCII armor trail (depending on the headerline).

An ASCII armor headerline consists of the appropriate headerline text and five dashes on either side of the headerline text. The headerline text, in turn, is chosen based upon the type of data that is being armored, and how it is being armored. Headerline texts include the following strings:

- `BEGIN PGP MESSAGE` is used for digitally signed, encrypted, or compressed files;
- `BEGIN PGP MESSAGE, PART X/Y` is used for multi-part messages, where the ASCII armor is split into Y files, and the current part comprises the Xth file out of Y.
- `BEGIN PGP PUBLIC KEY BLOCK` is used for transferring public keys;

The second option — namely to split a message into pieces — is required because some e-mail systems or system components are restricted to a maximum message length (e.g., 50 KB). Any message longer than that must be broken up into smaller pieces, each of which is mailed separately. To accomodate this restriction, PGP automatically subdivides a message that is too large into segments that are small enough to be delivered by the e-mail system. In fact, the segmentation is done after all other processing, including the radix-64 encoding. Consequently, the encrypted session key(s) and digital signature(s) appear only once, at the beginning of the first segment. It is up to the recipient to strip off all header information and to reassemble the entire block before performing all other operations.

Similar to RFC 822 headers, the ASCII armor headers are pairs of strings that can give the recipient information about how to decode or use the message. The headers are a part of the armor, not a part of the message. Consequently, they should not be used to convey any important information, since they can change in transit. As examples we saw `Version` and `Comment` ASCII armor headers earlier in this chapter.

The ASCII armor checksum refers to a 24-bit cyclic redundancy check (CRC) to detect transmission errors. The CRC is computed using the generator `0x864CFB` and an initialization of `0xB704CE`. The accumulation is done on the data before it is radix-64 encoded. The CRC is converted to four bytes of radix-64 encoding that are prefixed with an equal sign (=) to form the ASCII armor checksum. For example, in the PGP/MIME examples given earlier in this chapter the ASCII armor checksums are `=PDDf` and `=z5tV`.

Finally, the ASCII armor trail is composed in the same manner as the ASCII armor headerline, except the string `BEGIN` is replaced by the string `END`.

7.5 CRYPTOGRAPHIC KEYS

PGP specifies and implements a cryptographic system. As such, it makes use of the following types of cryptographic keys:

- One-time session keys;
- Passphrase-based encryption keys;
- Public key pairs (public and private keys).

As discussed next, these types of cryptographic keys have different requirements with regard to their generation and management.

7.5.1 Session Keys

One-time session keys used in PGP are secret keys (i.e., keys from a secret key cryptosystem). The most important requirement for session keys refers to the need to generate them in a way that is unpredictable for an outsider.

In essence, PGP generates random numbers from the content and timing of user keystrokes, and pseudorandom numbers using an algorithm that is based on the one specified in ANSI X12.17. Contrary to this ANSI standard, however, PGP uses CAST-128 instead of 3DES for encryption. The entire processes for generating random and pseudorandom numbers are fully described in appendix 12C of [11] and not repeated in this book.

7.5.2 Passphrase-Based Encryption Keys

Similar to one-time session keys, passphrase-based encryption keys as used by PGP are secret keys (keys from a secret key cryptosystem). Passphrase-based encryption keys are used to encrypt and protect the private keys that are used in PGP. More specifically, we will see in the subsequent chapter that private keys are stored in encrypted form only, and that the encryption key is derived from a user-selected passphrase using the SHA-1 algorithm. This is an efficient and effective scheme. Note, however, that its security depends on the security of the passphrase (like any scheme based on shared secrets, such as passwords).

It is fairly obvious that passphrases should never be written down. To avoid the temptation to write it down, the user should use a passphrase that is not easily guessed but that is easily remembered. If a passphrase consists of a single word, it can be easily guessed by having a computer try all the words in a dictionary until it finds the correct word (a so-called "dictionary attack"). That's why a passphrase is generally much better than a password. However, it is only fair to mention that there is not sufficient statistical material available to determine how much a passphrase is better (i.e., more secure) than a password.

7.5.3 Public and Private Keys

As discussed in this chapter, PGP makes use of public key cryptography. Consequently, there are public and private keys that need to be stored and managed in a systematic way for efficient and effective use. According to [12], the

> "... whole business of protecting public keys from tampering is the single most difficult problem in practical public key applications. It is the Achilles' heel of public key cryptography, and a lot of software complexity is tied up in solving this one problem."

The scheme used in PGP is to provide a pair of data structures for each user, one to store his public key pairs and one to store the public keys of other users. In PGP terminology, these data structures are referred to as *private key ring* and *public key ring*. We elaborate on these data structures in the following chapter.

Furthermore, we mentioned previously that PGP uses a unique way to manage public keys and public key certificates. Remember that a trust model refers to the set of rules a system or application uses to decide whether a public key certificate is valid, and that the trust model used by PGP has historically been called a "web of trust." PGP's web of trust is further addressed in the following chapter.

REFERENCES

[1] T. ElGamal, "A Public Key Cryptosystem and a Signature Scheme Based on Discrete Logarithm," *IEEE Transactions on Information Theory*, IT-31(4), 1985, pp. 469 – 472.

[2] W. Diffie, and M.E. Hellman, "New Directions in Cryptography," *IEEE Transactions on Information Theory*, IT-22(6), 1976, pp. 644 – 654.

[3] D. Atkins, W. Stallings, and P. Zimmermann, "PGP Message Exchange Formats," Request for Comments 1991, August 1996.

[4] J. Callas, L. Donnerhacke, H. Finney, and R. Thayer, "OpenPGP Message Format," Request for Comments 2440, November 1998.

[5] M. Elkins, "MIME Security with Pretty Good Privacy (PGP)," Request for Comments 2015, October 1996.

[6] J. Galvin, S. Murphy, S. Crocker, and N. Freed, "Security Multiparts for MIME: Multipart/Signed and Multipart/Encrypted," Request for Comments 1847, October 1995.

[7] S. Crocker, N. Freed, J. Galvin, and S. Murphy, "MIME Object Security Services," Request for Comments 1848, October 1995.

[8] P. Deutsch, "DEFLATE Compressed Data Format Specification version 1.3," Request for Comments 1951, May 1996.

[9] P. Deutsch, and J-L. Gailly, "ZLIB Compressed Data Format Specification version 3.3," Request for Comments 1950, May 1996.

[10] J. Ziv, and A. Lempel, "A Universal Algorithm for Sequential Data Compression," *IEEE Transactions on Information Theory*, May 1977.

[11] W. Stallings, *Cryptography and Network Security: Principles and Practice*, 2nd Edition, Prentice Hall, Upper Saddle River, NJ, 1998.

[12] P.R. Zimmermann, *The Official PGP User's Guide*, The MIT Press, Cambridge, MA, 1995.

Chapter 8

Web of Trust

In this chapter, we elaborate on PGP's unique trust model and the resulting web of trust. More specifically, we overview and discuss PGP certificates in Section 8.1, PGP key rings in Section 8.2, the establishment of trust in Section 8.3, key revocation in Section 8.4, and the use of PGP key servers in Section 8.5. Finally, we draw some conclusions in Section 8.6.

8.1 PGP CERTIFICATES

In Chapter 4, we mentioned that there are two practically relevant formats for digital or public key certificates, namely PGP certificates and X.509 certificates, and that PGP makes use of PGP certificates,[1] whereas S/MIME makes use of X.509 certificates. In this section, we overview and discuss PGP certificates. X.509 certificates are further addressed in Chapter 13, which mainly focuses on the PKI requirements of S/MIME. In Chapter 4, we also mentioned that a distinguishing feature of the PGP certificate format is that it allows potentially multiple identities (user IDs) and signatures per certificate. What this basically means is that a PGP certificate is issued for a public key and that multiple user IDs can be associated

[1]Since version 6.5.1, PGP also supports X.509 certificates.

with this key. Furthermore, multiple signatures can certify the fact that a specific user ID is associated with the public key. Consequently, there is a one-to-many relationship between the public key of a PGP certificate and the user IDs associated with it, and there is another one-to-many relationship for each of these user IDs and the signatures that are associated with it. Contrary to that, the X.509 certificate format is simpler. It allows only one user ID associated with a public key and one signature that certifies this association. The situation is illustrated in Figure 8.1. The left side illustrates the structure of a PGP certificate, whereas the right side illustrates the comparably simple structure of an X.509 certificate.

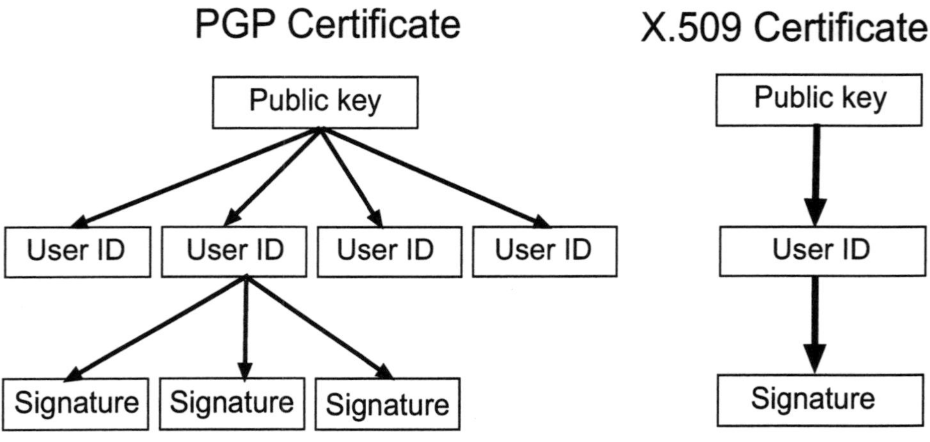

Figure 8.1 The structures of PGP and X.509 certificates.

Technically spoken, a PGP certificate is a data structure that includes the following fields:

- *Version number:* This field is used to identify which version of PGP was used to create the public key pair (of which the public key is associated with the certificate).
- *Public key:* This field is used to hold the public key and a corresponding algorithm identifier (e.g., RSA, Diffie-Hellman, or DSS).
- *Certificate owner information:* This field is used to hold identity information about the certificate owner and the holder of the corresponding private key. As discussed above, it may include several identities and signatures.

- *Self-signature:* This field is used to hold a self-signature for the certificate. As its name suggests, a self-signature is generated by the certificate owner using the private key that corresponds to the public key associated with the certificate.

- *Validity period:* This field is used to determine the start and expiration date and time of the certificate. As such, it specifies the certificate's validity period or lifetime.

- *Preferred encryption algorithm:* This field is used to identify the encryption algorithm of choice for the certificate owner (e.g., CAST, IDEA, or 3DES).

One may think of a PGP certificate as a public key with one or more labels attached to it. For example, several user identifiers (user IDs) may be attached to a PGP certificate or public key, each of which contains different means of identifying the certificate owner (e.g., the certificate owner's name and corporate e-mail address or the certificate owner's first name and private e-mail address). Typically, a user ID includes the name of the user and one of his e-mail addresses put in angle brackets (< and >), such as `Rolf Oppliger <rolf.oppliger@esecurity.ch>`. Also, one or several photographs may be attached to a PGP certificate or public key to simplify visual authentication processes.

As mentioned above, the association of a user ID with a PGP certificate or public key may be testified by one or several people, each of them generating a digital signature that is attached to the corresponding user ID in the PGP certificate. In fact, many people may sign a PGP certificate to attest to their own assurance that the public key included in the certificate actually belongs to the claimed user ID. Later in this chapter we will elaborate on PGP key servers. If you have a look at such a server, you may notice that certain certificates, such as the one of Philip R. Zimmermann, contain many signatures from different people. Note, however, that the list of signatures attached to each user ID may differ, and that a signature simply attests to the authenticity that one label belongs to the public key, not that all the labels on the key are authentic. This should alwys be considered with care when discussing the authenticity of a public key employed by PGP.

8.2 KEY RINGS

As mentioned in the previous chapter, PGP uses a private key ring to store the public key pairs of its user (including the private keys) and a public key ring to store the public keys of the other users. In a typical PGP installation, the public key ring is called `pubring.pkr` and the private key ring is called `secring.skr`. In either key ring, entries can be indexed by user IDs and/or key IDs.

PGPkeys is the utility program of PGP that can be used to manage key rings (both the private key rings and the public key rings). Figure 8.2 illustrates the GUI of PGPkeys. Each entry in the list refers to a public key or a public key pair (there are three public key pairs). If the entry refers to a public key pair, the corresponding private key is stored in the private key ring. Each entry in the list can be expanded by clicking at the plus sign on the left side. The expanded format shows the user IDs and photographs that are associated with the public key. For example, Figure 8.2 shows my principal PGP key in expanded format (the sign on the left side turns into a minus). As of this writing, there are five user IDs and one photograph associated with this key. In addition, the user IDs can be expanded by clicking at the plus sign. In this case, the expanded format shows the signatures that are associated with the user ID, and that provide credentials that the user ID actually belongs to this public key (the expanded format is not shown in Figure 8.2).

PGPkeys

File Edit View Keys Server Groups Help

Keys	Vali...	Trust	Size	Description	Key ID	Creation	Expiration
Philip R. Zimmermann <prz@pgp.com>			2048/1024	DH/DSS public key	0xFAEBD5FC	08.04.97	Never
Rolf Oppliger <rolf.oppliger@esecurity.ch>			1024	RSA key pair	0xD88E4C4D	24.01.00	Never
Rolf Oppliger <rolf.oppliger@esecurity.ch>			512	RSA key pair	0x82DB00A3	24.01.00	Never
Rolf Oppliger <rolf.oppliger@esecurity.ch>			2048/1024	DH/DSS key pair	0x0AC29A5B	14.09.98	Never
Rolf Oppliger <rolf.oppliger@esecurity.ch>				User ID			
Photograph				Photograph			
Rolf Oppliger <rolf.oppliger@acm.org>				User ID			
Rolf Oppliger <rolf.oppliger@isb.admin....				User ID			
Rolf Oppliger <oppliger@computer.org>				User ID			
Rolf Oppliger <rolf.oppliger@bluewin.ch>				User ID			

Figure 8.2 GUI of the PGPkeys utility program. © 2000 Network Associates, Inc.

For each entry in PGPkeys's list of public keys and public key pairs, the Keys > Key Properties menu leads to a screen that summarizes the main properties of the corresponding public key or public key pair. For example, Figure 8.3 illustrates the screen for my principal PGP key pair. We mentioned in the previous chapter that the key ID of my principal PGP key is `8E50 BDB3 0AC2 9A5B` (written in hexadecimal notation), and that only the second half of this key ID — namely `0AC2 9A5B` — is actually displayed by PGP. This part of the key ID is shown in the first field. The type of the key is DH/DSS and the lengths of the corresponding keys are 2,048 bits (for Diffie-Hellman or ElGamal) and 1,024 bits (for DSS). The key pair was created on September 14, 1998, and is not expected to expire on a specific date. The encryption algorithm of choice for this key pair is CAST (this is the default value). Finally, note that the key pair is implicitly trusted and considered to be valid (as explained later in this chapter).

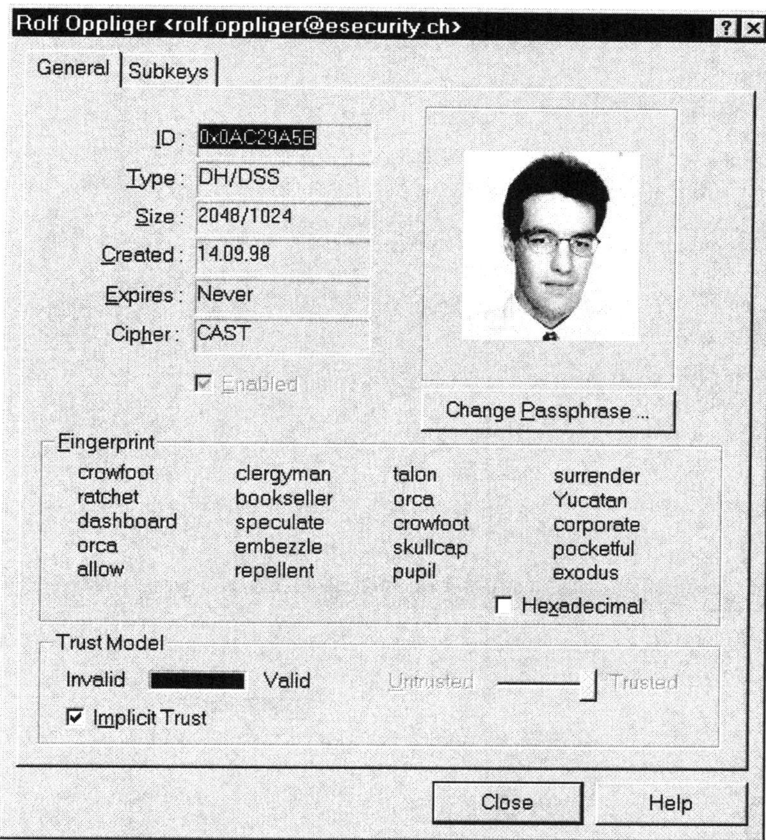

Figure 8.3 General properties of a PGP key as illustrated by PGPkeys. © 2000 Network Associates, Inc.

Although it is intended that the private key ring be stored only on the computer system of the user that created and owns the private key, and that it is accessible only to that user, it makes sense to make the value of the private key as secure as possible. Consequently, the private key(s) is (are) stored in encrypted form in the private key ring. By default, the encryption algorithm is CAST, but optionally other algorithms may be configured (e.g., IDEA or 3DES).

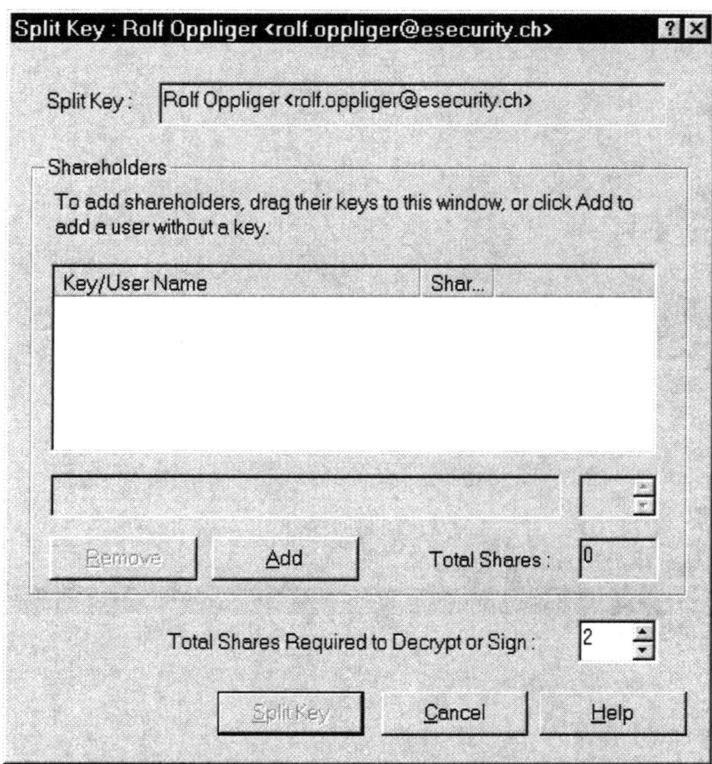

Figure 8.4 The Keys > Share Split menu of PGPkeys for a PGP key. © 2000 Network Associates, Inc.

In either case, the encryption key is taken from the one-way hash value of a user-selected passphrase. Each time a user wants to access the private key ring and employ one of his private keys, he must provide the correct passphrase. PGP will retrieve the encrypted private key, generate the hash value of the passphrase (using SHA-1), and decrypt the encrypted private key with this value. The user, in turn, can configure the use of passphrase caching for a certain amount of time. This configuration is done in the General panel of the Edit > Preferences menu of the PGPkeys utility.

To provide a higher level of security, PGP provides support for a secret sharing scheme [1,2]. Consequently, the private key can be split into multiple parts (so-called "shares") in a way that the reconstruction of the private key (to decrypt or digitally sign data) requires at least a certain number of shares. Figure 8.4 illustrates the Keys > Share Split menu of the PGPkeys utility program for my principal PGP key. You can add an arbitrary number of shareholders and define a threshold on how many shares must be provided to reconstruct the private key (default value is two shares). The use of secret sharing schemes to recover secret or private keys is useful and highly recommended for any system that makes use of cryptographic keys. As such, it is possible and very likely that future S/MIME implementations will employ similar schemes. In fact, the use of secret sharing schemes is good practice for any system that makes use of cryptographic keys.

Finally, note that in addition to the information mentioned so far, each entry in a key ring is also assigned a key legitimacy field (KEYLEGIT), a signature trust field (SIGTRUST), and an owner trust field (OWNERTRUST). These fields are internally used to determine the trustworthiness of signatures attached to user IDs, and to determine the legitimacy of public keys and PGP certificates accordingly. The corresponding procedures to establish trust are discussed next.

8.3 ESTABLISHMENT OF TRUST

As discussed so far, user A must have a public key ring that basically contains the public keys of the users she wants to securely communicate with. Suppose that A's public key ring contains a public key associated with B but that the key is, in fact, owned by C (meaning that C knows the corresponding private key). This could happen, for example, if A is careless and accepts the key from an untrusted source without proper validation of B's identity. In this situation, there basically exist two threats:

- First, C can send messages to A and forge B's signature, so that A will accept the messages as being originated by B;

- Second, any encrypted message from A to B can be read by C.

An attack in which an intruder replaces the proper public key of a principal with its own public key is a special form of a man-in-the-middle attack.[2] In general, a number of approaches are possible to protect against this form of man-in-the-middle attack, and to minimize the risk that a user's public key ring is fed with spoofed public keys. Let's assume that A wishes to obtain an authentic copy of B's public key. Against this background, the following are some approaches that could be used:

- First, A could personally (and physically) get an authentic copy of the public key from B. For example, B could store his public key k_B on a floppy disk and hand the disk over to A. A, in turn, could load the key into her system from the floppy disk. Obviously, this is a fairly secure approach but has some practical limitations and shortcomings (e.g., A and B must meet in person).

- Second, if A personally knows B and can recognize the voice of B on the phone, she can also authenticate B's public key. For example, A could call B and ask him to spell the key (in radix-64 encoded form) over the phone. As a more practical alternative, B could transmit his key in an e-mail message to A. A, in turn, could use a one-way hash function to compute a message digest for the key (a so-called "fingerprint"). A could then call B and ask him to spell the fingerprint of the key over the phone. If the two fingerprints match, the key is assumed to be authentic. Note, however, that this approach only works if A can recognize and authenticate the voice of B.

- Third, A could obtain B's public key from a trusted individual D (sometimes also referred to as an "introducer"). For this purpose, D must create a signed certificate for B's public key. The signed certificate could be sent directly to A by B or D, or it could also be made publicly available on a directory service, bulletin board, or Web-based repository.

- Fourth, A could obtain B's public key from a (trusted) CA.

It is obvious that the first two approaches do not scale to the size of the Internet, and that any scheme for secure messaging on the Internet must use either the third or fourth approach. It is also obvious that the third and fourth approach are conceptually similar (in the fourth approach, the CA simply plays the role of the

[2]More generally spoken, a man-in-the-middle attack includes interception, insertion, deletion, and modification of messages, reflecting messages back to the sender, replaying old messages, and redirecting messages.

introducer in the third approach). In fact, one of the major differences between PGP and S/MIME is that the former follows the third approach (using "introducers" to authenticate public keys), whereas the latter follows the fourth approach (using CAs to authenticate public keys). In either case, it is up to the user to decide which introducers or CAs he ultimately trusts.

Consequently and contrary to all other schemes for secure messaging on the Internet (including, for example PEM, MOSS, and S/MIME), PGP originally did not make use of CAs and PKIs to establish trust. It did, however, provide a convenient scheme of using trust, associating trust with public keys, and exploiting trust information to validate public keys. This scheme is based on PGP's cumulative trust model that is also called "web of trust." More recently, PGP has been extended to additionally make use of CAs, PKIs, and corresponding certificates (i.e., X.509 certificates).

To better understand PGP's cumulative trust model and the resulting web of trust, it is important to note that trust as a property is not necessarily transferable. What this basically means is that if A trusts B not to lie and B trusts C not to lie, this does not necessarily mean that A also trusts C not to lie. The same is true with users authenticating other users. You may trust your friend to reliably authenticate the owners of public keys, but you may not trust the ones that have been authenticated by your friend to be comparably reliable. Put in other words: Your friend's friends are not necessarily your own friends. In daily life, we are accustomed to this limited transferability of trust, and PGP's cumulative trust model adheres to this limitation.

Against this background, how does PGP judge the validity of a public key? There are two questions that must be answered in the affirmative:

- First, has the public key been digitally signed (and certified)?

- Second, has the public key been digitally signed (and certified) by somebody who is trusted to certify other people's public keys?

Obviously, PGP and other software packages can automatically answer the first question (assuming that enough information is provided), but there is no possibility to automatically answer the second question. This question involves trust and must be decided by each user individually. The use of official CAs and PKIs seemingly solves the problem, but it only moves the problem to the question of how to decide whether a given CA or PKI is trustworthy. Again, we come to the situation in which the user must decide whether a source of certificates is trustworthy from his individual point of view.[3]

PGP does not make use of CAs and PKIs (at least in its basic form without trusted introducers and meta-introducers as explained below). Instead, a user must autonomously decide whether a given key holder (user) is considered trustworthy, and whether he or she accepts that key holder as an introducer accordingly. This decision is not necessarily binary and may be fuzzy. For example, a PGP user can designate a key holder as unknown, untrusted, marginally trusted, or completely trusted to certify other public keys. Having assigned these trust levels to key holders, a public key certificate is considered to be valid if at least one of the following two conditions hold:

- The certificate is digitally signed by at least one completely trusted key holder whose certificate is valid;
- The certificate is digitally signed by at least two of the marginally (or cumulatively) trusted key holders whose certificates are all valid.

Consequently, if a certificate is digitally signed by an unknown or untrusted key holder it is not considered to be valid. This makes a lot of sense, since if we do not know or do not trust a key holder, we cannot say anything about the trustworthiness of the certificates he digitally signs and issues.

As a result of this trust assignment procedure and certificate validation scheme, each user establishes his own web of trust and there is no notion of a globally trusted party. As mentioned above, this approach contrasts sharply with other standards-based public key management schemes, such as the one employed by S/MIME, which are based on a centralized or hierarchical notion of trust. In fact, the standards-based public key management schemes all rely on CAs that collectively decide whom users should trust.

PGP's decentralized and probabilistic method for determining public key legitimacy is the centerpiece of its public key management scheme. PGP lets the user choose who he trusts, putting him at the top of his own certification hierarchy. As expressed in [3], "PGP is for people who prefer to pack their own parachutes," and this statement hits the point.

[3]Note that many Internet software packages (e.g., Web browsers) are distributed with lists of preconfigured CAs that are considered to be trustworthy. In this case, the user does not have to decide whether a CA is trustworthy from his point of view, because the software vendor has already decided on his behalf.

To implement the PGP's cumulative trust model or web of trust, some additional fields are required and associated with the entries in the key rings (we briefly mentioned the fields in the previous section):

- First, each key (public key or public key pair) is associated with a key holder (owner) and a corresponding *owner trust* field (OWNERTRUST). The owner trust field, in turn, indicates the degree to which this owner is trusted by the user to sign other public keys (and to serve as an introducer accordingly). More specifically, there are three levels of trust that can be assigned to an owner trust field of a key:

  - Complete trust (completely trusted key);
  - Marginal trust (marginally trusted key);
  - No trust (untrusted key).

  If the user generated a public key pair and his private key ring holds the corresponding private key, the public key pair is implicitly and completely trusted. Contrary to that, if a key is not included in either of the key rings, it is unknown (rather than untrusted).

- Second, each key (public key or public key pair) is associated with zero or more signatures that the owner of the corresponding key ring has collected so far. Each signature, in turn, has associated with it a *signature trust* field (SIGTRUST). This field indicates the degree to which the user trusts the creator of the signature to certify public keys. The value of this field is inherited from the owner trust field of the corresponding signer (e.g., complete trust, marginal trust, or no trust). Note that the signature trust fields can also be thought of as cached copies of the owner trust field from another entry in the key ring.

- Third, each key (public key or public key pair) is associated with a *key legitimacy* field (KEYLEGIT) that indicates to what extent the user trusts that this key is valid and belongs to its claimed owner. This field is also known as "validity" field, and there are currently three levels of validity:

  - Valid;
  - Marginally valid;

– Invalid.

The value of a key's legitimacy field is computed (and periodically recomputed) by PGP based on the signature trust field values that have been collected for that key.

When user A inserts a new public key on his public key ring, PGP must assign a value for the owner trust field of that particular key. If A generated the public key pair and owns the corresponding private key (meaning that the private key is included in the private key ring), then a value of implicit trust is automatically assigned to the owner trust field. Otherwise, PGP must ask the user for his assessment regarding the trust level of the owner of the key, and the user must select a desired value (i.e., unknown, untrusted, marginally trusted, or completely trusted). Also, one or more signatures may be attached to the new public key (more signatures may be added later). For each signature that is attached to the public key, PGP searches the public key ring to see if the corresponding signer is among the known key holders:

- If the signer is among the known key holders, the value of the corresponding owner trust field is assigned to the signature trust field;
- Contrary to that, if the signer is not among the known key holders, an unknown user value is assigned for the signature.

Finally, the value for the new public key's legitimacy field is computed by PGP on the basis of the signatures attached to the key (and the values of the corresponding signature trust fields). If at least one signature attached to the public key is completely trusted (because the owner trust field of the corresponding key holder is completely trusted), then the value of the legitimacy field is set to valid. Otherwise, PGP computes a weighted sum of the signature trust values. A weight of $1/X$ is given to signatures that are completely trusted and $1/Y$ to signatures that are marginally trusted, where X and Y are system parameters (e.g., $X = 1$ and $Y = 2$ in current implementations). When the total of weights of the public key reaches 1, it is considered to be trustworthy, and the key legitimacy value is set to valid. Thus, in the absence of ultimate trust, at least X (e.g., $X = 1$) signatures that are completely trusted or Y (e.g., $Y = 2$) signatures that are marginally trusted or some combination is needed to declare a key valid.

Periodically, PGP processes the public key ring in a top-down process to achieve consistency. For each owner trust field, PGP scans the public key ring for all signatures provided by that owner and updates the corresponding signature trust field values to equal the owner trust field value. This process starts with keys for which there is ultimate trust. Afterwards, all key legitimacy fields are computed on the basis of the attached signatures as discussed above.

In general, there are several possibilities to visualize the PGP trust model and the process of establishing trust in the resulting web of trust. For example, [4] introduces a graphical notation to illustrate the content of a PGP public key ring and the way in which signature trust and key legitimacy are related.[4] Another graphical tool is a Web-based service for authenticating PGP public keys that was designed and developed by Michael K. Reiter and Stuart G. Stubblebine a couple of years ago, and named PathServer [5]. The tool works by enabling a user to find certificate paths from a key he trusts to a key he wants to learn about. The primary technical challenges result from allowing the user to specify properties of paths that he finds desirable, including independence and length properties that make locating a sufficiently large set of such paths NP-hard or worse. If PGP (or at least PGP's trust model) were deployed on a large scale, tools like PathServer would be very important for the user to visualize and better understand the notion of trust with regard to public keys and public key certificates.

More recently (since version 6.5.1), NAI has extended PGP's trust model to additionally support X.509 certificates. Note, however, that this does not change PGP's characteristic web of trust. X.509 certificates are only used as a replacement for the signatures associated with a public key and user ID pair in PGP. It is still possible to use several user IDs for a public key, and to associate several signatures to each of these user IDs. Consequently, the use of X.509 certificates in PGP does not change the web of trust. It does, however, simplify convergence between the two approaches for secure messages on the Internet (this point is further addressed in Chapter 17). Taken into account the effort that is being made to establish and run X.509-based PKIs on a global scale, the feature of PGP to understand and make use of X.509 certificates has become very important.

8.4 KEY REVOCATION

In general, PGP certificates are created with a specific validity period and lifetime (defined by a start date and time and an optional expiration date and time), and each certificate is expected to be usable during its entire lifetime. However, there are situations in which it is necessary to invalidate a certificate prior to its expiration

[4]The notation is credited to Philip R. Zimmermann.

date, such as when a certificate owner terminates employment with a company or suspects that the certificate's corresponding private key has been compromised.

The process of invalidating a certificate prior to its expiration date is called *certificate* or *key revocation*. Note that a revoked certificate is much more dangerous than an expired certificate, because the fact that it has been revoked is not detectable by simply looking at the certificate (the fact that a certificate has expired is detectable by simply looking at its expiration date and time).

It is commonly agreed that certificate or key revocation is the hard problem when it comes to the large-scale deployment of public key cryptography in general, and PKIs in particular. For example, Aviel D. Rubin, Daniel Geer, and Marcus J. Ranum argued that much of the implied cost savings of public key cryptography over secret key cryptography is nothing more than an illusion [6]. To further clarify this point, they argued that the sum of the cost for cryptographic key issuance and the cost for cryptographic key revocation is more or less constant (for both public key cryptography and secret key cryptography). There seems to be some truth in this statement, considering the difficulty and pain we experience today in establishing fully operational PKIs that provide support for certificate revocation. Most importantly and worrisome, any viable solution to address the certificate or key revocation problem makes it mandatory to (re)introduce some online components (for otherwise offline CAs). These components, however, have originally been thought to become obsolete due to the use of public key cryptography.

To make things worse, PGP follows a decentralized and fully distributed approach with regard to certificate and trust management, and this approach makes the key revocation problem even more difficult to address. This is because there is no single authority that keeps track and may hold a list of recently revoked keys and corresponding certificates. In addition, there is a fundamental difference between revoking signatures in the X.509 world and revoking signatures in the PGP world:

- With X.509 certificates, a revoked signature is practically the same as a revoked certificate given the fact that the only signature on the certificate is the one that made it valid in the first place (the signature of the CA). Consequently, only the issuer of an X.509 certificate should be able to revoke it.

- Contrary to that, PGP certificates can be signed multiple times and anyone who has signed a certificate can also revoke his signature. A revoked signature, in turn, indicates that the signer no longer believes the public key and user ID belong together, or believes that the certificate's public key or the corresponding private key has been compromised.

In addition to the possibility of revoking single signatures, PGP also provides the feature that a user can revoke his entire certificate (not just the signatures on it) if he feels that the certificate has been compromised. Note, however, that only the certificate's owner (the holder of the corresponding private key) or someone whom the certificate's owner has designated as a revoker can revoke a PGP certificate. In short, it is revoked by issuing a *key revocation certificate* and disseminating this certificate as widely as possible. A key revocation certificate, in turn, is similar to a normal certificate but includes an indicator that the purpose of this certificate is to revoke the use of its public key. As such, it is digitally signed either by the certificate owner or one of its designated revokers. Note that designating one (or several) revoker(s) is a useful practice, as it's often the loss of the passphrase for the certificate's corresponding private key that leads a PGP user to revoke his certificate. At least it is the suggested way of revoking keys and PGP certificates in large organizations.

When a PGP certificate is revoked (by issuing a key revocation certificate), it is important to make potential users of the certificate aware that it is no longer valid. With PGP certificates, the most common way to communicate that a certificate has been revoked is to post it on a certificate or key server so others may be warned not to use that public key. PGP key servers that can also be used to post key revocation certificates are overviewed next.

8.5 PGP KEY SERVERS

In short, a certificate or key server refers to a server that provides its users with public key certificates, meaning that they can submit and retrieve public key certificates. Similarly, a PGP certificate or key server can be used to submit and retrieve PGP certificates.

In the last couple of years, many *PGP key servers* have been established to provide online certificate repositories for PGP users. The repositories can be accessed with LDAP or HTTP. For example, MIT distributes a PGP Certificate Server freeware software package (currently version 2.5.1) for Windows NT, Windows 2000, and Sun Solaris platforms.[5] This software package can be used to set up and run a PGP key server (it comes packaged with a comprehensive Administrator's Guide).

By default, the PGP software is configured with the following two PGP key servers:

- `ldap://certserver.pgp.com`;

[5] `http://web.mit.edu/network/pgp.html`

- http://pgpkeys.mit.edu:11371.

In addition, the PGPadmin utility can be used to customize a PGP package with other preconfigured PGP key servers.

The use of PGP key servers is simple and straightforward. In addition, Brian A. LaMacchia[6] maintains Web-based information about PGP key servers.[7] Among other useful information, the site includes a list of servers and a frequently asked questions (FAQ) document.

8.6 CONCLUSIONS

In this chapter, we overviewed and discussed the procedures and the rationale behind PGP's cumulative trust model and the resulting web of trust. More specifically, we saw that PGP's trust model is appropriate for communities in which users can decide in one way or another whether other users are trustworthy. Given the current state and experience, it is not clear whether the model scales, meaning that it is not clear whether the model is appropriate for large communities in which only a few users know each other. In such communities, it seems to be very difficult to establish trust according to the decentralized and fully distributed approach followed by the trust model of PGP. Consequently, the scalability properties of PGP remains an open question for further research. In the meantime, however, one can reasonably argue that for very large communities, hierarchical trust models, such as the ones employed by X.509 and S/MIME, provide some advantages. Fortunately, the two trust models are not mutually exclusive and it is possible and very likely that we will see hybrid trust models and corresponding certification and validation schemes in the future (or at least products that support both trust models).

Against this background, a final word is due to the relationship between PGP's notion of an introducer (a completely trusted key holder) and a CA or X.509-style PKI. In PGP parlance, an introducer who is commonly trusted (i.e., trusted by all employees within an organization) is called a *trusted introducer*. The trusted introducer concept, in turn, can be used to model a hierarchical two-level X.509-style PKI. In this case, a trusted introducer acts as a CA for a large number of individual key holders. People trust the trusted introducer or CA to establish the validity for all certificates. This means that everyone relies upon the trusted introducer or CA to go through the whole manual validation process for them. This is fine up to a certain number of users or number of sites. Beyond that number,

[6]When Brian A. LaMacchia started the PGP public key server project he was with MIT.

[7]http://pgp5.ai.mit.edu/

however, it is generally required to add other validators to maintain the same level of quality. This is where the concept of a *meta-introducer* comes into play. Similar to a king who hands his seal to his trusted advisors so they can act on his authority, the meta-introducer enables others to act as trusted introducers. These trusted introducers can validate keys to the same effect as that of the meta-introducer. They cannot, however, nominate and create new trusted introducers. The meta-introducer concept can be used to model a hierarchical three-level X.509-style PKI. In this case, the meta-introducers are located on the top, trusted introducers are located in the middle, and individual key holders are located at the bottom.

Both concepts — trusted introducers and meta-introducers — are particularly helpful if PGP-like webs of trust and X.509-like PKIs must be configured in a way to interoperate and complement each another. In reality, there is hardly any situation that requires more than three levels in a PKI hierarchy. Consequently, trusted introducers and meta-introducers seem to provide enough flexibility to model any practically relevant PKI structure.

In practice, the PGP administration utility (i.e., PGPadmin) can be used to configure a corporate signing key (CSK) for the PGP software packages that are distributed within an organization. The private key of the CSK pair, in turn, can then be used to digitally sign and certify the public keys of the parties that are assumed to be trusted introducers within the organization. Consequently, the holder of the private key of the CSK pair is acting as a meta-introducer. Obviously, this important key can also be split into multiple shares in a way that the provision of a digital signature requires the agreement of multiple parties.

REFERENCES

[1] A. Shamir, "How to share a secret," *Communications of the ACM*, 22(11), November 1979, pp. 612 – 613.

[2] G.R. Blakley, "Safeguarding cryptographic keys," *Proceedings of the AFIPS National Computer Conference*, 1979, pp. 313 – 317.

[3] P.R. Zimmermann, *The Official PGP User's Guide*, The MIT Press, Cambridge, MA, 1995.

[4] W. Stallings, *Cryptography and Network Security: Principles and Practice*, 2nd Edition, Prentice-Hall, Upper Saddle River, NJ, 1998.

[5] M.K. Reiter, and S.G. Stubblebine, "Path Independence for Authentication in Large-Scale Systems," *Proceedings of the 4th ACM Conference on Computer and Communications Security*, 1997, pp. 57 – 66.

[6] A.D. Rubin, D. Geer, and M.J. Ranum, *Web Security Sourcebook*, John Wiley & Sons, Inc., New York, NY, 1997.

Chapter 9

Standardization and Products

In this chapter, we overview the standardization of PGP and the products that conform to and support the resulting standards. More specifically, we address PGP standardization in Section 9.1, and overview some products from NAI and alternatives in Section 9.2.

9.1 STANDARDIZATION

As of this writing, the standardization work related to PGP is primarily driven by NAI and the participants of the IETF OpenPGP WG.[1] The relevant RFC documents produced by the IETF OpenPGP WG are as follows (in chronological order):

- RFC 1991 [1], entitled "PGP Message Exchange Formats," specifies the message format for PGP (using the so-called "old packet format");
- RFC 2015 [2], entitled "MIME Security with Pretty Good Privacy (PGP)," specifies the use of PGP with MIME (PGP/MIME);

[1] `http://www.ietf.org/html.charters/openpgp-charter.html`

- RFC 2440 [3], entitled "OpenPGP Message Format," specifies the message format for OpenPGP (using the so-called "new packet format").

In addition to these RFC documents, there are several Internet-Drafts being written and published on the IETF OpenPGP WG's homepage. We mentioned some of these Internet-Drafts in earlier chapters. Most importantly, there is a pair of Internet-Drafts[2] that collectively specify the use of OpenPGP with MIME (also known as "OpenPGP/MIME"). We already mentioned that these Internet-Drafts will probably have become Internet standard track RFC documents by the time you read this book. Eventually, there will also be some other Internet-Drafts being published as RFC documents.

It is highly recommended to periodically visit the homepage of the IETF OpenPGP WG (mentioned in footnote one of this chapter) and to look for the latest protocol specifications (both RFC documents and Internet-Drafts). For example, during the writing of this book there is an Internet-Draft[3] being written that extends and possibly will replace RFC 2440 in the future.

9.2 PRODUCTS

First of all, it is important to note that the PGP effort is mainly driven by NAI and its PGP Security business unit (remember from Chapter 6 that the company Pretty Good Privacy, Inc. was acquired by NAI in December 1997, and that PGP Security is now a business unit of NAI). This is true for both standardization within the IETF OpenPGP WG (as mentioned above) and product development. Consequently, most products that conform to the PGP specifications (either PGP or OpenPGP) are developed and marketed exclusively by NAI.

In this section, we provide a rough overview about the most important implementations of PGP and OpenPGP (both NAI and alternative products). More complete information about the various PGP products and product versions is available from the PGP Interactions page at URL `http://rmarq.pair.com/pgp/`.

9.2.1 NAI Products

NAI and its PGP Security business unit provide several (commercial and noncommercial) products and software packages related to PGP. Depending on the version and legal status, the software packages are called PGP Personal Privacy,

---

[2] `draft-ietf-openpgp-mime-*.txt` and `draft-ietf-openpgp-multsig-*.txt`

[3] `draft-ietf-openpgp-rfc2440bis-*.txt`

PGP Business Security, PGP Desktop Security, or something similar. There is even a freeware version of PGP available from NAI and distributed internationally called PGP Freeware. In this chapter, we use the term "PGP" to collectively refer to the commercial software packages and the term "PGP Freeware" to refer to the freeware versions thereof.

PGP is primarily available for Microsoft platforms (e.g., Windows 95/98, Windows NT, and Windows 2000). According to the International PGP Home Page, there are noncommercial versions of PGP Freeware available for the following platforms (the latest release as of March 2000 is indicated in brackets):

- Amiga (PGP 5.0i);
- Atari (PGP 5.0i);
- BeOS (PGP 5.0i);
- MS-DOS (PGP 5.0i);
- MacOS (PGP 6.5.2a or PGP 6.5.1i);
- OS/2 (PGP 5.0i);
- Psion 5 (PGP 2.6.3ia beta 1.0);
- Unix (PGP 6.5.1i);
- Windows 3.x (many shells for MS-DOS PGP);
- Windows 95/98/NT/2000 (PGP 6.5.3).

As of this writing, the latest release of PGP and PGP Freeware is version 6.5.3.[4] It provides plug-ins for the following UAs (the last three plug-ins are available separately):[5]

- Microsoft Exchange;
- Microsoft Outlook 97/98/2000;
- Microsoft Outlook Express 4.x and 5.x;

[4]As already mentioned in Chapter 6, NAI publicly released PGP Desktop Security 7.0 in September 2000.

[5]Refer to the NAI Web site to get the latest information about supported UA versions.

- Qualcomm Eudora 3.x and 4.x;
- Novell Groupwise;
- Lotus Notes 4.5.x, 4.6.x, and 5.0;
- Claris Emailer for Apple Macintosh.

Using one of these UA plug-ins, it is very convenient to use PGP (since PGP's functionality is fully integrated into the UA interface). The look-and-feel for each of these plug-ins depends on the UA in use. For example, the plug-in for Microsoft Outlook Express is integrated into the Tools menu of the New Message composition window (as illustrated in Figure 9.1). Note that Microsoft Outlook Express natively supports S/MIME, so the user must decide which scheme to use to secure (i.e., encrypt and/or digitally sign) a message.

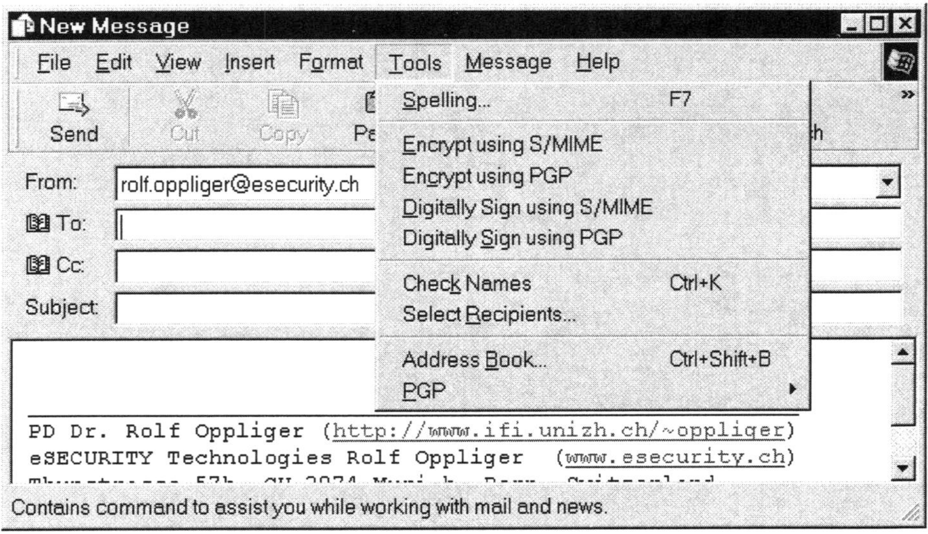

Figure 9.1 The Tools menu of the New Message Composition window in Microsoft Outlook Express. © 2000 Microsoft Corporation.

Users of UAs that are not supported by PGP plug-ins can still make use of PGP's functionality by using the PGPtray[6] menu and its commands. Using these

[6]The PGPtray is the main menu of PGP and PGP Freeware. It is usually placed on the bottom

commands, it is possible to encrypt and/or digitally sign or decrypt and verify the content of the current window or the system clipboard.

In addition to the UA plug-ins and PGPtray commands mentioned above, PGP also provides support for some new tools and features that go beyond a tool for secure messaging. Examples include PGPtools, PGPdisk, and PGPnet:

Figure 9.2 GUI of PGPtools. © 2000 Network Associates, Inc.

- PGPtools provides a GUI to incorporate several utility programs. The GUI of PGPtools is illustrated in Figure 9.2. From left to right the icons refer to the following utility programs:

  - The PGPkeys utility (further addressed in Chapter 8);
  - A file encryption utility, including a feature to create self-decrypting archives (SDAs);
  - A file authentication utility (using digital signatures);
  - A file encryption and authentication utility;
  - A file decryption and signature verification utility;
  - A file wiping utility;
  - A freespace wiping utility (as explained on the introductory screen for the PGP Free Space Wiper utility illustrated in Figure 9.3).

  Note that PGP's freespace wiping utility allows its user to use the Windows Task Scheduler to schedule periodic secure wiping of the freespace on his disk. This ensures that previously deleted files are securely wiped from time to time.

---

right of the window screen and is represented with an icon that symbolizes a lock.

- *PGPnet* is a "bump-in-the-stack" implementation of the IPsec suite of security protocols [4 – 6]. It can be used to build virtual private network (VPNs) connections between peer entities or between a PGPnet entity and a corporate firewall (also implementing the IPsec suite of security protocols). For example, the IPsec implementation that comes along with Checkpoint's Firewall-1 interoperates with PGPnet. This book is not about IPsec and virtual private networking. Consequently, we are not going to delve into the technical details of IPsec and the corresponding PGPnet implementation thereof.

Figure 9.3 Introductory screen for the PGP Free Space Wiper utility. © 2000 Network Associates, Inc.

- *PGPdisk* is a file encryption utility that allows a user to define partitions on a local drive that are transparently encrypted and decrypted. The corresponding encryption and decryption processes are fed with a key that is derived from a user-selected passphrase. Consequently, each time the user wants to write to or read from a PGPdisk-protected partition, he has to enter the corresponding passphrase (the passphrase, in turn, is cached for the entire session). PGPdisk is particularly useful to encrypt and protect the contents of the local drives of a mobile station, such as a laptop or notebook. Note, however, that the PGPdisk utility is only included in the commercial versions of PGP.[7]

In addition, a PGPadmin utility can be used to configure and customize a PGP software distribution package for an organization (e.g., a company). Several parameters can be configured and customized using PGPadmin, such as PGP key servers, additional decryption keys (ADKs) for incoming and/or outgoing messages, or *corporate signing keys* (CSKs). The CSKs, in turn, are used to specify meta-introducers (entities that are authorized to certify trusted introducers) for the organization. The PGPadmin utility simplifies the installation, configuration, and use of PGP considerably. As such, it is highly recommended for organizations that want to deploy PGP for internal use.

Finally, NAI and its PGP Security business unit also markets the following auxiliary products and software packages (related to PGP):

- The PGP Certificate Server can be used to set up and operate a PGP key server within a corporate environment;
- The PGP Software Development Kit (SDK) can be used by developers to incorporate PGP functionality into their applications;
- The PGP Policy Management Agent for SMTP can be used to set up and enforce security policies on standard SMTP-based mail servers.

Note that Network Associates International B.V. has packaged the various PGP components differently for the international market. Also note that NAI and its PGP Security business unit also provide other network security products (in addition to PGP), including, for example, the Gauntlet Firewall (for both UNIX and Windows NT), the Cybercop security scanner and intrusion detection software, as well as an IPsec-compliant PGP VPN software. Various product sheets are available and can be downloaded from PGP Security's homepage.[8]

---

[7]The PGPdisk utility is also available in PGP Freeware version 6.0.2 that is still in use today.

[8]`http://www.pgp.com`

9.2.2 Alternative Products

There are only a few alternative products that conform to either the PGP or OpenPGP specification. Most importantly there are many shells that make use of PGP to provide a more sophisticated and convenient GUI. Most of these shells are available for the Windows 3.x platform that's no longer in widespread use.

There are some plug-ins mainly for Microsoft messaging products (e.g., Microsoft Exchange and Microsoft Outlook) that implement the OpenPGP specification. Examples include the CryptoEx OpenPGP CryptoEngine from Glück & Kanja[9] and iT_SEC_outlook from the IT-Sec IT-Security AG.[10] Note that the iT_SEC_outlook plug-in implements S/MIME in addition to OpenPGP.

An interesting alternative to NAI products is being developed in Germany. More specifically, the German Federal Ministry of Economics and Technology issued a DM 250,000 grant to the *GNU Privacy Guard* (GPG) project on November 19, 1999. The aim of this project is to further develop the GnuPG software, a free and open source implementation of the OpenPGP specification. Because GnuPG does not use IDEA or RSA, it can be used without any legal restriction. The software is currently available only as a command line program (a GUI version is planned for the future). Further information about the GPG project in general, and the GnuPG software in particular, is available at `http://www.gnupg.org`.

REFERENCES

[1] D. Atkins, W. Stallings, and P. Zimmermann, "PGP Message Exchange Formats," Request for Comments 1991, August 1996.

[2] M. Elkins, "MIME Security with Pretty Good Privacy (PGP)," Request for Comments 2015, October 1996.

[3] J. Callas, L. Donnerhacke, H. Finney, and R. Thayer, "OpenPGP Message Format," Request for Comments 2440, November 1998.

[4] R.J. Atkinson, "Towards a More Secure Internet," *IEEE Computer*, Vol. 30, January 1997, pp. 57 – 61.

[5] R. Oppliger, "Security at the Internet Layer," *IEEE Computer*, Vol. 31, No. 9, September 1998, pp. 43 – 47.

[6] S. Frankel, *Internet Security: De-mystifying the IPsec Puzzle*, Artech House, Norwood, MA, forthcoming.

[9] `http://www.glueckkanja.de`

[10] `http://www.it-sec.com`

Chapter 10

Conclusions and Outlook

In this chapter, we conclude Part II of the book and elaborate on some possible future developments related to PGP. More specifically, we summarize the use of PGP for secure messaging in Section 10.1, provide a rough security analysis in Section 10.2, elaborate on future developments in Section 10.3, and point to some sources of further information in Section 10.4.

10.1 SUMMARY

In this part of the book, we addressed the use of PGP for secure messaging on the Internet. More specifically, we elaborated on the history and development in Chapter 6, overviewed the conceptual and technological approach employed by PGP in Chapter 7, discussed the trust model of PGP and the resulting web of trust in Chapter 8, and summarized the standardization related to PGP and the products that conform to the evolving standards in Chapter 9.

In summary, PGP provides a simple and straightforward approach and product line to provide basic message protection services for the Internet. It uses specific packet and message formats and a handcrafted transfer syntax. The unique feature of PGP, however, is its trust model (the "web of trust") that provides an alternative way to address the public key certificate management problem as compared to

X.509-based PKIs. The web of trust is appropriate for relatively small user communities, but it is an open question and research problem whether it also scales to large communities and communities in which users hardly know each other. Because of its questionable scalability properties and the fact that many X.509-based PKIs are being established and deployed today, the latest versions of PGP additionally provide support for X.509 certificates. This is an important prerequisite for PGP and S/MIME to eventually converge in the long term (this point is further discussed in Chapter 17).

Another distinguishing feature of PGP is its support for additional security-related functions discussed in Section 9.2 (including, for example, PGPtools, PGPnet, PGPdisk, and others). This trend is likely to continue, and NAI has already announced the incorporation of a personal firewall and a personal intrusion detection system (IDS) into version 7 of PGP. Note that the use of PGPnet for virtual private networking and remote access leads to a situation in which mobile stations, such as laptop computers and notebooks, are connected to the firewall of an organization through cryptographically protected IP tunnels. If these mobile stations are successfully attacked, they may become a remote access point for the organization's intranet. This situation is dangerous (to say the least). If the security of a mobile station breaks, the attacker can easily access the intranet through that station (independent from any cryptographic protection for the IP tunnel that interconnects the station with the firewall). In principle, the mobile station becomes a logical part of the firewall, and as such it extends the perimeter of the firewall protection in a way that is beyond the responsibility of the firewall administrator. NAI has recognized this potential vulnerability (of any remote access mechanism) and has developed a set of corresponding security mechanisms to effectively protect the mobile stations against security exploits. As mentioned above, this set includes a personal firewall and a personal IDS.

In summary, the general trend (and the marketing strategy of NAI) is to turn PGP into an entire security solution for desktop systems and mobile stations. As such, PGP is going to incorporate many security-related functions, most of them going far beyond a tool or software product for secure messaging. Note, however, that most of the security-related functions provided by PGP are not specific for PGP and can also be implemented for S/MIME. Consequently, it is possible and very likely that future implementations of S/MIME will provide identical or similar functions.

10.2 SECURITY ANALYSIS

In this section, we provide a rough security analysis for PGP. More specifically, we address cryptanalysis, physical security, and some real threats.

Before we start, it's important to note that PGP does not care and does not protect against traffic analysis attacks. In short, traffic analysis refers to the inference of information from observation of external traffic characteristics (e.g., presence, absence, amount, direction, and frequency of data traffic). If a PGP-protected message is sent from one user to another, anybody can see a message flow between them (or their UAs respectively). The content of the message may not be visible (since it is encrypted), but the mere existence of the message is recognizable for an eavesdropper. As already mentioned in Chapter 1, protection against traffic analysis attacks is a difficult problem that is only briefly addressed in Chapter 17.

10.2.1 Cryptanalysis

The first question that arises immediately when it comes to a public discussion about the security properties of PGP is whether the cryptographical primitives and algorithms used and employed are sufficiently strong to protect against contemporary cryptanalytical attacks. As we discussed in previous chapters of this book, PGP employs cryptographically strong primitives and algorithms. This is true for all major versions of PGP. For example, the feasibility of cryptanalytical attacks against the algorithms used in earlier versions of PGP (e.g., MD5, IDEA, and RSA) is investigated in a PGP attack FAQ document.[1] The document concludes with the insight that the algorithms seem to be sufficiently strong (in a cryptanalytical sense). No cryptanalytical attack is publicly known that could be launched to successfully attack any of the cryptographic algorithms used in later versions of PGP (e.g., ElGamal, DSS, 3DES, CAST, ...). Consequently, given the current state of the art and knowledge in the open literature, it seems to be too expensive to successfully attack and cryptanalyze PGP. This is good news. However, there is also bad news:

- First, it may be the case that some intelligence agencies can successfully attack and cryptanalyze some of the algorithms employed by PGP (either through the use of a brute force attack or through the use of another type of attack);
- Second and more importantly, there are other ways to break the security of a cryptographic system rather than to cryptanalyze it.

[1] `http://axion.physics.ubc.ca/pgp-attack.html`

Unfortunately, it is not possible to say more about the first point (since hardly any outsider reliably knows the current state of the art and knowledge of intelligence agencies), so we focus on the second point. As a general rule of thumb, it is important to note and keep in mind that no security system (that is of any use for real applications) is absolutely secure and impenetrable, and that all security systems can be circumvented in one way or another. This is equally true for cryptographic systems, such as PGP. For example, the Unix version of PGP 5.0i had a serious bug in its use of the `/dev/random` device to generate pseudorandom numbers. This bug led to a situation in which the session keys generated by PGP were predictable (as argued in Chapter 4, the use of a weak pseudorandom number generator is very dangerous and may break the security of any system). Similar bugs and vulnerabilities exist in every system and may be exploited by attackers to gain illegitimate acces.

10.2.2 Physical Security

One should not get lulled into a false sense of security simply because one uses a cryptographic software like PGP. For example, cryptographic techniques may protect data only while they are employed, and encryption protects data only while it's encrypted. If the same data is stored in unencrypted form on a multi-user system, it is generally much simpler (and cheaper) to attack the data there. All the attacker has to do is to circumvent or break the security of the access control system. In general, the simplest (and cheapest) way to break the security of a system is to compromise its physical security. We address three points related to physical security next.

Multi-User Systems

First of all, it is important to note that PGP was originally designed for single-user systems, such as personal computers running the MS-DOS operating system. These systems are fairly simple to secure if they are located in physically protected environments, such as private homes and apartments. But PGP also runs on multi-user systems, such as UNIX or Windows NT, and on these systems there are much greater risks of sensitive data being exposed.

File Deletion

A potential security problem is caused by how most operating systems delete files. When you encrypt a file and then delete the original plaintext file, most operating systems do not physically erase the data. Instead, they merely mark the corresponding disk blocks as logically deleted, allowing the space to be reused later. The disk blocks still contain the original plaintext data you wanted to erase, and will probably eventually be overwritten by new data at some later point in time. If, however, an attacker reads the deleted disk blocks soon after they have been deallocated, he can recover the original plaintext data. The situation is comparable to sensitive paper documents that are put in the paper recycling bin instead of the shredder. The digital analog to the paper shredder is to physically erase and wipe the memory space that has been occupied by the data. As mentioned in Chapter 9, the PGPtools comprise file and free space wiper utilities (the number of passes to overwrite a file during the wipe process is configurable with a default value of eight). If users employed these utilities, they would be reasonably secure against the reconstruction of logically erased files. Unfortunately, users seldom employ them.

Tempest

It is possible and technically feasible to remotely detect the electromagnetic signals produced by a computer system when keystrokes are transmitted from the keyboard or video signals are transmitted to the screen. This type of attack frequently occurs in computer espionage and information warfare. Again, we must say that protection against this type of attack requires some form of physical security. For example, one possibility is to properly shield computer equipment and network cabling so that it does not emit sufficiently strong electromagnetic signals. This shielding technology has been named "Tempest." It is mainly used by government agencies and defense contractors.

PGP is a software product. As such, there is no possibility to incorporate physical security mechanisms. Nevertheless, some newer versions of PGP can display decrypted messages using a specially designed font that minimizes the physical strength of the electromagnetic signals produced by the video screen. This may make it more difficult for the signals to be remotely detected. This special font is available in PGP versions that support the "Secure Viewer" feature. For users who deal with sensitive data, this software-based Tempest scheme is certainly appropriate to use.

10.2.3 Real Threats

The three most important threats against PGP are related to man-in-the-middle, passphrase guessing, and malicious software attacks.

Man-in-the-Middle Attacks

In any scheme that uses public key cryptography, a major vulnerability exists if public keys are tampered with. We discussed this point and elaborated on PGP's unique approach to address the problem: the PGP web of trust. Since it's up to the legitimate PGP user to control her web of trust, this vulnerability can be countered on an individual user's basis. Note, however, that it is not simple for a casual user to understand PGP's notion of trust and key legitimacy. Also note that there are many possibilities to misconfigure PGP in a way that completely breaks the security of the overall scheme. Consequently, there is need for education and properly explaining the rationale behind PGP's web of trust.

Passphrase Guessing Attacks

Since PGP uses passphrases to derive secret keys that are used to encrypt private keys, the security of the passphrase scheme in use is an upper limit to the overall security of PGP. There are several points to make:

- First, users may write down passphrases;
- Second, users may choose easily guessable passphrases;
- Third, when a user enters his passphrase it is susceptible to computer viruses, Trojan horses, and other software-related attacks. These kinds of attacks are further addressed below.

These points are very similar to passwords and lead to a situation in which passphrase-protected systems may still be successfully attacked (even if the cryptography employed by the systems is strong). Note that there are many investigations that address the security of password schemes, whereas there are only a few of them addressing the security of passphrase schemes. You may take this as a research challenge.

Malicious Software Attacks

The most likely attack against the passphrase protection scheme of a user's private key(s) would involve malicious software, such as Trojan horses, computer viruses, or worms. For example, the Caligula Word 97 macro virus was released by a virus exchange group called the "Codebreakers" and was found in many companies a couple of years ago. When executed, the virus tried to open the registry of a

Windows NT system and looked for the registered PGP path where it eventually found the user's secret key ring (i.e., the file `secring.skr`). The virus then copied this file to a file called `secringXXXX.skr`, where each `X` refers to an integer ranging from 0 to 7, for example, `secring4321.skr`. Finally, the virus tried to upload this newly created file to an FTP site (`ftp.codebreakers.org` or `209.201.88.110`) and to store it in the incoming directory. Any file uploaded to this directory could then be attacked by offline passphrase guessing. In the case of the Caligula Word 97 macro virus, there are many possibilities to counter the threat. For example, most commercially available antivirus software packages are able to detect and remove the macro virus. Also, since the virus registers itself in the Windows NT registry, its existence can be detected there. Finally, since the virus tries to establish an FTP connection to upload the copied file, it can be detected by a properly configured and running intrusion detection system.

In spite of the fact that the Caligula Word 97 macro virus has been properly countered by the security community, its mere existence has shown that it is possible to use malicious software to attack the secret keys of PGP users. In addition to stealing private key rings and launching offline passphrase guessing attacks, it is also possible to create malicious software that captures passphrases when they are entered by users, and send these passphrases to an attacker's site (for example, using SMTP or HTTP).

Defending against these types of attacks falls under the category of protecting against malicious software in general, and computer viruses in particular. PGP has no defenses against malicious software, so the user must rely on the underlying operating system or use antivirus products that are commercially available (another business unit of NAI is selling antivirus products). To make sure that nobody has tampered with PGP, the software should be downloaded from a reliable site and the digital signature that comes along with the PGP distribution package should be verified accordingly.

10.3 FUTURE DEVELOPMENTS

In this section, we elaborate on some future developments related to PGP. In fact, there are currently two processes and two trends that occur in parallel:

- First, the process of integrating PGP and OpenPGP with MIME continues (the resulting message formats are called PGP/MIME and OpenPGP/MIME).
- Second, the process of integrating X.509 certificates with PGP's web of trust continues (this is particularly important for the deployment of PGP in large

companies and organizations).

- Third, the designers and developers of network applications generally tend to use ASN.1 to specify message formats. Consequently, the packet and message formats of PGP, OpenPGP, PGP/MIME, and OpenPGP/MIME may eventually be specified using ASN.1.

- Fourth, various applications outside the scope of secure messaging are starting to make use of PGP and the infrastructure that is being established with the deployment of PGP. For example, PGP-CCI was an early attempt to link the functionality of PGP to a Web browser to provide transaction security [1].[2]

The net result of these processes and trends is a further deployment of PGP and PGP-enabled applications software on the one hand, and a long-term convergence of PGP and S/MIME on the other hand. Again, the second point is further addressed in Chapter 17.

Finally, it is important to note that no security mechanism or feature will actually be used in practice if it is not usable. Consequently, usability is a prerequisite for any security mechanism or feature to be useful at all. Against this background, Alma Whitten and Doug Tygar empirically investigated the usability of PGP software at Carnegie Mellon University (CMU). In short, they found rather pessimistic results that indicate that PGP is still far too complicated to be usable in practice by casual users [2,3]. For example, the majority of the participants of empirical tests were unable to sign and encrypt a message using PGP 5.0 within 90 minutes. Against this background, it is possible and very likely that the design of mechanisms and features that are secure and usable will become an important field of study for future application developers.

10.4 FURTHER INFORMATION

As mentioned before, further information about PGP is available from the homepage of the PGP Security business unit of NAI,[3] the homepage of Network Associates

[2]The PGP-CCI application was based on and made use of the common client interface (CCI), which was an early attempt at extending the functionality of common Web browsers. Now largely abandoned, CCI was an experimental protocol that allowed some versions of the NCSA Mosaic WWW browser to be controlled by an HTTP server. Today, many of the more useful functions of CCI are present in the Java and JavaScript languages.

[3]`http://www.pgp.com`

International B.V.,[4] and the international PGP homepage.[5]

In addition to the information available on these homepages, the PGP software distribution also comes with the following documents that are recommended reading:

- *An Introduction to Cryptography*;
- *PGP Command Line User's Guide*;
- *PGP User's Guide.*

More recently, Philip R. Zimmermann also initiated an NAI newsletter named *Zimmermann Telegram*[6] to serve as "a forum for technical material about cryptography and current PGP and PGP-compatible product information." The *Zimmermann Telegram* is recommended reading for anybody seriously using PGP. Further information (including instructions to subscribe to the newsletter) about the *Zimmermann Telegram* is available from the homepage of Network Associates International B.V. mentioned above. Eventually, the *Zimmermann Telegram* will also be distributed on NAI's or PGP Security's homepage in the future.

REFERENCES

[1] J.D. Weeks, A. Cain, and B. Sanderson, "CCI-Based Web Security – A Design Using PGP," *Proceedings of 4th International World Wide Web Conference*, December 1995, pp. 381 – 395.

[2] A. Whitten, J.D. Tygar, "Why Johnny Can't Encrypt: A Usability Evaluation of PGP 5.0," *Proceedings of 8th USENIX Security Symposium*, August 1999.

[3] A. Whitten, J.D. Tygar, "Usability of Security: A Case Study," CMU-CS-98-155, December 1998.

[4] `http://www.pgpinternational.com`

[5] `http://www.pgpi.org`

[6] The newsletter is named for both its initiator and the famous "Zimmermann Telegram" of World War I. The Zimmermann Telegram, an encrypted German diplomatic communication, was intercepted and cryptanalyzed by British intelligence agencies. Its content helped draw the United States into the war against Germany.

Part III

S/MIME

Chapter 11

History and Development

Earlier in this book we mentioned that PEM was an early IETF-initiated Internet standardization effort for secure messaging that suffered from two major limitations and shortcomings (namely the incompatibility with the MIME message formats and the far too restrictive PKI requirements), and that MOSS was an attempt to overcome them. In parallel with the development of MOSS in the mid-1990s, however, an industry working group led by RSA Security, Inc.[1] started to develop another specification for conveying digitally signed and/or encrypted and digitally enveloped data in accordance to the MIME message formats and some of the earlier specified public key cryptography standards (PKCSs). Remember from our discussion in Chapter 5 that the PKCS specifications are developed by another industry working group also led by RSA Security, Inc. Consequently, RSA Security, Inc. had a vital interest promoting the PKCS specifications and applying them in the field of secure messaging.

The approach and protocol specification that was developed by the industry working group was named *Secure Multipurpose Internet Mail Extensions*, or *S/MIME* in short. Similar to PEM and MOSS, S/MIME refers to a specification rather than a product (such as PGP), and similar to MOSS, S/MIME was also

[1]The former name of the company was RSA Data Security, Inc.

designed to add security to e-mail messages that make use of the MIME message formats. Consequently, S/MIME cannot be used with UAs that do not provide support for MIME (contrary to PGP). Unlike PEM and MOSS, however, S/MIME has been successfully deployed on the global marketplace. That is why we make it a substantial part of this book.

While the goals of MOSS and S/MIME were largely the same, the final solutions ended up being quite different. This is primarily due to the fact that S/MIME is built on top of some PKCS specifications, whereas PEM, MOSS, and PGP all use character-encoding style of protocols. Note, however, that this is not a fundamental difference, but rather an implementation issue. Also note that using established encoding schemes is certainly good practice, since any security analysis does not have to start from scratch.

As of this writing, there are three versions of S/MIME, of which only versions 2 and 3 are used in practice:

- S/MIME version 1 was specified and officially published in 1995 by RSA Security, Inc. [1].
- S/MIME version 2 was specified in a pair of informational RFC documents — RFC 2311 [2] and RFC 2312 [3] — in March 1998.[2]
- The work was continued in the IETF S/MIME Mail Security (SMIME) WG and resulted in S/MIME version 3 in June 1999. S/MIME version 3, in turn, is specified in a set of five related RFC documents (RFC documents 2630 to 2634 [4 – 8]). As such, S/MIME version 3 has been submitted for consideration as an Internet standards track protocol. The changes between version 2 and version 3 are not fundamental, and it is generally recommended that S/MIME version 3 implementations should attempt to have the greatest interoperability possible with S/MIME version 2 implementations.

Since the very beginning of the standardization effort, many vendors of Internet messaging products (including, for example, Microsoft and Netscape Communications) have actively supported S/MIME. This commitment and strong vendor support has not changed so far and is likely to continue in the future.

In the past, S/MIME has had some difficulties receiving consideration as an Internet standards track protocol due to its use of patented technologies and algorithms. Historically, all standards approved by the IETF must use only public

[2]The pair was complemented by three informational RFC documents that specify PKCS #1 (RFC 2313), PKCS #7 (RFC 2314), and PKCS #10 (RFC 2315). Refer to Chapter 5 to get the references for these RFC documents.

domain technologies and algorithms, so anyone can implement them without paying royalties to patent holders. Unfortunately, this is not the case with some public key algorithms. For example, we already mentioned in Chapter 4 that the RSA public key algorithm was (and still is) protected by U.S. Patent No. 4,405,829 "Cryptographic communications system and method," granted to MIT in September 1983. Also, other public key algorithms are protected by patents.[3] As mentioned above, S/MIME makes use of PKCS #1, PKCS #7, and PKCS #10. Although the PKCS specifications are freely available, any developer who wants to use the algorithms described therein (e.g., the RSA algorithm), whether he uses RSA Security's own toolkits or not, is required to pay RSA Security, Inc. royalties, at least for products created and distributed in the United States.[4] Because of this situation, Internet standardization for S/MIME version 2 has been blocked and the pair of informational RFC documents is historical material being published for the public record. Meanwhile, the situation has improved mainly for two reasons:

- First, S/MIME version 3 provides more flexibility with regard to the cryptographic algorithms that must be supported (as discussed in the following Chapter);

- Second, most public key patents either have expired (e.g., the patent for the Diffie-Hellman key exchange algorithm expired in 1997) or are about to expire (e.g., the patent for the RSA algorithm expired on September 20, 2000).

Consequently, it is possible and very likely that the situation is going to improve and that Internet standarization for S/MIME version 3 will speed up considerably.

Finally, due to the fact that S/MIME version 3 has been submitted for possible consideration as an Internet standards track protocol, interoperability has become a major issue. Vendors participate in S/MIME compliance and interoperability testing programs conducted over the Internet. As such, they put their application programs through S/MIME test suites that include online certification, digitally signed and digitally enveloped message creation, as well as verification and decryption of received messages. For example, RSA Security, Inc. runs an S/MIME interoperability center and we further elaborate on S/MIME compliance and interoperability testing in Chapter 14.

[3]Most public key algorithms are protected by U.S. patents (and not international patents as, for example, some of the earlier secret key algorithms).

[4]Outside the United States, the development and marketing of public key cryptography is not restricted.

REFERENCES

[1] RSA Data Security, Inc., *S/MIME Implementation Guide*, Interoperability Profile, Version 1, August 1995.

[2] S. Dusse, P. Hoffman, B. Ramsdell, L. Lundblack, and L. Repka, "S/MIME Version 2 Message Specification," Request for Comments 2311, March 1998.

[3] S. Dusse, P. Hoffman, B. Ramsdell, and J. Weinstein, "S/MIME Version 2 Certificate Handling," Request for Comments 2312, March 1998.

[4] R. Housley, "Cryptographic Message Syntax," Request for Comments 2630, June 1999.

[5] E. Rescorla, "Diffie-Hellman Key Agreement Method," Request for Comments 2631, June 1999.

[6] B. Ramsdell (Ed.), "S/MIME Version 3 Certificate Handling," Request for Comments 2632, June 1999.

[7] B. Ramsdell (Ed.), "S/MIME Version 3 Message Specification," Request for Comments 2633, June 1999.

[8] P. Hoffman (Ed.), "Enhanced Security Services for S/MIME," Request for Comments 2634, June 1999.

Chapter 12

Technological Approach

In this chapter, we overview and discuss the conceptual and technological approach employed by S/MIME. More specifically, we introduce the topic in Section 12.1, address message formats, supported algorithms, and message processing in Sections 12.2 to 12.4, and elaborate on the management of cryptographic keys in Section 12.5.

12.1 INTRODUCTION

First of all, it is important to note that S/MIME uses digital signature, data encryption, and digital envelope mechanisms to provide basic message protection services.[1] As such, the technological approach employed by S/MIME is conceptually similar to the one employed by PGP (and most other secure messaging schemes). Also, the cryptographical strength of the algorithms employed by S/MIME are comparable to the ones employed by PGP.

Contrary to these similarities, however, there are (at least) two fundamental differences between PGP and S/MIME:

[1]More specifically, basic message protection services include data origin authentication, connectionless confidentiality, connectionless integrity, and nonrepudiation services with proof of origin.

- First, PGP and S/MIME use different message formats;
- Second, PGP and S/MIME handle public keys and public key certificates in fundamentally different ways:
  - PGP relies on users to exchange public keys and PGP certificates in order to establish trust in each other;
  - Contrary to that, S/MIME relies on X.509 certificates that are issued by CAs and eventually distributed by directory services.

  We elaborated on PGP's web of trust in Chapter 8, and we address the management of X.509 certificates and the corresponding public key infrastructure (PKI) requirements for S/MIME in the following chapter.

In either case, both differences lead to a situation in which PGP and S/MIME implementations do not interoperate.[2] In Chapter 17, we elaborate on the possibility for the two technologies to eventually converge in the future. In the meantime, however, we have to live with a situation in which two competing standards for secure messaging on the Internet are evolving and coexist.[3]

As its name implies, the aim of S/MIME is to secure MIME entities. A MIME entity, in turn, may be a message subpart, a set of subparts, or an entire e-mail message (with all of its subparts but without the message header). In either case, S/MIME defines how to cryptographically protect a MIME entity (i.e., using digital signatures and/or digital envelopes) according to PKCS #7. Again, refer to Chapter 5 for more information related to the PKCS specifications in general, and PKCS #7 in particular.

12.2 MESSAGE FORMATS

S/MIME is based on the cryptographic message syntax (CMS) specified in RFC 2630 [1]. The CMS, in turn, is derived from PKCS #7 version 1.5 specified in RFC 2315 [2]. CMS values are generated using ASN.1 and encoded as octet strings according to BER. Again, refer to Chapter 5 for a brief overview about ASN.1 and BER.

[2]Note that recent versions of PGP provide support for X.509 certificates. This does not, however, solve the different message formats problem.

[3]This is more evidence for the generally bad shape of contemporary standardization bodies for the IETF, including the IETF.

More specifically, the CMS describes an encapsulation syntax to cryptographically protect and enhance MIME entities. As such, it provides support for digital signatures, message authentication codes (MACs), and message encryption using digital envelopes. The syntax allows recursive structures, so one encapsulation envelope may be nested inside another. For example, it is possible to encapsulate some previously signed MIME entity, or it is possible to digitally sign some previously encapsulated entity. Furthermore, the syntax allows arbitrary attributes, such as timestamps, to be signed along with MIME entities, and provides for other attributes, such as countersignatures, to be associated with signatures.

In theory, the CMS is general enough to be useful for the definition of many protection content types. RFC 2630, however, only defines one protection content type. The aim of this type is to encapsulate an identified content type, and this identified content type may provide further encapsulation. The ASN.1 specification for the protection content type `ContentInfo` is as follows:

```
ContentInfo ::= SEQUENCE {
  contentType ContentType,
  content [0] EXPLICIT ANY DEFINED BY contentType
}
```

Consequently, a value of protection content type `ContentInfo` consists of two components: `contentType` that identifies the content type and refers to a value of type `ContentType`, and `content` that comprises the actual content value.

As of this writing, RFC 2630 defines the following six content types (additional content types may be defined outside the scope of RFC 2630 and S/MIME):

- The `data` content type (ASN.1 type `Data`) is intended to refer to arbitrary data, such as ASCII text, which may or may not have an internal structure. In either case, the interpretation of the data is left to the application.

- The `signed-data` content type (ASN.1 type `SignedData`) consists of content of any type, such as `data`, and zero or more signatures (including all the required information, such as algorithm identifiers, certificates, certificate revocation lists, and other signer-related information).

- The `enveloped-data` content type (ASN.1 type `EnvelopedData`) consists of an encrypted content of any type, such as `data` or `signed-data`, and encrypted content-encryption keys for one or more recipients.[4]

[4] As further addressed in Chapter 4, the combination of the encrypted content and one encrypted content-encryption key for a recipient represents a digital envelope for that recipient.

- The `digested-data` content type (ASN.1 type `DigestedData`) consists of content of any type and a message digest for this content. Typically, the `digested-data` content type is used to provide data integrity services, and the result generally becomes input to the `enveloped-data` content type.

- The `encrypted-data` content type (ASN.1 type `EncryptedData`) consists of encrypted data of any type. Contrary to the `enveloped-data` content type, however, this content type includes neither recipient information nor any encrypted content-encryption key. Instead, keys must be distributed and managed out-of-band by other means.

- The `authenticated-data` content type (ASN.1 type `AuthenticatedData`) consists of content of any type, a MAC, and encrypted authentication keys for one or more recipients.

An implementation that conforms to the CMS must at least implement the protection content, `ContentInfo`, and the `data`, `signed-data`, and `enveloped-data` content types. The other content types are optional and may be implemented at will. The full ASN.1 specifications for the content types itemized above are provided in RFC 2630 and are not replicated in this book.

Table 12.1
MIME Content Types and Subtypes Employed by S/MIME

Type	Subtype	"Smime-type" Parameter
`multipart`	`signed`	
`application`	`pkcs7-mime`	`signed-data`
	`pkcs7-mime`	`enveloped-data`
	`pkcs7-mime`	`certs-only`
	`pkcs7-signature`	
	`pkcs10-mime`	

Based on the CMS specified in RFC 2630 [1], RFC 2633 [3] defines how to create a MIME entity that is cryptographically protected and enhanced according to the CMS. More specifically, RFC 2633 introduces and explains the use of the `multipart/signed` content type defined in 1847 [4], as well as several new subtypes of the MIME `application` content type. The MIME content types and corresponding subtypes employed by S/MIME are summarized in Table 12.1. The use of the additional "smime-type" parameter is explained next.

Table 12.2
MIME Types and File Extensions

MIME Type	"Smime-type" Parameter	File Extension
`application/pkcs-7-mime`	`signed-data`	`.p7m`
	`enveloped-data`	`.p7m`
	`certs-only`	`.p7c`
`application/pkcs-7-signature`		`.p7s`

Looking at Table 12.1, it is intuitively clear that the most important MIME content type for S/MIME is `application/pkcs7-mime`.[5] In fact, this content type is used to carry CMS objects of several types, including digitally signed data (indicated with the "smime-type" parameters `signed-data` and `certs-only`) and digitally enveloped data (indicated with the "smime-type" parameter `enveloped-data`). More specifically, the `application/pkcs7-mime` type has a couple of optional parameters:

- As discussed above, the "smime-type" parameter is used to indicate whether the `pkcs7-mime` content is digitally signed or enveloped (possible values are `enveloped-data`, `signed-data`, `certs-only`, or any other CMS content types).
- The "name" and "filename" parameters are used to specify a filename (limited to eight characters) with an appropriate extension (limited to three characters).[6] Refer to Table 12.2 for an overview of the relevant MIME types and the corresponding file extensions. The filename base `smime` is often used to indicate that the MIME entity is associated with S/MIME. According to this convention, the filename `smime.p7m` is used to refer to a MIME entity that carries a CMS object that is either digitally signed or digitally enveloped. The use of these parameters will become clear when we look at exemplary S/MIME messages later in this section.

In addition to the `application/pkcs7-mime` content type (with the "smime-type" parameter set to `signed-data`), the `multipart/signed` and the `application/pkcs7-signature` MIME types can also be used to indicate a digital signature (as further explained below). Finally, the `pkcs10-mime` content type

[5]Note that some UAs use `application/x-pkcs7-mime` instead of `application/pkcs7-mime`. This is only for historical reasons and the two MIME content types are in fact equivalent.

[6]The "filename" parameter is sent together with the `Content-Disposition` header.

can be used to declare a certificate request message according to the PKCS #10 specification.

S/MIME provides one format for enveloped-only data, several formats for signed-only data, and several formats for signed and enveloped data. In either case, a single procedure is used to prepare a MIME entity to be signed, enveloped, or both signed and enveloped. Roughly speaking, the procedure comprises the following five steps:

- First, the MIME entity is prepared according to the normal rules for MIME message preparation;
- Second, the leaves of the MIME entity are converted to canonical form;[7]
- Third, the MIME entity plus some security-related information, such as algorithm identifiers or certificates, are processed by S/MIME to produce a PKCS object;
- Fourth, the PKCS object is treated as message content and wrapped in MIME. During this wrapping process, additional MIME headers may be prepended to the message;
- Fifth, the resulting message is sent to its intended recipient(s) using the MTS.

The procedure is further addressed in Section 3.1 of RFC 2633 [3]. Typically, canonicalization and transfer encoding are performed by the nonsecurity part of the UA rather than the S/MIME implementation (since they are not security relevant).

In the subsections that follow, we address the creation procedures and formats of enveloped-only, signed-only, signed and enveloped, and certificates-only MIME entities. More information is available in the RFC document referenced above. Furthermore, you may look at the details of arbitrary S/MIME messages to get more complete examples.

12.2.1 Enveloped-Only MIME Entities

First of all, it is important to note that enveloped-only MIME entities are not protected in terms of message origin authentication and data integrity, and that it is possible to replace ciphertext in such a way that the processed MIME entity will still be valid, but the meaning is changed. Consequently, enveloped-only MIME

[7]The exact details of this canonicalization step depend on the actual MIME type and subtype of an entity. Consequently, the standard for the particular MIME type should be consulted. For example, canonicalization for MIME type `text` involves converting the line endings to the pair of characters `<CR><LF>` and choosing a registered character set.

entities should only be used in situations where message origin authentication and data integrity are not relevant or can be provided by other means.

Taking these preliminary comments into account, the procedure to create an enveloped-only MIME entity includes the following three steps:

- First, the MIME entity to be enveloped is prepared for S/MIME processing (more specifically, it is converted to canonical form and transfer-encoded as mentioned above).
- Second, the MIME entity and other required data is processed into a CMS object of type `enveloped-data` (the corresponding procedure is explained in Section 12.4).
- Third, the CMS object is inserted into a MIME entity of type `application/pkcs7-mime`. Furthermore, the "smime-type" parameter is set to `enveloped-data` and the "name" and "filename" parameters are set to something like `smime.p7m` (the extension `.p7m` is mandatory).

Finally, the resulting MIME entity is encapsulated into an e-mail message (with proper message headers) and sent to the recipient(s).

The skeleton of a resulting S/MIME message that is digitally enveloped looks as follows:

```
From:     ...
To:       ...
Subject: ...
MIME-Version: 1.0
Content-Type: application/pkcs7-mime;
     smime-type=enveloped-data;
     name="smime.p7m"
Content-Transfer-Encoding: base64
Content-Disposition: attachment;
     filename="smime.p7m"

...
```

The three dots at the bottom of the message skeleton refer to the base-64 encoded enveloped data (note that the data is separated from the message header with an empty line).

12.2.2 Signed-Only MIME Entities

As mentioned above, S/MIME provides two different formats for digitally signed MIME entities:

- The first format uses the `application/pkcs7-mime` MIME type with the "smime-type" parameter set to `signed-data`.
- The second format makes use of and combines the `multipart/signed` and `application/pkcs7-signature` MIME types.

There are no fixed rules when a particular format should be applied. In fact, this decision depends on the capabilities of all the recipients and the relative importance of recipients with S/MIME facilities being able to verify the signature versus the importance of recipients without S/MIME facilities being able to view the message. More specifically, messages signed using the second format (using the `multipart/signed` and `application/pkcs7-signature` MIME types) can always be viewed by the recipients whether they have S/MIME-enabled UAs or not. This format is therefore also sometimes referred to as the "clear-signing format." Contrary to that, messages signed using the first format (using the `application/pkcs7-mime` MIME type and corresponding parameters set to the appropriate values) cannot be viewed by a recipient unless he has a S/MIME-enabled UA. Since this causes problems in certain environments, the second format is usually preferred in practice. The two formats are further addressed next.

Application/pkcs7-mime Signatures

Using the `application/pkcs7-mime` MIME type, the procedure to create a signed-only MIME entity is as follows:

- First, the MIME entity to be signed is prepared for S/MIME processing (as discussed above);
- Second, the MIME entity and other required data is processed into a CMS object of type `signed-data` (again, the corresponding procedure is explained in Section 12.4);
- Third, the CMS object is inserted into a MIME entity of type `application/pkcs7-mime`. Furthermore, the "smime-type" parameter is set to `signed-data` and the "name" and "filename" parameters are set to something like `smime.p7m` (again, the extension `.p7m` is mandatory).

Finally, the resulting MIME entity is encapsulated into an e-mail message (with proper message headers) and sent to the recipient(s).

The skeleton of a resulting S/MIME message that is digitally signed looks as follows:

```
From:    ...
To:      ...
Subject: ...
MIME-Version: 1.0
Content-Type: application/pkcs7-mime;
     smime-type=signed-data;
     name="smime.p7m"
Content-Transfer-Encoding: base64
Content-Disposition: attachment;
     filename="smime.p7m"

...
```

Again, there are three dots at the bottom of the message (separated with an empty line). In this case, the dots refer to the base-64 encoded digitally signed MIME entity.

Multipart/signed and Application/pkcs7-signature Signatures

Alternatively, the sender can also use the clear-signing format (using the `multipart/signed` and `application/pkcs7-signature` MIME types) to create a signed-only MIME entity. In this case, the resulting `multipart/signed` MIME entity has two parts:

- The first part contains the MIME entity that is digitally signed (in the clear).
- The second part contains a detached signature CMS object of type `signed-data` (with no encapsulated content). The CMS object, in turn, is encapsulated into a MIME entity of type `application/pkcs7-signature`, and the "name" and "filename" parameters are set to something like `smime.p7s` (the extension `.p7s` is mandatory).

The procedure to create a signed-only MIME entity using the clear-signing format includes the following five steps:

- First, the MIME entity to be signed is prepared for S/MIME processing (as discussed above).
- Second, the MIME entity is inserted into the first part of a `multipart/signed` MIME entity.
- Third, the MIME entity is subjected to CMS processing in order to obtain a detached signature of type `signed-data` (again, the procedure to compute the digital signature is explained in Section 12.4).
- Fourth, transfer encoding is applied to the detached signature. As such, it is inserted into a MIME entity of type `application/pkcs7-signature`.
- Fifth, the MIME entity of type `application/pkcs7-signature` is inserted into the second part of the `multipart/signed` entity.

As discussed in Chapter 7, the `multipart/signed` MIME type has two parameters: the "protocol" parameter and the "micalg" parameter.

- The "protocol" parameter must be set to `"application/pkcs7-signature"` (the quotation marks are required because MIME requires that the slash character in the parameter value must be quoted).
- The "micalg" parameter must be set to the message integrity check (MIC) algorithm in use, such as `md5` for MD5 or `sha1` for SHA-1.

Finally, the resulting MIME entity is encapsulated into an e-mail message (with proper message headers) and sent to the recipient(s).

The skeleton of a resulting S/MIME message that is digitally signed using the clear-signing format looks as follows:

```
From:     ...
To:       ...
Subject: ...
Date:     ...
MIME-Version: 1.0
Content-Type: multipart/signed;
     protocol="application/pkcs7-signature";
     micalg=sha1;
     boundary="foo"
```

```
--foo
Content-Type: text/plain

This is a test message to demonstrate the clear-signing format
for signed-only messages.

--foo
Content-Type: application/pkcs7-signature;
     name="smime.p7s"
Content-Transfer-Encoding: base64
Content-Disposition: attachment;
     filename="smime.p7s"

...
--foo--
```

In this case, the three dots at the bottom of the message body part refer to the base-64 encoded detached signature for the test message.

12.2.3 Signed and Enveloped MIME Entities

Input and output to S/MIME processing are always MIME entities (whether secured or not). Consequently, signing and enveloping can also be iterated and nested. In general, it is possible to either sign or envelope the message first:

- When a message is first signed and then enveloped, the signature(s) is (are) securely obscured by the digital envelope. In this case, the only way a passive attacker (e.g., an eavesdropper) can determine the sender of an S/MIME message is by looking at the `From` field in the message header, which may or may not be correct. Consequently, sender anonymity may be achieved in this case.

- Contrary to that, when a message is first enveloped and then signed, the signature(s) is (are) exposed, but it is possible to verify it (them) without removing the envelope. This may be particularly useful in situations where automatic signature verification must be used to take appropriate actions before the message ever reaches the recipient (since no private key is required to verify a signature).

Both possibilities are technically feasible, and it is up to the implementor and user to choose between them.

12.2.4 Certificates-Only MIME Entities

Finally, a certificates-only MIME entity may be used to transport public key certificates, such as in response to a registration request. The same format can also be used to convey certificate revocation lists (CRLs).

The procedure to create a certificates-only MIME entity includes the following two steps:

- First, the certificate is made available to the CMS generating process which creates a CMS object of type `signed-data`.
- Second, the CMS object is enclosed in an `application/pkcs7-mime` MIME entity with the "smime-type" parameter set to `certs-only` and a file extension of `.p7c`.

The algorithms supported by S/MIME for digital signatures and digital envelopes are overviewed next.

12.3 SUPPORTED ALGORITHMS

The CMS is quite general, and an S/MIME-compliant UA may support multiple message digest, data encryption, key encryption, and digital signature algorithms:

- With regard to message digest algorithms, the S/MIME version 2 specification mandates support for SHA-1 and MD5 for receiving UAs, and recommends the use of SHA-1 for sending UAs.[8] Similarly, the S/MIME version 3 specification requires that (sending and receiving) UAs must support SHA-1 and should still support MD5.
- With regard to data encryption algorithms, the S/MIME version 2 specification mandates support for 40-bit RC2[9] and recommends support for DES and 3DES. Prior to the liberalization of the U.S. export controls, many software vendors have used 40-bit RC2 in the international versions of their UAs, whereas they have additionally used DES and 3DES in the domestic versions of their UAs. According to the S/MIME version 3 specification, however, support for 3DES is required and a corresponding UA may additionally support 128-bit RC2.

---

[8] As mentioned in Chapter 4, there is justifiable concern about the security of MD5, so SHA-1 is clearly the preferred alternative.

[9] Note that RC2 is an encryption algorithm that can be used with variable key sizes.

- With regard to key encryption algorithms (for digital envelopes), the S/MIME version 2 specification mandates support for the RSA encryption algorithm with a variable key size (between 512 and 1024 bits[10]). In addition to this RSA-based key transport, the S/MIME version 3 specification also requires support for the Diffie-Hellman key agreement method (as further specified in an RFC document of its own [5]).

- Finally, with regard to digital signature algorithms, the S/MIME version 2 specification mandates support for RSA, whereas the S/MIME version 3 specification mandates support for the digital signature algorithm (DSA) and declares that implementations may additionally provide support for the RSA algorithm.

Note that the algorithms mandated by either version of S/MIME are comparable to the ones proposed for PGP and OpenPGP. Also note that implementors are free to provide support for additional algorithms (mainly data encryption algorithms). For example, many implementations (e.g., the iT_SEC_outlook plug-in) additionally provide support for the International Data Encryption Algorithm (IDEA).

If a sending UA has to encrypt and digitally envelope a message for a specific recipient, it must know in one way or another what data encryption algorithms the recipient supports and must choose among them. Consequently, the relevant S/MIME specifications also include a discussion of the procedure for deciding which encryption algorithm to use. In fact, the sending UA may have to make two decisions:

- First, it must determine if the receiving UA is capable of decrypting using a given encryption algorithm;

- Second, if the receiving UA is only capable of accepting weakly encrypted content, the sending UA must decide if it is acceptable to send the message using weak encryption.

To enable and support this decision, a sending UA may announce its decrypting capabilities in form of a capability attribute. A capability attribute, in turn, allows a sending UA to announce its decrypting capabilities in order of preference (the highest preference first). A receiving UA may store this information for future use.

According to the relevant S/MIME specification, the following rules, in the given order, should be followed by a sending UA to determine the decrypting capabilities of the receiving UA and to send out a message accordingly:

[10]Note that the key size is determined by the private key holder and the key generation process.

1. If the sending UA has a capability attribute (list of preferred decrypting capabilities) from the receiving UA, it should choose the first capability on the list that it supports.

2. If the sending UA has no capability attribute from the receiving UA but has received one or more messages from the receiving UA, the outgoing message should use the same encryption algorithm as was used on the last signed and encrypted message received from that UA.

3. If the sending UA has no knowledge about the decrypting capabilities of the recipient and is willing to risk that the recipient may not be able to decrypt the message, it should use 3DES.

4. If the sending UA has no knowledge about the decrypting capabilities of the receiving UA and is not willing to risk that the recipient may not be able to decrypt the message, it should use 40-bit RC2.

When an S/MIME-compliant UA sends an e-mail message to multiple recipients, some of the recipients may not be able to decrypt a strongly encrypted message (e.g., a message encrypted with 3DES). In this case, the sending UA may decide to use weak encryption for those recipients and strong encryption for the others. An eavesdropper listening to the data traffic, however, can determine the content by simply decrypting the message that was encrypted with the weak algorithm. In this case, strong encryption may not provide any added value over weak encryption.

12.4 PROCESSING MESSAGES

As mentioned above, a MIME entity that is to be secured with S/MIME must be prepared according to the normal rules for MIME message preparation. The MIME entity plus some security-related information, such as algorithm identifiers and public key certificates, must then be processed by an S/MIME implementation to produce a CMS object. The CMS object, in turn, must be treated as message content and wrapped in MIME (provided with appropriate MIME headers). The steps we have not addressed so far include the creation and verification of digital signatures, as well as the use of digital envelopes. These steps are overviewed next.

12.4.1 Digital Signatures

In general, the use of digital signatures requires at least one message digest algorithm and at least one public key algorithm (that can be used to digitally sign and verify messages). We mentioned some possible algorithms in the previous section.

On the sender's side, the procedure to digitally sign a MIME entity includes four steps that can be summarized as follows:

- First, the sender uses a one-way hash function to generate a message digest.
- Second, the sender encrypts the message digest using one of his private keys (the encrypted message digest represents the digital signature for the MIME entity).
- Third, the sender prepares a block of sender information (a value of the ASN.1 type `SignerInfo`) that contains the sender's public key certificate, an identifier for the message digest algorithm, an identifier for the public key algorithm (that is used to encrypt the message digest), and the encrypted message digest.
- Fourth, the MIME entity and the block of sender information are concatenated to form a CMS object of type `signed-data`.

As such, the CMS object is treated as message content, wrapped in MIME (using either one of the two formats for signed-only entities), and transmitted to the recipient(s).

On the recipient's side, the procedure to verify the digital signature prepended to a message includes two steps that can be summarized as follows:

- First, the recipient decrypts the digital signature using the sender's appropriate public key (the appropriate key is extracted from the block of sender information) to reveal the message digest.[11]
- Second, the recipient generates a new message digest for the received message and compares it to the revealed message digest. If both message digests match, the digital signature is verified and the message is accepted as being authentic.

When an S/MIME-compliant UA receives a message with a digitally signed MIME entity, it needs to have a valid certificate chain for the message sender to verify the signature. This issue is further addressed in the following chapter.

[11] Optionally, the status of the provided public key may be checked at this point in time (using CRL or OCSP).

12.4.2 Digital Envelopes

As mentioned previously, S/MIME uses the MIME content type `pkcs7-mime` with the "smime-type" parameter set to `enveloped-data` to transfer an encrypted and digitally enveloped message to its recipient(s).

On the sender's side, the procedure to digitally envelope a MIME entity includes five steps that can be summarized as follows:

- First, the sender (pseudo)randomly generates a content-encryption key that is appropriate for the encryption algorithm of choice (the encryption algorithm may be any one of the algorithms mentioned in the previous section).
- Second, the sender encrypts the MIME entity with the content-encryption key.
- Third, for each recipient, the sender encrypts the content-encryption key with the recipient's public key.[12]
- Fourth, for each recipient, the sender prepares a block of recipient information (a value of ASN.1 type `RecipientInfo`) that contains the sender's public key certificate, an identifier of the algorithm used to encrypt the session key, and the encrypted content-encryption key.
- Fifth, the encrypted MIME entity and the block(s) of recipient information are concatenated to form a CMS object of type `enveloped-data`. In addition, a copy of the content-encryption key should also be encrypted for the sender and included in the enveloped data.

As such, the CMS object is treated as message content, wrapped in MIME, and transmitted to the recipient(s).

On the recipient's side, the procedure to decrypt the MIME entity includes two steps that can be summarized as follows:

- First, the recipient decrypts his block of recipient information using his private key.
- Second, the recipient decrypts the message content with the session key.

Obviously, the second step reveals the message content to the recipient.

[12]Optionally, the status of the recipient's public key may be checked at this point in time.

12.5 CRYPTOGRAPHIC KEYS

Similar to PGP, S/MIME employs several cryptographic keys that must be managed in an appropriate way. Most of the things we said for PGP in Section 7.5 are equally true for S/MIME. Most importantly, the private key of a user must be secured and this can be achieved either by storing the private key locally in encrypted form or using smartcards. Against this background, the use of PKCS #11- and PKCS #15-compliant hardware tokens is getting increasingly important for S/MIME. As discussed before, the use of smartcards is advantageous but also more expensive.

Furthermore, S/MIME can support a variety of architectures for the management of X.509 certificates, such as the one defined by the IETF PKIX WG. This topic is further explored in the following chapter.

REFERENCES

[1] R. Housley, "Cryptographic Message Syntax," Request for Comments 2630, June 1999.

[2] B. Kaliski, "PKCS #7: Cryptographic Message Syntax, Version 1.5," Request for Comments 2315, March 1998.

[3] B. Ramsdell (Ed.), "S/MIME Version 3 Message Specification," Request for Comments 2633, June 1999.

[4] J. Galvin, S. Murphy, S. Crocker, and N. Freed, "Security Multiparts for MIME: Multipart/Signed and Multipart/Encrypted," Request for Comments 1847, October 1995.

[5] E. Rescorla, "Diffie-Hellman Key Agreement Method," Request for Comments 2631, June 1999.

Chapter 13

Public Key Infrastructure

In this chapter, we elaborate on the public key infrastructure (PKI) requirements for S/MIME. More specifically, we introduce the topic in Section 13.1, overview the work that is being done within the relevant IETF working group in Section 13.2, focus on the establishment of trust in Section 13.3, address certificate revocation in Section 13.4, elaborate on a few exemplary certification service providers in Section 13.5, and conclude with some final remarks in Section 13.6. Parts of this chapter are taken from [1] and Chapter 8 of [2]. Further information can also be found in [3,4].

13.1 INTRODUCTION

In Chapter 4, we introduced the notion of a digital or public key certificate and briefly overviewed the two formats that are in use today: PGP and X.509. In Chapter 8 we addressed PGP certificates and in this chapter we discuss X.509 certificates and their use for secure messaging with S/MIME.

More specifically, S/MIME makes use of X.509 certificates [5]. The current version of X.509 is version 3. The ASN.1 specification of a corresponding `Certificate` type is as follows:

```
Certificate ::= SEQUENCE {
    tbsCertificate          TBSCertificate,
    signatureAlgorithm      AlgorithmIdentifier,
    signature               BIT STRING
}
TBSCertificate ::= SEQUENCE {
    version            [ 0 ] Version DEFAULT v1(0),
    serialNumber             CertificateSerialNumber,
    signature                AlgorithmIdentifier,
    issuer                   Name,
    validity                 Validity,
    subject                  Name,
    subjectPublicKeyInfo     SubjectPublicKeyInfo,
    issuerUniqueID      [ 1 ] IMPLICIT UniqueIdentifier OPTIONAL,
    subjectUniqueID     [ 2 ] IMPLICIT UniqueIdentifier OPTIONAL,
    extensions          [ 3 ] Extensions OPTIONAL
}
Version ::= INTEGER { v1(0), v2(1), v3(2) }
CertificateSerialNumber ::= INTEGER
Name ::= SEQUENCE OF RelativeDistinguishedName
RelativeDistinguishedName ::= SET OF AttributeValueAssertion
AttributeValueAssertion ::= SEQUENCE {
    attributeType            OBJECT IDENTIFIER,
    attributeValue           ANY
}
Validity ::= SEQUENCE {
    notBefore                UTCTIME,
    notAfter                 UTCTIME
}
UniqueIdentifier ::= BITSTRING
Extensions ::= SEQUENCE OF Extension
Extension ::= SEQUENCE {
    extnid                   OBJECT IDENTIFIER,
    critical                 BOOLEAN DEFAULT FALSE,
    extnValue                OCTETSTRING
}
```

Consequently, an X.509v3 certificate refers to a value of type `Certificate`.

Such a value, in turn, includes a `TBSCertificate` value and a digital signature for this value. The digital signature, in turn, consists of an algorithm identifier and a bit string that represents the actual signature. Furthermore, the `TBSCertificate` value consists of the following fields and components:

- The `version` field refers to a value of type `Version` which is basically an integer value. The value represents the version of the X.509 recommendation the certificate conforms to. Note that the version numbers are one less than the actual X.509 version because in ASN.1 one starts counting from 0 (instead of 1).
- The `serialNumber` field refers to a serial number for the certificate which is basically an integer value. The value should be unique for each certificate issued by a CA.
- The `signature` field contains the algorithm identifier for the signature algorithm used by the CA to sign the certificate. It is specified as an object identifier (OID) value.
- The `issuer` field is used to encode an X.500 distinguished name (DN).
- The `validity` field defines the time interval in which the certificate is considered to be valid. The start and expiration times are specified as values of type `UTCTIME`.
- The `subject` field contains the X.500 DN for the certificate owner.
- The `subjectPublicKeyInfo` field is used to carry the public key (that is certified) and identifies the algorithm with which the key is used (the format of the field actually depends on the algorithm).
- The `issuerUniqueID` field is optional and may include further information related to the issuer.
- The `subjectUniqueID` field is optional and may include further information related to the subject.
- Finally, the `extensions` field is also optional. It provides a way to associate additional information for subjects, public keys, and managing certificates. As such, X.509v3 extension fields enable communities and organizations to define their own extensions and encode information specific to their needs in certificates. ITU-T and ISO/IEC have developed and published a set of standard extension fields.

In spite of the fact that X.509 is specified with ASN.1, the recommendation is somewhat vague and open-ended. Consequently, every nontrivial group which has any reason to work with X.509 certificates has to produce a profile which nails down many features which are left undefined in X.509. The difference between a specification (e.g., ITU-T X.509) and a profile is that a specification does not generally set any limitations on what combinations can and cannot appear in various certificate types, whereas a profile sets various limitations, for example by requiring that signing and confidentiality keys be different.

According to [6], the major certificates and PKI profiles in use today are the following ones:

- The PKIX profile for the Internet developed by the IETF WG of the same name (overviewed in the next section);
- The Federal PKI (FPKI) profile for the U.S. government;
- The MISSI profile specified by the U.S. DoD;
- The profile specified in ISO 15782;
- The profile used in the Automotive Network Exchange (ANX) project;
- The German MailTrusT profile for TeleTrusT;
- The German profile to implement the German digital signature law;
- Many other profiles that are developed and promoted by national bodies.

Also, the Microsoft profile could be mentioned here (although it is not a real profile, the software is widespread enough and nonstandard enough that it constitutes a significant de facto profile). Unfortunately, there is (currently) no way to mark a certificate to indicate that it should be processed in a manner conformant to a particular profile, which makes it difficult for a relying party to know how their certificate will be processed by a particular implementation.

An S/MIME certificate is basically a certificate that conforms to the X.509v3 format, with the additional requirement that the e-mail address of the subject (i.e., the certificate owner) should appear in the `subjectAltName` extension field. This is the long-term solution. In the meantime, however, the e-mail address is still encoded in the subject field most of the times. For example, Figure 13.1 illustrates the certificate details panel of one of my public key certificates (issued by VeriSign,

Inc.) for Microsoft Outlook Express. According to this figure, the e-mail address `rolf.oppliger@esecurity.ch` is encoded in the certificate's subject field.

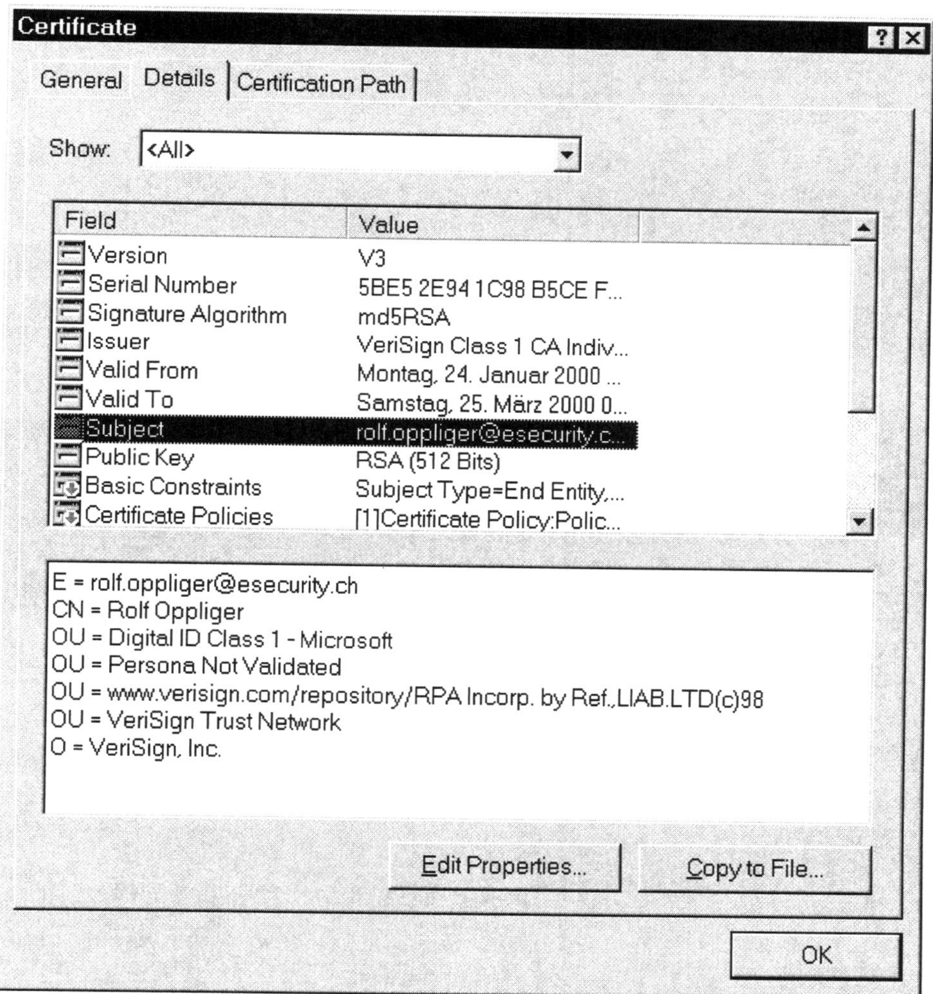

Figure 13.1 Certificate Details panel of Microsoft Outlook Express. © 2000 Microsoft Corporation.

Sending and receiving S/MIME-compliant UAs behave differently with regard to the `subjectAltName` extension field:

- On the one hand, sending UAs should ensure that the e-mail address specified in the `From` header of an e-mail message matches the e-mail address specified in the `subjectAltName` extension field of the signer's certificate.

- On the other hand, receiving UAs must recognize e-mail addresses in the `subjectAltName` extension fields. More specifically, a receiving UA should check that the e-mail address specified in the `From` header of an incoming e-mail message matches the e-mail address specified in the `subjectAltName` extension field of the signer's certificate.

Unfortunately, if a user has multiple e-mail accounts and wants to send digitally signed e-mail messages from all of them, he needs to have an S/MIME certificate for each account.

In addition, S/MIME requires certificates to conform to the specifications developed by the IETF PKIX WG (as discussed in the following section) and the requirements defined in RFC 2632 [7]. More specifically, RFC 2632 requires that receiving UAs must support PKIX v1 and PKIX v3 certificates, and that they should also support X.509 attribute certificates. In fact, receiving UAs should support the decoding of X.509 attribute certificates included in CMS objects. All other issues regarding the generation and use of attribute certificates are outside the scope of RFC 2632 and this book. Note, however, that attribute certificates may become an important building block for future e-commerce applications [2,8]. Last but not least, a receiving UA needs to provide some certificate processing that is further addressed in Sections 13.3 and 13.4.

13.2 IETF PKIX WG

S/MIME gains a lot from the work that has been done within the IETF Public Key Infrastructure X.509 (PKIX) WG. In short, the IETF PKIX WG has been tasked to design and build a PKI for the Internet community based on the ITU-T recommendation X.509.[1] As such, it has come up with a family of RFC documents that address the management of ITU-T X.509v3 public key certificates and corresponding certificate revocation lists (CRLs).

[1]`http://www.ietf.org/html.charters/pkix-charter.html`

The operational model of the IETF PKIX WG consists of subjects and end entities,[2] CAs, and registration authorities (RAs).[3] The functions which the RA may carry out will vary from case to case but may include personal authentication, token distribution, certificate revocation reporting, name assignment, key generation, and key archival. In any PKI architecture, RAs are optional components that are transparent to the end entities (when they are not present, the CA is assumed to be able to carry out the RAs' functions so that the PKI management protocols are the same from the end entities' point of view). Finally, the certificates generated by the CAs may be made publicly available in certificate repositories (e.g., network services that are available online).

According to this operational model, the family of RFC documents produced by the IETF PKIX WG can be summarized as follows (note that some RFCs are submitted for the Internet standards track, whereas other RFC documents are just for informational purposes):

- Standards track RFC 2459 [9] profiles the format and semantics of X.509v3 certificates and X.509v2 CRLs for use on the Internet. As such, it describes in detail the X.509v3 certificate format and its standard and Internet-specific extension fields, as well as the X.509v2 CRL format and a required extension set. Finally, the RFC also describes an algorithm for X.509 certificate path validation and provides ASN.1 specifications for all data structures that are used in the profiles.

- Standards track RFC 2510 [10] describes the various certificate management protocols that are supposed to be used in an X.509-based PKI for the Internet.

- More specifically, standards track RFC 2511 [11] specifies the syntax and semantics of the Internet X.509 certificate request message format (CRMF) that is used to convey a request for a certificate to a CA (possibly via an RA) for the purpose of X.509 certificate production. The request typically includes a public key and some related registration information.

- Informational RFC 2527 [12] presents a framework to assist the writers of certificate policies and certificate practice statements (CPSs) for CAs and PKIs. More

[2] In the specifications of the IETF PKIX WG, the term "end entity" is used rather than the term "subject" to avoid confusion with the X.509v3 certificate field of the same name.

[3] Other terms are used elsewhere for the functionality of an RA. For example, the term local registration agent (LRA) is used in ANSI X9 standards, local registration authority (also acronymed as LRA) is used in [4], organizational registration agent (ORA) is used in certain U.S. government specifications, and registration agent (RA) has also been used elsewhere.

specifically, the framework provides a comprehensive list of topics that potentially need to be covered in a certificate policy definition or CPS. Note that the framework needs to be customized in a particular operational environment.

- Informational RFC 2528 [13] profiles the format and semantics of the field in X.509v3 certificates containing cryptographic keys for the KEA.[4]

- Standards track RFC 2559 [14] addresses requirements to provide access to certificate repositories for the purpose of retrieving PKI information and managing that information. The mechanism is based on the Lightweight Directory Access Protocol (LDAP) as specified in RFC 1777 [15], defining a profile of LDAP for use within the X.509-based PKI for the Internet. In addition, RFC 2587 [16] defines a minimal schema to support PKIX in an LDAPv2 environment, as defined in RFC 2559.

- Standards track RFC 2585 [17] specifies the conventions for using FTP and HTTP to obtain certificates and CRLs from certificate repositories.

- Finally, standards track RFC 2560 [18] specifies a protocol useful in determining the current status of a digital certificate.

In summary, the above-summarized family of RFC documents (most of them specifying proposed standard protocols) specifies an X.509-based PKI for the Internet. This evolving PKI is sometimes also referred to as *Internet X.509 public key infrastructure* (IPKI).

The number of RFC documents that specify various aspects of the IPKI will certainly grow in the future, since a lot of work is being done to further refine the IPKI and its operational protocols and procedures. In fact, the number of RFC documents specifying the IPKI will certainly have increased by the time you read this book (e.g., for the provision of certificate validation and timestamping services). Refer to the IETF PKIX WG homepage that is indicated in footnote 2 to get a comprehensive overview about the RFC and Internet-Draft documents currently available. The current trend in industry is to make commercial PKI products "PKIX compliant," and this trend is most likely to continue.

[4]The KEA is a key exchange algorithm that was originally proposed by NIST for use together with the Skipjack encryption algorithm in Clipper and Fortezza chips. Refer to `http://csrc.nist.gov/encryption/skipjack-kea.htm` for a specification of the Skipjack and KEA algorithms.

13.3 ESTABLISHMENT OF TRUST

In Chapter 8 we overviewed and discussed PGP's trust model and the resulting "web of trust." More specifically, we saw that a PGP certificate is valid if it is digitally signed by a completely trusted individual whose certificate is valid, or if it is digitally signed by a set of marginally (or cummulatively) trusted individuals whose certificates are all valid.

Contrary to that, an X.509 certificate is valid if there is a certificate path to a certificate for a trusted individual, where each certificate in the path is valid [19]. A *certificate path*, in turn, refers to an ordered list of certificates, with succeeding certificates signed by the private keys corresponding to preceding certificates. For example, a certificate path for A → B → C → D may look as follows:

$$A \ll B \gg, B \ll C \gg, C \ll D \gg$$

X.509-based PKIs are typically based on a hierarchical trust model. What this basically means is that top-level CAs issue certificates, which in turn can be used to issue other certificates, and so on, resulting in hierarchies of certificates. For example, the PEM specifications promoted a hierarchy consisting of three layers. Contrary to that, the S/MIME specifications do not require a specific hierarchical structure.

When an S/MIME-compliant UA receives a message with a digitally signed MIME entity, it needs to have a valid certificate chain and related certificate status information for the sender to verify the signature. The certificate chain and related certificate status information can be provided either as a part of the message (in-band provision) or outside the scope of the secure messaging scheme (out-band provision). The two possibilities are overviewed next.

13.3.1 In-Band Provision

With in-band provision, the certificate chain and related certificate status information are provided as a part of the message that is digitally signed. Consequently, the sending UA must include the relevant certificate information into the message. The relevant certificate information, in turn, may include the entire certificate chain and related certificate status information or only the certificate chain. In the second case, however, the recipient must have access to certificate status information to validate the certificate chain and to make sure that the certificates used have not been revoked (or suspended) meanwhile.

In summary, in-band provision has the advantage that it provides the recipient(s) with all information required to validate a certificate chain. However, in-band provision has the disadvantage that a certificate may occupy 1 to 3 kilobytes of data, and that a chain of certificates may require several kilobytes of data for transfer and storage. The situation gets worse if a message is sent to a large number of people (e.g., the message is posted to a newsgroup or a mailing list). Including CRL information with an e-mail message is even more worrisome because CRLs can become quite large.

13.3.2 Out-Band Provision

One alternative to including certificate information with a digitally signed message is to provide a recipient with a reference to a location where such information can be found. The recipient can then decide whether to verify the signature and can download the signer's certificates from the designated location. Virtual business cards (if supported by UAs) can be used to provide a recipient with this type of certificate and CRL location information.

With out-band provision, the certificate chain and related certificate status information are not provided as a part of the message and must be provided entirely outside the scope of the secure messaging scheme. In this case, the recipient must have some certificate information retrieval mechanism in order to gain access to the sender's certificate or certificate chain. As discussed in the following section, there are many ways to implement certificate retrieval mechanisms.

In summary. the decision to include certificates with a digitally signed e-mail message depends on a variety of factors, such as the capabilities of a recipient for storing certificates, the capabilities of a recipient to access a directory service, and the size of the group of e-mail users. In a small group, one can reasonably expect that users have already stored other users' certificates locally on their computers. In larger groups, however, including certificates or reference locations where certificates can be found is certainly more appropriate.

13.4 CERTIFICATE REVOCATION

The term *certificate revocation* refers to the process of publicly announcing that a certificate has been revoked and should no longer be used. In practice, there may be several reasons that require certificate revocation. For example, a user's or a CA's private key may be compromised, or a user may no longer be registered and certified by a particular CA.

In general, the certification and revocation of (public key) certificates involves three parties:

- The certificate-issuing authority (namely the CA);
- The certificate repository, such as a networked directory service (that may even be replicated several times);
- The users of the CA and the certificate repository.

In this setting, the CA does not necessarily provide online certificate status information to the users. Instead, it may operate offline and update the certificate repository only on a periodic basis. The certificate repository, in turn, operates online and is permanently available and accessible to the users. In general, it must be assumed that the CA is trusted, whereas the certificate repository and the users may not be. A user who contacts the directory does not only want to retrieve a certificate, but may also want to get some kind of proof of validity for the certificate.

From a theoretical point of view, certificate revocation refers to a challenging problem, and there are several approaches to address it:

- The first approach is to make certificates automatically time out after a certain amount of time and to require periodic renewals of certificates;
- The second approach is to list all nonrevoked certificates in an online directory service, and to accept only certificates that are found there;
- The third approach is to have CAs periodically issue CRLs that itemize the certificates that have been revoked and should no longer be used;
- Finally, the fourth approach is to provide an online certificate status checking mechanism that informs users whether a specific certificate is still valid or has been revoked.

Note that the approaches are not mutually exclusive, but can be combined to come up with more efficient or more effective certificate revocation schemes. Also note that all approaches have advantages and disadvantages. For example, the first approach has the advantage of not requiring explicit certificate revocation (since the certificates time out after a certain amount of time). The disadvantages of this approach are due to the fact that time-outs only provide a slow revocation mechanism, and that it depends on servers having accurate clocks. Someone who can trick a server into turning back its local clock can still use expired certificates (the security of the certificate revocation mechanism thus depends on the security of the timing service). Similarly, the second approach has the advantage that it is almost immediate, whereas the disadvantages are that the availability of authentication is only as good as the availability of the directory service, and that the security of the certificate revocation mechanism as a whole is only as good as the security of the directory service. Furthermore, users tend to cache certificates they have retrieved from the directory service for performance reasons, and the use of such a cache actually defeats the original purpose of the directory service (to provide timely status information).

For all practical purposes, the third and fourth approaches are the ones that are being followed and most widely deployed. For example, the ITU-T recommendation X.509 follows the third approach,[5] and recommends that each CA periodically issues a CRL that itemizes all certificates that have been revoked and should no longer be used. A user receiving a certificate would first check in the appropriate CRL whether the certificate has been revoked. In addition to the use of CRLs as proposed in the ITU-T recommendation X.509, the IETF PKIX WG is specifying and standardizing an Online Certificate Status Protocol (OCSP). CRLs and the use of OCSP are further addressed in the remaining part of this section. Afterward, we mention some alternative certificate revocation schemes that are primarily of theoretical interest.

13.4.1 CRLs

The classical and simplest solution to the certificate revocation problem is the use of CRLs. As mentioned above, this approach is being followed by the ITU-T recommendation X.509 [5]. In this approach, a CA periodically issues and digitally signs a message that lists all certificates that have been revoked and should no longer be used. This message is called a CRL and it is made available through the certificate repository. Users who want to make sure that a particular certificate has not been revoked must query the repository and retrieve the latest CRL. If the CRL does not include the certificate, the user can assume that the certificate has not been revoked (at least until the time the CRL was issued and digitally signed).

If a CRL is getting too large, the use of delta CRLs may be appropriate. In short, a delta CRL lists all certificates that have been revoked and should no longer

[5]The X.509 CRL format is an ITU-T and ISO/IEC standard, first published in 1988 as version 1 (X.509v1 CRL). Similar to the ITU-T X.509 certificate format, the X.509v1 CRL was subsequently modified to allow for extension fields, resulting in X.509 version 2 CRL (X.509v2 CRL) format.

be used since the latest breakpoint. Consequently, the set of all revoked certificates at a given point in time consists of all certificates listed in the most recent CRL plus all certificates listed in the delta CRLs that have been published meanwhile.

The major advantage of using CRLs (together with delta CRLs) is simplicity. A user of a certificate is required to retrieve the latest CRL from the appropriate CA or the repository and check whether the certificate has been revoked. Only if the certificate is not included in the CRL (and has not been revoked accordingly) is the user authorized to accept and use the certificate. Obviously, the consequence of this scheme is that the user has to periodically retrieve the latest CRLs from all of the CAs he uses and accepts certificates from. This introduces some communication costs between the CA and the certificate repository, and high communication costs between the repository and the users (since CRLs may be very long). Another disadvantage is that a user does not receive succinct proof for the validity of a particular certificate.

Finally, note that a CRL is a negative statement. It is the digital equivalent of the little paper books of bad checks or bad credit cards that were distributed to cashiers in the 1970s and before. These have been replaced in the retail world by positive statements in the form of online validation of a single check, ATM card, or credit card. The digital equivalent to this online validation of a certificate is provided by the OCSP (or a similar protocol).

13.4.2 OCSP

Instead of, or as a supplement to, checking against periodically issued CRLs, it may be necessary to obtain timely information regarding a certificate's current status. Examples include high-value funds transfer or large stock trades. Consequently, the IETF PKIX WG has specified and standardized an OCSP in RFC 2560 [18]. In short, the OCSP enables a user to determine the status of an identified certificate. An OCSP client issues a status request to an OCSP responder and suspends acceptance of the certificate in question until the responder provides a response (whether the certificate in question is good, revoked, or is in an unknown state for the responder). A certificate-issuing authority can either respond to OCSP requests directly or have one (or several) delegated OCSP responder(s) providing OCSP responses to the requesting entities on its behalf.

As of this writing, the use of OCSP is not yet widely deployed on the Internet.[6]

[6]Note that browsers do not currently check the revocation status of any certificate at all. The only time a browser knows that a site certificate has been revoked is when it eventually expires. It is possible and very likely that this behavior will change in the future, and that

Nevertheless, it is assumed and very likely that future CAs and certificate repositories will provide support for both certificate revocation mechanisms (CRLs and OCSP queries). It is also possible and very likely that the value of an e-commerce transaction will finally determine whether a check in a CRL is sufficient enough, or whether an OCSP query must be invoked.

13.4.3 Alternative Certificate Revocation Schemes

We have seen that the use of CRLs introduces some communication costs between the CA and the certificate repository, and high communication costs between the repository and the users (since CRLs may be very long), and that using CRLs, a user does not receive succinct proof for the validity of a particular certificate. We have also seen that the OCSP can be used to address the second problem.

More recently, some alternative certificate revocation schemes have been proposed that try to address both problems mentioned above. Chapter 8 of [2], for example, overviews and discusses Silvio Micali's certificate revocation system (CRS) [20], Paul Kocher's certificate revocation trees (CRTs) [21], and a certificate revocation and update scheme proposed by Moni Naor and Kobbi Nissim [22]. These discussions are not repeated in this book. The alternative certificate revocation schemes are interesting mainly from a theoretical point of view (they are not relevant in practice).

13.5 CERTIFICATION SERVICE PROVIDERS

There are many companies that provide CA products and services for S/MIME. Examples include VeriSign and Entrust in the United States and Canada, Baltimore Technologies in Europe, and Swisskey in Switzerland. Also, many software packages, such as Netscape Navigator and Microsoft Internet Explorer, are distributed with a set of preconfigured CAs that users accept and trust by default if they do not explicitly disable them.

In this section, we overview the offerings of two exemplary certification service providers that can be used for secure messaging with S/MIME (VeriSign and Swisskey). Note, however, that there are other companies that offer similar or comparable certification services to the general public. In fact, the number of commercial certification service providers is expected to increase in the future (as public key cryptography is being deployed in more applications).

---

certificate revocation checking will be adapted in one way or another. For example, Netscape has implemented a preliminary and incomplete version of OCSP.

13.5.1 VeriSign

Historically, the first commercial certification service provider was VeriSign, Inc.[7] located in Mountain View, California. VeriSign was founded by RSA Security, Inc. in 1995, when the first version of Netscape Navigator with SSL support appeared on the marketplace. The mission of VeriSign was and still is "to provide public key infrastructure (PKI) and digital certificate solutions to enable trusted commerce and communications over private and public networks." As such, VeriSign has been offering digital certificates (digital IDs) to the general public for many years. As of this writing, VeriSign has issued over 215,000 Web site digital certificates and over 3.9 million digital certificates for individuals. Note, however, that VeriSign is also issuing free certificates for marketing purposes, and that these certificates are also included in these numbers.

In the recent past, VeriSign has shifted away from a provider of digital certificates to a solution provider that has many products and services to offer for a company or organization that wants to make use of a PKI.[8] Most importanly, VeriSign has a Go Secure! program for many applications, such as IPsec and VPNs, intranet messaging (e.g., Microsoft Exchange and Lotus Notes), electronic payment systems (e.g., SET transactions), and applications that make use of the wireless application protocol (WAP). Furthermore, VeriSign also has an OnSite program that offers distributed certificate management services. What this basically means is that VeriSign provides the infrastructure for a corporate PKI, whereas the customer of the OnSite service manages his own data and certificates on this infrastructure (you may refer to this service as "PKI hosting"). A design of a similar distributed certificate management service is also described in [23].

In spite of these additional services, VeriSign is still offering individual digital certificates and server digital certificates, as well as code signing certificates:

- *Individual digital certificates* (class 1 digital IDs) are intended for Web and e-mail users. They are tied to a unique e-mail address and are suitable for securing correspondence to that address. As of this writing, a class 1 digital ID is priced at $14.95 (U.S. dollars) per year.

- *Server digital certificates* (server IDs) are primarily intended for Web servers. There are several categories of server digital certificates, ranging from some hundreds of U.S. dollars to more than a thousand. Also, pricing depends on the number of server IDs that are actually bought. Refer to URL

[7] `http://www.verisign.com`

[8] `http://www.verisign.com/products/`

`http://www.verisign.com/server/` for a comprehensive overview of the various classes of server IDs available from VeriSign.

- Finally, *code signing certificates* are available for individual (class 2 digital IDs) and commercial software publishers (class 3 digital IDs). Individual software publisher digital IDs are currently available only in the United States and are priced at $20.00 (U.S. dollars) per year, whereas commercial software publisher digital IDs are globally available and priced at $400.00 (U.S. dollars) per year. Code signing certificates are available for Microsoft Authenticode, Microsoft Office 2000/VBA Signing, Netscape Object Signing, and Marimba Castanet.[9]

In addition, VeriSign is offering insurance protection against economic loss caused by corruption, loss, or misuse of digital IDs (NetSure), as well as smartcard support (Litronic NetSign smartcards).

13.5.2 Swisskey

Swisskey Ltd.[10] was established in the spring of 1998 as a joint-venture between Swisscom, Telekurs Holding,[11] and DigiSigna.[12] Since October 1998, Swisskey has been selling digital certificates in Switzerland to the general public.

Table 13.1
Categories of Swisskey Certificates and Prices

Certificate Category	Price
Personal ID	CHF 35
Corporate ID	CHF 90
Server ID	CHF 495
Code ID	CHF 550

As summarized in Table 13.1, Swisskey is offering several categories of certificates. More specifically, Swisskey is offering Personal ID, Corporate ID, Server ID,

[9]In short, Marimba's Castanet is a set of technologies which distributes and maintains applications and services within a corporate intranet or across the Internet. It ensures that subscribers always and automatically have the most up-to-date tools and information available at their desktops.

[10]`http://www.swisskey.com`

[11]The Telekurs Holding is owned by the Swiss banks.

[12]DigiSigna is an association of the chambers of commerce throughout Switzerland and Lichtenstein.

and Code ID certificates. Personal ID cerificates are aimed for personal use, whereas Corporate ID certificates are aimed for professional use. As such, it is ensured that the name of the certificate owner's organization (e.g., company) is included in the Corporate ID certificate. Furthermore, Server ID certificates can be used by Web service providers to authenticate their servers to clients, whereas Code ID certificates can be used by software developers and publishers to authenticate their code to clients.

The prices for Swisskey certificates can also be found in Table 13.1. Except Personal ID certificates, the prices of all Swisskey certificates decrease with the number of certificates. For example, for 100 (1000) Corporate ID certificates the price decreases to CHF 33.10 (26.40). Detailed pricing information is available from Swisskey's homepage.

In addition to the four categories of certificates mentioned above, Swisskey is also offering customer-branded CA services. With these services, customers can make use of Swisskey's infrastructure to issue and revoke certificates according to their own CPSs. Consequently, certificates issued by a customer-branded CA are digitally signed with a private key that actually belongs to the customer (contrary to Corporate ID certificates that are digitally signed by Swisskey). Finally, Swisskey is also offering a smartcard called SafeCard and a Swisskey certificate management system (SCMS) to its customers.

Unlike VeriSign and other commercial certification service providers that operate on a global scale, Swisskey requires its customers to appear at a physical RA for proper authentication (using some legitimate passport or picture identification card). Currently, there are a number of chambers of commerce that act as RAs for Swisskey. Furthermore, the branches of two major banks in Switzerland serve as RAs for Swisskey (the Credit Suisse and UBS). It is currently not clear whether the branches of the Swiss Post (the now private postal delivery service in Switzerland) will also serve as RAs for Swisskey.

13.6 CONCLUSIONS

In this chapter, we overviewed and discussed the procedures and the rationale behind the X.509-based hierarchical trust model and the resulting PKI for S/MIME. As already mentioned in Chapter 8, an X.509-based PKI seems more appropriate for large communities in which only few users know each other. Consequently, the Internet PKI (IPKI) as specified in the RFC documents produced by the IETF PKIX WG [9 – 18] and RFC 2632 [7] are very useful for the use and deployment of S/MIME. In fact, S/MIME is certainly one of the major driving forces behind the establishment of an IPKI (the other major driving forces are SSL/TLS and virtual private networking).

REFERENCES

[1] R. Oppliger, "Managing Certificates in a Corporate Environment," *Les Annales des Télécommunications*, 2000.

[2] R. Oppliger, *Security Technologies for the World Wide Web*, Artech House Publishers, Norwood, MA, 2000.

[3] W. Ford, and M.S. Baum, *Secure Electronic Commerce: Building the Infrastructure for Digital Signatures & Encryption*, Prentice Hall PTR, Upper Saddle River, NJ, 1997.

[4] J. Feghhi, J. Feghhi, and P. Williams, *Digital Certificates: Applied Internet Security*, Addison-Wesley Longman, Reading, MA, 1999.

[5] ITU-T, Recommendation X.509: The Directory — Authentication Framework, 1988.

[6] P. Gutmann, "X.509 Style Guide," September 1999, electronically available document at `http://www.cs.auckland.ac.nz/~pgut001/pubs/x509guide.txt`.

[7] B. Ramsdell (Ed.), "S/MIME Version 3 Certificate Handling," Request for Comments 2632, June 1999.

[8] R. Oppliger, "Authorization Methods for E-Commerce Applications," *Proceedings of IEEE Symposium on Reliable Distributed Systems*, October 1999, pp. 366 – 371.

[9] R. Housley, W. Ford, W. Polk, and D. Solo, "Internet X.509 Public Key Infrastructure Certificate and CRL Profile," Request for Comments 2459, January 1999.

[10] C. Adams, "Internet X.509 Public Key Infrastructure Certificate Management Protocols," Request for Comments 2510, March 1999.

[11] M. Myers, C. Adams, D. Solo, and D. Kemp, "Internet X.509 Certificate Request Message Format," Request for Comments 2511, March 1999.

[12] S. Chokhani, and W. Ford, "Internet X.509 Public Key Infrastructure Certificate Policy and Certification Practices Framework," Request for Comments 2527, March 1999.

[13] R. Housley, and W. Polk, "Internet X.509 Public Key Infrastructure Representation of Key Exchange Algorithm (KEA) Keys in Internet X.509 Public Key Infrastructure Certificates," Request for Comments 2528, March 1999.

[14] S. Boeyen, T. Howes, and P. Richard, "Internet X.509 Public Key Infrastructure Operational Protocols — LDAPv2," Request for Comments 2559, April 1999.

[15] Y. Yeong, T. Howes, and S. Kille, "Lightweight Directory Access Protocol," Request for Comments 1777, March 1995.

[16] S. Boeyen, T. Howes, and P. Richard, "Internet X.509 Public Key Infrastructure LDAPv2 Schema," Request for Comments 2587, June 1999.

[17] R. Housley, and P. Hoffman, "Internet X.509 Public Key Infrastructure Operational Protocols: FTP and HTTP," Request for Comments 2585, May 1999.

[18] M. Myers, R. Ankney, A. Malpani, S. Galperin, and C. Adams, "X.509 Internet Public Key Infrastructure Online Certificate Status Protocol — OCSP," Request for Comments 2560, June 1999.

[19] Network Associates, Inc., "PGP and X.509: A Practical Comparison of Trust Models and Validation Mechanisms for E-Business Applications," 1999.

[20] S. Micali, "Efficient Certificate Revocation," Massachusetts Institute of Technology (MIT), Technical Memo MIT/LCS/TM-542b, 1996.

[21] P. Kocher, "A Quick Introduction to Certificate Revocation Trees (CRTs)," article electronically available at `http://www.valicert.com/pdf/Certificate_revocation_trees.pdf`.

[22] M. Naor, and K. Nissim, "Certificate Revocation and Certificate Update," *Proceedings of 7th USENIX Security Symposium*, January 1998.

[23] R. Oppliger, A. Greulich, and P. Trachsel, "A Distributed Certificate Management System (DCMS) Supporting Group-based Access Controls," *Proceedings of Annual Computer Security Applications Conference (ACSAC '99)*, 1999, pp. 241 – 248.

Chapter 14

Standardization and Products

In this chapter, we overview and briefly discuss the standardization process and products related to S/MIME. More specifically, we overview the S/MIME standardization process in Section 14.1, address some products that conform to the S/MIME specifications in Section 14.2, and elaborate on S/MIME interoperability testing in Section 14.3. Note that due to its claimed multivendor support, interoperability testing has become an increasingly important topic and area of concern.

14.1 STANDARDIZATION

In Chapter 11, we mentioned that the two first S/MIME specifications (version 1 and 2) were developed by an industry working group led by RSA Security, Inc., and that the work was later continued by the IETF S/MIME Mail Security (SMIME) WG. As such, the current S/MIME version 3 is specified in the following set of related RFC documents:

- RFC 2630 [1], entitled "Cryptographic Message Syntax," describes the CMS used to compose S/MIME messages.

- RFC 2631 [2], entitled "Diffie-Hellman Key Agreement Method," specifies the use of one particular variant of the Diffie-Hellman key exchange algorithm for S/MIME. The variant is based on X9.42 drafted by the X9F1 working group of the American National Standards Institute (ANSI).

- RFC 2632 [3], entitled "S/MIME Version 3 Certificate Handling," elaborates on the certificate processing requirements for S/MIME (in addition to the ones specified in the RFC documents of the IETF PKIX WG).

- RFC 2633 [4], entitled "S/MIME Version 3 Message Specification," focuses on the algorithms and procedures that are employed by S/MIME to add cryptographic protection to MIME entities.

- RFC 2634 [5], entitled "Enhanced Security Services for S/MIME," describes some optional service extensions for S/MIME.

The topics addressed in RFC 2630 to RFC 2633 are covered in the previous chapters of this book (most importantly in Chapters 12 and 13). In addition, RFC 2634 describes the following four optional security service extensions for S/MIME:

- *Signed receipts:* Returning a signed receipt provides to the sender of a message a proof of delivery that allows him to prove to a third party (e.g., a judge in court) that the recipient was actually able to verify the signature of the original message. In essence, the recipient signs the entire original message (including the sender's original signature) and appends a new signature to form the new message.

- *Security labels:* A security label is a set of security information regarding the sensitivity of data in general, and S/MIME encapsulated data in particular. Consequently, the sensitivity information in a security label can be compared with a user's privileges to determine if the user is allowed to access the content that is protected by S/MIME encapsulation.

- *Secure mailing lists:* When a S/MIME UA sends a message to multiple recipients, a certain amount of per-recipient processing is required, including, for example, the use of each recipient's public key. The agent can be relieved of this work by employing the services of an S/MIME mail list agent (MLA). In short, an MLA can take a single incoming message, perform the recipient-specific processing for each recipient, and forward the message (preventing, for example, mail loops[1]).

[1]A mail loop occurs if one mailing list is a member of a second mailing list, and the second mailing list is also a member of the first mailing list. Consequently, a message will go from one

- *Signing certificate attributes:* There are some concerns related to the fact that the certificate that the signer of a message wants to be bound into the signature verification process is not cryptographically linked to the signature. This service extension addresses this issue by creating a signing certificate attribute that is digitally signed by the signer and transmitted together with the message.

The first three services itemized above provide functionalities that are similar to the Message Security Protocol used for the Secure Data Network System (SDNS) [6]. As such, they are useful in many environments. We are not going to delve into the technical details of the optional security service extensions for S/MIME in this book (since this is ongoing work). Instead, we briefly address some products that conform to the S/MIME specifications next.

14.2 PRODUCTS

First of all, it is important to note that S/MIME (like MIME) requires new message headers and new content be inserted into the body part of an e-mail message. This makes it difficult if not impossible to support S/MIME with a separate stand-alone application program (as is possible with PGP). Consequently, there is need to either use a plug-in to add S/MIME functionality to an existing non-S/MIME-compliant UA, or to use an S/MIME-compliant UA — sometimes also called S/MIME agent — in the first place. In fact, an increasingly large number of UAs directly support S/MIME (version 2 and/or version 3).

In this section, we briefly overview and discuss the most important S/MIME plug-ins and S/MIME-compliant UAs that are available today. Note that this situation changes rapidly, as more and more vendors are implementing and integrating S/MIME into their products (basically turning their UAs into S/MIME agents). Also note that many vendors provide toolkits for developers looking to build S/MIME functionality into their products. Examples include the RSA BSAFE S/MIME-C Software Developer Kit (SDK[2]) from RSA Security, Inc., or the Secure Messaging Toolkit (SMT[3]) from Baltimore Technologies. Again, these and similar toolkits are not addressed in this book (since this book does not focus on the development of PGP or S/MIME-compliant software).

---

list to the other in a rapidly cascading succession of messages that will also be distributed to all other members of both lists.

[2] `http://www.rsa.com/products/bsafe/smimec.html`

[3] `http://www.baltimore.com/products/smt/`

14.2.1 S/MIME Plug-ins

There are many plug-ins that can be used to add S/MIME functionality to existing non-S/MIME-compliant UAs. Due to the U.S. export controls, many of these plug-ins have been developed and are being marketed outside the United States, most importantly in Europe. In this subsection, we briefly itemize the most important S/MIME plug-ins. Refer to the corresponding vendors' homepages for further information about their products.

- *iT_SEC_outlook* is an S/MIME (and PGP) plug-in for Microsoft Outlook developed and marketed by the Swiss company IT-Sec IT-Security AG.[4] The plug-in runs on Windows 95/98 and Windows NT (version 4.0 or above) and is aimed at being used with smartcards to store private keys (the company also provides corresponding chipcards and chipcard readers). It implements and makes use of the IDEA algorithm for data encryption (using 128-bits keys) and the RSA algorithm for digital signatures. Public key pairs that are generated with iT_SEC_outlook can be certified and stored according to X.509 or PGP.

- *TrustedMIME* is an S/MIME plug-in developed and marketed by the Irish Siemens company Secure Solutions Experts (SSE).[5] As of this writing, the plug-in is available for Microsoft Exchange, Microsoft Outlook, and Lotus Notes. It provides support for strong encryption (RC2 and 3DES with 128-bits keys, as well as RSA key lengths of 512, 1024, and 2048 bits). Furthermore, TrustedMIME supports many personal security environments (PSEs), including, for example, floppy disks and several smartcards.

- *MailSecure* is an S/MIME plug-in developed and marketed by the Irish company Baltimore Technologies plc. In addition to Microsoft Exchange, Microsoft Outlook, and Lotus Notes, MailSecure also comes along with a plug-in for Qualcomm Eudora and a client for other e-mail systems. Similar to the other S/MIME plug-ins, MailSecure provides support for strong cryptography.

- *CryptoEx SECUDE S/MIME CryptoEngine* is an S/MIME-compliant plug-in that is developed and marketed by the German company Glück & Kanja.[6]

- Finally, *SafeGuard Sign&Crypt* is an S/MIME-compliant plug-in that is developed and marketed by the German company Utimaco Safeware AG.[7] In addition

[4] `http://www.it-sec.com`
[5] `http://www.sse.ie`
[6] `http://www.glueckkanja.de`
[7] `http://www.utimaco.de`

to the S/MIME specifications, SafeGuard Sign&Crypt is also compliant to the German MailTrusT specification. As such, it also conforms to the Act on Digital Signature in Germany.

In summary, there are several S/MIME-compliant plug-ins that provide support for strong cryptography.

14.2.2 S/MIME-Compliant UAs

The need for S/MIME plug-ins is slowly disappearing as more and more vendors directly support S/MIME in their UA products. Furthermore, some vendors have announced plans for making S/MIME-compatible versions of their products available to the public domain. Consequently, one can reasonably expect that S/MIME will be one of the dominant standards for secure e-mail in the future, and that users will be able to choose from a variety of interoperable software packages that conform to the S/MIME specifications (most likely version 3).

In this subsection, we briefly elaborate on the most widely used S/MIME-compliant UAs (Netscape Messenger and Microsoft Outlook Express). Refer to the corresponding vendors' homepages for further information about their products. Alternative S/MIME-compliant UAs include the WorldSecure client,[8] OpenSoft Express Mail,[9] and Entrust/Express.[10]

Netscape Messenger

The *Netscape Messenger* is Netscape Communications's S/MIME-compliant UA that comes bundled with Netscape Communicator. For quite a long time, the Netscape Messenger supported domestic and export-level encryption, whereas the export-level encryption was restricted to 40-bit RC2. More recently (as discussed in Chapter 4), however, the United States liberalized their export controls and Netscape Communications is now allowed to distribute its Netscape Messenger software with strong encryption put in place on a worldwide basis.

The user interface and certificate management procedures for Netscape Messenger are fully discussed in Chapter 5 of [7] and not repeated in this book. Figure 14.1 only illustrates the Netscape Messenger Security Info panel. Note that the user can configure the Netscape Messenger to encrypt and/or digitally sign e-mail

[8] `http://www.worldtalk.com/Products/WSC/wsclient.shtm`

[9] `http://www.opensoft.com/products/expressmail/`

[10] `http://www.entrust.com/express/`

messages and news messages by clicking on the corresponding checkboxes. Also, the user can choose a certificate to be used by Netscape Messenger. Finally, the user can configure his cipher preferences.

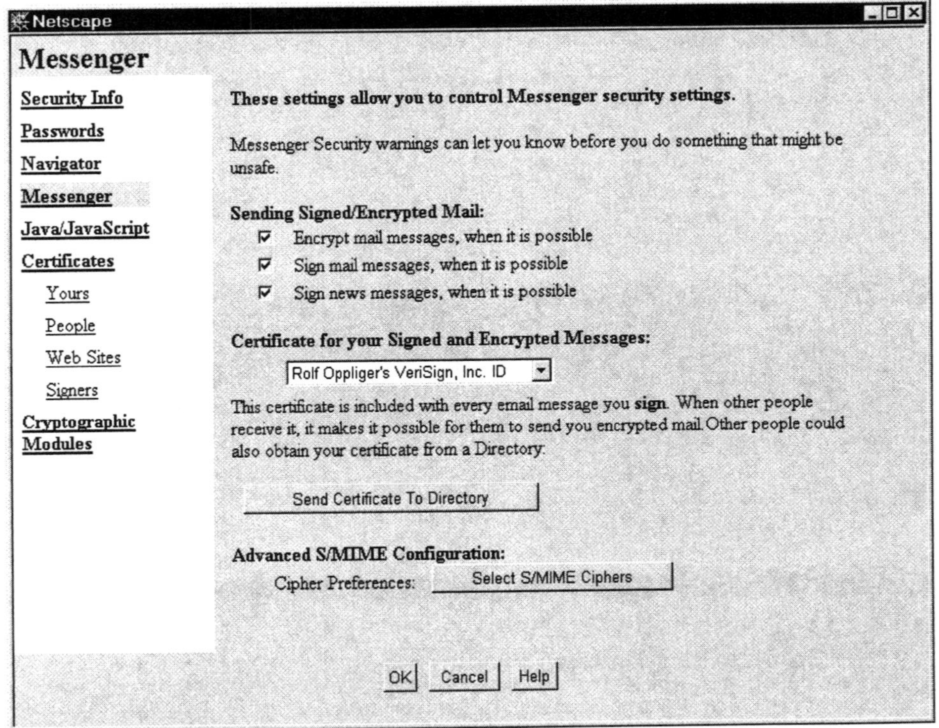

Figure 14.1 Netscape Messenger Security Info. © 2000 Netscape Communications Corporation.

Figure 14.2 illustrates the corresponding panel, in which the user can enable the Netscape Messenger's S/MIME implementation to support the following encryption algorithms:

- 3DES;
- 128-bits RC2;
- DES;

- 64-bits RC2;
- 40-bits RC2.

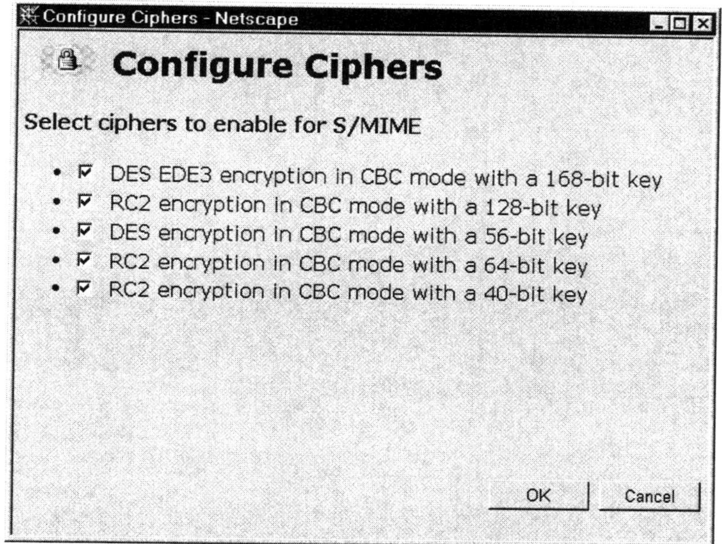

Figure 14.2 Netscape Messenger Cipher Preferences. © 2000 Netscape Communications Corporation.

Microsoft Outlook Express

Similar to Netscape Communications, Microsoft provides support for S/MIME in several of its messaging products (including, for example, Microsoft Exchange, Microsoft Outlook, and Outlook Express). Outlook Express is the UA that comes as part of the standard installation of Microsoft Internet Explorer. It is compatible with S/MIME versions 2 and 3, and supports the following encryption algorithms:

- RC2 (40-bit and 128-bit);
- DES (56-bit);
- 3DES (168-bit).

Until early in 2000, the RC2 40-bit encryption algorithm was the only algorithm available for international versions of Outlook Express. More specifically, the international version could decrypt messages that have been encrypted, but it could not actively encrypt and send out messages using any one of the strong encryption algorithms (e.g., 128-bit RC2, 56-bit DES, and 112-bit 3DES).

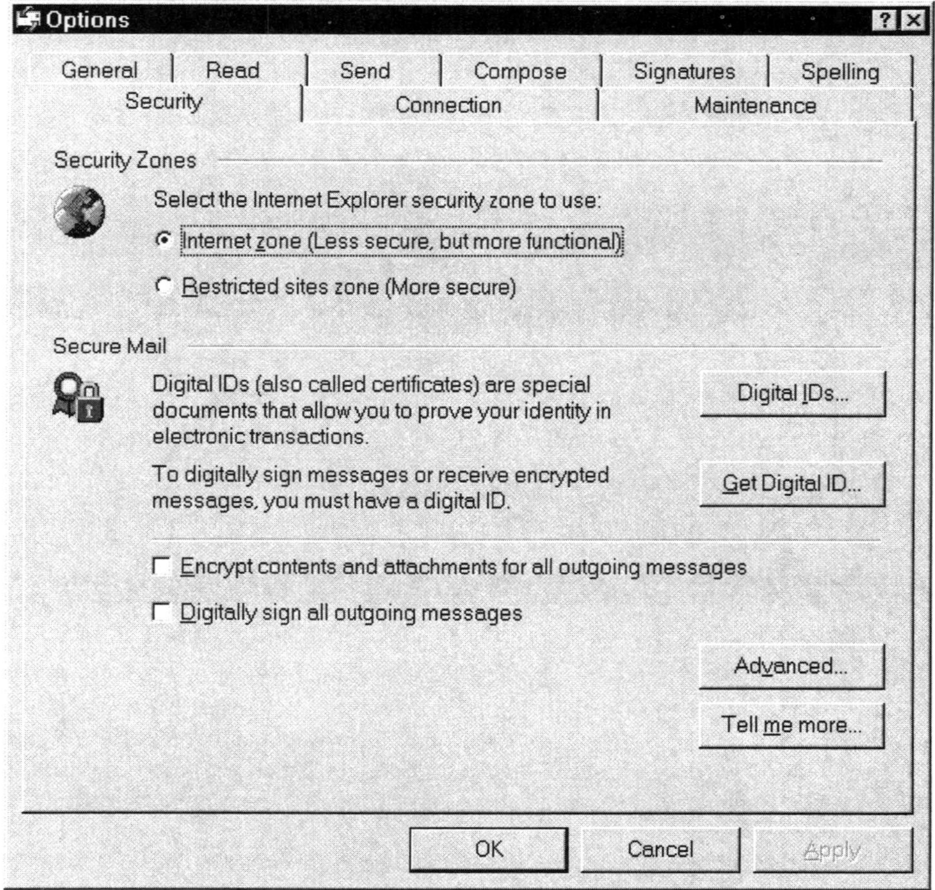

Figure 14.3 Security Options panel of Microsoft Outlook Express. © 2000 Microsoft Corporation.

Due to the liberalization of the U.S. export controls, Microsoft can now make available strong encryption in its retail encryption products.[11] Most importantly, Microsoft freely distributed Internet Explorer Encryption Packs[12] that can be used to upgrade the cryptographical strength of both Internet Explorer and Outlook Express that comes bundled with it.

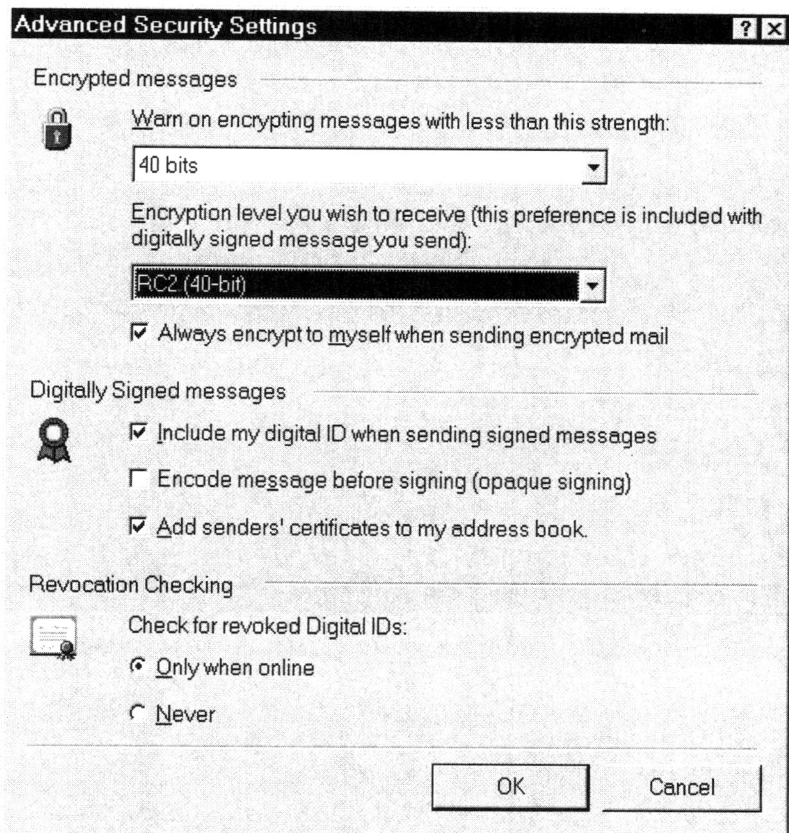

Figure 14.4 Advanced Security Settings panel of Microsoft Outlook Express. © 2000 Microsoft Corporation.

[11] `http://www.microsoft.com/exporting/EncProds.htm`

[12] `http://www.microsoft.com/windows/ie/download/128bit/intro.htm`

To digitally sign and verify messages, Outlook Express uses SHA-1 and RSA. The bit length of the private key varies, depending on the CA from which a user obtains a public key certificate. A CA that uses the Microsoft Enrollment wizard will generate private keys that are at least 512 bits in length. Optionally, Outlook Express supports certificate revocation checking (at least if the UA is online).

Again, the user interface and certificate management procedures for Outlook Express are fully discussed in Chapter 5 of [7] and not repeated in this book. Figure 14.3 illustrates the Options Security panel of Microsoft Outlook Express (that can be found in the Tools menu), and Figure illustrates the Advanced Security Settings panel that appears when the Advanced... button is pressed on the Options Security panel.

14.3 INTEROPERABILITY TESTING

The S/MIME specification was originally designed to promote interoperable secure messaging in a way that two compliant implementations would be able to communicate securely with one another. However, because the specification still allows multiple interpretations and implementations, and is sometimes open in key aspects that affect interoperability. This situation has resulted in several S/MIME compliant products that are not fully interoperable with respect to secure messaging.

However, and due to the fact that S/MIME version 3 has been submitted for possible consideration as an Internet standards track protocol, interoperability has become a major issue. Vendors participate in S/MIME compliance and interoperability testing programs conducted over the Internet. As such, they put their products through S/MIME test suites that include online certification, digitally signed and digitally enveloped message creation, as well as verification and decryption of received messages. As mentioned in Chapter 11, RSA Security, Inc. runs an S/MIME Interoperability Center.[13] This Interoperability Center was established in 1997. Products that have successfully completed the S/MIME interoperability testing earn the "S/MIME-Enabled" seal from RSA Security. As of this writing, the interoperability test procedure is as follows:[14]

- Before beginning the online interoperability testing, the vendor must make sure that he has self-tested the product (he should both download a copy of the World-Secure client to test against, and use the Entrust Autoresponder).

[13] `http://www.rsasecurity.com/standards/smime/interop_center.html`

[14] `http://www.rsasecurity.com/standards/smime/procedure.html`

- The vendor must complete an interoperability test application (using an online form).
- The vendor must generate an RSA key pair, using a modulus size of 512 bits.
- The vendor must obtain a digital certificate for the public key by following the "VeriSign Class 1 S/MIME Web-based CSR Submit Interface Specification."[15]
- The vendor must send a digitally signed message to `smime-test@smime.org`, with a subject field set to `S/MIME Interop Test: <vendorname>'s Certificate`.
- In response, the vendor will receive two messages: One message will be digitally signed and enveloped using RSA 512, RC2 40, and SHA-1, and the other message will be digitally signed and enveloped using RSA 512, 3DES, and SHA-1. These messages will be constructed using a CMS `signed-data` object, nested inside an `enveloped-data` object.
- When these messages are decrypted, the vendor will find two secret phrases, unique to his company. These secret phrases must be kept for the next step.
- The vendor must prepare and send two messages to `smime-test@smime.org`: One message must be digitally signed and enveloped using RSA 512, RC2 40, and SHA-1, and the other message must be digitally signed and enveloped using RSA 512, 3DES, and SHA-1. In the body of each message, the secret phrases from the previous step must be included. The subjects should be `S/MIME Interop Test: <vendorname>'s RC2 40` and `S/MIME Interop Test: <vendorname>'s 3DES`, respectively. Again, the messages must be constructed using a PKCS #7 `signedData` construct, nested inside a PKCS #7 `envelopedData` construct. Vendors may also create additional messages using the `multipart/signed` construct, although this will not be required for interoperability compliance.
- Upon successful recovery of the secret phrases, the vendor will receive a test completion notice from RSA Security's S/MIME Interoperability Center. Results will then be posted on the S/MIME Interoperability Center Web page.

Products that have earned the "S/MIME-Enabled" seal should be interoperable, meaning that one user can send an encrypted and digitally signed message from one

[15] `http://www.verisign.com/smime/`

product to a recipient who uses another product, and that the recipient can still verify and decrypt the message.

Note that RSA Security's interoperability testing, while providing useful information, is limited in scope. In fact, it does not test the ability of an S/MIME implementation to interact with a certificate repository or PKI. Furthermore, it does not test the ability to process certificates issued by different CAs or the ability to process CRLs. Since the implementations are tested with a reference implementation, it also does not follow that they successfully test with each other.

Against this background, the U.S. National Institute of Standards and Technology (NIST) has also become active in the field of S/MIME interoperability testing (as part of its PKI initiative), and has launched an S/MIME Laboratory[16] to "test the interoperability and overall functionality attained using current S/MIME products." As such, the activities of the S/MIME laboratory are intended to complement RSA Security's interoperability testing and its "S/MIME-Enabled" seal. More specifically, the S/MIME laboratory conducts interoperability experiments using commercial off-the-shelf (COTS) S/MIME-compliant products. In addition to the interoperability between peer S/MIME applications, the S/MIME laboratory also tests the interoperability between S/MIME applications and PKIs and directory services. For example, the S/MIME version 2 specification makes use of a single certificate for both signing outgoing messages and decrypting incoming messages. Consequently, many S/MIME implementations support a single certificate for the local user running the UA. S/MIME version 3, however, supports the use of separate certificates for digital signatures and digital envelopes, and few S/MIME implementations actually implement this two-certificate scheme. As a result, an S/MIME implementation that only supports a single certificate may be unable to communicate securely with a peer entity that supports a two-certificate scheme. Similar and related characteristics and attributes that affect S/MIME product interoperability are summarized in [8].

REFERENCES

[1] R. Housley, "Cryptographic Message Syntax," Request for Comments 2630, June 1999.

[2] E. Rescorla, "Diffie-Hellman Key Agreement Method," Request for Comments 2631, June 1999.

[3] B. Ramsdell (Ed.), "S/MIME Version 3 Certificate Handling," Request for Comments 2632, June 1999.

[16] `http://csrc.nist.gov/pki/smime/`

[4] B. Ramsdell (Ed.), "S/MIME Version 3 Message Specification," Request for Comments 2633, June 1999.

[5] P. Hoffman (Ed.), "Enhanced Security Services for S/MIME," Request for Comments 2634, June 1999.

[6] "Secure Data Network System (SDNS) Message Security Protocol (MSP) 4.0," Specification SDN.701, Revision A, 1997-02-06.

[7] J. Feghhi, J. Feghhi, and P. Williams, *Digital Certificates: Applied Internet Security*, Addison-Wesley Longman, Reading, MA, 1999.

[8] J. Mulvenna, et al., "Characteristics and Attributes that affect S/MIME Product Interoperability," draft report available at `http://csrc.nist.gov/pki/smime/welcome.htm`.

Chapter 15

Conclusions and Outlook

In this chapter, we conclude Part III of the book and elaborate on some possible future developments related to S/MIME. More specifically, we summarize the use of S/MIME for secure messaging in Section 15.1, provide a rough security analysis in Section 15.2, elaborate on future developments in Section 15.3, and point to some sources of further information in Section 15.4.

15.1 SUMMARY

In this part of the book, we addressed the use of S/MIME for secure messaging on the Internet. More specifically, we elaborated on the history and development of S/MIME in Chapter 11, overviewed the conceptual and technological approach employed by S/MIME in Chapter 12, discussed the PKI requirements of S/MIME in Chapter 13, and summarized the standardization of S/MIME and the products that conform to the evolving standards in Chapter 14.

In summary, S/MIME provides a thoroughly designed and widely deployed technological approach to provide basic message protection services for the Internet. It is entirely specified using ASN.1 and makes use of a hierarchical trust model based on the ITU-T recommendation X.509. Most importantly, S/MIME is strongly supported by all major vendors of UA products. As such, it is possible and very likely that S/MIME will become the predominant technology for secure messaging on the Internet. This is certainly true for the business world. For private use, however, PGP provides a viable alternative that is simpler to deploy due to its decentralized public key and certificate management procedures.

15.2 SECURITY ANALYSIS

Most of the things we said when we analyzed the security of PGP in Section 12.2 also apply for S/MIME. This is particularly true for the real threats related to password guessing attacks and software-based attacks. Because of this situation, many vendors of S/MIME-compliant UAs are looking into possibilities to make use of smartcards or USB tokens to protect the users's private keys and the computational processes performed with these keys. For example, one of the distinguishing features of the iT_SEC_outlook plug-in is its strong support for smartcards.

15.3 FUTURE DEVELOPMENTS

The standardization effort has temporarily slowed down with the release of S/MIME version 3. The corresponding specifications are being implemented and deployed. It will be interesting to see whether version 3 of S/MIME is sufficiently complete, or whether another version will be necessary.

Furthermore, it is important to note that the application of S/MIME is not at all restricted to e-mail. Instead, S/MIME can be used to secure any system that transports MIME entities. For example, HTTP can also make use of S/MIME to securely transfer MIME entities between a Web server and a browser. Also, S/MIME can be used to securely exchange digitally signed EDI messages over the Internet. It is possible and very likely that we will see alternative applications of S/MIME on the Internet, as well.

15.4 FURTHER INFORMATION

The best place to start with is the homepage of the IETF SMIME WG.[1] Other places to get further information about and related to S/MIME are the homepages of the following organizations and laboratories:

- The NIST S/MIME Laboratory;[2]

[1] http://www.ietf.org/html.charters/smime-charter.html
[2] http://csrc.nist.gov/pki/smime

- The S/MIME Central of RSA Security, Inc.;[3]
- The Internet Mail Consortium.[4]

If you want to get updated information about S/MIME, these homepages are certainly good places to start with.

[3]`http://www.rsasecurity.com/standards/smime`

[4]`http://www.imc.org`

Part IV
EPILOGUE

Chapter 16

Comparison

In this book, we elaborated on secure messaging with PGP and S/MIME. More specifically, we introduced the notion of "secure messaging" and elaborated on two conceptual and technical approaches to provide basic message protection services for Internet messaging: PGP and S/MIME.

While the two approaches are designed to perform similar tasks, they are different and incompatible with each other from a technical, practical, and policy point of view and will likely remain that way in the near future. More specifically, we elaborated on two technical differences that lead to a situation in which PGP and S/MIME implementations do not interoperate:

- First, PGP and S/MIME use different message formats;
- Second, PGP and S/MIME handle public keys and public key certificates in fundamentally different ways (as discussed in Chapters 8 and 13).

In the following chapter we discuss the likelihood of the two approaches to eventually converge in the long term. In the meantime, the two approaches coexist, and it is up to a company or organization that wants to make use of secure messaging to choose between them (and to invest money accordingly).

In the rest of this chapter, we provide some background information and arguments that can be used to choose between PGP and S/MIME. The arguments are related to security, scalability, usability and convenience in use, availability, costs, and future prospects.

Security: In Chapters 10 and 15, we provided rough security analyses for PGP and S/MIME. According to these analyses, the security properties of PGP and S/MIME are comparable. Both technologies provide basic message protection services at the discretion of a user, and both technologies use cryptographic algorithms that are assumed to be practically secure (given the current state of the art in cryptanalysis). In fact, none of the algorithms in use have been successfully cryptanalyzed, and all have had many years of peer review, public scrutiny, and testing. The major security threats related to PGP and S/MIME are still poorly chosen passphrases (to protect the users' private keys) and software-based attacks (e.g., Trojan horses to "steal" the private keys). The use of tamper-resistant hardware tokens (e.g., smartcards and "secure" smartcard readers) to hold and use the secret keys is appropriate in either case to provide a higher level of security. Finally, note that PGP attempts to provide a most comprehensive security solution for desktop and laptop systems, whereas S/MIME only addresses the secure messaging part. This is particularly true for the upcoming version 7 of the PGP software that will also include a personal firewall and a personal IDS (in addition to the additional security features that are already available today, such as disk encryption and virtual private networking).

Scalability: In addition to security, scalability is another important requirement for any software package for the Internet. Against this background, the use of X.509 certificates and corresponding PKIs is particularly useful. Note that PGP certificates are appropriate for environments in which users know each other. If there is no relationship between users, there is hardly any chance that they can act as introducers for each other. In this situation, the use of CAs acting as TTPs is very useful. Since S/MIME initially made use of X.509 certificates and the latest versions of PGP also support X.509 certificates, S/MIME and PGP are comparable with regard to their scalability properties. One may even argue that PGP is advantageous, because it can handle both trust models.

Usablity and Convenience in Use: As also mentioned in Chapter 10, the usability and convenience in use of security software is an important issue that must be considered with care. Any security software that cannot be used by casual users is not immediately useful. Again, PGP and S/MIME are very comparable with regard to their usability and convenience in use. Any solution that is fully integrated into the UA software is advantageous (as compared to stand-alone applications or UA plug-ins). Against this background, large companies, such as Microsoft, have the advantage that they are able to fully integrate S/MIME functionalities into their UA products.

Availablity: PGP and S/MIME are supported on all major platforms that are used for Internet messaging (either integrated into the UA software or as a plug-in to extend the functionality of the UAs). Refer to Chapters 9 and 14 for a corresponding overview.

Costs: Costs are an important issue when it comes to the evaluation of a secure messaging solution. Obviously, any solution in which the UA software comes bundled with PGP and/or S/MIME support is advantageous. Against this background, S/MIME-enabled UAs, such as Microsoft Outlook, Microsoft Outlook Express, or Netscape Messenger, are particularly cost-effective. Alternatively, many commercial plug-ins for PGP and S/MIME are available.

Future Prospects: First of all, it's important to note that both PGP and S/MIME are on the Internet standards track, and that both protocols will eventually emerge as Internet standards. Since the IETF does not mandate a single standard for a technology category (e.g., secure messaging), it is possible and very likely that both protocols will be adopted. However, due to its history and industrial focus, S/MIME has been able to garner a significant amount of industry support and is recognized as the protocol of choice to bring secure messaging to the business world. Consequently, it is possible and likely that PGP will be the secure messaging standard for private use, whereas S/MIME will be the secure messaging standard for business use. Fortunately, both technologies can make use of X.509 certificates.[1]

Taking into account these arguments, the use of UA software that comes bundled with PGP and/or S/MIME support is particularly advantageous and cost-effective. For example, a company or organization that is already using Microsoft Outlook for messaging is well-advised to employ the S/MIME features of Outlook to provide support for secure messaging.

A final word is due to the fact that secure messaging is an end-to-end security technology, and as such it makes it impossible (or at least very difficult) for a company or organization to decrypt the e-mail messages that are originated or

[1] As mentioned several times in this book, PGP supports X.509 certificates since version 6.5.1.

received by its employees. If an employee intentionally destroys his private key, the company or organization is no longer able to decrypt the archived messages (note, however, that this is already the case if the user intentionally destroys the encrypted files). Similarly, the use of virus scanning software at the edge of an intranet (e.g., the SMTP proxy server) is no longer possible, since it only has access to encrypted data. Consequently, there is some recent interest in having key recovery facilities for the professional use of secure messaging schemes. For example, there are some products available that decrypt and optionally re-encrypt e-mail messages as they enter the intranet environment (i.e., at the e-mail gateway that is operated on the firewall system). In the future, we will certainly see more products that provide key recovery facilities for companies and organizations, and that combine message delivery with message archival services.

Chapter 17

Outlook

In this chapter, we address some final points that are relevant for secure messaging on the Internet. More specifically, we discuss the possible convergence of PGP and S/MIME in Section 17.1, elaborate on Web-based secure messaging schemes in Section 17.2, overview and briefly discuss some additional security services in Section 17.3, and address current research efforts related to trust management in Section 17.4.

17.1 CONVERGENCE

Having discussed PGP and S/MIME to a certain extent, it may be interesting to ask whether it is possible or even likely that the two primary technologies for secure messaging on the Internet (i.e., PGP and S/MIME) eventually converge in the medium or long term. We mentioned several times that from a technical point of view, there are (at least) two fundamental differences between PGP and S/MIME:

- First, PGP and S/MIME use different message formats.
- Second, PGP and S/MIME handle public keys and public key certificates in fundamentally different ways (PGP uses a web of trust, whereas S/MIME uses an X.509-based PKI).

Obviously, the first difference could be easily removed by having the two relevant IETF WGs — the IETF OpenPGP WG and the IETF SMIME WG — cooperate to come up with a standardized message format. This is difficult but not impossible. Using ASN.1 in future specifications for PGP would certainly be a first step in that direction.

The second difference is more challenging from a technical point of view. We overviewed and fully discussed PGP's web of trust in Chapter 8 and the X.509-based PKI for S/MIME in Chapter 13. Based on these discussions, it seems obvious that the two approaches differ fundamentally in the way they handle public keys and public key certificates. However, three points are worth mentioning:

- First, NAI has extended the PGP trust model to additionally support X.509 certificates. Consequently, PGP applications can issue X.509 certificate requests and send them to CAs. Furthermore, NAI has introduced the notion of trusted introducers and meta-introducers that can be used to model a PKI.

- Second, the PGP certificate format is being added to several network security standard protocols, such as IPsec and SSL/TLS, that have previously only used X.509 certificates. Note, however, that this standardization effort is mainly driven by NAI, and that it is not at all clear whether the resulting specifications will be adopted and implemented by other companies.

- Third, there is no need for a UA to be restricted to only one trust model and corresponding class of certificates. In fact, a UA can simultaneously provide support for different trust models and classes of certificates (e.g., PGP certificates and X.509 certificates).

Consequently, one can reasonably expect an increasingly large number of UA software packages and plug-ins for UAs that provide support for both PGP and S/MIME. Examples include the iT_SEC_outlook and the CryptoEx Security Suite from Glück & Kanja, as well as software provided by PowerMail Technologies, Inc.[1]

17.2 WEB-BASED SECURE MESSAGING

Due to the increase in user mobility, Web-based messaging is getting increasingly important and popular. Exemplary Web-based messaging schemes and services

[1] `http://www.powermailtech.com`

include GMX,[2] Hotmail,[3] Yahoo! Mail,[4] and many ISPs that provide similar services (e.g., BlueMail and Freesurf in Switzerland). The big advantage of Web-based messaging schemes and services is related to the fact that a commercial off-the-shelf (COTS) browser is generally sufficient to read and create e-mail messages. More specifically, instead of having to install and configure UA software, a user can simply use a Web browser to access his e-mail account. Furthermore, Web-based messaging schemes are particularly useful if the exchanged messages are very large (since they do not have to be downloaded in sequential order).

It is obvious that the security concerns related to Internet-based messaging also apply for Web-based messaging (refer to Chapter 1 for an overview of these security concerns). In addition, the fact that the messages are kept on the server's side also raises some new security concerns. Against this background, the providers of Web-based messaging services are trying to secure their offerings. For example, it is fairly simple to use the SSL/TLS protocol to secure the communications between the Web browser and the Web server. Several companies, including, for example, Tumbleweed Communications[5] provide products and corresponding services in this area.

In addition to SSL/TLS-enhanced Web-based messaging systems, there are also some other Web-based secure messaging schemes and services available today. As mentioned in Chapter 1, examples include HushMail[6] and ZipLip.[7] HushMail, for example, works as follows:

- During the e-mail account initialization process, the following steps are performed:

  1. The user downloads the NewAccount Java applet from the HushMail Web site, and picks an e-mail address;
  2. The user is asked to move his mouse to seed a pseudorandom number generator;
  3. A public key pair is generated, using a 1024 bit ElGamal scheme (with fixed constants that are encoded into the applet);
  4. The user enters, and confirms his self-created passphrase;

[2] `http://www.gmx.net`
[3] `http://www.hotmail.com`
[4] `http://www.yahoo.com`
[5] `http://www.tumbleweed.com`
[6] `http://www.hushmail.com`
[7] `http://www.ziplip.com`

5. The passphrase, seen as a key, is used to symmetrically encrypt the private key;

6. Finally, the encrypted private key and the plaintext public key are sent to the HushMail server.

- When a user wants to send a message, the following steps are performed:

1. The user enters his e-mail address, and downloads the HushApplet;

2. The HushApplet, running on the client machine, requests the user's passphrase;

3. The passphrase is entered, and it is then securely hashed. Part of this hash is sent to the HushMail server for user validation;

4. Only if the partial hash is valid, the HushMail server sends the client HushApplet the user's plain text public key and encrypted private key;

5. The HushApplet uses the passphrase to decrypt the encrypted private key into its plaintext form;

6. The user enters the system and can do things such as view mail headers, create address aliases, and compose mail;

7. When the user composes and sends a message, the HushApplet contacts the HushMail server and downloads the recipient's public key;

8. If the recipient is in the sending user's address book, the HushApplet compares the public key values for extra security;

9. The body of the e-mail message being sent is encrypted with a pseudorandomly generated session key;

10. Using the recipient's public key, the random session key is asymmetrically encrypted to the recipient;

11. The entire message is sent to the HushMail server, which sends the message out via SMTP;

12. When a message is first read by a recipient, the recipient's private key will decrypt the session key, which will yield access to the plain text message itself.

In summary, the Web-based secure messaging schemes and services do not provide anything substantially new except for the possibility of having the private key stored on the server side in cryptographically protected form. This idea can also be used for PGP and S/MIME. In fact, it would be possible and technically feasible to implement a Java applet that provides support for PGP and/or S/MIME, and that can be downloaded to an arbitrary Web browser. It is very likely that such products and services will appear on the marketplace in the future. They may already be available by the time you read this book.

17.3 ADDITIONAL SECURITY SERVICES

In this book, we used the term "secure messaging" to refer to a messaging scheme that is able to provide the basic message protection services summarized in Chapter 1:

- Data origin authentication services;
- Connectionless confidentiality services;
- Connectionless integrity services;
- Nonrepudiation services with proof of origin.

Furthermore, we mentioned that enhanced message protection services do more than simply protect single messages as stand-alone objects. Examples include confirmation services that provide secure notifications back to a message originator that the message was actually delivered to an intended recipient or, at least, reached some other point on the message delivery path. Unfortunately, confirmation services require major modifications in the messaging infrastructure or e-mail systems. There are, however, some other security services that go beyond the basic message protection services without requiring major modifications in the messaging infrastructure or e-mail systems. Some of these security services are overviewed and briefly discussed next (others will be invented and provided in the future).

17.3.1 Nonrepudiation of Receipt Services

In spite of the fact that e-mail is becoming increasingly important for e-commerce and e-business applications, the Internet does not provide a reliable message delivery service. Consequently, the sender of an e-mail message cannot be sure and does not receive any evidence if his message was actually delivered to its intended recipient(s). The lack of evidence for the message delivery is actually a missing piece in the infrastructure required for the professional use of e-mail. This may change one day when a delivery status notification (DSN) or message tracking mechanism (as discussed in Chapter 3) is actually put in place. There is, however, a long way to go. Note that not only the sending and the receiving UAs must support a DSN mechanism, but all MTAs along the message delivery path.

A lot of research and development activities currently address the problem of certified mail and the design of corresponding cryptographic protocols. Any protocol for certified or registered mail must be able to provide both nonrepudiation services in a fair way:

- *Nonrepudiation with proof of origin:* The recipient of an e-mail message must have some way of proving that the sender actually originated the message (if the sender later tries to deny it);
- *Nonrepudiation with proof of receipt:* The sender of an e-mail message must have some way of proving that the recipient actually received the message (if the recipient later tries to deny it);

Obviously, a nonrepudiation service with proof of origin is fairly simple to provide by using digital signatures. Contrary to that, a nonrepudiation service with proof of receipt is much harder to provide, and the problem related to certified mail addresses this issue. Furthermore, the fairness property requires that the proper execution of the protocol ensures that the proof of origin and the proof of receipt are available to the recipient and sender, respectively. The protocol must be fail-safe in the sense that incomplete execution of the protocol will not result in a situation where the proof of receipt is available to the sender but the message is not available to the recipient, or vice versa.

One way to address the proof of delivery problem is to look at the paper world and draw some conclusions from there. Registered or certified paper mail uses the notion of a signed receipt. More specifically, the Post Office will not release a message unless the recipient signs a corresponding receipt. This receipt, in turn, is either returned to the sender or archived by the Post Office for later use. In either case, it can be used as a piece of evidence to prove that the sender actually sent a message to the recipient. Note, however, that it is still up to the judge to value the piece of evidence. Also, note that the piece of evidence only certifies that the sender sent out some message to the recipient not a particular message. This weak binding between the piece of evidence and the message being certified or registered is pervasive through all paper authentication methods and one major drawback and shortcoming of handwritten signatures as compared to digital signatures.

The problem of certified mail is basically a problem of simultaneous exchange of an e-mail message and a proof of receipt between two parties (the sender and the recipient) that do not trust each other. Protocols for certified mail based on simultaneous secret exchange schemes have been studied extensively in the cryptographic literature [1 – 9]. In a simultaneous secret exchange scheme, it is assumed that two parties, A and B, each possess a secret a and b (each n-bits long). It is further assumed that both secrets represent some value to the other party and that they are willing to trade secrets with each other. In essence, a simultaneous secret exchange protocol is executed in the following two phases:

- In the first phase, A and B commit to their secrets by exchanging $f(a)$ and $g(b)$ for some predefined one-way functions f and g. Consequently, A cannot recover b from $g(b)$ and B cannot recover a from $f(a)$.
- In the second phase, A and B release a and b bit-by-bit (until all n bits are released).

For such a protocol to be useful, it must be correct and fair. More specifically, the correctness of each bit exchanged must be verifiable for each recipient to ensure that his secret has not been traded for garbage. Furthermore, the fairness property must ensure that the computational effort required from the parties to obtain each other's remaining part of the secret should be approximately equal at any stage during the execution of the protocol.[8] In summary, certified mail protocols based on simultaneous secret exchange are theoretically interesting since they enable two distinct parties to simultaneously exchange an e-mail message and its receipt in absence of a trusted third party (TTP). However, the protocols are highly interactive and are not appropriate for asynchronous applications, such as e-mail.

Another class of certified mail protocols relys on trusted software to provide a fair exchange between the message and its receipt. These protocols are particularly popular among companies that attempt to make a business out of certified message delivery. According to these protocols, the sender of a registered mail sends the mail in encrypted form via a special software program that will not allow the recipient to read it until he sends a receipt back to the sender. These protocols are susceptible to reverse-engineering attacks and hacking, and cannot provide any real assurance and

[8]Note that this fairness definition on equal computational complexity makes sense only if the two parties have equal computing power, an often unrealistic assumption [10].

useful evidence of message delivery. Consequently, they are not further addressed in this book.

The most promising class of certified mail protocols for the Internet, however, makes use of a TTP in one way or another. As discussed in [11], there are certified mail protocols that make use of inline, online, or offline TTPs. All protocols have specific advantages and disadvantages. From a practical point of view, the use of certified mail protocols that make use of online TTPs are appropriate. An architecture for a certified mail system (CMS) implementing two certified mail protocols is described in [11]. The CMS is currently being prototyped.

In addition, there are several services provided on the Internet that also make use of a TTP (i.e., an SSL/TLS-enabled Web server). Examples include the following services:

- *CertifiedMail* is an SSL/TLS-based message delivery and tracking service that is provided for free to registered users.[9] When a user wants to send a message, he logs into the Web server using his login ID and password. On successful login, the user is able to prepare a message for a specific recipient. The server, in turn, stores the message and records it with the user's identity. In addition, the server creates a separate mailbox for the recipient, generates a unique URL for the recipient to retrieve the message, and sends a message to the recipient that includes the unique URL. The recipient is asked to log into the server to retrieve the message. The server records the date and time as to when the recipient viewed the message as well as the IP address of the recipient and stores this information with the user's identity. Finally, the server sends a notification message to the sender informing him that the message has been viewed by the recipient.
- Similar to CertifiedMail, *ReturnReceipt* is an SSL/TLS-based message delivery and tracking service that is provided for free to registered users.[10]
- Contrary to CertifiedMail and ReturnReceipt, *CertMail* is a certified mail and archival service that is provided on a commercial basis.[11] In short, messages are sent to the CertMail server and forwarded to the intended recipient(s). Also, response messages are sent to the CertMail server and forwarded to the sender of the original message. Either message is archived by the CertMail server. For users who want to protect the privacy of their messages, CertMail provides additional encryption utilities that can be applied on an end-to-end basis.

[9] `http://www.certifiedmail.com`
[10] `http://www.returnreceipt.com`
[11] `http://www.caprica.com/ certmail/`

The point to make is that most currently available TTP-based certified mail protocols and systems require the user to completely trust the TTP (not to misuse or reveal the message content). This is not true for the CMS described in [11]. In this system, the certified messages remain confidential and can only be read by the intended recipients.

17.3.2 Anonymity Services

As discussed in [12], there are three types of anonymous communication properties that can be provided individually or combined:

- Sender anonymity;
- Receiver anonymity;
- Unlinkability of sender and receiver (connection anonymity).

In short, *sender anonymity* means that the identity of the party who sent a particular message is hidden, while its receiver and the message itself might not be. Similarly, *receiver anonymity* means that the identity of the receiver is hidden, while its sender and the message itself might not be. Finally, *unlinkability of sender and receiver* (also referred to as *connection anonymity* in the remaining parts of this chapter) means that though the sender and receiver can each be identified individually as participating in some communication, they cannot be identified as communicating with each other.

A second aspect of anonymous communication is the adversary against which sender and receiver anonymity, as well as unlinkability of sender and receiver, must be provided, and ensured. In short, the adversary might be an eavesdropper who can observe some or all messages sent or received, collaborations consisting of some senders, receivers, and other parties, as well as variations thereof. It is important to know the capabilities of a potential adversary against which one wants to protect privacy (this knowledge is sometimes made explicit in a threats model).

There is previous work in providing anonymity service for e-mail. For example, `anon.penet.fi` was a simple and easy-to-use anonymous e-mail forwarding service (a so-called *anonymous remailer*) that was operated by Johan Helsingius in Finland.[12] In short, the `anon.penet.fi` anonymous remailer was provided by a simple SMTP proxy server that stripped off all header information of incoming

[12]According to a press release on February 20, 1995, over 7,000 messages were forwarded daily, and the alias database contained more than 200,000 entries.

e-mail messages before forwarding them toward their destination. In addition, if not already assigned, an alias for the sender of an e-mail message was created. In the outgoing message, the real e-mail address of the sender was replaced by the alias that allowed the recipient(s) of the message to reply to the sender without knowing his real identity or e-mail address. Consequently, `anon.penet.fi` provided sender anonymity by simply keeping the mapping between real e-mail addresses and their aliases anonymous. The downside of this simple approach was that any user of `anon.penet.fi` had to unconditionally trust the service provider not to reveal his real identity or e-mail address. This level of trust may or may not be justified.[13] In either case, it is difficult for a user to judge the trustworthiness of a particular service provider. Today, there are several anonymous remailers available for public use on the Internet, and a corresponding list has been compiled by Raph Levien (refer to `http://www.cs.berkeley.edu/~raph/remailer-list.html`).

A more sophisticated approach to provide anonymous e-mail forwarding services was originally developed and proposed by David Chaum in the early 1980s [13]. In essence, Chaum combined cryptographic and some other privacy enhancing technologies to provide anonymity services in a *Chaum mixing network*. According to this terminology, a *Chaum mix*, or *mix* in short, refers to an anonymous remailer that is able to decrypt messages with its private key, before forwarding the decrypted messages toward their final destination. In addition to forwarding incoming e-mail messages, a Chaum mix may also try to hide the relationship between incoming and outgoing traffic. To achieve this, it typically reorders, delays, and eventually pads data traffic to disable or at least complicate traffic analysis attacks.

In a Chaum mixing network, the sender of an anonymous e-mail message first chooses a route through a series of mixes, $M_1, \ldots, M_n$, to the intended recipient, and wraps some extra layers of data around the message. To form the innermost layer, the name of the last mix M_n — the mix one hop away from the destination — is concatenated with the original message (which may be encrypted with the public key of the recipient), and the result is then encrypted with the public key of the second-to-last mix, M_{n-1}, in the route. Consequently, the resulting bundle has one layer of routing data prepended to the original message, and it's encrypted with a key possessed only by M_{n-1}. If the bundle were to somehow arrive at M_{n-1}, it could be decrypted there, and the one layer of remaining routing data would be enough to route the message to M_n and from there to its final destination.

[13]On February 8, 1995, based on a burglary report filed with the Los Angeles police, transmitted by Interpol, the Finish police presented Helsingius with a warrant for search and seizure. Bound by law, he complied, thereby revealing the real e-mail address of a single user.

This sort of message encapsulation can be repeated, the next time with the third-to-last mix, namely M_{n-2}. The result is a bundle that can be decrypted only by M_{n-2}. Once decrypted, the interior can be forwarded to M_{n-1}. At the same time, however, M_{n-2} cannot read the interior of the bundle, since that part is encrypted with the public key of M_{n-1} (of which the corresponding private key is known only to M_{n-1}). The result of this message encapsulation scheme is illustrated in Figure 17.1. Each layer of gray refers to one additional layer of encryption. In short, a message for the final destination is encrypted with the public key of the last mix M_n in the route and addressed accordingly. Afterward, the result is encrypted with the public key of the second-to-last mix M_{n-1} and addressed accordingly. This continues until finally the bundle is encrypted with the public key of the first mix M_1 and addressed accordingly. One can think of this encapsulation scheme as an onion that is prepared by the sender. On the forward route to the destination, each mix peels off one layer of encryption (by decrypting the message with its private key).

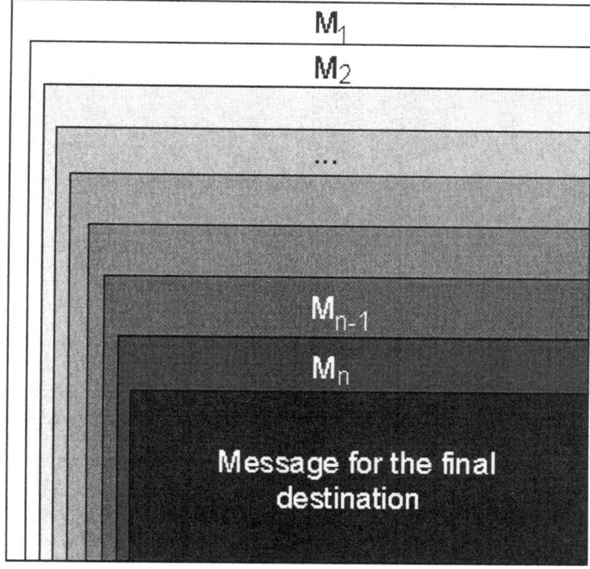

Figure 17.1 The message encapsulation scheme of a Chaum mixing network.

If a Chaum mixing network were used to transmit e-mail messages only through one mix, this mix would have to be trusted not to reveal the senders' and receivers' identities (since it sees both of them). Consequently, most people forward e-mail messages through two or more mixes in an attempt to protect themselves against a single mix that may see both the sender and the receiver identities of a particular message. In other words, using two or more mixes keeps the sender anonymous to every mix but the first and the receiver anonymous to every mix but the last. Consequently, a user's identity is best hidden if he runs his own Chaum mix and directs all of his outgoing e-mail messages through it.

If you were worried about an adversary powerful enough to monitor several Chaum mixes in a network simultaneously, you would also have to worry about timing and other correlation attacks. In an extreme case, consider the situation in which a Chaum mixing network is idle until a message is sent out. Then even though an adversary cannot decrypt the layered encryption, he can still locate the route just by watching the active parts of the network and analyzing the data traffic accordingly. Chaum mixing networks have been designed to resist such attacks using queues to batch, reorder, and process incoming messages. In fact, each mix may keep quiet — absorbing incoming messages but not retransmitting them — until its outbound buffer overflows, at which point the mix emits a randomly chosen message to its next hop. Note that this only works because e-mail is an asynchronous application without real-time constraints.

One question arises immediately with regard to the use of anonymous remailer services: how can the receiver of an (anonymous) e-mail message reply to the sender? The answer is that the receiver cannot unless explicitly told how to do so. A simple technique is to tell the receiver to send a reply to a certain newsgroup, such as `alt.anonymous.messages`, with a specific subject field, such as `12345example`. The reply can then be grabbed by the sender from the appropriate newsgroup. This approach of replying is yet untraceable but also expensive and unreliable. A more sophisticated technique uses the knowledge of how to build an untraceable forward route from the sender to the receiver, to build an inverse untraceable backward route from the receiver to the sender. In general, the forward and backward routes are independent (they can be completely identical, partially identical, or completely disjunct). According to this technique, the sender computes a block of information that is used to anonymously return a reply from the receiver to the sender. This additional block of information is sometimes also referred to as a *return path information* (RPI) block. The RPI block is prepended to the original message and padding data that is sent from the sender to the receiver. It is then used by the receiver to build a corresponding backward route or return path.

The use of Chaum mixes to provide anonymous e-mail forwarding and RPI-based reply services was prototyped by Ceki Cülcü and Gene Tsudik at the IBM Zürich

Research Laboratory in Switzerland. In fact, they utilized the scripting language Perl (version 5.0) and PGP version 2.6 to build a system called BABEL [14].

17.3.3 Protection Against Spam

In Chapter 1 we introduced the term "spamming" as referring to the act of sending "junk" e-mail messages to advertise a product or service. Spamming is facilitated by the fact that it is easy to obtain a list of valid e-mail addresses and use it without the corresponding user's consent. Note that many people (including myself) publish their e-mail address or give them to Web sites where they open accounts. Newsgroups provide another good source to collect a large number of valid e-mail addresses. Also note that up to a relatively large number, there is no cost associated with generating and sending spam messages.

Unfortunately, a recipient of an e-mail message cannot easily distinguish between a personal message and an unsolicited spam message. There is no characteristic envelope or sender's address that facilitates easy recognition of spam messages. In fact, the recipient must open the message and read it before deleting it. As such, spam messages fill the recipient's mailbox and necessitate time-consuming examination prior to message removal. Consequently, there is a lot of interest in providing technologies and tools to protect e-mail accounts against spam [15,16]. According to [17], all currently available tools use one (or a combination) of the following methods for detecting and removing spam:

- Spam messages can be filtered according to a blacklist of known spammer e-mail addresses (*source address filtering*);
- Spam messages can be filtered according to a blacklist of keywords often found in spam messages (*keyword filtering*);
- A user can change his or her e-mail address when his mailbox is constantly overloaded with spam messages (*address change*).

Unfortunately, source address filtering can be circumvented by spammers that disguise their true address by various means and frequently "mutate" among various bogus return addresses. Also, keyword filtering is only a heuristic and may lead to the removal of some valid messages. Furthermore, spammers have started to adapt to keyword filtering by changing the vocabulary of their messages. Finally, address change may serve only as a tedious, last-resort operation.

Against this background, a group of researchers at Bell Laboratories introduced a method to protect against spam messages via a new kind of e-mail address, called an *extended e-mail address* [17,18]. It enables a user to use his core e-mail address with different extensions and consequently classify incoming e-mail messages according to the extension they were sent to. It is possible and very likely that protection against spam will become more important in the future.

17.4 TRUST MANAGEMENT

In this book, we elaborated on two fundamentally different approaches to manage trust in a networked or distributed system:

- On the one hand, PGP uses a completely decentralized and distributed notion of trust;
- On the other hand, S/MIME makes use of formally recognized CAs that are commonly trusted.

These are only two possibilities to manage trust in a networked or distributed system, and there are certainly many other possibilities to address trust management. In fact, a lot of research is going on to study and better understand the notion of trust and to come up with more appropriate approaches for trust management. For example, a lot of research in this area is done in Ueli M. Maurer's information security and cryptography group[14] at the ETH Zürich, Switzerland:

- In [19], Pierre Schmid and Maurer proposed a calculus of channel properties which allows analyses and comparisons of secure channel establishment protocols at a high level of abstraction. In addition to its properties (i.e., whether a channel provides authenticity and/or confidentiality), a channel is also characterized by its direction and time of availability. Cryptographic primitives and trust relationships can then be interpreted as transformations for channel properties, and cryptographic protocols can be viewed as combinations of such transformations. A cryptographic protocol thus allows transformation of a set of secure channels established during an initial setup phase, together with a set of insecure channels available during an operational phase of the system, into a set of secure channels specified by the security requirements. More specifically, Maurer and Schmid gave necessary and sufficient requirements for establishing a secure channel between two entities in terms of secure channels to be made available during the initial setup phase, and in terms of trust relations between users, or users and TTPs.

[14] `http://www.inf.ethz.ch/department/TI/um/`

- In [20], Maurer proposed an approach to modeling and reasoning about a PKI from a user's point of view. More specifically, Maurer used the notion of a "recommendation." In short, a recommendation can be thought of as a signed statement about the trustworthiness of another entity and is similar to a certificate. Note that recommendations are of fundamental importance in our society, because it is not possible to personally know all the people one has to rely on. According to Maurer's model, the view of a user consists of certificates and recommendations, as well as statements about which public keys the user believes to be authentic and which entities he believes to be trustworthy. Whether given information provides sufficient evidence for a user of the authenticity of another user's public key depends on various parameters to be set by the user, including his own assumptions about the trustworthiness of certificate-issuing entities, the authenticity of the public keys stored in his database, and the security requirements of the application in which the public key is going to be used. The model includes confidence values (values measured on a continuous scale between 0 and 1) for statements and can exploit arbitrary certification structures containing multiple intersecting certification paths to achieve a higher confidence value than for any single certification path. This argument is similar to the one that led to the development of the PathServer, as briefly mentioned in Chapter 8.

- In [21], Reto Kohlas and Maurer proposed a calculus for deriving conclusions from a given entity's view (e.g., a user or a judge) consisting of evidence and inference rules valid in this entity's world.

- In [22], the same authors formalized the assignment and the valuation of confidence values in the general context of reasoning based on uncertain evidence, and proposed a set of principles for confidence valuation in a PKI.

In addition to Maurer's work, a group of researchers at AT&T broadened the scope of trust management to design and build a PKI that also supports security policies, credentials, access control, and authorization (in addition to authentication). They prototyped their ideas in a system called *PolicyMaker* [23,24]. According to this system, a trust management system consists of five basic components:

- A mechanism for identifying principals;

- A language for describing actions (operations with security consequences that are to be controlled by the system);

- A language for specifying application policies (policies that govern the actions that principals are authorized to perform);
- A language for specifying credentials (data records that allow principals to delegate authorization to other principals);
- A compliance checker (component that provides a service to applications for determining how an action requested by one or several principals should be handled, given a policy and a set of credentials).

Any application that makes use of a trust management system can ask the compliance checker whether a requested action should be allowed. More recently, the AT&T researchers also designed a simple and flexible trust management system to work with various TCP/IP-based applications. The resulting trust management system was named *KeyNote*. Version 2 of the KeyNote trust management system is further described in an informational RFC document [25].

REFERENCES

[1] M. Blum, "How to exchange (secret) keys," *Proceedings of STOC '83*, 1983, pp. 440 – 447.

[2] M. Luby, S. Micali, and C. Rackoff, "How to simultaneously exchange secret bit by flipping a symmetrically-biased coin," *Proceedings of FOCS '83*, 1983 pp. 23 – 30.

[3] S. Even, O. Goldreich, and A. Lempel, "A randomized protocol for signing contracts," *Communications of the ACM*, Vol. 28, 1985, pp. 637 – 647.

[4] A. Yao, "How to generate and exchange secrets," *Proceedings of FOCS '86*, 1986, pp. 162 – 167.

[5] E.F. Brickell, D. Chaum, I. Damgard, and J. Van de Graaf, "Gradual and verfiable release of a secret," *Proceedings of CRYPTO '87*, 1987, pp. 156 – 166.

[6] R. Cleve, "Controlled gradual disclosure schemes for random bits and their applications," *Proceedings of CRYPTO '89*, 1989, pp. 573 – 588.

[7] J. Kilian, *Use of Randomness in Algorithms and Protocols*, MIT Press, Cambridge, MA, 1990.

[8] I. Damgard, "Practical and provably secure exchange of digital signatures," *Proceedings of EUROCRYPT '93*, 1993, pp. 200 – 217.

[9] T. Okamoto, and K. Ohta, "How to simultaneously exchange secrets by general assumptions," *Proceedings of the ACM Computer and Communications Security*, 1994, pp. 184 – 192.

[10] M. Ben-Or, O. Goldreich, S. Micali, and R. Rivest, "A fair protocol for signing contracts," *IEEE Transactions on Information Theory*, Vol. 36, 1990, pp. 40 – 46.

[11] R. Oppliger, "A Certified Mail System (CMS) for the Internet," eSECURITY Technologies Rolf Oppliger, 2000.

[12] A. Pfitzmann, and M. Waidner, "Networks without user observability," *Computers & Security*, Vol. 2, No. 6, pp. 158 – 166.

[13] D. Chaum, "Untraceable Electronic Mail, Return Addresses and Digital Pseudonyms," *Communications of the ACM*, Vol. 24, No. 2, February 1981, pp. 84 – 88.

[14] C. Cülcü, and G.Tsudik, "Mixing Emails with BABEL," *Proceedings of ISOC Symposium on Network and Distributed System Security*, February 1996, pp. 2 – 16.

[15] A. Schwartz, S. Garfinkel, and D. Russell, *Stopping Spam*, O'Reilly & Associates, Sebastopol, CA, 1998.

[16] G. Mulligan, *Removing the Spam: Email Processing and Filtering*, Addison-Wesley, 1999.

[17] E. Gabber, M. Jakobsson, Y. Matias, and A. Mayer, "Curbing Junk E-Mail via Secure Classification," *Proceedings of Financial Cryptography*, 1998.

[18] D. Bleichenbacher, E. Gabber, P. Gibbons, Y. Matias, and A. Mayer, "On Secure and Pseudonymous Client-Relationships with Multiple Servers," *Proceedings of USENIX Workshop on Electronic Commerce*, 1998.

[19] U.M. Maurer, and P.E. Schmid, "A Calculus for Secure Channel Estabishment in Open Networks," *Proceedings of European Symposium on Research in Computer Security (ESORICS)*, 1994, pp. 175 – 192.

[20] U.M. Maurer, "Modelling a Public-Key Infrastructure," *Proceedings of European Symposium on Research in Computer Security (ESORICS)*, 1996, pp. 325 – 350.

[21] R. Kohlas, and U.M. Maurer, "Reasoning About Public-Key Certification: On Bindings Between Entities and Public Keys," *Proceedings of Financial Cryptography*, 1999.

[22] R. Kohlas, and U.M. Maurer, "Confidence Valuation in a Public-Key Infrastructure based on Uncertain Evidence," *Proceedings of the International Workshop on Practice and Theory in Public-Key Cryptography*, 2000.

[23] M. Blaze, J. Feigenbaum, and J. Lacy, "Decentralized Trust Management," *Proceedings of IEEE Conference on Security and Privacy*, 1996, pp. 164 – 173.

[24] M. Blaze, J. Feigenbaum, and M. Strauss, "Compliance-Checking in the PolicyMaker Trust-Management System," *Proceedings of Financial Cryptography*, 1998, pp. 251 – 265.

[25] M. Blaze, J. Feigenbaum, J. Ioannidis, and A. Keromytis, "The KeyNote Trust-Management System Version 2," Request for Comments 2704, September 1999.

Glossary

Access The ability of a principal to use the resources of a(n information) system.

Access control The prevention of unauthorized access to resources of a(n information) system, including the prevention of their use in an unauthorized manner.

Access control list A list of principals who are authorized to have access to a resource, together with their corresponding access rights.

Access control service Security service that is used to control access to resources.

Access right The right to access a resource.

Accountability The property that ensures that the actions of a principal may be traced uniquely to this particular principal.

Accounting The process of measuring resource usage of a principal.

ActiveX Marketing name for a set of technologies, protocols, services, and application programming interfaces based on Microsoft's Component Object Model (COM). As such, ActiveX is also a system for downloading executable code over the Internet. The code is bundled into a single file called ActiveX control. In general, a file carrying an ActiveX control has the extension `.ocx`.

Adversary Commonly used to refer to an intruder, opponent, enemy, or any other mischievous person who desires to compromise someone else's security.

AES The Advanced Encryption Standard (AES) is a data encryption algorithm that will replace DES in the future.

Anonymous remailer Anonymous e-mail forwarding service (provided through an anonymizing SMTP proxy server).

Application gateway An internetworking device that interconnects one network to another for a specific application. An application gateway can either work at the application or transport layer. If the gateway works at the application layer, it is usually called an application-level gateway or proxy server. If the gateway works at the transport layer, it is usually called a circuit-level gateway.

ASCII Standard character set.

ASN.1 Formal specification language and notation of choice for the OSI reference model and its communication protocols. It is specified in the multipart standard ISO/IEC 8824 that has also been approved by the ITU-T in a series of recommendations (ITU-T X.680 to X.683).

Attack An exploitation of a vulnerability by an intruder.

Attribute authority Authority that issues (and eventually revokes) attribute certificates.

Attribute certificate Data record that provides an attribute for a principal. It is rendered unforgeable by appending a digital signature from an attribute authority.

Audit trail Evidence, in documentary or other form, that enables a review of the functioning of elements of a(n information) system.

Authentication The process of verifying the claimed identity of a principal.

Authentication context Information conveyed during a particular instance of an authentication process.

Authentication exchange A sequence of one or more messages used and sent for authentication.

Authentication information Information used for authentication.

Authorization The process of assigning rights, which includes the granting of access based on specific access rights.

Authorization policy Part of an access control policy by which access by subjects to objects is granted or denied. An authorization policy may be defined in terms of access control lists, capabilities, or attributes assigned to subjects, objects, or both.

Availability The property that ensures a resource is available and accessible for authorized principals.

Base-64 encoding scheme Scheme to encode arbitrary 8-bit data into a restricted character set (also known as radix-64 encoding scheme).

Binary mail attachment Attachment to an e-mail message that contains binary data and may encode anything (from random data to executable program code).

Biometrics The science of using biological properties to identify individuals, such as fingerprints, retina scans, or voice recognition.

Bit Binary digit (either 1 or 0).

Blind signature scheme Digital signature scheme that allows one party to have a second party sign a message without revealing information about the message to the second party.

Block cipher An encryption algorithm (cipher) that encrypts a message by breaking it into blocks and encrypting each block individually. A block, in turn, is a sequence of bits of fixed length.

Block cipher based MAC A message authentication code (MAC) algorithm that is performed by using a block cipher as a keyed compression function.

Blowfish Secret key cryptosystem.

Brute force attack Attack that requires trying all (or a large fraction of all) possible values until the right value is found. This attack is sometimes also called an exhaustive search.

Capability Data record that can serve as an identifier for a resource such that possession of it confers access rights for that particular resource.

Capability attribute List of preferred decrypting capabilities used by PGP.

CAST Secret key cryptosystem.

Certificate path An ordered list of certificates, with succeeding certificates signed by the private keys corresponding to preceding certificates.

Certificate practice statement Written statement that specifies the policies and practices of a CA with regard to issuance and maintenance of (public key) certificates.

Certificate profile Specification of certificate contents in terms of the required syntax and semantics of each field.

Certificate revocation Process of publicly announcing that a certificate (either a public key certificate, an attribute certificate, or any other form of certificate) has been revoked and should no longer be used.

Certificate revocation list A list of certificates that have been revoked before their expiration date.

Certificate revocation tree A binary hash tree built from one (or several) certificate revocation list(s).

Certification authority Trusted third party that creates, assigns, distributes, renews, and possibly revokes public key certificates.

Certification authority certificate Public key certificate used to hold the public key of a CA.

Channel Information transfer path.

Ciphertext Data produced through the use of encryption (encryption transforms plaintext into ciphertext).

Ciphertext-only attack A form of cryptanalysis where the cryptanalyst has some ciphertext but nothing else.

Client A process that requests and eventually obtains a service. A client is usually acting on a specific user's or principal's behalf.

Collision Two values x and y form a collision of a function f if $x \neq y$ but $f(x) = f(y)$.

Collision resistance Property of a hash function that makes sure that collisions are hard to find.

Communication compromise Result of the subversion of a communication line within a computer network or distributed system.

Communication security Field of study that aims to protect data during its transmission in a computer network or distributed system.

Communication security service Security service that is used to protect communications within and between networks. According to the terminology of the OSI security architecture, communication security services include authentication, data confidentiality and integrity, as well as nonrepudiation services.

Compression function A function that takes a fixed length input and returns a shorter output of fixed length.

Computational complexity Measures the amount of resources (space and time) that are required to solve a problem. In this context, space refers to spatial (memory) constraints involved in a certain computation, and time refers to the temporal constraints.

Computer network Interconnected collection of autonomous computer systems.

Computer security Field of study that aims to preserve computing resources against unauthorized use and abuse, as well as to protect data that encodes information from accidental or deliberate damage, disclosure, or modification.

Confidentiality The property that ensures that information is not made available or disclosed to unauthorized parties.

Connection anonymity Property that ensures that though the sender and receiver can each be identified as participating in some communication, they cannot be identified as communicating with each other.

Countermeasure A feature or function that either reduces or eliminates one (or more) system vulnerabilities or counters one (or more) threats.

Credentials Data that is needed to establish the claimed identity of a principal.

Cross-certifying CA Certification authority (CA) that is trusted to issue certificates for arbitrary principals and other CAs over which it may not have immediate jurisdiction.

Cryptanalysis The art and science of breaking encryption or any form of cryptography. In short, it embodies the analysis of a cryptographic system and its inputs and outputs to derive confidential variables or sensitive data including the plaintext.

Cryptographic algorithm Algorithm defined by a sequence of steps precisely specifying the actions required to achieve a specific security objective.

Cryptographic protocol Distributed algorithm defined by a sequence of steps precisely specifying the actions required of two or more entities to achieve a specific security objective.

Cryptography The art and science of using mathematics to secure information. More specifically, cryptography refers to the study of mathematical techniques related to aspects of information security such as confidentiality, data integrity, entity authentication, and data origin authentication.

Cryptology Science of secure communications. As such, it also refers to the branch of mathematics concerned with cryptography and cryptanalysis.

Cryptosystem An encryption and decryption algorithm (cipher), together with all possible plaintexts, ciphertexts, and keys.

Daemon Program that runs in the background to perform a specific network service. Unlike other programs that execute and exit, a daemon performs its work and waits for more.

Decryption The creation of plaintext from ciphertext.

Denial-of-service attack The prevention of authorized access to a shared resource or the delaying of a time-critical operation.

DES Data Encryption Standard (DES) that was developed by IBM and the U.S. government in the 1970s as an official federal information processing standard (FIPS).

Detached signature A digital signature that may be stored, processed, and transmitted separately from the message it signs.

Dictionary attack A brute force attack that tries passwords and/or keys from a precompiled list of possible values (e.g., a dictionary of words). This is often done as a precomputation and offline attack.

Differential cryptanalysis A chosen plaintext attack relying on the analysis of the evolution of the differences between two plaintexts.

Diffie-Hellman key exchange A key exchange protocol allowing the participants to agree on a key over an insecure channel.

Digest Commonly used term to refer to the output of a hash function.

Digital signature Data appended to or a cryptographic transformation of a data unit that allows a recipient of the data unit to prove the source and integrity of the data unit and to protect against forgery, for example, by the recipient.

Digital timestamp A record mathematically linking a document to a time and date.

Discrete logarithm problem The problem of given a and y in a group, to find x such that $a^x = y$. For some groups, the discrete logarithm problem is a hard problem that can, for example, be used in public key cryptography.

Distributed system Multiple autonomous computer systems connected together via a network that cooperate to perform a task.

Dual-homed firewall Firewall configuration containing a dual-homed host.

Dual-homed host Host with two interfaces that interconnect to different networks. Usually, the IP routing function is disabled on the dual-homed host.

Dual signature Digital signature in which two parts of a message are dually signed by first hashing them separately, then concatenating the two hash values, and finally digitally signing the result.

EBCDIC Character set developed and deployed by IBM.

Electronic commerce The use of an open and public network, such as the Internet, to market goods and services without having to be physically present at the point of sale. The Internet may serve several purposes, including marketing, services, and sales.

Electronic payment system System that provides support for payments using electronic means.

Elliptic curve cryptosystem A public key cryptosystem based on the properties of elliptic curves.

E-mail message Message composed or read on a computer system and exchanged between users (or user agents, respectively).

Encryption The cryptographic transformation of plaintext into an apparently less readable form (called ciphertext) through a mathematical process. The ciphertext may be read by anyone who has the key that decrypts the ciphertext.

Exhaustive search Checking every possibility individually until the right value is found.

Extranet Network based on the TCP/IP communications protocol suite that connects an intranet to network segments of partners, suppliers, and customers.

Factoring problem The problem of breaking down an integer into its (prime) factors.

Fingerprint A hash value of a public key (in PGP terminology).

Firewall A blockade between a privately owned and protected network (that is assumed to be secure and trusted) and another network, typically a public network or the Internet (that is assumed to be nonsecure and untrusted). The purpose of a firewall is to prevent unwanted and unauthorized communications into or out of the protected network.

Gateway Internetworking device that operates at any layer higher than the network layer in the OSI reference model. Typically, a gateway operates at the application layer.

GnuPG A free and open source implementation of the OpenPGP specification.

Hard problem A problem that is computationally difficult to solve.

Hash function A function that takes a variable length input and returns a shorter output of fixed length. As such, it iteratively applies a compression function.

Host Addressable entity within a computer network or distributed system. The entity is typically addressed either by its name or its network address.

Host compromise The subversion of an individual host within a computer network or distributed system.

IDEA (International Data Encryption Algorithm) Secret key cryptosystem.

Information Data with meaning (concerning a particular fact or circumstance in general).

Information technology Technology that deals with information.

Integrity The property that ensures that data is not altered undetected.

Internet Globally interconnected set of networks that use the TCP/IP communications protocol suite.

Internet-Draft Working document of the IETF, its areas, and its working groups. As such, it is valid for a maximum of six months and may be updated, replaced, or obsoleted by other documents at any time.

Internet Society International nonprofit membership organization formed in 1992 to promote the use of the Internet for research and scholarly communication and collaboration.

Intranet Corporate or enterprise network based on the TCP/IP communications protocol suite.

Introducer Completely trusted PGP key holder.

IPsec Internet layer security protocol suite.

ISO The International Organization for Standardization (ISO) is a non-governmental, worldwide federation of national standards bodies established in 1947. The mission of the ISO is to promote the development of standardization and related activities in the world with a view to facilitating the international exchange of goods and services, and to developing cooperation in the spheres of intellectual, scientific, technological, and economic activity.

ISO/IEC 8859 Family of character sets standardized by the International Organization for Standardization (ISO) and International Electrotechnical Committee (IEC).

ISO/IEC 10646-1 Multi-octet character set standardized by the International Organization for Standardization (ISO) and International Electrotechnical Committee (IEC).

ITU The International Telecommunications Union (ITU) is a branch of the United Nations within which governments and the private sector coordinate global telecommunications networks and services. ITU activities include the coordination, development, regulation, and standardization of telecommunications (abbreviated as ITU-T).

Java Programming language developed by Sun Microsystems. In essence, Java is an object-oriented, general-purpose programming language that has a syntax similar to C^{++}, dynamic binding, garbage collection, and a simple inheritance model.

Kerberos A symmetric encryption-based authentication and key distribution system developed at the Massachusetts Institute of Technology (MIT).

Key A sequence of symbols that controls the operations of plaintext encipherment and decipherment.

Key agreement A shared secret is derived by two (or more) parties as a function of information contributed by, or associated with, each of these, (ideally) such that no party can predetermine the resulting value.

Key establishment A process or protocol used by two or more parties to establish a shared secret key, for subsequent cryptographic use. Key establishment may be broadly subdivided into key transport and key agreement.

Key management The generation, storage, distribution, deletion, archiving, and application of keys in accordance with a specific security policy.

Key pair The full key information in a public key cryptosystem, consisting of a set of a public and private key that belong together.

Key recovery A special feature of a key management scheme that allows a secret or private key to be recovered even if the original key is lost.

Keyspace The set of all possible keys for a given cryptosystem.

Key transport One party creates or otherwise obtains a secret value, and securely transfers it to the other(s).

Label Information associated with an object (may be security-relevant or not).

Limitation Feature that is not as general as possible.

Link Physical connection between two hosts.

Man-in-the-middle attack Attack that includes interception, insertion, deletion, and modification of messages, reflecting messages back to the sender, replaying old messages, and redirecting messages.

Masquerade The unauthorized pretense by a principal to be a different principal.

Meet-in-the-middle attack A known plaintext attack against double encryption with two separate keys where the attacker encrypts a plaintext with a key and decrypts the original ciphertext with another key and hopes to get the same value.

Message Data unit that originates from and is ultimately received by a user.

Message authentication code The result of applying a function that takes a variable length input and a key to produce a fixed-length output.

Message digest The result of applying a one-way hash function to a message.

Meta-introducer Trusted introducer who can nominate and create other trusted introducers.

MOSS Protocol specification for secure messaging.

Multihomed host Host with multiple network interfaces. Similar to the dual-homed host, the routing function is usually disabled on a multihomed host.

Network security policy Document that describes an organization's network security concerns and specifies the way network security should be achieved in that organizational environment.

Nonrepudiation The property that enables the receiver of a message to prove that the sender did in fact send the message even though the sender might later deny ever having sent it.

Number theory A branch of mathematics that investigates the relationships and properties of numbers.

One-time pad A secret key cryptosystem in which the key is a truly random sequence of bits that is as long as the message itself, and encryption is performed by XORing the message with the key. The resulting cryptosystem is perfectly secret (unconditionally secure).

One-way function Function that is easy to compute but hard to invert, meaning that it is computationally infeasible to find the input from the output.

One-way hash function A one-way function in which the output is usually much smaller than the input.

Open system System that conforms to open system standards (meaning that the details about the open system are available for anyone to read and use, ideally without even paying royalities).

Open system standard Standard that specifies an open system, and that allows manufacturers to build corresponding component parts.

Originator User who originates a message.

OSI reference model Preeminent model for structuring and understanding communication functions in computer networks and distributed systems. The reference model for open systems interconnection was originally proposed by the ISO/IEC JTC1 in 1978.

Packet filter A multiported internetworking device that applies a set of rules to each incoming IP packet in order to decide whether it will be forwarded or dropped. IP packets are filtered based on information that is found in packet headers.

Password Authentication information that is typically composed of a string of characters.

Password guessing The process of correctly guessing the password of a legitimate user.

Patent The sole right, granted by the government, to sell, use, and manufacture an invention or creation.

PathServer A Web-based service for authenticating PGP public keys.

PEM Protocol specification for secure messaging.

Perfect forward secrecy A protocol has perfect forward secrecy if compromise of long-term keying material does not compromise session keys that have been established in the past (assuming that the keys have been deleted after use).

Personal certificate Public key certificate used to authenticate a particular user.

Personal proxy server A trimmed-down proxy server intended for individual use.

PGP Software package and protocol specification for secure messaging.

Plaintext The input of an encryption function or the output of a decryption function. Decryption transforms ciphertext into plaintext.

Plug-in A module that is loaded directly into the address space of an application program and is automatically run when documents of a particular type are received.

Precomputation attack An attack where the adversary precomputes a look-up table of values used to crack encryption or passwords.

Primality testing A test that determines, with varying degree of probability, whether or not a particular number is prime.

Principal Human or system entity that is registered in and authenticable to a computer network or distributed system.

Principal identifier Identifier used to uniquely identify a principal.

Private key Cryptographic key used in public key cryptography to sign and/or decrypt messages.

Process Instantiation of a program running on a particular host.

Proprietary system System that does not conform to open system standards (meaning that the system is created, developed, and controlled by a single company).

Protocol Specification of the syntax and semantics as well as the relative timing of a finite sequence of messages.

Protocol stack Selection of protocols from a protocol suite to support a particular application or class of applications.

Protocol suite Set of protocols that fit a particular network model.

Proxy server Application-specific software that runs on an application-level gateway to deal with external servers on behalf of internal clients and internal servers on behalf of external clients. As such, the proxy (server) acts both as a server as well as a client: the proxy is a server to the client connecting to it, and a client to servers to which it connects.

Public key Cryptographic key used in public key cryptography to verify signatures and/or encrypt messages.

Public key certificate Data record that provides the public key of a principal, together with some other information related to the principal, and the certification authority that has issued the certificate. The certificate is rendered unforgeable by appending a digital signature from a certification authority (CA).

Public key cryptography standards A suite of specifications that address various aspects related to the implementation of public key cryptography.

Public key infrastructure Infrastructure to issue and revoke public keys and public key certificates. As such, it comprises a set of agreed-upon standards, certification authorities, structures between multiple CAs, methods to discover and validate certificate paths, operational and management protocols, interoperable tools, and supporting legislation.

RC2, RC4, RC5, and RC6 Secret key cryptosystems.

Receiver anonymity Property that ensures that the identity of a party who received a particular message is hidden, while its sender and the message itself might not be.

Recipient User who receives a message.

Replay attack An attack that comprises the recording and replaying of previously sent messages or parts thereof. Any constant authentication information, such as a password, a one-way hash of a password, or electronically transmitted biometric data, can be recorded and replayed.

Repudiation Denial by a principal of having participated in a communication.

Root CA Certification authority that bears a self-signed certificate (the term is sometimes also used to refer to the "CA of the root of a trust" or "the most trusted CA").

Router Internetworking device that operates at the network layer in the OSI reference model and the Internet layer in the Internet model.

RSA Public key cryptosystem invented by Rivest, Shamir, and Adleman.

Salt A string of random (or pseudorandom) bits concatenated with a key or password to foil precomputation attacks.

Screening router A router with packet filtering capabilities.

Secret key The key used in a symmetric cryptosystem that is shared between the communicating parties.

Secret sharing Splitting a secret (e.g., a private key) into many pieces such that any specified subset of n pieces may be combined to form the secret.

Secure Sockets Layer Transport layer security protocol.

Security architecture A high-level description of the structure of a system, with security functions assigned to components within this structure.

Security attribute A piece of security-related information that is associated to a principal in a distributed system.

Security audit An independent review and examination of system records and activities in order to test for adequacy of system controls, to ensure compliance with established policy and operational procedures, to detect breaches in security, and to recommend any indicated changes in control, policy, and procedures.

Security audit message A message generated following the occurrence of an auditable security-related event.

Security audit trail Data collected and potentially used to facilitate a security audit.

Security domain A set of machines under common administrative control, with a common security policy and security level.

Security mechanism A concrete mechanism or procedure used to actually implement one or several security services.

Security scanner A program that is able to probe a system for known security holes and configuration weaknesses.

Security service A quality of a system present to satisfy a security policy.

Security zone A group of Web sites in which a user has the same level of trust.

Self-certified public key Public key that is certified with its corresponding private key.

Sender anonymity Property that ensures that the identity of a party who sent a particular message is hidden, while its receiver and the message itself might not be.

Server Process that provides a network service.

Session hijacking Attack in which a connection is taken over after a legitimate user has authenticated himself.

Session key A temporary and ephemeral secret key shared between two or more principals, with a limited lifetime (e.g., the duration of a session).

Site certificate Public key certificate used to authenticate a particular Web site.

S/MIME Protocol specification for secure messaging.

S/MIME agent User agent software that conforms to the S/MIME specification.

SOCKS A circuit-level gateway that is in widespread use.

Software patent Patent applied to a computer program.

Software publisher certificate Public key certificate used to authenticate a particular software publisher (an individual programmer or a commercial software company).

Spamming The act of sending "junk" e-mail messages to advertise a product or service.

Standard A documented agreement containing technical specifications or other precise criteria to be used consistently as rules, guidelines, or definitions of characteristics to ensure that materials, products, processes, and services are fit for their purpose.

Swisskey A commercial certificate service provider located in Switzerland.

TCP/IP protocol suite Suite of data communications protocols. The suite gets its name from two of its most important protocols, namely the Transmission Control Protocol (TCP) and the Internet Protocol (IP).

Threat Circumstance, condition, or event with the potential to either violate the security of a system or to cause harm to system resources.

Traffic analysis The inference of information from observation of external traffic characteristics (presence, absence, amount, direction, and frequency of data traffic).

Traffic padding The generation of spurious instances of communications, spurious data units, or spurious data within data units, usually to counteract traffic analysis.

Transform Specification of the details of how to apply a specific algorithm to data.

Transport Layer Security Transport layer security protocol.

Trusted introducer Introducer who is commonly trusted (e.g., by all employees within an organization).

Trusted third party A security authority or its agent, trusted by other entities with respect to security-related activities.

Trust model The set of rules a system or application uses to decide whether a certificate is valid.

Tunneling Technique of encapsulating a data unit from one protocol inside another, and using the facilities of the second protocol to traverse parts of the network.

Unicode Character set developed by the Unicode Consortium.

User Principal who is accountable and ultimately responsible for his or her activities within a computer network or distributed system.

User agent Software that implements the Internet messaging protocols.

UU encoding scheme Scheme to encode arbitrary 8-bit data into a restricted character set. The restricted character set, in turn, comprises only characters that are likely to be transferable in most systems.

VeriSign A commercial certificate service provider located in the United States.

Virtual private network Network that consists of a collection of hosts that have implemented protocols to securely exchange information.

Vulnerability A weakness that could be exploited by an intruder to violate a system or the information it contains.

Web of trust Trust model used by PGP.

World Wide Web A virtual network that is overlaid on the Internet. It comprises all clients and servers that communicate with one another using the Hypertext Transfer Protocol (HTTP).

Abbreviations and Acronyms

AA	attribute authority
ADK	additional decryption key
AES	Advanced Encryption Standard
ANSI	American National Standards Institute
ANX	Automotive Network Exchange
API	application programming interface
ASCII	American Standard Code for Information Interchange
ASN.1	Abstract Syntax Notation 1
bcc	blind carbon copy
BER	basic encoding rules
BXA	Bureau of Export Administration
CA	certification authority
CBC	cipher block chaining
cc	carbon copy
CCI	common client interface
CCITT	Consultative Committee on International Telegraphy and Telephony (now ITU-T)
CFB	cipher feedback

CMS	cryptographic message syntax
CMU	Carnegie Mellon University
COM	component object model
COTS	commercial off-the-shelf
CR	carriage return
CRL	certificate revocation list
CSI	Computer Security Institute
CSK	corporate signing key
CSS	contents scrambling system
DAC	discretionary access control
DAP	Directory Access Protocol
DARPA	Defense Advanced Research Projects Agency
DCA	Defense Communications Agency
DDoS	distributed denial-of-service
DER	distinguished encoding rules
DES	Data Encryption Standard
DFA	differential fault analysis
DH	Diffie-Hellman
DIT	directory information tree
DM	Deutsche Mark
DMS	defense messaging system
DN	distinguished name
DNA	deoxyribonucleic acid
DNS	domain name system
DNSsec	domain name system security
DoC	Department of Commerce
DoS	denial-of-service
DPA	differential power analysis
DSA	Digital Signature Algorithm
DSN	delivery status notification
DSS	Digital Signature Standard
DVD	digital versatile disc
EAR	Export Administration Regulations
EBCDIC	extended binary coded decimal information code
ECB	electronic code book
ECC	elliptic curve cryptography

E-commerce	electronic commerce
EHLO	extended HELLO
E-mail	electronic mail
ESMTP	Extended SMTP
FAQ	frequently asked questions
FIPS	Federal Information Processing Standard
FSUIT	Federal Strategy Unit for Information Technology
FTP	File Transfer Protocol
FYI	for your information
GMT	Greenwich mean time
GPG	GNU Privacy Guard
GSS-API	generic security service API
GUI	graphical user interface
HTML	Hypertext Markup Language
HTTP	Hypertext Transfer Protocol
IAB	Internet Architecture Board
IANA	Internet Assigned Numbers Authority
IBM	International Business Machines Corporation
ICMP	Internet Control Message Protocol
IDEA	International Data Encryption Algorithm
IDS	interdomain service
IEAK	Internet Explorer administration kit
IEC	International Electrotechnical Committee
IEEE	Institute of Electrical and Electronic Engineers
IESG	Internet Engineering Steering Group
IETF	Internet Engineering Task Force
IGP	interior Gateway Protocol
IMAP	Internet Message Access Protocol
IP	Internet protocol
IPsec	IP security
IRSG	Internet Research Steering Group
IRTF	Internet Research Task Force
IS	international standard
ISO	International Organization for Standardization

ISOC Internet Society
ISP Internet service provider
IT information technology
ITSEC information technology security evaluation criteria
ITU-T International Telecommunication Union —
Telecommunication Standardization Sector
IV initialization vector

JTC1 Joint Technical Committee 1

kB kilobyte
kbps kilobit per second
KDC key distribution center
KDS key distribution server
KEA key exchange algorithm
KEK key encryption key
KTC key translation center

LAN local area network
LDAP Lightweight Directory Access Protocol
LF line feed
LLC logical link control
LRA local registration agent
local registration authority
LSB least significant bit

MAC message authentication code
MAN metropolitan area network
MD message digest
MDC modification detection code
MHS message handling system
MIB management information base
MIC message integrity check
MIME Multipurpose Internet Mail Extensions
MIT Massachusetts Institute of Technology
MLA mail list agent
MOSS MIME object security services
MSP Message Security Protocol

MTA	message transfer agent
MTS	message transfer system
NAI	Network Associates, Inc.
NAS	network access server
NIST	National Institute of Standards and Technology
NLSP	Network Layer Security Protocol
NMS	network management station
NNTP	Network News Transfer Protocol
NSA	National Security Agency
NSP	network security policy
NTP	Network Time Protocol
OCR	optical character recognition
OCSP	Online Certificate Status Protocol
OFB	output feedback
OID	object identifier
OpenPGP	open specification for PGP
OSI	open systems interconnection
PC	personal computer
PEM	privacy enhanced mail
PEP	Protocol Extension Protocol
PER	packet encoding rules
PGP	Pretty Good Privacy
PIN	personal identification number
PKCS	Public Key Cryptography Standard
PKI	public key infrastructure
PKIX	public key infrastructure X.509
POP	Post Office Protocol
	point of presence
PPP	Point-to-Point Protocol
PPPEXT	PPP extensions
PSE	personal security environment
RA	registration agent
	registration authority

RFC	Request for Comment
RSA	Rivest, Shamir, and Adleman
RTF	rich text format
SAML	send and mail
SCMS	Swisskey certificate management system
SDA	self-decrypting archive
SDK	software development kit
SDSI	simple distributed security infrastructure
SHA-1	secure hash algorithm 1
SHS	secure hash standard
SLIP	serial line IP
SMIME	S/MIME mail security
S/MIME	Secure MIME
SMS	service management system
SMT	Secure Messaging Toolkit
SMTP	Simple Mail Transfer Protocol
SNMP	Simple Network Management Protocol
SOML	send or mail
SPKAC	signed public key and challenge
SPKI	simple public key infrastructure
SSE	Secure Solutions Experts
SSL	Secure Sockets Layer
STD	Internet standard
TCB	trusted computing base
TCP	Transport Control Protocol
TCSEC	trusted computer system evaluation criteria
TFN	Tribe Flood Network
TIS	Trusted Information Systems
TLI	transport layer interface
TLS	Transport Layer Security
TLSP	Transport Layer Security Protocol
TNI	trusted network interpretation
TTL	time to live
TTP	trusted third party
UA	user agent

UC	University of California
UCS	Universal Character Set
UK	United Kingdom
URL	uniform resource locator
U.S.	United States
UTC	universal time coordinated
VPN	virtual private network
WAP	Wireless Application Protocol
WG	Working Group
WISP	Working Party on Information Security and Privacy
WWW	World Wide Web
W3C	World Wide Web Consortium
XML	Extensible Markup Language

About the Author

Rolf Oppliger (`http://www.ifi.unizh.ch/~oppliger`) received M.Sc. and Ph.D. degrees in computer science from the University of Berne, Switzerland, in 1991 and 1993, respectively. After spending one year as a postdoctoral researcher at the International Computer Science Institute (ICSI) in Berkeley, California, he joined the Swiss Federal Strategy Unit for Information Technology (FSUIT) in 1995, and continued his research and teaching activities at several universities and polytechnics in Switzerland and Germany. Early in 1999, he received the Venia legendi from the University of Zürich, Switzerland. He also became an Artech House series editor for computer security and founded eSECURITY Technologies Rolf Oppliger (`http://www.esecurity.ch`) to provide scientific and state of the art consulting, education, and engineering services related to information technology(IT) security. He has published numerous scientific papers, articles, and books, mainly on security-related topics. He's a member of the Swiss Informaticians Society (SI) and its Working Group on Security, the Association for Computing Machinery (ACM), and the IEEE Computer Society. He also serves as vice-chair of the International Federation for Information Processing (IFIP) Technical Committee 11 (TC11) Working Group 4 (WG4) on Network Security.

Index

Recent Titles in the Artech House Computing Library

Advanced ANSI SQL Data Modeling and Structure Processing, Michael M. David

Advanced Database Technology and Design, Mario Piattini and Oscar Díaz, editors

Business Process Implementation for IT Professionals and Managers, Robert B. Walford

Configuration Management: The Missing Link in Web Engineering, Susan Dart

Data Modeling and Design for Today's Architectures, Angelo Bobak

Electronic Payment Systems, Donal O'Mahony, Michael Peirce, and Hitesh Tewari

Future Codes: Essays in Advanced Computer Technology and the Law, Curtis E. A. Karnow

Global Distributed Applications With Windows® DNA, Enrique Madrona

A Guide to Software Configuration Management, Alexis Leon

Guide to Standards and Specifications for Designing Web Software, Stan Magee and Leonard L. Tripp

Information Hiding Techniques for Steganography and Digital Watermarking, Stefan Katzenbeisser and Fabien A. P. Petitcolas, editors

Internet Commerce Development, Craig Standing

Internet and Intranet Security, Rolf Oppliger

Managing Computer Networks: A Case-Based Reasoning Approach, Lundy Lewis

Metadata Management for Information Control and Business Success, Guy Tozer

Multimedia Database Management Systems, Guojun Lu

Practical Guide to Software Quality Management, John W. Horch

Practical Process Simulation Using Object-Oriented Techniques and C++, José Garrido

Secure Messaging with PGP and S/MIME, Rolf Oppliger

Security Fundamentals for E-Commerce, Vesna Hassler

Software Verification and Validation: A Practitioner's Guide, Steven R. Rakitin

Strategic Software Production With Domain-Oriented Reuse, Paolo Predonzani, Giancarlo Succi, and Tullio Vernazza

Systems Modeling for Business Process Improvement, David Bustard, Peter Kawalek, and Mark Norris, editors

User-Centered Information Design for Improved Software Usability, Pradeep Henry

For further information on these and other Artech House titles, including previously considered out-of-print books now available through our In-Print-Forever® (IPF®) program, contact:

Artech House
685 Canton Street
Norwood, MA 02062
Phone: 781-769-9750
Fax: 781-769-6334
e-mail: artech@artechhouse.com

Artech House
46 Gillingham Street
London SW1V 1AH UK
Phone: +44 (0)20 7596-8750
Fax: +44 (0)20 7630-0166
e-mail: artech-uk@artechhouse.com

Find us on the World Wide Web at:
www.artechhouse.com

Pathologies of Speech and Language: Advances in Clinical Phonetics and Linguistics

Pathologies of Speech and Language

Advances in Clinical Phonetics and Linguistics

Edited by

BEN MAASSEN and PAUL GROENEN
Medical Psychology/Child Neurology/ENT, University Hospital
Nijmegen, The Netherlands

Whurr Publishers Ltd
London

First published 1999 by
Whurr Publishers Ltd
19b Compton Terrace, London N1 2UN, England

Reprinted 2002 and 2003

British Library Cataloguing in Publication Data
A catalogue record for this book is available from the British Library.

ISBN: 1 86156 122 9

Contents

List of Contributors

H. Ackermann, Neurological Clinic, University of Tübingen, Germany

S. Awan, Department of Communication Disorders and Special Education, Bloomsburg University, USA

D. Axmann-Krcmar, Department of Prosthetic Dentistry, University of Tübingen, Germany

M. Bacher, Department of Orthodontics, University of Tübingen, Germany

R. Bastiaanse, Department of Linguistics, University of Groningen, The Netherlands

R. Berndt, Neurological Clinic, University of Tübingen, Germany

R. Berry, Speech Pathology and Audiology, Richard Stockton College of New Jersey, USA

S. Bharadwaj, Callier Center for Communication Disorders, University of Texas at Dallas, USA

V. Boucher, Audiology and Speech-Language Pathology Program, University of Ottawa, Canada

T. Bressman, Klinitum rechts der Isar, München, Germany

C. Bried, École d'Orthophonie, Faculté de Médecine et de Pharmacie, Université de Besançon, France

P. van den Broek, Department of Otorhinolaryngology, University Hospital Nijmegen, The Netherlands

K. Bryan, Department of Human Communication Science, University College London, UK

R. Burger, Utrecht Institute of Linguistics, Utrecht University, The Netherlands

D. Burton Koch, Department of Communication Sciences and Disorders, Northwestern University, USA

R. Catizone, Department of Computer Science, University of Sheffield, UK

C. Core, Linguistics Program, University Park Campus, Florida International University, USA
L. Crampin, Glasgow Dental Hospital, Glasgow, UK
T. Crul, Department of Otorhinolaryngology/Childrens' Audiology, University Hospital Nijmegen, The Netherlands
M. Daly, LDMM Corporation, Dallas, Texas, USA
R. Daniloff, Department of Speech and Hearing Sciences, University of North Texas, USA
S. Davis, Department of Linguistics, Indiana University, USA
D. Dinnsen, Department of Linguistics, Indiana University, USA
M. Elbert, Department of Speech and Hearing Sciences, Indiana University, USA
B. Elsendoorn, Institute for the Deaf, Sint-Michielsgestel, The Netherlands
T. Flowers, Department of Speech and Hearing Sciences, University of North Texas, USA
S. Frischmuth, Sektion Phoniatrie-Pädaudiologie der Universitäts-HNO-Klinik, Freiburg, Germany
L. Gagnon, Centre de Recherche, Institut Universitaire de Gériatrie de Montréal, Canada
H. Garratt, National Hospital for Neurology and Neurosurgery, London, UK
E. Gerrits, Utrecht Institute of Linguistics, Utrecht University, The Netherlands
F. Gibbon, Department of Speech and Language Sciences, Queen Margaret College, Edinburgh, UK
M. Gósy, Research Institute for Linguistics, Budapest, Hungary
P. Goulet, Centre de Recherche, Institut Universitaire de Gériatrie de Montréal, Canada
G. Göz, Department of Orthodontics, University of Tübingen, Germany
P. Groenen, Department of Otorhinolaryngology, University Hospital Nijmegen, The Netherlands
M. Hägg, Linguistics, University of Joensuu, Finland
W. Hardcastle, Department of Speech and Language Sciences, Queen Margaret College,Edinburgh, UK
L. Harvey, Dundee Royal Infirmary, Dundee, UK
M. Henoch, Department of Speech and Hearing Sciences, University of North Texas, USA
I. Hertrich, Department of Neurology, University of Tübingen, Germany.
B. Heselwood, School of Applied Social Sciences, Leeds Metropolitan University, UK
M. Holm, Pädaudiologische Sprachtherapeutin, Freiburg, Germany

H. Horch, Klinitum rechts der Isar, München, Germany
H. Horn, School of Dental Medicine, Eberhard-Karls-University of Tübingen, Germany
D. Huot, École d'orthophonie et d'audiologie, Université de Montréal, Canada
K. Huttunen, Department of Finnish, Saami and Logopedics, University of Oulu, Finland
Y. Joanette, Centre de Recherche, Institut Universitaire de Gériatrie de Montréal, Canada
A. Jochmann, Clinical Neuropsychology Research Group, City Hospital Bogenhausen, Munich, Germany
K. Kao, Department of Speech and Hearing Sciences, University of North Texas, USA
W. Katz, Callier Center for Communication Disorders, University of Texas at Dallas, USA
S. Kelly, Electronic Engineering Laboratory, University of Kent, UK
S. Kohn, Moss Rehabilitation Research Institute, Philadelphia, USA
P. Körkkö, Department of Finnish, Saami and Logopedics, University of Oulu, Finland
N. Kraus, Department of Communication Sciences and Disorders, Northwestern University, USA
B. LeBlanc, Centre de Recherche, Institut Universitaire de Gériatrie de Montréal, Canada
G. Le Dorze, École d'orthophonie et d'audiologie, Université de Montréal, Canada
W. Levelt, Max Planck Institute for Psycholinguistics, Nijmegen, The Netherlands
P. van Lieshout, ENT Clinic, Department of Speech and Voice Pathology, University Hospital Nijmegen and Nijmegen Institute for Cognition and Information (NICI), University of Nijmegen, The Netherlands
J. Luther, Department of Orthodontics, University of Tübingen, Germany
B. Maassen, Child Neurology Centre, University Hospital Nijmegen, The Netherlands
A. Main, Electronic Engineering Laboratory, University of Kent, UK
G. Manley, Canterbury and Thanet Community Healthcare Trust, UK
J. Maxim, Department of Human Communication Science, University College London, UK
T. McGee, Department of Communication Sciences and Disorders, Northwestern University, USA
M. Merk, Institute for Communication Engineering, Federal Armed Forces University, Munich, Germany

A. Meyer, Max Planck Institute for Psycholinguistics, Nijmegen, The Netherlands

V. Mildner, Department of Phonetics, University of Zagreb, Croatia

C. Miller, Department of Special Education, Murray State University, USA

I. Moen, Department of Linguistics, University of Oslo, Norway

M. Nairn, Department of Speech and Language Sciences, Queen Margaret College, Edinburgh, UK

K. Neijenhuis, Department of Otorhinolaryngology/Childrens' Audiology, University Hospital Nijmegen, The Netherlands

C. Newton, Department of Human Communication Science, University College London, UK

J. Niemi, Linguistics, University of Joensuu, Finland

I. Peers, Department of Human Communication Sciences, University of Sheffield, UK

W. Peeters, Utrecht Institute of Linguistics, Utrecht University, The Netherlands

M. Perkins, Department of Human Communication Sciences, University of Sheffield, UK

T. Powell, Department of Communication Disorders, Louisiana State University Medical Center, USA

R. Razzell, Royal Hospital for Sick Children, Edinburgh, UK

W. Renier, University Hospital Nijmegen, The Netherlands

B. Reynolds, Royal Aberdeen Children's Hosptial, Aberdeen, UK

N. Roussel, Department of Communication Disorders, University of Southwest Louisiana, USA

E.B Ruigendijk, Department of Linguistics, University of Groningen, The Netherlands

J. Ryalls, Department of Communicative Disorders, University of Central Florida, USA

R. Sader, Klinitum rechts der Isar, München, Germany

S. Scarpino, Susquehanna Health System, Williamsport, USA

N. Schiller, Max Planck Institute for Psycholinguistics, Nijmegen, The Netherlands

T. Scholl, Neurological Clinic, University of Tübingen, Germany

A. Simard, Centre de Recherche, Institut Universitaire de Gériatrie de Montréal, Canada

A. Snik, Department of Otorhinolaryngology, University Hospital Nijmegen, The Netherlands

M. Sorri, Centre for Wellness Technology and Department of Otolaryngology, University of Oulu, Finland

T. Spickler, Department of Special Education, Murray State University, USA

K. Sundet, Department of Psychosomatic and Behavioural Medicine, The National Hospital, Oslo, Norway

S. Terrell, Department of Speech and Hearing Sciences, University of North Texas, USA

I. Ueda, Department of Area Studies, Osaka University of Foreign Studies, Japan

W. Vieregge, Department of Language and Speech, University of Nijmegen, The Netherlands

S. Vinter, École d'Orthophonie, Faculté de Médecine et de Pharmacie, Université de Besançon, France

B. Wells, Department of Human Communication Science, University College London, UK

F. Wijnen, Utrecht Institute of Linguistics, Utrecht University, The Netherlands

Y. Wilks, Department of Computer Science, University of Sheffield, UK

M. Yavas, Linguistics Program, University Park Campus, Florida International University, USA

W. Ziegler, Clinical Neuropsychology Research Group, City Hospital Bogenhausen, Munich, Germany

A. Zierdt, Clinical Neuropsychology Research Group, City Hospital Bogenhausen, Munich, Germany

R. Van Zonneveld, Department of Linguistics, University of Groningen, The Netherlands

Preface

This volume contains recent advances in clinical phonetics and linguistics for the study, diagnosis and remediation of pathologies of speech and language.

The contents of this volume reflect the continued ICPLA-tradition to cover topics related to language, speech, aphasia, language development and measurement techniques, in both adults and children. In particular, contributions related to hearing impairment and central auditory processing disorders (including their consequences for speech production and speech development) were welcomed, to counterbalance a relative scarcity of papers in this field during previous ICPLA-conferences. We are very happy with the nine outstanding chapters collected in Part II.

The 44 chapters of this book are divided into four parts. In Part I: Phonology and Developmental Disorders, chapters include topics such as phonological representation in aphasia, perception in children with apraxic speech disorders, evaluation of language comprehension processes, syntax in children with specific language impairment, and stuttering as a phonological encoding defect. Part II deals with Hearing Impairment and Central Auditory Processing Disorders. The biology of speech sound perception and linguistic experience is one of the main chapters in this part. In addition, topics such as speech perception tests, electrophysiology as a means to assess speech perception processes, listener judgements of diphthongs by deaf speakers, and criteria for cochlear implantation are discussed. In Part III, chapters about aphasia and neurological conditions are presented. A major contribution concerns brain lateralization and the semantic processing of words. Moreover, research in subjects with agrammatic aphasia, Broca's aphasia, left and right brain damage, apraxia of speech, supranuclear palsy, and cerebellar dysarthria is presented. In the final part, Part IV, methods in clinical linguistics are discussed. How is the neurologist involved in diagnosis and therapy in speech pathology? Do IPA transcriptions of speech add to the diagnosis of speech problems? What is the role of computers in contemporary speech and voice analysis? How can new electromagnetic articulography help in solving theoretical issues in speech production? What are the technical novelties with regard to investigation and treatment of speech disorders associated with cleft palate? These are just a few questions that are addressed in this part.

The reader is presented with a huge variety of scientific and clinical topics. In our opinion, this variety reflects the strength and importance of the booming field of clinical linguistics and phonetics, a field that is characterized by an abundant diversity of different specialisms. Readers can only benefit from the multitude of approaches and themes. It offers the perfect opportunity to look beyond that which is already known and expected from within one's own specialism. Greater insights may well trade off in unexpected ideas and, as a consequence, increase expertise in the diagnosis and treatment of communication disorders.

The papers published in this volume were presented at the Sixth Annual Conference of the International Clinical Phonetics and Linguistics Association (ICPLA) in Nijmegen, psycholinguistically a big city in a small country, 13–15 October 1997

Ben Maassen
Paul Groenen

Acknowledgements

The conference that lies at the heart of this book was organized by the Department of Medical Psychology, the Interdisciplinary Child Neurology Centre and the Institute of Otorhinolaryngology of the University Hospital Nijmegen, in collaboration with the Interfaculty Research Unit for Language and Speech of the University of Nijmegen and the Department of Linguistics of the University of Groningen.

The conference and this volume could not have been realized without the help of several people. We would particularly like to thank Yvonne Flokstra and Jacob Wijnia for their executive assistance, and the people of the Max Planck Institute for Psycholinguistics for their hospitality and research demonstrations.

We are grateful for substantial grants from the Royal Netherlands Academy of Arts and Sciences (KNAW) and the Mgr J.C. van Overbeekstichting, and also very much appreciate the considerable contributions from the the Generale Bank, Veenhuis Medical Audio and Electro Medical Instruments.

Finally, we wish to thank all authors for their contributions to this volume.

PART I

Phonology and Developmental Disorders

Chapter 1
The Status of Phonological Representation in Fluent Aphasia

SUSAN E KOHN

Introduction

The term aphasia refers to any kind of language impairment in an adult that follows some kind of brain damage. Clinicians and researchers have various ways to categorize aphasic individuals. One major variable involves speech fluency. Patients can be described as primarily fluent or non-fluent. Fluent aphasics tend to speak in complete sentences and with no apparent articulatory difficulty. However, their speech is not always phonologically accurate. This paper focuses on phonological breakdown in the speech output of English-speaking adults who have developed a fluent aphasia following a cerebral vascular accident to the posterior portion of their left hemisphere. Findings of several studies are presented both to provide more information about the phonological output deficits of fluent aphasics, and to argue for the role of formal phonological theory in framing this programme of investigation. The information is presented in an order that reflects some of the basic steps I took in developing the model of lexical-phonological production that currently guides my research. Retracing these steps provides a means for motivating some of the major decisions made along the way.

Developing a model of lexical-phonological breakdown

Before we begin to systematically examine properties of the phonological speech errors of fluent aphasics, let us look at the kinds of errors they produce. In the extreme, the errors can look like the following: /pɛpɚmekə/, /mɛkədɑIvɚz/, /vʌrdəbɛn/, /kɛlʃʌræ/. These errors were produced by four different English-speaking fluent aphasic subjects, trying to name a picture of an elephant. These extreme errors of phonological distortion are often referred to as *neologisms*. Phonological errors can be less extreme, where the targets are recognizable. Here again are some examples drawn from a corpus of picture-naming errors: elephant> /mɛlopæ t/, kite > /krɑIt/, accordion > /əgordlufIn/, pumpkin > /krʌŋkən/. These errors are typically called *phonemic paraphasias*.

The phonological errors produced by fluent aphasics are articulated with ease, or with no real hint of an articulatory struggle, and hence these errors have been associated with phonological breakdown at an abstract level – at a level of accessing and/or processing a stored lexical-phonological representation for output. I have spent much of my research career attempting to verify this clinically-based notion, and to try to understand what it means to have such a deficit in terms of a model of cognitive processing.

The first step in exploring the nature of the phonological deficits in fluent aphasia is to adopt a model of lexical-phonological processing. In this way, clear hypotheses can be generated that are based on an independent framework. As a way to motivate the theoretical framework that I have gradually adopted, more specifically, to motivate the incorporation of formal phonological theory into processing models, let us consider the state of the aphasia research world in the early 1980s, when I began this endeavour. It helps to understand how studies involving aphasic subjects were conducted at that time, and to see what kinds of models of cognitive processing were available. Note that I was coming to this field as an experimental neuropsychologist.

First of all, researchers were almost exclusively conducting group studies back in the early 1980s, and grouping their subjects by clinical diagnostic categories. The relevant classifications for the current discussion are *conduction* and *Wernicke's* aphasia. These terms refer to different types of fluent aphasia. Patients with either classification produce well-articulated speech that can contain errors like the ones shown above. A diagnosis of Wernicke's versus conduction aphasia often hinges on the status of the patient's auditory comprehension. The practice is to assign a diagnosis of Wernicke's aphasia when there is impairment in this domain.

In the research conducted in the 1980s, there was some clinical intuition that conduction and Wernicke's aphasics are not similar in terms of the source of their phonological output errors. However, possible varieties of phonological output deficits amongst these aphasic speakers were obscured by a number of practices. First, there was (and still is) the practice of reclassifying a Wernicke's aphasic as a conduction aphasic if his or her auditory comprehension deficit resolves sufficiently. This has made group studies comparing Wernicke's and conduction aphasics difficult to interpret. In addition, the presence of a semantic deficit in Wernicke's aphasics was argued to be responsible for making their output more distorted phonologically (e.g. Burns and Canter,

1977) so that neologisms produced by Wernicke's aphasics were said to reflect a combination of semantic and phonological problems. In this way, differences between conduction and Wernicke's aphasics in terms of the nature of their phonological output errors need not be attributed to differences in their phonological deficits. Consequently, while in the 1980s there may have been some clinical intuition that there were varieties of abstract phonological deficits among fluent aphasics, there was little experimental support.

The kind of cognitive model of lexical processing that was popular in neuropsychological research at this time involved a series of boxes and arrows, in which different types of lexical information were divided into different modules (e.g. Howard and Franklin, 1988; Kohn, 1989). The relevant boxes for the current discussion are the *phonological output lexicon* and the *phonological output buffer*. These models specified little if any detail about the nature of lexical representations. To the extent that a model of this type did specify some aspects of the entries stored in the phonological output lexicon, these representations were said to involve a string of phonemes, or segments. These phoneme strings were accessed and held passively in the output buffer while they were being programmed into some kind of articulatory form. This general approach to lexical-phonological processing was echoed in the normal literature at that time, and that had evolved from the study of normal slips-of-the-tongue (e.g. Shattuck-Hufnagel, 1979). On the basis of the normal slips-of-the-tongue, such as reversing the initial consonants of words (red book > bed rook), the role of the phonological output buffer was considered to be less passive: while words were purportedly stored as ordered sets of segments in the phonological output lexicon, it was argued that these strings of segments were reordered at the time of production into awaiting syllabic slots. This counterintuitive move, rearranging already ordered segments for production, was made to account for normal speech errors in which the initial consonants of words are exchanged or erroneously copied (Kohn and Smith, 1990).

This type of model suggests two basic types of abstract phonological deficits: impaired access to stored phonological representations, and impaired phonemic planning of those representations (Kohn, 1989; Kohn and Smith, 1994, 1995). My early work focused largely on attempting to distinguish these two basic types of deficits in aphasic behaviour. I used the above type of model to generate a set of contrasting features expected with breakdown at each level, and examined different fluent aphasics to test for these sets of contrasting features.

Identifying two levels of phonological breakdown

In order to illustrate the types of variables I used to assess the deficits responsible for phonological errors in the speech of different fluent aphasics, let us consider the full set of responses produced by two fluent aphasics while trying to name a picture of *dominoes* (Kohn and Smith, 1994). Before doing so, however, note that these aphasic speakers had much in common. They produced phonological errors in their speech, which was, nevertheless, well articulated. Both had suffered left-sided temporoparietal neurological damage. They were both tested around the same time following their stroke (i.e. between seven and eight months). Finally, they achieved similar scores on various single word production tests, indicating similar levels of word production difficulty. Nevertheless, while both aphasics produced many phonological attempts in the course of trying to correctly name the picture of dominoes, a careful examination of the full set of their naming attempts suggests that they are suffering different types of phonological impairment.

Consider, first, CM's performance, noting that the responses ending in dashes were produced in a manner suggesting false starts:

> CM: /dɑmIk, dɑmIk, dɑn-, dɑn-nʌ-nIk/, [comment], /dʌ-, dʌ-, don-, domə-, dom-ɛ-nik/, a /dʌ-/... oh, /dɑm-, dɑm-, dɑmInik/.

There is a term for such a series of successive approximations – *conduite d'approche* (Kohn, 1984). If we consider his set of responses as a whole, CM seems to have recovered a great deal of phonological information about the target. In several of his responses, he produced the correct number of syllables and the correct alternating pattern of consonants and vowels. However, he appears to have difficulty organizing phonemic-level information, particularly for the final syllable.

This contrasts with LW's attempt to name the same picture. The differences, shown below, are all the more striking insofar as the two aphasic speakers achieved almost identical scores on the picture naming test from which these data were drawn: LW 20/30, CM 21/30. LW's full set of attempts to name the picture of dominoes is as follows:

> LW: /fImәlaʊ/, [untranscribable neologism, comment], /fIlә/, a /fIlәbʌmθ/, playing the, um, /dɑmәli, dɑmlәfɛloz, dɑm-, dɑmәfɛloz/, play, play /bɑm-/, play /bɑr-/, playin' /bɑfIns/.

In contrast to CM, LW seems unclear about the basic syllabic structure of the target, and is more uncertain about the target phonemes. While LW's initial attempt basically preserves the CV (consonant-vowel) structure of the target, she persists in repeating the incorrect segments in her subsequent responses. When she finally produces the first syllable accurately, she incorporates extraneous material (/dɑmәfɛloz/), and, in fact, her last attempt shows far less resemblance to the target, perhaps because of interference from another lexical entry ('ball').

So one might suspect that LW's word production system is breaking down at the level of accessing stored phonological representations. CM, on the other hand, produces attempts that are consistently close to the target. His fragments and exaggerated syllable breaks indicate an attempt to focus on particular segments. So one might suspect that CM's primary source of error is due to a subsequent level of breakdown where stored phonological representations are being segmentally encoded.

Serial order and segmental errors in the two phonological output deficits

The above examples provide an impression of the behavioural differences that might signal breakdown at the level of lexical-phonological access versus segmental planning. Let us now turn to results of one experimental study that tried to systematically explore the differences between these two levels of phonological breakdown (Kohn and Smith, 1995). The purpose of this study was to test a variable that was hypothesized to be able to further discriminate between these two types of patients: the distribution of segmental errors across individual responses.

It was at this point in my research that I began to question the concept of phonemic planning as a stage where a stored string of phonemes is purportedly reordered for output. I started to consider the idea that the role of phonemic planning may be to complete a stored, underspecified representation. Phonological theory provided a framework for making such a change to the production model. The concept of *underspecification* has been developed in linguistics to capture properties of the most basic phonological description of a word (Paradis and Prunet, 1991). Put simply, it refers to the notion that the information stored in a lexical-phonological representation is arbitrary and non-redundant, and that predictable information is filled in subsequently by rules (see below).

In the study presented below, this general proposal was used to make some predictions about expected patterns of consonant errors in aphasic speakers with breakdown at the level of lexical-phonological access versus phonemic planning. It was speculated that the phonemic planning process involved in fully specifying a phonological representation might occur in a linear fashion, from the beginning to the end of a word, while it was not clear that the accessing of the underlying stored form should have any particular directionality. This suggested the following pair of hypotheses concerning the distribution of consonant errors within incorrect word production responses: impairment at the level of lexical-phonological access should be associated with a random distribution of segmental errors across a response, while a phonemic planning problem should be associated with an increase in errors from left to right.

To test these predictions, we (Kohn and Smith, 1995) examined the performance of three subjects with 'impaired lexical-phonological access' and three subjects with 'impaired phonemic planning'. They had been experimentally 'diagnosed' on the basis of a set of features that had been tested in previous studies (e.g. Kohn and Smith, 1994). They were asked to name a set of pictured objects and read aloud a set of nouns. The analyses focused on their non-word errors (i.e. phonemic paraphasias and neologisms) with the correct number of syllables, involving multisyllabic targets, as in the following examples: balloon > /bərun/, umbrella > /ɛmbɛlow/, faucet > /fɔsIst/, guitar > /kədɑnk/, dominoes > /fIləbʌmθ/. We calculated the distribution of segmental errors across the syllables of the responses, considering phoneme substitution, omission, and addition to an existing syllabic constituent. So, in the response to *balloon*, above, there is a consonant substitution at the end of the second syllable. The response to *faucet* contains a consonant added towards the end of the second syllable. The response to *guitar* is more distorted. There is one error in the first syllable, and three in syllable two.

The results for the pattern of consonant errors across the paraphasic attempts of each deficit group are presented in Figure 1.1. In summary, the two expected patterns emerged and were associated with the expected deficit group. The distribution of errors for the three subjects with impaired lexical-phonological access, displayed on top, form essentially a straight line. Thus, no position effects emerged in terms of the locus of their consonant errors, a pattern expected if the segmental errors are randomly distributed. By contrast, the distribution of errors for the three subjects with impaired phonemic planning displays a pattern of increasing number of errors by syllable from left to right. We had expected this pattern with a deficit in completing the phonological representation.

Further specifying the phonological output deficits

More generally, the above results supported the notion that phonological processing during word production is divided into two basic stages, lexical-phonological access and phonemic planning, and that some fluent aphasics suffer breakdown primarily at one stage and other fluent aphasics suffer breakdown primarily at the other stage. At this point, my research efforts turned towards examining these deficits with more detailed notions as to how these stages of processing are structured and operate. This shifted my orientation from focusing on distinctions between these two levels of phonological breakdown to examining how aspects of current phonological theory can inform our understanding of properties of fluent aphasic speech errors, regardless of the particular point in the phonological process at which the responsible deficit arises.

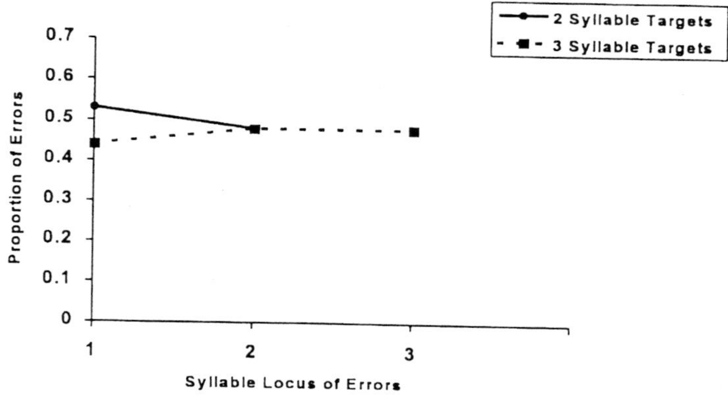

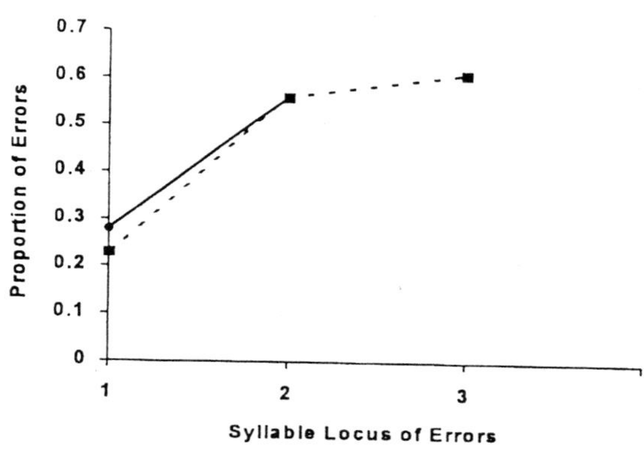

Figure 1.1. The locus of consonant errors within the non-word picture naming and oral reading errors of six fluent aphasics (three in each deficit group).

By way of illustration, findings from two studies will be discussed that represent our first pass efforts at exploring two areas of phonological theory: consonant harmony (Kohn et al., 1995), and feature geometry (Kohn et al., 1998). In order to motivate and then describe our study involving consonant harmony (Kohn et al., 1995), we need to discuss further the concept of ***underspecification***. Recall that underspecification refers to the notion that underlying phonological representations are underspecified for certain information, such as features of phonemes. There are different versions of underspecification theory (UST) in the formal phonological literature. For our study involving consonant harmony effects in fluent aphasic speakers, we adopted a universal markedness version of UST. Universal markedness refers to the notion that across languages, the different values of a feature, such as [+voice] versus [-voice] (/b/ versus /p/), have different statuses in the phonological system (Chomsky and Halle, 1968; Kean, 1975). For each feature class, one value is designated as unmarked, and the other value, or values, is designated as marked, on the basis of such empirical information as distributional patterns of features across languages and their articulatory-phonetic characteristics. The values we considered for our study to be unmarked and marked according to a universal markedness version of UST are presented below:

	Unmarked	*Marked*
Place:	[+ant, +coronal]	[+velar], [+labial]
Voice:	[-voice]	[+voice]
Manner:	[-continuant]	[+continuant]

Notice that /t/ is comprised entirely of unmarked feature values. According to a universal markedness version of UST, marked values are specified underlying, while unmarked values are not specified at the most basic level of phonological description, because they represent default values.

Phonological representations can become fully specified through two basic types of processes: (1) harmony (or assimilation) rules, which copy marked features, or those features specified in the lexicon; and (2) default rules, which add unmarked features. At the lexical-phonological level, harmony involves feature copying within a restricted domain – the domain being adjacent consonants, and is triggered by the process of affixation (i.e. the adding of prefixes and suffixes). English has a rule of voice harmony, determining the phonological variants of several common inflectional suffixes. The suffixes for plural, present tense, and past tense conform to the voicing value of the last consonant of the root morpheme (e.g. seed+/z/ versus book+/s/). This is really the only productive context for harmony in English.

The status of consonant harmony in fluent aphasic speech

We wanted to examine whether a rule based on consonant harmony processes could be responsible for a subset of the segmental errors produced by fluent aphasics. This research would serve two basic purposes: (1) test the validity of a processing model based on underspecification theory; and (2) explore how fluent aphasics produce speech based on faulty lexical-phonological information.

It has often been observed that the phonological errors produced by fluent aphasics generally conform to the phonotactic constraints of the speaker's language. This observation suggests that, while production may be based on faulty information about stored lexical representations, the rules of the phonological system in these patients may be relatively preserved, and these rules may be used, in part, to compensate for missing lexical information. So the general hypothesis we were testing was the following: are particular rule-governed processes that constitute part of the normal phonological system relied on as a compensatory mechanism for completing a deficient phonological representation? Specifically, we wanted to know if consonant harmony was one of those compensatory rules.

To test the status of consonant harmony in English among fluent aphasic speech errors, we asked eight English-speaking fluent aphasics to name a set of pictured objects (Kohn et al., 1995). Analysis focused on their phonemic paraphasias. For example, in one attempt to name a picture of a *vest*, the initial consonant was devoiced: /fɛst/. In a response to *igloo*, place of articulation was substituted for the first consonant: /Idlu/. To systematically identify the responses with clear phonological overlap with the target, we employed a set of criteria that have been used in a number of studies (e.g. Kohn, 1989; Kohn and Smith, 1994, 1995). The responses had to minimally match the target for a stressed vowel, consonant cluster, or complete onset and coda of a particular syllable. Across their phonemic paraphasias (n = 543) we identified 143 consonant substitutions that differed by only one feature from the intended target.

Consonant substitutions were analysed to determine whether the pattern of *feature* substitutions matched predictions based on consonant harmony, as follows. (1) If a feature substitution involves a marked value, the feature should match that of a consecutive target consonant, or the next consonant in either direction. (2) If a feature substitution involves an unmarked value, the feature should randomly match another target consonant. The first prediction reflects our working definition of harmony. We extended the environment of feature copying to allow an intervening vowel. This move enlarged our data set, and seemed justified for an initial study on harmony for theoretical reasons. The distinction between consecutive consonants and those separated by a vowel disappears if we adopt the three-dimensional representation of Autosegmental Phonology (Goldsmith, 1979), as does virtually all work on underspecification, and assume further that features for consonants and vowels are assigned to separate tiers (McCarthy, 1979). In addition, examples of consonant harmony errors produced by young children seem to occur in simple CVCs (Stemberger and Stoel-Gammon, 1991; Stoel-Gammon and Stemberger, 1994). The second prediction, above, follows from the argument that unmarked features are added via default rules (see above). Because default rules are not contextually constrained, an unmarked feature substitution *could* match the feature of another target segment, but only by chance.

Finally, it should be noted that our stimuli were monomorphemic. As illustrated by the above description of voice harmony in English, consonant harmony does not apply to words consisting of simple root morphemes. Rather, it is triggered by affixation of a derivational or inflectional morpheme. In this study, subjects were asked to name pictures associated with monomorphemic words. Thus, we also relaxed the domain in which this phonological rule applies. This modification, as well as the one related to the potential segmental environment in which harmony applies, seemed reasonable, when we consider that we were investigating whether a common phonological rule can serve as the basis for a compensatory device for dealing with missing featural information.

First we determined how often different features were substituted. *Manner* was rarely substituted in isolation, so these errors were not considered for further analysis. Analyses focused on the substitutions involving *voice* and *place of articulation* that matched a feature value found anywhere else in the target word (calendar>/gæləvIn/, igloo> /Idlu). These *within-target* errors represent the broadest set of feature substitutions that should be considered for possible harmony effects, since they can broadly be described as involving feature copying, though not necessarily under the constraints of a universal markedness version of underspecification theory.

For these feature errors, we determined: (1) if the substituted feature involved a marked value, and (2) if the substituted feature matched a consecutive target consonant. If the answer to both questions was yes, the error conformed to our definition of harmony. Thus, there were four categories of errors, depending on whether the feature change was marked versus unmarked, and matched a consecutive versus nonconsecutive target consonant. Data for the voice errors were entirely consistent with our predictions. All marked voicing errors involved copying between consecutive consonants. By contrast, marked *place* errors were as likely to match the feature of a consecutive as a nonconsecutive consonant, suggesting no clear contextual influences ($\chi^2 = 0.185$, df = 1, $p = 0.68$). Also consistent with our predictions, the data for the unmarked substitutions for both voice and place did not differ significantly from chance in terms of matching the value of a consecutive consonant.

We acknowledge that this study must be followed up to explore inherent differences between voice and place of articulation that could have contributed to the results. Nevertheless, the fact that only the voicing errors appeared to be constrained by consonant harmony makes sense, given that our aphasics were English-speaking, and that the only productive harmony rule in English involves voice, as stated earlier. If these English-speaking aphasics are adapting phonological rules of their language to compensate for missing lexical-phonological information, they may only have access to a harmony rule involving the feature *voice*.

This picture can be reconciled with the reports of harmony errors involving place and manner features during language acquisition (Stemberger and Stoel-Gammon, 1991; Stoel-Gammon and Stemberger, 1994). It may be the case that these developmental errors reflect difficulty at a more articulatory level, while we are hypothesizing breakdown at an abstract phonological level in fluent aphasics. One would then predict to find evidence of place and manner harmony in non-fluent aphasics who display evidence of a phonetic-articulatory disturbance. At a more general level, our findings encourage us to adopt the notion of underspecification when building models of lexical-phonological processing, especially in the context of exploring the source of phonological breakdown in fluent aphasia.

The role of feature geometry in accounting for fluent aphasic speech errors

The final study to be discussed examines another dimension of the feature substitution errors produced by fluent aphasics, by exploring another aspect of formal phonological theory – feature geometry. Feature geometry refers to the general relationship amongst different features, namely that they are organized hierarchically, reflecting natural groupings according to articulatory and acoustic properties (e.g. Paradis and Prunet, 1991). The exact ordering of features within such a hierarchy is still under scrutiny, but it is generally accepted that the feature *sonorant* sits at the top, dividing all consonants into two categories: [+sonorants] (e.g. /m/, /n/) and [-sonorants] (e.g. /b/, /s/). [+Sonorant] segments have a resonant acoustic quality, and are produced with a vocal tract configuration that permits a degree of airflow that is sufficiently unimpeded to allow for, what has been called, 'spontaneous voicing' (Kenstowicz, 1994). The status of the feature sonorant as a *major class* feature is based on the fact that it rarely functions independently in assimilation, or copying, processes (like harmony), in contrast to lower level features – such as place and voice – and plays an important role at the syllable level, determining how strings of segments are organized into syllables (Kohn et al., 1998).

In accordance with the status of the feature sonorant in the feature hierarchy, we hypothesized that this feature should be substituted the least often and rarely in isolation in the phonologically distorted speech of fluent aphasics. To test this prediction, we examined the single word repetition of two fluent aphasics. Results were based on a total of 123 feature substitution errors, involving consonant substitutions in which one or more features could have changed (e.g. rebels > /dəbɛls/, gem > /dʒɛn/). We tabulated the proportion of consonant substitutions involving the features sonorant, voice, continuant and place, separately for the two fluent aphasics. As displayed in Figure 1.2, the results for the two subjects are remarkably similar. For both subjects, sonorant errors were rare – only 13 over all, and in all but one case, the sonorant substitution occurred without involving a change in value of another feature of the affected consonant (boot > /mut/; note that in our analysis system we ignored the privitive feature nasal). Because of the strong constraints that sonority places on the possible arrangements of consonants within onsets and codas (Clements, 1988), it is important to note that a majority of their consonant substitution errors were located in syllabic positions where the sonorant value could vary freely: simple onset, codas, and medial clusters (AB = 0.87, RD = 0.86). Thus the rarity of sonorant substitution errors was not due to a limited potential for such errors. Place of articulation figured quite differently in the error data. Not only were there many more place errors, but unlike the sonorant substitutions, most occurred in isolation, or without changes to the value of other features of the affected consonant (0.88 for AB and 0.77 for RD).

These results lend some preliminary support to the notion that a feature's status within a model of feature geometry is one variable that helps us understand that feature's susceptibility to error in the context of impaired lexical-phonological processing. As with the data presented on consonant harmony, we have findings that are consistent with our predictions, but which require further study to determine if the data are reliable, and to explore certain aspects in more detail (e.g. why sonorant substitutions rarely occur in isolation).

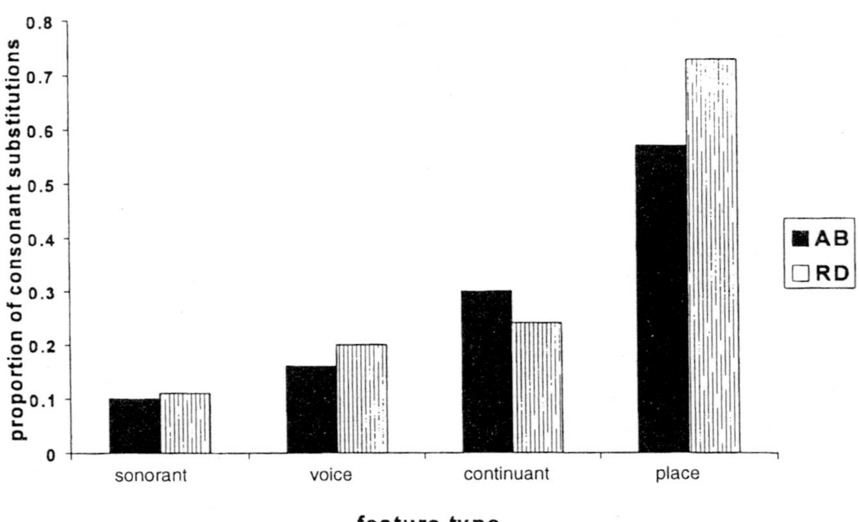

Figure 1.2. The distribution of feature substitution errors according to feature type in the single word repetition errors of two fluent aphasics (AB and RD).

Conclusions

In conclusion, by incorporating aspects of formal phonological theory, we can build a more detailed picture of the phonological deficits associated with fluent aphasics. I have tried to argue that a greater understanding can be gained by considering basic lexical-phonological processing to encompass two basic stages:

1. Lexical-phonological access, which involves the accessing of an underspecified entry from the phonological lexicon.
2. Phonemic planning, which involves the application of rules to fully specify the representation.

I have tried to argue, further, that the phonological speech errors produced by fluent aphasics result from breakdown somewhere in the process of accessing an underspecified lexical-phonological representation and completing it in preparation for phonetic-articulatory encoding. While I have been working within a representational framework, staying close to the form provided by theoretical linguistics, the kinds of information and rules being examined can be ultimately accommodated by the kinds of network models that researchers are constructing for work that focuses on error simulation.

Summary

A common feature of fluent aphasia is the production of phonological errors in speech. These errors are typically well-articulated and conform to the phonotactic constraints of the speaker's language. Accordingly, it has been argued that the phonological speech errors of fluent aphasics are based on faulty information about lexical-phonological representations, in the face of preserved rules of the phonological system. Nevertheless, little research has been conducted in the context of a sufficiently detailed language processing model to confirm and fully explain the nature of phonological breakdown in fluent aphasic speech. The purpose of this paper was twofold. Findings from several studies were presented both to provide more information about the phonological output deficits of fluent aphasics, and to argue for the role of formal phonological theory in framing this programme of investigation.

In the early 1980s, research in aphasic word production was generally guided by box-and-arrow models, with some influence from models based on normal slips-of-the-tongue. My early research used this kind of model to draw a distinction between fluent aphasics with deficits primarily at the level of accessing stored lexical-phonological representations versus phonemically planning these representations for production. By way of illustration, a study examining the distribution of consonant substitutions across the picture-naming errors of fluent aphasic speakers was presented to argue that each level of breakdown is associated with a distinct error pattern (Kohn and Smith, 1995).

The goal of my more recent work has been to flesh out these abstract phonological output deficits, by turning to formal phonological theory as an independent means for generating specific research questions. Results of two studies were presented to illustrate this approach. On the basis of consonant substitution data, we discussed how consonant harmony, a common rule-governed process of feature copying, may operate as a compensatory device for completing phonological representations in fluent aphasia (Kohn et al., 1995). Finally, the role of feature geometry was considered as a variable in determining the relative susceptibility of different segmental features to error (Kohn et al., 1998). The general conclusion drawn from these studies is that we can build a more detailed picture of the phonological deficits associated with fluent aphasics by incorporating aspects of formal phonological theory into our processing models.

Acknowledgements

This work was supported, in part, by research grant 1 RO1 DC 02517 from the National Institute on Deafness and Other Communication Disorders, National Institutes of Health. It should be noted that the studies reported involve highly collaborative efforts with my co-authors, in particular, Katherine Smith and Janis Melvold.

References

Burns MS, Canter GJ (1977) Phonemic behavior of aphasic patients with posterior cerebral lesions. Brain and Language, 4, 492–507.

Chomsky N, Halle M (1968) The Sound Pattern of English. New York: Harper and Row.

Clements GN (1988) The role of the sonority cycle in core syllabification. Working Papers of the Cornell Phonetics Laboratory, No. 2. Ithaca, NY.

Goldsmith J (1979) Autosegmental Phonology. New York: Garland.

Howard D, Franklin S (1988) Missing the Meaning? A Cognitive Neuropsychological Study of Processing of Words by an Aphasic Patient. Cambridge, MA: MIT Press.

Kean M-L (1975) The theory of markedness in generative grammar. PhD dissertation, MIT, Cambridge, MA.

Kenstowicz M (1994) Phonology in Generative Grammar. Cambridge, MA: Blackwell.

Kohn SE (1984) The nature of the phonological disorder in conduction aphasia. Brain and Language, 23, 97–115.

Kohn SE (1989) The nature of the phonemic string deficit in conduction aphasia. Aphasiology, 3, 209–39.

Kohn SE, Melvold J, Shipper V (1998) The preservation of sonority in the context of impaired lexical-phonological output. Aphasiology, 12, 375–98.

Kohn SE, Melvold J, Smith KL (1995) Consonant harmony as a compensatory mechanism in fluent aphasic speech. Cortex, 31, 747–56.

Kohn SE, Smith KL (1990) Between-word speech errors in conduction aphasia. Cognitive Neuropsychology, 7, 133–56.

Kohn SE, Smith KL (1994) Distinctions between two phonological output deficits. Applied Psycholinguistics, 15, 75–95.

Kohn SE, Smith KL (1995) Serial effects of phonemic planning during word production. Aphasiology, 9, 209–22.

McCarthy JJ (1979) Theoretical issues in semitic phonology and morphology. PhD dissertation, MIT, Cambridge, MA.

Paradis C, Prunet J-F (eds) (1991) Phonetics and Phonology. Vol. 2. The Special Status of Coronals: Internal and External Evidence. NY: Academy Press.

Shattuck-Hufnagel S (1979) Speech errors as evidence for a serial-ordering mechanism in sentence production. In Cooper WE, Walker ECT (eds) Sentence Processing: Psycholinguistic Studies Presented to Merrill Garrett. Hillsdale, NJ: Erlbaum.

Stemberger JP, Stoel-Gammon C (1991) The underspecification of coronals: Evidence from language acquisition and performance errors. In Paradis C, Prunet J-F (eds) Phonetics and Phonology, Volume 2. The Special Status of Coronals: Internal and External Evidence. NY: Academic Press.

Stoel-Gammon C, Stemberger JP (1994) Consonant harmony and phonological underspecification in child speech. In Yavas M (ed.), First and Second Language Phonology. San Diego, CA: Singular Publishing Group.

Chapter 2 Sonority, Glottals and the Characterization of [Sonorant]

BARRY HESELWOOD

Introduction

Like the syllable, everyone knows what sonority is but, as Christman (1992) points out, nobody has offered a fully satisfactory definition. Whatever definition might in due course emerge needs to take account not only of the common occurrences of sonority but also of less common ones.

An example of an uncommon kind of sonority is the substitution by some deaf speakers of nasals by voiced implosives, which in phonetic theory would normally be classed as obstruents. As discussed more fully in Heselwood (1998b) the salient part of a voiced nasal consonant is the hold phase, the time during which the articulators are in contact, when there is a complete closure in the mouth and a periodic pressure wave is created. In general, the salient part of an oral stop is the release phase, the time when the pressure difference in the vocal tract is equalized and a transient pressure wave is created. Voicing during the hold phase of a plosive, for example, typically decreases in amplitude as a function of time due to the progressive reduction in the transglottal pressure differential. With a voiced implosive, however, the extensive descent of the larynx retards or even reverses the reduction in the pressure differential and there is 'either a gradual increase in the amplitude of the voicing . . . or, in other cases, a level, fairly large amplitude' (Lindau, 1984); this difference is evident in the tokens produced by the present author in Figure 2.1 where they are compared to the waveform of a nasal). If, therefore, we focus on the acoustics of the hold phase of a voiced implosive we can explain its use as a substitute for a nasal – the voicing resembles the nasal murmur, and there is also presence of damped higher formants. The substitution thus combines the target's sonority and its articulatory closure and can be said to have much the same phonetic content as the target. In terms of the classification put forward in Heselwood (1998a), it is an example of structural deviance.[1] In this case any audible release of the voiced implosive is merely redundant phonetic 'noise'.

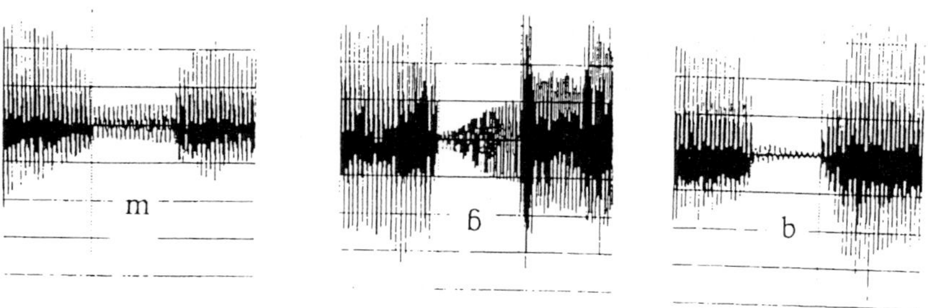

Figure 2.1. Waveforms of [ɑmɑ] [ɑɓɑ] and [ɑbɑ] as spoken by the author. Note the similarity in amplitude between the first two compared with the third.

Glottals

This section considers certain properties of glottal stops and how they might relate to the notion of sonority in order to begin to explain some occurrences of these stops in contexts where they would not perhaps be expected.[2]

Table 2.1 contains examples of words collected from an English-speaking girl of 4;08 during a phonological assessment. For this speaker there appears to be a constraint on the content of the second mora of a syllable such that only a vowel, nasal, lateral or a glottal stop can occupy it; the glottal stop occurs in place of all obstruent targets.

Table 2.1. Sample of words produced by a girl of 4;08 showing that only sonorants and glottal stop occur in the second mora of the syllable

Target	Realization	Target	Realization
sun	sʊn	pig	pɪʔ
hill	hɪl	wash	wɒʔ
lamb	lam	tap	taʔ
sea	siː (sii)	shed	ʃɛʔ
cow	kaʊ	grass	gɹaʔ

Not all authors have agreed with Chomsky and Halle's (1968) classification of glottal stop as a sonorant and the arguments against it as given, for example, by Ladefoged (1971) have to be taken seriously.

Nevertheless, many phonologists seem happy enough with it (e.g. Stemberger, 1993) and if we can find a plausible phonetic basis for including it in the sonorant class then the data in Table 2.1 become much easier to explain, i.e. the constraint is that only a sonorant may occur in the second mora. That is to say, there is no sudden downward deflection of the sonority slope of the kind found with obstruent consonants in that position. Of course this explanation only works if a glottal stop is a very different kind of phonetic object than stops at other places of articulation.

Glottal stop versus supralaryngeal plosives

Stemberger (1993) has claimed that 'glottals are not specified for place of articulation features' and that this is a phonological matter, nothing to do with their phonetics. However, there are a number of suggestive phonetic differences between glottal stops and supralaryngeal stops which are worth considering.

Formant transitions

In the acoustic signal of a vowel+supralaryngeal plosive there are formant transitions that begin about 60 or 70 ms before the articulatory closure. As is well known, the particular pattern of positive and negative transitions is an important perceptual cue to the place of articulation of the plosive, so for example in the sequence [ɑk] the speech perception system of a listener is being primed for recognition of a [k] during that 60–70 ms period (see Figure 2.2). In the case of a vowel+glottal stop there are, by contrast, no formant transitions and thus no priming of the listener's perception prior to the glottal occlusion: it arrives unannounced except perhaps for a pulse or two of creak. In light of this it might be better to think of the difference between e.g. [ɑ] and [ɑʔ] as a difference between, respectively, a gradual and an abrupt transition to silence, a slow and a rapid decay time. That is to say, the glottal stop does not disturb the sonority level of the preceding vowel any more than would the silence of a pause, and would account for the distribution of the glottal stop in Table 2.1.

Release burst

Another important perceptual cue to the place of articulation of a supralaryngeal plosive is the spectrum of the release burst (Blumstein and Stevens, 1979). Even where the plosive has a voice onset time (VOT) value of 0 ms the burst spectrum is sufficiently dissimilar to the spectrum of a glottal pulse to stand out perceptually. This is not the case with the release spectrum of a glottal stop, which is very similar to that of a single pulse of voicing. It may make better sense with some data to regard a prevocalic glottal stop as an abrupt onset in contrast to a gradual onset without a glottal stop, i.e. rapid and slow amplitude rise times.

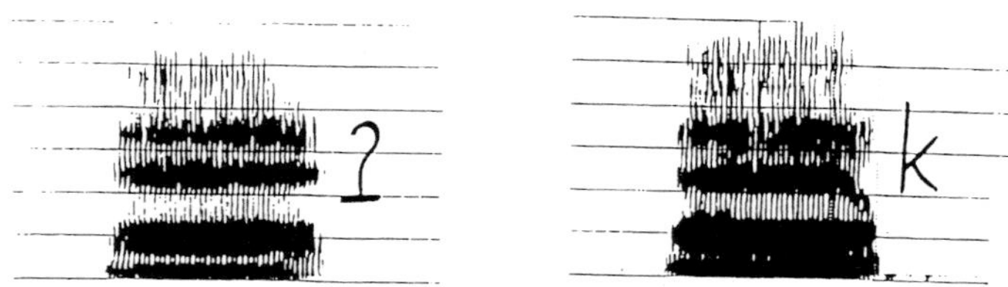

Figure 2.2. Spectrograms of [ɑʔ] and [ɑk]. Information as to the place of articulation of the stop begins to be available c.65 ms before closure in the latter, but not the former.

Taking this suggestion with the one in the previous subsection, there is perhaps a sense in which it is true to say that in these initial and final positions the glottal stop is not really there, at least not from a perceptual point of view. This may help to explain why students beginning their training in practical phonetics often miss glottal stops in these positions in listening exercises.

In Hausa glottal stops occur redundantly in two contexts: 'word-initially before vowels and pre-pausally after short vowels' (Lindsey et al., 1992). In the latter context – the same syllabic position for the glottal stop as in the data in Table 2.1 – an abrupt termination prevents neutralization of the short–long vowel opposition without priming the listener's expectation of a stop consonant. In both contexts the glottal stops function as markers of juncture types and this may be a common function for them cross-linguistically; it is rare to find supraglottal plosives having only this function in any context, if it is found at all.

Mowrer and Fairbank (1991) present data from a dysfluent speaker who inserts glottal stops varying in duration between c.50–150 ms into the vowels of tonic syllables approximately one-third of the way through their course. If this is analysed as abrupt termination and onset then even though the acoustic signal of the vowel has been interrupted perhaps we should not say that its sonority has, i.e. the sonority slope has not descended in the interval but bridges the gap, so to speak.

The source-filter model

Vocal tract resonance, a phenomenon intimately connected with the concept of sonority, is usually modelled in terms of a tube open at one end and closed at the other with formant resonances explained in terms of perturbations within the tube (Fant, 1960). Formant transitions come about as responses to the perturbations caused by articulators moving to sites of constriction. A glottal stop has no transitions because the closed end of the tube cannot be also a perturbation *within* the tube. This fact gives a clear phonetic interpretation to Stemberger's claim that glottals lack a place of articulation.

Glottal states

Connected with the previous point is the fact that for glottal sounds the site of what has traditionally been thought of as their articulation is in the glottis and therefore, unlike other sounds, the articulation and the glottal state cannot vary independently. Furthermore, there is in effect a continuum from complete glottal occlusion through creak phonation to modal voice and other phonatory types of which speakers can take advantage. In Arabic, for instance, the 'ayn phoneme is variously realized as a pharyngealized glottal stop, a pharyngeal glide with creak, and a pharyngeal glide with modal voice (see Figure 2.3). We might venture to propose that each of these allophones manifests sonority in acoustically and articulatorily different ways but nevertheless maintains it at a functionally equivalent level. The glottal stop variant results in the same break in the signal as in the data discussed by Mowrer and Fairbank.

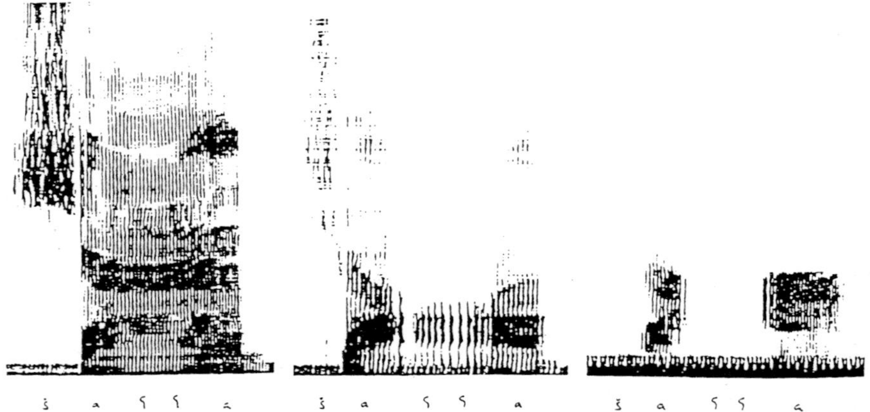

Figure 2.3. Spectrograms of three geminate realizations of Arabic 'ayn in the word \ʃaʕʕa\ 'to disperse'. From left to right: pharyngealized glide with modal voice (speaker from Hebron, West Bank); pharyngealized glide with creak (speaker from Khan Younis, Gaza Strip); pharyngealized glottal stop (speaker from Damascus, Syria). Data from Heselwood (1992).

An understandable objection to this proposal, and to those relating to Mowrer and Fairbank's data and the data in Table 2.1, is to point out the incoherence of a concept of 'silent sonority'. We should, however, consider the possibility that this glottal occlusion silence is perceived via a phonetic processing system tuned to speech, not a non-speech auditory mode of signal processing, and there is evidence adduced in support of the motor theory of speech perception that short silences are processed differently according to whether they are taken to be integral parts of the speaker's articulatory behaviour or not (Borden et al., 1994).

The feature [sonorant]

If a plausible phonetic basis can be found for including glottal stop in the class of sonorants then the feature [sonorant] has to be characterized in such a way as not to exclude them, nor must the voiced implosive substitutes for nasals be left out. Here it is useful to differentiate between the usage of the terms 'sonority' and 'sonorant'. A certain degree of sonority is a sufficient but not necessary condition for a sound to be classed as a sonorant, i.e. the sound must be at or above a given point on the so-called sonority hierarchy (see Laver, 1994: 503–5 for a recent discussion of the hierarchy); sounds at or above this point have in common that there is only a (quasi)periodic sound source in the glottis and no supraglottal sound source. This characterization, while accommodating the hold phase of voiced implosives does, however, exclude glottal stops. What glottal stops have in common with sounds possessing sonority is an absence of a supralaryngeal sound source; in the case of glottal stops this can be expressed, as was discussed above, as an absence of a place of articulation. One way, then, to characterize [sonorant] is disjunctively: sonorants have *either* sonority *or* no place feature. An added bonus is that the open [a] vowel can be said to be sonorant on both counts and can therefore be characterized as the sonorant sound par excellence; it does not, however, exclude the voiceless glottal fricative [h]. There is no room here to discuss whether or not this should be considered a sonorant, but if it should not then an alternative is to characterize [sonorant] in terms of the continuum of glottal states referred to above. A variable that comes close to defining the continuum is the measure known as the closed quotient (Qx) in laryngography, i.e. the proportion of the voicing cycle during which the vocal folds are in contact along their length. A glottal stop could be conventionally assigned the numerical maximum (but impossible) Qx value of 100%, the modal voice state has a range of values typically between about 45 and 60% (Abberton et al., 1989) and the fully voiceless state could be conventionally assigned the minimum (and also impossible) value of 0%. By establishing an appropriate threshold on this scale of values, and excluding all sounds with supralaryngeal sound sources, it might be possible to define [sonorant] satisfactorily.

A further alternative is to take Stemberger's notion of glottal transparency and apply it to sonority. That is to say, a glottal stop has no effect on the sonority profile of its syllable. This is perhaps an attractive idea but to investigate it further would require studying the cross-linguistic clustering potential of glottal stops compared with other oral stops. In Ait Alloui Berber, a Tachlhiyt variety, a sound involving a glottal closure (represented here as [ʔ] but it may also involve epiglottal articulation) occurs in clusters such as [ʔqəd] 'be careful', [ʔsɑn] 'security', [ʔfən] 'they forgive' (examples from Alouane, 1993). If glottal stops are transparent to sonority then these glottal stops will have the sonority value of the following obstruent.

Notes

1 If the implosive is phonologically opposed to a plosive in the speaker's system then the glottalic ingressive mechanism has distinctive function and therefore there is also functional deviance (Heselwood, 1997).

2 By 'glottal stop', in this chapter, is meant a full glottal occlusion without the possibility of any phonatory activity during the hold phase. Allophones of glottal stop phonemes that show creaky or even modal voice (see e.g. Ladefoged and Maddieson, 1996) are excluded from the term.

References

Abberton E, Howard D, Fourcin AJ (1989) Laryngographic assessment of normal voice. Clinical Linguistics and Phonetics, 3, 281–96.

Alouane M ben Salah (1993) An account of the Berber dialect of Ait Alloui. Unpublished DPhil thesis, University of Ulster.

Blumstein S, Stevens KN (1979) Acoustic invariance in speech production: evidence from measurements of the spectral characteristics of stop consonants. Journal of the Acoustical Society of America, 66, 1001–17.

Borden GJ, Harris KS, Raphael LJ (1994) Speech Science Primer. Baltimore: Williams and Wilkins.

Chomsky N, Halle M (1968) The Sound Pattern of English. New York: Harper & Row.

Christman SS (1992) Uncovering phonological regularity in neologisms: contributions of sonority theory. Clinical Linguistics and Phonetics, 6, 219–47.

Fant G (1960) Acoustic Theory of Speech Production. The Hague: Mouton.

Heselwood B (1992) Extended axiomatic–functionalist phonology: An exposition with reference to modern standard arabic. Unpublished DPhil thesis, University of Ulster.

Heselwood B (1998a) A phonetically–based feature geometry for the analysis and classification of disordered pronunciation. In Ziegler W, Deger K (eds) Clinical Phonetics and Linguistics. London: Whurr, 115–22.

Heselwood B (1998b) An unusual kind of sonority and its implications for phonetic theory. In Leeds University Working Papers in Linguistics and Phonetics.

Ladefoged P (1971) Preliminaries to Linsuistic Phonetics. Chicago: University of Chicago Press.

Ladefoged P, Maddieson I (1996) The Sounds of the World's Languages. Oxford: Blackwell.

Laver J (1994) Principles of Phonetics. Cambridge: University of Cambridge Press.

Lindau M (1984) Phonetic differences in glottalic consonants. Journal of Phonetics, 1, 147–55.

Lindsey G, Hayward K, Haruna A (1992) Hausa glottalic consonants: a laryngographic study. Bulletin of the School of Oriental and African Studies, University of London, vol 55, part 3.

Mowrer DE, Fairbank C (1991) A case report of within–vowel glottal stop insertion in the speech of an adult male. Journal of Fluency Disorders, 16, 55–69.

Stemberger JP (1993) Glottal transparency. Phonology, 10, 107–38.

Chapter 3
Constraint-based Analysis of Japanese Rhotacism

ISAO UEDA and STUART DAVIS

Introduction

Although the acquisition of Japanese 'r' poses many problems and the early substitution of other phonemes for 'r,' termed 'rhotacism', is notably well-known in Japanese first language acquisition, it has seldom been a subject matter for phonological analysis. In this chapter we first take a look at the two representative types of rhotacism by observing some descriptive acquisitional data. We then point out theoretical deficits of a previous derivation-based account and reanalyse the same data under Optimality Theory. It is argued that the optimality-theoretic account provides a better explanation and characterization of rhotacism and that the distinction between the two representative types of rhotacism can be reduced to the difference in constraint ranking.

Data

The phoneme 'r' is one of the segments that is acquired relatively late in phonological development and is very frequently replaced by other sounds (Ishikawa, 1930; Umebayashi and Takagi, 1965; Sakauchi, 1967; Nishimura, 1979). Japanese 'r' in the earlier stage of development exhibits two distinct distributional patterns as reported in Murata (1970), which will be referred to as Type A in Table 3.1 and as Type B in Table 3.2.

Facts and problems

It is obvious that in Type A rhotacism [d] and [ɾ] are distributed complementarily; [d] and [ɾ] behave like two allophones of a phoneme. The allophonic status of [d] and [ɾ] is illustrated in the following.

(1) Allophonic status of [d] and [ɾ]

/d/ → [d] / #____

/d/ → [ɾ] / V____V

On the contrary, in Type B target /ɾ/ is misproduced as [d] irrespective of the position in the word. Some intriguing questions arise here: what is the difference between these two types of rhotacism? In what respect is rhotacsim different from normally developing phonological systems? Further, how should rhotacism be characterized in any linguistically significant way? To answer these questions, we first examine a previous derivation-based account in the next section.

Previous derivation-based account

The only phonological analysis of rhotacism available thus far is provided by Ueda, Ito and Shirahata (1997). Given that [d] and [ɾ] are

Table 3.1. Type A (six subjects, aged 3;6–5;0)

	Phonetic forms	Target forms	Gloss
	Word-initial position		
(a)	Phonetic forms	Target forms	Gloss
	dap̆pa	ɾappa	trumpet
	doosakɯ	ɾoosokɯ	candle
	demoŋ	ɾemoŋ	lemon
	disɯ	ɾisɯ	squirrel
	(Target /ɾ/ is misproduced as [d])		
(b)	Phonetic forms	Target forms	Gloss
	daɾɯma	daɾɯma	tumbler
	doobɯtsɯeŋ	doobɯtsɯeŋ	zoo
	denʃa	denʃa	tram car
	(Target /d/ is correctly produced as [d])		
	Word-medial position		
(b)	Phonetic forms	Target forms	Gloss
	paɾaʃɯɯto	paɾaʃɯɯto	parachute
	gɯɾoobɯ	gɯɾoobɯ	glove
	teɾebi	teɾebi	television
	soɾa	soɾa	sky
	(Target /ɾ/ is correctly produced as [ɾ])		
(a)	Phonetic forms	Target forms	Gloss
	dʒiɾooʃa	dʒidooʃa	automobile
	namiɾa	namida	tear
	bɯɾoo	bɯdoo	grape
	(Target /d/ is misproduced as [ɾ])		

Table 3.2. Type B (one subject, aged 3;6)

	Phonetic forms	Target forms	Gloss
		Word-initial position	
(a)	Phonetic forms	Target forms	Gloss
	dappa	ɾappa	trumpet
	doosakɯ	ɾoosokɯ	candle
	demoŋ	ɾemoŋ	lemon
	disɯ	ɾisɯ	squirrel
	(Target /ɾ/ is misproduced as [d])		
(b)	Phonetic forms	Target forms	Gloss
	daɾɯma	daɾɯma	tumbler
	doobɯtsɯeŋ	doobɯtsɯeŋ	zoo
	denʃa	denʃa	tram car
	(Target /d/ is correctly produced as [d])		
		Word-medial position	
(b)	Phonetic forms	Target forms	Gloss
	padaʃɯɯto	paɾaʃɯɯto	parachute
	gɯdoobɯ	gɯɾoobɯ	glove
	tedebi	teɾebi	television
	soda	soɾa	sky
	(Target /ɾ/ is misproduced as [d])		
(a)	Phonetic forms	Target forms	Gloss
	dʒidooʃa	dʒidooʃa	automobile
	namida	namida	tear
	bɯdoo	bɯdoo	grape
	(Target /d/ is correctly produced as [d]))		

differentiated from each other in terms of the feature [flap], they claim the following. First, [d] and [ɾ] are underspecified underlyingly as in Figure 3.1.

Ueda, Ito and Shirahata (1997) further claim that the default is [-flap] (namely [d]), and the realization of intervocalic [ɾ] is a lenition process with the spreading of vocalic quality from the adjacent vowel as in Figure 3.2.

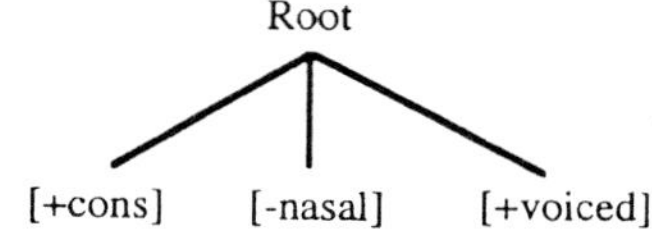

Figure 3.1. Underlying representation of [d] and [ɾ].

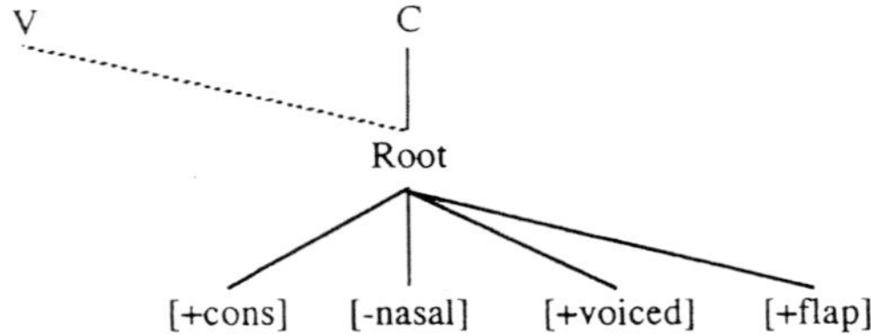

Figure 3.2. Realization of intervocalic [ɾ].

The Type B children produce only [d] whether the target is /d/ or/ɾ/. Ueda et al. (1997) claim that two distinct underlying representations are needed to explicate this; namely that of [d] produced for the target /d/ and that of [d] produced for the target /ɾ/. The representation in Figure 3.1 is postulated again for the underlying representation of [d] produced for the target /d/ in Type B. The coronal stop [d] is the 'default' voiced consonant in this case and hence there is no specification with respect to [flap]. For the underlying representation of [d] produced for the target /ɾ/, Ueda et al. (1997) introduce the notion of 'shadow-specification' (Dinnsen, 1993; Dinnsen and Chin; 1995). The 'shadow-specification' is a modified version of radical underspecification whereby a sound may actually be specified for the default value. In this particular case, the default value is [-flap], which is actually (and therefore wrongly) specified in the child's underlying representation for [d] for the target /ɾ/ as in Figure 3.3.

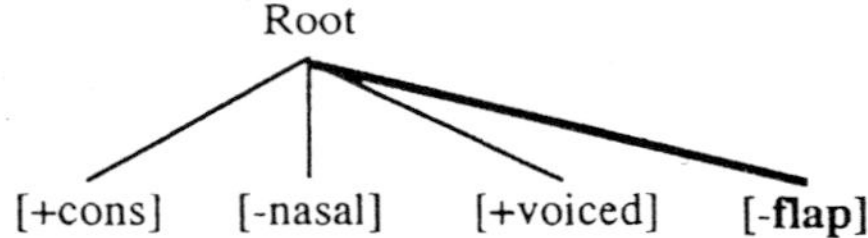

Figure 3.3. 'Shadow-specified' underlying representation of [d] for target /ɾ/.

Problems of the previous account

First, according to this analysis, the realization of word-medial [ɾ] in Type A is the result of the spreading of vocalic quality from the preceding vowel as in Figure 3.2. However, Figure 3.2 means that what spreads from the vowel is the feature [flap], with the value specified as plus. It is not at all clear that vowels have the feature specification [+flap], and for that matter, it is reasonable to regard that vowels have nothing to do with, and therefore do not have, the feature [flap]. Although this might be one of many common intervocalic weakening processes, feature geometry, as utilized here as an analytic tool, has no way to formalize the process.

The second problem is associated with the context. In this analysis, the default is word-initial [d] and the word-medial [ɾ] is a result of a rule. However, Dinnsen (1996) puts forth convincing arguments that the default value can and should be different according to the context; the segment can be radically underspecified but only in a context-sensitive fashion. If so, the default value in this case is [-flap] word-initially, but [+flap] word-medially. There is no spreading of vocalic quality from the preceding vowel. Only default rules fill the default values later in derivation. It is not very easy to decide on one way or the other, but if we adopt this context-sensitive model, we somehow have to specify the context where [d] and [ɾ] appear.

Analysis under Optimality Theory

Optimality Theory, set out by Prince and Smolensky (1993), rests on the following principles. First, Universal Grammar largely consists of a set of constraints on representational well-formedness, out of which individual grammars are constructed. Second, in general, the constraints in a grammar need not be mutually consistent (i.e. they can be contradictory) and are not true without exception; the constraints often have conflicting requirements. Third, a grammar consists of constraints together with a general means of resolving conflicts in favour of analyses that best satisfy, or least violate, the conflicting constraints. There are no rules (Trask, 1996; 249). In the case of rhotacism, we assume the following three universal constraints at work.

(2) Three constraints at work
(a) No Onset 'r' (*r-ons): segments with high sonority like 'r' are avoided in the syllable-onset position.
(b) Intervocalic Weakening (IW): segments in intervocalic position are weakened.
(c) Feature Faithfulness (FF): features that make up the input should be realized in the output.

Let us see how these constraints interact in the phonological system of normally developing Japanese children, or in that of adults, by considering their ranking.

(3) Constraint ranking in adult systems
FF >> * r-ons, IW

This shows that FF outranks *r-ons and IW, which means that the underlying input, be it /d/ or /ɾ/, is properly realized as the same form in the output whether it is in the syllable-onset position or the intervocalic position; the output is 'faithful' to its input. If *r-ons outranks FF, no [ɾ] is allowed to appear, at least syllable-initially, and if IW outranks FF and *r-ons, then no [d] is allowed word-medially

Let us examine Type A rhotacism. The word-initial output of Type A is realized as [d] regardless of the target. The fact suggests that *r-ons is higher ranked than FF. This ranking is formalized in (4) below. (We use [a] as representing all vowels throughout the discussion.)

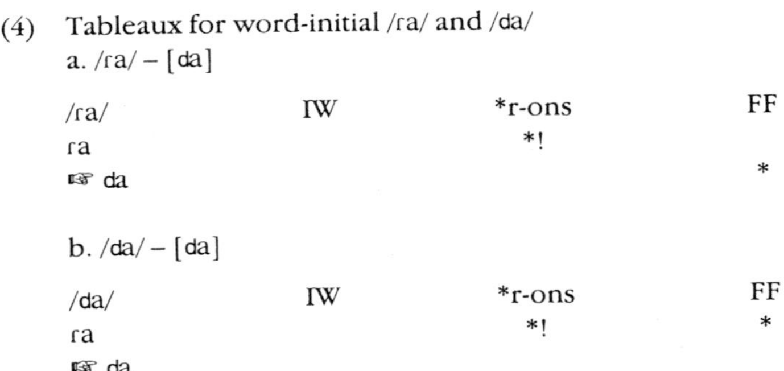

(4) Tableaux for word-initial /ɾa/ and /da/

a. /ɾa/ – [da]

/ɾa/	IW	*r-ons	FF
ɾa		*!	
☞ da			*

b. /da/ – [da]

/da/	IW	*r-ons	FF
ɾa		*!	*
☞ da			

The two tableaux in (4) demonstrate that *r-ons plays a crucial role in determining the output. The violation of FF matters relatively less. Thus, *r-ons is ranked higher then FF, resulting in the unfaithful output [da]. Therefore, the constraint ranking here is: *r-ons >> FF, with IW being irrelevant in this case.

In the word-medial position, the constraint IW, in turn, is at work, resulting in the targets /d/ and /ɾ/ being both realized as [ɾ]. This is formalized in the two tableaux in (5) below.

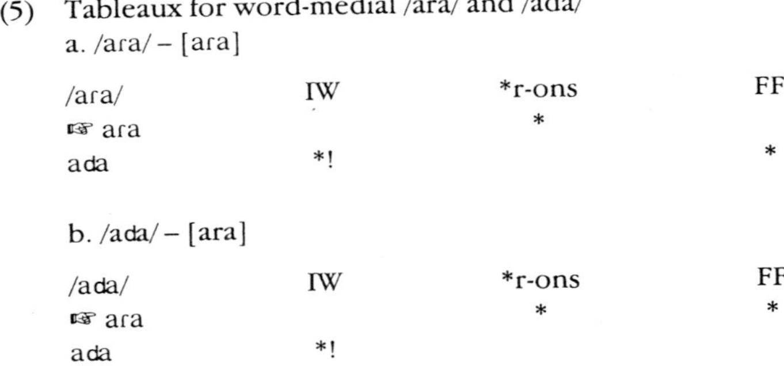

(5) Tableaux for word-medial /aɾa/ and /ada/

a. /aɾa/ – [aɾa]

/aɾa/	IW	*r-ons	FF
☞ aɾa		*	
ada	*!		*

b. /ada/ – [aɾa]

/ada/	IW	*r-ons	FF
☞ aɾa		*	*
ada	*!		

The tableaux in (5) exhibit that IW plays a crucial part in this case. IW must outrank *r-ons or else [ada] would wrongly surface as the output in (5). Because IW outranks *r-ons and FF, the word-medial [ɾ] is generated as the output both for target /d/ and target /ɾ/. Thus we have the ranking of IW ranked higher than *r-ons and FF.

In (4) *r-ons is higher than FF. In (5) it is IW that is ranked higher than *r-ons and FF. We can integrate these two rankings and get the final ranking of IW ranked highest, with *r-ons coming next and FF ranked lowest as in (6) below. This is the ultimate constraint ranking of Type A.

(6) Constraint ranking in Type A
IW >> *r-ons >> FF

Let us consider how these constraints are interacting in Type B. In Type B, the targets /d/ and /ɾ/ are produced as [d] irrespective of the position in the word. Here, *r-ons is predominant syllable-initially either word-initially or word-medially. The tableaux for word-initial /ɾa/ and /da/ and word-medial /aɾa/ and /ada/ are shown in (7) and (8) respectively.

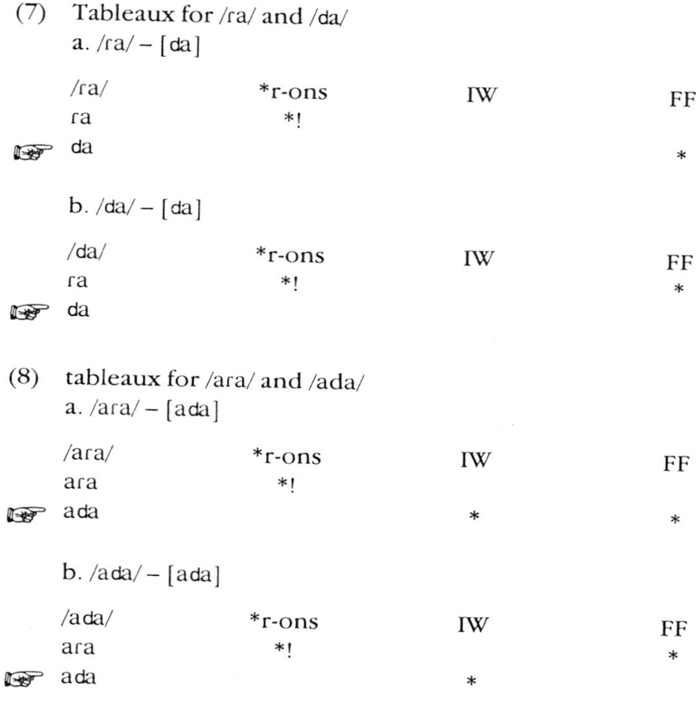

(7) Tableaux for /ɾa/ and /da/

a. /ɾa/ – [da]

/ɾa/	*r-ons	IW	FF
ɾa	*!		
☞ da			*

b. /da/ – [da]

/da/	*r-ons	IW	FF
ɾa	*!		*
☞ da			

(8) tableaux for /aɾa/ and /ada/

a. /aɾa/ – [ada]

/aɾa/	*r-ons	IW	FF
aɾa	*!		
☞ ada		*	*

b. /ada/ – [ada]

/ada/	*r-ons	IW	FF
aɾa	*!		*
☞ ada		*	

In the tableaux in (7), both inputs /ɾa/ and /da/ are realized as [da]. The violation of FF is overridden by that of *r-ons, which is ranked higher than FF; if the ranking is reversed, [ɾa] is incorrectly chosen as the output. Also in (8), the inputs /ara/ and /ada/ are both realized as [ada]. The ranking is the same with this instance. Note that in the first tableau of (8) the [ada] form violates both IW and FF but these violations are overridden by that of *r-ons. The overall ranking in Type B is the one in which *r-ons is ranked higher than FF and IW, which is shown in (9) below.

(9) Constraint ranking in Type B
*r-ons >> IW, FF

Discussion

Examining rhotacism under the Optimality Theory has brought some advantages that overcome the theoretical deficits in the derivation-based analysis. In the derivation-based analysis mentioned above, we have to appeal to the specification (or non-specification) of the untenable feature [flap]. The spreading of [+flap] from the preceding vowel was notably a problem; vowels do not have the feature specification [+flap]. Under Optimality Theory, we do not have to make reference to the feature as such.

We have also raised the issue of context-sensitivity, to which the notion of default is closely related. The problem of context-sensitivity arises from two different default values in two different contexts. In Type A we would have to state the default values as in (10).

(10) Default values in two different contexts
1. The default is [-flap] word-initially.
2. The default is [+flap] word-medially.

However, under Optimality Theory we can get rid of this complex statement. For example, *r-ons is a constraint that governs segments only in the syllable-onset position, and IW is a constraint that is relevant only intervocalically; there is no need to make any direct reference to the context per se, independent of the universal constraints.

In the derivation-based analysis, rhotacism occurs when the feature [flap] becomes specified. Under Optimality Theory we have seen that both in Type A and B, FF, which is supposed to be ranked highest in fully-developed systems, is ranked lower than IW or *r-ons. Thus, we can characterize rhotacism as in (11).

(11) Characterization of rhotacism
Rhotacism is the result of constraint ranking whereby FF, which is ranked highest in the fully-developed system, is ranked lower than either IW or *r-ons.

Bearing this definition in mind, let us consider the phonological knowledge to be learned. The child displaying rhotacism already has the three constaints. They have the proper, ambient-like input representations. All they have to learn is that FF should be ranked highest among the three constraints. The difference between Type A and Type B is simply reduced to the statement that IW is ranked highest in Type A, whereas *r-ons is ranked highest in Type B. We can state the difference between the two types without any reference to underspecification. Optimality Theory thus allows us simpler characterizations both in the definition of rhotacism itself and in the difference between the two types.

Acknowledgements

We are grateful to Dan Dinnsen, Mafuyu Kitahara and John Matthews for their helpful comments and suggestions on earlier versions of this chapter. The first author gratefully acknowledges grants from the Japan-United States Educational Commission and from the United States Council for International Exchange of Scholars.

References

Dinnsen D (1993) Underspecification in phonological disorders. In Eid M, Iverson G (eds) Principles and Prediction: The Analysis of Natural Language. Philidelphia: John Benjamins.

Dinnsen D (1996) Context-sensitive underspecification and the acquisition of phonemic contrasts. Journal of Child Language, 23, 57–79.

Dinnsen D, Chin S (1995) On the natural domain of phonological disorders. In Archibald J (ed.) Phonological Acquisition and Phonological Theory. Hillsdale, NJ: Lawrence Erlbaum.

Ishikawa S (1930) Hatsuonhattatsu no bunsekiteki kenkyu. Aichiken jido kenkyusho kiyou, 5, 115–33.

Murata K (1970) Yoji no kotoba to hatsuon. Tokyo: Baifukan.

Nishimura B (1979) Koonshogaiji no koonkino kakutoku. In Sasanuma S (ed.) Kotoba no shogai 3. Tokyo: Taishukan, pp. 100–32.

Prince A, Smolensky P (1993) Optimality Theory: Constraint Interaction in Generative Grammar. Boulder: University of Colorado and New Brunswick: Rutgers University.

Sakauchi T (1967) Kodomo mo koonnoryoku ni tsuite. Gengoshogai kenkyu, 68, 13–26.

Trask R (1996) A Dictionary of Phonetics and Phonology. London: Routledge.

Ueda I, Ito T, Shirahata T (1997) A paradox in progress-based analysis. In Ziegler W, Deger K (eds) Clinical Phonetics and Linguistics. London: Whurr Publishers.

Umebayashi N, Takagi S (1965) Gakureimae no kodomo no koonnoryoku ni kansuru ichikenkyu. Onseigengo igaku, 6, 17–18.

Chapter 4
Feature Geometry, Underspecification and Child Substitutions

MEHMET YAVAS and CYNTHIA W. CORE

Introduction

Current phonological models view the segmental structure as a hierarchically arranged featural organization. Such a hierarchical representation is given in articulatorily based tree structures and is known as feature geometry.

The basic idea of feature geometry is that features are organized around six active articulators that reflect the anatomical structures involved in the production of speech. These are the glottis, the soft palate, the lips, the tongue blade, tongue body and the tongue root. Most features are the sole responsibility of a particular articulator. For example, [labial] is uniquely related to the lips, while [nasal] is the exclusive responsibility of the soft palate. Such features are called articulator-bound features. On the other hand, some other features are not dedicated to a particular articulator and can be executed by several different articulators. These features, which are called 'articulator-free', fall into two groups: the major class features [consonantal] and [sonorant] which are placed at the root of the tree, and the stricture (manner) features [continuant], [strident] and [lateral].

Root features [consonantal] and [sonorant] jointly define the major classes of sounds and create the linkage of the segment to the prosodic tiers above. Among the four possible combinations of these two features, one [-consonantal, -sonorant] is excluded, because it is an impossibility.

The remaining combinations define the following major classes:

	obstruents	liquids, nasals	glides, vowels
consonantal	+	+	–
sonorant	-	+	+

Manner (stricture) features [continuant], [strident] and [lateral] come directly from the root and thus are classified as articulator-free. One of the cavity nodes, Laryngeal, defines the glottal characteristics of the segment such as voicing and aspiration, while the other cavity node, Supralaryngeal, dominates two class nodes, [soft palate] and [oral place]. Here the first one determines the difference between nasal and non-nasal segments, and the second one [oral place] dominates the articulator nodes [labial], [coronal] and [dorsal]. Unlike most other features, the articulator features – [labial], [coronal] and [dorsal] – are privative (one valued), rather than binary. The reason for this is that phonological rules operate only on the positive values of these categories. For example, as mentioned above, while there are rules and processes involving labial and coronal segments, no generalization seems to be made on the [-labial] or [-coronal] groups. Finally, articulator class nodes dominate binary valued features. The labial place is related to lip articulations, bilabials and labiodentals /p, b, m, w, f, v/, rounded vowels and /r/. It dominates the binary value [round]. The coronal place is related to articulations with the tongue tip or blade which covers interdentals, alveolars, palato–alveolars and palatals /θ, ð, t, d, s, z, n, r, l, ʃ, z, tʃ, dʒ, j/. It dominates the terminal features [anterior] and [distributed]; the former separates palatals [-anterior] from the rest [+anterior], and the latter isolates the interdentals via [+distributed]. Coronal place is considered the universally unmarked (default) place (Paradis and Prunet 1991). Dorsal place is related to articulations of the back of the tongue. It covers velar consonants /k, g, ŋ/ and vowels, and dominates terminal features [high], [low] and [back]. The applied feature tree is based on Halle (1992).

Underspecification

Another trademark of current approaches is the concept of underspecification, which states that the underlying representations of segments need not include the values of certain distinctive features that can be predicted.

Certain properties of a sound are predictable from its other properties. Such predictable redundancies are part of every language, and, instead of being part of the underlying form, they can be given as redundancy rules. For example, [+low] implies [-high] universally, as it is impossible for a segment to be made with both low and high tongue position at the same time. Also, if a segment is [+sonorant], it is more than likely that it will be [+voiced]. The feature [coronal] is taken as the universal unmarked (unspecified) place of articulation, whereas [labial] and [dorsal] are specified. As far as the manner of articulation is concerned, continuants are treated as marked, thus specified, whereas non-continuants are unmarked (unspecified). The reason for this is that stops are much more common than fricatives in the languages of the world. Resulting from these, /t/, a coronal non-continuant, is the least specified stop, and /s/, a coronal continuant is the least specified fricative. When the two are compared, however, /t/ is less specified than /s/, because it is not specified for continuant.

Besides these universal relationships, there are also some language specific redundancies. English and Sindhi stops made in the same place of articulation provide a familiar example for this. If we consider the bilabial stops, both English and Sindhi have voiceless unaspirated, voiceless aspirated, and voiced, [p, p^h, b]. However, there is a fundamental difference in their phonological organization. In Sindhi, these three sounds are used contrastively, as in [pənu] 'leaf', [p^hənu] 'snake hood', and [bənu] 'forest'. In English, on the other hand, there is no contrast between the voiceless aspirated and the voiceless unaspirated stops; [p] and [p^h] are allophones of the same phoneme, and their distribution is predictable. Thus, aspiration is non-distinctive (predictable, redundant) in English and does not have to be shown in the underlying representations. In Sindhi, on the other hand, aspiration has to be indicated in the underlying representations. Table 4.1 gives the specifications for English consonants (Bernhardt and Stoel-Gammon 1994).

Table 4.1. Specification for English consonants

Segment	Root Node	Laryngeal Node	Place Node
/b/	[+consonantal]	[+voice]	Labial
/t/	[+cons]		
/d/	[+cons]	[+voice]	
/k/	[+cons]		Dorsal
/f/	[+cons], [+cont]		Labial
/v/	[+cons], [+cont]	[+voice]	Labial
/θ/	[+cons], [+cont]		Coronal:[+distrib]
/ð/	[+cons], [+cont]	[+voice]	Coronal:[+distrib]
/s/	[+cons], [+cont]		
/ʃ/	[+cons], [+cont]		Cor:[–anterior]
/w/	[+sonorant]		Labial:[+round]
/j/	[+sonorant]		
/l/	[+cons],[+sonorant]		
/r/	[+cons], [+son]		Lab + Cor place or [-anterior]

From Bernhardt and Stoel-Gammon, 1994.
Features specified in the underlying representation of each segment are indicated.

Feature geometry and underspecification have implications for phonological development. Using feature geometry, we expect that more deeply embedded features in the tree such as place features would be learned later than the features that appear at higher nodes, especially those at the root node that define major classes. As a corollary, common child substitutions would involve mismatches in features that are lower in the tree. Also, since underspecification is tied to relative markedness of segments, we would expect a relationship between underspecified and preferred segments in development. In child substitutions, the replacements would be less specified (less marked) than the targets that are more specified. A further hypothesis is that in unusual substitutions, the above principles would be violated. In the following we look at data from child substitutions and see if feature geometry and underspecification has a principled way of separating common (normal) substitutions from unusual (idiosyncratic) ones.

Common substitutions

The substitutions that are looked at here are basically from English, though similar cases are frequently cited for many other languages. Our analytical framework is relational with adult-like underlying representations posited. We also would like to point out that these substitutions are all non-assimilatory (context-free) in nature. The exclusion of the so-called assimilatory substitutions is due to the fact that there would be no way to clearly observe the interplay of features because of the surrounding assimilatory environments. The following common processes (Grunwell, 1987; Stoel-Gammon and Dunn, 1985) were analysed:

Liquid gliding:	/r/ → [w]	*rabbit* → [wæbɪt]
	/l/ → [j]	*leaf* → [jif]
Stopping:	/s/ → [t]	*sun* → [tʌn]
	/ð/ → [d]	*that* → [dæt]
Fronting:	/k/ → [d]	*key* → [ti]
	/ʃ/ → [s]	*shoe* → [su]
Fricative simplification:	/θ/ → [f]	*thick* → [fɪk]
	/θ/ → [s]	*thick* → [sɪk]

Analysis of these common substitutions reveal that they generally involve more specified targets and less specified substitutes. They also generally reflect changes in low level nodes in the feature tree.

These can be illustrated in the following /ʃ/ → [s] substitution.

/ʃ/	→	[s]
[+cons]		[+cons]
[+cont]		[+cont]
Cor: [-ant]		

In this substitution, a less specified substitute replaces a more specified target.The feature cor:[-ant], which changes in the substitute, is a low-level feature on the tree. Table 4.2 summarizes the relationships between the target and the substitute in terms of these two parameters.

Table 4.2. Common processes

	Liquid Gliding		Stopping		Fronting		Fricative Simplification	
	r → w	l → j	s → t	ð → d	k → t	ʃ → s	θ → f	θ → s
More specified → Less specified	+	+	+	+	+	+	Ø	+
Lower level feature → Higher level feature	+	Ø	Ø	+	Ø	+	+	+

Plus signs (+) indicate that the parameter contributes to a substitution. The Ø symbol indicates that the parameter does not contribute to a substitution.

In the table, a Ø indicates that that particular factor is not contributing to the change, and a (+) indicates that the factor is contributing to the substitution according to the expectations. As we observe, in each of these common substitutions, at least one of these parameters has the (+) assigned. Thus, we can conclude that normal substitutions should have at least one (+) and no (–) in their designations.

Unusual substitutions

The validity of these observations receives support from another group of substitutions that are called 'unusual' or 'idiosyncratic'. This group is exemplified by the following substitutions (Stoel-Gammon and Dunn, 1985; Grunwell, 1987).

Gliding of fricatives:	/f/ → [w]	*fig* → [wɪg]
Stopping of glides:	/w/ → [b]	*will* → [bɪl]
Frication of approximants:	/l/ → [ð]	*lock* → [ðɔk]
Frication of stops:	/b/ → [v]	*ban* → [væn]
Backing:	/t/ → [k]	*pat* → [pæk]
Stopping of liquids:	/r/ → [d]	*rake* → [dek]

Unusual processes, contrary to what we have seen in the common processes, generally involve targets that are less specified than the substitutes. Also, these substitutions are expected to have changes in higher nodes. Using the same (+), (–), and Ø markings that we used in Table 4.2, we can show the situation for the unusual substitutions in Table 4.3.

For the two parameters we have been considering, the expected values should be (–) because these should reveal exactly the opposite situation to the common processes. There are, however, several exceptions to this. In /f/ → [w], /l/ → [d], /r/ → [d], there are no (–) signs. In fact one of these, /r/ → [d], with two (+) signs, looks like a normal

Table 4.3. Unusual processes

	Gliding of Fricatives	Stopping of Glides		Frication of Approximants		Frication of Stops	Backing	Stopping of Liquids	
	f → w	w → b	j → t	l → ð	w → v	b → v	t → k	l → d	r → d
More specified → Less specified	+	–	–	–	–	–	–	Ø	+
Lower level feature → Higher level feature	Ø	Ø	Ø	–	Ø	Ø	–	Ø	+

Plus signs (+) indicate that the parameter contributes to a substitution. The (–) signs indicate that the opposite occurs for a parameter. The Ø symbol indicates that the parameter does not contribute to a substitution.

substitution marking. What this substitution and several other unusual substitutions show, however, is that the feature [sonorant] is affected. This is never the case for common substitutions. Thus, this condition has to be included in the identification of common/uncommon separation. Actually, in the order of importance, this ranks higher than any other factor. We can say that if the [sonorant] feature is affected, then the substitution is unusual. However, this is a unidirectional implication in that not all unusual substitutions involve the feature [sonorant]. If [sonorant] is not affected, then the other two factors have to be considered.

In summary, the hypotheses were supported by most of the data; feature geometry and underspecification could account for most substitutions. However, the type of feature that is affected in the substitution also needed to be considered. In general, normal substitutions involved lower level place features, while unusual substitutions involved higher level features, especially [sonorant]. Normal substitutions did not involve this feature. The importance of [sonorant] seems to be in accord with its high position in the feature hierarchy and might even suggest that it be given a more prominent position than [consonantal].

References

Bernhardt B, Stoel-Gammon C (1994) Nonlinear phonology: Introduction and clinical application. Journal of Speech and Hearing Research, 37, 123–43.

Grunwell P (1987) Clinical Phonology, 2nd edn. Baltimore, MD: Williams and Wilkins.

Halle M (1992) Phonological Features in International Encyclopedia of Linguistics, Vol 3. Oxford: Oxford University Press, pp. 207–12.

Paradis C, Prunet JF (eds) (1991) Phonetics and Phonology: Vol 2: The Special Status of Coronals: Internal and External Evidence. San Diego, CA: Academic Press.

Stoel-Gammon C, Dunn C (1985) Normal and Disordered Phonology in Children. Baltimore, MD: University Park Press.

Chapter 5
Identification and Discrimination of Vowels in Children with Apraxic Speech Disorders

PAUL GROENEN, BEN MAASSEN and THOM CRUL

Introduction

Apraxic speech disorders are considered a developmental disorder in the ability to perform purposeful speech movements (Hall et al., 1993). The explanation of articulatory problems as an output speech disorder does not preclude the possibility that children may demonstrate related language problems (Marion et al., 1993; Groenen et al., 1996b). In the present study, the perception of speech sounds in the etiology and maintenance of apraxic speech disorders was examined.

Data on the auditory perceptual skills of children with apraxic speech problems are scarce (Hall et al., 1993) and inconclusive (Guyette and Diedrich, 1981; Edwards, 1984). This inconclusiveness may reflect the lack of differentiation of speech perception into distinct processes. In the present study, an attempt was made to distinguish between the different processes in the perception of speech. This was accomplished by administering identification and discrimination tasks. An identification task requires a phonemic judgement, and thus decisions are based primarily on the phonetic properties and features represented in phonetic short-term memory. In a discrimination task, however, not only phonetic information is used but the listener can also base perceptual judgements on information in auditory memory.

Groenen et al. (1996b) showed that children with developmental apraxia of speech showed auditory processing problems of consonants. They found that speech perception problems manifested themselves more easily in auditory processing than in phonetic processing. A straightforward conclusion could be that these children did not have problems in phonetic processing. However, an alternative explanation could be that the type of stimulus (consonants) had a too high identifiability and speech cues were perceptually too salient. Vowel misarticulations are associated with apraxic speech problems. The sensitivity of both identification and discrimination tasks may be enhanced by utilizing vowels instead of consonants in the assessment of speech perception problems. Therefore, we decided to use vowels instead of consonants.

To sensitively assess phonetic processing, stimuli were chosen with relatively low identifiability. In addition, to sensitively assess speech perception processes, vowel stimuli were chosen with a low level of redundancy, that is, vowels that approached the 'neutral-vowel position' while preserving vowel identity.

The perceptual abilities of a group of articulation-disordered children and a control group of children in response to a vowel continuum /i/-/I/ was studied. Both the children with articulation problems and the control children were administered an identification and a discrimination task. The main questions were: (1) do children with apraxic speech problems exhibit problems in the perception of vowels?; and (2) are potential speech perception problems of phonetic or auditory origin?

Method

Subjects

The purpose was to form a homogeneous group of children whose main articulation problem was apraxic in nature. The subjects with apraxic speech problems were 11 children (mean age 8;0 years, range 6;11–9;6 years) attending special schools for children with language and speech disorders in a Dutch city. The criteria for inclusion were: (1) high rates of speech sound errors; (2) inadequate diadochokinetic profile for the production of multisyllabic sequences; (3) posturing and groping of the articulators; (4) periods of highly unintelligible speech; (5) difficulties with or inability to produce complex phonemic sequences; (6) high incidences of context-related sound substitutions (e.g. metathetic errors); and (7) an inconsistent speech performance. In addition, each child had to be unequivocally diagnosed by certified speech-language pathologists as having apraxic speech problems. This diagnosis was made through classification based on spontaneous speech production and speech and sentence imitations.

Each selected child (1) had no structural problems in the speech organs that could be held responsible for their speaking problems; (2) did not have otorhinolaryngologic problems; and (3) did not suffer from severe attention deficits. Each articulation-disordered child functioned within a normal range of intelligence (performance IQ on WISC-R test of intelligence was above 85).

The control children were 12 subjects (mean age 8;1 years, range 7;0– 9;8 years) attending a regular elementary school. The children did not have evidence of learning disabilities, a history of hearing problems, speech and language problems, or speech-limiting structural abnormalities. Based on school performance and information from the classroom teachers, normal levels of cognitive, motoric and perceptual functioning could be assumed. The control children were gender matched to the young children with articulation problems and were in the same school grade, so the educational level was the same across groups.

The children in both groups also met the following selection criteria: (1) absence of hearing loss on bilateral pure tone audiometric testing with air-conduction thresholds at 250, 500, 1000, 2000, 4000 Hz; the maximally allowed hearing loss was 25 dB HL for either ear; (2) no previous exposure to resynthesized speech; and (3) Dutch as the native language.

Stimuli: Generating the two continua

To degrade vowel cues, the spectral characteristics of a 'neutral-vowel position' had to be determined. This was done by analysing five natural male utterances of each of 12 Dutch monophthongs (/i/, /I/, /e/, /ɛ/, /a/, /ɑ/, /ɔ/, /o/, /u/, /y/, /ø/ and /œ/) spoken in isolation, and computing the centroid for this specific speaker. After A/D conversion, the Computerized Speech Lab (CSL Model 4300, V5.05) was used for analysing the spectral structure of the speech tokens. To compute the position of the neutral vowel, the grand average across all vowels was computed. This speaker centroid served as the reference position for determining the specific areas of vowel degradation.

The endpoint tokens of the continuum were chosen by taking vowel stimuli with formant frequencies that elicited above 75% correct responses in children with normal hearing. The formant frequencies associated with these critical levels were considered most sensitive and taken as composing the spectral structure of the endpoint tokens of the continuum. In Figure 5.1, the /i/-/I/ continuum based on these critical levels is plotted in the vowel space determined by the first two formants.

The LPC Parameter Manipulation/Synthesis Program (ASL Model 4304, V1) was used for manipulating and resynthesizing the spectral structure of the signal. For each vowel, one utterance was analysed using a pitch-asynchronous autocorrelation method (pre-emphasis factor: 0.95, Hamming window, frame length: 150 points, filter order: 12). The locations of the spectral peaks, their bandwidths, and their intensities were estimated by transforming the reflection coefficients to autoregressive coefficients and then performing a fast Fourier transformation (FFT). Sampled data were resynthesized with a pitch-asynchronous synthesis procedure by transforming the manipulated reflection coefficients to inverse filter coefficients. The total length of each stimulus was cut back to 200 ms, a value proven to be typical for isolated vowels in

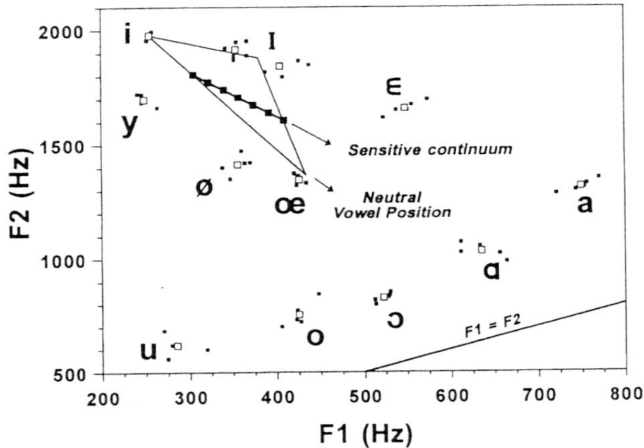

Figure 5.1. Representation of the optimally sensitive vowel continuum /i/-/I/ in the vowel space determined by F1 and F2.

speech production (Koopmans-van Beinum, 1980) and to preserve the speechlike aspects of the vowel (see Repp, 1984).

Procedure

The stimuli were recorded and played back using a portable DAT recorder. Presentation was via a Beyerdynamic closed headphone (Type DT770). The playback level was set at the level judged as comfortable by the subject (always close to 70 dB HL).

Each subject was administered an identification and a discrimination task. The identification task consisted of a two–alternative forced choice response to a single auditory stimulus. Ten repetitions of each of the seven stimuli of the continuum were presented in a random order consisting of five blocks of 14 stimuli each. The stimuli were separated by interstimulus intervals of 3000 ms. The subjects could identify the stimulus by pointing to one of two pictures: a picture of a man named Piet (/pit/), representing the stimulus /i/, and a picture of a pit (/pIt/), representing the stimulus /I/.

The AX discrimination task required a response of 'same' or 'different' on each trial. In order to obtain a bias-free measure of discriminability, the tasks were set up in such a way that signal detection measures could be applied. For this, each task contained physically different as well as identical pairs. The subjects listened to two series of 21 discrimination pairs. Each series contained two repetitions of the physically identical pairs 2-2, 3-3, 4-4, 5-5, 6-6, 7-7, and three repetitions of the physically different pairs consisting of stimulus 2, the so-called 'anchor' stimulus for which the 'just noticeable difference' (JND) was being measured; this resulted in pairs 2-3, 2-4, 2-5, 2-6 and 2-7. The 'anchor' stimulus was always in first position in the pair. All pairs in one series were randomly ordered with an intrapair interval of 400 ms and an interpair interval of 3000 ms. The subjects were asked to point to a picture containing a triangle and a circle when the words in the pair they heard sounded different and simply not to respond when the words in the pair they heard sounded the same.

Results

Identification

In Figure 5.2, the mean identification curves for the groups are displayed along with the individual identification curves of the experimental group. The articulation-disordered children were much more variable in their performance than the control children.

To compare the identification results of both groups for each articulation-disordered subject, a measure of response variability was established. For this, the mean probit curve of the control group was taken to predict prototypical identification values. For each subject, then,

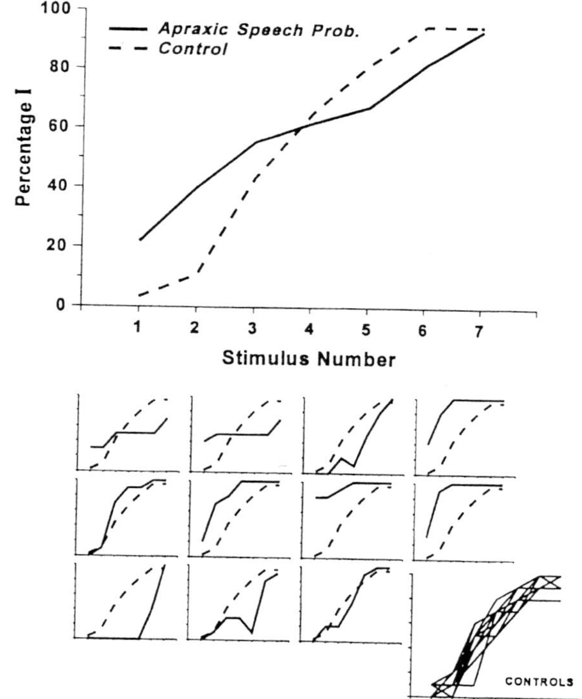

Figure 5.2. Mean percentages 'I' responses as a function of stimulus number for the children with apraxic speech problems and control children along with the individual identification curves.

response variability was calculated by taking the sum of squared errors (actual percentage minus prototypical predicted percentage) across stimuli and dividing it by the total number of stimuli in the continuum. The resulting value was considered a penalty score of response variability. A low response variability value reflects close to normal identification performance, whereas a high response variability value reflects unstable or deviant identification performance.

Student *t*-tests were performed to test for differences in means between the groups. The *t* statistic was computed taking into account the equality or unequality of variances. There was a significant difference in response variability between both groups. Higher response variability values were found for the children with apraxic speech problems ($t(10.1) = 4.86, p < 0.001$). The articulation-disordered children showed a high amount of interindividual variation in response variability. In addition, the articulation-disordered group showed more variation in response variability than the control group ($F(10,11) = 256.0, p<0.001$).

Discrimination

Discrimination results for each pair were expressed with the non-parametric estimate of d', yielding -ln eta scores (discriminability). The mean -ln eta results, as a function of stimulus pair, are shown in Figure 5.3 along with the individual discrimination curves. The articulation-disordered children demonstrated much more variability in their discrimination performance than the control children. For both conditions, the articulation-disordered group seemed to demonstrate shallower discrimination functions than the control group. To substantiate this, for each subject JND measures of sensitivity were computed. Linear regression analyses were performed on the individual discrimination functions. JNDs could be determined by computing the interpair difference that provided a discriminability of 50% of the maximum discriminability value.

Again *t*-tests were performed to test for differences between the groups. There were significant differences in JND between both groups. Higher JNDs were found for the children with apraxic speech problems ($t(11.9) = 2.85, p = 0.01$). Children with apraxic speech problems required a greater acoustic difference between two stimuli in order to differentiate between them than control children. In addition, the articulation-disordered group showed a higher amount of interindividual variation in JND values than the control group ($F(10,11) = 9.59, p<0.001$).

Clinical value of perceptual measures

To substantiate the apparent clinical value of perceptual measures, randomization testing was used on the total group of subjects (including

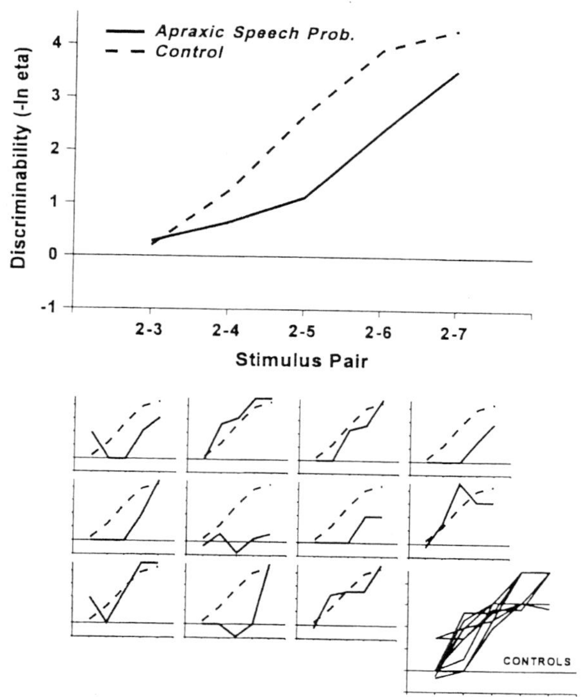

Figure 5.3. Mean discrimination scores as a function of stimulus pair for the children with apraxic speech problems and control children along with the individual discrimination curves.

both articulation-disordered and control children, i.e. N = 23) to single out the poorest performing cases based on a combination of their identification and discrimination performance. Exhaustive randomization testing was performed on a combination of response variability for identification and JND. All possible solutions for the selection of a subgroup of 3–11 poorest performing children were tested (the test statistic used was equivalent to F for MANOVA). The result was a set of subgroups ranging from 3 to 11. The subjects in each subgroup showed coherence and differed maximally from the rest of the group.

For each subgroup, the number of children with apraxic speech problems was counted. This result converted to percentage was considered an expression of the clinical value. For example, when taking a combination of measures of response variability and JND to establish an optimal objective division (using a criterion of the highest F statistic from multiple randomization tests) of the total group of subjects (including all children with apraxic speech problems and all control children, i.e. N = 23) consisting of subgroups of 11 and 12 subjects (1 out of 1 352 078 possibilities), 10 out of the 11 (i.e. a clinical value of 91%) subjects in one subgroup were children with apraxic speech problems.

For subgroups up to 10 subjects, the clinical value was 100%, because the 10 poorest performing subjects in perception, all had apraxic speech problems. The clinical value slightly decreased with subgroups greater than 10 subjects but never went below 91%. This suggests that (1) most of the articulation-disordered children showed perceptual problems, and (2) a combination of perception measures (identification and discrimination) have a high clinical value for the assessment of children with apraxic speech problems.

Discussion

The main conclusions from this study were twofold. First, the group of children with apraxic speech problems demonstrated poorer perception vowels than the control children. This was found on two levels: (1) they demonstrated a shallower mean identification function and a higher mean response variability than the control children, indicating poorer phonetic processing; and (2) higher JNDs were found for the children with apraxic speech problems. Children with apraxic speech problems showed a need for acoustic speech redundancy and required a greater auditory difference between two stimuli in order to differentiate them than control children. The children with apraxic speech problems demonstrated poorer discrimination than the control children, which indicates poorer auditory processing.

Second, a combination of perception measures (identification and discrimination) proved to have a high clinical value for the assessment of children with apraxic speech problems.

Central auditory processing disorders of speech sounds tend to manifest themselves in perceptually aggravated conditions. It has been suggested that degradation of the stimuli with non-linguistic information (e.g. adding noise, reducing spectral richness) does not tap into speech perception problems because of the potentially marginal relation to the speech signal and the specific processes of speech perception. The manipulations lack psycholinguistic relevance.

Instead of reducing the redundancy of the speech signal without reference to psycholinguistic dimensions, in the present study the redundancy of the vowel stimuli was reduced by decreasing vowel contrast and partly neutralizing the spectrum in an ecologically valid way. Moving the vowel formants to a 'neutral-vowel position' can be considered a type of reduction of the redundancy of the speech signal directly concerning entities that have psycholinguistic value. The results with this type of reduction confirmed suggestions made in Groenen et al. (1996a, 1996b) about reductions of the redundancy based on dimensions with psycholinguistic relevance to tap more easily into central auditory processing problems of speech sounds than reductions of the redundancy of the speech signal based on dimensions without psycholinguistic relevance.

The present study shows that auditory perception of vowels in children with apraxic speech problems is affected. They demonstrate poorer auditory and phonetic processing. The articulation-disordered children exhibit a high amount of interindividual variation in both identification and discrimination. A combination of perception measures (identification and discrimination) proves to have a high clinical value for the assessment of children with apraxic speech problems. These facts must be considered in the diagnosis of apraxic speech disorders and in the development of therapy.

References

Edwards M (1984) Disorders of Articulation. New York: Springer Verlag, pp. 77–97.

Groenen P, Crul Th, Maassen B, Van Bon W (1996a) Perception of voicing cues in children with early otitis media with and without language impairment. Journal of Speech and Hearing Research, 39, 43–54.

Groenen P, Maassen B, Crul Th, Thoonen G (1996b) The specific relation between perception and production errors for place of articulation in developmental apraxia of speech. Journal of Speech and Hearing Research, 39, 468–82.

Guyette TW, Diedrich WM (1981) A critical review of developmental apraxia of speech. In Lass NJ (ed.) Speech and Language: Advances in Basic Research and Practice. New York: Academic Press, pp. 1–47.

Hall PK, Jordan LS, Robin DA (1993) Developmental Apraxia of Speech. Austin, TX: Pro-ed.

Koopmans-van Beinum FJ (1980) Vowel Contrast Reduction. PhD thesis. Amsterdam: Academische Pers.

Marion MJ, Sussman HM, Marquardt TP (1993) The perception and production of rhyme in normal and developmentally apraxic children. Journal of Communication Disorders, 26, 129–60.

Repp BH (1984) Categorical perception: Issues, methods, findings. In Lass NJ (ed.) Speech and Language: Advances in Basic Research and Practice. New York: Academic Press, pp. 243–335.

Chapter 6
Evaluation of Speech Perception and Comprehension Processes of Children: Description and practical results

MÁRIA GÓSY

Introduction

Speech perception and comprehension processes are of crucial importance for both language acquisition and literacy acquisition. However, while evaluation of the decoding processes is impossible by simple observation, a language-specific test-package can provide reliable information on these subprocesses. Such a test-package has been developed for the evaluation of the decoding mechanism for children who are speakers of Hungarian, and which can be applied to evaluate subprocesses ranging from hearing up to the highest levels of comprehension. The exact analysis of the decoding mechanism is necessary (1) in the early detection of central auditory disorders, i.e. perception deficits; (2) in the detection, prevention, and correction of dysphasic children and of children with diverse speech defects, with reading/writing/learning difficulties, as well as with attention and behaviour problems; and (3) in planning corrective methods for children suffering from decoding problems. When testing the perception and comprehension processes, answers should be obtained for the following questions:

- Do the speech perception and comprehension mechanism of the child meet the age-specific requirements?
- Where are the actual deficits located within the perception mechanism?
- What is the size and the extent of the disorder?
- What are the compensation strategies of the child?
- What are the disorders that co-occur in any given child?

The delayed or disturbed speech perception and comprehension processes lead to consequences that negatively affect all of a child's activities. The most frequent consequences are as follows: speech defects, restrictions in the ways of thinking, false decoding of the verbal messages followed by false reactions, difficulties in acquiring reading, writing, spelling, learning disability, difficulties in the solution of both verbally set and written tasks, failures in everyday communication, behavioural and psychological problems.

The GMP test-package was developed in order to evaluate speech perception, comprehension and related processes of children between the ages of 3 and 13. The aim was to define age-specific values for correct performances. In compiling the test-package, efforts were also made to obtain information on the operations of each level of the decoding mechanism quasi-separately (cf. Gósy, 1989; 1992). The test-package was first published in 1989 (after a 10-year experimental and standardization procedure with the participation of 8000 children between the ages of 3 and 10), and since that time has been widely used in Hungary, primarily by speech therapists and psychologists. The evaluation procedure and the actual use of the test-package is taught at the Training College for Teachers of Handicapped Children in Budapest.

About 200 children are tested yearly at the Phonetics Laboratory. In this chapter the results of the author's eight-year experience using the test-package will be discussed.

A brief description of the GMP test-package

The test-package contains 20 subtests; there are subtests specifically for schoolchildren and others for kindergarten children only. GMP20 is a subtest for testing dysphasic and/or autistic children. The evaluation procedure is relatively quick, it takes about 30 minutes. The examiner has the right to choose an order of subtests appropriate to the age, developmental phase, behaviour, etc. of the child in question (cf. Manual of the GMP Diagnostics, Gósy, 1995). Some of the listening tests (recorded speech materials) should be administered to the children through a loudspeaker (in a silent room) while others should be through headphones (monosyllables for hearing screening and dichotic tests).

GMP1: Hearing screening by means of the Gósy-Olaszy-Hearing (G-O-H) hearing screening device. The identification of synthesized meaningful monosyllables – separately administered to the right and left ear, at the intensity levels of 45 and 55 dB – provides information on hearing capacity on the one hand and, in the case of normal hearing, on the operations of acoustic cues for word perception (Gósy et al., 1987; Gósy, 1992).

GMP2: Evaluation of acoustic-phonetic perception using sentences. In everyday communication the spoken message is frequently covered by noises of various types and intensities. For successful communication to take place the speech understanding process should work correctly even under noisy circumstances. The 'cocktail-party problem' arises especially for children because they do not have as much practice in understanding speech as adults do. The present task of the GMP test-package is to identify 10 well-formed sentences masked by white noise. The signal/noise ratio is 4 dB. The average intensity level used during the examination was 65 dB. Both the vocabulary and the syntax of the sentences were familiar to the children.

GMP3: Evaluation of acoustic-phonetic perception using words. This subtest is similar to the previous one but, instead of sentences, 10 frequent words masked by white noise should be identified by the child.

GMP4: Evaluation of acoustic-phonetic perception using filtered sentences. This subtest is the identification of sentences filtered by pass-band filtration with a slope of 36 dB. After filtration all sentences were confined to the frequency range of 2.2 to 2.7 kHz. In the case of this filtration, identification can be made only on the basis of secondary acoustic cues; which means that the operations at the phonetic level will be uncertain and decisions at all perceptual levels will become of utmost importance. Both the vocabulary and the syntax of the sentences were familiar to the children.

GMP5: Evaluation of phonetic and phonological speech perception using speeded-up sentences. Identification of speeded-up sentences, with the normal tempo being electrically speeded up to 130% of the original version, gave us an opportunity to detect central perceptual problems in decoding a speech signal. The actual speech tempo of the 10 sentences is 15 sounds/s on average. The first signs of a disturbed speech perception/comprehension mechanism very often appear when the process is forced to work for time-compressed speech, i.e. in a narrower time structure (Shriner and Daniloff, 1970). Children with severe articulation problems have been shown to have difficulty in accurately processing time-compressed speech. The vocabulary and the syntax of the sentences are partly familiar to the children, though they partly might be somewhat difficult even for the 6-year-olds.

GMP6: Sentence identification subtest for young children using natural sentences. Naturally pronounced and recorded sentences containing three, four or five words (i.e. 9, 12 or 14 syllables/sentence) without any distortion are to be identified by young children. Both the vocabulary and the syntax of the sentences are already familiar to the 3-year-old children.

GMP7: Evaluation of visual information integration: lip-reading ability. Visual speech perception ability, i.e. lip-reading or (as it is frequently called) speech reading is very important for verbal communication. Visual information, i.e. the reinforcement of articulatory gestures by eye, is also of crucial importance during language acquisition both for speech perception and production. The children are asked to identify the names of 10 well-known animals on the basis of the examiner's lip-movements. The names of the animals consist of two and three syllables. The examiner is asked to practise mouthing the animals' names (without vocal cord vibration).

GMP8 and 9: Evaluation of verbal and visual short-term memories. Both verbal and visual short-term memories are of crucial importance for a successful working of the decoding mechanism. The standard values for recalling random items are 7±2 (Lenneberg, 1971). Twelve words familiar to children (monosyllables, bi- and tri-syllabic words) are used in this subtest told by the examiner, while 12 colour pictures (on an A/5 size sheet) are used for the visual STM.

GMP10: Evaluation of serial perception. Serial perception is examined by 10 nonsense words of two, three, and four syllables that meet the phonotactic rules of Hungarian. They are pronounced by the examiner and has to be faithfully repeated by the child. The skill being tapped in this subtest is that of breaking words down into their components, a necessary skill for language and literacy acquisition. This skill is based on the verbal seriality processes taking place at the phonetic level of the speech perception mechanism: categorization and definition of the order of the speech sounds without any semantic or syntactic information.

GMP11: Activation of the mental lexicon. It is a very difficult methodological problem to assess the size of a child's mental vocabulary although there are several methods (all of them involving some uncertainty) for finding out the possible size of children's active and passive vocabularies. For this subtest a word-detection method was used to explore the child's ability to activate his or her vocabulary. Results provide information about the working of the active vocabulary by means of a word completion task (cf. naming tests). The child has to expand the syllable he has heard into a normal word, like *mo* → *money, monkey*, etc. The number of words he says – without too much time to think – can be compared with the average for his age-group. From these recalled words, only independent roots are accepted, further inflected versions of the same root are discounted.

GMP12: Evaluation of text comprehension. A short tape-recorded story is played in order to assess the child's inferential comprehension. The comprehension of the story is checked by questions answered by the subject. Responses to the carefully prepared questions highlight the successful comprehension processes and strategies. The questions touch upon various facts of the text: location, time, object, action, instrument, characters, cause/effect, problem/solution, etc. and also interrelations. There is only one correct answer for each question (the manual of the test-package contains the correct answers for scoring).

GMP13: Evaluation of handedness and direction identification. Hand dominance is checked by a series of eight short subtests: (1) touching the ears, (2) crossing the arms, (3) crossing the fingers, (4) using a zip on the table (down and up), (5) imitating hammering a nail, (6) picking up small things from the table and putting them into a small bag, (7) comparing the size of the fingernails of the lefthand and righthand thumb, and (8) drawing a house.

The correct identification of directions is checked simply by asking the child to turn right or left and to raise his or her hands towards right and left. The child's ability to handle 'up' and 'down', as well as 'where' versus 'where from' versus 'where to' on a paper sheet on the table is checked in a similarly simple fashion (directions meet special grammatical forms in Hungarian that are supposed to be known by the age of 6).

GMP14: Evaluation of verbal rhythm perception. Rhythmic repetition of two Hungarian sentences of two poems (quantity) provides information about the children's abilities for perceiving and articulating long and short syllables of a sentence according to the examiner's rhythmic articulation.

GMP15: Evaluation of the central auditory synthesizing ability. A dichotic test has been developed to obtain information about the children's auditory synthesizing ability. The two parts of well-known Hungarian compound words are administered to the children's ears at the same time (e.g. test word: *shoehorn* – right ear: *shoe*, left ear: *horn* at the same time). The child's task is to 'synthesize' the compound word and repeat the original *hornshoe*.

GMP16: Evaluation of the sentence comprehension. Three sets of 10 sentences and 10 picture pairs have been developed according to the first-language acquisition processes of the Hungarian-speaking monolingual children. Normal sentences were created to be understood by normally developed 4-, 5-, 6- and 7-year-olds. Both the semantics of the sentences and also their opposite meaning could be drawn. (For example, one of the test sentences for 4-year-olds: *The rabbit is eating the carrot*. One of the pictures demonstrates this scene. The other picture shows *a rabbit that is not eating the carrot* (the carrot is actually lying in front of the rabbit). The examiner says the sentence and the child has to show the picture that demonstrates the meaning of the heard sentence.

GMP17: Evaluation of the speech sound discrimination ability. Pairs of meaningless sound sequences are said. The members of each pair differ with one phoneme. The child's task is to decide whether the two sound sequences heard were equal or not.

GMP18: Evaluation of the transformational perception of children. Transformational perception is the basis for sound/letter correspondences and some other transformational processes that are necessary for the operations of the whole perceptual mechanism. Twelve small colour cubes are used in the test (three red, three black, three green and three yellow). The child has to identify the colour cube with a speech sound he has just been told. Four subtests provide information (within 2 minutes) about the (1) operation of the transformational perception of the child; (2) serial identification process together with transformational correspondences; and (3) correct directions of transformations.

GMP19: Evaluation of hemispheric dominance (lateralization). A dichotic test containing monosyllables and bisyllabic meaningful words has been developed to obtain information about the children's hemispheric dominance.

GMP20: Evaluation of decoding and related processes of young dysphasic children whose vocabulary is limited to up to 10 words (3-, 4-year-olds). This subtest aims at obtaining information about the child's ability in hearing, speech perception (if available), comprehension and articulation (if available). Most of the tasks of this subtest do not require the child's verbal reactions.

Results with the GMP test-package

Three groups of tested children – whose IQ-values fell into the normal range – and their speech perception and comprehension performances will be briefly discussed (for the results of the verbal speech decoding mechanism of dysphasic children see Gósy, 1997).

Group 1

Children between the ages of 3 and 6 years often suffer from temporary hearing losses for a variety of reasons (such as adenoid vegetation, allergy or repeated catarrh). In these cases their threshold curves are at 20, 30 or 40 dB, particularly at lower frequencies, either with one or with both ears. These hearing deficits often last for 2 or 3 years. Our hypothesis was that these temporary hearing losses (1) cause deficits in the speech perception process, (2) have long-lasting consequences, and (3) are detectable even after several years. A total of 537 children (girls and boys, aged 5–9 years), who had been reported as suffering from catarrh for more than a year, were tested in order to evaluate their speech perception processes.

The acoustic, phonetic and phonological levels of these children's speech perception processes, as well as their serial perception, show extremely severe problems in all age groups (see Tables 6.1 and 6.2). The data show that most children could not recover from the processing failures even by the ages of 8 and 9 years. The performances of their serial perception show significant backwardness by 2 or 3 years. Our data have supported the claim that temporary auditory deficits result in slight or severe disorders in almost all decoding subprocesses, and cause long-lasting perceptual problems with older children as well.

Table 6.1. Children's acoustic-phonetic-phonological perception performances

Age groups	Average of correct speech perception (%)			
	noisy sentences	filtered sentences	speeded-up sentences	standard
5-year-olds	70	87.1	62.7	70/100/80
6-year-olds	73.6	90.9	52.7	90/100/90
7-year-olds	75.4	90.9	66.3	100 (for each)
8-year-olds	86.9	99	71	100 (for each)
9-year-olds	88	99	75	100 (for each)

Group 2

In *language impaired children*'s speech perception and comprehension processes, some delay and/or disorders are expected to exist. The performances of 800 children (aged 6–10) who had had various speech defects supported this claim. For this chapter, data were selected of those children who showed no more language impairment at the time of testing by the GMP test-package. Results obtained show deficiencies in almost all areas of these children's decoding mechanism that are significantly different from those exhibited by normally developed children. Table 6.2 summarizes the sound discrimination results of the tested children. The deficiencies seem to accumulate and lead to a complete breakdown of age-required performance both in speech perception and in comprehension.

Short-term visual memories are better than short-term verbal memory results with these children; however, both performances are poorer than the age-required values. There were only 60 children out of the 800 whose speech perception and comprehension mechanism was appropriate to the age-required norms. Severe speech perception and/or comprehension problems often come to light only when the child first goes to school.

Table 6.2. Sound discrimination performances of language-impaired children

Age groups	Correct sound discrimination (%)		
	mean	range	standard
6-year-olds	60.5	50–80	90
7-year-olds	72.4	50–90	100
8-year-olds	76.1	60–100	100
9-year-olds	86.3	70–100	100
10-year-olds	86.2	70–100	100

Group 3

Children with reading/writing/spelling difficulties as well as with learning disability show severe delays and/or disorders in their speech perception and comprehension processes (see also Vellutino, 1980). Identification of noisy, filtered, and fast sentences as well as of meaningless sound sequences showed significant backwardness ($p<0.001$, see Table 6.3). Disorders of the transformational perception lead to basic problems of reading and writing acquisition (Figure 6.1).

Table 6.3. Speech perception performances of children with reading difficulties

	Correct identification (%)			
Test groups	noisy sentences	filtered sentences	speeded-up sentences	nonsense words
7-year-olds	67.8	96.7	53.5	46.5
8-year-olds	72.8	100	65.4	58.9
9-year-olds	81.2	100	71.6	79.2
10-year-olds	84.3	100	79.8	81.3

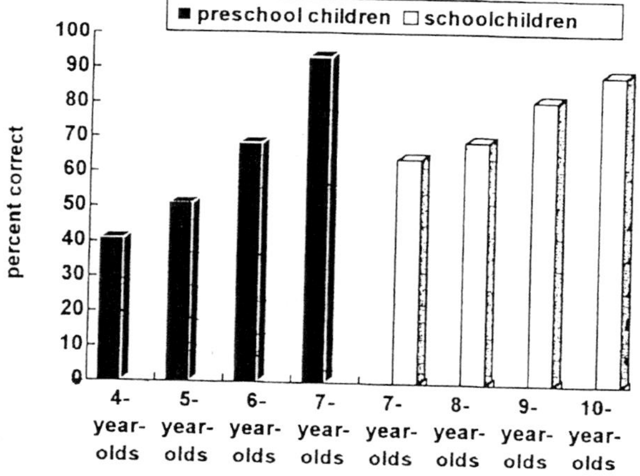

Figure 6.1. Performances of transformational perception of normally developed young children and schoolchildren suffering from reading difficulties.

These children's sentence comprehension was better than their text comprehension on average but all the data obtained show a significantly poorer performance compared with those of normally developed children of the same ages ($p<0.0001$), see Figure 6.2. Children with poorer sentence comprehension than text comprehension had problems in decoding short messages, and verbal or written descriptions of various tasks. Children with poorer text comprehension than sentence comprehension had severe problems with almost all subjects in school, with reading comprehension, as well as with learning.

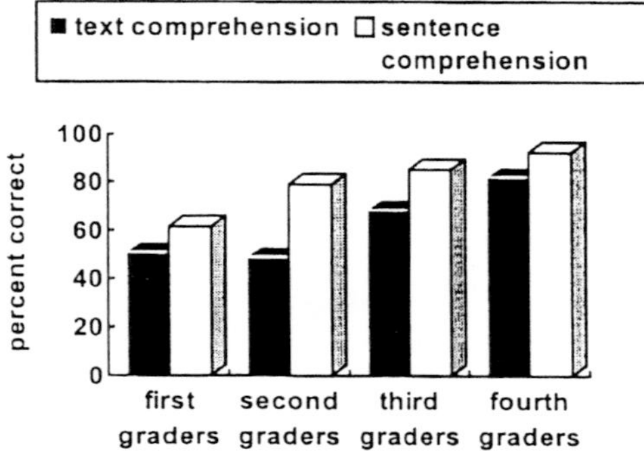

Figure 6.2. Sentence and text comprehension of schoolchildren with reading difficulties (age-required values: 100%).

Conclusions

The results obtained by the GMP test-package suggest that the tested children with various problems have common perception and comprehension difficulties. Due to their communicative experience, good logic, intelligence and various compensatory strategies, they are usually able to hide these difficulties. The 'hidden' deficiencies of some component(s) of their speech perception/comprehension mechanism will lead to further problems, e.g. reading, writing and learning difficulties.

The results (1) highlight the actual decoding deficiencies of the child, (2) provide an opportunity to predict the consequences, and (3) indicate and define the treatment procedure.

References

Gósy M (1989) GMP - Beszédészlelési és beszédmegértési teljesítmény. Tesztcsomag. [GMP Speech perception and comprehension performance. Test-package.] Budapest: Logo-Press.

Gósy M (1992) Speech Perception. Frankfurt: Hector.

Gósy M (1995) GMP - Diagnosztika. [Manual of GMP diagnostics.] Budapest: Nikol.

Gósy M (1997) Speech perception and comprehension of dysphasic children. In Ziegler W, Deger K (eds) Clinical Phonetics and Linguistics. London: Whurr Publishers, pp. 29–37.

Gósy M, Olaszy G, Hirschberg J, Farkas Z (1987) Phonetically based new method for audiometry: the G-O-H measuring system using synthetic speech. Hungarian Papers in Phonetics, 17, 84–102.

Lenneberg EH (1971) The importance of temporal factors in behavior. In Horton DL, Jenkins JJ (eds) The Perception of Language. Columbus, Ohio: Merrill, pp. 174–85.

Shriner T, Daniloff R (1970) Reassembly of segmented CVC syllables by children. Journal of Speech and Hearing Research, 13, 537–47.

Vellutino F (1980) Perceptual deficiency or perceptual inefficiency. In: Kavanagh JF, Venezky RL (eds) Orthography, Reading, and Dyslexia. Baltimore: University Park Press, pp. 251–71.

Chapter 7 The Influence of Sampling Context upon Young Children's Production of Fricative CV and CCV Syllables

CREIGHTON J MILLER, TRISTA B SPICKLER, RAYMOND DANILOFF and RICHARD BERRY

Introduction

Children's abilities to control relative timing and accuracy of production for speech sounds across varying contexts are known to differ from adult norms (Kent, 1982; Hawkins, 1984; Goodell and Studdert-Kennedy, 1993). However, published data on this topic continue to present contradictory interpretations of the nature and extent of these differences and the manner in which they change as children's speech and language skills mature (see especially Hawkins, 1979; Weismer and Elbert, 1982; Vihman, 1996). In this study we asked whether the nonsense syllable imitation tasks most commonly used in such studies (including our own) might contribute to patterns of variability observed in children's utterances. Our rationale for studying contextual effects is rooted in historical disputes about the 'speech mode' and its putative influence upon the perceptual and productive 'set' of experimental subjects (Morrison and Schreiberg, 1992). The present study analyses the influence of context upon spatial and temporal control factors in children's production of fricatives in CV and CCV contexts.

Method

Subjects

Ten children aged 36–48 months, were selected as candidates for participation in this study. The children were enrolled in a Headstart preschool programme in Western Kentucky, and were screened for inclusion via parent/teacher questionnaires and LAPD scores (Learning

Accomplishment Profile – Developmental, Sanford and Zelman, 1981) to verify normal cognitive, auditory and speech-language development. Each of the children participated in a recording session with the second author in a quiet area within the preschool facilities.

Procedures

Audio recordings of the children's speech were produced with a Sony ECM-50 electret microphone attached to a Marantz PMD 221 cassette recorder. During the recording session the microphone was clipped to the child's shirt collar and the interviewer utilized a popular trademarked hand puppet as a focus, asking the children to 'say silly sounds to Barney'. Each child was prompted to produce two sets of three exemplars, each, for the fricative CV and CCV syllables, /si/, /sa/, /su/, /sti/, /sta/ and /stu/, in. two distinct eliciation contexts. The two production contexts were designed to probe the influence of adult models upon the children's speech behaviour.

Immediate imitation of nonsense syllables

In this task children were cued to repeat trisyllable token sets immediately after presentation of a target by the experimenter, e.g. 'sa-sa-sa'. In this context an acoustic model immediately precedes the child's effort, thus emphasizing auditory memory and placing only minimal demands on the child's communication skills. Models for the children to imitate were the CV syllables /si/, /sa/, /su/ and the CCV syllables /sti/, /sta/, /stu/.

Delayed imitation of nonsense syllables

Following completion of the immediate imitation task, the children were asked to produce nonsense syllables embedded in the carrier phrase, 'I can say [token]'. The goal of this strategy was to reduce the effect of the adult model by introducing a time delay between adult and child speech acts. It was anticipated that this might also allow a greater influence from the child's own phonological competence.

Prior to acoustic analyses, the audio recordings were screened by the first and second authors, to judge overall task performance, phonetic accuracy and acoustic quality of the children's syllable productions. From these screenings it was obvious that the two imitation tasks were more difficult for children in the 3–4 year age group than had been anticipated. All of the children showed some evidence of classic phonological processes such as consonant omission (e.g. /sa/ for /sta/), substitution (e.g. /ʃi/ for /si/) and order reversal (e.g. /tsu/ for /stu/), voicing and articulatory errors or distortions, etc. The interviewer also encountered considerable difficulty in eliciting some utterances from most of the children and in fact could not elicit the full range of prompted utterances from several of the children. From the initial group of 10 participants, six children, four females and two males, were judged to have produced at least a few acceptable and analysable syllables in each of the elicitation contexts (immediate versus delayed imitation for each of the six CV and CCV exemplars).

Acoustic analyses

Acoustic analyses compared spectral and temporal characteristics for /s/ in CV and CCV syllables produced in the two testing contexts. All tokens were digitized (16-bit, 16 kHz) and subsequently analysed with a PC-based acoustic analysis system that allows graphical comparisons of oscillographic, spectral and spectrographic representations (Miller, 1991).

Spectral measures

Automated spectral calculations of the 'first moment' (Forrest et al., 1988) were calculated as the power weighted means for DFT spectra at the midpoint of all fricatives produced by the subjects in the study. Used in this fashion, the first moment provides an estimate of centre frequency for the fricative spectrum. We chose this measure with the expectation that central tendencies and variances for first moment data would provide a measure of the subjects' articulatory precision and consistency in fricative production.

Temporal measures

Consonantal closure durations were calculated for each syllable as the interval, in milliseconds, separating fricative onset and voicing onset in each syllable. We envisioned this as a measure of the coordination of sequential articulatory gestures during syllable production.

Results

A full data set of six repetitions was obtained for only 30 of the 72 conditions in our experiment (6 subjects x 6 syllables x 2 contexts); however, at least three repetitions were obtained from the participants in 65 of the 72 conditions. Each of the six subjects reported in these results did produce at least one measurable exemplar for each test condition in the study. From these raw data, representative averages were determined for each subject in each condition, and these values were then entered as cells in all subsequent analyses described in this report.

Calculated means for fricative CV and CCV closure durations are summarized in Table 7.1 and presented graphically in Figure 7.1. Since the temporal measure of closure duration encompassed two phonetic units in CCV syllables (frication and stop closure) and only one phonetic unit in CV syllables (frication), absolute durational differences for syllable type include a measurement artefact and do not of themselves indicate a main effect in the data.

Table 7.1. Summary mean durations (msec) for consonantal closure in fricative CV and CCV syllables

		Immediate 'see, see, see'	Delayed 'I can say "see"'	Percentage change
	/si/	187	235	25.7
CV	/sa/	195	230	17.9
	/su/	191	258	35.1
	Mean CV	191.0	241.0	26.2
	/sti/	294	382	29.9
CCV	/sta/	304	323	6.2
	/stu/	328	333	1.5
	Mean CCV	308.7	346.0	12.1
	Overall	249.8	293.5	17.5

As is obvious in Figure 7.1, consonant closure durations for all six of the CV and CCV syllables in the study were longer for the delayed imitation context than they were for the immediate imitation context, with an average disparity of 17.5%. Context-mediated differences in closure duration were also consistently greater for CV syllables than for CCV syllables (26.2% versus 12.1%, respectively). It seems likely that the smaller duration changes for CCV syllables may be attributable to fricative duration reduction effects which are known to intervene in CCV versus CV environments. Durational effects by vowel type across context are also observable in the comparisons; however, no clear pattern is apparent.

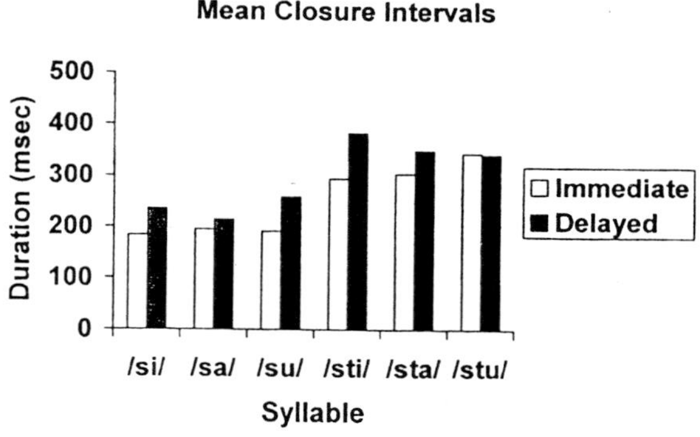

Figure 7.1. Mean durations (msec) for consonantal closure intervals in fricative CV and CCV syllables. Means are grouped by testing context and syllable type.

Although the durational effects of context are clear in the trends represented in Figure 7.1 and Table 7.1, a repeated measures analysis of variance for the data from the six subjects in the study did not reveal significant main effects ($F(1, 5) = 3.55, p = 0.118$).

Table 7.2. Summary means data (Hz) for spectral 'first moment' analyses of /s/ produced by six subjects in CV and CCV contexts

		Immediate 'see, see, see'	Delayed 'I can say "see"'	Percentage change
	/si/	4385	4244	–3.3
CV	/sa/	4630	4410	–4.8
	/su/	4710	4824	+2.4
	Mean CV	4575.0	4492.7	–1.8
	/sti/	4823	4468	–7.4
CCV	/sta/	4730	4341	–8.2
	/stu/	4150	4511	+8.7
	Mean CCV	4567.7	4440.0	–2.8
	Overall	4571.3	4466.3	–2.3

Mean data for fricative spectra are summarized in Table 7.2 and presented graphically in Figure 7.2. As can be seen in those presentations of the spectral data, average first moment estimates of fricative centre frequency ranged between 4.5 kHz and 4.6 kHz for all conditions in the study. Standard error calculations from summary statistics indicated variabilities for individual estimates in the range of 0.33–0.36 kHz. No patterns indicative of syllable type or data elicitation context are apparent in these data.

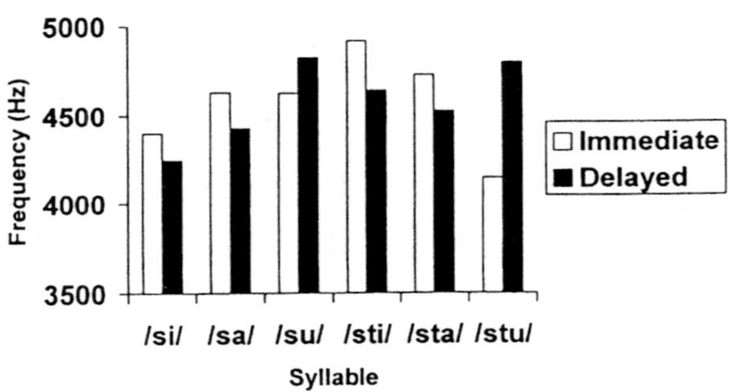

Figure 7.2. Mean frequencies (Hz) for fricative spectra in CV and CCV syllables. Means are grouped by testing context and syllable type.

Repeated measures analyses of variance revealed no significant differences at any level in the spectral analyses of the data from the six subjects in the study ($F(1, 5) = 0.09, p = 0.781$). From these results it is clear that the effects of context did not influence the precision of fricative articulation for the children in this study.

Discussion and conclusions

The results of this study did not reveal statistically significant effects for sampling context upon young children's productions of nonsense CV and CCV syllables. However, the fact that the tabulated durational results showed clear differences in the two tested contexts suggests that children's speech timing may, indeed, be susceptible to external influences like those initially contemplated in our rationale. We anticipate that a larger data set collected from more children might well reveal statistically significant effects for the token elicitation context, at least for temporal factors in children's imitations of adult forms. Accordingly, it seems prudent at least to consider that differences in published findings on young children's articulatory and phonetic abilities may be contaminated by differences in experimental procedure.

Since contextual influences are not reflected in the spectral data for the children in this study, it is our inference that articulatory precision (e.g. phonetic targets) and the temporal coordination of articulatory gestures (e.g. rhythm and segment coproduction) may have been differentially affected by our experimental procedures. This leads us to suspect that different, relatively independent processes, may underlie these separate aspects of syllable production, and further that these processes may mature in differential fashion as young children progress towards the acquisition of adult-like speech skills. It is tempting, though perhaps overly simplistic, to suppose that young children may initially learn and rigidly implement production targets quite early, while developing coordinated temporal control over the articulatory mechanism somewhat later, at a slower pace. While these latter interpretations are highly speculative, the results of this study directly support our initial inference that some of the contradictory findings reported for gestural control in the speech of young children may be attributable to methodological factors.

Note

1 Portions of this research were reported at the 1995 and 1996 Annual Conventions of the American Speech-Language-Hearing Association.

References

Forrest K, Weismer G, Milenkovic P, Dougall RN (1988) Statistical analysis of word-initial voiceless obstruents: Preliminary data. Journal of the Acoustical Society of America, 84, (1),115–23.

Goodell E, Studdert-Kennedy M (1993) Acoustic evidence for the development of gestural coordination in the speech of 2-year-olds: A longitudinal study. Journal of Speech and Hearing Research, 36, 707–27.

Hawkins S (1979) Temporal coordination of consonants in the speech of children: Further data. Journal of Phonetics, 7, 235–67.

Hawkins S (1984) The development of motor control in speech. In Lass, N (ed.) Speech and Language: Advances in Basic Research and Practice. Vol. II. New York: Academic Press.

Kent RD (1982) The psychobiology of speech development: Co-emergence of language and a movement system. Presented to Miniseminar on Language and Movement, UCLA, February. (Unpublished.)

Miller CJ (1991) WAVEDIT: General purpose program for Waveform Capture/Manipulation/Analysis. Users' Manual. Baton Rouge: Author.

Morrison J, Schrieberg L (1992) Articulation testing versus conversational speech sampling. Journal of Speech and Hearing Research, 35, 259–73.

Sanford A, Zelman JG (1981) Learning accomplishment profile – developmental. Winston-Salem, NC: Kaplan Press.

Vihman M (1996) Phonological Development: The Origins of Language in the Child. Cambridge, MA: Blackwell.

Weismer G, Elbert M (1982) Temporal characteristics of 'functionally' misarticulated /s/ in 4- to 6-year-old children. Journal of Speech and Hearing Research, 25, 275–87.

Chapter 8 The Development of Between-word Processes in the Connected Speech of Children Aged Between 3 and 7 Years

CAROLINE NEWTON and BILL WELLS

Introduction

Until recently, most research involving the speech production of children has concentrated on isolated words. One consequence of this has been that phonological assessment of child speech has focused almost exclusively on single word production. While this concentration is predictable, given the great number of prosodic phenomena affecting this length of utterance by children, most normal children will very quickly begin to use utterances of two words or more, and one-word utterances will become uncommon (Stemberger, 1988). Multi-word utterances present new challenges to children and further investigation related to the production of longer utterances is appropriate. Furthermore, it is evident that children with phonological difficulties are generally more difficult to understand in connected speech contexts, and may have particular difficulties in 'glueing' words together in the appropriate way (Wells, 1994). In order to achieve a more comprehensive approach to the assessment of children's phonological difficulties it is therefore important to investigate normal development of between-word phonological processes.

There has been particularly little research carried out on these between-word processes of connected speech in relation to the system known to exist in adult speech. This 'system' and the classification of individual phenomena within it have been discussed by various researchers, such as Gimson (1989), Barry (1985) and Brown (1990). The research project reported here concentrated on a small number of phenomena widely agreed to be the most common or 'central' forms of between-word processes in adult speech. This chapter presents the procedures used for, and some results from, the project, which was aimed at determining whether any developmental trend for the use of these processes exists between the ages of 3 and 7 years.

One hypothesis is that the connected speech processes of adult English are 'natural' in the same sense as the developmental simplification processes described by Stampe (1979) for single words, and also described for the child's first two-word utterances by Donahue (1986), Matthei (1989) and Stemberger (1988). For example, consonant harmony/assimilation occurs within and between words in many children's early productions, presumably as a result of articulatory and/or perceptual immaturity, but is subsequently 'suppressed'. In the same way, it might be hypothesized that the assimilation of final alveolars in adult English represents simplification in articulatory and/or perceptual terms, and so will be present as soon as the child begins to produce word sequences that contain the relevant environments. The difference is that this type of assimilation, unlike 'velar harmony' for example, does not get suppressed as the English-speaking child matures. This hypothesis would be supported if we were to find no age-related increase in the incidence of connected speech processes such as assimilation. Such a finding would support the interpretation that the processes operate at a phonetic level, such as coarticulation.

An alternative hypothesis is that children have to learn the connected speech processes that are specific to English. If this were the case, one would expect younger children initially to produce words in their full forms in connected speech, and only gradually to start using assimilation, elision and liaison. Such a finding would suggest that the processes represent language-specific phonological rules that have to be acquired.

Method

Participants

Fourteen 3-year-olds and 20 children in each of the following age groups: 4, 5, 6 and 7 years were selected to participate in this project. Subjects were monolingual English-speakers, with no history of speech, language or hearing problems and no reported reading difficulties. They attended local schools and nurseries in the City of Hereford, which lies in the West of England, just east of the border with Wales.

Stimuli

Researchers have determined a great number of between-word processes occurring in adult connected speech. As mentioned above, this project concentrated on a small subset of the most common phenomena. These are:

- Assimilation, where alveolar /t, d, n/ assimilate to following word-initial bilabial or velar oral and nasal stop consonants, and alveolar /s, z/ assimilate to following /S/. For example, 'one cloud': ['wʌŋklaʊd].
- Consonant cluster reduction (elision), where /t/ and /d/ elide in the environment /C_#C/. For example, 'just like': ['dʒʌslaIk].
- Liaison, where glides /j, w, r/ are inserted over the word boundary between 2 vowels. For example, 'near a': ['nIərə].
- Production of 'adult-like' definite and indefinite articles when preceding vowel-initial nouns. For example, 'an ice-cream' [ən'aIskrim] versus 'a banana': [əbə'nɑnə].

Two-word environments, containing the relevant strings of segments that might provide sites for the processes, were devised and included in the two tasks, which are described below.

Tasks

Two sets of tasks were specifically designed for this study, to facilitate investigation into the occurrence of processes in different speech 'styles'. A sample of spontaneous speech was also elicited from each child, giving three conditions: sentence repetition, story re-telling and spontaneous speech.

Sentence repetition

Six sets of 15 short sentences were created, which the child would be asked to repeat quite quickly and then slowly and carefully. In order to avoid the effects of tonic stress placement, as far as possible, this element was positioned in all sentences to the right of the two-word site. For example,

> This train goes to 'HEreford
> Jane gave me an 'ICE-cream

No environments were included where the two words of the process site crossed a major syntactic boundary. Two token sentences were created for each 'item'. See the examples above for tokens for /n/ -> /ŋ/ before word-initial /g/.

Story re-telling

Each one of five short stories was told to each child who then was asked to re-tell it immediately. Each story was accompanied by a set of pictures, in the style of Renfrew's (1988) 'Bus Story'. The text below is an excerpt from one of the stories:

Soon they were tired, so they stopped walking and sat down near a brown bench for a drink.
Peter and John saw that there were some white clouds in the sky.
Peter thought one cloud looked just like an ice-cream

In addition to these tasks, three formal standardized tests were administered, to ensure a relatively homogeneous sample. These were: the *Edinburgh Articulation Test* (Antony et al., 1971); the *Bus Story* (Renfrew, 1988) and the *Goodenough-Harris Drawing Test* (Goodenough, 1963).

Scoring

The data collected (on digital audio tape) from the children was transcribed and scored by the investigator. Each potential environment for a between-word process was identified and then scored one of three values:

0	:	process definitely occurring; a clear case of closed junction
1	:	intermediate value, which was intended to cover instances such as the 'partial assimilation' observed by Wright and Kerswill (1989)
2	:	process definitely not occurring; a clear case of open junction

For the main analysis of results, the proportion of score 0 as opposed to otherwise was calculated for each subject, for all 'items' included, in each of the three conditions. These scores were then collated into age groups, for each condition, to be used for further analysis.

Results

Developmental trend

The use of the appropriate form of the more 'morphological' type of process – definite and indefinite articles – could clearly be seen to increase with age (see Figure 8.1). Results of a Mann Whitney U Test indicate that the most statistically significant difference between consecutive age groups occurs between the ages of 4 and 5, suggesting that a 'jump' from the more child-like productions to those more 'adult-like' occurs at around this time, for both definite and indefinite articles.

The results for the articles contrast strikingly with those for the strictly phonological processes: assimilation, elision and liaison. Figure 8.2 shows over 70% use of these phenomena for all ages, and an absence of any developmental trend. Furthermore, no statistically significant differences were found between any age groups.

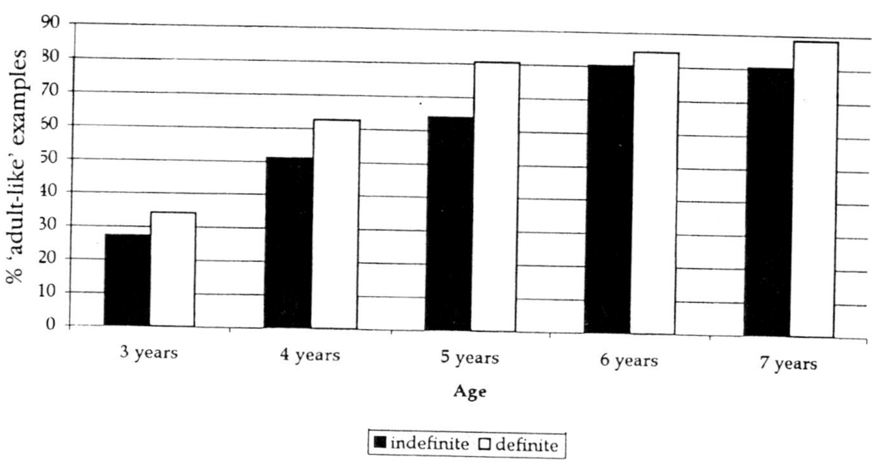

Figure 8.1. Developmental trend for definite and indefinite articles.

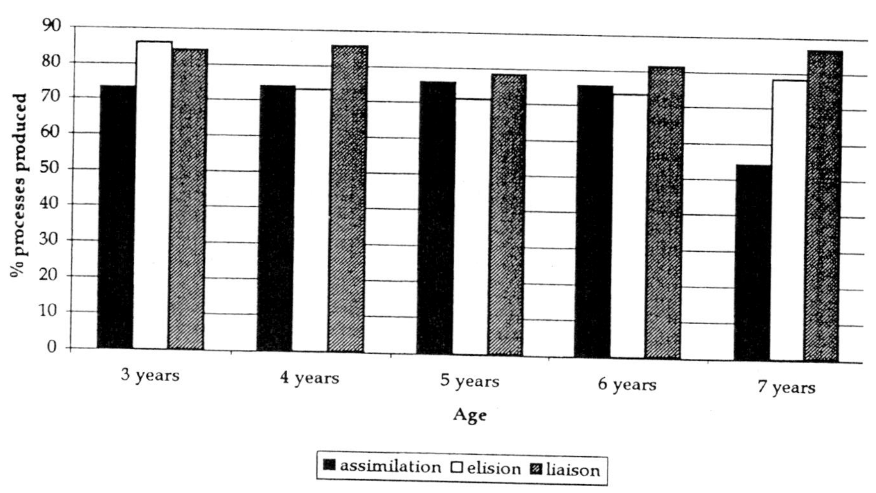

Figure 8.2. No developmental trend for other processes.

Conditions

Results suggest a statistically significant hierarchy for the susceptibility to between-word processes, including the articles in the order: spontaneous speech – sentence repetition – story re-telling (see Figure 8.3). Though results of various Mann Whitney U Tests (for example, for individual age groups) indicate such a hierarchy, Figure 8.3 also shows that this is not a consistent trend across all processes.

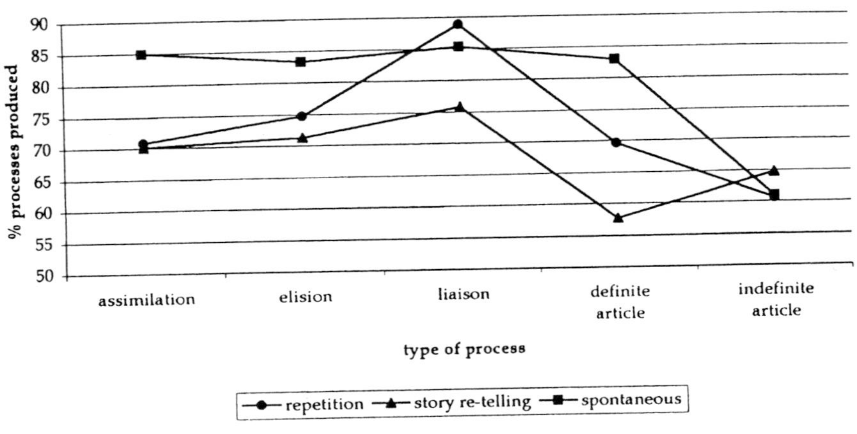

Figure 8.3. The effect of 'condition' on the occurrence of between-word processes.

'Items'

For individual age groups, the application of a Mann Whitney U Test to the data showed no significant differences between any items of any type of between-word process. However, Figures 8.4a, 8.4b and 8.4c, over all the ages, indicate that there are at least some slight differences between them (that is, liaison specifically involving /j/, for example). Figure 8.4a shows that for all the age groups /d/ is the least likely to be assimilated (with statistically significant differences between it and /n, t, S/), /t/ is the most likely to be assimilated.

Figure 8.4b shows that /t/ is generally also more likely to be elided than /d/ (Mann Whitney U Test, $p = 0.0011$).

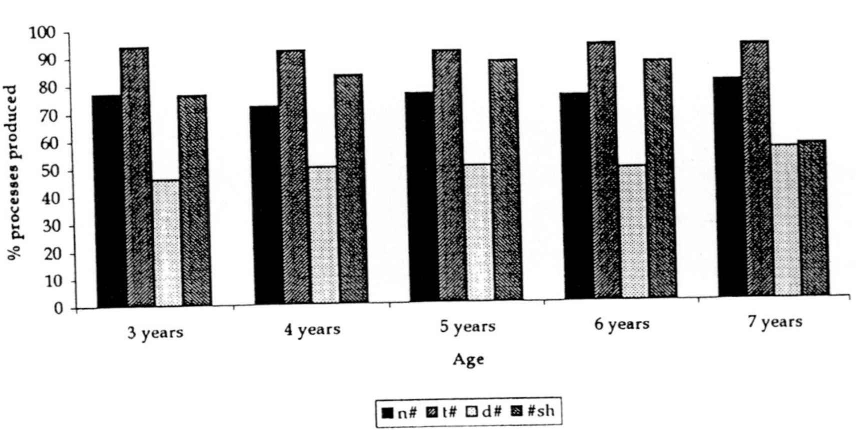

Figure 8.4a. Percentage different assimilation items produced.

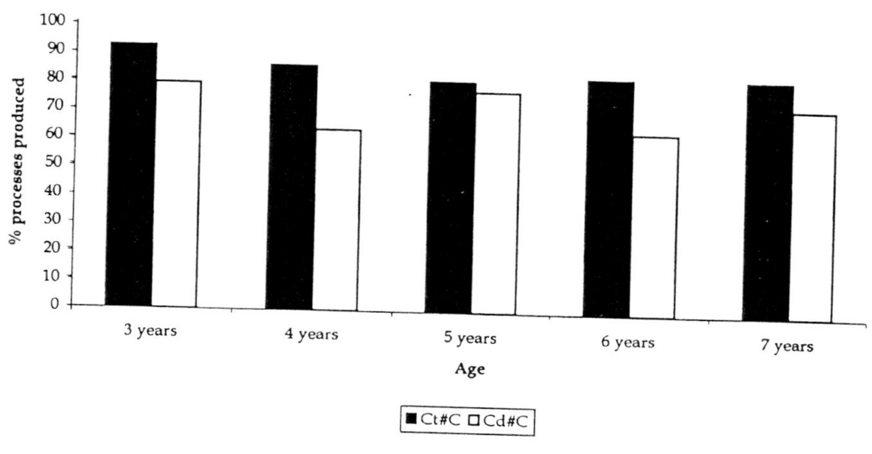

Figure 8.4b. Percentage different elision items produced.

Figure 8.4c shows that liaison with /r/ is the least common form of liaison over all ages, with /j/ the most common (the difference between the two is statistically significant, $p = 0.0032$).

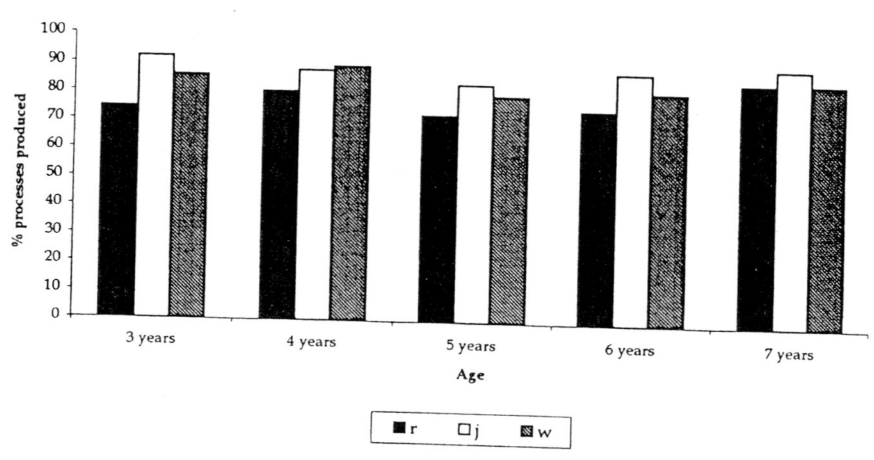

Figure 8.4c. Percentage different liaison items produced.

Conclusions

Lack of a developmental trend for the phonological between-word processes: assimilation, elision and liaison, indicates that children treated these differently from the 'morphological' type of definite and indefinite articles. Furthermore, a number of idiosyncratic productions of the articles (for a time, one child produced the definite article as /ði/

whether followed by vowel or consonant) occurred at around the age of 4, when the 'jump' to more 'adult-like' productions seems to occur. These results suggest that, as might be expected, children have to learn the correct form of the allomorph for definite and indefinite articles. This would be expected, since the alternations involved (the insertion of alveolar nasal before vowel for the indefinite article; the use of a front vowel in the definite article before a following vowel) are in no sense natural from a phonetic perspective. On the other hand, the absence of developmental change in the between-word processes of assimilation, elision and liaison suggests that these may not be 'acquired' as phonological rules, but instead happen as a result of coarticulatory factors. However, this conclusion can only remain tentative on the basis of the research reported here. An alternative possibility is that the between-word processes are learnt, but that the learning is largely complete before the age of around 40 months, the age of the youngest children in the present study. In order to pursue this hypothesis, we are currently undertaking a longitudinal single case study of a child between 2;4 and 3;4, to track any changes in the child's realization of the between-word junctions where, in the adult language, assimilation, elision or liaison might be expected to occur. Furthermore, it may be the case that developmental changes in between-word processes do in fact occur between 3 and 7 years, but that these do not constitute quantitative shifts of the type analysed in this study. In order to pick up any such changes, more qualitative analysis would be needed.

In summary, on the basis of this study, we can conclude that no gross changes in the occurrence of between-word processes are found between the ages of 3 and 7; and in this respect, these processes contrast with the development of the use of allomorphic variants for the definite and indefinite articles, over the same period.

In general, speakers did apply the processes differentially in the different conditions (with the highest proportion in spontaneous speech, and the lowest in story re-telling). This suggests that children of this age consider some conditions to require more careful production than others. It seems possible that the speakers may have felt a greater need to speak more 'clearly' when telling a story to the investigator, which would not be necessary for the immediate reproduction of the investigator's utterance in sentence repetition. Therefore, 'style' – as reflected in these three conditions – has an effect on the production of these processes. It can also be observed in the results of this study that speakers do make distinctions between subgroups of processes, i.e. for individual 'items'.

This account of normal development of between-word processes provides control data against which production of children with speech or language difficulties may be measured. These results also raise questions concerning when and how between-word processes develop from the time children start to produce two-word utterances.

References

Antony A, Bogle D, Ingram TTS, McIsaac MW (1971) Edinburgh Articulation Test. Harlow: Churchill Livingstone.

Barry M (1985) Connected Speech: Processes, Motivations, Models. In Nolan F (ed.) Cambridge Papers in Phonetics and Experimental Linguistics 3. Cambridge: Department of Linguistics, University of Cambridge.

Brown G (1990) Listening to Spoken English. London: Longman.

Donahue M (1986) Phonological constraints on the emergence of two word utterances. Journal of Child Language, 13, 209–18.

Gimson AC (1989) An Introduction to the Pronunciation of English, 4th edn. London: Edward Arnold.

Goodenough FL (1963) The Goodenough-Harris Drawing Test. New York: Brace, Harcourt Jovanovich.

Matthei E (1989) Crossing boundaries: more evidence for phonological constraints on early multi-word utterances. Journal of Child Language, 16, 41–54.

Renfrew C (1988) The Bus Story - a test of continuous speech. Oxford: C. Renfrew.

Stampe D (1979) A Dissertation on Natural Phonology. New York: Garland.

Stemberger JP (1988) Between-word processes in child phonology. Journal of Child Language, 15, 39–61.

Wells B (1994) Junction in developmental speech disorder: a case study. Clinical Linguistics and Phonetics, 7, 1–25.

Wright S, Kerswill P (1989) Electropalatography in the analysis of connected speech processes. Clinical Linguistics and Phonetics, 3, 49–57.

Chapter 9
Syntax at Late Stages of Acquisition: Experiments with Normal and SLI Children

JUSSI NIEMI and MINNA HÄGG

Introduction

The later stages of acquisition of language, especially those of complex syntactic patterns, have become increasingly important as empirical studies have shown that adult-like processing is not acquired as early as generally predicted (see e.g. Nippold, 1998). It has been, inter alia, shown that the degree of animacy and word-order affect the assignment of thematic roles in simple transitive noun-verb-noun (NVN) sentences (Bever's 1970 NVN strategy; Slobin's 1973 Operational Principle C; Harris, 1978; Slobin, 1982; Harley, 1995). Knowing this as well as the structure of Finnish, the data-source of the present study, we have focused on thematic role assignment in simple NVN sentences presented either as main sentences or embedded clauses. The word-order of Finnish is grammatically free, although the canonical word-order is subject-verb-object (SVO) (e.g. Hakulinen et al., 1980). Thus this language enables us to study such novel aspects of sentence processing related to word-order that have until now been unexplored.

Assignment of thematic roles in unambiguous NVN sentences

In these off-line tasks the subjects' task was to assign the thematic roles of actor and undergoer to unambiguous SVO/object-verb-subject (OVS) sentences, e.g. 'The dog bites the cat', where, in Finnish, the NPs are typically morphologically marked for their syntactic functions (*Kissa* [nominative] *puree koira+a* [partitive]). The order of the subject and object as well as the pragmatic plausibility of the NP roles were controlled for. The noun referents and actions were of high frequency and they represented picturable entities and actions. The sentences were divided into the following subgroups: (1) Pragmatically irreversible: *Kalle potkaisee seinää*, 'Kalle kicks wall'; (2) Pragmatically reversible: *Kissa puree koiraa*, 'Cat bites dog'; (3) Semi-irreversible (a) high probability: *Kissa puree kalaa*, 'Cat bites fish', (b) low probability: *Kala puree kissaa*, 'Fish bites cat'; (4) Anomalous: *Seinä potkaisee Kallea*, 'Wall kicks Kalle'.

The test was administered to 17 8–9-year-old ('younger normal group') and 27 10–11-year-old ('older normal group') children and eight 8–11-year-old SLI speakers. The sentences were both read aloud by the examiner and simultaneously given in their written form, one at a time. The task of the subjects was to respond in balanced conditions, in writing (normals) or orally (SLI), to elliptical questions like *Kumpi lyö?* 'Who/which (is) hit(ting)?' or *Kumpaa lyödään*? 'Who/which is (being) hit?', with a single word. The focus of the question (actor or undergoer) was systematically varied.

The main results are presented in Figure 9.1 and Table 9.1. As expected, overall, the older normal group succeeded best and made the fewest number of errors in interpreting sentences with an overall 93% success rate against the younger normal group's 87% and the SLI group's 72%.

An intriguing tendency is, however, that the *younger normal group relied mainly on pragmatics* (see especially sentence type 2 OVS, Type 4 OVS and Type 3b), whereas the main strategy of the *older normal group was to use the canonical SVO strategy* (see Types 4 and 3a and b OVS), with only slight reliance on the morphological cues. In Types 4

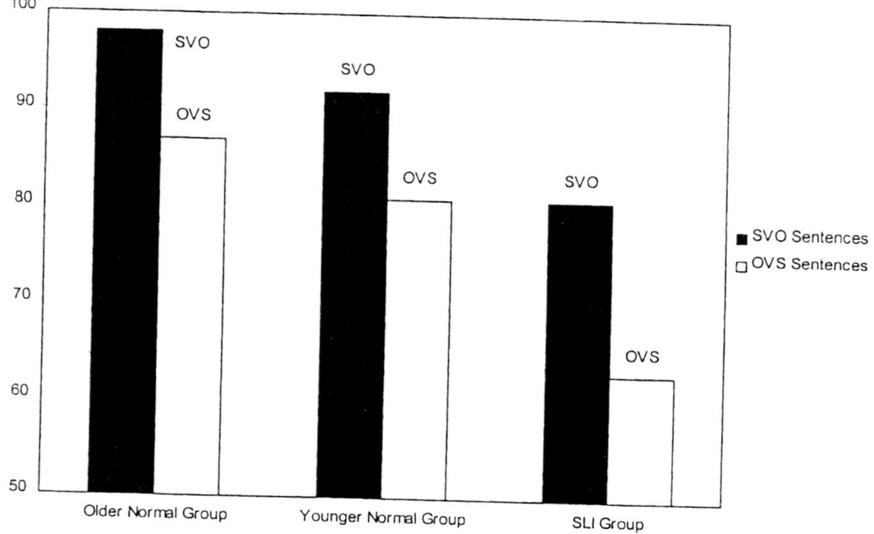

Figure 9.1. The overall performance of normal children and SLI group in unambiguous sentences task – percentages of correct answers.

Table 9.1. Unambiguous sentences assessed by normal children and SLI group – percentages of correct answers

	SVO Older normals	SVO Younger normals	SVO SLI	OVS Older normals	OVS Younger normals	OVS SLI
1. Pragmatically irreversible sentences	100	100	92	94	88	83
2. Pragmatically reversible sentences	99	98	81	94	74	53
3a. Semi-irreversible sentences, high probability	94	93	94	79	85	75
3b. Semi-irreversible sentences, low probability	96	82	69	83	81	41
4. Anomalous sentences	100	88	67	83	78	63

and 3b, where the second noun is the more plausible actor/undergoer, the SLI children scored especially low, and in Type 2 OVS their performance was at chance level.

In summary, the direction of the normal development from 8- to 11-year-olds is *from pragmatics to canonical*, but not yet to the level of fully grammatically-driven syntax. (We assume that normal adults would make only occasional, 'noise' type, e.g. fatigue-induced errors in this very simple task.)

Assignment of thematic roles in ambiguous NVN sentences

As the Finnish plural nominative and accusative noun forms are homophonous (e.g. *vauva+t* 'babies') and word-order is grammatically free, sentences can be constructed where the assignment of the roles of the NPs is not at all grammatically determined, as in the pragmatically reversible sentences like (5) *Tädit näkevät sedät*, 'Aunts see uncles' or 'Aunts are seen by uncles'. In pragmatically reversible, isolated sentences like (5) normal adults tend to rely on the SVO pattern. These and pragmatically more or less irreversible sentences like (6) *Äidit kantavat vauvat*, 'Mothers carry babies' or 'Mothers are carried by babies' and (7) *Vauvat kantavat äidit*, 'Babies are carried by mothers' or 'Babies carry mothers' were presented to the same children as the unambiguous sentences task, and using a similar procedure.

The results are seen in Figure 9.2. Especially interesting are the results of sentence Type 7, 'Babies carry mothers'. In these sentences, which pragmatically would have been interpreted as OVS, the older normal group chose to overuse an SVO strategy.

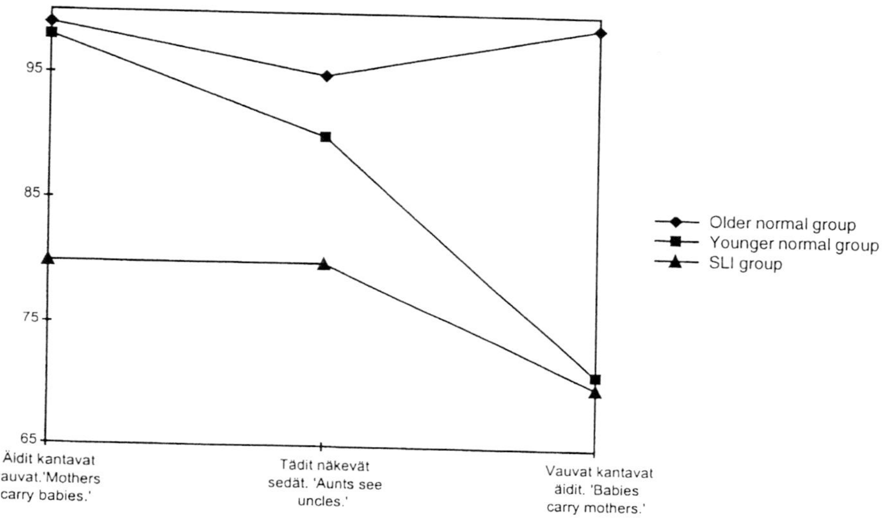

Figure 9.2. Ambiguous sentences assessed as SVOs.

Interestingly enough, in the SLI group, the SVO strategy was not highly prevalent in any of the sentence types used, not even in the case of 'Mothers carry babies', where both pragmatics and canonical word-order would support an SVO interpretation.

Centre-embedded relative sentences

The test sentences of the present centre-embedding task consisted of a matrix sentence noun phrase, a centre-embedded relative clause and a matrix verb phrase. The noun referents and actions were of high frequency and referentially concrete. The first verb (embedded sentence verb) was a transitive verb of perception and the matrix sentence verb was an intransitive verb of motion. The word-order of the relative sentences varied systematically. Sentences were divided into the following complex sentence quadruplets: (8) Subject relative, SVO embedding: *Tyttö, joka näkee pojan, juoksee nopeasti*, 'Girl, who sees boy(acc), runs fast'; (9) Subject relative, SOV embedding: *Tyttö, joka pojan näkee, juoksee nopeasti*, 'Girl, who boy(acc) sees, runs fast'; (10) Object relative, OVS embedding: *Tyttö, jonka näkee poika, juoksee nopeasti*, 'Girl, who sees boy, runs fast'; (11) Object relative, OSV embedding: *Tyttö, jonka poika näkee, juoksee nopeasti*, 'Girl, whom boy sees, runs fast'. These sentences were presented to the normal group (9 years of age) and the SLI group, using the same procedure as in the ambiguous and unambiguous sentences tasks.[1]

Both normal and SLI children gave random responses in the OVS embeddings (Table 9.2). A most probable reason is that these were the only stimuli to involve the processing of two full propositions (e.g. BOY RUNS, GIRL SEES).

Table 9.2. Centre-embedded sentences assessed by normal and SLI group – percentages of correct answers

	Normal group (9 yrs of age)	SLI group (8–11 yrs of age)
$S_{REL}VO$ *Poika, joka näkee tytön, juoksee nopeasti* 'Boy, who sees girl(ACC), runs fast'	90	66
$S_{REL}OV$ *Poika, joka tytön näkee, juoksee nopeasti* 'Boy, who girl(ACC) sees, runs fast'	88	69
$O_{REL}VS$ *Poika, jonka näkee tyttö, juoksee nopeasti* 'Boy, who sees girl, runs fast'	52	44
$O_{REL}SV$ *Poika, jonka tyttö näkee, juoksee nopeasti* 'Boy, whom girl sees, runs fast'	59	38

Concluding remarks

Our results, first of all, show that role assignment mastery undergoes quantal improvement during the few years that separate the present speaker groups. Furthermore, our findings enrich the developmental path schematized by Givón (1995), according to whom syntax develops, both phylogenetically and ontogenetically, from another communicative mode, i.e. a pragmatic-paratactic one. On the basis of the present ontogenetic data we hypothesize that the pragmatic and syntactic stages are bridged by a frequency/canonicality/typology based one.

We would like to summarize our results with a set of operational principles relating to the ontogenesis of syntactic processing in a free word-order language:

Stage 1: Language is used to communicate plausible events. Let pragmatics overrun morphosyntax.

Stage 2: This is an SVO language. Let canonical word-order overrun morphosyntax.

Stage 3: The world and people are what they are. Take grammar seriously.

Acknowledgement

We would like to thank Marja Virmajoki-Tyrväinen (Pihlajapiha School, Joensuu) and the staff at the Kanervala School (Joensuu), who were kind enough to assist us in recruiting the subjects and providing us an opportunity to run the experiments with their pupils.

Note

[1] In our poster we also discussed the associated data derived from chronometric lexical decision paradigm with adults (using the PsyScope program, see e.g. Cohen et al., 1993).

References

Bever T (1970) The cognitive basis for linguistic structures. In Hayes J (ed.) Cognition and the Development of Language. New York: John Wiley & Sons.

Cohen JD, MacWhinney B, Flatt M, Provost J (1993) PsyScope: A new graphic interactive environment for designing psychology experiments. Behavioral Research Methods, Instruments and Computers, 25, 257–71.

Givón T (1995) Functionalism and Grammar. Amsterdam: John Benjamins.

Hakulinen A, Karlsson F, Vilkuna M (1980) Suomen tekstilauseiden piirteitä: Kvantitatiivinen tutkimus. Publications of the Department of General Linguistics, University of Helsinki.

Harley TA (1995) The Psychology of Language: From Data to Theory. Hove, East Sussex: Erlbaum.

Harris M (1978) Noun animacy and the passive voice: A developmental approach. Quarterly Journal of Experimental Psychology, 30, 495–504.

Nippold M (1988) (ed.) Later Language Development: Ages Nine Through Nineteen. Boston, MA: Little, Brown and Co.

Slobin D (1973) Cognitive prerequisites for the development of language. In Ferguson C, Slobin D (eds) Studies in Child Language Development. New York: Holt, Rineholt & Winston.

Slobin D (1982) Universal and particular in the acquisition of language. In Wanner E, Gleitman LR (eds) Language Acquisition: The State of the Art. Cambridge: Cambridge University Press.

Chapter 10
A Follow-up Study of the Linguistic and Intellectual Abilities of Children Who Were Phonologically Disordered

THOMAS W POWELL, MARY ELBERT and DANIEL A DINNSEN

Introduction

Disorders affecting speech sound production are among the most common of handicapping conditions during the preschool years; however, many questions remain regarding the long-term prognosis for children with this type of communication disorder. Moreover, it has been suggested that much diversity exists among children with speech sound production disorders (Dodd, 1995; Shriberg, 1997). For some of these children, problems affecting the phonological system are resolved during the preschool years and they may be indistinguishable during follow-up from children with no history of speech disorder. Other children, however, are likely to present with residual disorders of communication or certain types of specific learning disabilities (Shriberg and Kwiatkowski, 1988; Felsenfeld et al., 1992).

Despite inherent design limitations, follow-up studies can provide important information regarding the nature and course of communication disorders (Weiner, 1985). The present follow-up study was undertaken to extend our understanding of the linguistic and intellectual sequelae of phonological disorders in young children. Specifically, the project sought to describe group trends and to identify patterns of linguistic and intellectual abilities that distinguish subgroups of these children.

Method

Participants

The 21 children (7 females, 14 males) who participated in this study represented a subset of the 40 phonologically disordered children described by Dinnsen, Chin, Elbert and Powell (1990). On average, the interval between the original assessment and follow-up was 4;9 (SD = 12 months). The average age of the participants at follow-up was 9;2 (SD = 17 months). The numbering conventions used by Dinnsen et al. (1990) to identify participants have been retained to facilitate comparison with previously published results.

Instrumentation

During the follow-up, a series of cognitive-communicative tests was administered to each child using standardized procedures. Included in this test battery were norm-referenced measures of language and intellectual abilities.

Linguistic skills were assessed using the *Clinical Evaluation of Language Fundamentals – Revised* (CELF-R; Semel et al., 1987). This individually administered test was designed to assess a variety of vocabulary, (morpho)syntactic, and memory skills. For each child, a total language score was computed as a global measure of linguistic ability. In addition, two scores were computed to compare tasks emphasizing language comprehension (the receptive language score) against those emphasizing linguistic formulation (the expressive language score).

Intellectual measurement was achieved by administering the 14-subtest extended scale of the *Woodcock-Johnson Tests of Cognitive Ability - Revised* (WJTCA-R; Woodcock and Johnson, 1989). The WJTCA-R provided a global measure of intelligence (*Broad Cognitive Ability: Extended Scale* or BCA:ES) and seven cluster scores assessing discrete cognitive abilities associated with Horn and Cattell's Gf-Gc theory (Woodcock, 1990; Horn, 1991). The seven cognitive clusters were (1) long-term retrieval – Glr, (2) short-term memory – Gsm, (3) processing speed – Gs, (4) auditory processing – Ga, (5) visual processing – Gv, (6) comprehension – knowledge – Gc, and (7) fluid reasoning - Gf.

All CELF-R and WJTCA-R test scores were transformed into age-referenced standard scores, with a mean of 100 and a standard deviation of 15 prior to statistical analysis. Finally, a parent of each participant completed a questionnaire relating to the children's speech and language proficiency, academic placement in school, and scholastic achievement.

Results

Group results

Language skills

During follow-up, this group of children performed in the average range of language functioning, with a mean CELF-R total language score of

93.3 (SD = 15.7). The mean receptive language (mean = 97.0, SD = 17.4) and expressive language (mean = 90.8, SD = 14.6) scores were also in the average range. The 6.2-point discrepancy between the group's receptive and expressive language scores approached, but did not meet, statistical significance (t = 2.074, df = 20, p = 0.051).

Intellectual skills

As a group, the children's scores were in the average range on the global measure of intelligence (BCA:ES mean = 104.6, SD = 16.4) as well as on all seven cognitive ability clusters. The lowest cluster score was obtained on the auditory processing cluster (Ga: mean = 92.5, SD = 10.4) and the highest score was obtained on the fluid reasoning cluster (Gf: mean = 111.4, SD = 14.1) There was considerable overlap among the cluster score distributions (see Figure 10.1).

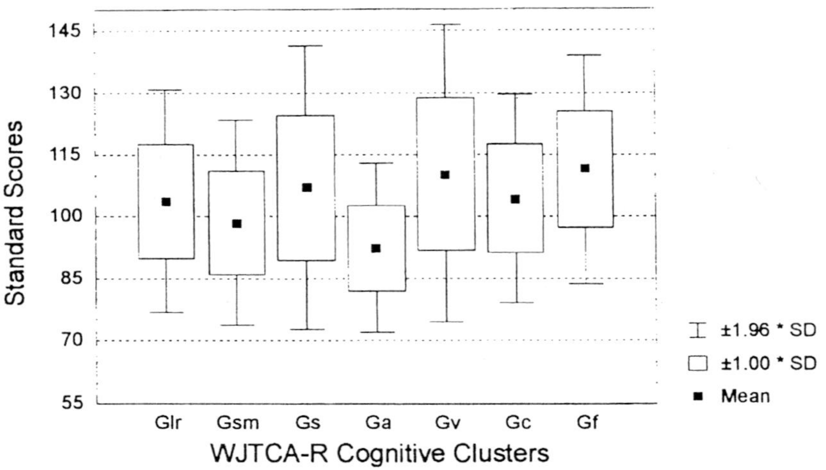

Figure 10.1. Box and whisker plot of group score distributions for the seven WJTCA-R cognitive clusters.

Individual results

Although group summaries allow identification of trends, they may obscure potentially important individual differences. Therefore, the diversity of performance among individual participants was examined.

Language skills

Each participant's total language score was classified using procedure described by Wiig (1989), and the frequency of cases corresponding to each diagnostic category is presented in Table 10.1. Although most children earned scores that were well within normal limits, eight of the 21 children (38%) earned total language scores that were consistent with some degree of language disorder.

Table 10.1. CELF-R total language score distribution (broken down by severity level)

TLS* Range	Description	Frequency
>85	Within normal limits	13
78–85	Mild-to-moderate language disorder	3
70–77	Moderate language disorder	5
<70	Severe language disorder	0

*CELF-R total language score

The statistical significance of receptive and expressive language score discrepancies was also evaluated (Powell, 1993). For most children (71%), the difference between the two language scores was not significant. In five cases (24%), the receptive language score was significantly greater than the expressive language score (cases 4, 6, 8, 14, 22). In only one case (5%) did the expressive language score significantly exceed the receptive language score (case 33). Significant discrepancies do not imply pathology; of the six children with significant receptive and expressive language score discrepancies, only three (cases 8, 22, and 33) met generally accepted criteria for linguistic disability (e.g. Wiig, 1989).

Intellectual skills

The WJTCA-R classification scheme was used to assess each individual's global performance. Most children were in the 'average' or 'high average' range, but four individuals performed in the 'low average' and 'low' ranges (see Table 10.2).

Profile analysis procedures were used to evaluate and describe patterns of performance among the seven WJTCA-R cognitive clusters. Specifically, the intra-cognitive discrepancy score procedure described by Hessler (1993: 83–5) was used. This procedure entails statistical comparison of each cluster score with a predicted standard score, which is then compared against discrepancy norms. Following the rationale presented by McGrew (1994: 144), discrepancy scores were considered significant if they deviated from the mean by ≥ 1.5 SD. The most commonly occurring profiles involved a solitary relative strength in fluid reasoning (i.e. Gf), a relative strength in one area and a relative weakness in one other area, or a flat profile. These three patterns accounted for 71% of the children (see Table 10.3).

Table 10.2. Global cognitive score distribution (broken down by WJ-R classification)

BCA:ES* Range	Description	Frequency
131+	Very superior	1
121–130	Superior	2
111–120	High average	7
90–110	Average	7
80–89	Low average	2
70–79	Low	2
≤ 69	Very low	0

*WJTCA-R broad cognitive ability: extended scale

Table 10.3. Summary of WJTCA-R profile analysis based on intra-cognitive discrepancy scores

Relative strengths	Relative weaknesses	N of subjects (percentage)
1	0	6* (28.5)
1	1	5 (23.75)
0	0	4** (19)
1	2	3 (14.25)
0	1	1 (4.75)
2	1	1 (4.75)
0	2	1 (4.75)

*Gf was strength in all cases
**'Flat' profile

Residual communication disorders and reading disability

Many children with moderate-to-severe speech sound production disorders continue to evidence some degree of disability through later childhood and even into adulthood (Felsenfeld et al., 1992). Furthermore, children with a history of phonological disorder are at-risk for later reading problems (Dodd et al., 1995). Therefore, the data were analysed to determine the incidence of residual speech errors and reading disability among the children under study.

According to parental report, 10 of the 21 children (48%) exhibited some degree of communication disorder at the time of follow-up. Four children (cases 3, 4, 8, and 25) reportedly had difficulty producing [r]. Other children had general 'difficulty with pronunciation', or 'occasional difficulty producing more complex two-syllable words'. One child (case 33) was reported to stutter, while another (case 22) used 'inappropriate words to express herself'. Parents of seven children (33.3% of the sample) said their child had reading problems that were sufficiently severe as to warrant retention, special placement in school, or tutoring.

Subgroups of children

As noted previously, children with disorders of speech sound production are a diverse group. To differentiate subgroups of children with different ability patterns, a hierarchical cluster analysis of the linguistic and intellectual data was undertaken. This procedure sought to identify groupings of individuals that are relatively homogeneous in their patterning of scores. The complete linkage method was used, with distances between observations expressed in simple Euclidean distance.

A vertical dendrogram was plotted to illustrate the cluster structure that emerged from the data (see Figure 10.2). Individuals dominated by a common node are maximally similar, whereas individuals who are subordinate to different nodes are less similar in their pattern of scores. The subject pool is first subdivided into two major groups. The 11 individuals on the left side of the diagram (cases 32–3) earned scores at the high end of the range (mean ≥ 104.66). Individuals on the right (cases 40–2) earned lower scores (mean ≤ 98.33). The majority of children with residual speech problems were among those with lower scores. Indeed, nine of the 10 children with lower scores evidenced some communication disability according to parental report.

Each major branch is subdivided into three smaller clusters, and these six clusters are labelled on the figure. Although these clusters were determined solely by a computer program searching for statistical

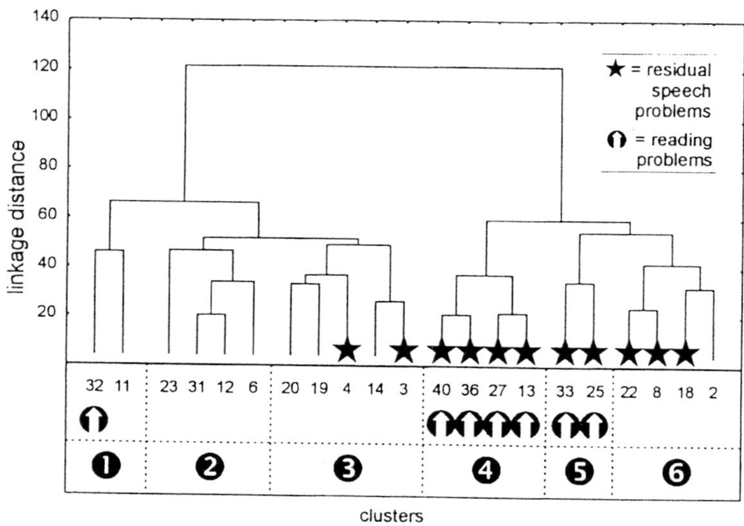

Figure 10.2. Vertical dendrogram summarizing cluster analysis results. Participants with residual speech errors are identified by stars; arrows denote children with reading problems.

patterns that underlie the test scores, they provide insight into the nature of the sample: clusters 4 and 5 included six of the seven children with reading problems.

A stepwise discriminant analysis was performed to identify the variables that distinguished among clusters. Poor performance on three variables differentiated the children in clusters 4 and 5 from all others: processing speed (Gs), CELF-R receptive language score, and long-term retrieval (Glr). The children in cluster 4 earned, on average, the lowest scores on all the norm-referenced tests. The children in cluster 5 earned low scores on most tests, but earned relatively high scores on three cognitive clusters: visual processing (Gv), comprehension knowledge (Gc) and fluid reasoning (Gf).

The remaining child with problems in the language arts (case 32) was assigned to cluster 1 by the computer. This assignment reflects the fact that his test performance differed markedly from the other children with reading problems. Indeed, he was the highest scoring child in this study (mean score of 122 across the variables under study). Clearly, consideration of additional variables would be necessary to identify a viable hypothesis regarding his reading disability.

Finally, severity of the initial phonological disorder emerged as a poor predictor of later reading problems. Case 4 evidenced the most limited range of phonological competence when his speech was assessed by Dinnsen et al. (1990). His phonetic inventory at age 3;7 was severely restricted (limited to vowels, glides, nasals, and voiced anterior stop consonants); his percentage of consonants correct score (PCC; Shriberg and Kwiatkowski, 1982) was 27% (i.e. severe). During follow-up, this child continued to have difficulty producing [r]; however, he reportedly excelled in reading and earned scores between the 90th and 95th percentile in all areas measured by a standardized statewide achievement testing programme.

Discussion

As a group, these 21 children performed in the average range on standardized tests of language and intellect, but diversity was apparent among individuals. Almost half of the children presented with some residual disorder of communication and one-third of the children were described as having difficulty in the language arts. These findings replicate and extend the findings of other researchers (e.g. Shriberg and Kwiatkowski, 1988; Dodd et al., 1995).

The use of cluster analysis in the present study provided a means of identifying certain subgroups of children, and attested to the validity of using psychoeducational assessment procedures with this population. It is true, however, that differentiating variables should not be interpreted as causal. For example, poor performance on the processing speed variable differentiated the poor readers (clusters 4 and 5) from all other children. While poor skills in this area could contribute to a reading disability, it is also possible that a reading disability would negatively impact performance on these tasks. A child with reading problems may earn a low score due to slow execution of the tasks in an attempt to compensate for reading imprecision. Clearly, additional research is needed in this area.

Finally, it is important to note that despite reports of residual speech and reading problems, many of the parental reports were encouraging. In fact, 71% of the children were reported to excel in at least one academic area, most commonly mathematics (43%) and reading (28%). As additional research becomes available, it is hoped that we will one day be able to isolate the variables that will enable earlier identification and treatment of children with phonological disorders who are at greatest risk for long-term disability.

Summary

Twenty-one children were seen for follow-up approximately five years after they were diagnosed with phonological disorder. Nearly half of the sample presented with some residual communication impairment (typically of a mild nature), and one-third of the sample was reported to have difficulty with the language arts, especially reading. Group trends, as well as individual variability, in linguistic and intellectual abilities are described, and a hierarchical cluster analysis was completed to identify relatively homogeneous subgroupings of children on the basis of their linguistic and intellectual performance on norm-referenced tests.

Acknowledgement

This work was supported in part by a grant to Indiana University from the National Institutes of Health, No. NS20976.

References

Dinnsen DA, Chin SB, Elbert M, Powell, TW (1990) Some constraints on functionally disordered phonologies: phonetic inventories and phonotactics. Journal of Speech and Hearing Research, 33, 28–37.

Dodd B (1995) Differential Diagnosis and Treatment of Children with Speech Disorder. London: Whurr.

Dodd B, Gillon G, Oerlemans M, Russell T, Syrmis M, Wilson H (1995) Phonological disorder and the acquisition of literacy. In Dodd B (ed.) Differential Diagnosis and Treatment of Children with Speech Disorder. London: Whurr, pp. 125–46.

Felsenfeld S, Broen PA, McGue M (1992) A 28-year follow-up of adults with a history of moderate phonological disorder: linguistic and personality results. Journal of Speech and Hearing Research, 35, 1114–25.

Hessler GL (1993) Use and Interpretation of the Woodcock-Johnson Psycho-Educational Battery – Revised. Chicago: Riverside.

Horn JL (1991) Measurement of intellectual capabilities: A review of theory. In McGrew KS, Werder JK, Woodcock RW (eds) WJ-R Technical Manual. Chicago: Riverside.

McGrew KS (1994) Clinical Interpretation of the Woodcock-Johnson Tests of Cognitive Ability - Revised. Boston: Allyn and Bacon.

Powell TW (1993) Critical values for evaluating CELF-R receptive and expressive language score discrepancies. Perceptual and Motor Skills, 76, 367–70.

Semel E, Wiig EH, Secord W (1987). Clinical Evaluation of Language Fundamentals – Revised. San Antonio, TX: The Psychological Corporation.

Shriberg LD (1997) Developmental phonological disorders: One or many? In Hodson BW, Edwards ML (eds) Perspectives in Applied Phonology. Gaithersburg, MD: Aspen.

Shriberg LD, Kwiatkowski J (1982) Phonological disorders III: a procedure for assessing severity of involvement. Journal of Speech and Hearing Disorders, 47, 256–70.

Shriberg LD, Kwiatkowski J (1988) A follow-up study of children with phonologic disorders of unknown origin. Journal of Speech and Hearing Disorders, 53, 144–55.

Weiner PS (1985) The value of follow-up studies. Topics in Language Disorders, 5(3), 78–92.

Wiig EH (1989) The interpretation of CELF-R results: a process. CELF-R Update, 2, 8–12.

Woodcock RW (1990) Theoretical foundations of the WJ-R measures of cognitive ability. Journal of Psychoeducational Assessment, 8, 231–58.

Woodcock RW, Johnson MB (1989) WJ-R Tests of Cognitive Ability. Chicago: Riverside.

Chapter 11
Language Performance of Black Children as a Function of Their Cultural Mistrust, Race of Examiner, Nature of Reinforcement and Language Task

SANDRA L TERRELL, RAYMOND G DANILOFF, MIRIAM A HENOCH and TERRY J FLOWERS

Introduction

In multiethnic communities, cultural minorities may experience directly or vicariously negative reactions to them because of their race. Terrell and Terrell (1981, 1996a,b) created an instrument to assess cultural mistrust exhibited by blacks toward whites in the United States of America. Their Cultural Mistrust Inventory (CMI) for adults proved to correlate strongly with willingness to participate in therapy (Watkins et al., 1989; Nickerson et al., 1994). Highly mistrustful blacks had lower expectations for outcomes of therapy and showed lower scores on intelligence tests (Terrell et al.,1981).

In order to explore the possible influence of cultural mistrust on the scholastic and social behaviours of black children, Terrell and Terrell (1996a, b) created the Children's Cultural Mistrust Inventory (CCMI). Barnes (1972) has suggested that mistrust originates early in childhood, a contention seemingly supported by Terrell, Terrell and Golin (1977) who found that black children talked less in the presence of white children than when in the company of other black children. Terrell, Taylor and Terrell (1978) found that when groups of black children were offered tangible reinforcers (candy), traditional social reinforcers, or culturally relevant social reinforcers during administration of the

Weschler Intelligence Scale for Children-Revised (WISC-R), scores were significantly higher for the culturally relevant social rewards than for either the tangible or traditional social rewards. When groups of black adolescent college freshmen partitioned into high and low mistrust subgroups and were administered the Weschler Adult Intelligence Test (WAIS) by either black or white examiners, the high mistrust groups scored higher on the WAIS for black examiners than for white. The low mistrust groups scored significantly better than the high mistrust group for the white examiners (Terrell et al., 1981). The findings of the above studies were applied to black children receiving the WISC-R short form intelligence test with black and white examiners using traditional social reinforcers, culturally relevant social reinforcers, or tangible reinforcers (Terrell and Terrell, 1983). Significantly higher intelligence quotient scores were elicited by culturally relevant social reinforcement. A significant interaction revealed that significantly higher scores were elicited by black examiners administering culturally relevant reinforcers than by white examiners giving traditional social reinforcers. These results, in turn, suggested the present study, which is one of a series of ongoing investigations.

Statement of the problem

Language performance of children is a socio-cognitive as well as a linguistic task. Language screening for educational placement has dramatic impact on subsequent therapeutic intervention. It is of clinical importance to determine whether black children who are screened for language status by black or white examiners will perform differently on the examinations as a function of the race of the examiner, type of reinforcement used, and level of children's mistrust. Candid language samples taken at the same time would reflect self-initiated versus elicited differences in performance. Based on the literature cited, one would predict that mistrustful black children presented with white examiners who used traditional social reinforcement would perform least successfully on standardized language tests and language productivity during conversation.

Method

Subjects

Forty-five young black children between the ages of 6;0 and 7;11, enrolled in St Philip's School and Community Center in Dallas, Texas (USA), were recruited as subjects. St Philip's is a private school with an all-black student enrollment. All subjects were performing satisfactorily in their academic studies and passed screening tests for normal hearing and articulation. Children were taken in roughly equal numbers from grades K (kindergarten) to 2, with nearly equal numbers of males and females. Socioeconomic status of the subjects' families could not be consistently ascertained, but according to the school's executive director, children came from families in a wide range of socioeconomic levels.

Examiners

Two speech-language pathology graduate students, both females with more than 450 hours of practicum experience each, served as examiners. Each had received prior experiences with providing clinical services to both black and white children and each exhibited a friendly, relaxed style of interaction with children.

Experimental task

One to three weeks prior to the language testing, all participants were given the Terrell and Terrell (1996a, b) Children's Cultural Mistrust Inventory (CCMI), a 19-item inventory that asks respondents to indicate the extent to which they trust whites in various situations. High scores reflect a tendency to mistrust whites; low scores indicate a tendency to trust whites. Participants are asked to respond to each item using a three-point scale that includes '1' = no; '2' = sometimes; and '3' = yes. Some illustrative items are as follows: 'Most white children will give your toys back if you lend them to him or her', and 'White policemen will accuse you of something you didn't do'. The CCMI was scored and the median was calculated. Children whose scores were above the median consisted of the high cultural mistrust group and those below the median composed the low cultural mistrust group. Through random selection, children in the two mistrust groups were assigned in equal numbers to the white or black examiner and to receive either the traditional social reinforcers or the culturally relevant social reinforcers from their assigned examiner. This division resulted in eight groups of children, four children per group.

One to three weeks following the CCMI, the children were administered the language tests individually. Each child was seated at a table in a quiet room facing the examiner who told them that they would be tested for their 'language'. The Clinical Evaluation of Language Functions-3 (CELF-3) (Semel et al., 1995) was administered. The CELF-3 is an examination consisting of '11 subtests that provide differentiated measures of selected receptive and expressive language skills in the areas of morphology, syntax, semantics, and memory' (Semel et al., 1995: 1, CELF-3 Technical Manual) for children, adolescents, and young adults aged 6–21 years. At intermittent intervals during the test, according to the assigned groups, traditional social reinforcers such as 'that's nice', 'okay', and 'good job' were used with half of the children and culturally relevant social reinforcers, such as 'nice job home-boy/girl', 'way to go little brother/sister', and 'that's sweet' were used for the other children. After the test, tape recordings were made as the examiner asked the children to talk about their favourite television shows, vacation trips, their favourite food, etc. This candid sample was used to measure mean length of utterance (MLU).

Results

Tests were scored and the candid speech sample was phonetically transcribed and MLU computed. A 2 x 2 x 2 factorial ANOVA was used to assess the main and interactive effects of three variables. The three independent variables were race of examiner, reinforcement type, and mistrust level. The language reception subtest (CELF-R), the language expression subtest (CELF-E), the combined total (CELF-T) and MLU measures comprised the four dependent variables tested by the ANOVAs.

For cultural mistrust level and for MLU there were no significant main or interactive effects among the three independent variables. For the three CELF test scores, only the main effect of RACE of examiner produced significance (CELF-R: $F(1, 15) = 9.304$, $p < 0.006$; CELF-E: $F(1, 15) = 8.679$, $p < 0.007$; CELF-T: $F(1, 15) = 7.987$, $p < 0.009$). Pearson product-moment correlations between mistrust scores and MLU, CELF-R, CELF-E, and CELF-T scores were all non significant, less than $\pm r = 0.22$.

Discussion

We expected that culturally relevant social reinforcement coupled with black examiners and high cultural mistrust would elicit the best overall language test and MLU performance by young black children. This was not the case, nor was there a significant race of examiner by bias interaction as might have been expected as was observed in the results of previous studies with IQ testing. Therefore, the explanation must rest with the characteristics of the black children and their environment. For example, we would predict that performance on IQ tests administered by black and white examiners in the very same private school would yield little or no race of examiner effect.

The black private school from which the subjects were drawn was special in that it had a racially integrated teaching staff and a formal, high-visibility programme of cultural self-esteem in operation as a major component of the curriculum. The children demonstrated highly positive feelings about themselves and their culture, which was witnessed by the examiners and experimenters during class periods, official activities and encounters outside the classroom. It is quite possible that these children could judge individual trustworthiness without relying on blanket judgements of individual untrustworthiness based on an individual's race. The integrated nature of the faculty and staff certainly reduced cultural stereotyping, adding to the neutralization of mistrust of the white examiner.

Lest the reader suspect that the issue of socioeconomic status contributed to the outcome, bear in mind that St Philip's School and Community Center is a neighbourhood 'oasis', one in which the children could trust that anyone entering the school was there for a worthwhile, and, therefore, trustworthy purpose. The school recruited students from all socioeconomic levels of black society as well. And, while the children used Black English in the gym and dining hall, as we witnessed, they used Standard English during all educational activities as a point of school policy and self-esteem. Further, parental participation in school-day activities was mandatory. It is highly likely that the nature of this private school resulted in the lack of significance in language performance between the white and black examiners and level of mistrust.

It is also possible that the characteristics of the black and white examiners influenced the results. The white examiner was 10 years older than the black examiner and had four years of experience working in a racially mixed Head-Start programme. Therefore, the white examiner may have presented a more relaxed and effective impact on the children than her younger black confrère even though both had similar lengths of professional training (two years as speech-language pathology graduate students).

In conclusion, our results support the notion that language testing may provide relatively trustworthy results if the educational setting promotes self-esteem and cross-cultural interaction and acculturation that is not stereotyped and is not built on transferred or direct negative racial-cultural experiences. For this reason, it is important to extend this research to other cultural groups in the United States of America and in other countries.

Summary

Language test scores and MLUs for candid speech samples were examined for primary school-age black youngsters as a function of three culturally sensitive variables: (1) race of the examiner, (2) traditional versus culturally relevant social reinforcement, and (3) level of cultural mistrust evidenced by the black primary school children tested. Children were screened using the CELF-3 language test, an MLU measure derived from a candid language sample, and scores derived from the CCMI. A pair of speech-language pathology graduate female students, one black and one white, administered all tests. Neither cultural mistrust scores nor type of reinforcement produced significant differences in language scores. Race of examiner was significant insofar as the white examiner elicited higher scores than the black examiner. Social-educational factors were used to explain the failure of cultural mistrust to interact significantly with race of examiner or the nature of the examiner's reinforcement.

Acknowledgements

We thank Athena Reese and Melanie Busby for their assistance with this project. We also wish to thank Lynn Flint-Shaw and the faculty, staff, students, and parents of St Philip's School and Community Center. The authors also wish to thank UNT science librarian Mr Edward Gonzalez for his technical and research support. This study was supported by a University of North Texas Faculty Research Grant awarded to the first author.

References

Barnes E (1972) Cultural retardation or shortcomings of assessment techniques. In Jones R (ed.) Black Psychology. New York, NY: Harper and Row, pp. 66–76.

Nickerson KJ, Helms JE, Terrell F (1994) Cultural mistrust, opinions about mental illness, and black students attitudes towards seeking psychological help from white counselors. Journal of Counseling Psychology, 41, 378–85.

Semel E, Wigg EH, Secord WA (1995) Clinical Evaluation of Language Fundamentals Third Edition. San Antonio, TX: The Psychological Corporation.

Terrell F, Terrell S (1981) An inventory to measure cultural mistrust among blacks. Western Journal of Black Studies, 5, 180–5.

Terrell F, Terrell S (1983) The relationship between race of examiner, cultural mistrust, and the intelligence test performance of black children. Psychology in the Schools, 20, 367–9.

Terrell F, Terrell S (1996a) The cultural mistrust inventory: development, findings, and implications. In Jones R (ed.) Handbook of Tests and Measurements for Black Populations, Vol 1. Hampton, VA: Cobb and Henry Publishers, pp. 321–31.

Terrell F, Terrell S (1996b) An inventory for assessing cultural mistrust in black children. In Jones R (ed.) Handbook of Tests and Measurements for Black Populations, Vol 2. Hampton, VA: Cobb and Henry Publishers, pp. 245–7.

Terrell F, Terrell S, Golin S (1977) Language performance in black versus white situations. Language and Speech, 20, 377–83.

Terrell F, Taylor J, Terrell S (1978) Effect of type of social reinforcement on the intelligence test performance of lower-class black children. Journal of Consulting and Clinical Psychology, 46, 1538–9.

Terrell F, Terrell S, Taylor J (1981) Effect of race of examiner and cultural mistrust on the WAIS performance of black students. Journal of Consulting and Clinical Psychology, 49, 570–1.

Watkins CE, Terrell F, Miller F, Terrell S (1989) Cultural mistrust and its effects on expectation variables on black client, white counselor relationships. Journal of Counseling Psychology, 36, 447–50.

Chapter 12
Stuttering as a Phonological Encoding Defect?

REMCA BURGER and FRANK WIJNEN

Introduction

The primary symptoms of stuttering are the repetition and the (tensed) prolongation of speech sounds, and/or blocking. The speaker knows what to say (including the words and their order), but is not capable of doing so at that moment.

There are numerous indications (Bosshardt, 1990; Postma et al., 1990) that stuttering may be related to a perturbation of the speech planning process. Psycholinguistic models, notably Levelt's (1989), divide the planning of speech into three components: conceptualization, formulation and articulation. The conceptualizor generates the pre-verbal message. The formulator creates a linguistic form for this message; the words are selected and ordered in a syntactic structure (grammatical encoding). During the phonological encoding (also a part of the formulation stage), the phonetic plan is formed, which consists of the information needed for the articulation of speech (e.g. order of phonemes, intonation patterns). This phonetic plan is not yet overt speech, and can be seen as internal speech. During the articulation, the phonetic plan is translated into audible speech. Levelt's model also includes a speech monitor, which enables the speaker to check his speech for errors and correct them. Besides audible speech, this monitor is able to check internal speech as well. An important question is during which phase the errors arise that cause stuttering.

According to Kolk (1991), stuttering is caused by a phonological encoding problem. In phonological encoding segments (phonemes) are selected for syllable frames. Segments are considered to be nodes in an activation spreading network. Several segments may compete for a particular syllable slot. The segment that is most activated is selected. Kolk has proposed that in stutterers activation spreading is slower than in non-stutterers. As a consequence, several elements are active for a longer period of time. This, in combination with the speaker's wish to speak at a 'normal' speaking rate, increases the chance of misselection. The speech monitor detects and corrects this error before it is uttered. These covertly repaired errors interfere with speech delivery and surface as dysfluencies. This explanation, which relates dysfluencies (including stuttered dysfluencies) to repair processes during speech production, is called the 'covert repair hypothesis' (Postma and Kolk, 1993).

The covert repair hypothesis does not by itself account for the observation that stressed syllables have a much higher probability of being involved in dysfluency than unstressed syllables (e.g. Prins et al., 1991). Wingate (1988) suggested on the basis of this observation that stutterers have particular difficulty with computing the prosodic parameters of the articulatory plan. This relates particularly to the rhyme, i.e. the part of the syllable that captures the vowel and the following consonants, since the rhyme is the stress bearing part of the syllable.

Wijnen and Boers (1994) combined the hypotheses of Kolk and Wingate, by suggesting that stutterers have difficulty in the phonological encoding of, in particular, the rhyme. The prototypical stuttering symptoms are interpreted as attempts to start speaking before the articulatory plan has been completely specified. To investigate this, they conducted a phonological priming experiment. The reasoning behind their experiment was as follows: 'if we could somehow influence phonological encoding in such a manner that the specific problem is (partially) reduced, the stutterer's behaviour would approximate that of normal speakers. However, if we interfered similarly *without* affecting the specific problem area (i.e. the syllable rhyme), we would fail to obtain a positive effect' (Wijnen and Boers 1994: 5). They used a speech production task, developed by Meyer (1988).

On each trial, the subject had to utter a response word, upon visual presentation of a (semantically) related cue word. In the homogeneous condition, the response words shared either the initial consonant (C) or the initial consonant and subsequent vowel (CV). Following Meyer (1988), the phonologically related response words were expected to prime each other. In the heterogeneous condition the response words were phonologically unrelated. The response words were disyllabic, with stress on the first syllable. Non-stutterers were faster in the homogeneous condition than in the heterogeneous condition. This 'priming effect' was larger for words with an identical consonant and subsequent vowel than for words with only an identical consonant. In the stutterers, a priming effect was found only when the response words shared both the consonant and the vowel. The results were taken to indicate that stutterers have a specific problem with the encoding of the rhyme of a syllable. However, the overall effect was representative for only four out of nine stuttering subjects. The others patterned with the non-stutterers.

Wijnen and Boers's experiment served as a starting point for this investigation. First, we attempted to replicate these results with a new set of stimulus words and a larger group of subjects. Second, although Wijnen and Boers's results are compatible with their hypothesis, their experiment does not constitute a strong test, since only response words that were stressed on the first syllable were used. In this study, words with initial stress were compared with words with final stress in order to determine whether stress is a crucial variable.

Four conditions were created by crossing stress position (first or second syllable) with prime type (word-initial C or word-initial CV). For the response words stressed on the first syllable, the results are expected to match Wijnen and Boers's findings. Following Wingate's hypothesis and Wijnen and Boers's assumption described above, priming (with word-initial elements) of response words with final stress will not speed up the stutterers' reaction times, since in that condition the stressed syllable, which is supposedly problematic, is not primed.

Method

Subjects

Fifteen non-stutterers (mean age: 25 years) and 15 moderate to severe stutterers (mean age: 24 years) participated in this experiment. Both groups consisted of 10 men and 5 women, and the subjects were all native speakers of Dutch. All subjects' stuttering was reported to have started in childhood. Most of the stutterers had been in therapy or were still in therapy during the investigation. The nature of the experiment made it impossible to use any strategies learned in therapy.

Procedure and design

In this investigation the implicit phonological priming procedure of Meyer (1988) was used. Before starting a section of the experiment (a 'block', see below), subjects learned five cue word–response word combinations. These combinations were semantically related to simplify the learning. The subjects were allowed to take as much time as they needed for learning the combinations. They were taught to utter the right response word as fast as possible upon visual presentation of the cue word.

In the homogeneous condition the word sets were phonologically related. They had either an identical first phoneme (C) or identical first and second phonemes (CV). In the heterogeneous condition the word pairs from different homogeneous sets were mixed. As a result, there is no phonological relation between the response words. The difference (in reaction time) between these conditions is referred to as the priming effect. The strength of this design is that each word pair serves as its own control. The dependent variable was the time between the visual presentation of the cue word and the onset of articulation of the response word (speech onset latency). After every 25 trials the mean reaction time and the number of late responses (longer than 1000 ms) was displayed on the screen. Blocks of trials were alternated with breaks.

The trials were structured as follows: warning beep, 600 ms pause, presentation cue word for 150 ms, 1050 ms pause, beginning of the following trial. When the reaction time exceeded 1000 ms, a second warning beep was presented and the next trial started after 200 ms.

Stimuli

All response words were disyllabic, and had a CV–CVC structure (e.g. kavel). Each block consisted of five different word pairs. Each word pair was presented five times, so one block consisted of 25 trials. The order was randomized, but a word pair never appeared in two successive trials. Five of such blocks (first consonant: p, k, s, f, t) were presented in both the homogeneous and the heterogeneous condition. The whole of 10 blocks was presented three times for each of the four combinations of the factors 'prime type' (C or CV) and 'stress position' (1st or 2nd syllable). This resulted in 120 blocks (120 x 25 = 3000 trials). Each subject was tested on all blocks. The presentation order of the blocks was balanced across subjects.

Apparatus

The experiment was run on an Indy workstation (Silicon Graphics). A 17" computer screen (Samtron) was used for presenting the cue words. Reaction times were registered by the computer, using a voice-key for determining the speech-onset times.

Results

Part of the data was excluded from the analysis (e.g. late responses, wrong responses, dysfluent responses). For the non-stutterers 8.8% and for the stutterers 17.7% of the total responses were invalid. The data were analysed by means of a five-way ANOVA, with stress position, prime type, and condition as within group variables, and group (non-stutterers, stutterers) and subject as between group variables. Subject was nested under group and treated as a random factor. A significance level of 5% was used.

Main effects

Table 12.1 gives the average reaction times and standard deviations for the several manipulated variables (main effects), and their p values.

Table 12.1. Average reaction times and standard deviation in ms

	Mean RT	
non-stutterers	634 (σ = 141)	$F_{(1,28)} = 4.55, p < 0.05$
stutterers	675 (σ = 141)	
homogeneous	634 (σ = 144)	$F_{(1,28)} = 60.92, p < 0.000$
heterogeneous	673 (σ = 138)	
C-prime	663 (σ = 140)	$F_{(1,28)} = 20.93, p < 0.000$
CV-prime	644 (σ = 144)	
stress 1st syllable	645 (σ = 142)	$F_{(1,28)} = 8.21, p < 0.01$
stress 2nd syllable	662 (σ = 142)	
subject		$F_{(1,28)} = 533.28, p < 0.000$

As can be seen from Table 12.1, non-stutterers responded significantly faster than stutterers. Further the homogeneous condition yielded significantly faster reaction times (RTs) than the heterogeneous condition across subjects. This difference is the priming effect. CV-prime primed significantly better than C-prime. Moreover, subjects responded significantly faster to words with stress on the first syllable than to words with stress on the second syllable.

Interaction effects

The factor subject interacted with all other main variables. This was visible in the significant two-way, three-way and four-way interactions of subject (within group) with stress position, prime type and condition. These effects show that there are very large differences between the subjects. To illustrate this, Table 12.2 shows the mean reaction time, the priming effect (heterogeneous minus homogeneous) across stress position divided up into prime type (C, CV) and the effect of stress position across prime type for every subject.

As Figure 12.1 shows, the expected interaction of group, condition and prime type (no effect or a significantly smaller effect of C-priming in stutterers than in non-stutterers) did not show up in these data. The pattern of the interaction of condition and prime type is the same for the two groups of subjects. Moreover, stress position did not affect the two subject groups differently.

Figure 12.2 is suggestive of a difference between the non-stutterers and the stutterers in the interaction of condition, stress position and prime type. It seems as if stutterers are more sensitive to the stress manipulation than non-stutterers, but this difference is far from significant.

Table12.2. Mean RT, priming effect (heterogeneous - homogeneous), and RT by stress position per subject

Subject	Mean RT	Priming effect C-prime	CV-prime	Mean RT Stress 1st syllable	Stress 2nd syllable
Non-stutterers					
1	504	3	30	504	503
2	636	18	66	620	652
3	664	10	1	668	660
4	682	54	77	705	659
5	657	31	66	643	671
6	612	37	63	610	615
7	649	–10	62	621	679
8	609	34	42	594	623
9	673	32	93	659	687
10	628	47	80	639	618
11	611	33	73	617	606
12	708	51	24	735	683
13	647	–14	38	630	662
14	595	23	65	567	623
15	647	21	36	638	656
Stutterers					
16	667	6	14	676	657
17	596	48	86	596	596
18	754	–5	–11	756	751
19	719	42	70	712	725
20	781	–15	3	773	788
21	731	72	175	696	765
22	667	28	28	623	714
23	590	7	60	560	620
24	601	3	70	597	605
25	659	7	17	647	671
26	640	38	68	639	641
27	730	46	47	708	752
28	680	4	23	664	697
29	606	62	93	605	606
30	767	14	34	752	783

Conclusions

This study was conducted primarily to replicate Wijnen and Boers's findings. They found an interesting interaction of group, prime type and condition, which suggested that stutterers have difficulty with the phonological encoding of the rhyme. In this study, this effect did not show up. The reaction times as function of the interaction between prime type and condition showed the same pattern in stutterers and non-stutterers. However, stutterers had overall larger speech-onset

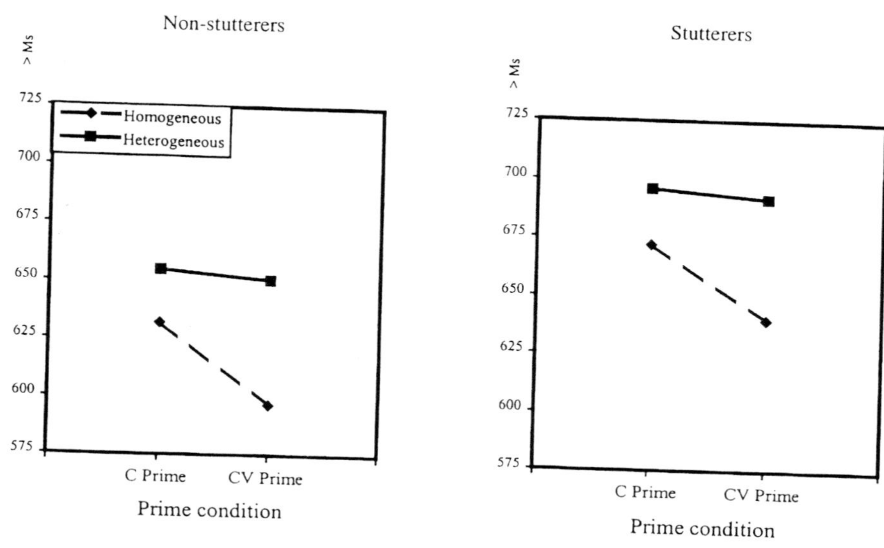

Figure 12.1. Mean RT by group, condition and prime condition.

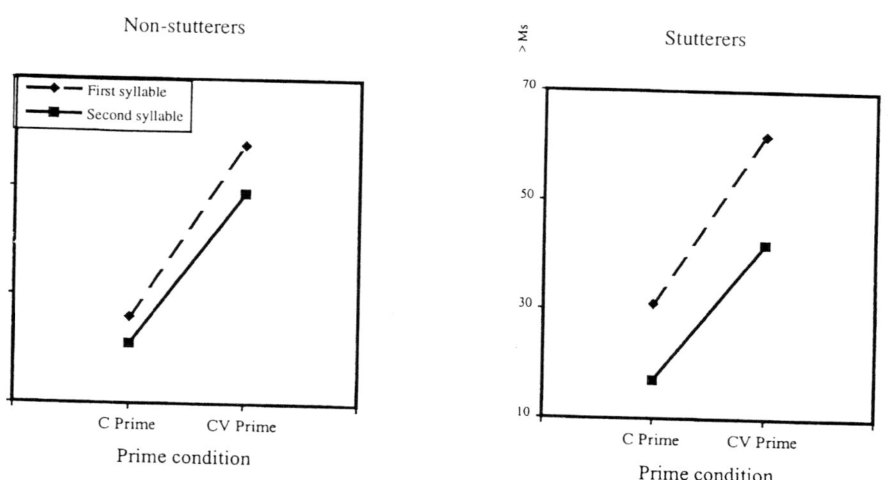

Figure 12.2. Priming effect (heterogeneous – homogeneous) by group, stress position and prime condition.

latencies than non-stutterers. This is compatible with a phonological planning problem for stutterers, but also with other explanations. Another purpose of this experiment was to examine the influence of stress upon the phonological encoding. We expected stress to influence stutterers and non-stutterers differently. This was not the case, no interaction was found between group and stress position. In conclusion, these results do not support the hypothesis that stuttering is specifically related to a difficulty in the phonological encoding of the stress-bearing part of the syllable. Apparently, the problem that Wingate speculates on is related to (sentential) accent, not to (word-level) stress.

A closer look into the data suggests that the difference between Wijnen and Boers's results on the one hand, and the outcome of this study on the other, is due to the vast interindividual variations in stutterers. An individual based examination of these data seems more appropriate.

Summary

A phonological priming experiment was conducted, primarily to replicate Wijnen and Boers's (1994) findings, which suggested that stutterers have difficulty with the phonological encoding of the syllable rhyme. The average response times in stutterers were significantly longer than in non-stutterers, but the crucial effect, i.e. an interaction of prime type (C versus CV) and subject group (stutterers versus non-stutterers) was not reliable. Another purpose of this experiment was to examine the influence of stress upon phonological encoding in non-stutterers and stutterers. No significant interaction between subject group and stress position was found. In conclusion, these results do not support the hypothesis that stuttering is specifically related to a difficulty in the phonological encoding of the stress-bearing part of the syllable.

References

Bosshardt HG (1990) Subvocalization and reading rate differences between stuttering and nonstuttering children and adults. Journal of Speech and Hearing Research, 33, 776–85.

Janssen P (1994) De etiologie van stotteren: theorieën, modellen, hypothesen en speculaties. Stem-, Spraak- en Taalpathologie, 3, 3–41.

Kolk H (1991) Is stuttering a symptom of adaptation or of impairment? In Peters HFM, Hulstijn W, Starkweather CW (eds) Speech Motor Control and Stuttering. Amsterdam: Elsevier/Excerpta Medica, pp. 131–40.

Levelt WJM (1989) Speaking: From Intention to Articulation. Cambridge, MA: Bradford Books/The MIT Press.

Meyer AS (1988) Phonological Encoding in Language Production. Doctoral dissertation, University of Nijmegen.

Postma A, Kolk H (1993) The covert repair hypothesis: prearticulatory repair processes in normal and stuttered disfluencies. Journal of Speech and Hearing Research, 36, 472–87.

Postma A, Kolk H, Povel DJ (1990) Speech planning and execution in stutterers. Journal of Fluency Disorders, 15, 49–59.

Prins D, Hubbard CP, Krause M (1991) Syllabic stress and the occurrence of stuttering. Journal of Speech and Hearing Research, 34, 1011–16.

Wijnen F, Boers I (1994) Phonological priming effects in stutterers. Journal of Fluency Disorders, 19, 1–20.

Wingate ME (1988) The Structure of Stuttering. New York: Springer.

Chapter 13
Perceptual Properties of Truncated Infant Protosyllabic CV-syllables

NANCYE ROUSSEL, RAYMOND DANILOFF, MICHAEL DALY, KUEN KAO, CREIGHTON MILLER and RICHARD BERRY

Introduction

The present experiment extends the work of Miller, Pirolli, Zlatin-Laufer, Daniloff (1998) who studied the acoustic clues in monosyllabic CV infant utterances produced during quiet, solitary play during months 6–15 of infancy. They found little acoustic evidence for developmental change in those CV monosyllables; in addition, the acoustic clues were rather impoverished vis-à-vis adult speakers. These findings of developmentally static CV utterances supplement those of Konopczynski (1997) and Konopczynski and Vinter (1997) who observed that deafened French infants produced frequent non-directed polyvocalic 'gibberish' during quiet play, which exhibited little developmental change. The present study examined perceptual properties of the set of 60 CV-utterances studied by Miller et al. (1998). This investigation derived the percentage of correct psychometric functions of the syllables as successively larger chunks were deleted from either the front or rear of each token. Critical perceptual intervals centred on the transitions (Furui, 1986; Warner, 1997) were computed as well as patterns of perceptual error and departures from prototypical adult CV perception in an attempt to discern adult–child differences and possible developmental change in perceptual properties not mirrored in the acoustic findings.

Procedures

Speech stimuli

Sixty CV monosyllabic stop plus vowel (six stops, 11 vowels) CV utterances used by Miller et al. (1998) represented calm, non-directed vocalizations of two normal first-born infants engaged in quiet play over months 6–15 of life. Three phoneticians identified the syllables reliably. The CV tokens were filtered at 36 dB/octave for a 0.15–10 kHz pass band, digitized at 20 KHz, and manipulated in a digital waveform/spectral analyser. Tokens were amplitude normalized, and each token was subjected to a truncation procedure during which successive 15 ms segments were deleted in unidirectional steps from the onset or the offset of each syllable until nothing remained of the torso of the token, yielding roughly 1200 different syllable remnants for perception. Zero axis-crossing truncations were made to minimize disruptive transients at the onset or the offset of the truncated syllable remnants. Thus, an initial truncation of a 150 ms syllable would produce 16 stimuli, respectively 150, 135, 120, 105, . . . , and 15 ms long.

Listening task

The syllable fragments were transferred to audio tape for presentation. One stimulus set consisted of truncated syllables cut in one direction only, which differed in duration by no more than 45 ms. Each stimulus set was repeated nine times, and tokens were presented in random order with respect to fragment length, speaker and token identity. All stimuli uttered within a single two-month developmental stage by the infants were used for a single set of stimuli to be labelled. All final truncations were presented first, starting with longest fragments, ending with the shortest.

Stimuli were presented in sets of three identical tokens with 800 ms ISIs followed by a 5 s response interval following each stimulus triplet. Subject responses consisted of 6-stop consonant, 11-vowel forced choice identifications. The listeners were two faculty persons with normal hearing who were experienced transcribers of infant/toddler vocalization. Stimuli were presented at roughly 80 dBA at a distance of 2 m from an Advent loudspeaker in a quiet room. Numerous rest periods were taken at 15–20 minute intervals because of the tediousness of the identification task. Each subject identified more than 24 000 stimuli.

Results

Percentage correct (PC) psychometric functions were developed for the consonant (PCC) and vowel (PCV) identifications for each listener for each direction of truncation at each developmental level for each of 60 syllables. Two point smoothing was used to compute the PC functions. For well-behaved PC functions, the 'perceptually critical point' in each CV transition was centred on the CV transition using Furui's (1986) protocol. Using forward truncation, PCV was expected to remain near 100 PCV throughout, whereas PCC should fall smoothly towards chance level within three to five 15 ms steps after CV onset. For final truncations, both PCC and PCV should remain near maximum until both begin smooth declines, PCV first, and PCC following, four or five steps from the syllable onset. Overall, only 44.8% of CV tokens yielded PC functions that were ideal; initially truncated vowel PCVs were most often ideally monotonic, see Figure 13.1.

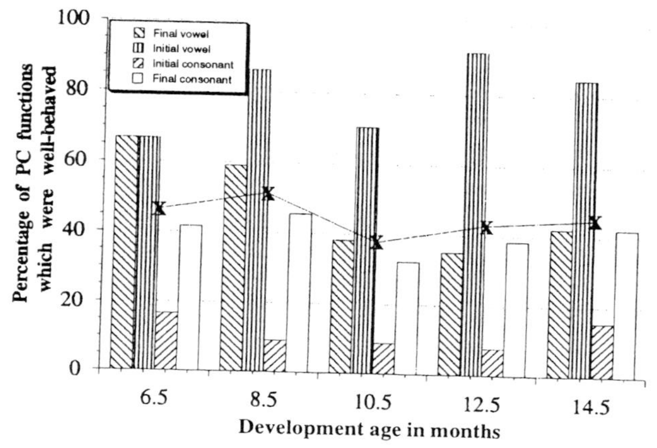

Figure 13.1. Percentage of total psychometric functions which were well-behaved during initial or final truncations.

On average, more initial truncation PCC/PCV were well behaved (45%) than were final truncations (19.8%). Only satisfactory initial PCV functions revealed a mild increase across developmental age (see Figure 13.1). The other PC functions were lower, declined, or showed no change across developmental age.

Table 13.1 reveals that anomalously shaped PC functions remained frequent across developmental age, 7.1–41%.

Monotonic PC functions, which exhibited asymptotic, maximum PC values below 75%, were most frequent during the first two developmental stages (5–6 and 7–8 months). The early developmental stages, months 5–8, displayed substantial incidence of non-monotonic PC functions as high as 66.6%, falling to 25% and 0% for initial and final truncations at months 11–15. A third frequent PC anomaly scattered across middle and late stages of development involved PC functions that exhibited no crossover; PC remained high throughout. For initial PCC functions, the consonant cues could not have been coproduced throughout the entire remaining vowel. This phenomenon was more frequent in final than in initial truncations throughout the developmental range.

Critical interval comparisons

For initial truncations, all monotonic, reasonably asymptotic PC functions were aligned at the interpolated 60 PC point. Furui suggested

Table 13.1. Percentage of total aberrant PC functions divided into four subtypes for consonant and vowel errors as a function of developmental age

	Developmental age (in months)									
	6.5		8.5		10.5		12.5		14.5	
Segment	C	V	C	V	C	V	C	V	C	V
Total anomalous errors PC	16	14	11	33	30	57	16	39	12	39
% error type										
1. No crossover	–	50	–	45.5	20	66.6	18.7	38.4	58.3	64.1
2. Wrong location crossover	–	–	–	–	10	–	–	–	–	–
3. PC function too low	66.6	42.9	63.6	24.2	30	19.3	56.3	20.6	25	–
4. Anomalous shape of PC function	33.3	7.1	36.4	30.3	40	14.1	25	41	–	25.6

80 PC for this point but we were forced to use 60 PC for consonant transitions because the maximum identification for infant utterances asymptoted at 80–85 PC. On average, the PCC fell from 85% to 45% or less as the PC crossed the perceptually critical (PC 60%) point, declining to 28 PC with one additional truncation. Our well-behaved infant PC functions resembled Furui's PC functions for Japanese adult speakers, although the infant PCC scores neither began at 100% nor declined as low and so rapidly as shown in his data.

The critical interval was computed as the temporal interval between the initial and final truncation derived critical points; these data are shown in Table 13.2.

Table 13.2. Critical interval: Mean duration between syllable onset and perceptual critical point for initial and final truncations as a function of developmental level

Developmental level (months)	Initial		Final		Critical interval (ms)
	Mean	SD	Mean	SD	
6.5	41.00	25.62	52.50	8.66	11.50
8.5	60.00	47.96	100.71	39.42	40.47
10.5	64.09	43.00	94.29	49.53	30.20
12.5	49.50	46.93	97.50	44.64	48.00
14.5	43.33	27.50	73.33	39.29	30.00
Average	54.20	40.69	86.10	41.80	31.90

Although the months 5–6 critical interval was only 10.8 ms, subsequent critical intervals were as large as 48.0 ms, about *four* times as large as Furui's adult values. There was no developmental trend, Kendall's tau = 0.2, which was non-significant in these data. The average critical interval of 31.9 ms (as opposed to Furui's 13 ms average adult interval) testifies to developmental articulatory stasis. When separated into bilabial, alveolar and velar stop critical intervals, the infant intervals could not be ranked in terms of duration (according to place of articulation) to match Furui's ranking.

Identification function analysis

Figure 13.1 presents mean PCV and PCC scores as a function of developmental age. Notice that vowels are approximately 2–3 times more accurately identified as their accompanying consonants, a ratio that did not vary systematically with developmental age. Correlation coefficients between the averaged maximum attained PCV and PCC scores for initial and for final truncations. Overall, there were modest, mostly positive correlations between the much more intelligible vowels and less intelligible consonants. Initial truncation PC functions produced no significant PCV-PCC correlations. For final truncations there were significant positive correlations at age levels 10–11, r = 0.365, p = 0.033 and 12–13, r = 0.514, p = 0.007, between final truncation scores.

The data were arranged in multidimensional contingency tables, one for each fragment of the truncated CV token perceived, and tested for departures from the expected distribution of correct identifications based on the 'ideal' PC functions, using the G statistic. The G statistic resembles a multidimensional χ^2, but it makes no assumptions about the a priori distribution of cell entries – any a priori distribution will suffice. The statistic operates on any set or row(s) and/or column(s) within a contingency table and establishes the significance of departures from the a priori expected distribution The results are converted to standard probability values for G, which are derived from a χ^2 random variable having the same degrees of freedom. The resulting statistic, G, (Lewis, 1962; Ku and Kallbach, 1974) was computed for all the response matrices prepared for C and V identification at each step of truncation. The results reveal that for consonants, roughly 50–70% or more of consonant confusion matrices across developmental ages reveal a significant scatter of incorrect identification responses. This result also occurred for a G analysis based on correct identification of place of articulation, where there were somewhat fewer significant G scores, that is, more successful transmission of information. There appeared to be no developmental trend toward increased truncated consonant intelligibility.

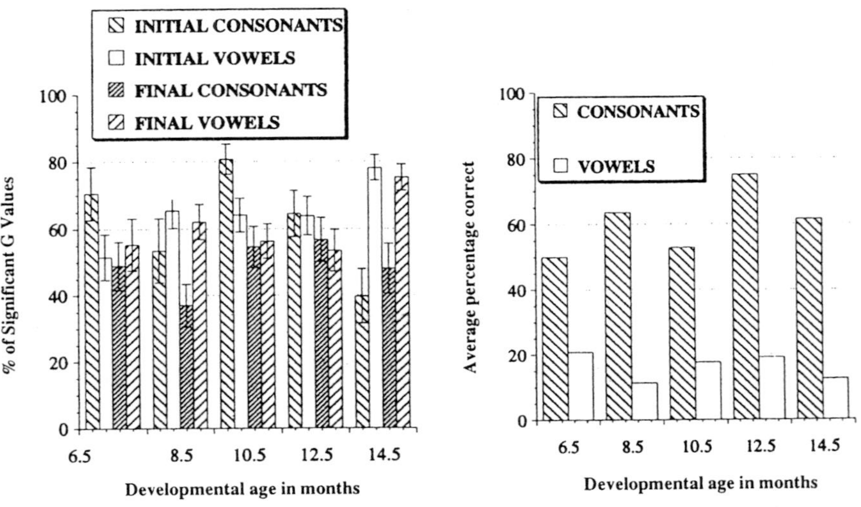

Figure 13.2. Percentage of significant estimates of perceptual confusion (G) for consonants and vowels as a function of developmental age.

For vowels, Figure 13.2 demonstrates that between 12.5% and 20.8% of vowels studied elicited statistically significant perceptual error, a rate one half to one third the error rate for consonants. As with the consonants, there was no discernible developmental trend in the G statistic across developmental age. In a final analysis, a χ^2 test was used to analyse the contingency of consonant and vowel G scores when taken from the same syllables across developmental stages. The results shown reveal a significant departure from random association for all but the first developmental stage: age 6;5, $\chi^2 = 2.36$, ns; age 8;5, $\chi^2 = 7.95$, $p = 0.01$; age 10;5, $\chi^2 = 6.74$, $p = 0.01$; age 12;5, $\chi^2 = 6.12$, $p = 0.0$; age 14;5, $\chi^2 = 8.07$, $p = 0.01$. Inspection of data showed that pairs of G scores indicating high consonantal and low vowel uncertainty, and mutually low consonant and vowel uncertainty predominate.

Discussion

The results of this study appear to confirm Miller et al.'s (1998) conclusions derived from acoustic analyses of the same syllables. The 'quiescent' monosyllabic utterances of normal children produced during quiet play (which are usually not directed at an interlocutor but generally toward a toy or nothing in particular) present acoustic and perceptual characteristics which do not appreciably change across the 6–15 month span of development. It appears that normally developing infants (the two infants studied now hold PhDs) produced developmentally static CV stop-vowel utterances during solitary, unaroused play . Thus a second non-developing phonetic form, albeit, a fairly sophisticated one as compared with the much more primitive polyvocalic 'gibberish' utterances of deafened infants (Konopczynski, 1997; Konopczynski and Vinter, 1997), has been identified. During much of this developmental period increasingly sophisticated canonical and variegated polysyllabic utterances were emitted by the two infants during aroused dialogue with an adult or with a toy or implement in hand or in view. When dialogue was extinguished and intent to communicate subordinated to private play, the children often reverted to the non-developmental, sparsely cued CV monosyllables, which we studied. They also produced polysyllabic quiescent utterances that we did not examine. Vowels were better defined acoustically and much better perceived than the stop consonants, but the perception of the infant CV monosyllables rarely elicited the near 100 PC values characteristic of Furui's Japanese adult speaker–listener performance and some of Warner's (1997) English speakers–listeners. In fact, less than 50% of infant PC functions were normal in shape and analysable. The critical transition intervals, defined by Furui to contain enough cues to enable perception at nearly 80% correct levels for consonant and vowel, were nearly three times as wide for our infants.

The lack of strong PCV-PCC correlations at any developmental level suggests that consonant targeting and coproduction with vowels does not appreciably advance for this type of utterance between months 5 and 15. In the absence of a need to shape acoustic form to enhance dyadic vocal interaction, we speculate that the child may be defaulting to the early mastered, prototypical stop+vowel CV form observed for normal infants in most languages about age 4–5 months (Vihman, 1996). It is possible that the infant directs efforts at articulatory learning toward the interlocutor-directed, highly social utterance characteristic of the mutual play and dyadic caretaker–child interaction using the ubiquitous speech forms of canonical and variegated babble. The quiescent syllables may be 'stranded articulatory forms', which disappear with the arrival of lexically, interlocutor dominated utterances at about age 14–16 months. Until that crucial point the infants may feel no pressure to discard these simple, self-referential monosyllables.

Summary

This investigation explored the developmental, perceptual properties of fragments of infant monosyllabic, stop plus vowel, 'quiescent' monosyllabic CV utterances. The 'quiescent' CVs represented calm utterances not directed to an interlocutor, recorded as two unaroused infants played quietly with toys, between months 6–15 of infancy. Utilizing Furui's (1986) protocol, the CV syllables were subjected to systematic truncation (deletion) of successive 15 ms bits of syllable cut sequentially from either the head or the tail end of the CV syllable until nothing but a single 15 ms fragment remained to be perceived. Two listeners then labelled all of the fragments of varying length produced by truncating each of 60 syllables in 15 ms steps.

The shape and absolute levels of the percentage correct vowel (PCV) and consonant (PCC) psychometric functions were calculated and critical perceptual intervals centred on the CV transitions were computed from the psychometric functions. Neither the shape or absolute performance levels of the psychometric functions nor the critical intervals showed any developmental change, confirming previous acoustic findings of Miller et al. (1998) who observed sparse acoustic cues with little change across developmental age. The infant CV monosyllables exhibited slower transitions with much wider critical intervals; fewer than 40% of syllables presented smooth, monotonic PC functions. For the syllabic fragments presenting orderly, monotonic PC functions, there appeared to be little developmental change in the PC functions except for an improvement in consonant identification when the first one or two 15 ms bits of consonant were deleted in a front-to-back direction. The percentage of non-standard PC functions did not decline over time. The 'quiescent' proto-syllables appeared to change very little over time in contrast with the rapidly evolving canonical and variegated interlocutor-directed babble being produced by these children during the same period of development.

Acknowledgement

The authors wish to thank UNT science librarian Edward Gonzalez for his technical and research support.

References

Furui S (1986) On the role of spectral transition for speech perception. Journal of the Acoustical Society of America, 80, 1016–25.

Konopczynski G (1997) Interactive developmental intonology: prosody of emergent language (French) in different situational contexts. Abstract #220. Sixth Annual Conference of the ICPLA, 13–15 October, Nijmegen, Holland.

Konopczynski G, Vinter S (1997) Constructing a voice from babbling: a comparison of hearing and profoundly deaf children. Abstract #224. Sixth Annual Conference of the ICPLA, 13–15 October, Nijmegen, Holland.

Ku HH, Kullbach S (1974) Log-linear models in contingency table analysis. American Statistician, 28, 115–22.

Lewis BN (1962) On the analysis of interaction in multidimensional contingency tables. Journal of the Royal Statistical Society (Series A), 125, 88–117.

Miller CJ, Pirolli J, Zlatin-Laufer M, Daniloff RG (1998) Acoustic analysis of infant CV proto syllables. In Ziegler W, Deger K (eds) Clinical Phonetics and Linguistics. London: Whurr Publishers.

Vihman MM (1996) Phonological Development. London: Blackwell.

Warner N (1997) Spectral transition in the perception of English segments. Abstract #2ASc20. 134 Meeting of the Acoustical Society of America, San Diego, CA.

Part II

Hearing Impairment and CAPD

Chapter 14
Biology of Speech Sound Perception and Linguistic Experience

NINA KRAUS, THERESE J McGEE and DAWN BURTON KOCH

Introduction

In this paper, three areas relevant to the central auditory representation of speech are reviewed. First, the representation of acoustic speech elements are represented by different neuronal firing patterns at different levels of the auditory system. The transformation of those patterns along the auditory pathway indicate the distinctive roles of the midbrain, thalamus, and cortex in speech processing. Differences between activity on the two sides of the pathway indicate the specialization of the left side for neuronal speech representation.

Second, relationships should exist between the representation of sound in the central auditory pathways and behavioural perception. Current knowledge about links between the neurophysiology and perception are presented, focusing in particular on the effects of altered central sensory representation on speech perception and communication abilities.

Last, the role of plasticity in speech sound perception is discussed. Auditory experience and speech perception training may be effective in altering the central auditory representation of sound.

Speech representation in the auditory system (thalamus and cortex)

Aggregate responses and patterns

Speech is a complex acoustic signal that changes rapidly in the frequency, amplitude and time domains. Consequently, the spectral and temporal complexity of speech inherently elicits responses from a broad neural population, and the pattern of activity changes constantly. Moreover, it is the pattern itself that is of importance. The response of an individual neuron is meaningful only insofar as it contributes to the overall pattern.

There are several methods one might use to examine the pattern of neural activity elicited by a speech stimulus. For example, imaging techniques permit visualization of neuronal patterns, but provide a limited view of the neural representation of speech. Specifically, imaging requires averaging over several minutes yet the acoustic speech signal changes continually in the millisecond time range. Measuring single neuron responses also can reveal patterns of neuronal activity. These measurements provide good resolution in time, but many neurons must be sampled and analysed, making the experiments extremely time consuming.

On the other hand, multi-unit or evoked potentials provide ready access to the patterns of neuronal activity elicited by speech signals. These responses depend upon neural synchrony and reflect precise and synchronous response patterns across a population of neurons. More importantly, auditory evoked potentials are one of the few ways of looking at neural activity in people. They can provide a bridge between what is known about single neuron physiology in animal subjects and what is reflected in behavioural studies of speech perception in human subjects. By using aggregate neural responses, it is possible to assess the central sensory representation of key acoustic elements that are important for speech perception.

Neural representation of speech sounds

Speech sound perception involves various bottom-up (ear) and top-down (cognitive) processes. The aspect of speech sound processing that is the focus in this chapter is the *central sensory representation* of speech sounds, which occurs after peripheral sensory encoding and is largely independent of conscious perception (attention, cognition, linguistic ability).

Because central sensory representation of sound occurs automatically and without conscious awareness, a good deal of information can be derived from experiments with anesthetized animals. The neural representation of voice-onset-time is an example of how speech sounds are represented in the central pathways. What distinguishes /da/ from /ta/, or /ba/ from /pa/, is that in the voiced consonants (/ba/ and /da/) the voicing begins at the start of the phoneme. In the voiceless consonants (/pa/ and /ta/), however, there is an initial aspiration followed by a short silence until the voicing begins for the following vowel. This period of silence is called the voice-onset-time, or VOT. Variations in VOT are used by normal listeners to distinguish one phoneme from another.

By measuring multiple unit activity in the monkey auditory cortex and using current-source-density analysis, Steinschneider and co-workers (1994) described response patterns that reflected VOT. Auditory cortex neurons showed two distinct peaks in response to the voiceless stimulus /ta/ (corresponding to the aspiration and the onset of voicing). In contrast, the response to /ba/ was a single peak. Interestingly, the point at which the neurons changed from a double to a single response peak corresponds to the human perceptual category boundary for /ta/ and /da/. Correspondingly, the representation of VOT can be visualized in the activity recorded from single cat neurons to the stimulus /ta/ (Eggermont, 1995). Responses recorded from hundreds of single neurons indicate that neurons fired first in response to the aspiration at the beginning of the syllable and that the timing of the next burst of activity reflected VOT (which was varied in the experiment).

Guinea pig evoked potentials also reflect VOT. In experiments by McGee and colleagues, VOT was varied using four stimuli in which voicing reached maximum amplitude at 15, 20, 25, or 30 ms after the aspiration (McGee et al., 1996). Figure 14.1 shows that the latency of peak A (which reflects the activity of auditory cortex (see Kraus and McGee, 1995, for a review)) corresponded to the onset of energy for a /pa/ stimulus. The latencies of successive peaks suggested that the first peak was elicited by the aspiration while the second peaks were elicited by the onset of voicing. Specifically, the latency of the second peak increased monotonically with increasing VOT while the latency of the first peak remained constant. For a VOT of 15 ms, only the first peak was observed, indicating that the temporal spacing between the aspiration and voicing was below the minimum needed to obtain a well-defined second positivity. Interestingly, human listeners perceived the 15 ms VOT stimulus as /ba/, while the rest of the stimuli in the continuum were perceived as /pa/. Finally, the representation of VOT also has been observed in cortical potentials recorded from human subjects (Kurtzberg, 1989; Koch et al., 1997).

Thus animal and human experiments indicate that neuronal activity can reflect acoustic aspects of the speech signals such as variations in voice-onset-time. Moreover, the responses show a physiologic discontinuity that may be associated with the phonemic categorization of voiced and voiceless stop consonants.

Repackaging of information: thalamus/cortex/right/left

Several lines of evidence suggest that different acoustic parameters may be encoded distinctively along the auditory pathway. Animal data demonstrate that acoustic parameters are represented differently at different levels of the auditory system (Whitfield and Evans, 1965; de Ribaupierre et al., 1972; Kiang and Moxon, 1974; Creutzfeldt et al., 1980; Rouiller et al., 1981; Steinschneider et al., 1982; Sachs et al., 1983; Delgutte and Kiang, 1984; Mendelson and Cynader, 1985; Phillips et al.,

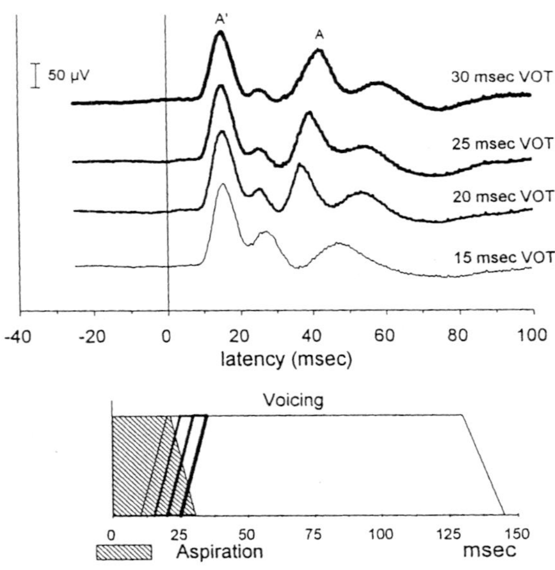

Figure 14.1. Average responses to four stimuli on a /ba/-/pa/ continuum. All stimuli had an initial burst of aspiration at $t = 0$ ms. Voice-onset-time varied in 5-ms steps. At VOT = 15 ms, no was observed. For VOT = 20, 25, 30 ms, A latency showed a monotonic shift, while A' was unchanged. From McGee et al., 1996.

1985; Carney and Geisler, 1986; Mäkelä et al., 1987; Schreiner and Langner, 1988; Phillips and Hall, 1990; Steinschneider et al., 1990; Eggermont, 1991; Heil et al., 1992; Phillips, 1993a; Phillips, 1993b; Shamma et al., 1993; Steinschneider et al., 1994; Mainen and Sejnowski, 1995; King et al., 1997). In addition, the perception of acoustic contrasts is not uniformly impaired in humans with auditory processing problems. Some sounds are more vulnerable to disruption than others (Phillips and Farmer, 1990; Shannon, 1993; Sharma et al., 1994; Koch et al., 1997). For example, the perception of certain consonants is specifically impaired in people with auditory cortex lesions. In general, steady-state or slowly changing acoustic parameters (which provide information about pitch, vowels and intonation) are better represented at lower levels of the auditory system. On the other hand, precisely timed transient elements (which may characterize certain stop consonants, place of articulation, and VOT) continue to be well represented more centrally, for example, in auditory cortex. As an example, Figure 14.2 contrasts the representation of an amplitude modulated signal in the midbrain, thalamus, and over the auditory cortex. It is evident that the same stimulus elicits different neuronal activity in the different areas and that the representation of transient elements (that is, stimulus onsets) is salient at the more central locations.

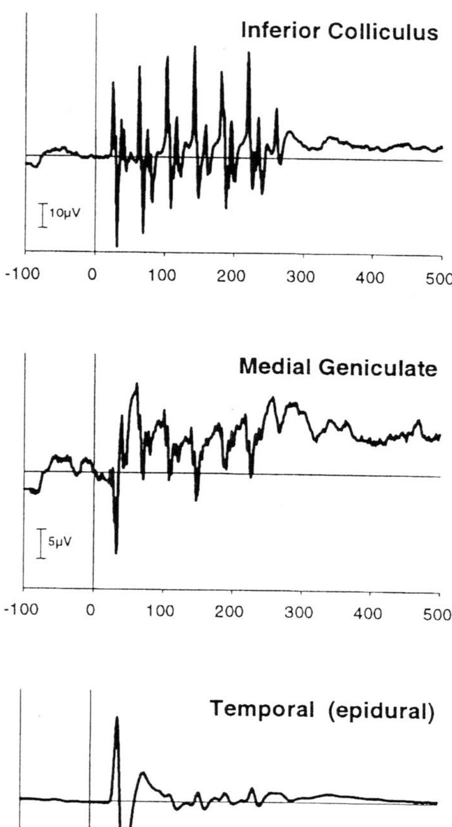

Figure 14.2. Aggregate neural responses obtained from the auditory midbrain, thalamus and over auditory cortex to a tone embedded in amplitude modulated noise. The response to the stimulus onset continues to be well represented at central levels.

The stimulus-dependent contribution of specific pathways can be examined using an evoked response termed the mismatch response (or MMN) (see Näätänen et al., 1978 and Näätänen and Kraus, 1995, for reviews). The mismatch response reflects a physiologic response to an acoustic change in an ongoing sequence. It can be elicited by any acoustic contrast, for example, a simple change in intensity, frequency or duration, or a change in a complex sound like a chord, a speech syllable, or an auditory pattern. The MMN can be elicited by very small acoustic changes, and it appears to reflect discrimination near or approximating psychophysical threshold (Sams et al., 1985). Because speech inherently consists of acoustic changes, this physiologic response may provide considerable insight into the biology of speech sound representation. Moreover, the MMN is thought to reflect echoic memory (Näätänen, 1986), which is also essential to the perception of fluent speech.

Any acoustic change will result in a mismatch response that can be recorded from the cortical surface. Yet in animals, when MMNs are recorded from within thalamic and cortical structures, an interesting differentiation of responses occurs depending on the stimulus (Kraus et al., 1994a). For various theoretical reasons (based on the single neuron and perceptual data mentioned above), the physiologic representation of the contrasts /ba/-/wa/ and /da/-/ga/ have been explored by Kraus and colleagues. Figure 14.3 shows mismatch responses to the /da/-/ga/ and /ba/-/wa/ contrasts at the epidural surface (midline) in the guinea pig. However, depth recordings in the auditory thalamus show a mismatch response to the /ba/-/wa/ contrast but not to the /da/-/ga/ contrast. These data suggest that representation of the /da/-/ga/ contrast occurs at a location other than the thalamus. The contribution of auditory cortex must be required for the representation of the acoustic change present in the /da/-/ga/ stimulus pair.

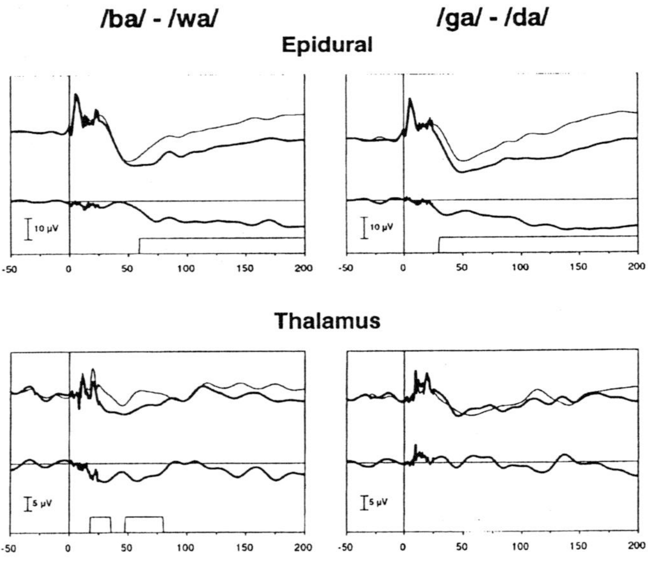

Figure 14.3. Grand average mismatch responses recorded from the epidural midline (top) and from the thalamus, specifically the caudomedial subdivision of the medial geniculate nucleus (bottom). Significant mismatch activity was evident in response to both /ba/-/wa/ and /da/-/ga/ contrasts at the epidural surface. In contrast, there was mismatch activity evident only in response to the /ba/-/wa/ contrast in the thalamus. Significant mismatch activity is indicated by the box under the difference waves. Modified from Kraus et al., 1994b.

Right versus left brain specialization

Right/left brain asymmetries for language are well known (Geshwind, 1972; Gazzaniga, 1983). Evidence also indicates that right/left differences also occur in the basic physiologic representation of complex signals such as speech (Sharma and Kraus, 1995; King et al., 1997; Tremblay et al., 1997). For example, the aggregate evoked response to /da/ in the auditory thalamus of the guinea pig differed in response magnitude on the left compared with the right side (Figure 14.4). Responses to /da/ also were larger over the left compared with the right auditory cortex, suggesting greater response synchrony on the left side. The mismatch response, which reflects a higher-level response to stimulus changes, also reflected brain asymmetry, yielding a larger response when the right ear (left hemisphere) was stimulated than when the left ear (right hemisphere) was stimulated. Thus, a left-side specialization for speech may be evident even in the representation of the most basic acoustic parameters of speech.

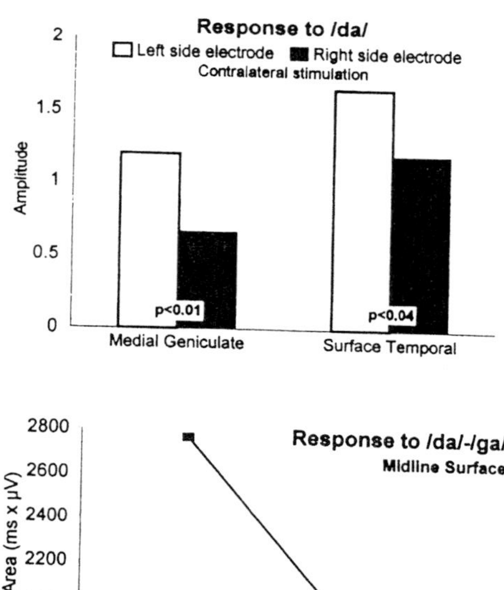

Figure 14.4. Top: Magnitude of aggregate neural responses to /da/ recorded from thalamus and epidural primary auditory cortex. Responses recorded from the left side (right ear stimulation) were larger in amplitude than those recorded from the right side (left ear stimulation). Bottom: Midline surface MMN responses to a /da/-/ga/ contrast. The response area (duration x onset latency – offset latency) is greater for right ear stimulation than for left ear stimulation.

In summary, the physiologic encoding of signals with the spectral and temporal complexity of speech must involve a pattern of response across the neural population. These aggregate neuronal responses can represent acoustic elements of the speech signal. Furthermore, physiologic continuities and discontinuities in those representations may provide insight into phonetic perception. The auditory pathway shows a specialization of processing in that certain acoustic discriminations require processing at the cortical level. In addition, left versus right specialization may be evident in the representation of complex signals even at the thalamic level.

Speech sound representation and learning disorders in children

Based upon knowledge of how speech sounds can be represented in the brain, the next step is to link that representation with perception. Taken together with the observations that speech sound perception is altered by lesions of auditory central pathways, it may be inferred that speech sound perception problems may arise (at least in some cases) from faulty representation in central auditory centres at an automatic level. There is some direct evidence for this relationship in studies of children with learning problems. Data show that neurophysiologic responses reflect speech perception abilities in normal-learning and learning-disabled children.

Research from the fields of psychoacoustics, speech perception and learning disabilities indicates that some learning disabled children have deficits in what has been called 'phonologic awareness' (Godfrey et al., 1981; Tees and Werker, 1987; Reed, 1989). These children have difficulty discriminating between certain speech syllables even though their hearing sensitivity is normal. For example, certain children have difficulty perceiving small acoustic differences and require larger spectral changes to discriminate speech sounds than normal children (Elliott and Hammer, 1988; Elliott et al., 1989). Other children exhibit deficits in the ability to process rapidly presented acoustic information in general (Tallal, 1981; Tallal et al., 1985; Tallal et al., 1993), or brief sounds in some contexts (Wright et al., 1997). More to the point, they experience difficulties with tasks fundamental to learning and communication processes.

Kraus and colleagues are investigating the underlying physiology of these acoustic-level auditory processing disorders in order to better understand the biological bases of auditory perceptual deficits. In a project called 'Listening, Learning and the Brain', they are investigating how elemental speech sounds are encoded in normal and learning-disabled children. Concurrently, they are examining the relationship among psychophysical speech discrimination (listening), standardized measures of learning and academic achievement (learning), and neurophysiology (the brain).

An interesting relationship emerged between the mismatch response and behavioural discrimination of selected speech sounds in normal-learning and learning-disabled children (Kraus et al., 1996). First, both groups of subjects were asked to discriminate behaviourally along two continua of contrasts, /da/-/ga/ and /ba/-/wa/, which had been equated for discriminability. The selection of those contrasts was based upon aforementioned single neuron studies in animals (which show that different neuronal pathways encode specific acoustic contrasts), and upon behavioural research in humans (which demonstrates that perception of different speech sounds are differentially disrupted (Phillips and Farmer, 1990; Sharma et al., 1994)). The results indicated that learning-disabled children found it more difficult to discriminate a /da/-/ga/ contrast than a /ba/-/wa/ contrast (Figure 14.5).

Then the mismatch response was evaluated in two subgroups of subjects – one composed of 'good' /da/-/ga/ perceivers and one composed of 'poor' /da/-/ga/ perceivers. A mismatch response was evident in 'good' /da/-/ga/ perceivers in response to just-perceptibly different variants of /da/ and /ga/. (The stimulus pair represented a d' of 0.86 in a group of normal-hearing adults.) In contrast, the 'poor' /da/-/ga/ perceivers had no mismatch response (Figure14.6). Notably, both 'good' and 'poor' /da/-/ga/ perceivers could discriminate the /ba/-/wa/ contrast easily and both groups had a robust mismatch response to a /ba/-/wa/ contrast. Thus the neurophysiologic responses to both contrasts reflected the behavioural discrimination abilities of the children.

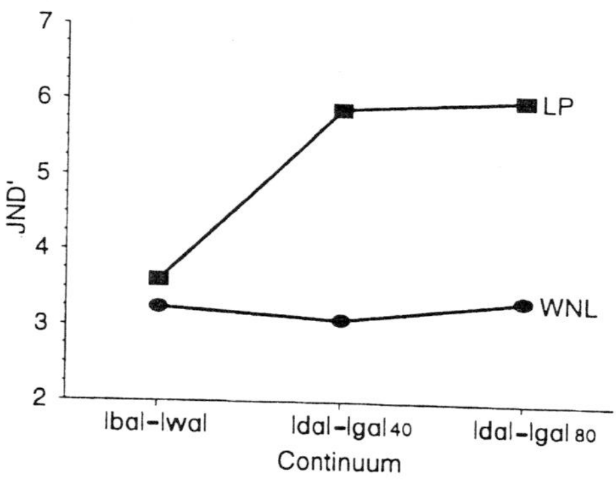

Figure 14.5. Mean JND' scores for normal-learning children (WNL) and children with learning problems (LP) for the /ba/-/wa/ and /da/-/ga/ continua. Discrimination thresholds were obtained for two separate /da/-/ga/ continua with formant transition durations of 40 and 80 msec. Modified from Kraus et al., 1996.

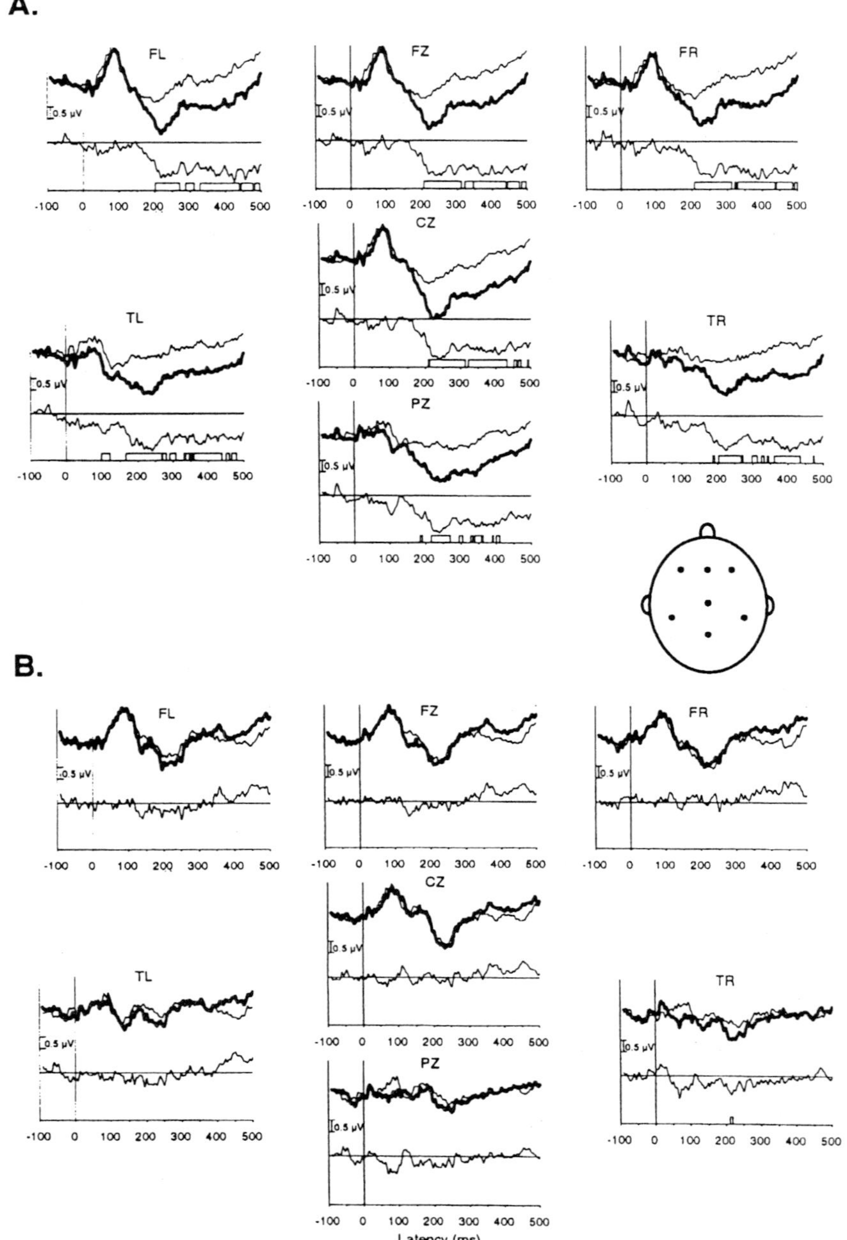

Figure 14.6. Grand-average MMN responses elicited by a /da/-/ga/ contrast at seven scalp recording locations in (A) 'good' /da/-/ga/ perceivers and (B) 'poor' /da/-/ga/ perceivers. The schematic head indicates electrode positions. The top thin line is the response to the /da/ stimulus when it was presented alone. The thick line is the response to the /da/ stimulus when it signalled an acoustic change in a sequence of /ga/ stimuli. The mismatch response is seen in the difference wave (lower thin line) as a deflection below the zero line. The boxes below indicate the latency ranges over which a significant mismatch response occurs ($p < 0.01$). Scale bars = 0.5 μV. From Kraus et al., 1996.

In order to further investigate the precise acoustic features of stop consonants that pose perceptual difficulties for these children, discrimination thresholds for normal-learning and learning-disabled children were compared along two separate synthetic /da/-/ga/ continua that differed only in the duration of the formant transition (Bradlow et al., 1998). Results showed that simply lengthening the formant transition duration from 40 to 80 ms did not result in improved discrimination thresholds for the learning-disabled children (Figure 14.5). Similarly, mismatch responses were diminished in these children regardless of the transition duration. This finding suggests that the brevity of the consonant transitions is not the sole acoustic factor contributing to the observed perceptual deficits. Thus, signal processing techniques aimed at enhancing perception of stop consonants need to address the effects of other acoustic features, such as relative amplitude and frequency characteristics, instead of (or in addition to) consonant-vowel transition duration.

To summarize, these data suggest that there is a biological basis for speech sound perception deficits in some children with learning problems. In the total subject population to date, about 30% of the children with learning problems have speech sound perception deficits that are revealed in biological responses that reflect unconscious, pre-attentive processes. Furthermore, the selective disruption of the neurophysiologic response is related to behavioural speech sound perception. Consequently, these neurophysiologic responses may provide an objective means to identify children with central sensory deficits that exist either independently or concurrently with language or cognitive problems.

If one could determine which children have impairment at this central sensory representation level, it would be easier to recommend appropriate therapeutic strategies. For example, focused listening training (which in reality trains the brain) might benefit these children, particularly since it is known that the auditory system exhibits significant plasticity.

Auditory system plasticity

The plasticity of the human auditory system is inherent. Throughout their lives, people learn to identify new voices, to speak new languages, to sing new songs. Hearing-impaired individuals learn to understand speech through hearing aids or cochlear implants. However, the neurophysiologic mechanisms underlying that auditory plasticity and learning – especially for speech – is far from understood.

It is clear that people can learn to hear speech sounds that they could not hear before training. For example, Pisoni and colleagues have shown that Japanese adults can be trained to distinguish between /r/ and /l/ phonemes that are not used in their native language (Bradlow, 1997; Pisoni et al, 1982). Importantly, the training effects generalized to listening situations outside the laboratory. Similar results have been demonstrated in children with learning problems (Bradley and Bryant, 1983; Lundberg et al., 1988; Ball and Blachman, 1991; Byrne and Fielding-Barnsley, 1993; Shankweiler et al., 1995; Merzenich et al., 1996; Tallal et al., 1996). For example, children were trained to distinguish sounds (tones and speech syllables) through a series of video games. Their discrimination abilities on the experimental tasks improved, as did their scores on benchmark tests of speech discrimination, language comprehension and grammar (Merzenich et al., 1996; Tallal et al., 1996).

Thus, behavioural studies in both adults and children indicate that speech perception abilities can be modified with training and that learning can generalize to other listening contexts. Those results undoubtedly reflect an underlying plasticity in the central auditory system. However, the specific neurophysiologic mechanisms underlying speech sound perceptual learning and plasticity are unknown. Animal experiments indicate that there is neuronal plasticity in the central auditory pathways. For example, tonotopic reorganization of the cortex occurs following cochlear lesions (Reale et al., 1987; Robertson and Irvine, 1989; Merzenich et al., 1991; Harrison et al., 1993), and single unit response characteristics and firing patterns will change after targeted acoustic stimulation (Buchwald et al., 1966; Halas et al., 1970; Olds et al., 1972; Oleson et al., 1975; Kraus and Disterhoft, 1982; Weinberger et al., 1984; Recanzone et al., 1993). People also show reorganization of cortical and behavioural activity after sensory deprivation (Neville et al., 1983; Gatehouse, 1992; Miyamoto et al., 1993).

Interestingly, neuronal plasticity is a characteristic predominately of non-primary pathways in the auditory thalamus and cortex (Kraus and Disterhoft, 1982; Weinberger et al., 1984; Edeline and Weinberger, 1991), although it is observed along the primary auditory pathways (Reale et al., 1987; Robertson and Irvine, 1989; Harrison et al., 1993; Rajan et al., 1993). Because the mismatch response also reflects non-primary central auditory system function (Scherg and Picton, 1990; Kraus et al., 1994a, 1994b) (although the extent to which its generating system involves primary and non-primary auditory cortex has not been determined (Hari et al., 1984; Näätänen and Picton, 1987; Csépe et al., 1988, 1993; Giard et al., 1990; Javitt et al., 1992; Alho, 1995)), it provides a means for examining auditory plasticity in human subjects.

For example, both neurophysiologic changes and speech perceptual abilities can be altered by listening training (Kraus and McGee, 1995). Specifically, young normal-hearing adults were trained to discriminate just-perceptibly-different variants of /da/ and /ga/. The discrimination was difficult and the subjects performed at chance level prior to training. After training, there were significant improvements in discrimination that were maintained one month after the last training session.

Importantly, changes in neurophysiologic responses were also observed in the group. Figure 14.7 shows a small grand-average mismatch response prior to training, and a much larger response after training. The changes in the grand-average response were representative of the individual subject data.

It also was of interest whether training effects generalized to other speech sounds and if neurophysiologic plasticity was limited to the training stimuli (Tremblay et al., 1997). Using a psychophysical paradigm developed by McClaskey et al. (McClaskey et al., 1983), normal-hearing English-speaking adults were trained to discriminate

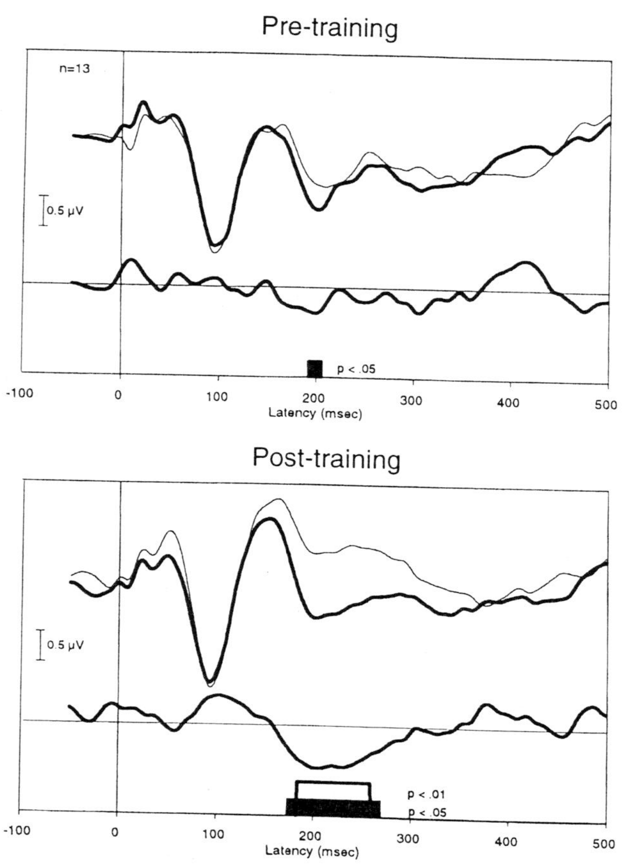

Figure 14.7. Grand-average mismatch responses to just-perceptively-different variants of /da/. The top thin line is the response to the stimulus /da/$_2$ when it was presented alone. The thick line is the response to the same stimulus when it signalled an acoustic change in the stimulus sequence. The MMN is seen in the difference wave (lowest trace) as a deflection below the zero line. The MMN was larger post-training compared with pre-training. Modified from Kraus and McGee (1995) latency – offset latency is greater for right ear stimulation than for left ear stimulation.

and identify a voicing contrast that does not occur in English but is phonetically salient in Hindi and Eastern Armenian. They were trained to hear that voice-onset-time distinction in a bilabial context, but were evaluated before and after training on their ability to discriminate and identify the voicing contrast both in the bilabial context (training condition) and an alveolar context (transfer condition). Electrophysiologic responses were evaluated before and after training for voicing contrasts in both contexts.

After training, the subjects could identify and discriminate both the training and transfer contrasts behaviourally. In other words, the ability to hear the non-native voicing contrast in the training stimuli transferred to the non-training stimuli. Training and generalization effects also were evident in the neurophysiologic responses. Grand-average mismatch responses were enhanced after training for both the training and transfer stimuli, although the effect was greater for the trained than the transfer stimuli. Most of the individual subjects showed an increase in duration and area for the mismatch response. Interestingly, learning-associated neurophysiologic changes were more pronounced over the left than over the right frontal cortex, further suggesting that a left-hemisphere specialization for speech may occur at a pre-attentive sensory level.

This study revealed that neuronal plasticity (as well as behavioural ability) occurred in response to the 'transfer' stimuli as well as to the 'trained' stimuli. Because discrimination of acoustic changes and generalization of learning underlies normal speech perception, these cortical evoked responses reflect processes essential to speech understanding. From a rehabilitative perspective, discrimination training for well-chosen acoustic elements of speech might generalize to other acoustic contexts.

Further insight into biologic processes underlying perceptual learning was gained by combined assessment of behavioural and neurophysiologic responses throughout the course of training to the same speech stimuli (Tremblay et al., 1998). Neurophysiologic change was apparent before behavioural improvement was evident. This suggests that auditory training altered the neural activity that underlies coding of the speech stimuli *before* those changes were incorporated into conscious behaviour. One can envision clinical applications for the objective monitoring of changes occurring during (re)habilitation in the communicatively impaired.

In summary, auditory evoked potentials are one of the few ways available for evaluating speech-elicited neural activity in people. These responses provide a bridge between single-neuron physiology in animals and speech perception in humans. Neurophysiologic changes associated with speech sound perception, training, and generalization can be measured in humans, thereby indicating that central sensory representation is plastic. Furthermore, learning-associated neurophysiologic responses reflect unconsious processes that are not confounded by higher-level linguistic skills, attention and cognition. Therefore, these neurophysiologic responses provide a window for viewing the biologic processes that underlie the plasticity of the central auditory system.

Summary

Historically, auditory research has focused predominately upon how relatively simple acoustic signals are represented in the neuronal responses of the auditory periphery. However, in order to understand the neurophysiology underlying speech perception, the ultimate objective is to discover how speech sounds are represented in the central auditory system and to relate that representation to the perception of speech as a meaningful acoustic signal. This paper reviews three areas that pertain to the central auditory representation of speech, (1) the differences in neural representation of speech sounds at different levels of the auditory system, (2) the relation between the representation of sound in the auditory pathway and the perception/misperception of speech, and (3) the plasticity of speech sound neural representation and speech perception.

Acknowledgments

This work was supported by National Institute on Deafness and Other Communication Disorders R01 DC01510 and R01 DC01906. This paper is a modified version of a publication by the same authors in Audiology and Neuro-Otology (1998). The scientific contributions of Trent Nicol BS, Cynthia King PhD, Kelly Tremblay MS, Jenna Cunningham MA, and Tom Carrell, PhD are gratefully acknowledged.

References

Alho K (1995) Cerebral generators of mismatch negativity (MMN) and its magnetic counterpart (MMNm) elicited by sound changes. Ear and Hearing, 16, 38–51.

Ball EW, Blachman BA (1991) Does phoneme awareness training in kindergarten make a difference in early recognition and developmental spelling? Reading Research Quarterly, 26, 49–66.

Bradley L, Bryant PE (1983) Categorizing sounds and learning to read – a causal connection. Nature, 30, 419–21.

Bradlow AR (1997) Training Japanese listeners to identify English /r/ and /l/: IV. Some effects of perceptual learning on speech production. Journal of the Acoustical Society of America, 101, 2299–310.

Bradlow AR, Kraus N, Nicol T, McGeeT, Carrell T (1998) Speech-sound perception in normal and learning-disabled children: Effect of lengthened CV transition duration. Journal of the Acoustical Society of America, 103, 2985.

Buchwald J, Halas E, Schramm S (1966) Changes in cortical and subcortical unit activity during behavioural conditioning. Physiological Behaviour, 1, 11–22.

Byrne B, Fielding-Barnsley R (1993) Evaluation of a program to teach phonemic awareness to young children: A 1-year follow-up. Journal of Educational Psychology, 85, 104–11.

Carney HL, Geisler CD (1986) A temporal analysis of auditory-nerve fiber responses to spoken stop consonant-vowel syllables. Journal of the Acoustical Society of America, 79, 1896–914.

Carrell T, King C, Littman T, Nicol T (1994a) Discrimination of speech-like signals in auditory thalamus and cortex. Journal of the Acoustical Society of America, 96, 2758–68.

Creutzfeldt OD, Hellweg FC, Schreiner CE (1980) Thalamocortical transformation of responses to complex auditory stimuli. Experimental Brain Research, 39, 87–104.

Csépe V, Karmos G, Molnár M (1988) Subcortical evoked potential correlates of sensory mismatch processing in cats. Advances in Bioscieces, 76, 43–6.

Csépe V, Pantev C, Hoke M, Hampson S, Ross B (1993) Evoked magnetic responses of the human auditory cortex to minor pitch changes: localization of the mismatch field. Electroencephalopathy and Clinical Neurophysiology, 84, 538–48.

de Ribaupierre F, Goldstein M, Yeni-Komshian G (1972) Cortical coding of repetitive acoustic pulses. Brain Research, 46, 205–25.

Delgutte B, Kiang NYS (1984) Speech coding in the auditory nerve. I. Vowel-like sounds. Journal of the Acoustical Society of America, 75, 866–78.

Edeline JM, Weinberger NM (1991) Subcortical adaptive filtering in the auditory system: associative receptive field plasticity in the dorsal medial geniculate body. behavioural Neurosciene, 105, 154–75.

Eggermont JJ (1991) Rate and synchronization measures of periodicity coding in cat primary auditory cortex. Hearing Research, 56, 153–67.

Eggermont JJ (1995) Representation of a voice onset time continuum in primary auditory cortex of the cat. Journal of the Acoustical Society of America, 98, 911–20.

Elliott LL, Hammer M (1988) Longitudinal changes in auditory discrimination in normal children and children with language-learning problems. Journal of Speech and Hearing Disorders, 53, 467–74.

Elliott LL, Hammer M, Scholl M (1989) Fine-grained auditory discrimination in normal children and children with language-learning problems. Journal of Speech and Hearing Research, 32, 112–9.

Gatehouse S (1992) The time course and magnitude of perceptual acclimatization to frequency responses: evidence from monaural fitting of hearing aids. Journal of the Acoustical Society of America, 92, 1258–68.

Gazzaniga MS (1983) Right hemisphere language following commissurotomy: a twenty-year perspective. American Psychology, 38, 525–37.

Geshwind N (1972) Language and the brain. Scientific American, 226, 76–83.

Giard M, Perrin F, Pernier J, Bouchet P (1990) Brain generators implicated in the processing of auditory stimulus deviance: a topographic event-related potential study. Psychophysiology, 27, 627–40.

Godfrey JJ, Syrdal-Lasky AK, Millay KK, Knox CM (1981) Performance of dyslexic children on speech perception tests. Journal of Experimental Child Psychology, 32, 401–24.

Halas E, Beardsley J, Sandie M (1970) Conditioned neuronal responses at various levels in conditioning paradigms. Electroencephalopathy and Clinical Neurophysiology, 28, 468–77.

Hari R, Hämäläinen M, Ilmoniemi R, Kaukoranta E, Reinikainen K, Salminen J, Alho K, Näätänen R, Sams M (1984) Responses of the primary auditory cortex to pitch changes in a sequence of tone pips: neuromagnetic recordings in man. Neurosci Lett, 50, 127–32.

Harrison R, Stanton S, Ibrahim D, Nagasawa A, Mount R (1993) Neonatal cochlear hearing loss results in developmental abnormalities of the central auditory pathways. Acta Otolaryngology, 113, 296–302.

Heil P, Rajan R, Irvine DRF (1992) Sensitivity of neurons in cat primary auditory cortex to tones and frequency-modulated stimuli. II: Organization of response properties along the 'isofrequency' dimension. Hearing Research, 63, 135–56.

Javitt D, Schroeder C, Steinschneider M, Arezzo J, Vaughan Jr H (1992) Demonstration of mismatch negativity in monkey. Electroencephalopathy and Clinical Neurophysiology, 83, 87–90.

Kiang NYS, Moxon EC (1974) Tails of tuning curves of auditory nerve fibers. Journal of the Acoustical Society of America, 55, 620–30.

King C, Nicol T, McGee T, Kraus N (1997) Aggregate responses in the left and right thalamus and cortex to auditory stimulation. Abstr Assoc Res Otolaryngol, 20, 104.

Koch D, Tremblay K, Dunn I, Dinces E, Carrell T, Kraus N (1997) Speech-evoked N1 and mismatch neurophysiologic responses in cochlear-implant users and normal listeners. Abstr Assoc Res Otolaryngol, 20, 80.

Kraus N, Disterhoft J (1982) Response plasticity of single neurons in rabbit auditory association cortex during tone-signalled learning. Brain Research, 246, 205–15.

Kraus N, McGee T (1995) The middle latency response generating system. Perspectives in event-related potentials research. Electroencephalopathy and Clinical Neurophysiology, suppl. 44, 93–101.

Kraus N, McGee T, Carrell T, King C, Littman T, Nicol T (1994a) Discrimination of speech-like signals in auditory thalamus and cortex. Journal of the Acoustical Society of America, 96, 2758–68.

Kraus N, McGee T, Littman T, Nicol T, King C (1994b) Nonprimary auditory thalamic representation of acoustic change. Journal of Neurophysiology, 72, 1270–7.

Kraus N, McGee TJ, Carrell TD, Zecker SG, Nicol TG, Koch DB (1996) Auditory neurophysiologic responses and discrimination deficits in children with learning problems. Science, 273, 971–3.

Kurtzberg D (1989) Cortical event-related potential assessment of auditory and systems function. Seminars in Hearing, 10, 252–61.

Lundberg I, Frost J, Peterson O-P (1988) Effects of an extensive program for stimulating phonological awareness in preschool children. Reading Research Quarterly, 23, 263–84.

McClaskey C, Pisoni D, Carrell T (1983) Transfer of training of a new linguistic contrast in voicing. Perception and Psychophysics, 34, 323–30.

McGee T, Kraus N, King C, Nicol T (1996) Acoustic elements of speechlike stimuli are reflected in surface recorded responses over the guinea pig temporal lobe. Journal of the Acoustical Society of America, 99, 3606–14.

Mainen ZF, Sejnowski TJ (1995) Reliability of spike timing in neocortical neurons. Science, 268, 1503–6.

Mäkelä J, Hari R, Linnakivi A (1987) Different analysis of frequency and amplitude modulations of a continuous tone in human auditory cortex: A neuromagnetic study. Hearing Research, 27, 257–64.

Mendelson JR, Cynader MS (1985) Sensitivity of cat primary auditory cortex (AI) to the direction and rate of frequency modulation. Brain Research, 327, 331–5.

Merzenich M, Grajski K, Jenkins W, Recanzone G, Peterson B (1991) Functional cortical plasticity: cortical network origins of representational changes. Cold Spring

Harbor Symp Quant Biol, 55, 873–87.

Merzenich MM, Jenkins WM, Johnston P, Schreiner C, Miller SL, Tallal P (1996) Temporal processing deficits of language-learning impaired children ameliorated by training. Science, 271, 77–81.

Miyamoto R, Osberger MJ, Todd S, Robbins A, Karasek A, Dettman D, Justice N, Johnson D (1993) Speech perception skills of children with multichannel cochlear implants. Paper presented at 3rd International Cochlear Implant Conference, Innsbruck.

Näätänen R (1986) Neurophysiological basis of the echoic memory as suggested by event-related potentials and magnetoencephalogram. In Klix F, Hagendorf H (eds) Human Memory and Cognitive Capabilities. Amsterdam: Elsevier, pp. 615–28.

Näätänen R, Picton T (1987) The N1 wave of the human electric and magnetic response to sound: a review and an analysis of the component structure. Psychophysiology, 24, 375–425.

Näätänen R, Kraus N (1995) Mismatch Negativity as an Index of Central Auditory Function: Special Issue. Ear and Hearing, 16, 1–146.

Näätänen R, Gaillard A, Mäntysalo S (1978) Early selective-attention effect on evoked potential reinterpreted. Acta Psychologica, 42, 313–29.

Neville H, Schmidt A, Kutas M (1983) Altered visual-evoked potentials in congenitally deaf adults. Brain Research, 266, 127–32.

Olds J, Disterhoft J, Segal M, Kornblith C, Hirsh R (1972) Learning centers of rat brain mapped by measuring latencies of conditioned unit responses. Journal of Neurophysiology, 35, 202–19.

Oleson T, Ashe J, Weinberger N (1975) Modification of auditory and somatosensory system activity during pupillary conditioning in the paralyzed cat. Journal of Neurophysiology, 38, 1114–39.

Phillips DP (1993a) Representation of acoustic events in the primary auditory cortex. Journal of Experimental Psychology: Human Perception and Performance, 19, 203–16.

Phillips DP (1993b) Neural representation of stimulus times in the primary auditory cortex. Ann NY Acad Sci 682: 104–18.

Phillips DP, Farmer ME (1990) Acquired word deafness, and the temporal grain of sound representation in the primary auditory cortex. Behavioral Brain Research, 40, 85–94.

Phillips DP, Hall SE (1990) Response timing constraints on the cortical representation of sound time structure. Journal of the Acoustical Society of America, 88, 1403–11.

Phillips DP, Mendelson JR, Cynader MS, Douglas RM (1985) Responses of single neurons in cat auditory cortex to time-varying stimuli: frequency-modulated tones of narrow excursion. Experimental Brain Research, 58, 443–54.

Pisoni DB, Aslin RN, Perey AJ, Hennessy BL (1982) Some effects of laboratory training on identification and discrimination of voicing contrasts in stop consonants. Journal of Experimental Psychology, 8, 297–314.

Rajan R, Irvine DR, Wise LZ, Heil P (1993) Effect of unilateral partial cochlear lesions in adult cats on the representation of lesioned and unlesioned cochleas in primary auditory cortex. Journal of Computational Neurology, 338, 17–49.

Reale R, Brugge J, Chan J (1987) Maps of auditory cortex in cats reared after unilateral cochlear ablation in the neonatal period. Developmental Brain Research, 34, 281–90.

Recanzone G, Schreiner C, Merzenich M (1993) Plasticity in the frequency representation of primary auditory cortex following discrimination training in adult owl monkeys. Journal of Neuroscience, 13, 87–104.

Reed MA (1989) Speech perception and the discrimination of brief auditory cues in reading disabled children. Journal of Experimental Child Psychology, 48, 270–92.

Robertson D, Irvine D (1989) Plasticity of frequency organization in auditory cortex of guinea pigs with partial unilateral deafness. Journal of Computational Neurology, 282, 456–71.

Rouiller E, de Ribaupierre Y, Toros-Morel A, de Ribaupierre F (1981) Neural coding of repetitive clicks in the medial geniculate body of cat. Hearing Research, 5, 81–100.

Sachs M, Voigt H, Young E (1983) Auditory nerve representation of vowels in background noise. Journal of Neurophysiology, 50, 27–45.

Sams M, Paavilainen P, Alho K, Näätänen R (1985) Auditory frequency discrimination and event-related potentials. Electroencephalopathy and Clinical Neurophysiology, 62, 437–48.

Scherg M, Picton T (1990) Brain electric source analysis of mismatch negativity. In Brunia C, Gaillar A, Kok A (eds) Psychophysiological Brain Research, Vol I. Tilberg: Tilberg University Press, pp. 94–8.

Schreiner CE, Langner G (1988) Coding of temporal patterns in the central auditory nervous system. In Edelman GM, Gail WE, Cowan WM (eds) Auditory Function. New York: John Wiley & Sons, pp. 337–61.

Shamma S, Fleshman J, Wiser P, Versnel H (1993) Organization of response areas in ferret primary auditory cortex. Journal of Neurophysiology, 69, 367–83.

Shankweiler D, Crain S, Katz L, Fowler AE, Liberman AM, Brady SA, Thorton R, Lundquist E, Dreyer L, Fletcher JM, Stuebing KK, Shaywitz SE, Shaywitz BA (1995) Cognitive profiles of reading-disabled children: Comparison of language skills in phonology, morphology, and syntax. Psychological Science, 6, 149–56.

Shannon RV (1993) Quantitative comparison of electrically and acoustically evoked auditory perception: implications for the location of perceptual mechanisms. Progress in Brain Research, 97, 261–9.

Sharma A, Kraus N (1995) Effect of contextual variations in pitch and phonetic processing: neurophysiologic correlates. Abstr Assoc Res Otolaryngol, 729, 183.

Sharma A, Kraus N, Carrell T, Thompson C (1994) Physiologic bases of pitch and place of articulation perception: a case study. Journal of the Acoustical Society of America, 95, 3011.

Steinschneider M, Arezzo JC, Vaughan Jr HG (1982) Speech evoked activity in the auditory radiations and cortex of the awake monkey. Brain Research, 252, 353–65.

Steinschneider M, Arezzo JC, Vaughan Jr HG (1990) Tonotopic features of speech-evoked activity in primate auditory cortex. Brain Research, 519, 158–68.

Steinschneider M, Schroeder C, Arezzo J, Vaughan Jr H (1994) Speech-evoked activity in primary auditory cortex: effects of voice onset time. Electroencephalopathy and Clinical Neurophysiology, 92, 30–43.

Tallal P (1981) Language disabilities in children: perceptual correlates. International Journal of Pediatric Otorhinolaryngology, 3, 1–13.

Tallal P, Stark R, Mellitis F (1985) The relationship between auditory temporal analysis and receptive language development: Evidence from studies of developmental language disorder. Neuropsychologia, 23, 314–22.

Tallal P, Miller S, Fitch RH (1993) Neurobiological basis of speech: A case for the pre-eminence of temporal processing. Annals of NY Academy of Science, 682, 27–47.

Tallal P, Miller SL, Bedi G, Byma G, Wang X, Nagarajan SS, Schreiner C, Jenkins WM, Merzenich MM (1996) Language comprehension in language-learning impaired children improved with acoustically modified speech. Science, 271, 81–4.

Tees RC, Werker JF (1987) Speech perception in severely disabled and average reading children. Canadian Journal of Psychology, 41, 48–61.

Tremblay K, Kraus N, Carrell T, McGee T (1997) Central auditory system plasticity: Generalization to novel stimuli following listing training. Journal of the Acoustical Society of America, 102, 3762–73.

Tremblay K, Kraus N, McGee T, Zecker S (1998) The time course of learning: Neurophysiologic changes during speech training. Journal of the Acoustical Society of America, 103, 2981.

Weinberger NM, Hopkins W, Diamond DM (1984) Physiological plasticity of single neurons in auditory cortex of the cat during acquisition of the pupillary conditioned response. I: Primary field (AI). Behavioral Neuroscience, 98, 171–88.

Whitfield IC, Evans EF (1965) Responses of auditory cortical neurons to stimuli of changing frequency. Journal of Neurophysiology, 28, 655–72.

Wright B, Lombardino L, King W, Puranik C, Leonard C, Merzenich M (1997) Deficits in auditory temporal and spectral resolution in language-impaired children. Letters to Nature, 387, 176–8.

Chapter 15
Sensorineural Hearing Loss as a Filter in Word Comprehension

VESNA MILDNER

Introduction

According to the verbotonal theory (Guberina, 1972; Pansini, 1995) every sound, word and sentence has its optimal band of frequencies. With respect to sounds, this optimal is defined as the minimal frequency band necessary and sufficient to ensure full intelligibility of the particular sound to native speakers. In general, this band is an octave wide. In Croatian, examples of high sounds (optimal frequency bands above 3.2 kHz) are /i,s,z,ts/; of medium-frequency sounds (optimal frequency bands between 1 and 3.2 kHz) are /a,r,k/ and of low sounds (optimal frequency bands below 1 kHz) are /p,u,b/. Some sounds (particularly nasals) have a discontinuous optimal form, comprising two separate octaves. The optimal bands of sounds do not necessarily correspond to the frequency regions of the formants. For example, first and second formants of Croatian /i/ range, depending on speaker's gender and age, between 0.282–0.375 kHz and 2.192–3.033 kHz, respectively (Bakran, 1996), whereas its optimal frequency band was found to be the 3.2–6.4 kHz octave. Each language has its own set of optimal frequency bands for its sound repertoire, which can be experimentally determined in listening tests (Vuletić, 1980; Pozojević-Trivanović, 1984; Desnica-Žerjavić, 1990).

Outside its optimal octave a sound is perceived as different when compared with its emitted form. Its identification changes as a function of the frequency bands through which it has been passed (Horga and Mildner, 1996). Actually emitted sounds filtered through the optimal octave of another sound may be identified as that other sound (e.g. /i/ band-passed through the optimal octave for /u/ between 0.2 and 0.4 kHz is commonly identified as /u/). These findings have been widely used in correction of non-pathological pronunciation errors (e.g. in foreign language teaching) with the help of specially designed apparatus (Mildner, 1993).

Hearing impairment can be considered as a built-in filter that eliminates auditory information beyond the boundaries of residual hearing. This may be manifested in two ways: the patients are not able to detect and/or identify stimuli that are outside their auditory field; sounds with optimal frequency bands in regions that have been lost through impairment are confused and replaced with related sounds of optimal frequencies within the preserved region. Accordingly, in cases of hearing loss in the high-frequency region with more or less residual hearing in the low and mid-frequency regions, it can be expected that the words containing high sounds will not be identified or that the high sounds will be replaced with lower ones. In this context the *high–low* distinction refers to the characteristic frequency bands rather than to the tongue position relative to the palate. For instance, high vowel /i/ may be confused with the low vowel /u/, or high fricative /s/ (optimal frequency band between 6.4 and 12.8 kHz) may be replaced with the lower /ʃ/ (optimal frequency band between 1.6 and 3.2 kHz).

The purpose of this study was to examine actual responses of subjects with sensorineural hearing loss to isolated words with respect to sound content of the presented words including the most frequent sound confusions. In addition, it was determined how much above their speech audiometry thresholds maximum intelligibility was reached, and what was their intelligibility capacity of speech.

Material and method

Data collection

Data were gathered at the SUVAG clinic for the rehabilitation of hearing and speech in Zagreb. Pure-tone audiometry and speech audiometry were done as part of regular audiological testing sessions. Pure-tone audiometry covered frequencies between 0.125 and 8 kHz in one-octave steps, and intermediate frequencies (1.5, 3 and 6 kHz) where appropriate. Speech audiometry included standard material (word lists). During speech audiometry subjects' responses were written down to be analysed later for sound confusions.

Subjects

The subjects were chosen on the basis of their pure-tone audiograms. The sample consisted of six men and six women, ranging in age between 68 and 90 years (mean: 77) with mean sensorineural hearing loss (averaged over 0.5, 1 and 2 kHz) ranging between 40 and 77 dB (curves sloping down toward higher frequencies). Nine subjects were sensitive to pure tones within the entire tested range in both ears. Left ears of three subjects were somewhat less sensitive (one gave no response to 6 and 8 kHz, one to 8 kHz and one did not respond above 3 kHz). It is evident, however, that all were sensitive to pure tones within the range considered to be essential for speech. Subjects' data are summarized in Table 15.1.

Procedure

Apart from the usual data for the pure-tone and speech audiograms, such as hearing level range (range), mean at 0.5, 1 and 2 kHz (mean), speech reception threshold (SRT) and threshold of discomfort (TD), several other parameters were included in the analysis: (1) gain, expressed in dB, is the increase in intensity in speech audiometry needed to reach maximum intelligibility (maximum discrimination score) after the threshold has been found; (2) intelligibility peak (corresponding roughly to maximum discrimination score), expressed in %/dB, is the intensity at which maximum percentage of correct responses is reached; and (3) intelligibility field capacity (IFC) of speech, which is calculated so that the percentages of correct responses for each 5 dB increment in speech audiogram from the threshold to 100 dB are added up (Šindija and Perović, 1993). For unimpaired ears that value is 1850, and the subjects' values discussed in this study are expressed as a percentage of that maximum capacity. The advantage of using IFC is that it enables more exact comparison of different patients' abilities to process speech by means of a single measure, rather than descriptive analysis of the speech audiogram curves. All these data are presented in Table 15.1.

Results and discussion

In Table 15.1 are summarized subjects' data from their case histories as well as the results of gain, intelligibility peak and intelligibility field capacity calculations.

It can be seen from the table that average maximum discrimination score was quite high (93.75%) and that it was reached at the average intensity of 77.5 dB. Mean difference between speech-reception threshold and maximum discrimination score (gain) was 30.63 dB, which is significantly higher than in the hearing population. That measure, however, was not significantly correlated with the pure-tone audiograms. On the other hand, as expected, a more sensitive measure turned out to be IFC. It takes into account not only the intensity needed to reach maximum intelligibility, but also the entire field spanned by the speech audiogram, including the slope and some decrease in intelligibility occurring with intensities approaching the threshold of discomfort (TD). The average percentage of intelligibility capacity was only 39.21% of that of the unimpaired population, which is evidently significantly lower ($p = 0.000$).

Table 15.1. Summary of subjects' data

Initial (age)	Ear	Pure-tone audiometry Range (dB)	Mean (dB)	SRT (dB)	Speech audiometry TD (dB)	Gain (dB)	Intelligibility peak (%/dB)	IFC (%)
BN (72)	R	30–50	37	30	105	15	100/45	69.7
	L	25–75	48	35	110	20	100/55	61.1
CA (75)	R	45–100	63	55	100	30	70/85	21.6
	L	55–75	62	55	100	30	80/85	22.7
HP (79)	R	45–100	65	55	110	30	100/85	28.6
	L	60–90	67	60	105	30	100/90	23.8
JA (84)	R	30–100	52	40	110	25	100/65	45.9
	L	35–95	52	35	110	35	100/70	51.4
KB (80)	R	40–65	45	40	120	25	100/65	51.4
	L	45–70	58	50	115	30	90/80	26.5
LA (70)	R	40–105	70	65	125	30	80/95	34.1
	L	45–110	68	60	125	20	90/80	33.0
MR (78)	R	35–100	77	55	120	40	100/95	27.0
	L	30–105	73	55	125	45	70/100	23.2
MM (70)	R	40–95	67	55	115	45	100/100	37.3
	L	45–90	58	45	110	30	100/75	47.0
PV (74)	R	20–75	45	20	115	60	100/80	67.0
	L	45–90	72	45	120	40	70/85	19.5
PS (68)	R	35–95	48	35	105	20	100/55	48.6
	L	35–105	60	40	110	30	100/70	27.0
SJ (90)	R	30–90	62	45	120	30	100/75	44.9
	L	25–65	62	45	130	20	100/65	47.0
SV (88)	R	30–65	58	55	110	30	100/85	41.6
	L	40–70	55	50	105	25	100/75	41.1

A high negative (-0.84) and significant (p = 0.000) correlation was found in this study between mean hearing level values averaged over 0.5, 1 and 2 kHz and IFC, confirmed by a significant (p = 0.000) high positive (0.90) correlation between IFC and pure-tone hearing capacity calculated in a similar manner (Šindija and Perović, 1993) but significantly higher (p = 0.000) (data not shown). In other words, the higher the pure-tone audiometry threshold the lower pure-tone hearing capacity and IFC. The significant difference between the two capacities in this sample is indicative of speech processing disability due to causes beyond the level of peripheral filter. The correlations between pure-tone thresholds and speech reception thresholds and maximum discrimination scores (0.80 and 0.49 respectively) were significant at the 0.05 level. They were somewhat lower than Bamford et al. (1981) reported for hearing impaired children (0.88 and 0.53) but the differences may be attributed to the age factor and a slightly different way of expressing SRT.

Analyses of variance have shown no significant differences with respect to ear or the fact that half of the subjects were specifically diagnosed with presbyacusis and the rest only with sensorineural hearing loss.

With respect to errors in word identification, on the basis of pure-tone audiometry, and as a consequence of poor sensitivity to high frequencies, two types of errors could be expected: (1) along the lines of the verbotonal theory, and (2) in light of the widely accepted importance of higher frequencies for word recognition (see Bamford and Saunders (1994) for brief review and discussion). Based on the former it was expected that the highest percentage of correct responses would be elicited by very low to mid-frequency words, that the greatest number of errors would be found in high words, and that there would be only substitutions of high sounds with lower ones. According to the latter, it was expected that there would be more errors in consonants than in vowels, that vowels with high second formants (front vowels) would be incorrectly identified and possibly replaced with back ones, and that among consonants the most frequent errors would be place errors with relatively few manner errors and practically no voicing errors.

Most frequent word confusions are presented in Table 15.2. It is shown what the original sounds have been substituted with and the difference is characterized in terms of verbotonal theory (namely lower/higher) and subphonemic features of voicing, place and manner of articulation.

It can be seen from Table 15.2 that the substitutions did not occur as clearly or as neatly as expected. Analysis based on verbotonal theory yielded only slightly more substitutions of lower sounds for the high ones (18, i.e. 40.91%) than the other way around (16, i.e. 36.36%), with 10 (22.73%) substitutions within the same optimal frequency band. Because of their optimal frequency bands comprising two discontinuous octaves nasals were marked higher or lower only if both their octaves were higher or lower than the particular sound. Otherwise, if the sound was between the two octaves, the substitution was characterized as 'no difference'. As expected, high sounds were substituted by lower ones. This was true for those with the low cut-off point of their optimal frequency bands at or above 1.6 kHz (/s,z,ts,i, ɲ,j,e,t,ʃ,tʃ/). On the other hand, very low sounds (/p,b,u/), with the upper cut-off point of their optimal frequency bands at 0.4 kHz were substituted by higher ones. Even more unexpected were substitutions of low to medium sounds by those with optimal frequency bands in either direction.

In spite of that, when entire words were analysed for correct responses, those consisting predominantly of medium sounds fared the best (60.86% accuracy), followed by low words (57.35% accuracy), and the words consisting predominantly of high sounds elicited the lowest number of correct responses (54.28% accuracy). Among the 28 words eliciting 65%

Table 15.2. Most frequent sound confusions

Original sound	Substituted with	Differences	
		Verbotonal theory	*Subphonemic features*
u	o	higher	more front, more open
	i	higher	more front
o	a	higher	more front, more open
	e	higher	more front
a	o	lower	more back, more close
e	a	lower	more back, more open
	o	lower	more back
i	u	lower	more back
j	l	lower	place, manner
	m	lower	place, manner
ʋ	b	lower	place, manner
	d	higher	place, manner
	m	–	place, manner
	s	higher	place, manner, voicing
	k	higher	place, manner, voicing
l	m, ɲ	–	place, manner
	n	–	manner
m	b	–	manner
	r, ʋ	–	place, manner
ɲ	n	lower	place
s	ʃ	lower	place
z	ʒ	lower	place
	b, ʋ	lower	place, manner
ʃ	k	lower	place, manner
ʒ	z	higher	place
tʃ	k,p	lower	place, manner
	t	–	place, manner
ts	t	lower	manner
	k	lower	place, manner
p	b	–	voicing
	f	higher	place, manner
	k,t	higher	place
b	d	higher	place
	n, ʋ	higher	place, manner
	m	–	manner
t	k	lower	place
d	b	lower	place
	z	higher	manner
	s	higher	manner, voicing
k	p	lower	place
	t	lower	place
	ts,tʃ	higher	place, manner
g	ʋ	lower	place, manner
	b	lower	place
	d	higher	place

or more correct responses 13 (46.43%) were medium words, 9 (32.14%) were low words and 6 (21.45%) were high words. Among the 9 words eliciting 35% or less correct responses were 4 (44.44%) high words, 4 (44.44%) low words and only 1 (11.12%) medium word.

In summary, it can be said that high words elicited the lowest percentage of correct responses, but they fared better than expected, whereas low words elicited a lower percentage of correct responses than expected. Substitutions of sounds were in favour of those whose characteristic frequency bands are in the mid-frequency region: high sounds were substituted by lower, very low sounds were substituted by slightly higher ones. This may be, at least in part, accounted for by the narrowing of the optimal listening range toward mid frequencies found to be characteristic of presbyacusis (Perović, 1993). Although half of the subjects were not specifically diagnosed with presbyacusis, due to their age it is possible that they behave in the same way (as said above, they did not differ from those with diagnosed presbyacusis).

Analysis of subphonemic features involved in errors has shown that where consonants are concerned voicing is indeed the most robust feature (four substitutions, i.e. 9.09% included voicing errors). However, manner was not nearly as resistant to substitutions as stated in literature (Bamford and Saunders, 1994). Manner errors occurred in 29 substitutions (65.91%). As expected, place errors were present in almost all substitutions (81.82%). Vowels were not substituted only along the horizontal axis (front-back), as predicted by the subphonemic features theory, but also along the vertical axis (open-close).

Great variability in confusion errors, manifested as various words substituted for the presented ones, was found among subjects. This may be attributed to individual differences in aspects of peripheral auditory perception other than simple detection, as Rosen and Fourcin (1986) have found.

The obtained results may be explained in a number of ways, in addition to the above mentioned compression of optimal listening range into mid frequencies. First of them is redundancy, resulting in top-down processing, partially disregarding available auditory information. It has been found in a number of studies (e.g. Mildner, 1986) that subjects approach speech processing tasks with primarily top-down strategies, and failing to complete the task to their satisfaction, try to make sense of auditory data. Another possible reason for results not directly accountable on the basis of theory is the development of transfer, i.e. of the ability to transpose all listening to the residual hearing area, due to the gradual progression of hearing loss.

Conclusion

It is clear that sensorineural hearing loss cannot be regarded as a simple filter, and that other perceptual processes, rather than just detection are at work. These perceptual processes are variably impaired. One common feature shared by all subjects in the sample is compression of speech processing to a frequency region narrower than actual residual hearing area, positioned between 0.4 and 1.6 kHz. Intelligibility field capacity is a better measure of the (dis)ability to process speech than simple speech audiogram, because it takes into account the dynamics of speech processing at various intensity levels and enables numeric comparison of different response patterns.

Summary

The purpose of the study was to examine how subjects with sensorineural hearing loss comprehend isolated words with respect to necessary intensity re their pure-tone and speech audiometry thresholds as well as with respect to sound content of the presented words.

The study involved 12 subjects (mean age 77 years) with sensorineural hearing loss ranging between 40 and 77 dB in both ears, and pure-tone audiometry curves sloping down toward higher frequencies. The tests were performed using the pure-tone and speech audiometry apparatus and material.

The subjects reached maximum intelligibility (sample mean 94%) on the average 31 dB above the threshold of hearing in speech audiometry. With respect to sound content of the presented words it was found that words consisting of predominantly low sounds whose characteristic frequencies are up to about 1 kHz (*klupa*) were repeated with the 57.35% accuracy; mid-frequency words, containing sounds whose characteristic frequencies are between 1 and 3.2 kHz (*jaje*), were repeated with 60.86% accuracy, and high words, containing sounds whose characteristic frequencies are above 3.2 kHz (*zmija*), were repeated least correctly (54.28% accuracy).

Acknowledgement

This study was financially supported by grant no. 130721 of the Croatian Ministry of Science and Technology. The help of the SUVAG clinic staff is gratefully acknowledged.

References

Bakran J (1996) Zvuèna slika hrvatskoga govora (Sound image of Croatian speech). Zagreb: Ibis grafika.

Bamford J, Saunders E (1994) Hearing Impairment, Auditory Perception and Language Disability. London: Whurr Publishers.

Bamford JM, Wilson IM, Atkinson D, Bench J (1981) Pure tone audiograms from hearing-impaired children: Predicting speech-hearing from the audiogram. British Journal of Audiology, 15, 3–10.

Desnica-Žerjavić N (1990) Neke slušne osobine glasova (About some auditive properties of speech sounds). GOVOR, 7, 157–77.

Guberina P (1972) Case studies in the use of restricted bands of frequencies in auditory rehabilitation of the deaf. Zagreb: Institute of Phonetics.

Horga D, Mildner V (1996) Optimala glasa mjerena vremenom brzine reakcije (Response time as a measure of the sound optimal frequency band). SUVAG, 8(1), 13–22.

Mildner V (1986) Perception of filtered speech by native and non-native listeners. Unpublished MA thesis, University of Pennsylvania, Philadelphia.

Mildner V (1993) Od dijalekta do standarda preko korektivne optimale (From dialect to standard via corrective optimal). SUVAG, 6, 119–22.

Pansini M (1995) Univerzalnost verbotonalnih zasada (Universality of verbotonal principles). GOVOR, 12, 125–34.

Perović N (1993) Govorno polje kod prezbiakuzije (Speech field in presbyacusis). MA thesis, University of Zagreb.

Pozojević-Trivanović M (1984) Slušanje i govor (Listening and Speech). Zagreb: University of Zagreb.

Rosen SM, Fourcin AJ (1986) Frequency selectivity and the perception of speech. In Moore BCJ (ed.) Frequency Selectivity in Hearing. London: Academic Press.

Šindija B, Perović N (1993) Kapacitet polja razabirljivosti (KAPRA) govora (Intelligibility field capacity (IFC) of speech). SUVAG, 6, 37–42.

Vuletić B (1980) Gramatika govora (Grammar of Speech). Zagreb: GZH.

Chapter 16
Speech Perception Tests on the Internet: An Example Using Filtering to Simulate Reception in Hearing Impairment

P KÖRKKÖ, K HUTTUNEN and M SORRI

Introduction

Noise masking (e.g. Pekkarinen, 1988; Sommers and Humes, 1993) has been used in simulating and modelling various hearing impairments. In masking studies, for example, the frequency resolution capacity of noise-masked normally hearing subjects has been quite identical with the results obtained from hearing impaired subjects with comparable threshold elevations (Humes et al., 1988).

Also, when low-pass, high-pass and band-pass filtering has been used more and more to simulate hearing impairments, the speech reception results have agreed rather well with the hearing impaired subjects' performance (e.g. Phillips et al., 1994; Stuart et al., 1995). This has also been the case in studies concerning the Finnish language (Kiukaanniemi, 1980; Kiukaanniemi and Määttä, 1980).

The proliferation of Internet connections, together with recent technological advances in interactive multimedia on the World-Wide Web (WWW), have greatly enhanced the possibilities of using the net for speech perception studies in phonetics, audiology and related disciplines. Listening test material placed on a media server is readily available to potential subjects or informants; multimedia and audio technologies are also available to ensure smooth transmission of high-resolution sound stimuli. With proper control and recording of test parameters via interactive tools, even response data collection appears possible.

To gain experience of the practical issues pertaining to remotely conducted listening tests on the WWW, an online program or test interface, HI-SIM, was produced that initially allows access to speech material filtered to simulate reception in hearing impairment. The listening test multimedia program also serves as an online educational tool. Lacking many of the advantages offered by multimedia demonstrations, traditional classroom techniques often fall short of the goal of furnishing students and clinicians with an adequate 'ears-on' awareness of the nature and quality of speech received through defective hearing mechanisms.

The test/simulation interface

Multimedia authoring tool

In order to create an interactive test interface and to make the simulation interface available to informants and other clients on the WWW interested in the nature and effects of hearing impairment, the multimedia authoring tool Director (Macromedia, Inc) with its network lingo extensions was used. Shockwave Audio (SWA) which enables so-called 'streaming' of sound files from an Internet server at faster modem speeds was selected as the sound format.

Sound Files

Digital signal processing software tools SoundEdit 16 (Macromedia, Inc) with the Native Power Pack plug-in software package (KS Waves Ltd) were used to produce the test or simulation material. Audiogram

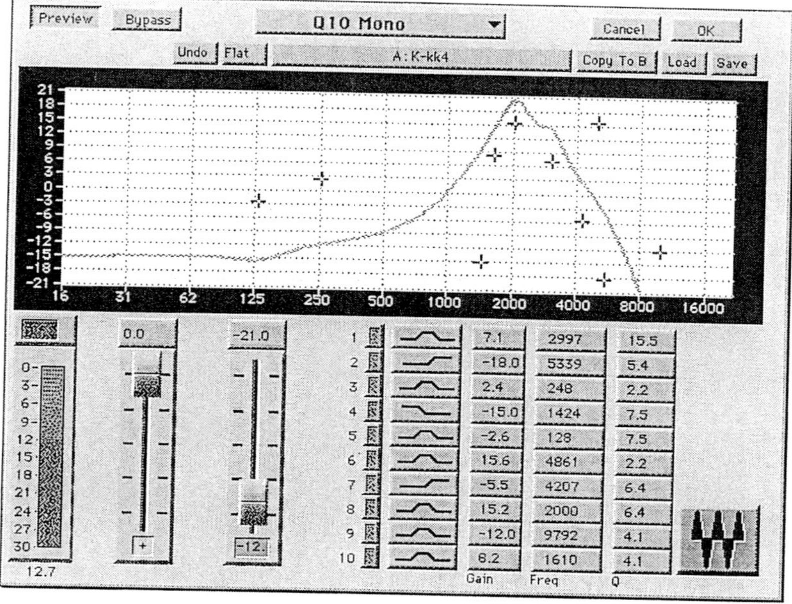

Figure 16.1. A sample view of the Q10 ParaGraphic Equalizer® window.

modelling and filtering of speech stimuli (word lists) were performed with the Q10 ParaGraphic Equalizer© software (Figure 16.1).

Listening test and simulation options

The simulation or test interface allows clients to simulate reception of speech in various types of hearing impairment such as hearing loss due to chronic otitis media, noise exposure or ageing. Also the effects on speech perception of differences in the type and level of background noise and in reverberation time can be assessed. In the interface (see Figure 16.2), subjects are presented with several test options: speech material (four options), grade of hearing impairment (four options), audiometric configuration (four options in each grade of hearing impairment), type (three options) and level (three options) of background noise and reverberation time (three options) as well as listening distance (two options).

Listening test procedures

Network informant set-up

To use the online listening test or simulation interface, a Macintosh or a Windows PC connected to the Internet and a WWW browser with the

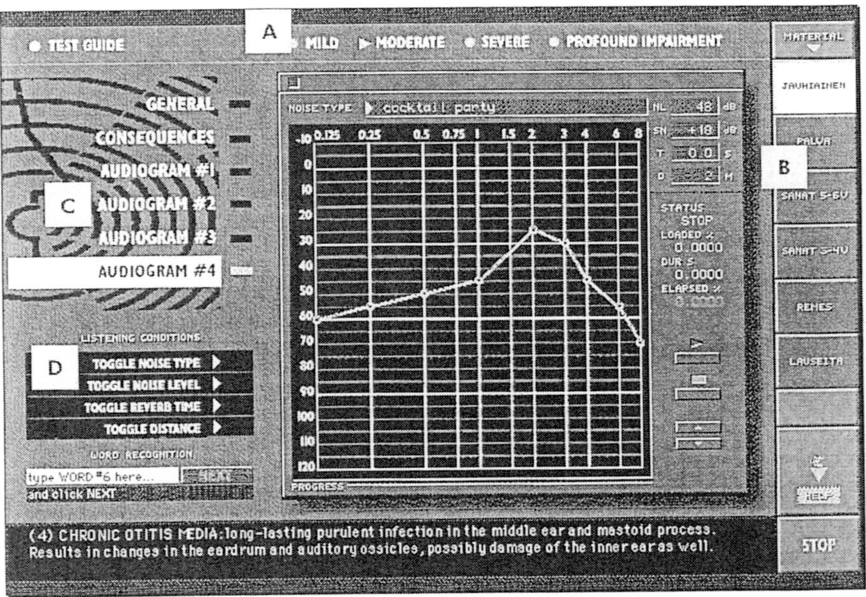

Figure 16.2. A sample view of the test/simulation interface; clickable menus and buttons are used for selecting the grade of hearing impairment (A), speech material (B), audiogram or filtering curve (C) and listening conditions (D).

Shockwave for Director plug-in (Macromedia, Inc) is required. The following hardware and software set-up is recommended: a Power Macintosh or a Pentium PC with an SVGA monitor capable of 8-bit colours, 16-bit audio hardware, a headphone set, a high-speed Internet connection (T1) and Netscape Navigator 3.0 with the Shockwave for Director plug-in installed. If only dial-up connections are available, modem speeds of 36 Kbps or higher must be used.

Word recognition tests

Conducting an online listening test involves a number of stages during which different tasks are performed to ensure the consistency of test conditions.

In stage 1, the WWW page with the embedded interactive test interface is loaded in the client's browser; the informant is guided to the instructions which are available through the TEST GUIDE menu item. In stage 2, the speech material and type of filtering are selected and the four parameters of the listening conditions are adjusted using the interface buttons. The selected parameter settings and options determine the stimulus file to be used in the test session. In stage 3, a listening test session is started by clicking the 'PLAY' button: the test file is downloaded, i.e. streamed from the test server to the client's computer and playback begins. During the playback the client records his or her responses and later, in stage 4, enters them in an editable text field in the test interface window or, alternatively, on a special WWW page loaded for response input. In stage 5, response data and all test parameter settings are saved in a text file, which is later uploaded to the appropriate directory on the test server.

In word recognition tasks, scores can be computed online by checking the informant's responses, which are entered in an editable text field using the computer keyboard, against a built-in database. Response data and test parameter settings can be saved in text files for subsequent processing.

Applications

Originally, this multimedia program to simulate hearing impairments, HI-SIM, was developed for the education of speech therapy students. Preliminary student feedback suggests that the interface and its speech material simulating reception in hearing impairment is a powerful educational tool. The program gives a rather realistic view of how a hearing impaired person hears. In addition to the effect of the hearing impairments themselves, the impact of difficult listening conditions, e.g. competing speech noise, can be simulated simultaneously. Of course, the program can be used in the education of other groups, such as audiologists, audiology assistants and virtually any personnel working with the hearing impaired. Furthermore, HI-SIM may also be used to demonstrate the effects of hearing impairments to the family members of the hearing impaired patients.

At present, HI-SIM may be used either on the Internet or as a CD-ROM version in the laboratory. When used on the Internet, the test (word) signal cannot be accurately calibrated. On the other hand, the S/N ratio, i.e. the level of the competing noise in relation to the speech signal is stable. Hence, the program is a very practical tool in collecting data on the effects of simulated hearing impairments and difficult listening conditions when piloting ordinary research projects, when first validated on real hearing impaired subjects. As a virtual test tool the program has obvious applications in the development and testing of amplification parameters for hearing aids.

References

Humes LE, Espinoza-Varas B, Watson CS (1988) Modeling sensorineural hearing loss. I. Model and retrospective evaluation. Journal of the Acoustical Society of America, 83, 188–202.

Kiukaanniemi H (1980) Speech Intelligibility in Hearing Losses Linearly Sloping to High Frequencies With Reference to Phonetic Aspects of Speech. Academic dissertation. Acta Universitatis Ouluensis, Series D, Medica No. 57, Ophthalmologica et oto-rhino-laryngologica No. 6, Oulu: University of Oulu (Finland).

Kiukaanniemi H, Määttä T (1980) Speech discrimination and hearing loss sloping to high frequencies. A phonetic approach. Scandinavian Audiology, 9, 235–42.

Pekkarinen E (1988) Effects of Noise and Reverberation on Speech Discrimination. Academic Dissertation, Annales Universitatis Turkuensis, Ser. D, Medica-Odontologica, 35, Turku: University of Turku (Finland).

Phillips DP, Rappaport JM, Gulliver JM (1994) Impaired word recognition in noise by patients with noise-induced cochlear hearing loss: Contribution of temporal resolution defect. The American Journal of Otology, 15(5), 679–86.

Sommers MS, Humes LE (1993) Auditory filter shapes in normal-hearing, noise-masked normal, and elderly listeners. Journal of the Acoustical Society of America, 93(5), 2903–14.

Stuart A, Phillips DP, Green WB (1995) Word recognition performance in continuous and interrupted broad-band noise by normal-hearing and simulated hearing-impaired listeners. The American Journal of Otology, 16(5), 658–63.

Chapter 17
Validation of a Central Auditory Speech Perception Test for Children

KARIN NEIJENHUIS, THOM CRUL, BEN MAASSEN and PAUL GROENEN

Introduction

In this experiment a central auditory speech perception test has been validated. The data proved that a psycholinguistic approach to central auditory processing disorders can provide additional information about speech perception processing.

Central auditory processing disorders (CAPD) are not a unitary diagnostic syndrome. The American Speech-Language-Hearing Association (ASHA) defines CAPD as an observed deficiency in one or more of the following functions (ASHA, 1996):

- Sound localization and lateralization;
- Auditory discrimination;
- Auditory pattern recognition;
- Temporal aspects of audition, including:
  - temporal resolution,
  - temporal masking,
  - temporal integration,
  - temporal ordering;
- Auditory performance decrements with competing acoustic signals;
- Auditory performance decrements with degraded acoustic signals.

From a behavioural point of view, children with CAPD often demonstrate difficulty comprehending speech in backgrounds of noise or competing speech; distractibility and hyperactivity; inattentiveness and short attention span; poor memory for auditory information, particularly for linguistically complex messages; difficulty understanding verbal directions; academic underachievement and reading difficulties because of auditory-phonetic confusions (Chermak and Musiek, 1992). In our view, *any* problem in the processing of auditory information – whether speech, music, or environmental sounds – that cannot be explained by peripheral hearing loss, is a CAPD.

There is a lack of standardization of central auditory tests and procedures. In clinical practice the available test battery is insufficient to diagnose all children who are referred by teachers and speech pathologists to an audiological department because of serious problems in listening to and understanding speech.

In various experiments it has been proven that children with primary and/or secondary language problems also have speech perception problems (Groenen et al., 1996a, 1996b, 1999). A psycholinguistic approach to CAPD has proven to be useful in these experiments. The present study compared this psycholinguistic approach with more classical (psychophysical) approaches to central auditory testing.

The aims of the study were:

1. To develop sensitive tests to detect and diagnose more children with problems in auditory speech processing as early as pre-school age.
2. To build from the available and newly developed tests a comprehensive test battery, which diagnoses central auditory problems in children, especially problems in the speech perception domain.
3. To validate the newly developed tests by comparing performances on these tests by children with auditory speech processing problems and normally developing children.

Method

A method to make a speech test more sensitive is to present the subject with so called degraded or low redundant speech. A psycholinguistic, as opposed to a psychophysical manner to reduce redundancy is based on the manipulation of critical cues in the acoustic speech signal, which normally brings about the perception of a specific speech contrast. We used a place-of-articulation contrast. For this contrast, a naturally spoken plosive consonant /b/ in the Dutch word /bɑk/ (meaning: 'box') was changed into the direction of the phoneme /d/ in /dɑk/ ('roof'), by manipulating in a stepwise manner the second and third formant transitions, yielding a speech continuum.

In previous studies we showed that children with a history of early otitis media with effusion (OME), children with developmental apraxia of speech and children with developmental dyslexia as a group perform poorer on speech continua than normally developing children, thereby demonstrating speech perception problems (Groenen et al., 1996a, 1996b, 1999).

Construction of the test battery

From a larger audiologic test battery, three tests that, based on previous studies, turned out to be the most sensitive and valid were selected (Simkens and van Velzen, 1993; van Velzen et al., 1995). These were the following, classical CAPD tests:

1. Filtered speech: low-pass filtered, cut-off frequency 500 Hz.
2. Fusion test: The speech signal was filtered in two bandpass-filters: a low band (350–450 Hz) and a high band (1950–2050 Hz).
3. Speech in noise: Two signal-to-noise ratios were used: S/N -5 dB and S/N -10 dB.

Added to this test battery were the following newly developed, categorical speech perception tests:

4. Identification of the stimuli of the place of articulation continuum /bɑk/ - /dɑk/.
5. Discrimination of pairs of stimuli from the place of articulation continuum /bɑk/ - /dɑk/.

Subjects

Fifty-one children attending a special school for the speech and language impaired were selected. These children showed serious problems in listening to and understanding speech, according to classroom teachers. A checklist was used to help the teachers detect the problems. The items on this list were selected from an observation profile, developed by Sanger and colleagues (Sanger et al., 1987).

Ages ranged from 5;6 to 8;6 years. A group of 30 normally developing children, matched on age, were selected from a primary school. All children had normal intelligence and normal hearing based on tympanometry and tone audiometry.

Results

We used different ways of analysing the data. For the classical CAPD-tests, ANOVA was used. The categorical perception test yielded two curves per subject: an identification curve and a discrimination curve. Figure 17.1 shows the ideal identification and discrimination curves.

To analyse the categorical speech perception data, we used Probit Analysis (Finney, 1971) to compute the slope and phoneme boundary of the identification curves. The slope and phoneme boundary data could be used in ANOVA to be compared with the data of the classical CAPD-tests. Also, the Categorical Score (Fourcin et al., 1978) was computed to categorize the perception curve in three different groups: (1) no categorization (0–0.5); (2) weak categorization (0.5–0.75); (3) good categorization (0.75–1.0). Figure 17.2 shows two identification curves, demonstrating 'good' and 'weak' categorization.

On the classical CAPD-tests as well as the categorical speech test /bak/-/dak/, the children in the experimental group scored significantly poorer than the normally developing children. In the experimental group, there were differential age effects, suggesting a developmental delay in CAPD children.

Looking at the Categorical Scores we found that of the experimental group, 50% showed 'no' or 'weak' categorization, compared with 13% of the control group.

Factor analysis showed that the test battery can be divided in functionally different groups of tests: (a) the classical CAPD-tests, (b) the

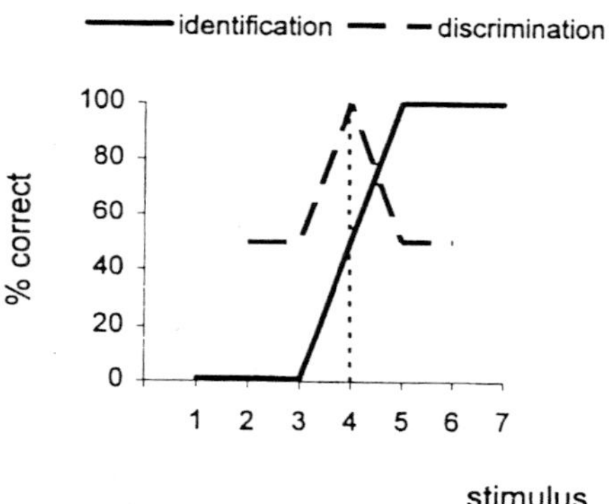

Figure 17.1. Ideal identification and discrimination curves as results of the categorical speech perception test. The vertical dashed line shows the phoneme boundary between /b/ and /d/.

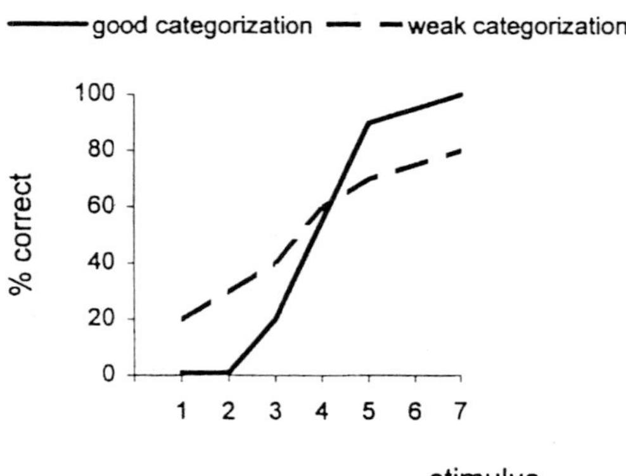

Figure 17.2. Identification curves of a 'good categorization' and a 'weak categorization'. The 'good categorization' curve shows a steeper slope.

categorical speech test. The classical CAPD tests seem to be testing at a higher level of speech processing than the categorical speech perception test. This is because at the classical tests, the lexicon is involved with repeating CVC-words. The categorical speech perception test involves smaller differences at phoneme level, which is at a lower level than the lexicon.

Conclusions

The conclusions from this study are:

1. A categorical speech perception test can discriminate children with CAPD from children without CAPD.
2. A categorical speech perception provides additional information about central auditory processing of speech.
3. Children with CAPD show a developmental delay in central auditory processing. Their auditory processing improves with age.

The results indicate that the psycholinguistic approach gives important additional information about central auditory processing of speech. We therefore suggest a combination of a psychophysical and a psycholinguistic approach to assess central auditory processing disorders. Together a valid CAPD test battery can be built.

Use of a central auditory test battery can be useful in diagnosing speech and language problems. Also, in the remediation of speech and language problems it is very important to know if there is a central auditory processing problem. Development of auditory training programmes following the administering of the suggested test battery needs further study.

Acknowledgements

We should like to thank the students from Hogeschool Arnhem en Nijmegen, speech-language therapy for administering the tests to the 81 children. Also we thank the children and their teachers of the dr Bosschool (Arnhem), Mgr Hanssenschool (Hoensbroek), De Horst (Eindhoven) and 't Veer for their participation. Finally, we thank our colleagues from Stichting Audiologisch Centrum Hoensbroeck (Hoensbroek) and Instituut Sint Marie (Eindhoven) for their help in setting up the experiment.

References

American Speech-Language-Hearing Association (1996) Central auditory processing: current research and implications for clinical practice. American Journal of Audiology, 5(2), 41–54.

Chermak GD, Musiek FE (1992) Managing central auditory processing disorders in children and youth. American Journal of Audiology, 1(3), 61–5.

Finney DJ (1971) Probit Analysis. Cambridge: University Press.

Fourcin A, Evershed S, Fisher J, King A, Parker A, Wright R (1978) Perception and production of speech patterns by hearing impaired children. Speech and Hearing. London: University College London, 174–204.

Groenen P, Crul Th, Maassen B, van Bon W (1996a) Perception of voicing cues by children with early Otitis Media with and without language impairment. Journal of Speech and Hearing Research, 39, 43–54.

Groenen P, Maassen B, Crul Th, Thoonen G (1996b) The specific relation between perception and production errors for place of articulation in developmental apraxia of speech. Journal of Speech and Hearing Research, 39, 468–82.

Groenen P, Maassen B, Crul Th, Assman-Hulsmans C (1999) Auditory and phonetic perception of voicing and place-of-articulation in developmental dyslexia. Submitted for publication.

Sanger DD, Keith RW, Maher BA (1987) An assessment technique for children with auditory-language processing problems. Journal of Communication Disorders, 20, 265–79.

Simkens H, van Velzen E (1993) Auditive Funktionen bei sprachbehinderten Kindern. In Plath P (ed.) Zentrale Hörstörungen. Essen: Geers-Stiftung, pp. 93–122

van Velzen ECW, Simkens HMF, Stollman MHP (1995) The value of central auditory tests in the detection of auditory processing disorders in language impaired children. In Schoonhoven R, Kapteyn T, de Laat J (eds) Proceedings European Conference on Audiology. Leiden: Nederlandse Vereniging voor Audiologie, pp. 247–53.

Chapter 18 Electrophysiological Event-related Indicators of Speech Perception Performance in Children Using a Cochlear Implant

PAUL GROENEN, AD SNIK and PAUL VAN DEN BROEK

Introduction

It is commonly recognized that objective measurements of event-related potentials can provide a neurophysiologic basis for the evaluation and the development of rehabilitation programmes for cochlear implant (CI) users (Kraus *et al.*, 1993; Ponton and Don, 1995). Most of the studies using objective measurements in subjects with a CI have focused on adult implant users. In our opinion, this typically is not the group that can benefit most from neurophysiologic objective measurements. The auditory neural system of deaf children may be degenerated or immature. Children with a CI are likely to benefit more from highly developed rehabilitation programmes than adults. There is a need for knowledge on neurophysiologic processes in children with CIs.

There is an increasing amount of literature on event-related potentials elicited in subjects with a CI. The P300 is elicited in an 'oddball paradigm', in which an unexpected stimulus occurs in a series of expected stimuli. It is an objective measure of the discrimination of stimulus differences. Event-related P300 measurements using tone bursts in subjects with a CI were performed in several studies (Kaga *et al.*, 1991; Kileny, 1991; Oviatt and Kileny, 1991; Groenen *et al.*, 1996). In all studies, significant P300 peaks were found. P300 measurements using speech in highly successful CI users showed no significant differences in P300 amplitude and latency between the group of CI users and a group of age-matched subjects with normal hearing (Micco *et al.*, 1995).

In the present experiment, P300s were elicited by tone and speech stimuli in a group of children with a CI. The tone contrast consisted of a

500 Hz and a 1000 Hz tone burst. A consonant place-of-articulation contrast /bɑ/-/dɑ/ was constructed, in which the target cue for auditory discrimination solely was the spectral transient of the second and third formant, the vowel characteristics where kept alike. Finally, a vocalic contrast /i/-/a/ was used, which was characterized by a speechlike difference in timbre. In addition to P300 responses, stimulus detection components N1 and P2 were examined and compared.

Method

Subjects

Subjects were nine children (five postlingually deaf: onset of deafness after the age of 2;5 yrs, and four congenitally deaf) with a Nucleus multichannel cochlear implant and an MSP processor. Their ages ranged from 9;11 to 16;10 years. In all the subjects, the electrode array was inserted into the cochlea over its full length. All the subjects were using the MPEAK speech processing strategy. The subjects were experienced users of CIs; they had been using one all day for several years. The control subjects were nine age-matched children with normal hearing.

Stimuli

For the tone contrast, a 500 Hz tone burst (20 ms linear rise and fall time, 80 ms plateau time) was used as the standard stimulus, whereas a 1000 Hz tone burst (with the same envelope) was used as a deviant stimulus. For the speech contrasts, the Computerized Speech Lab (CSL Model 4300, V5.05) was used for editing sound signals. The LPC Parameter Manipulation/Synthesis Program (ASL Model 4304, V1) was used for manipulating and resynthesizing the spectral structure of the signal. First, a place-of-articulation contrast /bɑ/-/dɑ/ was constructed, which was a contrast determined by spectral cues. By manipulation of the linear predictive coding (LPC) parameters and resynthesis of the result, the two syllables were constructed. The two speech tokens differed from one another in the starting value and slope of the transitions of the second and third formant. The transitions of the second and third formants were 45 ms in duration. All transitions were linear. The total length of each stimulus was 175 ms. Second, a vowel contrast /i/-/a/ was generated. This contrast was determined by formant frequencies of the first, second and, to a lesser extent, the third formant. A natural adult male voice formed the base of the speech token /i/. The two speech tokens differed from one another in the centre frequencies of the first, second and third formant.The total length of each stimulus was 150 ms.

Procedure

The stimuli were acoustically presented by a loudspeaker. The standard stimuli occurred at a probability rate of 85%; the deviant stimuli occurred at a probability rate of 15%. The presentation level at the position of the subjects' ears or CI microphone was approximately 70 dB(A). Recording electrodes were placed on the right mastoid (M2, reference) for the subjects with normal hearing and on the contralateral mastoid (Mc, refererence) for the CI users, on the forehead midline (Fz, active) and on the wrist (ground). The recordings were zero phase-shift low-pass filtered digitally off-line, with a cut-off frequency of 25 Hz. The inter-stimulus interval was set at 2 s.

For each sound contrast, evoked potentials were measured from two blocks of the stimuli. Each block comprised presentation of 20 standard stimuli, followed by 30 deviant stimuli pseudorandomly embedded in about 170 standard stimuli. Between two deviant stimuli at least three standard stimuli were presented. The subjects had their eyes closed during recording and were instructed to count the deviant stimuli.

Results and discussion

Reproducible P300 peaks were found in all control subjects for all sound contrasts. A reproducible P300 peak was found in all nine patients for the 500–1000 Hz contrast, eight out of nine subjects for the /i/-/a/ vowel contrast, and six out of eight subjects for the /ba/-/da/ consonant contrast. In Figure 18.1, a typical example of the waveforms is given for one of the children with a CI.

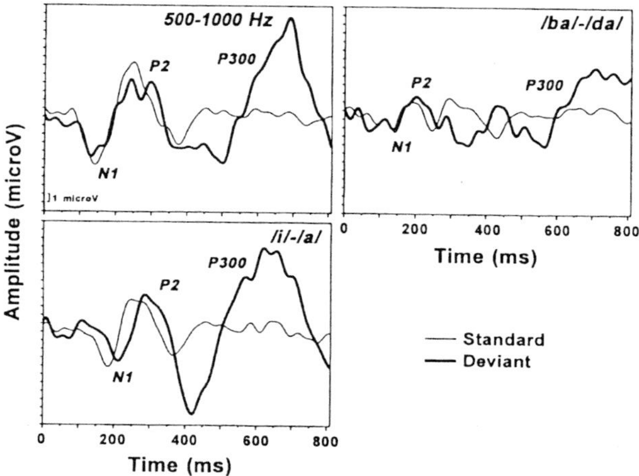

Figure 18.1. Typical example of event-related potentials in a child with a cochlear implantation.

Latencies and amplitudes of N1 and P2 were taken from the average trace of the standard signal. There were significant differences in N1 latency between both groups. Prolonged latencies were found for peak N1 for the CI users for all conditions (500–1000 Hz, $t(16) = 3.36, p = 0.004$; /bɑ/-/dɑ/, $t(16) = 2.21, p = 0.04$; /i/-/a/, $t(16) = 6.31, p < 0.001$). CI users showed prolonged latencies for peak P2 for all conditions (500–1000 Hz, $t(16) = 2.54, p = 0.02$; /bɑ/-/dɑ/, $t(15) = 3.74, p = 0.002$; /i/-/a/, $t(16) = 5.06, p < 0.001$).

In a previous study (Groenen et al., 1999), we reported prolonged latencies for peak P300 for adult CI users for tone and speech contrasts. In Figure 18.2, P300 latencies and amplitudes are displayed for the children. Children with a CI did not differ from children with normal hearing with regard to P300 latency or amplitude. Both groups did show a wide range in P300 latencies.

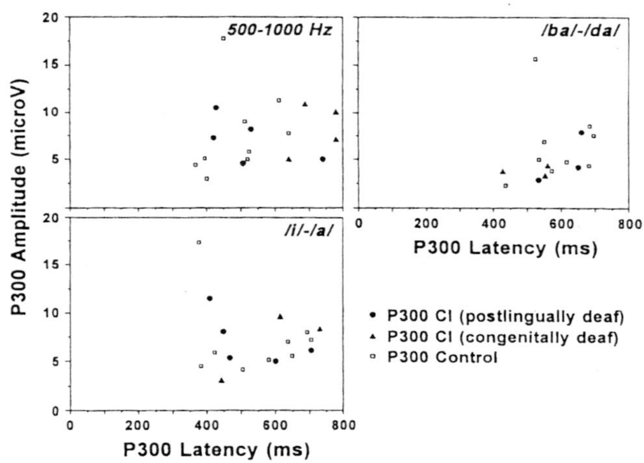

Figure 18.2. Latencies and amplitudes for P300 for both the CI children and the control children with normal hearing.

The number of subjects was rather small, so statistical comparison between the group of congenitally deaf children and postlingually deaf children was not possible. Still, it appeared that there was no difference in N1, P2, and P300 latencies and amplitudes between congenitally deaf and postlingually deaf children with a CI.

Electrophysiological measurements seem very useful in evaluating and monitoring the neural functionality of children with CIs. The P300 can help in fundamentally understanding the effects of electrical stimulation of the inner ear. It may help in adjusting and developing rehabilitation programmes for children with CIs. We agree with Micco *et al.* (1995) that electrophysiological assessment of event-related potentials may have potential as a clinical tool for evaluating processing on a cognitive level as well as on the level of auditory discrimination.

References

Groenen P, Makhdoum M, Van den Brink J, Stollman M, Snik A, Van den Broek P (1996) The relation between electric auditory brain stem and cognitive responses and speech perception in cochlear implant users. Acta Otolaryngologica (Stockholm), 116, 785–90.

Groenen P, Snik A, Van den Broek P (1999) The relation between cognitive tone and speech-evoked P300 potentials and speech perception ability in cochlear implant users. Submitted.

Kaga K, Kodera K, Hirota E, Tsuzuku T (1991) P300 response to tones and speech sounds after a cochlear implant: A case report. Laryngoscope, 101, 905–7.

Kileny PR (1991) Use of electrophysiologic measures in the management of children with cochlear implants: Brainstem, middle latency and cognitive (P300) responses. American Journal of Otology, 12, 37–42.

Kraus N, Micco AG, Koch DB, McGee T, Carrell T, Sharma A, Wiet RJ, Weingarten CZ (1993) The mismatch negativity cortical evoked potential elicited by speech in cochlear implant users. Hearing Research, 65, 118–24.

Micco AG, Kraus N, Koch DB, McGee TJ, Carrell TD, Sharma A, Nicol T, Wiet JR (1995) Speech-evoked cognitive P300 potentials in cochlear implant recipients. American Journal of Otology, 4, 514–20.

Oviatt DL, Kileny PR (1991) Auditory event-related potentials elicited from cochlear implant recipients and hearing subjects. American Journal of Audiology, 1, 48–55.

Ponton CW, Don M (1995) The mismatch negativity in cochlear implant users. Ear and Hearing, 16, 131–46.

Chapter 19
Listener Judgements of Diphthongs by Hearing and Deaf Speakers

ELLEN GERRITS, BEN AG ELSENDOORN and
WIM JM PEETERS

Introduction

Studies on deaf speech have shown that vowels and diphthongs produced by deaf speakers sound different from those produced by hearing speakers (Markides, 1970; Suonpää and Aaltonen, 1981; McGarr, 1983; Mencke et al., 1985). In an earlier production experiment (Elsendoorn et al., this volume, Chapter 20), differences in duration and formant pattern were found between diphthongs produced by deaf and hearing speakers. It would be interesting to find out if these deviant spectro-temporal cues in diphthongs are reflected in perceptual preference judgements.

Investigators have commonly used listening panels to rate the intelligibility of the speech of deaf speakers or had listeners actually recognise the speech. To ask listeners what they have heard is a time-consuming method, and although it can provide a measure of how much of the speech of deaf speakers is intelligible, it cannot reliably indicate why (Monsen, 1978). This method of analysis of deaf speech does not generally result in consistent and comparable results. Intelligibility scores range between 19% (Markides, 1970; Smith, 1975) and 76% (Monsen, 1974). One of the reasons for this difference is the use of different speech material. In Monsen's case it consisted of known monosyllabic words embedded in short sentences, and in the case of Smith of more natural sentences with a relatively complex grammatical structure. Apart from the differences in speech material, factors like age, degree and type of hearing loss, recording procedures, and different listener groups have their impact on analysis results. Monsen (1974) concluded that because intelligibility depends so strongly on what materials was said, to whom, and under what conditions, it is doubtful whether the notion of an average intelligibility score does have any significance at all.

A second, equally important, disadvantage of the use of rating of intelligibility is that it does not say anything about the acceptability of the speech. Speech can be intelligible without being acceptable. On the other hand, unintelligible speech will never be acceptable.

Because of these disadvantages, we used acceptability ratings. The aim of the current study was to assess if listeners prefer diphthongs based on original productions by deaf or by hearing speakers. In a series of experiments listeners were asked which of two diphthongs they found the more acceptable.

Method

Speakers

The speakers who provided the material that was to be used in the perception experiment were the ones who provided the production data described in Elsendoorn, Gerrits and Peeters (this volume, Chapter 20). One group consisted of four prelingually deaf (orally educated) high-school students of the Institute for the Deaf/IvD. They had an average hearing loss of 103 dB. The second group consisted of four students, untrained speakers, of Nijmegen University. The speakers were asked to pronounce the material using their normal, unmarked, speech rate.

Material

The speech material consisted of the diphthongs in the words [pɑuw] and [lʌy], digitized with a sampling frequency of 10 kHz. The diphthongs were segmented from the words, with an accuracy of one pitch period. To determine the beginnings and endings of the diphthongs, both visual and auditory feedback was used. Segmented diphthongs were stored in separate files. With LPC techniques the signal was analysed every 10 ms in terms of five formants, bandwidths, fundamental frequency and gain. The data of the first three formants and bandwidths, as well as the amplitude envelope were stored on disk.

Synthesis

In contrast to other studies the stimulus material did not consist of real speech, but of synthesized samples. The use of synthetic diphthongs was preferred, because it has the advantage of enabling the experimenter to vary certain parameters in a controlled fashion and of excluding any unwanted variation in the speech signal, such as, for example, fundamental frequency, intensity and bandwidth. The synthetic diphthongs were standardized, except for two parameters: duration and F1-F2 formant frequency.

The diphthongs were synthesized by using the allophone-based text-to-speech system developed at the Institute of Phonetics, University of Nijmegen (Loman *et al.*, 1989). The program controlling the synthesizer contains a great number of parameters that can all be changed. The default values of the synthesizer are as follows: a diphthong is represented as two segments. The formant pattern of a diphthong consists of three components: a steady-state part, followed by a transition, which is again followed by a steady state. The program contains values for the two steady-state segments. Three different types of stimuli were generated:

1. Diphthongs with speaker-specific durations;
2. Diphthongs with speaker-specific formant frequencies;
3. Diphthongs with speaker-specific durations *and* speaker-specific formant frequencies.

Synthetic diphthongs with speaker-specific duration

Diphthong component durations were measured by means of the plots showing the first three-formant tracks. The F1/F2 tracks were stylized by hand to emphasize the frequency changes in time. Next the formants were divided into two parts, i.e. the two segments, which was necessary to control the input to the synthesizer.

Formant frequencies and bandwidths for F1 and F2 were held constant in these stimuli, and were taken from the experiments by Peeters (1991). The default, monotonous 110 Hz fundamental frequency was changed, because isolated diphthongs are known to sound more natural when they have an intonation pattern (Peeters, 1991). Therefore the starting frequency for [ɑu] was 130 Hz, its end frequency 95 Hz; [ʌy] started at 135 Hz and ended at 110 Hz (values from Peeters, 1991). The other parameters used the default values of the synthesis program.

Synthetic diphthongs with speaker-specific formant frequencies

For the speaker-specific formant frequencies, the average formant frequencies of F1, F2, and F3 were determined for the two steady-state parts of the synthetic diphthong. The synthesis program determined the transition frequencies by linear interpolation.

Duration was held constant and was determined by averaging across the diphthong duration values found with hearing speakers in the open-word context. The total duration for [ɑu] and [ʌy] was set at 235 ms.

Synthetic diphthongs with speaker-specific duration and formant frequencies

This type of synthetic diphthong is a combination of the other two types. Speaker-specific values were determined as described above for the other two types.

For each of the diphthongs (both [ɑu] and [ʌy]) 24 different stimuli were generated; 2 (groups of speakers) x 4 (number of speakers per group) x 3 (types of synthetic diphthong). The synthesized versions were copied onto digital audiotape, with a sampling frequency of 48 kHz. This tape was fed into the computer on which the perception experiments would be run; the sampling frequency in this case was 22.5 kHz.

Listeners

Five subjects participated in this experiment. The listeners were students at the Faculty of Arts of Nijmegen University. Their average age was 25 years and they all had normal hearing.

Design

Listeners were asked to rate pairs of synthetic diphthongs in a two alternative forced-choice task, by indicating the preferred diphthong. An interactive computer program by Van Hessen (personal communication, April 1994) was used to run the perception experiments. By means of this program, diphthong pairs of the same type (type 1, 2, or 3) were generated at random, with the restriction that no pairs were made of diphthongs of speakers that belonged to the same speaker group. For instance, a stimulus with deaf speakers' values could be matched with one stimulus with hearing speakers' values, but two stimuli with deaf speakers' values were not allowed. All pairs were played back in both A-B and B-A order. Each pair was repeated once in the experiment. In total, subjects had to judge 64 pairs in one experiment.

For each type of diphthong a separate experiment was set up, three for [ɑu] and three for [ʌy]. All listeners participated in six experiments, which were presented in different order. The order of the [ɑu] and [ʌy] experiments was alternated across the listeners as well. The order of the stimulus pairs was completely random in each experiment for every listener.

Procedure

The subjects received written instructions about their task and the experiment. The material was played back through headphones. The interval between the two stimuli of each pair amounted to 300 ms. The response time for the listener was 2 s. In addition to the auditory information, the listener could see the number of the pair on the computer screen. After each stimulus pair the listener was asked to indicate the preferred stimulus by pressing the left (first stimulus) or the right (second stimulus) mouse button. The scores were automatically stored in a database. Preceding each experiment, six pairs were presented to train scoring with the mouse and to let the listener grow accustomed to the synthetic quality of the speech material. The experiments were carried out in a sound-treated booth at Nijmegen University. Every subject completed the six experiments within one day.

Results

The results of the listening experiment are displayed in Figures 19.1 and 19.2. The values in Figure 19.1 represent the percentage preference for a synthetic stimulus (/au/ = [ɑu], and /ui/ = [ʌy]), averaged over five listeners. In this figure it can be seen that listeners prefer a synthetic [ɑu] or [ʌy] with original hearing speakers' values. The synthetic diphthongs with the deaf speakers' values have the lowest preference score. The listeners' preference is independent of the diphthong type.

In Figure 19.2 the preference scores are shown separately for duration and formant frequency. The scores are averaged over both diphthongs, since the results for the [ɑu] and [ʌy] were the same.

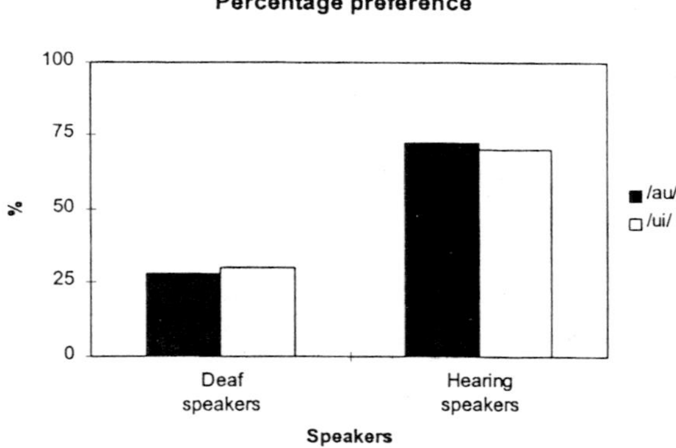

Figure 19.1. The percentage preferences of the listeners for the synthetic [ɑu] and [ʌy] with original values of the deaf and hearing speakers.

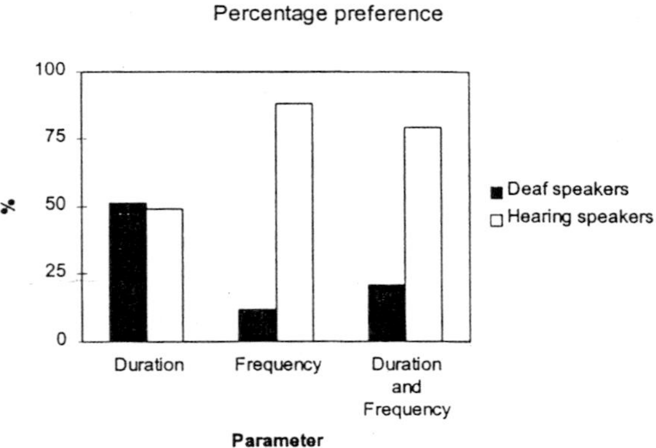

Figure 19.2. The percentage preferences of the listeners averaged over both synthetic diphthongs with original values of the deaf and hearing speakers, separated for each varied parameter.

A multivariate analysis of variance was performed on the data, with Diphthong(2) , Speaker(2), and Parameter(3) as independent variables. The factors Speaker and Parameter had a significant main effect ($F_{(1,48)}$ = 267.624, p = 0.000; $F_{(2,48)}$ = 7.63, p = 0.001 respectively).

There was also a significant interaction between the factors Speaker and Parameter ($F_{(2,48)}$ = 75.92, p = 0.000), which is shown in Figure 19.2. The synthetic diphthongs with the deaf speakers' duration values received relatively high scores compared with the other conditions. Apparently the listeners consider this duration acceptable, whereas the diphthongs with the frequency values and the combination of duration and frequency are judged as less acceptable. The influence of the parameter 'frequency' and the combination 'frequency and duration' is equally large in the judgements for the diphthongs with deaf and hearing speaker values.

Discussion

The results of the listening experiment show that listeners prefer the synthetic diphthongs generated with the original hearing speakers' productions. The scores diverge depending on the parameter that was varied. The durations of the diphthongs spoken by the deaf and hearing speakers are judged as equally acceptable, even though the duration of the deaf speakers' diphthongs was much longer. A possible explanation for this could be a general preference with the listeners for long stimuli to base their judgements on.

When the formant values are varied, a large discrepancy appears between the preference scores for the deaf and hearing speakers' values. Apparently a deviation of the formant frequency has a great impact on acceptability ratings. A low acceptability of the diphthong formants of deaf speakers had been expected due to a lack of dynamic change, which is characteristic of the formant pattern of diphthongs produced by hearing speakers (Peeters, 1991; Elsendoorn et al., this volume, Chapter 20).

Conclusion

In perception the diphthongs of deaf speakers are judged as deviant compared with diphthongs of hearing speakers. This is what may be expected on the basis of acoustic differences between the diphthongs of the speaker groups, found in a previous production experiment. The interaction results confirm the findings that the low preference scores are mainly caused by the anomalous formant frequencies.

Summary

In a series of perception experiments the influence of non-standard pronunciation of Dutch diphthongs on acceptability ratings was investigated. Deaf and hearing speakers had produced the original diphthongs (Elsendoorn et al., this volume, Chapter 20). Significant spectro-temporal differences were found between the two groups of speakers. These differences were superimposed on synthetic stimuli in order to establish the relative weight of non-standard diphthong duration, non-standard spectral composition and speaker. Deaf speakers' diphthongs were judged least acceptable, which is mainly caused by the deviant spectral composition.

References

Loman H, Kerkhoff J, Boves L (1989) A working environment for speech synthesis by rule. Proceedings of the Institute of Phonetics, University of Nijmegen, 13, 51–63.

Markides A (1970) The speech of deaf and partially hearing impaired children with special reference to factors affecting intelligibility. British Journal of Disorders of Communication, 5, 126–40.

McGarr NS (1983) The intelligibility of deaf speech to experienced and inexperienced listeners. Journal of Speech and Hearing Research, 26, 451–8.

Mencke EO, Ochsner GJ, Testut EW (1985) Distinctive-feature analyses of the speech of deaf children. The Journal of Auditory Research, 25, 191–200.

Monsen RB (1974) Durational aspects of vowel production in the speech of deaf children. Journal of Speech and Hearing Research, 17, 386–98.

Monsen RB (1978) Toward measuring how well hearing-impaired children speak. Journal of Speech and Hearing Research, 21, 197–219.

Peeters WJM (1991) Diphthong Dynamics. Doctoral Dissertation, University of Utrecht, the Netherlands, Kampen: Mondiss.

Smith CR (1975) Residual hearing and speech production in deaf children. Journal of Speech and Hearing Research, 18, 795–811.

Suonpää J, Aaltonen O (1981) Intelligibility of vowels in words uttered by profoundly hearing-impaired children. Journal of Phonetics, 9, 445–50.

Chapter 20
Durations and Formants Frequencies of Diphthongs by Hearing and Deaf Speakers

BEN AG ELSENDOORN, ELLEN GERRITS and WIM JM PEETERS

Introduction

Diphthongs are complex phonemes, which involve articulatory movements from an onset position towards an offset position. Because of their complexity diphthongs are often incorrectly pronounced by deaf speakers: they tend to prolong them and the articulation often results in a centralized diphthong or even a monophthong. In the present study deaf speakers' production of the three Dutch diphthongs [ɑu], [ʌy], and [ɛi] will be acoustically analysed in terms of temporal aspects, formant frequencies and formant tracks. The deaf speakers' diphthongs will be compared with diphthong productions by hearing speakers.

In a follow-up study the perceptual consequences of possible differences will be analysed (Gerrits et al., this volume, Chapter 19).

The production of vowels and diphthongs in deaf speech

It has been observed that 16% fewer errors are made in vowels than in consonants (Markides, 1970). However, incorrect vowel articulation often has a bigger negative effect on the intelligibility of deaf speech than incorrect consonantal articulation (Smith, 1975). The most common errors made are (Markides, 1970; Smith, 1975; Monsen, 1978; Geffner, 1980; Levitt et al., 1980; McGarr, 1983; Gulian et al., 1983; Maassen, 1985):

- Neutralization
- Diphthongization of monophthongs
- Substitution of a tense vowel, e.g. [i], for a lax one, e.g. [I]
- Vowel lengthening

Problems have been observed both in the temporal and in the spectral domain. With respect to the former, Monsen (1974) observed a consistent duration opposition between [i] and [I], whereas in normal speech this opposition is usually absent. For the spectral domain, it has been reported that deaf speakers produce the so-called back vowels, which have a relatively low F1, best. This may be due to a better acoustic or even tactile perception of these sounds (Geffner, 1980; Smith, 1975). Suonpää and Aaltonen (1981), McGarr and Gelfer (1983) and Gulian et al. (1983), however, found that the high or front vowels are pronounced best. Different analysis methods may be the cause of these diverging results.

There is agreement in the literature that there is a positive correlation between visual speech perception and the realization of phonemes by deaf speakers. This could explain the better intelligibility of the high or front vowels. In general, vowels spoken by deaf people show relatively small formant frequency variability, as a result of limited tongue movement (Angelocci et al., 1964; Monsen, 1978; Suonpää and Aaltonen, 1981; McGarr and Gelfer 1983; Gulian et al., 1983).

The pronunciation of diphthongs is even more problematic to deaf speakers than the pronunciation of 'normal' vowels is. The following types of articulation errors can be found in Markides (1970) and Levitt et al. (1980):

- Substitution for the diphthong of a neutral schwa
- Omission of the second component
- Excessive lengthening, which causes the diphthong to split into two separate sounds

Monsen (1978) analysed acoustic aspects of the American English diphthong [ɑI] as spoken by deaf speakers. This diphthong did not show the relatively quick upglide of the second formant which is characteristic of hearing speakers. The movement of the first formant was normal. Second formant variability showed a higher correlation with deaf speech intelligibility than did first formant variability. The explanation given is that lower frequencies, i.e. the first formant, are perceived better by deaf people; in hearing loss, high frequencies usually are more affected than low frequencies (Monsen, 1978; Gulian et al., 1983); this is in accordance with the better production of low-formant-frequency vowels by deaf people (Geffner, 1980). The second formant of diphthongs is less easy to perceive. Additionally, the quick upgliding movement of the tongue, which results in F2 change, is scarcely visible. So deaf people cannot imitate this articulatory movement properly (Gulian et al., 1983).

The diphthong

In the introduction it was said that diphthongs pose more difficulties to deaf speakers than vowels do. From the literature it has become clear that the diphthong in all respects is a complex sound: various terms and definitions are used, but there is no consistent diphthong concept (Lehiste and Peterson, 1961; Collier et al., 1982; Bond, 1982; Nearey and Assmann, 1986; Peeters, 1991). Collier et al. (1982) and Peeters (1991) distinguish 'genuine' and 'pseudo' diphthongs, the former always constituting single phonological entities, contrary to the latter. Collier et al. (1982) consider [ɑu], [ɛi] and [ʌy] as 'genuine' Dutch diphthongs. In this study the term diphthong is used to refer to these three phonemes.

Two important diphthong theories emerge from the literature, one being the 'Target Theory' (Lehiste and Peterson, 1961; Pols, 1977; Bond, 1982; Bladon, 1985; Nearey and Assmann, 1986): diphthongs are described by means of onset and offset frequencies. The other is called the 'Trajectory Theory' (Gay, 1968, 1970; Gerber, 1971; Pols, 1977; Nearey and Assmann, 1986): diphthongs are exclusively described by the direction and rate of formant movement. Recent research tries to combine both theories into a new diphthong definition, based on the temporal formant pattern (Manrique, 1979; Toledo and Antoñanzas, 1987; Yang, 1987; Cao, 1991; Peeters, 1991; Stollwerck, 1991; Nabelek et al., 1994). The idea behind this theory is that the integral formant pattern is needed for an adequate description of a diphthong.

In this study the temporal patterns of the formant tracks are regarded as important cues for diphthong identity. Because diphthongs pose specific articulatory problems to deaf people, we expect to find differences between the durations and the spectro-temporal patterns of the diphthongs produced by deaf and hearing speakers. An assessment is made of how deaf speakers produce their diphthongs in relation to the production of hearing speakers. The goals of the current study are: (1) to determine significant duration differences between the diphthongs produced by deaf and hearing speakers; (2) to ascertain significant differences between the temporal formant patterns of the diphthongs produced by deaf and hearing speakers.

Methods

Speakers

Two groups of male speakers participated in this experiment. One group consisted of four prelingually deaf (orally educated) high-school students of the Institute for the Deaf. They had an average hearing loss of 103 dB. The second group consisted of four students, untrained speakers, of Nijmegen University.

Material

The three Dutch diphthongs [ɑu], [ɛi] and [ʌy] were embedded in five words of the following type: CV (open context), and CVC, CVCV (closed context). The initial consonant was either a liquid [l], or the voiceless plosive [p] or [k]. The final consonant was either [p] or [t]. The intervocalic C was either an intervocalic glide, a voiceless plosive ([p] or [t]), or the voiced plosive [d]. The final vowel in the CVCV words was [ə].

Procedure

The deaf students were recorded in a sound-treated booth at the Institute for the Deaf. The hearing speakers were recorded in the sound studio of the Language and Speech Department of Nijmegen University. The recordings were made on digital audiotape with a sampling rate of 48 kHz.

All speakers were instructed (in writing) to read out the material at a normal speech rate. Each word was written on a separate card. The recording sessions started with speakers reading out four additional cards that were not part of the stimulus material.

Acoustic analysis

The speech material was digitized with a sampling frequency of 10 kHz. The diphthongs were segmented from the words, with an accuracy of one pitch period. To determine the beginnings and endings of the diphthongs, both visual and auditory feedback was used. Segmented diphthongs were stored in separate files.

With LPC techniques the signal was analysed every 10 ms in terms of five formants, bandwidths, fundamental frequency and gain. The data of the first three formants and bandwidths, as well as the amplitude envelope were stored on disk.

As the temporal patterns of the diphthongs were an important aspect of this research, each diphthong was divided into 10 time frames. This way the spectral data of the diphthongs were time-normalized. For each frame an average formant frequency and bandwidth were determined. With the description of each formant in 10 frames, the dynamic character of the diphthong was preserved (Gottfried et al., 1993). If an overall average frequency had been determined instead, essential information about the formant transitions would have been lost. This technique has also been reported in other studies (Peeters, 1991; Stollwerck, 1991; Holbrook and Fairbanks quoted in Gottfried et al., 1993), with a varying number of measuring points ranging from 5 to 12. In our study we chose 10 measuring points, as this seems to describe the diphthong formant track adequately.

Results

In the first part of this section the duration data will be presented. The second part will describe the results from the analyses of the formant trajectories.

Duration

The mean duration results for all three diphthongs are presented in Figure 20.1. The duration results are given separately for two contexts: open context, and closed context. There was no effect of diphthong type on duration; therefore averaged results are presented. The figure represents the mean duration of the diphthongs in the two different contexts as a function of type of speaker.

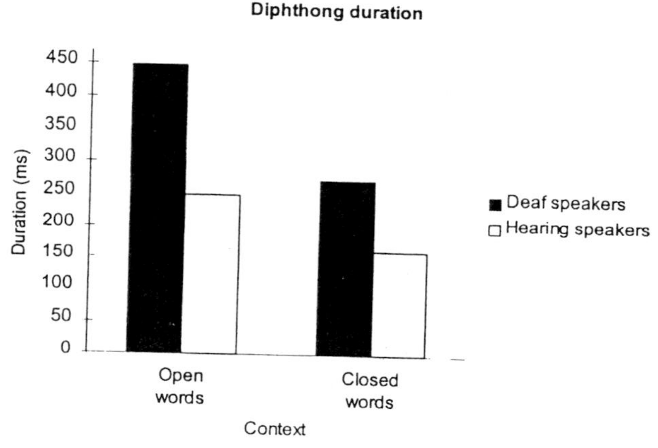

Figure 20.1. The mean duration results for all three diphthongs as a function of context and speaker.

Figure 20.1 shows that there is a difference between the duration values of the diphthongs of the deaf and the hearing speakers. The diphthongs of the hearing speakers are much shorter than those of the deaf speakers, especially in the open context. Duration is smallest in the closed context (Nooteboom, 1972). Both the deaf and hearing speakers follow this pattern. A multivariate analysis of variance with the variables Speaker (2), and Diphthong (3) showed that the Speaker factor had a significant effect ($F_{(1,18)} = 220416.7, p = 0.001$).

The differences in the closed context were tested for significance by a multivariate analysis of variance with the variables Speaker (2), Diphthong (3), and Word (4). Here, the variables Speaker and Word both had a significant main effect ($F_{(1,72)} = 134.54$, $p = 0.000$; $F_{(3,72)} = 4.39, p = 0.007$ respectively).

Formant trajectories

In order to compare and interpret the formant trajectories of the different groups of speakers, the formant frequencies were measured for each diphthong at 10 equidistant points. The frequency values of the first three formants of [ɑu], [ɛi] and [ʌy] were plotted for the closed context condition. An example of the differences between the temporal patterns produced by the deaf and the hearing speakers is presented in Figures 20.2 and 20.3.

A comparison of the formants in Figures 20.2 and 20.3 makes it clear that the formants of diphthongs produced by the hearing and deaf speakers follow different courses. What is most striking is the absence of any fast frequency movements in the trajectory of the second formant. To compute the effect of Speaker (2) on the formant trajectories of the

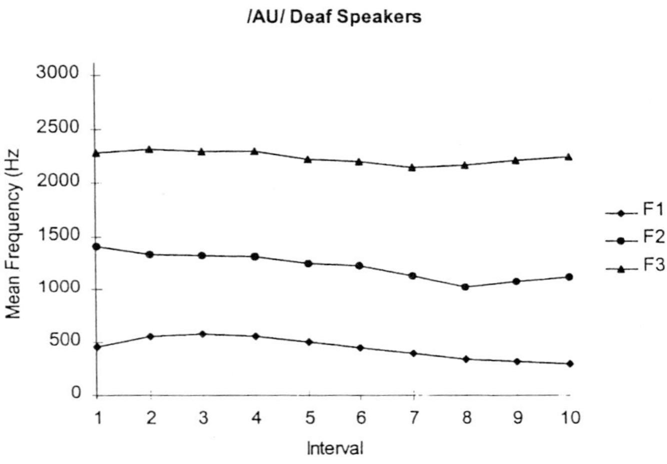

Figure 20.2. Diphthong formant tracks for [ɑu], produced in four closed context by four deaf speakers.

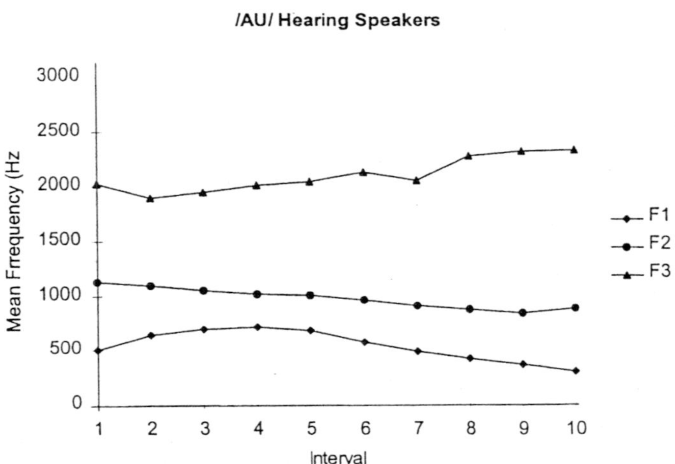

Figure 20.3. Diphthong formant tracks for [ɑu], produced in four closed context by four hearing speakers.

diphthongs, an analysis of variance was performed on each formant of the open context and closed context diphthongs.

In the open context data of the [ɑu], there proved to be a significant effect for Speaker in the first and second formant ($F_{(1,78)} = 5.20$, $p = 0.025$; $F_{(1,78)} = 110.61, p = 0.000$). For the [ʌy] in the open context, there was only an effect of Speaker in the first formant, $F_{(1,78)} = 21.59$, $p = 0.000$. The analysis of the open context data of the [ɛi] yielded the same effects as for [ɑu]: significant speaker effects in the first and second formant ($F_{(1,78)} = 12.41$, $p = 0.001$; $F_{(1,78)} = 29.97$, $p = 0.000$ respectively). In the closed context, there appeared to be a significant speaker effect on all formants, except on the third formant of [ɛi], and [ʌy]. There was no significant effect of Speaker on the third formant trajectories of any of the three diphthongs in the open context.

Discussion

Significant differences have been found between diphthong durations produced by deaf speakers and hearing speakers. The diphthongs of the deaf speakers have considerably longer durations. Whereas the hearing speakers had an average diphthong duration of 164 ms (closed context), durations by the deaf speakers amounted to 274 ms. These relatively long durations may influence intelligibility. Monsen (1978) found no significant relationship between speech rate and intelligibility. Monsen's results, however, refer to the overall intelligibility of deaf speech. Since the importance of the temporal aspects of diphthongs has been demonstrated (Peeters, 1991), we cannot state with any certainty that Monsen's conclusions will also hold for these diphthongs.

Spectro-temporal differences have also been found between deaf speakers and hearing speakers. The analyses of variance yielded significant effects of speaker on the first formant of the diphthong; however, the patterns in the first formants of both speaker groups were fairly similar. This is in contrast with the patterns of the second formant, which showed an absence of a fast rise in the deaf speakers' diphthongs. These results are in agreement with previous findings with English diphthongs (Monsen, 1978). According to Monsen (1978) it is a difficult task for many deaf speakers to produce enough difference in the second formant between different vowels; it is even more difficult to produce this change over a very short time period. In diphthongs, the frequencies of both formants must change rapidly within a few hundred milliseconds. When deaf speakers fail to produce diphthongs correctly, the most common deviation from normal is that the second formant shows only a small amount of frequency change (Monsen, 1976).

A possible explanation for the absence of the fast movement in the second formant pattern could be a deviant tongue movement during production. Movements of the second formant are heavily dependent on articulatory gestures of tongue height and forward-backward constriction, whereas increasing the area of mouth opening can bring about large changes in the frequency of the first formant. While the articulatory gestures of relative mouth opening are visible, the movements of the tongue in the oral cavity usually are not. In addition, changes in mouth opening can much easier be described and illustrated than changes in the shape of the tongue (Monsen, 1978).

Conclusions

The observations made on the basis of the data measured in this production experiment lead to the conclusion that diphthongs are differently realised by deaf speakers and hearing speakers of Dutch. The differences reside both in the temporal and the spectral domain. In a follow-up study, the perceptual relevance of these differences will be investigated (Gerrits, this volume, Chapter 19).

Summary

An analysis of deaf persons' speech production at the phoneme level often reveals a deviant pronunciation, which is very noticeable in diphthongs, which are intrinsically difficult to articulate. In a controlled study, Dutch diphthongs by hearing and deaf speakers are compared with regard to duration and formant frequencies. Results clearly show significant differences in diphthong duration between the two speaker groups. Distinct formant trajectories are also found: the second formant trajectories of the hearing speakers' diphthongs contain a fast rise in formant frequency, which is absent in the F2 of the diphthongs spoken by deaf speakers.

References

Angelocci A, Kopp G, Holbrook A (1964) The vowel formants of deaf and normal hearing eleven-to-fourteen year old boys. Journal of the Acoustical Society of America, 29, 156–70.

Bladon A (1985) Diphthongs: A case study of dynamic auditory processing. Speech Communication, 4, 145–54.

Bond ZS (1982) Experiments with synthetic diphthongs. Journal of Phonetics, 10, 259–64.

Cao J (1991) Temporal structure of diphthongal finals in Standard Chinese. Report of phonetic research. Institute of Linguistics, Chinese Academy of Social Sciences, 39–54.

Collier R, Bell-Berti F, Raphael LJ (1982) Some acoustic and physiological observations on diphthongs. Language and Speech, 25, 305–23.

Gay T (1968) Effect of speaking rate on diphthong formant movements. Journal of the Acoustical Society of America, 44 (6), 1570–3.

Gay T (1970) A perceptual study of American English diphthongs. Language and Speech, 13, 65–88.

Geffner D (1980) Feature characteristics of spontaneous speech production in young deaf children. Journal of Communication Disorders, 13, 443–54.

Gerber SE (1971) Perception of segmental diphthongs. Proceedings of the 7th International Congress on Phonetic Sciences, Montreal, 479–92.

Gottfried M, Miller JD, Meyer DJ (1993) Three approaches to the classification of American English diphthongs. Journal of Phonetics, 21, 205–29.

Gulian E, Hinds P, Fallside F, Brooks S (1983) Vowel learning and the vowel system of deaf children: Age and feedback related differences. Journal of Communication Disorders, 16, 449–69.

Lehiste I, Peterson GE (1961) Transitions, glides and diphthongs. Journal of the Acoustical Society of America, 33, 268–77.

Levitt H, Stromberg C, Smith C, Gold T (1980) The structure of segmental errors in the speech of deaf children. Journal of Communication Disorders, 13, 419–41.

Maassen B (1985) Artificial corrections to deaf speech. Doctoral dissertation, University of Nijmegen. Enschede: Sneldruk.

Manrique De AMB (1979) Acoustic analysis of the Spanish diphthongs, Phonetica, 36, 194–206.

Markides A (1970) The speech of deaf and partially hearing impaired children with special reference to factors affecting intelligibility. British Journal of Disorders of Communication, 5, 126–40.

McGarr NS (1983) The intelligibility of deaf speech to experienced and inexperienced listeners. Journal of Speech and Hearing Research, 26, 451–8.

McGarr NS, Gelfer CE (1983) Simultaneous measurements of vowels produced by a hearing-impaired speaker. Language and Speech, 26 (3), 233–46.

Monsen RB (1974) Durational aspects of vowel production in the speech of deaf children. Journal of Speech and Hearing Research, 17, 386–98.

Monsen RB (1976) A taxonomic study of diphthong production in the speech of deaf children. In Hirsh SK, Eldredge DH, Hirsh IJ, Silverman SR (eds) Hearing and Davis: Essays Honoring Hallowell Davis. St Louis: Washington University Press, pp. 281–90.

Monsen RB (1978) Toward measuring how well hearing-impaired children speak. Journal of Speech and Hearing Research, 21, 197–219.

Nabelek AN, Czyzewski Z, Crowly H (1994) Cues for perception of the diphthong /AI/ in either noise or reverberation. Part I. Duration of the transition. Journal of the Acoustical Society of America, 95(5), 2681–93.

Nearey TM, Assmann PF (1986) Modelling the role of inherent spectral change in vowel identification. Journal of the Acoustical Society of America, 80(2), 1297–308.

Nooteboom SG (1972) Production and perception of vowel durations. Doctoral dissertation, University of Utrecht, the Netherlands.

Peeters WJM (1991) Diphthong Dynamics. Doctoral dissertation, University of Utrecht, the Netherlands, Kampen: Mondiss.

Pols LCW (1977) Spectral Analysis and Identification of Dutch Vowels in Monosyllabic Words. Doctoral Dissertation, University of Amsterdam, the Netherlands, Amsterdam: Acade-mische Pers B.V.

Smith CR (1975) Residual hearing and speech production in deaf children. Journal of Speech and Hearing Research, 18, 795–811.

Stollwerck LE (1991) A Contrastive Study of the Dynamic Nature of the Diphthongs /ɑu/ and /ai/ in the Production of English and German Native Speakers. Unpublished master's thesis, University College London, London.

Suonpää J, Aaltonen O (1981) Intelligibility of vowels in words uttered by profoundly hearing-impaired children. Journal of Phonetics, 9, 445–50.

Toledo GA, Antoñanzas-Barroso N (1987) The influence of speaking rate in Spanish diphthongs. Proceedings of the 11th International Congress of Phonetic Sciences, Tallin, 3, 125–8.

Yang S (1987) An articulatory dynamic model for diphthongs in Chinese. Proceedings of the 11th International Congress of Phonetic Sciences, Tallin, 1, 239–42.

Chapter 21
Evaluation of Vocal Production and Hearing Abilities of 1–2-Year-Old Children. Criteria for an Early Cochlear Implantation

M HOLM, S FRISCHMUTH and S VINTER

Introduction

Evaluating vocal production in the first year of life

The research on prelinguistic vocal development shows that healthy infants pass through a predictable sequence of stages from cries and vegetative noises in the first months to jargon babble at the end of the first year. The emergence of canonical babbling between the sixth and eleventh month represents a culmination of a significant developmental process. It is the beginning of the use of well-formed syllables that occur in words. Studies focusing on the relation between babbling and speech show a strong link between the phonological patterns of late babbling and early meaningful speech (Oller, 1980; Papoušek, 1994).

Eilers and Oller (1994) studied the relationship between deafness and the absence of canonical babbling. They found that deaf children reduce or stop their vocal production in this period of time. Therefore the observation of the child's vocal production should become part of the diagnostic routine. The emergence of canonical babbling indicates a progressing language acquisition. The absence of canonical babbling indicates a possible severe hearing impairment.

Correlation of vocal production and hearing abilities

The early detection of a severe hearing impairment depends on the attentiveness of all of the baby's caretakers. Normally, parents not paediatricians suspect that there is something wrong with their child's hearing. Most of the parents report that between the sixth and the eighth month of life they noticed a lack of auditory attention. Healthy babies, without any risk factors, are able to compensate for auditory deficiencies by visual attentiveness. Thus they often slip through the preventive examinations and will not be detected as being deaf or hard of hearing in an early age. But only an early detection of hearing impairment can prevent the interruption of preverbal vocalizations and its devastating influence on the child's development of verbal and social communication skills. Therefore it is very important to guarantee an early fitting of hearing aids during the first year of life.

We studied the vocal development of French and German infants after the fitting of hearing aids during their first and second year of life (Holm et al., 1996). We found that the quality and quantity of vocal production highly depends on the amount of acoustic information the child receives due to hearing aids (Holm and Frischmuth, 1997). Evidently, the degree of hearing loss influences the gain from hearing aids. A close observation of the child's vocal production allows us to draw conclusions on sufficient or insufficient hearing ability for the acquisition of language. If the gain from hearing aids is not sufficient, a cochlear implantation can be discussed (Lenarz et al., 1994).

Case reports

To illustrate the effects of sufficient and insufficient hearing ability, we have chosen two German children with different degrees of hearing loss. Their early development was documented by regular long-term video recordings of parent–child interaction. This material was the basis for our analysis. The vocal production was analysed using spectrograms to show the emergence of syllabic organization and prosodic features.

SH

SH was born in August 1992. Hearing aids were fitted at the age of 6 months. He has no additional handicap. The audiological data show a hearing level of 95 dB in the better ear. After the fitting of hearing aids auditory attention developed continuously. Voicing was used for communicative purposes. About the age of 14 months, canonical babbling emerged (see Figure 21.1).

At the same time, verbal comprehension grew rapidly. At the end of the second year of life he apparently had a good comprehension of everyday conversation and had reached the two-word stage (Pivot grammar). He developed complex syntactical structures and an excellent auditory memory during the third year, learning rhymes by heart. Verbal conversation is an important part of his life.

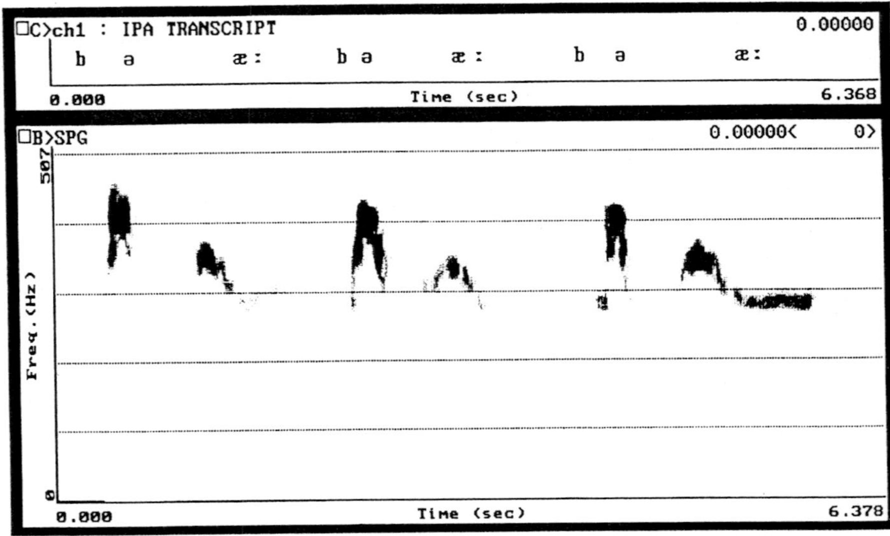

Figure 21.1. This is a typical consonant-vowel-combination with a visible syllabic structure and a vivid fundamental frequency.

AS

AS was born in November 1990. Hearing aids were fitted at the end of the first year. She has no additional handicap. The audiological data show a hearing level of 118 dB in the better ear.

After the fitting of hearing aids, the child did not develop any auditory awareness but was interested in all vibro-tactile sensations. She developed some marginal babbling with idiosyncratic meaning. Due to the absolute lack of auditory feedback, her voice remained monotonous (see Figure 21.2). She acquired a small vocabulary by lip-reading and reproduced it mostly by mute lip movements ('mouthing').

In January 1993, she received a cochlear implantation at the age of 2;2. She soon developed vocal play. She was very interested in listening to and imitating her mother's utterances. Voice and language developed simultaneously. At the end of the first year of hearing, she reached the two-word stage. At the end of the second year of hearing, she enjoyed singing and appeared to follow a near-to-normal language development. She communicates easily with hearing children of her age.

Conclusion

Both cases clearly show a strong relationship between the audiological data and the development of auditory behaviour, speech and language. This relationship can be observed in most of the children we followed.

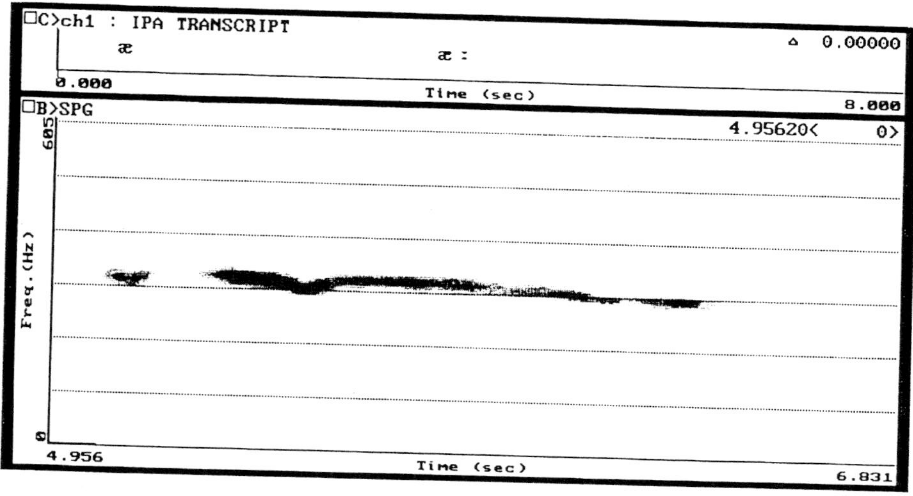

Figure 21.2. This spontaneous voicing is characterized by a very long duration and a monotonous fundamental frequency.

The children's speech and language development up to the age of two corresponds to their benefit from hearing aids. SH shows a near-to normal language development and sufficient hearing abilities with hearing aids. AS's verbal development corresponded to her absolute lack of auditory information. Therefore, she was a clear candidate for an early cochlear implantation.

We propose to observe and analyse the deaf child's vocal production closely. The segmental and suprasegmental structure of preverbal utterances gives information about the child's hearing ability. This should contribute to the decision for an early cochlear implantation. It is important to realize that the interval between the chronological age and the hearing age should be as short as possible.

References

Eilers R, Oller K (1994) Infant Vocalization and the Early Diagnosis of Severe Hearing Impairment. The Mailman Center for Child Development and the University of Miami, Florida: Mosby-Year-Book.

Holm M, Sauter-Bolz Ch, Frischmuth S (1996) Therapie nach Cochlear-Implant-Versorgung bei prälingual gehörlosen Kindern. Sprache-Stimme-Gehör 20.

Holm M, Frischmuth S (1997) Zur Bedeutung der Stimme in der kindlichen Sprachentwicklung. Vergleichende Beobachtungen und Analysen bei hörenden und hörbehinderten Kindern. Hörgeschädigten-Pädagogik 1/97.

Lenarz Th, Lehnhardt E, Bertram B (eds.) (1994) Cochlear-Implant bei Kindern. Stuttgart: Thieme Verlag.

Oller DK (1980) The emergence of the sounds of speech in infancy. In Yeni-Komshian GH, Kavanagh JF, Ferguson CA (eds) Child Phonology, Vol. 1: Production. New York: Academic Press.
Papoušek M (1994) Vom ersten Schrei zum ersten Wort. Bern: Huber.

Chapter 22
Interactive Developmental Intonology: Analysis Of Hearing Mother–Deaf Children Conversations

S VINTER, C BRIED and M HOLM

Introduction

In 1976, David Crystal submitted the methods for the study of the role of prosody in language development and proposed the concept of 'developmental intonology' that analyses the non-segmental (or suprasegmental) aspects of spoken language. In that framework, de Boysson-Bardies (1982) and Konopczynski (1986) studied the vocal, melodic and temporal aspects of the French child's emergent language.

In 1992, we proposed the concept of 'Interactive Developmental Intonology' (IDI), which includes the psycho-phonological and prosodic aspects of the mother–child conversation in a developmental perspective (Vinter 1992). It is a functional analysis of the developmental intonology that focuses on the child's production, the maternal responsiveness and the effects on the child's vocal and verbal behaviour and its evolution, and utilizes recent insights from the theoretical frameworks of discourse and conversation analysis.

The data (segmental and suprasegmental aspects) are examined within an integrated theoretical model of conversational interaction. The sounds, produced by the child, are examined not only as regards their form and their use, but also as regards their conversational value.

Researchers are particularly interested in the content of speech used with deaf children but not in prosodic aspects. However, several studies have shown that intonation can be perceived and even produced by hearing-impaired children with profound loss (Löhle's classification, 1991).

Method

This study is based on data concerning:

- the vocal productions of 25 profoundly deaf children (hearing loss > 90 dB), aged 4–31 months, in order to investigate the different stages these children pass through from the production of their first sounds to the first word combinations;
- the early communicative interactive processes between four profound deaf children (hearing loss > 100 dB) aged 2;5, who successfully acquired oral language, and their hearing mothers.

The following questions were addressed:

1. How does the vocal behaviour of the young deaf child affect the interaction between adult and child?
2. When did canonical babbling emerge?
3. When was the onset of the final lengthening in the babbling?
4. How do the sounds produced by the deaf child become linguistic signals?
5. What is the role of adult in all this?

The vocal behaviour of the young deaf

In previous research, Vinter (1992) pointed out that vocalizations appear only in interactional situations; there is no solitary gibber, the deaf child does not babble when alone. The loss of acoustic information has more effect on the quality than on quantity. In children, deaf from birth and who have never received any acoustic information, sounds are often limited to [oe]. In hearing children aged 3 months, Le Floch (1989) pointed out that these [oe], sounds of short duration and limited intensity, are imitated by the mother and integrated into a conversational framework. This is not always the case with deaf children who produce such sounds. Either these sounds are completely ignored by those around them or they do not become integrated into a conversation.

What is the effect of these productions on communication between the deaf child and his or her family?

We give one example: MI is 7 months and 20 days old and is a profoundly deaf child (hearing loss = 110 dB). Below is an extract of communication between him and his mother.

> Mother: Michaël
> Child: [oe]
> Mother: Go on my darling, come on, come sweetheart, go on, my little one. Talk to mummy!
> Child: [oehoe]
> Mother: Yes, that's it, come on, that's good, talk to mummy.

In this example, the mother calls the child. The mother's voice is ranged at level 2 and 3, between 360 Hz and 580 Hz. Pitch variations are very important. The mother emphasizes the [ka] in Michaël, (580 Hz with a lengthened vowel). The speaking rate is slow and corresponds with the syllabic length of the mother's. Three syllables last 750 ms (250 ms per syllable). Thus, the child produced an [oe] sound, which is so short that it was probably not 'picked up' by the mother. She continues to try to attract the child's attention, and it can noted that the prosody is particularly accentuated. The second sound that the child produces is longer at 380 ms, VCV, the consonant is not a true [oehoe], which seems like a syllable. How does the prosody in the mother's speech lead to the child producing this utterance, which could be said to represent the marginal babbling precursor of the canonical babbling in the hearing child?

The second sound the child emits is accepted by the mother not as a part of an exchange but as a correct response. The only importance for the mother is that the child has attempted to produce speech and it is this that produces feedback. The mother concentrates only on the sounds coming from the child's mouth.

Our studies show that the members of a deaf child's family focus most on his vocal behaviour. These basic sounds have to be maintained for their own sake as the basis for future spoken language. The inability to integrate the child's attempts at speech into a dialogue represents an additional factor which delays the process of developing conversational ability and, therefore, of mastering language. The non-speech-like characteristics of deaf childrens' vocalizations may affect interaction; it is not recognized and imitated by parents and integrated in social situations.

The onset of canonical babbling

The emergence of canonical babbling represents the culmination of a significant developmental process since it constitutes the beginning of the use of the well-formed syllables that occur in words.

The onset of the first syllables depends on the acoustic information the child receives. Canonical babbling with CV structures appears late in the profoundly deaf child; the higher the level of deafness, the later babbling appears. It is absent in the vocal productions of the children who have a hearing loss > 110 dB. The existence of babbling during the first 12 months of the deaf child's life can be questioned and the idea that audition plays no role in normal babbling is an error. However, in nearly all these cases, the hearing aids, and the cochlear implants, giving better acoustic information, help the child to improve the quantity and the quality of his or her babbling.

There is an interaction between auditory experience and production of canonical babbling. It can be concluded that *when a child produces no canonical babbling after 11 or 12 months, there may be a suspicion of deafness or the sign of possible important later dysfunctioning*. It is important to realize that the lack of babbling and structure dialogue may further delay the emergence of language and verbal dialogue.

The onset of the final lengthening in the babbling

The temporal structure of the French language, mainly characterized by a strong final lengthening (FL) is acquired very progressively, but not all deaf children acquire it. Some children, whose deafness was more profound than others' did acquire FL, some did not. It is not only due to physiological maturation. Language progress is rapid for children in whom FL is quickly established. In this population, FL is always correlated with the entrance in the syntactic stage. Among a population of 14 children aged between 11 and 32 months, seven who acquired FL acquired a good verbal language later.

From the cognitive point of view, the integration of the syllabic duration into the system can show the onset of a new stage in cognitive development marked by the appearance of a relational structure between the whole and its parts. But, it appears that its presence or absence does not depend on the hearing loss, but on other factors – perhaps the onset of turn taking. The final lengthening was in relation to the absence of overlapping in the interaction (according to a study based on data concerning 14 dyads). The onset of the final lengthening in the babbling indicates a strong predictor of entrance to the syntactic stage.

We observed:

- an interaction between the temporal structuration and and the turn-taking rules in dialogue; and
- an interaction between intonation and syntax.

Thus, it appears that prosodic cues are reliable predictors of later language development because they form a 'welcome structure', which has later to be filled with words. In consequence they can even help early diagnosis.

From sound to linguistic sign: analysis of two adult–deaf child dyads

Our analysis is based on two hearing adult–deaf child dyads. These particular two children were chosen because of their exceptional rate of oral language development, despite their considerable deafness.

From /mamama/ to /a mal/: First dyad: Hearing father–deaf child.

Hel is 33 months with a hearing loss > 110 dB (hearing age: 18 months). Below is an extract of her interaction with her father.

Child1: [aaa]
Father1: Il pleure le papillon ? Pourquoi?
(Is the butterfly crying ? Why is that?)
Child2: [amamama]
Father2: Comment?
(What's that?)
Child3: [amamamama]
Father3: Mamamama?
Child4: [ama] [ama]
Father4: Il a mal?
(He is hurt?)
Child5: [ama] [amama]
Father5: Il a mal à la main? Il a mal au doigt? Oh! Il pleure!
(He's hurt his hand? Has he hurt his finger? Ah ! He's crying!)
The father pretends to cry.
Child6 : [ama]
Father6: Ah sa main! Sa main! Attends.
(Oh it's his hand! His hand! Hang on.)

In this sequence, it's the child who initiates the sequence of exchanges. The adult is unable to interpret immediatly what the child is saying therefore he requests clarification: 'What's that?' The child, consequently, changes her vocal production slightly by adding an extra [ma] (Child3: [amamamama]). The syllables are produce with a flat contour and they have the same duration. The father, still unable to understand what the child has said, tries to reproduce the sounds the child has just made while requesting confirmation, the melody is rising. The fact that there is a repetition probably allows the child to adjust her vocalization to accord with her intention. She changes her utterance once again in Child4 [ama ama], placing the emphasis on the final [ma] which is accentuated and elongated. In the face of failure, infants may be pushed to produce new means. This leads the father to interpret the phrase as "il a mal?" (he is hurt?). The child is now able to continue the conversation by adding to what she has already said, and thus produced one or two utterances during her part of the exchange.

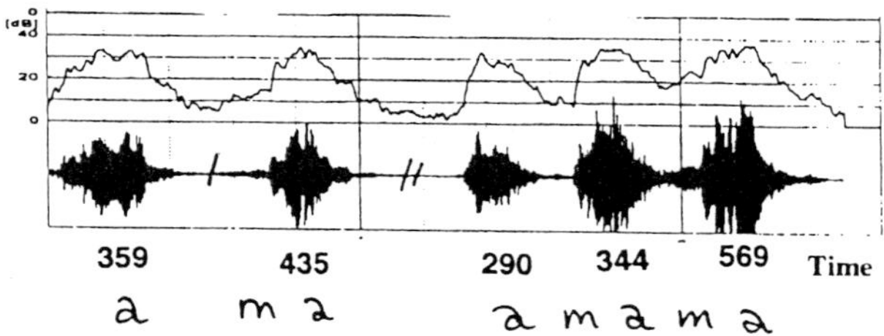

Figure 22.1. A deaf-child's production (duration in ms).

These utterances, structured on the temporal line with a final lengthening that forms perhaps two separate prosodic units, result in a complete phrase by the father 'il a mal à la main?' (he has hurt his hand?), with which the child seems to agree. The father then attemps to be more precise: 'Il a mal au doigt?' (Has he hurt his finger?) and continues speaking 'Oh! il pleure!' (Ah! He's crying!).

In this short dialogue, there are no overlaps. The father produces many utterances with a rising contour, which capture the child's attention. This example of 'negotiation of meaning' demonstrates the contribution that each partner makes in the construction and sharing of meaning; it takes two to develop the verbal concept. When the meaning is not transparent as here, it becomes necessary to negotiate the communication exchange; this is very important for a handicapped child. With very few sounds, the deaf child can nevertheless participate in a real dialogue with a help of an adult. The analysis demonstrates well how the adult allows the child to feel her own progress.

From /api/ to /ça pique/ and to /appuie/: the differentiation of lexical elements

Figures 22.2 and 22.3 concern Var (aged 25 months, with a hearing loss of 108 dB and a hearing age of 14 months) and her mother. In this example, we see how the mother's interjections, the fact that she adjusts the sounds and prosody of her voice and how she interprets, all lead the child progressively to be able to differentiate between lexical elements.

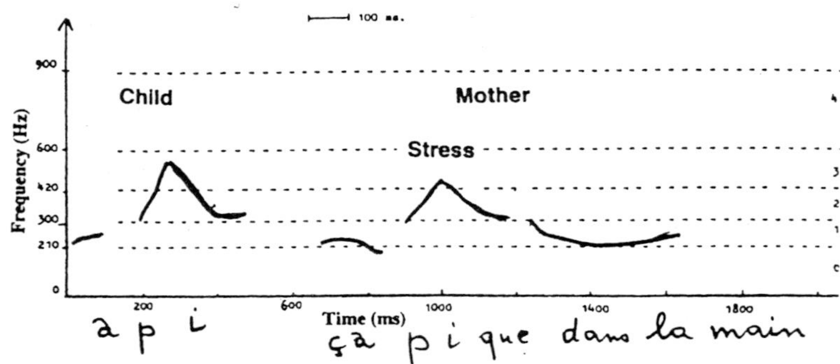

Figure 22.2. Interaction between a hearing mother and her deaf child.

The mother reproduces the high pitch of the child's voice (between 210 and 300 Hz for most of her speech and between 300 and 400 Hz for the part which is accentuated). The mother places the pitch of her voice in the same area of frequency as that of her daughter. The child produces a very high pitch sound (with a frequency over 500 Hz). This tonal break, resulting in very high pitched sound like [i] is common in the speech of deaf children. The mother reproduces and interprets this pathological trait. In her speech, the emphasis is placed on the word 'pique'.

The mother's reproduction is based equally on the rhythm; the syllabic lengths of mother and child are relatively similar.

The average duration of a syllable is about 250 ms for the child and 260 ms for the mother. The mother completely reformulates what the child has just said by giving it a phonetic and grammatically correct form (expansion).

During this interaction between the mother and her child (which includes 605 utterances from the mother and 370 utterances from the child), the two similar productions of the child [api] are interpreted in two different ways by the mother – according to each production and its context – either 'ça pique' or 'appuie'. Gradually, the child makes two productions, which can be differentiated by the length of the final [i], one being longer than the other. The [i] in the [api] understood as 'appuie' is lengthened while the [i] in the [api] which is understood as 'ça pique' is shorter. The child is able to differentiate two separate lexical elements because of the way that the mother has interpreted the child's utterances.

These analyses show the adults' efforts to structure and support their child's conversation. We have looked at one specific type of response by the adults; instead of responding globally to the child's vocalizations, they begin to reproduce or imitate sonoric and prosodic units, then they interpret vocalizations as if they were specific words. The observation of the last sequences show that mother (or father) and child engage in a joint activity based on the vocal material.

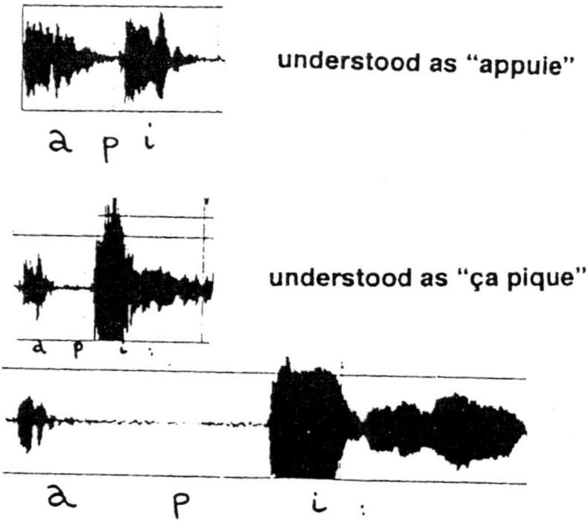

Figure 22.3. Three productions of Var, same sounds, different durations: two lexical elements.

These imitations of the segmental and suprasegmental features of the child's productions, by the mother, could be a means of:

- maintaining the interactions;
- taking into account the child's productions;
- focusing the joint attention of both mother and child on the same linguistic object;
- establishing a vocal relationship between the successive turn taking and finally faciliting the establishment of the first shared meanings. Without the caregiver's imitation of the infant's prosody, the infant might not have a reason to tune into the caregiver's message.

Conclusion

The intonational and rhythmic adaptation, which is such a common feature of these parents' utterances capture the child's attention and make it focus on what the parent is saying. Conversational turns are therefore linked by shared prosodic and sound features, which is one of the characteristics of verbal dialogue. In these exchanges, the two partners both focus their attention on the same prosodic and segmental content, and a sharing process is gradually built up.

The effects of prosody on the voice, language structures and onset of the conversational capacities of hearing-impaired children are little known. The analysis of the mother's and child's intonology based on the Interactive Developmental Intonology (IDI) theory suggest that these aspects play a vital role in the sharing of meaning in this population.

References

Boysson-Bardies B (de) (1982) Les bébés babillent-ils dans leur langue maternelle? La Recherche 129, 102–4.

Crystal D (1976) Developmental intonology. In Raffler-Engel W von, Lebrun V (eds) Baby Talk and Infant Speech. pp. 56–65.

Konopczynski G (1986) Du prélangage au langage: Acquisition de la structure prosodique. Thèse de Doctorat d'État, Strasbourg.

Holm M, Frischmuth S, Vinter S (1998) Hearing aids or cochlear implant? Criteria for evaluating the hearing abilities of deaf children aged 1–2 years: an introductory paper. Deafness and Education, 2(3), 9–17.

Le Floch M (1989) Étude exploratoire de la prosodie des interactions vocales entre la mère et son bébé âgé de 3 mois à 10 mois in Actes du 8ème Colloque Grofred, Lille, 131–9.

Löhle E (1991) Phoniatrische und pädaudiologische Ziele in der Erkennung Diagnostik und Therapie resthöriger Kinder. Int. Symposium Hohenems 1990, Hrsg: Stiftung zur Förderung körperbehinderter Hochbegabter, Liechtenstein.

Vinter S (1992) Mise en place des éléments prosodiques dans le langage émergent de l'enfant sourd: Rôle des stimulations acoustiques et des interactions sociales. Thèse de Doctorat, Besançon.

Part III

Aphasia and Neurological Conditions

Chapter 23
Single or Dual Semantics? Brain Lateralization and the Semantic Processing of Words

YVES JOANETTE, PIERRE GOULET, LOUISE GAGNON, BRIGITTE LEBLANC and ANNE SIMARD

Introduction

The availability of normal, efficient and relevant communicative abilities necessitates the integrity of both hemispheres. The conception of the respective roles of the two hemispheres for language is presently well accepted, as it was in the early nineteenth century. As we approach the dawn of the next millennium, however, we recall the dark age that once existed for one hemisphere with regard to its recognized participation in verbal communication. Indeed, for nearly 100 years, from Broca's (1865) popularization of the all-to-the-left theory to the clever clinical observations of neo-pioneers such as Joan Eisenson (1962), the so-called 'non-dominant' right-hemisphere has suffered from the loss of all consideration of its possible contribution to language, specifically, and to verbal communication, in general.

The sign of the end of this dark age for the right hemisphere came from many different and complementary sources. Thus, studies that examined right-hemispherectomized patient's language abilities (e.g. Smith, 1966), or the verbal capacities of split-brain patients with a disconnected right hemisphere (e.g. Zaidel, 1983) combined with the actual demonstration of the verbal communication deficits of right-hemisphere damaged right-handers (e.g. Critchley, 1962; Eisenson, 1962; Weinstein, 1964) all indicated that verbal communication was not to be considered an exclusive prerogative of the left hemisphere. Among all aspects of verbal communication that have been considered potential candidates for a right-hemisphere contribution, the semantic processing of words certainly stands out as one of the most widely studied. Not only has it been examined among all types of brain-damaged populations, but it has generated a wealth of studies with normal individuals – as long as undergraduate students in psychology are considered 'normal' if not representative of the general population – submitted to divided field studies.

It thus became obvious that the integrity of both hemispheres is required for the full and normal deployment of lexical-semantic abilities (Joanette et al., 1990; Joanette and Goulet, in press). However, there are still numerous unanswered questions pertaining to the respective and potentially complementary roles of the two hemispheres and the nature of their contribution to lexical-semantic processing. Among the most basic questions are the following:

- Given that the effects of left- and right-hemisphere lesions have long been recognized to result in word processing difficulties that are of distinct severeness, the first possibility would be that the distinction between both hemispheres is essentially *quantitative*.
- On the other hand, there are numerous indications in the literature according to which the exact nature of the effects of left- versus right-hemisphere lesions on word processing abilities can sometimes be distinct. For example, there are claims that a right-hemisphere lesion would interfere specifically with the processing of the metaphorical alternative meaning of words (Brownell et al. 1984). According to this scenario the difference between the two hemispheres would rather be *qualitative*.
- At the same time, and given that these two possibilities are certainly not mutually exclusive, it could well be that the difference between both hemispheres with regard to their contribution to lexical-semantic abilities would turn out to be both *quantitative* and *qualitative*.

The potential significance of a solely quantitative difference in the nature of the contribution of both hemispheres to lexical semantics is relatively straightforward. Such a quantitative difference could simply express a resource-linked phenomenon re-emphasizing the popular understanding that two hemispheres are better than one! However, if there are indeed qualitative differences between the two hemispheres, then we shall have to reconsider our conception of how we think the lexicon, or its semantic dimension, is represented in the brain. Indeed, qualitative differences could either express the fact that the functional properties of each hemisphere with regard to lexical-semantics are somewhat distinct and that the access they allow to a common semantic representation is influenced by these functional properties. In this case, a single semantic representation would be accessed distinctly by each hemisphere.

The second possibility refers to distinct semantic representations as suggested a long time ago by contributors such as Paivio. In this case, each hemisphere would have its own semantic representation. Though largely similar, and certainly mutually updated on-line, this representation would still be somewhat different in the right- and in the left-hemisphere. Such small variances could account for the claimed differences between the two hemispheres with regard to the privileged semantic relationships, for example. Indeed, according to some (Nocentini et al., in press), the left-hemisphere could be more sensitive to functional (e.g. airplane-cloud) than to categorical (e.g. airplane-boat) relationships. Though uneconomical, such an organization certainly offers higher security levels, for instance.

The question regarding the nature of the differences between the lexico-semantic abilities of the two hemispheres, thus, has tremendous impact on the way words are sustained by the brain. The evidence needed to disentangle this question can be viewed as contributing either to our understanding of the potential of each hemisphere or to its actual contribution. Indeed, all sources of evidence based on studies looking at the lexico-semantic abilities in the isolated right-hemisphere – this isolation may be physical (e.g. left hemispherectomy, split brain) or functional (e.g. divided field studies) – relate to the *potential* of the right-hemisphere to process words. It does not necessarily mean that this potential is actually required when both hemispheres are normally connected to each other, for example. Only the systematic analysis of the effects of an acquired right-hemisphere lesion, for example, can provide unquestionable evidence as to the *effective contribution* of the right hemisphere to the processing of words. Obviously, both sources should provide converging evidence but only the latter can be considered when one is interested in understanding the effective contribution of the right hemisphere to the processing of words in the normal brain.

This is the reason why the studies conducted by our group on the question of the possible quantitative and/or qualitative distinction between both hemispheres' contribution to the processing of words have essentially relied on the systematic analysis of lexico-semantic abilities in right-hemisphere-damaged patients. This approach certainly has its own limitations – such as the control brain-damaged populations (see Joanette and Goulet, 1990, for a full discussion) – but probably offers the greatest opportunities.

The goal here shall thus be to discuss the results obtained by our group in relation to three different lines of research having examined right-hemisphere-damaged patients and looked at different and complementary aspects of the question of right/left differences. The first line of research relates to the basic question with regard to left/right differences. This distinction is about the respective contribution of both hemispheres to the processing of properly lexical versus semantic dimensions of words through the use of a very simple, though powerful task. This task is known as *verbal fluency* in the traditional neuropsychometric literature while we refer to it as *oral naming*. The second line of research uses the priming paradigm and echoes the kind of question asked with regard to lexico-semantic impairments in aphasia, namely whether the impairment expresses a representation or an access to the representation deficiency. Finally the third line of research specifically questions the nature of the lexico-semantic impairments in right-hemisphere-damaged subjects, with one possible candidate for such a difference being the processing of the metaphorical meanings of words.

Oral naming and the effective contribution of the right hemisphere to lexico-semantic productions

Though initially introduced in neuropsychometry as some verbal equivalent of finger tapping and largely used in conjunction with the frontal semiology, verbal fluency, or oral naming, represents a very simple task used in order to look at lexico-semantic productive abilities. The task consists of asking the subject to name orally – in some cases, written – the largest number of words respecting a given criterion in a given amount of time, usually between one and two minutes. What this task measures depends largely on the nature of the criterion imposed. It can be either linked to the form of the word (e.g. words beginning with a given letter or starting with a given sound) or its meaning (e.g. categorical (animal) or situational (supermarket) semantic criteria). The comparison between formal and semantic criteria appeared to offer some direct testing of the basic assumption according to which the effective contribution of the right hemisphere to the processing of words relates more to its meaning than to its form. This assumption came from a large number of studies which demonstrated that the isolated right hemisphere has some capacities to process the meaning of words but very few to process its form (see Joanette et al., 1990, for a review).

We initially thought that the use of an oral naming task could shed some light on the question of the formal or semantic nature of the effective contribution of the right hemisphere to the processing of words. At the time we initiated our first study on this question, there was a large debate in the literature as to whether right-hemisphere-damaged right-handed (RHD) subjects would be impaired only on the semantic induced oral naming or on both formal and semantic inductions (see Joanette et al., 1990, for a review of the literature at that point in time). A first study revealed that RHD subjects, as compared with normal controls, were impaired only when the criterion was semantic, not when it was formal, namely orthographic in this study (Joanette and Goulet, 1986; see Figure 23.1). This result was highly satisfying and quite simple. It provided strong converging evidence as to the purely semantic nature of the effective contribution of the right hemisphere to the processing of words. The fact that there were no statistically supported differences between RHD and normal controls with regard to orthographic-induced oral naming confirmed the fact that the right hemisphere has very few capacities to process the form of the words and that consequently an acquired lesion of the right hemisphere does not interfere with the properly lexical processing.

It was, moreover, shown that the difference in performance between RHD and normal control subjects was not present throughout the task (Joanette et al., 1988). A time course analysis revealed that this difference only appeared in the last three-quarters of the two-minute long task (see Figure 23.2). Thus, there was no difference between RHD and

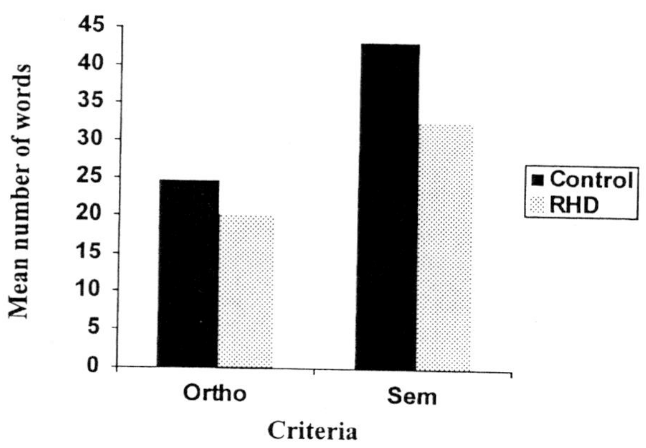

Figure 23.1. Mean number of words produced by control and right-hemisphere-damaged subjects (RHD) for orthographic (Ortho) and semantic (Sem) criteria.

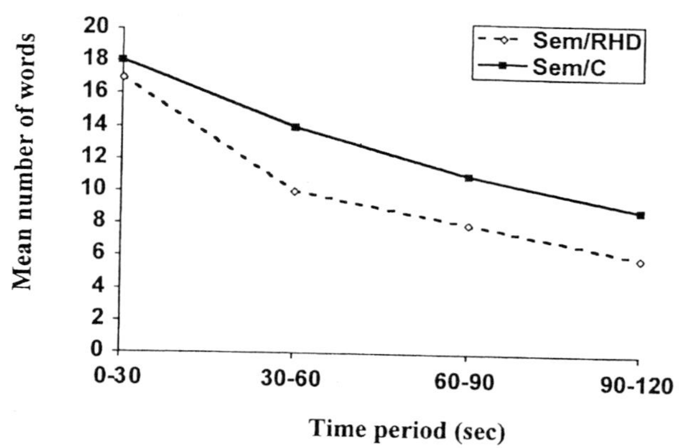

Figure 23.2. Mean number of words produced by control and right-hemisphere-damaged (RHD) subjects for semantic (sem) criterion for each of the 30-second time periods of the 2-minute long task.

normal controls during the first 30 s. However, after this initial period, performance became statistically different and remained different for the rest of the task. The interpretation of this phenomenon was more speculative. Its postulate related to the distinction made between the initial stage of such a task and the later stages. In fact, most if not all subjects confronted with a task asking them to provide animal names for two minutes will first resort to those names most easily activated by the superordinate 'ANIMAL'. In many cases, the most prototypical exemplars shall be produced, such as dog, cat, cow, horse and so on. It could be said that performance in this first phase necessitates an intact semantic representation and that spreading activation from the superordinate node to the most linked exemplars constitutes the bases of oral naming. In that sense, and despite the large time-scale, this first period could be conceived as more 'automatic' or less strategic/controlled. As time passes, however, the exemplars of the imposed superordinate have all been produced orally, yet the task is far from over. At this point, it seems that subjects have to use some kind of strategy in order to continue production: semantic clusters are identified – intentionally or not – and each of them is exploited. An analysis of RHD subjects' production did indeed indicate that such is the case (Joanette and Goulet, 1988). It was shown that RHD subjects exploit a smaller number of clusters and that each cluster is less exploited than in normal controls (Joanette and Goulet, 1988). Such an impairment probably expresses some lack in strategic/controlled processes on which the later stages of the task depend. In other words, the first stage relies more on automatic or less-controlled processes, while the later stages rely more on less automatic and more controlled, or effortful, processes. If such an interpretation is true, it can be hypothesized that the RHD subjects semantic oral naming impairment would more likely be attributed to some limitations in the strategic and controlled processes that allow access to the semantic representation rather than to a degradation of the semantic representation itself. Such a finding would then replicate for the right hemisphere what has been found in left-hemisphere-damaged aphasics in which the word processing impairment has been shown to be attributable to access limitations rather than to a degradation of the semantic representation itself. Not very original but rather reassuring, at this point.

The situation became more fuzzy, however, when we pursued trying to control for one small but very distinctive attribute of orthographic versus semantic criteria. Indeed, in most studies, the difference between orthographic and semantic criteria was considered unequivocal. This is not the case since most semantic criteria are much more productive than most orthographic criteria. For example, there are far more items to be readily produced for 'ANIMAL' than for the letter 'B'. It thus became uncomfortable to claim that RHD subjects were specifically impaired on semantic oral naming if productivity had not been controlled. Thus, in a

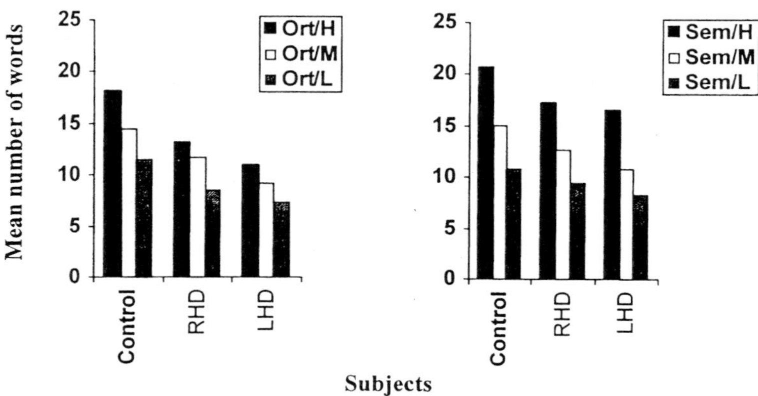

Figure 23.3. Mean number of words produced by control, right-hemisphere-damaged (RHD), and left-hemisphere-damaged (LHD) subjects for each of high- (H), medium- (M), and low- (L) level production for orthographic (Ort) and semantic (Sem) criteria.

subsequent study, we identified orthographic and semantic criteria which were truly comparable in terms of productivity (minimally, moderately and highly productive criteria). Results did not come out exactly as expected (Goulet et al., 1997): the specifically semantic impairment was replaced by one which was aspecific. Indeed, RHD subjects were impaired for both orthographic and semantic criteria, but only when they were highly productive (see Figure 23.3). This result suggested that all previous discussions based on the specifically semantic oral naming impairment had to be questioned and possibly replaced by an explanation likened to some difficulty scale. Indeed, minimally and moderately productive criteria, whether orthographic or semantic, do not seem to allow RHD control subjects to differentiate. However, highly productive criteria appear to offer control subjects the possibility of truly expressing their 'normalness' and performance whereas RHD subjects are limited. In any case, this second result suggests that the essence of the distinction between the two hemispheres with regard to the semantic processing of words is more quantitative than qualitative. But wait for the next episode.

The problems with the comparability of orthographic and semantic criteria inspired us to try to identify another way at looking at oral naming performance. We concluded that one possible way of looking at unbiased natural possible qualitative differences between the effective contribution of the two hemispheres would be to have subjects produce words without any imposed criterion. Such an unconstrained oral naming task would simply ask subjects to produce as many words – whatever they are – in a given period of time without these words forming sentences. The results we obtained comparing RHD, non- or mildly- aphasic left-hemisphere-damaged (LHD) subjects and normal controls were very interesting (Le Blanc and Joanette, 1996). Given that this unconstrained oral naming task is of the highest productivity possible, it confirmed the fact that RHD – as well as LHD – subjects had significantly impaired performance. Again, this result simply could lead to a reaffirmation of the aspecific contribution of the right hemisphere and the fact that there are no differences other than quantitative between the two hemispheres. However, an analysis of a number of characteristics of subjects' productions yielded interesting observations. Among these characteristics was the nature of the strategy used in order to produce items (formal or semantic) as well as the number and the extent of the clusters produced. All subjects had recourse to semantic strategies rather than formal ones. RHD and LHD subjects did not differ significantly in terms of number of clusters produced, nor in terms of mean words produced per cluster. However, the prototypicality index of the words produced by the RHD subjects was slightly – but significantly – smaller than that of both normal controls and LHD subjects, a result that is convergent to a finding by Grossman (1981). This result reactivates the possibility that, above and beyond the large quantitative difference between the effective contribution of the two hemispheres, there exists a smaller but still present qualitative difference such as indicated here.

Word semantic priming paradigms

Knowing that there can be a word semantic impairment following an acquired lesion of the right hemisphere, the next logical question pertains to the nature of such a deficit. Indeed, it is important and relevant to clinical management to know whether this deficit is attributed to limitations in access to the semantic representation, or if it expresses a degradation of the semantic representation itself. This question has already been raised with regard to the semantic impairments in vascular aphasia or in aphasia accompanying a dementia, for example. The seminal contribution of Milberg and Blumstein (1981) in this area has inspired many other groups. Milberg and Blumstein (1981) demonstrated that Broca's aphasics with lexico-semantic impairments had preserved priming abilities. Presuming that these priming abilities were only dependent on the spreading activation of the information in the semantic representation – namely realizing what is known as an *automatic* or *uncontrolled* priming condition – these authors concluded that the semantic representation of Broca's aphasics was intact. This meant that the lexico-semantic impairment was to be attributed to limitations in the cognitive processes allowing access to these representations.

However, the purely automatic nature of the experimental conditions such as the one used by Milberg and Blumstein (1981) was challenged (see Gagnon et al., 1994, for a review). Only a cost/benefit analysis, examining the respective effects of semantically-related, semantically-unrelated and neutral primes, makes it possible to disentangle the sources of the priming obtained. Indeed, an automatic unconscious condition is thought to be characterized by benefits associated to the presentation of semantically-related primes in the absence of any effect of unrelated primes by comparison to those of neutral primes. On the contrary, in the controlled or non-automatic condition, unrelated primes are the source of some costs by comparison to the neutral primes. Such a cost/benefit analysis applied to the results of a semantic priming task including the use of related, unrelated and neutral primes constitutes the only condition in which automatic (only benefits, no costs) or controlled (benefits and costs) priming effects are obtained. These two distinct priming effects are obtained by modifying some of the task's experimental conditions, such as the number of related primes, the stimulus onset asynchrony (SOA) and/or the instructions to the subjects that permit these two types of priming conditions. The use of automatic and controlled priming conditions in the context of a paired priming task (a task made up of a series of prime/target pairs) makes it possible to assess the representation/access debate. This is because automatic priming essentially depends on the intactness of the semantic representation, whereas controlled priming necessitates both intact semantic representations and intact voluntary and strategic access to this representation.

In a previous study, our group used the automatic/controlled pair-priming paradigm to study of lexico-semantic impairments in patients with right-hemisphere focal lesions (Gagnon et al., 1994). As in most other studies, subjects were instructed to operate a lexical decision choice on the target. The related primes to the word-targets were based on categorical co-hyponimic relationships. Automatic/controlled priming conditions were obtained though modifications of the percentage of related primes (25%/75%), length of the SOAs (short/long) and instructions to the subjects. Results were, to say the least, complex and, to a certain point, inconclusive. The main problems arose in the verification of the truly automatic or controlled nature of both priming conditions using a cost-benefit analysis. Indeed, this study has shown that it is very difficult to obtain an automatic semantic priming condition in which there are only benefits, without any costs. In the absence of such a confirmation, any interpretation based on the effective priming abilities of the patients in the two conditions is pure speculation. The reasons why automatic and controlled priming conditions appear to be difficult to achieve in brain-damaged subjects may be linked to the fact that nearly all the priming literature is based on studies conducted with young, non-brain-damaged subjects. Thus, the time-frames used in order to generate automatic and controlled conditions (e.g. SOAs) might be very different between a young normal population and older brain-damaged subjects. Other limitations come from the problems in trying to identify what would be a truly 'neutral' prime. Indeed, in most studies, the word 'BLANK' or a series of 'XXXXX' is used as a neutral prime. However, the reiteration of these peculiar stimuli could result in a special processing status which is probably far from being 'neutral'. Since the neutral primes are the point of reference in order to calculate costs and benefits, the problem is not trivial.

Some years ago, a new priming paradigm was introduced, which allowed researchers to truly ascertain the existence of an automatic priming condition. This new paradigm is called list-priming paradigm (LPP) (Prather, 1994). The essence of the LPP is to present the subject with a list of consecutively presented words forming a list. Without the subject being aware, some consecutive words form pairs, either related, or unrelated, while others are simply fillers. Using a basic lexical decision task, the difference between related and unrelated consecutive items enables the calculation of a priming effect. The automatic nature of this priming effect is ascertained by the fact that the effect increases with inter-stimulus interval to a certain point, after which any further increase in ISI results in a decrease in the priming effect. Such a pattern – increase, peak and decrease in priming effects as ISI are increased – is thought to express a truly automatic priming condition since controlled priming usually has a tendency to increase or be maintained with any increase in time allowing for strategic processing to fully express itself. The most interesting aspect of this paradigm is its adjustability feature to brain-damaged populations. Indeed, whether or not brain-damaged subjects are sensitive to the same time determinants of a given priming effect, the demonstration of an increase-peak-decrease pattern, whatever the exact ISI at which the peak expresses itself, shall constitute a demonstration of the automatic nature of the priming effect. Prather et al. (1992) used a LPP paradigm with a Broca's aphasic. The result was quite clear: the subject did show preserved automatic priming, but the peak was at 1,100 ms instead of 500 ms in normal-aged subjects.

Recently, our group obtained similar results with a right-hemisphere-damaged subject (Simard and Joanette, 1997). Using a similar LPP to that used by Prather et al. (1992), we showed that a RHD subject with mild lexico-semantic impairments had a preserved increase-peak-decrease pattern of priming effect following a steady increase in ISI (see Figure 23.4). This result suggests that semantic representation in RHD subjects with mild lexico-semantic impairments is largely unaffected. However, the LPP priming peak was obtained at an ISI of 800 ms, a notably longer ISI than what has been reported by Prather (1994) in normal-aged subjects (ISI of about 500 msec). The peak-ISI value obtained in the RHD subject submitted to the LPP paradigm is in fact intermediate between that found in normal-aged subjects on the one hand, and, on the other hand, that reported in the Broca's aphasic by Prather et al. (1992). This result is congruent with many results obtained in RHD subjects in which lexico-semantic performances are frequently intermediate between normal-aged and aphasic subjects. In any case, the results obtained by Simard and Joanette (1997) suggest that the semantic representation of RHD subjects is more or less intact, despite the presence of lexico-semantic impairments. However, the significance of the increased processing time needed to obtain an optimal priming effect still needs to be considered.

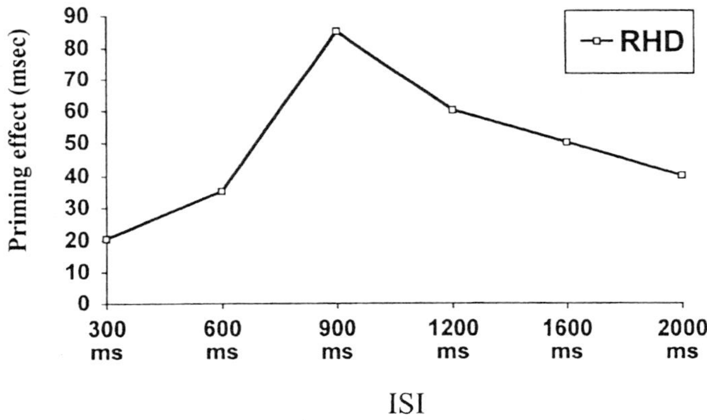

Figure 23.4. Magnitude of the priming effect according to inter-stimulus interval (ISI) for a right-hemisphere-damaged (RHD) subject.

The alternative metaphorical meaning of words

Many previous studies have suggested that a particularly specific effect of a right-hemisphere lesion would be its impact on the ability to adequately process the alternative metaphorical meaning of words (e.g. Brownell et al., 1984, 1990). In line with the suspected difficulties of RHD subjects to process various figurative linguistic material (for a review, see Joanette et al., 1990), it was proposed in the literature that the processing of the alternative metaphorical meaning of words might well reveal itself to become a specific effect of a right-hemisphere lesion on lexico-semantic abilities. Such a specific effect would then testify to the right hemisphere's specific contribution to the processing of words. However, due to the tasks used, the evidence available in the literature is not convincing that RHD subjects really exhibit a specific problem in the processing of the alternative metaphorical meaning of words rather than a mere inclination towards alternative non-metaphorical meanings.

Gagnon, Goulet and Joanette (1993) used two complementary tasks in order to ascertain that RHD subjects did exhibit a specific impairment in the processing of the alternative meaning of words. Subjects were thus submitted to both a triad- and a dyad task. The triad task was used in order to replicate the observation of Brownell et al. (1990) according to which RHD subjects would have a tendency to choose a word associated with its alternative non-metaphorical meaning rather than to its alternative metaphorical meaning. However, since the triad task simply indicates a preference of one relationship to the other, a second task – the dyad task – was also used. All alternative metaphorical and non-metaphorical relationships used in the triad task were thus re-introduced in the dyad task in order to see if RHD subjects were still capable of being sensitive to these relationships.

The main result of this study revealed the existence of a genuine deficit in RHD patients' ability to process the alternative metaphoric relationships of words, independently of the experimental task used (triad-word or dyad-word tasks). However, this deficit is also present among left-hemisphere-damaged (LHD) mild-to-moderate aphasic subjects and therefore cannot be considered specific to patients with a unilateral right-hemisphere damage. The absence of a double dissociation between LHD and RHD subjects regarding their capacity to apprehend metaphoric meaning at a lexical level contrasts with the results reported by Brownell et al. (1984, 1990). Therefore, this finding did not support the hypothesis of a specific contribution of the right hemisphere to the processing of metaphoric meaning at the word level. The meaning of the result obtained is, again, not obvious. However, it is noteworthy that normal control subjects did show a tendency for longer response time when they had to detect the presence of alternative metaphoric meanings as compared with non-metaphoric alternative meanings in the pilot studies carried out in preparation of the experiment. Consequently, lowered performance of both RHD and LHD subjects in the processing of an alternative metaphoric meaning of words could reflect a vulnerability to the most demanding conditions of cognitive processing, such as the processing of the metaphoric meaning of words. If this is indeed the case, it could then be said that the intactness of the right or the left hemisphere could be mandatory for the complete and successful processing of the metaphoric meaning of single words. The metaphorical meaning of words being the most resource demanding kind of processing, it would require the intactness of both hemispheres in order to be realized. In this particular case, the right hemisphere contribution would represent a quantitative rather than qualitative addition to the role played by the left hemisphere.

Right and left hemispheres: partners for life for an efficient and optimal processing of words

This chapter was intended to summarize a number of studies conducted by our group, which represent attempts at unveiling the effective contribution of the right hemisphere to the processing of words. Though the review was only centred on these contributions, and not on the numerous and relevant contributions made by colleagues around the world, the conclusion that can be made is probably representative of any attempt at summarizing the field at this point in time. Obviously, the full and efficient processing of words requires an intact brain, both left and right hemispheres considered. This apparently simplistic claim emphasizes the complementary nature of the contribution of each hemisphere to the processing of words. Indeed, the contribution of each hemisphere is probably not independent of the functional relationships it entertains with the other hemisphere. Thus, the capacities of the brain for the processing of words is certainly not the mere summation of the isolated capacities of the left and the right hemispheres put together. However, how the two hemispheres concur in the actualization of lexico-semantic abilities remains a mystery.

Our impression, looking at the evidence obtained over the past decade, is that the relationship entertained by the two hemispheres is much more than uni-dimensional. The first dimension uniting the two hemisphere is certainly quantitative. As seen in many of the experiments alluded to here, the integrity of the two hemispheres is needed for the full deployment of lexico-semantic abilities. The most effortful processing of words appears to require a largely spread neuro-biological substrate which appears to encompass both hemispheres. This purely quantitative contribution of the right hemisphere is not different from the one already well associated with the left hemisphere but still appears to be crucial. If the right hemisphere suffers a lesion, then the individual is left with word processing limitations determined by the task difficulties.

Whatever relative importance this first quantitative dimension has, there seems to be other dimensions linking the two hemispheres in their partnership. This second dimension of complementary between the two hemispheres could well be more qualitative. One example of such a qualitatively different complementary relationship is hinted at here by the specific effect of a right hemisphere lesion on the natural tendency to explore/access less prototypical meanings of words in an unconstrained oral naming task. Such a tendency is congruent, as noted before, with the general tendency of right-hemisphere-damaged patients to feel at ease with less predictable/plausible explanations, for example. Is the contribution of the right hemisphere to the processing of words qualitatively different – implying that the right hemisphere would allow for a specific kind of access or activation of the semantic representations – or would the overall lexico-semantic abilities of the individual be influenced by a general attitude towards unpredictability following a right-hemisphere lesion? An answer to this question is of course unavailable at this time, since the question is probably the expression of our lack of understanding of the real basic components of cognition. In any case, at this point in time, and until further negative evidence, it can be said that the complementary contributions of the two hemispheres appear to be both quantitative and qualitative. Only further studies shall allow us to disentangle these two distinct relationships between both halves of the brain whose total integrity seems to be crucial for the full deployment of its resources.

Aknowledgements

The studies here reported were made possible through grants to the first author (YJ) from the Canadian Medical Research Council as well as from the Québec FCAR with regard to financial support for students. The authors would like to acknowledge the collaboration of many clinicians including those at the following institutions: Institut de Réadaptation de Montréal, Hôpital Villa Medica, Hôpital Marie-Clarac, Centre François-Charron and many others. Many thanks to Elizabeth Ohashi for her help with the text and the figures. Many thanks also to Colette Cerny for her continuing contribution.

References

Broca P (1865) Sur faculté du langage articulé. Bulletin de la Société d'Anthropologie, 6, 337–93.

Brownell HH, Potter HH, Michelow D (1984) Sensitivity to lexical denotation and connotation in brain-damaged patients: a double dissociation? Brain and Language, 22, 253–65.

Brownell HH, Simpson TL, Bihrle AM, Potter HH, Gardner H (1990) Appreciation of Metaphoric Alternative Word Meanings by Left and Right Brain-Damaged Patients. Neuropsychologia, 28(4), 375–83.

Critchley M (1962) Speech and speech-loss in relation to duality of the brain. In Mountcastle VB (ed.) Interhemispheric Relations and Cerebral Dominance. Baltimore: John Hopkins Press, pp. 208–13.

Eisenson J (1962) Language and intellectuals modifications associated with right cerebral damage. Language and Speech, 5, 49–53.

Gagnon L, Goulet P, Joanette Y (1993) Processing of metaphoric word meanings by right-brain-damaged right-handers. Abstracts of the 31st Academy of Aphasia Annual Meeting, Tucson (USA), 24–26 October,.

Gagnon J, Goulet P, Joanette Y (1994) Activation of the lexical-semantic system in right-brain-damaged right-handers. Linguistische Berichte, 6, 33–48.

Goulet P, Joanette Y, Sabourin L, Giroux F (1997) Word fluency after a right-hemisphere lesion. Neuropsychologia, 35(12), 1565–70.

Grossman M (1981) A bird is a bird: Making reference within and without superordinate categories. Brain and Language, 12, 313–31.

Joanette Y, Goulet P (1986) Criterion-specific reduction of verbal fluency in right-brain-damaged right-handers. Neuropsychologia, 24, 875–9.

Joanette Y, Goulet P (1988) Word-naming in right-brain-damaged subjects. In Chiarello C (ed.) Right Hemisphere Contributions to Lexical Semantics. New York: Springer Verlag, pp. 1–18.

Joanette Y, Goulet P (1990) Narrative discourse in right-brain-damaged right-handers. In Joanette Y, Brownell HH (eds) Discourse Ability and Brain Damage: Theoretical and Empirical Perspectives. New York: Springer-Verlag, 131–53.

Joanette Y, Goulet P (1999) Right hemisphere and the semantic processing of words: Is the contribution specific or not? In Visch-Brink EG, Bastiaanse R (eds) Linguistic Levels in Aphasiology. San Diego: Singular, in press.

Joanette Y, Goulet P, Le Dorze G (1988) Impaired word naming in right brain-damaged right-handers. Error types and time-course analyses. Brain and Language, 34(1), 54–64.

Joanette Y, Goulet P, Hannequin D, with the collaboration of J Boeglin (1990) Right Hemisphere and Verbal Communication. New York: Springer-Verlag.

Le Blanc B, Joanette Y (1996) Unconstrained oral naming in left- and right-hemisphere-damaged patients: an analysis of naturalistic semantic strategies. Brain and Language, 55(1), 42–5.

Milberg W, Blumstein SE (1981) Lexical decision and aphasia: evidence for semantic processing. Brain and Language, 14, 371–85.

Nocentini U, Goulet P, Drolet M, Joanette Y (1999) Age-related evolution of the contribution of the right hemisphere to language: absence of evidence (submitted).

Prather PA (1994) The time course of lexical activation in fluent and nonfluent aphasia. Linguistics and Cognitive Neuroscience, 6, 128–44.

Prather PA, Zurif E, Stern C, Rosen TJ (1992) Slowed lexical access in nonfluent aphasia: A case study. Brain and Language, 43, 336–48.

Simard A, Joanette Y (1997) Activation automatique du savoir lexico-sémantique chez un cérébrolésé droit. Paper presented at the V Congreso Latinoamericano de Neuropsicologia/SLAN (Sociedad Latinoamericana de Neuropsicologia), Guadalajara (Mexico), 4–7 October.

Smith A (1966) Speech and other functions after left hemispherectomy. Journal of Neurology, Neurosurgery and Psychiatry, 29, 467–71.

Weinstein EA (1964) Affections of speech with lesions of the nondominant hemisphere. Research Publications of the Association for Research in Nervous and Mental Disease, 42, 220–8.

Zaidel E (1983) Disconnection syndrom as a model for laterality effects in the normal brain. In Hellige JB (ed.) Cerebral Hemisphere Asymmetry. Method, Theory and Application. Berlin: Praeger, pp. 95–151.

Chapter 24 Case Assignment in Agrammatism: Analysis of the Spontaneous Speech of Dutch and German Agrammatic Aphasics

ESTHER RUIGENDIJK, ROELIEN BASTIAANSE and RON VAN ZONNEVELD

Introduction

In Chomsky's case theory (Chomsky, 1986) a strong relationship is assumed between case assignment and verb production. It is known, from several studies, that verb production is poor in agrammatic speech. The number of lexical verbs may be reduced, and those verbs that are produced are often not inflected (Saffran et al., 1989; Bastiaanse et al., 1995). Based on this case theory, it is to be expected that the problems with verb production are reflected in problems with case assignment, surfacing as problems with determiners and pronouns, the word classes that may bear visible case. The present study evaluates the production of nouns, determiners and pronouns in the spontaneous speech of agrammatic aphasics, within the framework of Chomsky's case theory.

Theoretical background

According to case theory, all languages have an abstract case system, but languages differ in the morphological realisation of this system. Some languages realize case overtly, others only have covertly realized case. German, for example, has a rich overtly realized system, with overt case for pronouns and determiners, which are also specified for gender. In Dutch and English we only find overtly realized case in some forms of the pronoun.

Central in Chomsky's case theory is the so-called *case filter*:

Every phonetically realized NP must receive (abstract) case

When case is not realized overtly, in languages such as English or Dutch, it is still present, covertly, which means on an abstract level. By this case filter, sentences containing noun phrases without case are ruled out!

Case can be assigned in two ways: lexically, which is called *inherent* case, and syntactically, which is called *structural* case. Structural case assignment is configurational property, which solely depends on government. Inherent case is taken to be associated with government and θ-marking. Inherent case assigners (which can be verbs, adjectives, prepositions and nouns) can only assign case to NPs which they also θ-mark (Haegeman, 1991).

Structural or syntactic case is assigned under government, within functional Spec-head configurations.

The subject receives its case from I in [Spec,IP], the object receives its case from V [Spec,VP], as can be seen in Figure 24.1b. We assume the subject to be generated VP-internally. As case assignment takes place under Spec-head-agreement, the subject is moved to [Spec, IP], where it satisfies the agreement requirement with I (see Figure 24.1a). In Dutch and German root sentences, the finite verb is moved to I, which is the landing site of *verb second* (Figure 24.1a). The subject is assigned case in [Spec,IP].

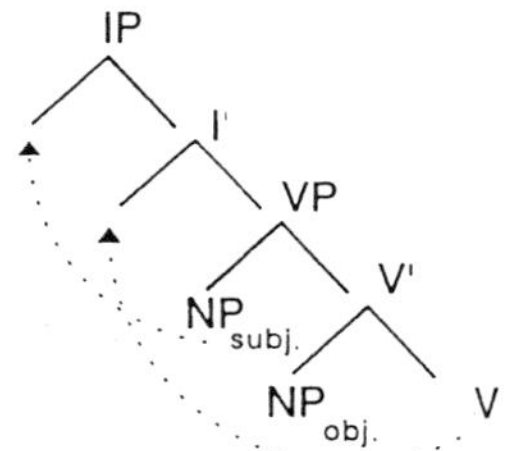

Figure 24.1a. Generation of a Dutch matrix clause: the subject NP is base-generated in VP and moved to [Spec, IP], the finite verb is moved to I, a movement rule called verb second.

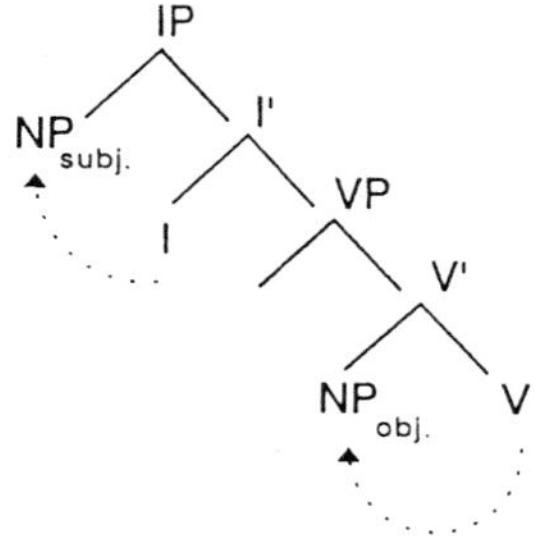

Figure 24.1b. Case assignment: nominative case is assigned to the subject by the finite verb, accusative case is assigned to the object by the verb.

This means that a nominative subject is dependent on the finite verb. Therefore, there can be no visible nominative subject in absence of a finite verb. Van Zonneveld (1994), however, observed that it is possible to construct sentences containing a subject and lacking a finite verb. He analysed sentences from Dutch cartoons, in which non-natives speak 'Black Dutch', which is characterized by omission of the finite verb.

Black Dutch:

(1) Dit geen gekke tekens, maar Afrikaanse letters zijn, en Sjimmie negertje, dus hij kunnen lezen!
These no crazy signs, but African letters be, and Sjimmie little Negro, so he can (non-finite) read!
These aren't crazy signs, but African letters, and Sjimmie is a little Negro, so he can read them!

This, of course, is deliberately broken language, but the point is that the mutilation is effectively carried out by leaving out the tense and agreement features of the verb. This phenomenon can also be found in Dutch exclamatives:

(2) Wat! Ik betalen en jij met de eer gaan strijken?! Dat nooit!
What! I pay and you the honour gain? Never!

The subjects are pronouns with nominative case, although there is no visible case assigner. This situation raises a conflict for the case theory of Government and Binding theory (GB), which we suggest solving by extending the theory with a default option:

(3) If the subject does not participate in a Spec-head configuration within I, it gets nominative case by default.
Elsewhere: the subject gets nominative case in [Spec,IP].

Case and agrammatism

There is hardly any literature on case assignment in relation to agrammatic speech. Given the fact that agrammatic patients show severe difficulties with verb second (Bastiaanse and van Zonneveld, 1998), we expect that these same patients perform poorly in terms of case assignment to the subject, as in absence of verb second the head I remains invisible. This leads to the following central question: Do we find NPs without a visible case assigner in the spontaneous speech of agrammatic aphasic patients? And if so, what is the case of these NPs without a case assigning head?

In dealing with this question, we use the *default* theory mentioned before, which states that subject NPs without an overt case assigner receive default case, which is nominative, for Dutch and German.

The question, then, is: what happens to an object without a verb? It should be noted that Van Zonneveld's default theory only covers for the assignment of *nominative* case to the subject NPs without a case assigner. According to Chomsky's and Van Zonneveld's case theories object nouns and pronouns will not occur if there is no verb, because then they are without case. An alternative strategy, at least for noun production, is to omit the case marker, i.e. to produce the bare noun stem without a determiner.

Therefore, if there is no case assigner, we expect to find default nominative NPs and/or the omission of visible case markers, i.e. determiners and suffixes that mark case, leading to the following hypotheses.

Hypothesis a

Nouns without a visible case assigner bear no visible case (that is, the determiner will be omitted and only the noun stem will be produced)

Hypothesis b

If there is no case assigner, subject pronouns and nouns with a determiner may receive nominative case by default; object nouns with a determiner (in German) and pronouns (in German and Dutch) will not occur.

Method

To test these hypotheses, the telegraphic speech of six Dutch and six German agrammatic Broca's aphasics was analysed. All patients participating in the present study spoke in so-called 'telegraphic speech'. The samples of the Dutch patients are from our database. The German samples are from different sources: Menn and Obler (1990), Schlenk, Schlenk and Springer (1995). Three of the samples were provided by a speech therapist.

From each of the patients a sample of the spontaneous speech was available. These samples were first analysed with regard to pronoun production. For each pronoun the case was examined and it was established whether or not a case assigner was present and whether case was assigned correctly. The same procedure was followed for nouns: which were counted and for which was established whether a determiner and a case assigner were present.

Results

In Table 24.1 the group results of the pronoun analysis are given. This table shows that the agrammatic patients produce pronouns with and without visible case assigner, showing that Chomsky's case theory is too strong. Our hypothesis with regard to pronouns was: any subject pronoun without case assigner is assigned nominative case by default.

This hypothesis is supported by the present data: only one pronoun without a case assigner is not a nominative: '*Wie ihn eine Keks*', which literally means 'how him a cookie'. The pronouns with case assigner are mostly in the subject position, which explains their nominative case. For all 18 pronouns in accusative and dative case, except the one mentioned, there is a case assigning verb present, as predicted by our hypothesis. Summarized: all pronouns without a case assigner are nominative, with one exception.

Table 24.1. Pronoun use (Dutch and German agrammatic aphasics)

	+ case assigner	- case assigner (NOM)	Total
Total	137	36	173
Mean	11.4	3	14.4
SD	4.3	1.1	4.5

Table 24.2. Nouns with and without determiner

Nouns with determiner

Dutch	+ case assigner	– case assigner	Total	German	+ case assigner	– case assigner	Total
Total	32	46	78		212	50	270
Mean	5.3	7.7	13		35.3	8.3	45
SD	2.4	1.8			67.0	4.6	

Nouns without determiner

Dutch	+ case assigner	– case assigner	Total	German	+ case assigner	– case assigner	Total
Total	44	184	236		41	43	86
Mean	7.3	30.7	39.3		6.8	7.2	14.3
SD	3.1	9.8			4.3	5.9	

Table 24.2 presents the group results of the Dutch and German agrammatics for the noun analysis. Our hypothesis predicts that (1) a noun without a visible case assigner bears no visible case, i.e. the determiner will be omitted, and the noun will be stripped from case-inflectional endings, and that (2) any noun without a visible case assigner is assigned nominative case by default. As shown in Table 24.2, these two hypotheses adequately predict the data. The first part of the hypothesis is supported by the Dutch agrammatic data: there is a strong significant tendency to leave out the determiner where no case assigner is produced. Because Dutch has no visible case, it is impossible to tell

whether in the remaining cases hypothesis (2) is valid. German patients leave out determiners as often as they produce them, if there is no case assigner. However, if they produce a determiner, it is in the nominative case, again with just one exception (*und da seinen Namen* = and there his (acc) name). These data confirm the second hypothesis. The German data show that accusative case is only assigned in the presence of a case assigner.

The errors concerning case are also considered, though only for the German data. From 270 produced nouns with a determiner, only 19 (7%) were incorrect. Only three of these errors were obvious case errors, while the other 16 may have been case or gender errors.

Discussion

All patients produced nouns and/or pronouns without a case assigner, which cannot be explained by Chomsky's case theory. If, however, this case theory is extended by Van Zonneveld's default theory, the agrammatic data are fully covered. The nouns (with overt case) and the pronouns produced without a case assigner, bear nominative case, with two exceptions, in both languages.

Regarding the use of determiners we found somewhat different results for Dutch and German. Dutch patients show a strong tendency to omit the determiner when there is no case assigner present. This was not found for the German patients, who equally produce and omit the determiner when there is no case assigner. This may be explained by the fact that in German the determiners are specified for case, gender and number (this is not the case in Dutch), which makes the 'connection' between the determiner and the noun stronger. Perhaps this stronger connection makes omission of the determiner 'less grammatical' than substitution of the determiner.

Using Chomskyan theory as a framework implies that we see the problem with grammatical morphemes concerning case as a structural problem, in which the relation between case morphemes and the verb (inflection) is crucial. Our data indicate that this relationship plays an important role: if a patient produces an object and marks it as an object, he will use a verb. This is exactly what we found: no accusative pronoun or determiner without a verb was found. On the basis of the spontaneous speech data it was impossible to tell if object NPs not marked for case are produced without a verb, because when there was no verb present it remained unclear whether an NP was an object or not. Of course, this needs further research.

If an agrammatic patient marks an NP for case, he will do so correctly. This means that agrammatics are sensitive to the relation between case assigner and case marker. A similar phenomenon has been observed for finite verbs (Bastiaanse and Van Zonneveld, 1998). In Dutch matrix clauses, the finite verb is in the second position and the non-finite verb is in clause final position. Dutch agrammatics are poor in the production of inflected verbs, but if they produce an finite verb, it is always in verb second position, whereas the non-finite verbs are always, correctly, in clause final position. This shows that agrammatics are sensitive to the relation between finiteness and structural position.

The results of this study have some serious implications for the clinical practice. When sentence production is trained, therapists should be aware of the strong relationship between NPs and the verb (inflection), even if case is only visible in pronouns (as in Dutch, English and French). If this relation is not emphasized, it is only the default strategy that is trained, and as the present data show: agrammatic aphasics are perfectly able to apply this default strategy; they assign nominative case to NPs that lack a case assigner.

Acknowledgements

We are grateful to Dirk den Ouden for his comments on an earlier version of this draft.

References

Bastiaanse R, Jonkers R, Moltmaker-Osinga U (1995) Aspects of lexical verbs in the spontaneous speech of agrammatic and anomic patients. In Jonkers R, Kaan E, Wiegel A (eds) Language and Cognition 5. Groningen: University of Groningen.

Bastiaanse R, Zonneveld R van (1998) On the relation between verb inflection and verb production in Dutch agrammatic aphasics. Brain and Language, 64, 165–81.

Chomsky N (1986) Knowledge of Language, its Nature, Origin and Use. New York: Praeger.

Haegeman L (1991) Introduction to Government and Binding Theory. Oxford: Blackwell.

Menn L, Obler LK (eds) (1990) Agrammatic Aphasia: A Cross-Language Narrative Source Book. Amsterdam: Benjamins.

Saffran EM, Berndt RS, Schwartz MF (1989) The quantitative analysis of agrammatic production: Procedure and data. Brain and Language, 37, 440 –79.

Schlenk C, Schlenk KL, Springer L (1995) Die Behandlung des Schweren Agrammatismus: Reduzierte Syntax Therapie. Stuttgart: Georg Thieme Verlag.

Zonneveld R van (1994) Kleine Syntaxis van het Nederlands. Dordrecht: ICG Publications.

Chapter 25 Production and Perception of Speech Prosody in Left- and Right-Brain-Damaged Adults

DANY HUOT, JACK RYALLS and GUYLAINE LE DORZE

Introduction

In an effort to understand the representation of speech and language in the human brain, there have been a considerable number of studies investigating speech prosody after neurological insult. While some studies have considered the production of speech prosody, others have investigated the perception of speech prosody. However, very few studies have investigated both perception and production.

A considerable number of studies have addressed speech prosody in patients with right-hemisphere damage, and a similar number of studies have considered prosody in left-hemisphere-damaged adults (overviews of this work can be found in Ryalls and Behrens (1988) and Van Lancker and Sidtis (1992)). Very few studies have compared both left- and right-brain damaged subjects on the same tasks.

Therefore the main thrusts of this study were to compare *both* production and perception of speech prosody and to compare the effects of left- *and* right-brain damage for the same prosodic tasks. We have previously gathered a rather substantial body of data from the speech prosody battery for 40 normal adults (Ryalls et al., 1995), and for patients with dysarthria (Le Dorze et al., 1994, 1998).

Method

A group of 16 patients with unilateral brain damage were recruited for the purpose of this study: eight patients with left-hemisphere lesions and eight with right-hemisphere lesions. All subjects were native speakers of French residing in Quebec. Left-hemisphere-damaged subjects were aphasics, mostly of the Broca type. In Table 25.1 the patient's characteristics such as age, lesion type and lesion site are presented.

Table 25.1. Subjects

	Gender	Age	Lesion type	Lesion site
Left hemisphere				
1	M	50	hypodensity	anterior
2	M	53	haemorrhage	anterior
3	M	55	ischemic	anterior
4	F	87	hypodensity	anterior
5	F	65	hypodensity	anterior
6	F	28	hypodensity	anterior
7	F	47	ischemic	anterior
8	F	70	small lesion	posterior
Right hemisphere				
1	M	64	hypodensity	anterior
2	M	82	haemorrhage	anterior
3	M	78	ischemic	anterior
4	M	18	infarct	posterior
5	M	70	hypodensity	posterior
6	M	68	hypodensity	posterior
7	F	50	lesion	posterior
8	F	80	lesion	posterior

We were interested in so-called rhetorical questions because they offer a tight control over word content. In this type of sentence, it is only the rising intonation contour that distinguishes the interrogative from the declarative sentence ; the word content is the same. (Example: 'It's nice out today.' versus 'It's nice out today?') Such sentences allow a unique opportunity to investigate speech prosody isolated from other aspects of speech production such as phonology, morphology and syntax.

First of all, the production of speech prosody was evaluated. In the production task, patients were presented with written versions of simple SVO (subject, verb, object) sentences varying from five to seven syllables in length, along with a card depicting either a period or a question mark. The task of the patient was to produce the particular sentence with the appropriate speech prosody. The patients' productions were recorded directly onto disk using IBM's SpeechViewer system. Measures were then derived of (1) the speech rate in syllables per second, (2) overall average fundamental frequency and (3) the fundamental frequency of the last word of the sentence. Finally, the difference in fundamental frequency for the last word of the statement and question versions of each sentence was calculated. This value gave us an objective measure of the subject's ability to differentiate these two types of sentences by means of speech prosody. Our research with normal speakers had shown us that this group average difference was 87 Hz for older normal female speakers and 65 for normal aged male speakers. Many dysarthric speakers only produce about half of the normal difference or less (Le Dorze et al., 1994).

Results

Production

Table 25.2 presents prosody production results in syllables per second for rate and in hertz for intonation difference. In almost all cases, the interrogative sentence was produced at a slightly faster rate than the declarative version of the same sentence. We had observed a similar difference among normal speakers (Ryalls et al., 1995). In fact, this difference was statistically significant. We consider this difference in speech rate by type of sentence to represent one of the ways by which neurologically-impaired subjects preserve normal speech prosody.

Table 25.2. Prosody results

	Gender	Rate D (syll/s)	Rate I (syll/s)	Intonation (Hz)	
Left hemisphere					
1	M	2.7	2.9	4	–
2	M	2.7	2.7	1	–
3	M	3.7	3.8	–2	–
4	F	2.8	2.9	10	–
5	F	4.1	4.3	79	+
6	F	2.5	2.5	63	+
7	F	4	4.6	4	–
8	F	3.1	3.3	88	+
Right hemisphere					
1	M	3.2	3.5	40	–
2	M	2.8	3	–2	–
3	M	3.6	3.5	20	–
4	M	4.6	5.4	52	+
5	M	3.2	3.4	0	–
6	M	4.5	4.5	32	–
7	F	3.6	3.7	8	–
8	F	4.1	4.3	88	+

However, most subjects spoke at a substantially slower-than-normal rate. We found the average rate for normal older subjects to be more than 4.6 syllables per second on the same speech task (Ryalls et al., 1995). This slower speech rate was evident in both left and right subject groups of the present study.

In the next-to-the-last column of Table 25.2 results are presented for the difference in fundamental frequency for the last syllable of the sentence. We refer to this difference as 'Intonation' in the table. It represents the amount of difference in fundamental frequency between the two types of sentences. There was quite a large amount of variation between individual subjects ranging from a fully normal degree of difference to no difference at all. Subjects who produced at least 50 Hz difference between question and statement versions of the sentence are indicated by a + symbol on in the last column of Table 25.2. You can see that three of the eight left-hemisphere-damaged patients produced at least 50 Hz difference; while there were only two of the eight right-hemisphere-damaged patients who produced such a difference.

Perception

Patients were also tested for their basic ability to perceive speech prosody – in this case, for their ability to discriminate declarative and interrogative sentences. A group of 10 declarative sentences and 10 interrogative sentences were recorded from the same speaker and presented to the subjects in mixed order. The task of the patient was to state whether the sentence was a statement or question. In Table 25.3, perception results are presented for each of these two sentence types. The number of correctly perceived sentences out of 10 presentations is indicated for each sentence type. As can be seen there was also considerable subject-to-subject variation ranging from only one sentence correct to perfect performance.

Table 25.3. Perception results

	Gender	D	I	Perception	Production
Left hemisphere					
1	M	3	6	–	–
2	M	10	10	+	–
3	M	4	8	–	–
4	F	10	0	–	–
5	F	10	8	+	+
6	F	9	10	+	+
7	F	10	1	–	–
8	F	10	10	+	+
Right hemisphere					
1	M	8	8	+	–
2	M	10	10	+	–
3	M	10	10	+	–
4	M	10	10	+	+
5	M	10	0	–	–
6	M	10	6	+	–
7	F	9	6	+	–
8	F	10	10	+	+

Since there are 20 sentences in all with a choice of two responses, a binomial test indicated that 15 or more correct responses represents better-than-chance performance. Subjects who correctly perceived 15 sentences or more of the 20 possible are indicated with a + sign. Only half of the left-brain-damaged patients performed this task at better-than-chance. In comparison, there was only one right-brain-damaged patient who performed worse than chance. We begin to get the impression that there is somewhat of a dissociation in perception performance between the two subject groups. That is, it seems that perception is more likely to be affected by left-hemsiphere damage than by right hemisphere damage. These results are of interest since most work on speech prosody has emphasized the role of the right hemisphere. Next, we wanted to compare subjects' performance on both the perception and production tasks. Of the left-hemisphere-damaged patients, there were no patients who did not perform well on the perception task but who were still able to produce a normal prosodic difference of at least 50 Hz. Among the left-hemisphere-damaged patients who did not perform at better-than-chance on the perception task, there were four patients (1, 3, 4, 7) who also did not produce an average of at least 50 Hz on the production task as well. One patient (2) had intact perception, but poor production. The remaining four patients performed well on both the perception task and on the production task.

In comparison, there was only one right-brain-damaged patient who did not perform well on the perception task (i.e. less than 15 sentences correct – subject 5). This patient did not detect a single interrogative sentence correctly, and produced virtually no difference between the two types of sentence in the production task.

Five other right-brain-damaged patients (1, 2, 3, 6, 7) performed well on the perception task, but produced less than 50 Hz average difference between sentence pairs. The other two right-brain-damaged patients (4 and 8) performed well on both perception and production tasks.

Discussion

Based on these results, two preliminary observations can be made in regard to the perception and production of speech prosody. First of all, it seems that left-hemisphere damage is more likely to affect perception of prosody than is right-hemisphere damage. Half of the left-brain-damaged patients performed poorly on the perception task, while there was only one such patient among the right-brain-damaged group. This finding is supported by some recently published research conducted by Pell and Baum (1997) who also found left-hemisphere patients to have problems in the perception of linguistic prosody. In our study, perception performance seems to be more predictive of production performance among the left-hemsiphere-damaged subjects. Second, right-brain damage seems more likely to result in a dissociation between perception and production. Among the right-hemisphere-damaged patients, five had intact perception but abnormal production (1, 2, 3, 6 and 7). One patient had poor perception and production (5). The two remaining right-brain-damaged patients performed well on both tasks (4 and 8).

In contrast, all four of the left-brain-damaged patients who performed poorly in the perception task also performed poorly on the production task (1, 3, 4 and 7). There was only one left-brain-damaged patient who performed well on the perception task, but who performed poorly on the production task (2). The remaining three left-brain-damaged patients performed well on both tasks (5, 6 and 8).

Although we have been able to make some preliminary predictions based on this limited group of subjects, these observations should be investigated in a much larger group of subjects to determine if they can be generalized to a wider population. Therefore, future studies should include many more subjects. It is also important that further experimentation take into consideration whether the lesion is anterior or posterior in the respective hemisphere. This would require more balanced subject groups.

While more difficult to conduct, we feel that studies which consider both perception and production of speech prosody stand to give us a much better understanding of the representation of prosody in the brain than the study of either of these aspects in isolation. We believe that poor production results may in many cases reflect a patient's poor perception, especially in the case of left-hemisphere damage.

References

Le Dorze G, Ouellet L, Ryalls J (1994) Intonation and speech rate in dysarthric speech. Journal of Communication Disorders, 27, 1–18.

Le Dorze G, Ryalls J, Brassard C, Boulanger N, Ratte D (1998) A comparison of prosodic characteristics of the speech of people with Parkinson's disease and Friedreich's ataxia with neurologically normal speakers. Folia Phoniatrica et Logopaedia, 50, 1–9.

Pell M, Baum S (1997) The ability to perceive and comprehend intonation in linguistic and affective contexts by brain-damaged adults. Brain and Language, 57, 80–94.

Ryalls J, Behrens S (1988) An overview of changes in fundamental frequency associated with cortical insult. Aphasiology, 2, 107–15.

Ryalls J, Le Dorze G, Lever N, Ouellet L, Larfeuil C (1995) The effect of age and sex on speech intonation and duration. Journal of the Acoustical Society of America, 95, 2274–6.

Van Lancker D, Sidtis J (1992) The identification of affective-prosodic stimuli by left- and right-hemisphere-damaged subjects: All errors are not created equal. Journal of Speech and Hearing Research, 35, 963–70.

Chapter 26
An Acoustic Investigation of Pitch Accent Contrasts in the Speech of a Norwegian Patient with a Left-Hemisphere Lesion (Broca's Aphasia)

INGER MOEN and KJETIL SUNDET

Introduction

The present study is an investigation of the distinction between the two Norwegian pitch accents in the speech of an East Norwegian patient with Broca's aphasia. Pitch accent languages and tone languages use differences in pitch for lexical purposes. In languages of this type there are minimal pairs of words with the same segmental phonological structure, but with different pitch patterns on one or more of their syllables. The difference between pitch accent languages on the one hand and tone languages on the other, is generally that in a tone language differences in pitch are associated with every syllable in a word, whereas in a pitch accent language differences in pitch are associated with only one syllable in a word (see for instance Cruttenden, 1986).

Investigations of the brain-damaged population seem to indicate that the tonal production in tone languages and in pitch accent languages may be disrupted after unilateral damage to the left hemisphere and that a tone production deficit is linked up with type and severity of aphasia. The evidence for disrupted tonal production following unilateral right-hemisphere damage is limited (for references see Moen and Sundet, 1996; Gandour et al., 1997). Moen and Sundet (1996) found that one of their right-hemisphere-damaged patients failed to produce a clear auditory distinction between the two Norwegian pitch accents in all instances. The auditory impression could not be verified acoustically, however, because the F_0 contours of the deviant productions were either too short to be revealing – accented syllables consisting of a short vowel followed by a voiceless consonant – or inconclusive.

The Norwegian pitch accent

Norwegian is a pitch accent language in the sense that every accented syllable will carry the pitch pattern of one of two possible tones, referred to as Accent1 and Accent2. The choice between these accents is normally lexically determined. That is, the accent must be listed in the lexicon together with the word's segmental phonological structure. There are a number of minimal pairs differing only in tone, the pitch pattern of their accented syllables, for instance the following pairs (the superscripts [1] and [2] indicate Accent1 and Accent2, respectively): *vannet* /[1]vane/ (the water) – *vanne* /[2]vane/ (to water); *skuffen* /[1]skufen/ (the drawer) – *skuffen* /[2]skufen/ (the shovel).

Both accents are associated with a low pitch level in East Norwegian. The difference between them is located in the beginning of the syllable, before the pitch reaches its lowest level. Accent2 involves an extensive fall in pitch from the beginning of the syllable to its lowest pitch level. Accent1 may either exhibit an initial narrow fall or a low level pitch. The pitch pattern may be described as high-low in Accent2 syllables and as low in Accent1 syllables. The pitch pattern of the syllable(s) following the accented syllable varies. This variation is not part of the tonal distinction, but belongs to the domain of sentence intonation and signals differences in the information structure of the utterance (see Figure 26.1). The pitch patterns in Figure 26.1 represent two words spoken in isolation, with focal accents. The final pitch patterns are therefore rising. In order for there to be a contrast between Accent1 and Accent2 the accented syllable must be followed by one or more unaccented syllables. When the accented syllable is not followed by an unaccented one, the opposition is neutralized and only Accent1 is used.

Previous acoustic investigations

There are two published acoustic investigations of the production of the Norwegian pitch accents in the speech of the brain-damaged population. Ryalls and Reinvang (1986) in an investigation of the tonal production of both left-hemisphere-damaged and right-hemisphere-damaged patients in a repetition test found that their left-hemisphere-damaged patients – patients with a non-fluent type of aphasia with good comprehension – did distinguish between the two pitch accents in minimal pairs of words, although the pitch contours differed from those of a control subject. The right-hemisphere-damaged patients' production was near normal.

Moen and Sundet (1996) in an acoustic investigation of a similar patient population as that of Ryalls and Reinvang found – based on a reading test of minimal pairs – that the three aphasic patients who took

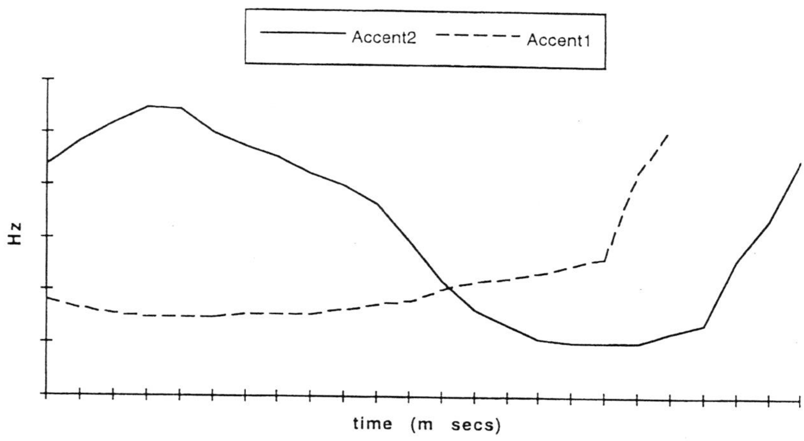

Figure 26.1. Fundamental frequency curves of the two Norwegian pitch accents.

part in the test, failed to distinguish between the two pitch accents in at least some of the pairs. The most impaired patient was a patient with Broca's aphasia, the same patient as that of the present study. The patient's auditory discrimination of the two pitch accents was also impaired. He only identified 50% of the words correctly. The auditory confusion of the two accents was bidirectional. The reason this patient is of particular interest is that in a reading test which did *not consist of minimal pairs* he produced a clear distinction between Accent1 and Accent2. The present paper compares and discusses the results of the two tests.

Patient

The patient is a 54-year-old man with 12 years of education who, except for a long lasting Reiter's disease, was in good health when he suffered a stroke which left him with dysarthric speech and coordination difficulties in his right arm and leg. Cerebral CT showed a small haemorrhagic infarction in his left hemisphere and evidence of thrombosis in the arteria cerebri media. EEG showed generalized dysrythmic activity as well as focal theta-delta activity in the left fronto-temporal region. Over the next two days the condition worsened and he developed complete hemiparesis of his right arm and leg, right-sided central facial paresis, and expressive aphasia. Control-CT showed a large infarction area in his left cerebral hemisphere (located to the fronto-temporal area), a thrombotic left arteria cerebri media and a highly stenotic left arteria carotis interna. The situation stabilized, and after four weeks he was referred to a rehabilitation hospital.

The patient was tested seven weeks after his stroke. At this time he could walk with a slight limp but was paralytic in his right arm. He managed alone in daily life activities (ADL score: 32 out of 36) and scored in the lower normal range with his left arm (T = 40) on a motor coordination test (Grooved Pegboard). His language profile on the Norwegian Basic Aphasia Assessment matched that of a Broca's aphasia with a total aphasia quotient of 194 (max. 217), placing him at the 70th percentile level in the aphasic reference group. On the Token Test he scored 15.5 out of 36.0, which suggested more difficulties with verbal comprehension than was evidenced at first hand. At the Similarities subtest from the WAIS he obtained an age-corrected standard score of four, which indicates major problems with verbal word finding. He showed no evidence of visual or visuo-spatial difficulties and obtained a normal score on the Raven's Coloured Progressive Matrices (34 out of 36).

Test 1

The patient was asked to read twelve words in a syntactic frame, *Det var . . . jeg sa* (It was . . . I said). The target word was presented by a drawing with the sentence written beneath the drawing. The test words represented by the drawings were chosen to form pairs, though not minimal pairs, of Accent1 and Accent2 words with the same, or similar, segmental structure in the accented syllable. In addition, these syllables should contain segments which could provide relatively long, unbroken F_0 contours – either a long vowel or a short vowel plus a voiced continuant. The words were also chosen on the basis of their 'picturability' since they were to be illustrated by means of drawings. Each sentence was read once by the patient in a quiet room in the hospital. A digital recording was made of the reading. Two normal controls, matched for age, sex and education, were tested and recorded in the same way.

Test results (1)

The patient had a reduced speech rate compared with the controls and lengthy pauses between the words in each sentence – features, which have frequently been noted in other investigations of Broca's aphasia.

The control subjects, as expected, read each sentence with one focal accent – on the word corresponding to the drawing – whereas the patient read each sentence with a focal accent on each word.

Although, as indicated above, the patient's prosody deviated from that of the normal controls, he did distinguish between the two pitch accents (see Figure 26.2). He only produced one of the 12 words with the wrong accent. The noun *lynet* – /^{1}ly:ne/(Accent1) was pronounced with the accent of the corresponding verb *lyne* – /^{2}ly:ne/(Accent2). But this mistake could just as well have been the result of wrong selection of word class as of wrong assignment of accent type.

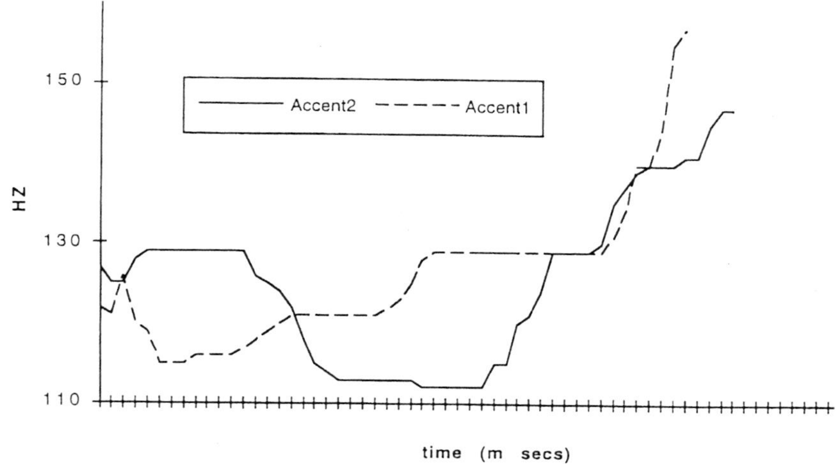

Figure 26.2. F_0 contours of the patient's articulation of *målet* (Accent1) and *måne* (Accent2).

Test 2

This is the test which has been reported in Moen and Sundet (1996). The stimuli consisted of six minimal pairs illustrated by drawings, with the target word written below each drawing. The patient was presented with one illustration at a time and asked to read the word written below the picture. Each member of a minimal pair was read once. The members of the same pair were not read consecutively. The patient was tested in the hospital in a reasonably quiet room in a single setting. The readings were recorded using a digital recorder. The recordings were then analysed acoustically.

The recordings were also presented to a group of five normal subjects, who functioned as judges, in order to see if they were able to identify the targets. They were asked to identify each word by pointing to the corresponding drawing.

Test results (2)

Five of the six minimal pairs were produced in such a way that the judges failed to identify a correct contrast. The judges were either uncertain as to which word was produced or identified both words of a minimal pair as the word with Accent1. The F_0 traces of the patient's pronunciation support the judges' impression. The F_0 traces of the accented syllables in ^{1}kammer/^{2}kammer, ^{1}bordet/^{2}borde, ^{1}tømmer/^{2}tømmer all show a narrow fall in the beginning of the accented syllable followed by a level contour, with or without a final rise – the typical Accent1 contour (see Figure 26.3).

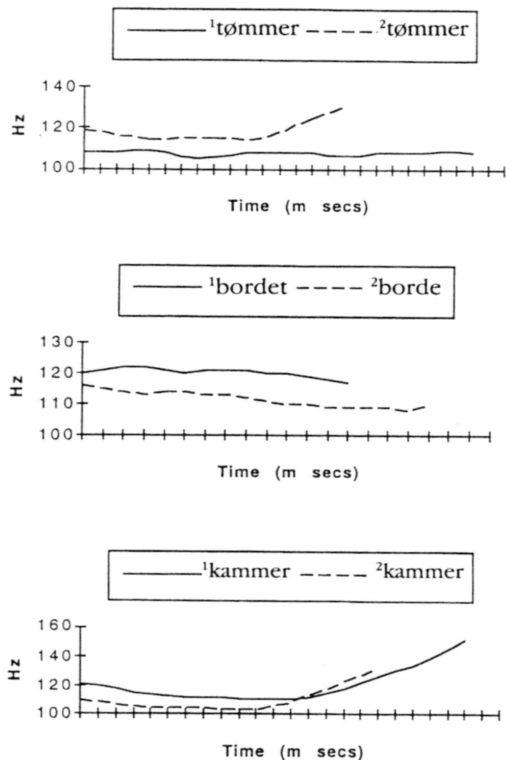

Figure 26.3. F_0 traces of the accented syllables in the patient's pronunciation of ^{1}tømmer/^{2}tømmer , ^{1}bordet/^{2}borde, ^{1}kammer/^{2}kammer.

Summary

1. The patient makes a distinction between Accent1 and Accent2 when tested on the production of words which are not members of minimal pairs.
2. When tested on the production of words which are members of a minimal pair, he tends to produce both members with an Accent1 contour.
3. The patient's problem seems to be a phonological one. There is no indication, on the basis of these tests, that the patient's ability to control pitch variation as such is reduced.

Discussion

It is noteworthy that most of the accent production mistakes involved the substitution of Accent1 for Accent2. Accent1 is the unmarked accent, the pitch pattern used when the opposition between the two accents is neutralized, and it is the accent given to new loanwords. Most of the accent substitutions thus involve the replacement of a marked feature by an unmarked one. According to the theory of phonological underspecification (see for instance Kenstowicz, 1994) only one of the accents, the marked one, will be specified in the lexical phonological representation. The patient's accent substitutions could then be accounted for by assuming that Accent2 words occasionally are retrieved from the mental lexicon without accent specification. These words will then, by default, be assigned Accent1.

But the theory of phonological underspecification cannot, at the same time, account for the fact that the patient does make a distinction between Accent1 and Accent2 when tested on the production of words which are not members of minimal pairs. If phonological underspecification was the only mechanism at work, one would expect some Accent1 contours on Accent2 words regardless of whether they were members of minimal pairs. In order to account for the difference in the patient's success rate between the production of minimal pairs and words that are not members of minimal pairs, a different theory must be invoked.

We suggest that a connectionist model of lexical access, in addition to the theory of phonological underspecification, might account for the observed difference. This type of model assumes that when a target word is accessed, at some stage in the process towards speech production the phonological structure of the target word, together with the structure of phonologically similar words, will be activated (see for instance Dell, 1988). If the target word is the member of a minimal accent pair, two identical segmental phonological structures with different prosodic patterns will be activated. The patient then has to choose between these two. When the target word is not a member of a minimal pair, the patient does not have to make a choice between two identical segmental structures with different pitch patterns. As a result, the correct accent is produced also on Accent2 words.

The present investigation focuses on the patient's pitch accent *production*, but it should be noted that neither the theory of phonological underspecification nor a connectionist model of lexical access can account for the patient's bidirectional failure to discriminate auditorily between the two pitch accents. It is still unclear what the mechanisms underlying the patient's pitch accent perception may be (Moen and Sundet, 1996).

Acknowledgement

We are indebted to Eva Hofft for assistance in connection with the collection of the data.

References

Cruttenden A (1986) Intonation. Cambridge: Cambridge University Press.

Dell GS (1988) The retrieval of phonological forms in production: Tests of predictions from a connectionist model. Journal of Memory and Language, 27, 124–42.

Gandour J, Ponglorpisit S, Potisuk S, Khunadorn F, Boongird P, Dechongkit S (1997) Interaction between Tone and Intonation in Thai after Unilateral Brain Damage. Brain and Language, 58, 174–96.

Kenstowicz M (1994) Phonology in Generative Grammar. Oxford: Blackwell Publishers.

Moen I, Sundet K (1996) Production and Perception of Word Tones (Pitch Accents) in Patients with Left and Right Hemisphere Damage. Brain and Language, 53, 267–81.

Ryalls J, Reinvang I (1986) Functional lateralisation of linguistic tones: Acoustic evidence from Norwegian. Language and Speech, 29, 389–98.

Chapter 27 Assessment of Auditory Word Comprehension in Aphasia

WOLFRAM ZIEGLER, ANGELA JOCHMANN and ANDREAS ZIERDT

Introduction

Patients with aphasic disorders of nearly all types may show comprehension problems at the level of auditory-phonetic processing (e.g. Basso et al., 1977). Such a deficit may also occur with almost no accompanying aphasic symptoms, a constellation which has been termed 'word sound deafness', 'word form deafness' or 'word meaning deafness', depending which level in a hierarchy of processing steps is impaired (e.g. Franklin, 1989). It may be true that many patients can cope with their speech processing problems by using lip-reading or different kinds of contextual information. Nevertheless, one should not underestimate the clinical relevance of acoustic-phonetic deficits, since they may interfere with the automatized nature of acoustic-phonetic processing, which allows normal subjects to allocate their attention to other cognitive tasks during speech decoding. Thus, aphasics compensate for their acoustic-phonetic problems at the expense of their parallel processing resources, which may lead to a breakdown of language comprehension in cognitively demanding situations.

Most conventionally, acoustic-phonetic processing in aphasia is assessed by phoneme discrimination or by phoneme identification tasks. Whereas in the former patients are required to decide whether two spoken syllables or words are the same or different, the latter requires them to relate a heard item to a linguistic category, e.g. a syllable or word written on a card. A finding which has often been replicated is that aphasic patients are more impaired in identification than they are in discrimination tasks (e.g. Blumstein et al., 1977; Gow and Caplan, 1996). This may mean that the basic processes of matching two acoustic patterns are preserved in aphasia, but the more advanced capacity of mapping acoustic input onto stable linguistic representations of phonemes or syllables can be impaired (Blumstein et al., 1977).

The study reported here focused on two aspects that have been neglected so far. The first is that we used a discrimination task including syllables spoken by *different talkers*. Earlier studies have rather tried to keep this source as constant as possible, in order to allow for the best control of the acoustic contrast between two items (for references see Gow and Caplan, 1996). However, one of the specific achievements of a listener in understanding speech is to separate the talker-related information in the speech signal from the phonetic information, thereby creating a constant percept in the face of considerable acoustic variability (Remez et al., 1997). Moreover, recent investigations into the nature of auditory speech processing have underscored the fact that talker-specific attributes of the speech signal interact with the phonetically relevant features during the decoding of speech (cf. Green et al., 1997). Based on this evidence we asked whether aphasic patients may be specifically impaired in the capacity of matching two acoustically different utterances for phonetic equivalence. To answer this question, we constructed a discrimination task involving comparisons of syllables spoken by talkers with maximally different acoustic patterns, i.e. children and adults.

A second focus was on the point that most of the identification tasks used in earlier studies were based on a matching of spoken and written syllables. Given that the processing of written language can be particularly impaired in many aphasic syndromes, this test format may introduce variance more related to written language processing than to speech decoding. In the identification task presented here we circumvented any orthographically-based decision modes by matching spoken words with pictured words. In order to be able to compare our results with those of earlier studies, a test based on matching of spoken and written materials was also administered.

Methods

Subjects

Twelve aphasic patients (2 women, 10 men, aged 20–68 years, median 48 years) and 20 neurologically and audiologically normal subjects (10 women, 10 men, aged 27–73 years, median 39 years) were examined. All consecutive aphasic patients who presented any input- or output-disturbances at the phonemic level were entered into the study, i.e. three Wernicke's aphasics, one Broca's aphasic, one conduction aphasic, one global aphasic, one transcortical-sensory aphasic and five non-classified aphasics. All patients, including the global aphasic, were able to comprehend the test instructions. Two patients had to be excluded from reaction time measurements since they were unable to use the mouse keys.

Test stimuli were spoken by four subjects with no known neurological or speech problems. Two adults (f, 27 years; m, 30 years) and two children (f, 10 years, m, 11 years) were chosen as speakers.

Discrimination task

A nonsense-syllable discrimination task based on minimal pairs was developed. In order to be compatible with earlier work (e.g. Gow and Caplan, 1996) we used the features *place* (represented by the pairs /fa/ – /ʃa/ and /ta/ – /ka/), *manner* (represented by the pairs /ba/ – /ma/ and /da/ – /la/), and *voice* (represented by the pairs /va/ – /fa/ and /ga/ – /ka/). Each of the test syllables was spoken twice by each of the four speakers.

Stimulus pairs were presented in (1) a *homogeneous* and (2) a *heterogeneous* condition. In the former, only stimuli of a single speaker were paired, resulting in one homogeneous block for each speaker. In the latter, stimulus pairs of the type *girl–male adult* and *boy – female adult* were formed, thereby maximizing the acoustic difference in the two stimuli of a pair. In each condition, each syllable was paired with itself ('same' pairs, e.g. ba – ba, ma – ma) and with its cognate ('different' pairs, e.g. ba – ma, ma – ba). 'Same' pairs of the homogeneous conditions were always composed of two different realizations of the same syllables by the same speaker.

The tests were controlled by a PC. The two syllables of a pair were presented over headphones with a one-second ISI, responses were given on the left or right mouse button for same or different pairs, respectively. Each stimulus combination was presented twice, resulting in a total of 192 homogeneous and 192 heterogeneous stimulus pairs. The four homogeneous subtests were administered blockwise, the heterogeneous subtest was divided into four equal parts. Thus, a total of eight subtests with 48 stimulus pairs each was administered to the subjects in two sessions, with sufficiently long pauses between two blocks and shorter pauses within each single block. The subjects received as many learning- and warm-up trials as they felt they required.

Identification tasks

Spoken – pictured

In this task, subjects were required to compare a spoken utterance with a picture presented 1.5 s later and to decide whether or not the two matched. Again, spoken and pictured words formed minimal pairs differing in the initial phoneme, using one-feature-distances with the same phonetic features as in the discrimination task. As an example for the *place*-feature, the word /fax/ ('drawer') was spoken and a picture of a chess-board (/ʃax/) was presented, requiring subjects to respond by pressing the 'different' key. Further, a second spoken cognate differing in more than one phoneme was selected for each pictured name (e.g. /kɔx/ 'cook' – /ʃax/ 'chess'), in order to control for the influence of phonetic distance. Each phoneme opposition, like /ʃ/ – /f/, was represented in two different orders (spoken /ʃ/ – pictured /f/ and vice versa). Two equal sets of *spoken-pictured* triples were constructed in this manner, one with spoken natural words and one with spoken non-words. Whereas in the former top-down lexical information might influence a subject's response, no such information is available from spoken non-words.

Overall, for each of the six phoneme oppositions mentioned above four sets of four tasks each (two 'same'-tasks, one *close-different* task and one *distant-different* task) were constructed, resulting in a total of 96 matching tasks. As in the heterogeneous condition, each word or non-word was spoken by each of the four speakers. Speakers and tasks were combined in a Latin-Square-design. Therefore, each speaker was presented 24 times overall. The whole test was administered twice, using different speaker-stimulus-combinations in two parallel blocks on two different days.

Spoken – written

This experiment was designed to replicate earlier studies based on a spoken-written matching task (e.g. Gow and Caplan, 1996). The stimulus materials were the same as in the discrimination task described above. One of the two syllables of a pair was spoken, and a written syllable was presented 1.5 s later on the computer screen. The spoken stimuli were delivered by only one speaker (the 10-year-old girl). Six syllable pairs were presented in four different combinations, resulting in a total of 48 matching tasks.

Results and Discussion

Discrimination task

The average discrimination error was 3% for the 20 controls and 17% for the 12 aphasics. Mean response delays were 776 ms for the controls and 1032 ms for the patients. One-way ANOVAs using response delays and discrimination errors as dependent variables and the four speakers as independent variables revealed no speaker-related differences. Moreover, the factor Phonetic Feature had no influence on either discrimination errors or reaction times. Figure 27.1 compares discrimination errors for the homogeneous and the heterogeneous tasks for each subject individually.

There was no task-related difference on the small error numbers of the control group (Wilcoxon matched pairs, $z = -1.72$, $p = 0.09$). However, the patients demonstrated consistently higher error rates on

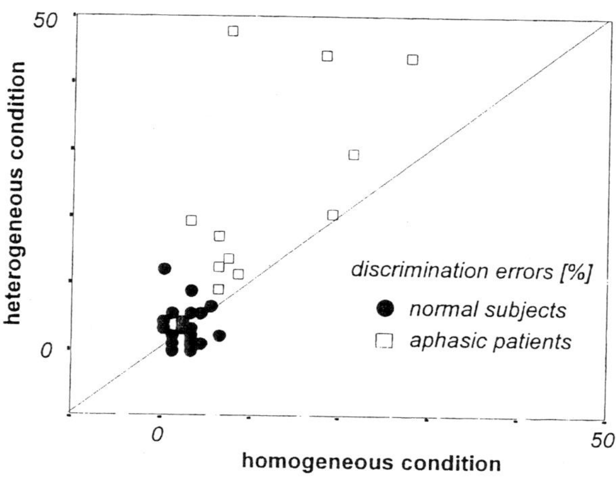

Figure 27.1. Comparison of discrimination errors in the homogeneous and the heterogeneous condition.

the heterogeneous as compared with the homogeneous condition (z = –2.90, p = 0.004). Response delays showed that in the controls, too, additional processing was required in the mixed-speaker condition, since average reaction times were increased by 148 ms (Wilcoxon matched pairs, z = –3.92, p = 0.0001). The difference was even higher in the patients, whose responses were slowed by an average of 184 ms when they matched syllables delivered by different speakers as compared with syllable pairs spoken by a single speaker (Z = –2.80, p = 0.005). This confirms the results of earlier studies on the role of talker information during phonetic perception in controls (Green et al., 1997). It further demonstrates that the patients had a particular deficit in matching the phonemic content of syllables spoken by two different speakers.

Identification tasks

Spoken – pictured

Subjects made consistently fewer errors on the spoken–pictured matching task than in phoneme discrimination. Normal error rates were 2.5% on average, with a mean reaction time of 522 ms. The patients made an average of 13 errors, with a mean response delay of 1020 ms. The aphasics made consistently more errors on the phonetically close pairs than on the distant pairs (Wilcoxon matched pairs, p = 0.003), which validates the construction of the test. As regards the influence of lexicality, no difference between words and pseudowords was obtained for identification rates or response delays in the controls or the patients as a group (α = 0.05). However, in single cases substantial differences were seen in either direction, which may indicate that lexical information was utilized rather individually in the 12 cases examined here. One of the Wernicke's aphasics, for instance, accepted 43% of all pseudowords as words, but was able to reject most of the non-matching word-word pairs. On the contrary, the conduction aphasic recognized 98% of all non-words as non-matching but made 16% errors on the words.

Spoken – written

On this task, control subjects were an average of 166 ms slower than on the picture-matching task, which had an otherwise identical format. Again, the controls made almost no errors (2%). Response errors for the patient group were 20%, which was substantially higher than in spoken-pictured matching. Further, the patients were also substantially slower on the task involving written words and non-words. These differences were attributable to a particularly poor performance of five patients who were obviously unable to match spoken with written words, but were much better at matching words with pictures. In these cases, conventional identification tasks as used, for instance, by Gow and Caplan (1996), would say more about the patient's processing of written materials than it would contribute to an assessment of his or her acoustic-phonetic performance.

Conclusions

The results of the phoneme discrimination task corroborated our expectation that aphasic subjects are specifically impaired in their capacity to 'normalize' spoken utterances for their talker-related variability. This capacity goes beyond that of comparing two utterances spoken by the same subject or generated by a computer, which is the requirement of conventional discrimination tasks reported in the literature. Therefore, our experiment has revealed a specific processing deficit in aphasic patients, which is located at an intermediate stage between the basic process of matching two acoustic patterns and the identification of a phoneme. This result may be of considerable clinical relevance since it may explain why aphasics often have particular problems in 'cocktail party' situations.

Regarding the relation between phoneme discrimination and identification we obtained a pattern opposite to that reported in the literature. This was only partly ascribable to the higher demands of our heterogeneous discrimination task. Several patients of our study made fewer errors in the matching of spoken and pictured items than in the more conventional spoken-written task. Therefore, earlier investigations into the relation between discrimination and identification in aphasic patients may have underestimated aphasics' identification performance through the use of an orthographic mode.

Acknowledgement

We would like to express our thanks to the four speakers who produced the materials, especially to Lucy and Julian. We are also indebted to our control listeners and to the 12 aphasic patients who participated in the study.

References

Basso A, Casati G, Vignolo LA (1977) Phonemic identification defect in aphasia. Cortex, 13, 85–95.

Blumstein SE, Baker E, Goodglass H (1977) Phonological factors in auditory comprehension in aphasia. Neuropsychologia, 15, 19–30.

Franklin S (1989) Dissociations in auditory word comprehension: evidence from nine fluent aphasic patients. Aphasiology, 3, 189–207.

Gow DW, Caplan D (1996) An examination of impaired acoustic-phonetic processing in aphasia. Brain and Language, 52, 386–407.

Green KP, Tomiak GR, Kuhl PK (1997) The encoding of rate and talker information during phonetic perception. Perception and Psychophysics, 59, 675–92.

Remez RE, Fellowes JM, Rubin PE (1997) Talker identification based on phonetic information. Journal of Experimental Psychology - Human Perception and Performance, 23, 651–66.

Chapter 28
Remediation of Apraxia of Speech Using Magnetometer-feedback Therapy

WILLIAM F. KATZ and SNEHA BHARADWAJ

Introduction

Adults with brain damage (particularly those with damage to the anterior or fronto-parietal regions of the cerebral speech zone) often present with slow, halting speech containing numerous sound- and meaning-based errors. Speech sounds may be distorted or appear to contain substituted phonemes, particularly for difficult or uncommon words. Moreover, the patient is typically aware of such errors yet may remain rather powerless to do much about them. This pattern is described in some taxonomies as a unique speech disorder unto itself ('apraxia of speech' or AOS), while others classify it as a common symptom of a non-fluent (or 'Broca's') aphasia syndrome. Extensive research has revealed much about how such disorders affect speech at the level of the phoneme, syllable and individual word (see Blumstein, 1995 for review). However, the exact underlying mechanisms involved in this disorder remain somewhat controversial. In addition, from a clinical perspective these symptoms are broadly considered to be rather difficult to treat.

Traditional treatment generally includes compensation strategies and motor-planning or motor-sequencing activities designed to promote voluntary control of the articulators (e.g. Rosenbek et al., 1984; Sarno, 1991). Clinical studies have indicated that progress may be made using such techniques (e.g. Wambaugh and Doyle, 1992). Other forms of therapy provide sensory information as an important means of improving speech production. For example, Square-Storer and colleagues (Square et al., 1985, 1986; Square-Storer and Hayden, 1989) propose a method known as 'PROMPT therapy'. In this method, the clinician places his or her fingers on the patient's face and jaw to provide a series of tactile 'prompts' or cues. These tactile cues, combined with the provision of a linguistic template, reportedly serve as input for correcting articulatory deficits, such as the spatial targeting of phonemes and the regulation of segment and syllable durations.

The present study is an attempt to develop a new means of remediating AOS symptoms using the recent technology of Electromagnetic Midsagittal Articulography (EMMA). Briefly, EMMA is a relatively non-invasive, on-line method of tracking speech articulator movement using low field-strength, alternating electromagnetic fields. There are at least three reasons to expect that EMMA may be used to assist patients with AOS. First, therapies which incorporate sensory feedback provided by a clinician (e.g. PROMPT therapy) have reported substantial success. These studies imply that precise visual feedback concerning real-time movement of the tongue provided by EMMA technology could be used to improve speech further. Second, in computer-guided biofeedback the patient can control the rate of stimulus presentation and complexity, with no interpersonal expectations or metalinguistic factors which might complicate the motor learning process. Third, evidence suggests kinematic biofeedback can assist individuals having other neurogenic speech disorders (e.g. Hardcastle et al., 1991; Volin, 1991; Goldstein et al., 1994). We therefore explored EMMA as a means of remediating AOS in the speech of an adult with Broca's aphasia. Specifically, we looked for improvement in both non-speech oral and speech motor behaviour.

Method

Participant

PA is a 63-year-old female, right-handed, monolingual, native speaker of American English. She had a CVA in 1989 subsequent to intracranial surgery. A recent CT report indicated a large middle cerebral artery infarct and a focus of decreased density along the anterior limb of the right internal capsule and right frontal periventricular white matter. PA was diagnosed as having Broca's aphasia. An apraxia battery taken at the time of testing indicated a slight buccofacial apraxia and moderate-to-severe apraxia of speech. PA had received intermittent speech therapy, both in individual and group settings, over the eight years since her stroke.

Design and procedure

Kinematic data were obtained using a Carstens AG-100 electromagnetic articulograph. An initial (baseline) speech assessment session, five treatment sessions, and a final assessment session were all held within a one-month period. We also conducted a long-term assessment session 10 weeks after the end of therapy. In the initial assessment session we obtained data concerning PA's speech errors, including recordings of the movement of the subject's tongue tip, tongue body and mandible. Coils placed on the upper incisors and on the nasal bridge served as anatomical references.

During assessment, PA repeated productions of single words and short phrases following auditory and written (4 x 6" flash cards) presentation given in randomized order by an experimenter. There was a total of 156 stimuli, including monosyllabic words, polysyllabic words and short functional phrases. The assessment items included a broad spectrum of consonantal contrasts in different syllable positions. From these data, as well as from PA's clinical records, we selected the [s]/[ʃ] distinction for subsequent remediation trials. Briefly, PA's clinical records consistently indicated poor performance with fricatives and affricates. For example, a recent report noted 40–50% accuracy in [s]/[ʃ] production. Also, our baseline assessment indicated clear problems with [s]/[ʃ], including distortions, substitutions and omissions. Finally, we selected the [s]/[ʃ] contrast for remediation because these phonemes involve an alveolar versus post-alveolar place-of-articulation distinction that can be readily tracked using an EMMA system.

Each therapy session included an experimental treatment (i.e. computer-guided biofeedback) and a foil treatment designed to control for possible motivational factors arising from computer-based therapy. The order of the experimental and foil treatments was counterbalanced between sessions. In the experimental treatment, PA sat in front of a monitor which displayed a real-time image of the midsagittal position of her tongue tip. Using a mouse, the investigators first mapped in 'target' zones along the palate corresponding with PA's perceptually-adequate [s]/[ʃ] productions. These target zones were subsequently displayed as large circles, each representing a region along the palate ranging from 0.6 to 0.8 cm in diameter. The computer then used this information to guide PA's tongue movements during training, and to record kinematic data for later analysis.

Each experimental session included a blocked series of four tasks arranged in the following order: (1) SILENT – silently move the tongue tip between the target zones; (2) HUMMING – move the tongue tip between the target zones while simultaneously humming; (3) NON-WORD – produce repetitions of the nonsense utterances [asa]/[aʃa]; (4) REAL WORD – produce repetitions of 'a sip'/'a ship'. In the SILENT and HUMMING tasks, PA was instructed to 'hit the target regions with your tongue tip'. During the actual experimental procedure, one target zone would light up green, indicating the subject should move the tongue-tip coil into that region. When successful, a pleasing tone would sound and a small 'balloon' image would rise on the computer monitor (to give the subject further visual feedback on her progress). Immediately after this target zone was hit, it turned red and the alternative target then lit up green. In this fashion, positive feedback for spatial positioning of the tongue was provided, and correct hits on desired targets were recorded.

In the NON-WORD and REAL WORD tasks, PA was required to complete a slightly more complex motor behaviour pattern before a positive feedback message was given. In these tasks it was necessary to let the tongue tip return to a lower, more central vocal tract position (necessary for producing the vowels of each utterance) before entering the correct (fricative) target space. The idea was to guide PA to produce appropriate vowel–consonant–vowel trajectories. This requirement was effected automatically by requiring the tongue-tip coil, after each hit, to return outside an 'active area' (marked by a large, external circle), before the next target would become active. Similar to the creation of the target zones, the 'active area' circle was designated at the beginning of each experimental session by the investigators using a special software tool. The size of this region was based on interactive observation of the subject's tongue tip movement during repeated production of sample utterances.

PA was required to successfully hit the target zones 80 times before being thanked (by the computer) for finishing each task. The four tasks were completed in serial order, with an entire experimental test session lasting approximately 30 minutes. The purpose of this procedure was to lead PA through progressively more complicated motor behaviour during each test session. In the foil treatment, a self-paced computer program delivered visual and auditory examples of word and phrase stimuli to the subject for simple repetition. As in the experimental treatment, the computer provided positive feedback and thanked PA for completing the experiment. The foil treatment addressed the feature of stop consonant voicing (i.e. [p t k b d g]) and contained no items used in the experimental treatment.

Results

Kinematic data

Visual inspection of PA's kinematic data during the experimental treatment sessions revealed substantial improvement in motor control as the sessions progressed. For example, Figure 28.1 shows sample tongue-tip traces for PA's [s] productions during the first and last experimental sessions. Each panel is a recording of tongue tip movement during the NON-WORD task (i.e. producing [asa]/[aʃa]). A trace indicates tongue tip movement toward the [s] target, and an 'X' marks current tongue tip position. Small circles denote the target regions that were designated by the experimenters at the start of each session (based on PA's tongue tip positioning for perceptually-adequate productions). Note that the size of these target zones has been decreased over the test sessions to make

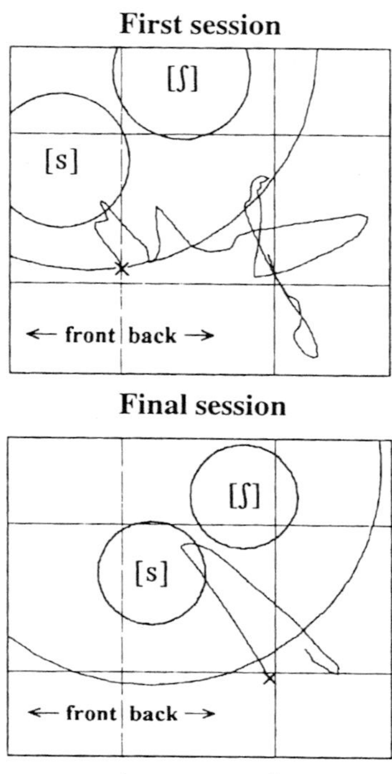

Figure 28.1. Sample tongue-tip movement patterns produced by PA in the first and final experimental treatment sessions for the NON-WORD task. Small circles mark the [s] and [ʃ] target zones. The active area is shown by the large, outer circle and the current position of the tongue-tip coil is marked with an 'X'.

the task increasingly challenging. A large, outer circle marks the border of the 'active area' required to activate targets. During the first experimental session, PA demonstrated poor lingual control, as may be seen in the large, irregular trajectories and repeated unsuccessful attempts. In contrast, by the final session the [s] target was hit after a single, direct attempt.

These kinematic patterns were quantified by computing the average tongue tip distance travelled per target 'hit'. This was done by first calculating the total tongue tip distance (in cm) traversed in a complete session (80 target hits), then dividing by the number of hits. These data, shown in Table 28.1, encompass at least three factors, including (1) the number of repeated attempts to target; (2) the variability of each trajectory to target; and (3) the variability of motions before or after hitting each target. Data were available for four out of the five sessions, and for all the tasks except for REAL WORD in session one (these data were lost due to recording errors).

Although this measure of PA's motor performance is somewhat general, the results nevertheless demonstrate remarkably consistent

Table 28.1. Mean distance (cm) per hit for tongue-tip coil in experimental treatment sessions 1–5, and ratio of means for first/last recorded sessions

Task	Mean tongue-tip distance (cm)/hit				Ratio: means first/last session
	Session				
	1	3	4	5	
silent	22.6	4.95	3.01	1.79	12.7
humming	6.05	1.95	1.47	1.23	4.92
non-word	19.5	11.3	8.35	8.21	2.37
real word	–	15.6	11.1	8.79	1.77

improvement across sessions. Specifically, all four conditions showed a decrease in tongue tip distance across the successive test sessions. Not surprisingly, the overall values for the REAL WORD and NON-WORD tasks were larger than for the SILENT and HUMMING tasks. This is because the REAL WORD and NON-WORD tasks required the tongue to travel greater distances (e.g. in and out of the 'active area') in order to activate the targets. However, over and above these absolute differences there also appeared to be task-specific differences in the amount of improvement noted: the SILENT task showed the largest reduction across sessions (i.e. 22.6–1.79 cm/hit), a 12.7-fold difference. This effect was smaller for the HUMMING task (ratio = 4.9); followed by NON-WORD (ratio = 2.4); then REAL WORD (ratio = 1.8). This apparent interaction suggests that PA improved in all tasks with practice, but her improvement was more marked for some tasks than for others.

Perceptual measures

Figure 28.2 shows PA's baseline, final, and long-term assessment data. These perceptual data are based on independent transcription of PA's productions by the two experimenters, with interrater reliability at 93%. Results of the experimental treatment data (indicated with solid bars) indicate improvement from 41% accuracy at the initial session to 66% accuracy by the final session, largely attributable to improved [ʃ] productions. Moreover, [s]/[ʃ] productions were completed with 65% accuracy at long-term assessment, well above baseline. The foil treatment data (i.e. [p t k b d g], indicated with striped bars) showed slight improvement from baseline to final sessions (61% and 72% respectively), with performance dropping back near baseline level (64%) at long-term assessment.

Discussion

The results suggest that visual biofeedback concerning tongue tip position helped improve [s]/[ʃ] articulation difficulties resulting from

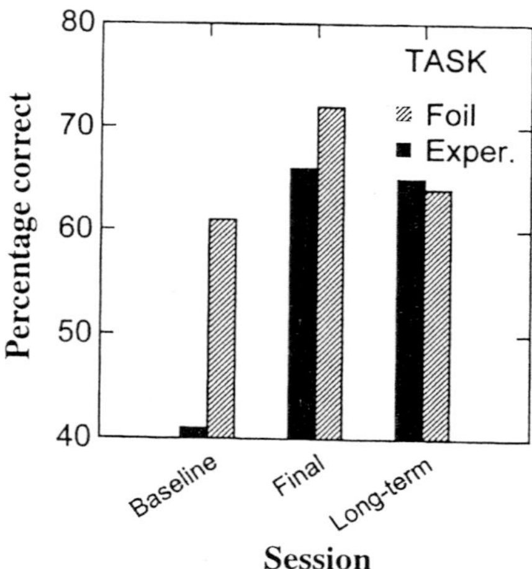

Figure 28.2. Perceptual adequacy of PA's productions treated by the experimental ([s]/[ʃ]) and foil ([p t k b d g]) treatments. Baseline, final and long-term (10 weeks post-treatment) assessment data are shown.

AOS in an adult with Broca's aphasia. Both kinematic and (to a lesser extent) perceptual data indicate that rapid and relatively lasting improvements resulted from the experimental treatment, while a carefully balanced control treatment produced only slight, impermanent effects. These results are particularly striking because the course of biofeedback therapy was quite brief, and PA had previously shown only limited improvement on the target phonetic contrast during years of therapy. However, these positive conclusions must be tempered with at least three reservations. First, perceptual data showed the effects of biofeedback therapy slightly diminished over time, with performance at 10 weeks post-treatment being lower than post-treatment values (although still higher than baseline). Second, the kinematic data showed greater improvement in non-speech than motor speech tasks. Third, the results of a single subject experiment can at best provide only tentative evidence for the efficacy of a new form of therapy. Future research should examine these issues. Moreover, future studies should investigate long-term retention and generalization, and the use of other articulators and kinematic parameters (e.g. velocity, acceleration) for biofeedback purposes.

Finally, even though the present research results are encouraging, the high cost and technical expertise needed to accurately use EMMA technology largely preclude its clinical utility at this time. In the meantime, basic research in biofeedback techniques should continue so that there will be scientifically-motivated clinical procedures available to meet patients' needs in the near future.

Summary

Electromagnetic midsagittal articulography (EMMA) was used to remediate [s]/[ʃ] articulation deficits resulting from apraxia of speech (AOS) in an adult with Broca's aphasia. Over a one-month period, two different treatments were given in a counterbalanced procedure: (1) visually-guided biofeedback concerning tongue tip position; and (2) a foil treatment in which a computer program delivered voicing-contrast stimuli for simple repetition. Kinematic and perceptual data suggest substantial and lasting improvement for the [s]/[ʃ] distinction treated by biofeedback. In contrast, the stimuli treated in the foil condition showed only marginal improvement during the therapy session, with performance dropping back to baseline 10 weeks post-treatment. Although preliminary, the findings suggest that visual biofeedback concerning tongue tip position can be used to treat non-speech oral and (to a lesser extent) speech motor behaviour in adults with AOS and Broca's aphasia.

Acknowledgements

This work was supported by an IDEA Program Grant (#97–13) from Texas Instruments. We thank Burkhard Carstens for assistance in developing the biofeedback software and Rebecca Nawy for help in data processing.

References

Blumstein SE (1995) The neurobiology of language. In Miller JL, Eimas PE (eds) Speech, Language, and Communication. San Diego, CA: Academic Press, pp. 339–70.

Goldstein P, Ziegler W, Vogel M, Hoole P (1994) Combined palatal-lift and EPG-feedback therapy in dysarthria: A case study. Clinical Linguistics and Phonetics, 8, 201–18.

Hardcastle WJ, Gibbon F, Jones W (1991) Visual display of tongue-palate contact: Electropalatography in the assessment and remediation of speech disorders. British Journal of Communication Disorders, 26, 41–74.

Rosenbek J, McNeil MR, Aronson A (1984) Apraxia of Speech: Physiology, Acoustics, Linguistics, Management. San Diego, CA: College Hill Press.

Sarno MT (1991) Recovery and rehabilitation in aphasia. In Sarno MT (ed) Acquired Aphasia. San Diego, CA: Academic Press, pp. 521–82.

Square P, Chumpelik D, Adams S (1985) Efficacy of the PROMPT system of therapy for the treatment of acquired apraxia of speech. In Brookshire R (ed) Clinical Aphasiology Conference Proceedings. Minneapolis, MN: BRK Publishers, pp. 319–20.

Square P, Chumpelik D, Morningstar D, Adams S (1986) Efficacy of the PROMPT system of therapy for the treatment of apraxia of speech: A follow-up investigation. In Brookshire R (ed) Clinical Aphasiology Conference Proceedings. Minneapolis, MN: BRK Publishers, pp. 221–6.

Square-Storer P, Hayden D (1989) PROMPT treatment. In Square-Storer P (ed) Apraxia of Speech in Aphasic Adults: Theoretical and Clinical Issues. Hillsdale, NJ: Erlbaum, pp. 190–219.

Volin RA (1991) Microcomputer-based systems providing biofeedback of voice and speech productions. Topics in Language Disorders, 11, 65–79.

Wambaugh JL, Doyle PJ (1992) Treatment for acquired apraxia of speech: A review of efficacy reports. In Lemme ML (ed) Clinical Aphasiology Vol. 22. Austin, TX: Pro-Ed, pp. 231–43

Chapter 29
Palilalia in Progressive Supranuclear Palsy: Failure of the Articulatory Buffer and Subcortical Inhibitory Systems

HELEN GARRATT, KAREN BRYAN and JANE MAXIM

Introduction

Progressive Supranuclear Palsy (PSP) is an acquired degenerative neurological disease. It is one of the 'Parkinson's plus' syndromes that are similar to Parkinson's disease but have additional features. PSP is the second most common cause of parkinsonism after Parkinson's disease. The first clinical report and the original naming of the disease was by Steele, Richardson and Olszewski in 1964. Neuropathology is seen in the basal ganglia, brainstem and cerebellum. Motor speech disturbances are common in PSP and can be the earliest manifestation of the disease (Tolosa et al., 1994) with a pattern of mixed dysarthria, most commonly spastic or hypokinetic dysarthria.

Palilalia is generally accepted as being a speech disorder characterized by 'compulsive repetition of a phrase or word with increasing rapidity and with a decrescendo of voice volume' (Boller et al., 1975) and may be reiteration of a word, phrase or short sentence. The number of times the utterance is reiterated varies, with reports of up to 52 times and with a pattern of decreasing volume and increasing rate (Critchley, 1927; Boller et al., 1975; Ackermann et al., 1989; Yasudo et al., 1990). LaPointe and Horner (1981) and Kent and LaPointe (1982) have described palilalia in the same patient, a 29-year-old man with no firm medical diagnosis. The data showed that 38% of recorded output was reiterated and the highest number of reiterations of a single item was 52. Speech tended to be most severely affected in verbal formulation tasks, and least affected in repetition. The authors suggested that the severity of effect was related to the meaningfulness of the communication. Little consistency was found in palilalia when comparisons were made across five readings of a passage.

Wallesch (1990) suggests that palilalia occurs at a peripheral stage in terms of cognitive models of language processing. However, models of speech production commonly become less explicit towards the end points of speech in specifying input to the articulators themselves (see Levelt (1989, 1991) for discussion of this issue). Levelt and Wheeldon (1994) suggest that, in phonological encoding, the word form is retrieved and is then represented in the form of its syllable structure, which is then associated with the segmental (phonemic) structure. The speaker then accesses a mental syllabary, a store of articulatory phonetic syllable programmes that are detailed enough to guide articulation. The input to the articulatory system is therefore in the form of syllables.

After formulation of a message, it is passed as a phonetic plan to the articulator which executes the phonetic plan but also has access to a storage device: the articulatory buffer which can hold the phonetic plan (the speech motor programme) as it develops. Levelt (1989) suggests that the motor planning units held in the buffer are 'stress groups' i.e. a small phonological phrase that has one stressed element.

The motor programme available to the speaker for articulation can include syllable, word or phrase-sized units. Laver (1980) suggests that the central nervous system handles a stretch of speech as a 'unitary behavioural act'. He suggests that the 'tone group' or 'phonemic clause' could be this 'stretch of speech'. This is a stretch of speech spoken with a single intonation contour. In palilalia, reiteration of syllables, words and phrases can occur. It would therefore appear that units of this size are involved in speech motor processing.

Models of language processing have provided us with a framework to explain how speakers read aloud and repeat. It is known that there are a number of routes available either via the lexicon or via sub-lexical processes which avoid having to access the semantic system. It would seem reasonable to suppose that there is a much lower processing requirement for these tasks and that the modules involved in these tasks would appear to be similar to those requiring automatic processing in Levelt's (1989) model. There are clearly higher processing demands (or at least more modules that need to be accessed) when producing self-formulated speech as opposed to reading aloud or repetition. It therefore seems possible that demands for a greater degree of cognitive processing 'tips the balance' for the palilalic speaker, which may result in greater numbers of palilalic episodes.

Under normal conditions, speakers do not continually reiterate parts of their speech. Information held in the articulatory buffer is passed on and articulated, to be replaced by the next 'chunk'. One possible explanation for reiteration is that speakers with palilalia may have some inability to clear the articulatory buffer of the syllable, word or phrase stored in it; hence the reiteration. In palilalia, another explanation may be that inhibitory action is not effective, and the utterance is therefore repeated over and over again. There is converging evidence from neuroscience research that language production involves a loop via the basal ganglia and ventral thalamus and that reiterative behaviour such as palilalia may reflect disruption of this loop (Wallesch, 1990).

This study considers two research questions: (1) What form does palilalia take in PSP? Is there a common pattern of palilalia across the subjects with PSP, and in which speech tasks will palilalia be more evident? (2) At what level of speech production does palialia occur?

Method

Three subjects with PSP who were also palilalic were assessed on: a test of cognitive status (The Mini Mental State Examination (MMSE) (Folstein et al., 1975)), an orofacial examination, a dysarthria classification, an intelligibility measure and a palilalia assessment consisting of a series of six speech tasks, adapted from LaPointe and Horner (1981). The palilalia assessment consisted of a verbal formulation task ('tell me how you would make a cup of tea'), conversation, picture description, reading aloud (words, non-words, phrases, paragraph), automatic speech and repetition (the same words, non-words and phrases were used as for the reading aloud tasks).

To analyse the palilalic output, the following schema was adapted from LaPointe and Horner (1981) and Horner and Massey (1983): counting the types of reiteration, the number of episodes of reiteration, and the number of reiterations per episode. Seven types of reiteration were observed: sound (s s slice), syllable (fi fi fi fill), word (I like racing racing racing), phrase (put it on the put it on the fire), sound reiteration within a word reiteration (. . . would w . . . would be more accurate), sound reiteration within a phrase reiteration (. . . o . . . on to the on to the cup) and word reiteration within a phrase reiteration (and allow and and allow it to brew).

The overall degree of palilalia was calculated in two ways. First (as in LaPointe and Horner, 1981), the total number of reiterations was divided by the total number of words (Measure 1). Second, the number of episodes was divided by the total number of words minus the number of words that had been reiterated (Measure 2). Measure 1 gives an overall frequency while Measure 2 is a severity rating. Subject SC first reported symptoms in 1990 at the age of 52 years. In 1993 he was described as having dysarthria and palilalia, a down gaze abnormality and minimal akinesia. In 1993 he reported difficulty in thinking of more than one thing at a time and PSP was diagnosed. Neuropsychological assessment showed a verbal IQ of 93 and a performance IQ of 92 on the WAIS, interpreted as reflecting a mild degree of general intellectual deterioration. Visual perception was well preserved with scores of 43/50 on face recognition, 19/20 on fragmented letters and 10/10 on cube analysis. Tests of frontal lobe functioning showed variable performance.

Subject PG presented with micrographia, clumsiness and slowness of the left hand in 1994. In 1995 he was noted to have palilalia, drooling, severe levator inhibition, reduced up and down gaze, a fine postural tremor of the hands, and mild spastic rigidity of the arms and legs. Neuropsychological assessment indicated mild intellectual underfunctioning, and performance was very slow on tasks requiring abstract reasoning. Performance on tests of frontal lobe functioning was reported as unremarkable. An MRI scan in 1995 showed cortical atrophy and decreased size of the dorsal part of the midbrain.

Subject BS had initial symptoms in 1989 of general slowing and diminished facial expression were noted. Medical examination in 1996 reported reduced blinking, except during speech when eye closure was excessive, vertical eye movements appeared slow, tone was increased in the limbs and akinesia of the left limbs was present.

Results

Analysis of palilalia for individual subjects

For subject SC, analysis of palilalia showed that the total number of words produced across all the speech tasks was 526. The total number of reiterative episodes was 37, the total number of reiterations was 61. Using Measure 1, the percentage of output reiterated was 12%, Measure 2 gave 7% of the output involved in reiterative episodes. The pattern of type of reiteration was predominantly phrase reiteration (46%), followed by word (35%), and then by much fewer sound reiterations (11%). Episodes of reiteration by type of reiteration for SC are shown in Table 29.1.

Table 29.1. Reiterations for subject SC

Type of reiteration	No. of episodes	Percentage of total episodes
phrase	17	46
word	13	35
sound	4	11
word within a phrase	3	8

An example of different types of reiteration from SC is '. . . wait for it to steep /unintelligible/ steep then pour the milk pour some milk into a cup / unintelligible / milk into a cup pour the teapot i. . .n into the into the cup . . .". The maximum number of reiterations in an episode was 10 word reiterations of 'no'. The conversation task produced the most reiterations followed by verbal formulation and picture description. Reading aloud and repetition tasks only led to one or two reiterations per task.

For subject PG, analysis of palilalia showed that the total number of words produced across all the speech tasks was 594. The total number of reiterative episodes was 48, the total number of reiterations was 234. Using Measure 1, the percentage of output reiterated was 39%. Using Measure 2, the percentage was 8%. The pattern for type of reiteration for PG revealed equal numbers of word, syllable and sound reiterations, which together accounted for 78% of the total reiteration episodes.

Table 29.2. Reiterations for subject PG

Type of reiteration	No. of episodes	Percentage of total episodes
phrase	7	16
word	12	26
syllable	12	26
sound	12	26
word within a phrase	1	2
sound within a phrase	2	4

Six of the episodes (sound) appeared to be related to difficulty initiating the word e.g. 'fi fi fi fill up the kettle with water put it on the put it on the fire.' The maximum number of reiterations in an episode was 55 reiterations of /p/ at the start of 'people'. The verbal formulation task produced the largest number of reiteration episodes (48%), followed by the conversation task (17%). There were no reiterations in automatic speech.

For subject BS, number of words produced across all the speech tasks was 747. The total number of reiterative episodes was 67, and the total number of reiterations was 75. On both Measures 1 and 2, the percentage of output reiterated was 10%. The pattern for type of reiteration was predominantly word (39%), followed by sound (26%) and by phrase (16%). Episodes of reiteration by type of reiteration for BS are shown in Table 29.3.

Table 29.3. Reiterations for subject BS

Type of reiteration	No. of episodes	Percentage of total episodes
phrase	11	16
word	26	39
syllable	3	4
sound	18	26
word within a phrase	3	4
sound within a phrase	6	9
sound within a word	1	2

The majority of sound reiterations were prolongations, produced with effort and appeared to be related to difficulty initiating the word: '. . . m most of my travelling these days Helen is to is to London and I and I come by train and I and I a . . . and I and I visit one or more customers . . .'. The maximum number of reiterations in an episode was six word reiterations of 'the'. The verbal formulation task produced the most episodes of reiteration (25/67), followed by conversation (20/67) and there were none in the automatic speech task.

Pattern of palilalia across subjects

There are some similarities in the pattern of palilalia between the three subjects but there are also clear differences. All three had more episodes of palilalia on the speech tasks that carried a greater propositional load, i.e. verbal formulation and conversation. All had phrase, word and sound reiterations which occurred at the beginning, middle and end of utterances. The phrase reiterations could be considered to be occurring within 'phonemic clauses'. However, the frequency of the different types of reiteration varied. SC had predominantly phrase reiterations, PG equally word, sound and syllable, and BS predominantly word reiterations. The initial sound of the word reiterated showed a different pattern for each subjects. SC had a greater number of singleton consonants than vowels, PG had all singleton consonants, and BS had nearly equal numbers of singleton consonants and vowels. Although all subjects had instances of sound prolongations and effortful initiation, these were most marked in PG and BS. The severity of the palilalia, indicated by the percentage of the output reiterated (Measure 2), showed little variation (SC 7%, PG 8% and BS 10%).

Discussion

The data from this study support the observation that palilalia is more frequent on tasks involving self formulated or more 'meaningful' speech. All subjects produced the most reiterations on the verbal formulation task. Familiar conversation, picture description and reading a passage appeared less demanding than verbal formulation but still produced a large proportion of reiterations. The degree of processing plays an important part in the degree of palilalia. Palilalia was not observed in 'automatic speech' tasks, and it could be argued that these tasks can be completed without demand on other processing resources. It was predicted that the subjects would make more reiterations on reading non-words than words as the processing demands are higher but subjects made very few errors on word level reading overall. Further assessment with longer and more complex words would be useful.

Extra processing demands appear to 'stress' the damaged motor speech system. While the potential for palilalia is a constant in the damaged system, in tasks requiring less processing, the system is able to inhibit the palilalia. This explanation of palilalia involves a failure of monitoring or, more likely, of inhibition. When questioned, the palilalic speakers in this study were aware that they were palilalic; one subject (PG) made active attempts to stop the palilalia, suggesting that monitoring abilities are still available.

Palilalia was primarily associated with hypokinetic dysarthria in the three subjects here. However, given the mild dysarthria present in these subjects and their ability to form a phonetic plan, it is suggested that palilalia is due to a failure of the speech motor processing system after formation of the phonetic plan, but before the level of muscle action. The most likely level of speech processing for palilalic reiterations is the articulatory buffer or in accessing the buffer. A possible neurological mechanism which may explain reiterations is the failure of sub-cortical inhibitory systems once the utterance begins.

Acknowledgements

Professor Niall Quinn, Dr Andrew Lees and Dr Andrew Churchyard for their help in referring subjects for this study.

References

Ackermann H, Ziegler W, Oertel WH (1989) Palilalia as a symptom of levodopa induced hyperkinesia in Parkinson's disease. Journal of Neurology Neurosurgery and Psychiatry, 52(6), 805–7.

Boller F, Albert M, Denes F (1975) Palilalia. British Journal of Disorders of Communication, 10, 92–7.

Critchley M (1927) On palilalia. Journal of Neurology and Psychopathology, 29, 23–32.

Folstein MF, Folstein SE, McHugh PR (1975) Minimental state: a practical method for grading the cognitive state of patients for the clinician. Journal of Psychiatric Research, 12, 189–98.

Horner J, Massey EW (1983) Progressive dysfluency associated with right hemisphere disease. Brain and Language, 18, 1–85.

Kent RD, LaPointe LL (1982) Acoustic properties of pathologic reiterative utterances: a case study of palilalia. Journal of Speech and Hearing Research, 25, 95–9.

LaPointe LL, Horner J (1981) Palilalia: a descriptive study of pathological reiterative utterances. Journal of Speech and Hearing Disorders, 46, 34–8.

Laver J (1980) Monitoring systems in the neurolinguistic control of speech production. In Fromkin VA (ed.) Errors in Linguistic Performance: Slips of the Tongue, Ear, Pen and Hand. London: Academic Press, 287–305.

Levelt WJM (1989) Speaking from Intention to Articulation. Cambridge, MA: Massachusetts Institute of Technology.

Levelt WJM (1991) Lexical access in speech production: stages versus cascading. In Peters FHM, Hulstijn W, Starkweather CW (eds) Speech Motor Control and Stuttering. Amsterdam: Elsevier.

Levelt WJM, Wheeldon L (1994) Do speakers have access to a mental syllabary? Cognition, 50, 239–69.

Steele JC, Richardson JC, Olszewski J (1964) Progressive supranuclear palsy; a heterogenous degeneration involving the brain stem, basal ganglia and cerebellum with vertical gaze and pseudobulbar palsy, trunchal dystonia and dementia. Archives of Neurology, 10, 333–59.

Tolosa E, Valleoriola F and Marti MJ (1994) Clinical diagnosis and diagnostic criteria of progressive supranuclear palsy (Steele-Richardson-Olszewski syndrome). In Tolosa E, Duvoisin R and Cruz-Sánchez (eds) Progressive Supranuclear Palsy: Diagnosis, Pathology and Treatment. New York: Springer-Verlag.

Wallesch CW (1990) Repetitive verbal behaviour: functional and neurological considerations. Aphasiology, 4, 133–54.

Yasuda Y, Akiguchi I, Ino M, Nabatabe H, Kameyama M (1990) Paramedian thalamic and midbrain infarcts associated with palilalia. Journal of Neurology Neurosurgery and Psychiatry, 53, 797–9.

Chapter 30 Acoustic Analysis of Coarticulation in Cerebellar Dysarthria

INGO HERTRICH and HERMANN ACKERMANN

Introduction

At least partially, coarticulation simply reflects biomechanical constraints of the speech motor system (Bell-Berti and Harris, 1981). In addition, however, motor planning (Whalen, 1990) and, at an even higher level, phonetic or phonological processing (Archangeli, 1988; Keating, 1988; Kohler, 1991; Lahiri and Jongman, 1990) seem to contribute to the context-dependent shaping of the acoustic signal.

It is unsettled so far which components of the central nervous system (CNS) control these various coarticulation effects. Studies of patients with circumscript brain damage or diseases restricted to a single functional CNS system provide a feasible approach to address this issue. Impaired anticipatory coarticulation has been documented in at least a subgroup of patients with apraxia of speech (AOS), a disorder usually attributed to a lesion of the anterior perisylvian language zone (Ziegler and von Cramon, 1985, 1986; Southwood et al., 1997). Ziegler and von Cramon considered deficient timing of the onset of a target gesture to be the relevant pathomechanism. However, other authors (e.g. Katz et al., 1990) emphasized articulatory distortions within the spatial domain. Apart from a few descriptive studies (Kent and Netsell, 1975; Netsell and Kent, 1976), systematic studies of coarticulation in other CNS lesions or disease processes are not yet available.

Besides dysphonia, cerebellar dysarthria comprises laboured and imprecise articulation, decreased speech rate, slowed orofacial movements, and a scanning speech rhythm (for a review see Cannito and Marquardt, 1997). First, this speech disorder may give rise to prolonged transition times due to slowed motor performance and, thus, increases perseverative coarticulation. However, reduced speech tempo, target undershoot, and 'scanning' speech rhythm may counteract these effects by reducing the quantitative influences of a target category on the acoustic properties of surrounding segments. Second, several lines of evidence indicate a contribution of the cerebellum to speech timing (Kent et al., 1979; Kent and Rosenbek, 1982; Ackermann and Hertrich, 1994, 1997; Ackermann et al., 1997). Assuming that delayed anticipatory coarticulation in AOS represents a timing deficit, deviant anticipatory coarticulation might be expected in ataxic dysarthria as well. In order to further elucidate the contribution of the cerebellum to coarticulation, the present study determined anticipatory vowel-to-vowel (VV), anticipatory vowel-to-consonant (CV), perseverative vowel-to-consonant (VC), as well as perseverative VV effects in ataxic subjects and in a control group.

Acoustic analysis of coarticulation has relied on a variety of approaches so far. Besides visual inspection of spectrograms (Öhman, 1966), algorithms have been developed to extract formants using linear predictive coding (LPC) concomitant with a decision logic. However, the validity of small differences in formant values with respect to coarticulation effects must be questioned. First, the number and frequencies of obtained formants largely depend on system parameter settings; second, the formant structure does not provide an exhaustive image of the overall spectral energy distribution; and in the presence of continuous formant trajectories crossing each other, third, logical numbering of formants is inconsistent with respect to vocal tract resonances (Schwartz et al., 1993). Therefore, the present study used averaged fast Fourier transform (FFT) spectra. FFT analysis is applicable to vowels as well as to consonants and, in contrast to LPC, does not imply any model assumptions with respect to source and filtering processes. Squared difference spectra were used as an estimate of coarticulation effects.

Methods

Participants

Nine individuals with cerebellar atrophy (CA; 5 female, 4 male; aged 30–68 years) and eleven healthy controls (NC; 7 female, 4 male; aged 26–73 years) participated in the present study. All cerebellar subjects had an ataxic syndrome comprising oculomotor disturbances, speech motor deterioration, and dyscoordination of voluntary upper and lower limb movements; none showed any signs of extracerebellar motor deficits, impaired somatosensory functions, or cognitive decline at clinical examination. Diagnosis was further confirmed by means of nuclear magnetic resonance imaging (MRI).

Speech material and procedure

The speech material comprised, among others, three nonsense words of the type [g̊ət^h]-V-[t^{h}ə] (V = [ɑ], [i], [u]) embedded into the German carrier phrase 'Ich habe $ge_1t_1Vt_2e_2$ gelesen'. Representing, first, the nucleus of the focus syllable and, second, a non-redundant phonological item within the series of stimuli, the three target vowels must be assigned a prominent position within the test sentences. In order to elicit these utterances, the target words, printed in bold letters on separate cards, were displayed 10 times each in randomized order. To account for group differences in speech rate, the control subjects were asked to produce 10 additional repetitions at a slowed speech rate. Subjects' utterances were recorded on a DAT tape (recorder PCM 2000, microphone C-48, Sony, Japan) in a sound-treated booth.

Data analysis and statistics

Using the Computerized Speech Lab CSL 4300 (Kay Elemetrics, USA), averaged FFT spectra were computed ('LTA' function of the CSL 4300 including higher-frequency preemphasis, Hamming window, 128-point FFT, frame length = 6.4 ms, frequency resolution = 156.25 Hz) from the intervals e1, t1, V, t2, and e2. Figure 30.1 displays the respective segments (for details see Hertrich and Ackermann, 1995). Each spectrum comprised 64 values corresponding to the intensity (in dB) of the respective frequency bands (B1 to B64) up to 10 kHz on a linear frequency scale. Altogether, 9 (subjects) x 5 (intervals) x 3 (targets) x 10 (repetitions) = 1350 averaged spectra were obtained from the CA group and 11 (subjects) x 5 (intervals) x 3 (targets) x 10 (repetitions) x 2 (speech rates) = 3300 from the controls.

After normalization of each spectrum for absolute sound intensity by subtracting its mean dB value from all bands, spectra were averaged across repetitions. As a measure of spectral dissimilarity induced by the different target vowel categories, squared differences ($D_{a\text{-}i}$, $D_{a\text{-}u}$, $D_{i\text{-}u}$) were calculated across the spectral bands B2 to B40 (frequency range 300–6000 Hz), for example:

$$D_{a\text{-}i} = \frac{1}{39} \sum_{j=2}^{40} (B_{aj} - B_{ij})^2 \qquad \{j = 2 \text{ to } 40\}\ ;$$

B_{aj}, B_{ij} = dB value of the frequency band j of a spectrum derived from a test item with target [ɑ] and [i], respectively; $D_{a\text{-}i}$ = squared distance between two spectra of homologous sounds corresponding to different target categories (e.g. the distance between the schwa preceding [ɑ] and the schwa preceding [i]).

These three distances, representing the three possible comparisons among the target vowel types [ɑ], [i], and [u], were collapsed to the measure:

$$D = \sqrt{D_{a\text{-}i} + D_{a\text{-}u} + D_{i\text{-}u}}.$$

The D-values obtained from the five considered segments (i.e. D_{e1}, D_{t1}, D_V, D_{t2}, D_{e2}) provide estimates of overall target-induced coarticulation.

As an objective parameter of speaking rate, in addition, the interval from vowel onset of the first to the offset of the final syllable of the target word was measured (*wordur*; see Figure 30.1).

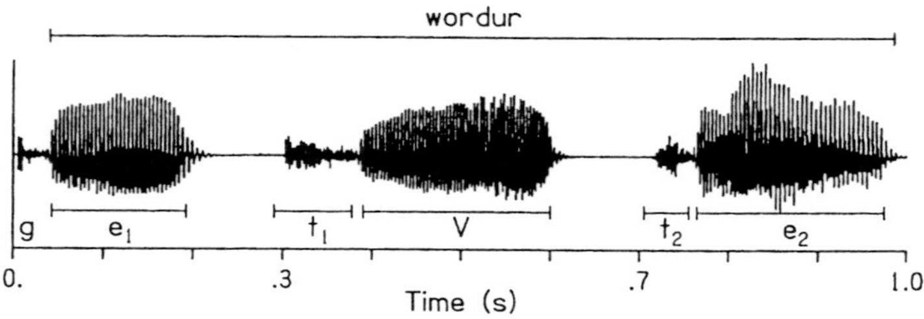

Figure 30.1. Acoustic signal of the target word 'getate' [g̊ətʰɑtʰə] produced by a cerebellar patient: Horizontal bars indicate word duration (*wordur*) and the five intervals for spectral analysis (e1, t1, V, t2, e2).

Results

As a test for overall differences in coarticulation between the cerebellar and the control subjects, a multivariate analysis was performed with the four spectral distance measures D_{e1}, D_{t1}, D_{t2}, and D_{e2} as dependent variables. GROUP {CA, NC} was considered the independent factor, and word duration (*wordur*) a covariate to statistically control for speech rate. A significant group effect emerged (Wilks' Lambda = 0.6427; $F(2,25) = 3.475$; $p < 0.05$). Furthermore, the coefficients of the canonical function related to the group effect differed in sign, indicating discrepancies in the direction of the various coarticulation effects. Using univariate ANOVAs, subsequent analysis considered the four coarticulation effects as well as the effect of the target category on the target spectra themselves. The group means are displayed in Figure 30.2.

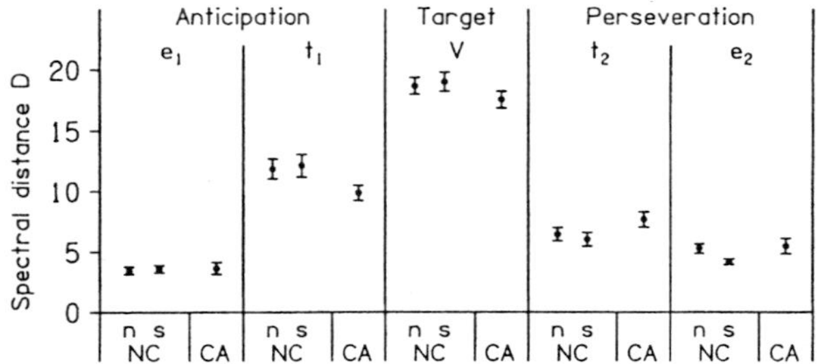

Figure 30.2. Groups means with standard errors of the target-induced spectral distance D for the five segments considered (e1, t1, V, t2, e2); n = normal rate; s = slow conditions; CA = cerebellar group; NC = controls.

Target vowel

As expected, the most pronounced effect of the target category refers to the spectra of the target vowels themselves (D_V). There was a tendency towards reduced D_V values in the ataxic group as compared with the controls (mid-panel of Figure 30.2).

Anticipatory VV effects

No remarkable group differences emerged with respect to anticipatory VV coarticulation (D_{e1}; leftmost panel of Figure 30.2; $p > 0.1$). Within the control group, D_{e1} did not significantly correlate with *wordur* ($p > 0.1$).

Anticipatory CV effects

The cerebellar group had a tendency ($p < 0.1$) toward lower D_{t1} values than the controls (Figure 30.2, second panel from the left). Within the control group, the correlations between *wordur* and D_{t1} ($r = -0.19$) failed significance ($p > 0.1$). Visual inspection of the spectra revealed the most consistent effect in the control group to be reduced intensity in the lower frequency bands of the stop consonant t1 preceding target [i]. This aspect of coarticulation seems to be less pronounced in the cerebellar group.

Perseverative VV effects

As concerns the strength of perseverative VV coarticulation, the control group exhibited a negative correlation between *wordur* and the spectral distance D_{e2} ($r = -0.60$, $p < 0.01$). In order to control for this systematic influence of speaking rate, *wordur* was used as a covariate in the tests for group effects. This analysis yielded significantly higher D_{e2} values in the CA group as compared with the controls ($F_{GROUP} = 4.69$, $p < 0.05$; Figure 30.2, rightmost panel).

Perseverative VC effects

Perseverative VC and perseverative VV coarticulation showed by a similar relation between the subject groups (Figure 30.2, second panel from right). However, the group comparisons failed significance for perseverative VC effects and, therefore, can be considered a tendency only.

Discussion

The present study revealed the degree of anticipatory VV coarticulation to vary across subjects, uncompromised by cerebellar dysfunctions and independent of speaking rate. Conceivably, this effect has to be understood in terms of a pre-motor representation of acoustic goals rather than low-level timing relations of articulatory gestures. The suggestion of preplanned structures rather than simple temporal overlap is also confirmed by the language-specific nature of these phenomena (Boyce, 1990; Manuel, 1990).

The ataxic patients of the present study seem to differ from the apraxic speaker described by Ziegler and von Cramon (1985, 1986a) with respect to anticipatory VV coarticulation. However, no definite conclusions can be drawn considering, first, the small number of individuals with apraxia of speech so far analysed and, second, the large inter-subject variability of VV coarticulation.

The strength of anticipatory CV effects was slightly reduced in the cerebellar group as compared with the controls at either speech rate instruction. Conceivably, these findings reflect the reduced distinctness of the three target sounds. Since speech rate did not influence anticipatory CV coarticulation, this effect may also arise from segment-linked planning.

In spite of reduced distinctness of the three target vowels, the ataxic speakers showed significantly increased perseverative VV effects as far as speech rate was taken into account statistically. A similar tendency was observed with respect to VC effects. Previous studies revealed slowed motor execution to represent a core feature of cerebellar dysarthria (Kent and Netsell, 1975; Ackermann et al., 1995). Perceptually, ataxic speech has been characterized as laboured and imprecise. Conceivably, the partial persistence of former targets into the following segments contributes to this impression. As concerns the strength of perseverative coarticulation effects, slow ataxic speakers were comparable to fast-speaking controls. These findings indicate perseverative coarticulation to be closely linked to the time available for the execution of articulatory gestures. Articulatory slowness may be inevitable in ataxic dysarthria, because it does not seem possible to improve ataxic speech without further slowing of speech rate (Simmons, 1983; Yorkston et al., 1990). The slow, scanning speech rhythm of cerebellar subjects, thus, might be an adjustment to avoid perceptual deterioration of speech by keeping perseverative coarticulation within the range of fast-speaking healthy subjects.

Summary

The present study investigated acoustic aspects of coarticulation in nine ataxic patients suffering from cerebellar atrophy and a control group. The test material consisted of three different target words ([g̊ət^h]-V-[t^{h}ə]; V = [ɑ], [i], [u]) embedded into a carrier sentence. Quantification of coarticulation effects of V on the surrounding [ə] and [t^h] segments relied on computation of the squared distances between averaged FFT spectra. In order to account for group differences in speech rate, the controls additionally produced the test sentences under a slow-speaking instruction. Anticipatory [ə]-to-V coarticulation turned out to vary across subjects, in the absence of significant effects of speech rate or cerebellar dysfunction. As compared with the controls, the cerebellar subjects showed slightly reduced anticipatory [t^h]-to-V coarticulation effects. Presumably, this effect can be explained by reduced distinctness of the three target vowels in the patient group. Perseverative V-to-[t^h] and V-to-[ə] coarticulation tended to be increased in the cerebellar group after correction for slowed speech rate. The results suggest a principal asymmetry of coarticulation mechanisms with higher-level processes underlying anticipatory and low-level motor phenomena accounting for perseverative effects.

References

Ackermann H, Gräber S, Hertrich I, Daum I (1997) Categorical speech perception in cerebellar disorders. Brain and Language, 60, 323–31.

Ackermann H, Hertrich I (1994) Speech rate and rhythm in cerebellar dysarthria: An acoustic analysis of syllabic timing. Folia Phoniatrica et Logopaedica, 46, 70–8.

Ackermann H, Hertrich I (1997) Voice onset time in ataxic dysarthria. Brain and Language, 56, 321–33.

Ackermann H, Hertrich I, Scharf G (1995) Kinematic analysis of lower lip movements in ataxic dysarthria. Journal of Speech and Hearing Research, 38, 1252–9.

Archangeli D (1988) Aspects of underspecification theory. Phonology, 5, 183–207.

Bell-Berti F, Harris KS (1981) A temporal model of speech production. Phonetica, 38, 9–20.

Boyce SE (1990) Coarticulatory organization for lip rounding in Turkish and English. Journal of the Acoustical Society of America, 88, 3584–95.

Cannito MP, Marquardt TP (1997) Ataxic dysarthria. In McNeil MR (ed.) Clinical management of sensorimotor speech disorders. New York: Thieme, pp. 217–47.

Hertrich I, Ackermann H (1995) Coarticulation in slow speech: durational and spectral analysis. Language and Speech, 38, 159–87.

Katz W, Machetanz J, Orth U, Schönle P (1990) A kinematic analysis of anticipatory coarticulation in the speech of anterior aphasic subjects using electromagnetic articulography. Brain and Language, 38, 555–75.

Keating PA (1988) Underspecification in phonetics. Phonology, 5, 275–92.

Keele SW, Ivry R (1990) Does the cerebellum provide a common computation for diverse tasks? A timing hypothesis. Annals of the New York Academy of Sciences, 608, 179–211.

Kent R, Netsell R (1975) A case study of an ataxic dysarthric: cineradiographic and spectrographic observations. Journal of Speech and Hearing Disorders, 40, 115–34.

Kent RD, Netsell R, Abbs JH (1979) Acoustic characteristics of dysarthria associated with cerebellar disease. Journal of Speech and Hearing Research, 22, 627–48.

Kent RD, Rosenbek JC (1982) Prosodic disturbance and neurologic lesion. Brain and Language, 11, 259–91.

Kohler KJ (1991) The phonetics/phonology issue in the study of articulatory reduction. Phonetica, 48, 180–92.

Lahiri A, Jongman A (1990) Intermediate level of analysis: features or segments. Journal of Phonetics, 18, 435–43.

Manuel SY (1990) The role of contrast in limiting vowel-to-vowel coarticulation in different languages. Journal of the Acoustical Society of America, 88, 1286–98.

Netsell R, Kent RD (1976) Paroxysmal ataxic dysarthria. Journal of Speech and Hearing Disorders, 41, 93–109.

Öhman SEG (1966) Coarticulation in VCV utterances: spectrographic measurements. Journal of the Acoustical Society of America, 39, 151–68.

Schwartz J-L, Beautemps D, Abry C, Escudier P (1993) Inter-individual and cross-linguistic strategies for the production of the [i] vs. [y] contrast. Journal of Phonetics, 21, 411–25.

Simmons NN (1983) Acoustic analysis of ataxic dysarthria: An approach to monitoring treatment. In Berry WR (ed.) Clinical Dysarthria. San Diego: College-Hill, pp. 283–94.

Southwood MH, Dagenais PA, Sutphin SM, Garcia JM (1997) Coarticulation in apraxia of speech: a perceptual, acoustic and electropalatographic study. Clinical Linguistics and Phonetics, 11, 179–203.

Whalen DH (1990) Coarticulation is largely planned. Journal of Phonetics, 18, 3–35.

Yorkston KM, Hammen VL, Beukelman DR, Traynor CD (1990) The effect of rate control on the intelligibility and naturalness of dysarthric speech. Journal of Speech and Hearing Disorders, 55, 550–60.

Ziegler W, von Cramon D (1985) Anticipatory coarticulation in a patient with apraxia of speech. Brain and Language, 26, 117–30.

Ziegler W, von Cramon D (1986a) Disturbed coarticualation in apraxia of speech: Acoustic evidence. Brain and Language, 29, 34–47.

Ziegler W, von Cramon D (1986b) Timing deficits in apraxia of speech. European Archives of Psychiatry and Neurological Sciences, 236, 44–9.

PART IV

Methods in Clinical Linguistics

Chapter 31
What the Neurologist can Contribute to Diagnosis and Therapy in Speech Pathology

WO RENIER

Introduction

In our society, communication is based largely on verbal signs and language symbols. The development of this communication system is unique to the human species. Speech is composed in the normal condition by a cooperation in harmony between hearing, language comprehension, cognition, planning of speech, respiration, voice and articulation. At all levels (kinesthetic, auditory, visual, emotional, cognitive) the nervous system contributes to the language-speech cascade process. Pathology of the nervous system can have deleterious effects on this process. Knowledge of the structure, development and functioning of the nervous system gives a better insight in speech and language pathology and in the possibilities and impossibilities of therapy. Because language is considered to act as a model for other cerebral functions in men, it is still important and interesting to study its biological and genetic basis, especially in the view of the new developments in functional neuro-imaging (magnetic resonance imaging, positron emission tomography, single photon emission tomography), neurophysiology (electroencephalography, magnetoencephalography, evoked potentials) and clinical genetics (chromosomal and DNA-analysis).

The study of the relation between language disorders and brain lesions goes back to the beginning of the nineteenth century. The observations, arguments and opinions reported in these early papers are still crucially important. These pioneers were neuropsychiatrists interested in the relation between brain and behaviour. As clinicians, they observed the mental and motor behaviour of their patients, sometimes over many years and from the later findings at autopsy they developed a concept on the organization of speech comprehension and production. From the beginning there were proponents and opponents of the localization theory: those who believed that brain functions can be precisely localized and others, who considered that the massive inter-neural connections render attempts at precise localization meaningless (Eling, 1994). In recent years, there is a gradual emergence of the opinion that both theories are complementary and that a more rigorous methodological approach is needed both in neurology and in clinical psychology. Every scientific theory is a child of the prevailing fundamental scientific trend of its era. The interdependence of general ideological and special scientific theories is particularly strong in the theories about nature and dynamics of language. This, also, is reflected in the theories of aphasia (Bay, 1969).

Within the concept of a dynamic view on the central nervous system, more hierarchical and age-dependent levels of information processing have been proposed. Primary motor and sensory areas, primary and secondary association areas and uni-, poly- and supramodal association areas in the cortex have been described (Pandya and Seltzer, 1982; Mesulam, 1983). The myelination rate determines when these areas are functional. It is necessary that the cortex and its connections are intact for normal information processing (Renier, 1985). Extrapolations from theories about the nature of aphasia in adults contribute little to the understanding of children's speech and language disorders. In the developing brain, neuropsychological functions are less well developed and localized. The symptomatology of neuropsychological disorders is closely related to the period of structural and functional development of the nervous system. The impact of plasticity in recovery is much larger in the very young than in the adult brain. Brain maturation follows a posterior-anterior direction or receptive-expressive time schedule. The pyramidal cells of the cerebral cortex are among the most complex nerve cells to have developed in the course of evolution. In particular, the first three years of maturation are very important. Lack of stimulation in the first years can have deleterious effects as unactivated synapses atrophy. Developmental speech disorders can be expressed at different levels and are age dependent (Bannatyne 1976; Rapin, 1982; Grunwell, 1990; Locke, 1990).

Looking at the central nervous system the neurologist tries to have insight in input, transformation and output of information and in the quality of the different systems involved. At the input side, hearing and visual perception of gestures and facial expression are primary in the language-speech cascade. Maturation and quality of the brain systems and their mutual cooperation determine the quantity and quality of the information that can be processed. The developmental and medical history of the patient can point to risk factors for the development of an encephalopathy. However, one should be careful in the interpretation of emotionally coloured information concerning delivery and birth and other traumatic events. An objectively determined dysmaturity (too low birth weight for age) or other acquired brain lesion has a great predictability for later dysfunctioning. Family history is of utmost value for evaluating genetic factors for speech and language impairment. By a careful neurological examination, the neurologist searches for dysfunctioning of the neurological in- and output systems (functioning of cranial nerves, pyramidal, extrapyramidal (hypo- or dyskinetic), cerebellar, or neuromuscular signs and symptoms). In close cooperation with the psychologist, the cognitive, emotional and attentional profile of the patient is mapped. Adjuvant techniques (neuroimaging, neurophysiology, neurogenetics and neurochemistry) complete the search for a possible etiology and prognosis of the neurological findings.

Speech and language disorders may be the expression of a restricted lesion in the classical speech-language areas of the brain, but can also be part of a larger or diffuse brain damage or of a syndrome. In traditional aphasiology, language is situated in the cerebral cortex. However, the cortex is not an isolated organ. There is a thalamo-cortical circuit that permanently interacts. That can explain why aphasia in thalamic lesions can resemble aphasia of cortical origin (van Lieshout et al., 1990).

In individual cases, diagnosing cerebral pathology does not necessarily predict type and severity of the neuropsychological dysfunction. Language disorders do not respect linguistic boundaries and typically more than one function is impaired. Different language aspects vary in their vulnerability to disruption. Phonology is the most vulnerable, next syntax and morphology, then semantics and finally comprehension being the least vulnerable.

Depending on the neurological system that is dysfunctioning, one can observe pyramidal, extrapyramidal (hypo- or dyskinetic), cerebellar, or neuromuscular elements in speech (Renier, 1979). Pronunciation acquisition involves concurrent development on levels ranging from the most central linguistic to the most peripheral or motoric. In dysarthrias, differentiating between these conditions can be problematic and can be complicated by the coexistence of pathology at different levels.

Until now the only unexplained speech disorder is the mutism occurring after surgical intervention on or trauma of the nervous structures in the posterior fossa and especially of the dopaminergic ascending system. Specific syndromes associated with speech disorders are well known in child neurology. A 'cocktail party speech syndrome' may be observed in patients with a hydrocephalus. Intellectual sequelae in non-obstructive hydrocephalus can be predicted by looking at the time of onset of speech (Op Heij et al., 1985).

In mental retardation, qualitative and quantitative abnormalities of the micro-architecture of the cortex at the synaptic level can help in explaining poor information processing by a macroscopically normal-looking brain. In some mental retardation syndromes (Angelman syndrome, Rett syndrome, mental retardation with lissencephaly, mental retardation with severe microcephaly), lack of speech is part of the syndrome and has consequences for treatment strategies (Renier et al., 1982; Laan et al., 1996).

More than one hundred years ago, Gowers stated that 'epilepsy is the great teacher' for neurologists. The epileptic discharges create a unique condition of transient brain dysfunction. Patients with left temporal lobe epilepsy have been described as showing the worst performance on the phonemic cued recall, poor performances on the delayed free recall and relatively intact performance on the semantic cued recall (Mungas et al., 1985). Naming problems are more prevalent with posterior than with anterior left temporal electroencephalographic abnormalities (Mayeux et al., 1980). In contrast to left-hemisphere lesions, right-hemisphere lesions produce profound alterations of functions that depend on visuospatial skills, directed attention, modulation of affect and paralinguistic aspects of communication, but also emotional and interpersonal difficulties and shyness (Weintraub and Mesulam, 1983). Unusual seizure disorders, particularly those originating from the frontal and temporal lobes, may account for part or all of speech and language disorders in patients with epilepsy. Regression of language skills is characteristic of intractable epilepsies of childhood. In the Landau-Kleffner syndrome or the acquired epileptic aphasia in childhood, verbal agnosia has an intriguing relation with a disturbed sleep-EEG pattern in childhood (Renier, 1993).

Many authors writing about language skills have commented that in some linguistic skills, there are small, often significant differences between males and females. Especially in the field of reading disabilities, auditory discrimination, hearing, verbal fluency, speech disorders and social immaturity, boys predominate. Females are superior to males in various automatic language skills, but this sex difference is not true for the conceptualizing aspects of linguistic content. Hormonal influence can be one of the determining factors. In general, endocrine pathology can threaten the mental state of a person. Neurons in many brain areas have been found to have highly specific receptors for hormonal substances. As the brain is no exception to the biological rule of inheritance, it is highly likely that many genes must contribute to the complex psychoneurophysiological structure of language. A verbal factor linked to the X-chromosome has been suggested (Lehrke, 1968; Renier et al., 1983).

Patients with disturbed speech and/or language and their families want a diagnosis, an estimate of prognosis and advice about management. Before any attempt to elaborate a cure and/or care programme for the speech disorder, a full neurological assessment and as precise a possible diagnosis are required. The therapeutic perspective is determined by the neuropathological substrate. The results of the neurological and neuropsychological investigations have to be explained as clearly as possible, but with care in the interpretation of the neurological, neuroimaging and neurophysiological findings.

Concerning treatment strategies, more individual instead of standard therapy is claimed. Therapy can consist of medication or exceptionally of neurosurgery in some cases. A critical attitude is obligatory when evaluating effectiveness of speech therapy. Some clinicians question if speech therapy is of any help. They believe in the spontaneous all or not complete recovery. In their opinion, speech therapy is more of psychological importance by stimulation and support. The current clinical opinion is that therapeutic nihilism has no place, especially when the patient is relatively young. Particularly in the very young child with speech delay, professional help can prevent psychosocial maladaptation. Training of other impaired functions in aphasic patients is still a matter of debate. Search for familial traits is of most interest, especially in specific speech and language disorders in children. However, the genetic expression in a family can be variable.

In conclusion, the contribution of the neurologist in a multidisciplinary approach of speech and language disorders is one of explaining the biological and genetic background and of giving therapeutic advice based on the neurological diagnosis. However, the neurologist should be aware that a lesion in a specific area of the cortex can cause disturbances in different functional systems and that problems with complex skills are not always explained by a simple local anomaly of the nervous system or by one specific anatomo-physiologic system. When looking for more insight into the relation between brain and behaviour, study in depth of individual cases by a multidisciplinary approach has advantages over lumping cases with more or less identical pathology.

References

Bannatyne A (1976) Language, Reading and Learning Disabilities. Psychology, Neuropsychology, Diagnosis and Remediation, 3th edition. Springfield, IL: Charles C Thomas.

Bay E (1969) Modern problems of aphasiology. Nederlands Tijdschrift voor Geneeskunde, 113, 314–19.

Eling P (ed.) (1994) Reader in the History of Aphasia. Classics in Psycholinguistics, vol.4. Amsterdam/ Philadelphia: John Benjamins Publishing Company.

Grunwell P (ed.) (1990) Developmental Speech Disorders. Edinburgh: Churchill Livingstone.

Laan LAEM, den Boer ATh, Hennekam RCM, Renier WO, Brouwer OF (1996) Angelman syndrome in adulthood. American Journal of Medical Genetics, 66, 356–60.

Lehrke RG (1968) Sex-linked mental retardation and verbal disability. Minneapolis, MN: Report to the Minnesota Association for Retarded Children.

Locke JL (1990) Structure and stimulation in the ontogeny of spoken language. Developmental Psychobiology, 23, 621–43.

Mayeux R, Brandt J, Rosen J, Benson DF (1980) Interictal memory and language impairment in temporal lobe epilepsy. Neurology, 30, 120–5.

Mesulam MM (1983) The functional anatomy and hemispheric specialization for directed attention; the role of the parietal lobe and its connectivity. Trends in Neurosciences, 6, 384–7.

Mungas D, Ehlers C, Walton N, Mc Cutchen (1985) Verbal learning differences in epileptic patients with left and right temporal lobe foci. Epilepsia, 26, 340–5.

Op Heij CPMO, Renier WO, Gabreëls FJM (1985)Intellectual sequelae of primary non-obstructive hydrocephalus in infancy: Analysis of 50 cases. Clinical Neurology and Neurosurgery, 87, 247–53.

Pandya DN, Seltzer B (1982) Association areas of the cerebral cortex. Trends in Neurosciences, 386–90.

Rapin I (1982) Children with Brain Dysfunction. Raven Press, New York.

Renier WO (1979) Taalontwikkeling bij neuromotorisch gestoorde kinderen (Language development in children with neuromotor disabilities). Tijdschrift voor Logopedie en Audiologie 4, 145–55.

Renier WO (1985) Neurologische aspecten van dyslexie (Neurological aspects of dyslexia). In van der Leij A, Stevens LM (eds) Dyslexie. Lisse: Swets and Zeitlinger, pp. 11–20.

Renier WO (1993) Het syndroom van Landau en Kleffner: de verworven epileptische afasie op kinderleeftijd (The Landau-Kleffner syndrome: the acquired epileptic aphasia in childhood). Epicare, 1993; 2, 12–20.

Renier WO, Gabreëls FJM, Jaspar HHJ, Hustinx TWJ, Geelen JAG, van Haelst UJG (1982) An X-linked syndrome with microcephaly, severe mental retardation, spasticity, epilepsy and deafness. Journal of Mental Deficiency Research, 26, 27–40.

Renier WO, Smeets DFCM, Scheres JMJC, Hustinx TWJ, Hulsmans CFC, Op Heij CPMO, Bomers AJAM, Gabreëls FJM (1983) The Martin-Bell syndrome: a psychological, logopaedic and cytogenetic study of two affected brothers. Journal of Mental Deficiency Research, 27, 51–9.

van Lieshout P, Renier W, Eling P, de Bot K, Slis I (1990) Bilateral language processing after a lesion in the left thalamic and temporal regions. Brain and Language, 38, 173–94.

Weintraub S, Mesulam MM (1983) Developmental learning disabilities of right hemisphere. Archives of Neurology, 40, 463–8.

Chapter 32
Clinical Computational Corpus Linguistics: A Case Study

MICHAEL R PERKINS, ROBERTA CATIZONE, IAN PEERS and YORICK WILKS

Introduction

This paper shows what can be gained by combining the methods and insights of clinical linguistics, corpus linguistics and computational linguistics. Although a great deal has been learned in recent years from the creation and analysis of large electronic corpora of natural language, attempts to extend such approaches to the study of disordered language have hardly begun. We briefly review below the progress made so far in the computational analysis of disordered corpora. A major limitation of all such approaches to date is the amount of time-consuming manual analysis required before computational analysis can take place. In the next part of the paper we present findings from a research project, based on a 65 000-word corpus of aphasic discourse, which addresses this limitation by focusing on devising a set of computational analytical tools which entirely eliminates manual analysis.

Approaches to the characterization of language disorders

Until relatively recently the principal way of characterizing pathologies of language has been in terms of anatomy, physiology and neurology – the so-called 'medical model'. Wernicke's aphasia and Broca's aphasia, for example, are named after a part of the brain which has sustained damage. An alternative approach which has made a great deal of progress over the last two decades or so is to focus instead on the patient's linguistic behaviour – the so-called 'behavioural model'. The labels 'fluent aphasia' and 'non-fluent aphasia', for example, are commonly used to subclassify aphasia in terms of its linguistic manifestations. Although linguistic behaviour is clearly neurologically based, our ability to identify causal links between, say, the production of a specific linguistic structure and some underlying neurological event is still extremely limited in spite of recent technological developments in brain imaging. For the time being, then, although the ultimate aim is to integrate both linguistic and neurological information, one of the main concerns of clinical linguists is to establish a typology of communication disorders based on their linguistic characteristics (Perkins and Howard, 1995). In order to achieve this, an extensive range of corpora of disordered language is essential.

Computational corpus linguistics

Over the last few years, important advances have been made in developing computer techniques for the analysis of large electronic corpora of natural language. This has led to a major increase in our understanding of a wide range of characteristics of normal language based, for example, on lexical and structural frequency and distribution and lexical collocation and concordances. However, in contrast to the proliferating number of multi-million word electronic corpora of normal language now available, there are virtually no machine-readable disordered language corpora currently in the public domain and those that do exist consist of no more than a few thousand words (Perkins, 1995). Nevertheless, as we hope to show here, the creation of large corpora of disordered language could have an enormous impact on linguistic and medical research.

Because of the paucity of corpora of disordered language, there have consequently been few computational tools specifically devised for their analysis. In those that do exist (e.g. CLEAR (Computerized Language Error Analysis Report) (Baker-van den Goorbergh and Baker, 1991), Computerized Profiling (Long and Fey, 1994), SALT (Systematic Analysis of Language Transcripts) (Miller and Chapman, 1982-1995)) computational procedures play only a secondary role. They are primarily used to collate data which have already been transcribed and coded by hand. In short, computational analysis of disordered language-corpora is barely in its infancy and future developments will require both the creation of much larger machine-readable corpora as well as the development of more sophisticated software to analyse them. In the next section we outline a project which begins to address these requirements.

Use of automatic processing methods to characterize fluent versus non-fluent aphasic discourse

As an illustration of the kinds of insights offered by what might be termed 'Clinical Computational Corpus Linguistics' (CCCL) we describe here some findings from a research project designed to investigate to what extent the spontaneous conversation of people with fluent aphasia

(FL) can be characterized and distinguished from that of people with non-fluent aphasia (NF), and also from that of an unimpaired interlocutor (R) on the basis of a limited set of characteristics. One aim of the project was to see to what extent it was possible to characterize the groups using only automated procedures, i.e. without any manual analysis of the data. A second aim was to see whether the FL and NF aphasics could be characterized as distinct and homogeneous groups on the basis of the linguistic characteristics used in the analysis and to what extent the groupings agreed with the diagnosis of the therapist. Our specific research questions were:

- Can FL and NF groups be distinguished on the basis of the linguistic characteristics of their spontaneous conversation alone?
- Which automated measures – either alone or in combination – are most effective in this regard?
- To what extent are the conversational characteristics of a normal interlocutor differentially affected when talking to the FL and NF groups and can these characteristics also be used as measures for distinguishing the groups?

Method

The corpus used consists of approximately 65 000 words of natural conversation between 20 aphasic individuals and a researcher (Perkins and Varley, 1996). Each of the aphasic individuals, 10 of whom had been diagnosed as 'fluent aphasics' (FL) by a speech and language therapist and 10 as 'non-fluent aphasics' (NF), spoke to the researcher (R) for 30 minutes. The conversation was initiated by R, who asked the aphasic person to describe how his or her illness had occurred and subsequently evolved naturally. Each session was transcribed and stored as a computer text file. The measures used in the analysis were chosen on the grounds that (1) the aphasiology literature suggested that they were likely to differentiate NF from FL aphasia and (2) it was possible to implement them computationally with no need for prior manual analysis. As well as being compared with each other, the conversation of FL and NF groups was also compared with that of R who acted as their interlocutor and as a normal control. Computer programs were written to extract a range of characteristics from the transcribed dialogues without any prior manual analysis. The programs identified a number of features from the contributions of both aphasic individual and researcher for each 30-minute dialogue. From these basic measures, a variety of both individual and group characteristics were derived, some of which are illustrated below.

Results

Differentiation of non-fluent and fluent aphasic groups

The NF and FL groups, as diagnosed by a speech and language therapist, were significantly differentiated by a combination index score consisting of the four measures: percentage of total words (PTW), percentage of words which were deictic pronouns (PWDP), lexical type-token ratio (LTTR) and degree of preseveration (CR3) (see Figure 32.1). They were also differentiated by a range of individual measures. The fluent group said more than the non-fluent group, both in terms of the number of words spoken over the 30-minute period and as a proportion of the total number of words spoken by both aphasic and researcher (Figure 32.2 and Table 32.1). The FL group also took markedly longer conversational turns than the NF. The FL group used a far higher proportion of deictic pronouns than the NF group, although the FL proportion was clearly not abnormal as it was virtually identical to that of the unimpaired interlocutor. The vocabulary of the NF group was far more restricted than that of the FL group. Finally, the NF group perseverated more than the FL group. For all of the above the Wilcoxon 2-sample test indicated significant differences at the 1% level for all mean comparisons.

The interlocutor's contribution

Both groups were also distinguishable by the amount of speech addressed to them by their interlocutor, i.e. the latter was consistently influenced by the differences in the nature of the NF and FL discourse ($p < 0.001$) (Figure 32.2). For other measures, it was possible to see the interlocutor as a normal control since she was remarkably consistent in

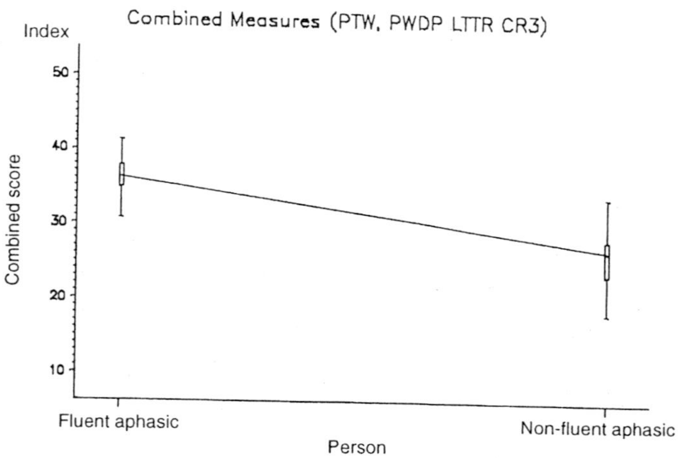

Figure 32.1. Differentiation of fluent and non-fluent aphasic groups by a combination of measures.

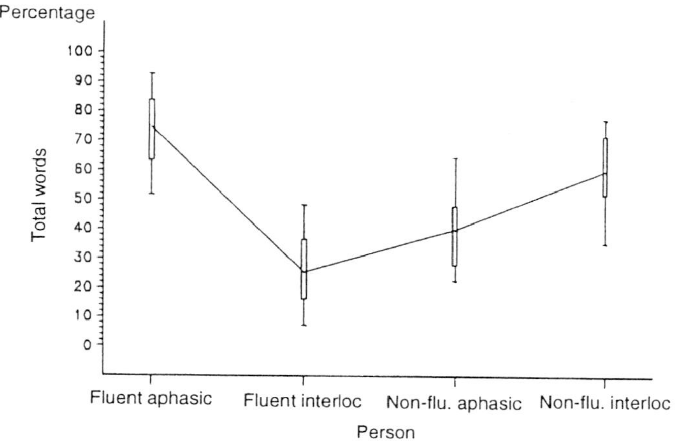

Figure 32.2. Percentage of total number of words spoken per half-hour session.

Table 32.1. Percentage of total number of words spoken by fluent and non-fluent aphasics and their interlocutor

Fluent				Non-fluent			
Patient		Interlocutor		Patient		Interlocutor	
Mean	SD	Mean	SD	Mean	SD	Mean	SD
73.1	14.2	26.8	14.2	39.8	13.6	60.1	13.6

terms of mean length of turn, use of deictic pronouns and lexical productivity, independently of whether her conversational partner was FL or NF.

Conclusions

Although the above measures are relatively simple in that they take no account of grammatical structure, they show that the NF and FL groups can be regarded as distinct both from each other, in accordance with the therapist's diagnosis, and from a normal speaker across a range of measures. Furthermore, these results are obtained completely automatically and require no prior manual analysis of the data. They also demonstrate that a client's communication disorder can be partially characterized in terms of the effect it has on their interlocutor's language.

Implications and future prospects

This study shows that fully automatic computerized analysis can provide a viable means of characterizing samples of disordered language. We are currently exploring the use of far more sophisticated computational analytical techniques, including the use of part of speech taggers and parsers, in the analysis of corpora of disordered language. Clinical Computational Corpus Linguistics (CCCL) holds out the prospect of ultimately being able to provide automatic assessment and diagnosis of a wide range of communication disorders based on computerized analysis of transcribed data samples.

Acknowledgements

This research was supported by a grant from the University of Sheffield Research Development Fund to Michael Perkins and Yorick Wilks. Thanks to Eric Iverson, Takahiro Wakao and Chunyu Kit for their work on earlier versions of the programs.

References

Baker-van den Goorbergh L, Baker K (1991) Computerised Language Error Analysis Report (CLEAR). Kibworth, Leics: FAR Communications.

Long SH, Fey ME (1994) Computerized Profiling. San Antonio, TX: The Psychological Corporation.

Miller JF, Chapman R (1982–1995) SALT: Systematic Analysis of Language Transcripts. Madison, WI: Language Analysis Laboratory, Waisman Centre on Mental Retardation and Human Development, University of Madison-Wisconsin.

Perkins MR (1995) Corpora of disordered spoken language. In Leech G, Myers G, Thomas J (eds) Spoken English on Computer: Transcription, Mark-up and Application. London: Longman, pp. 128–34.

Perkins MR, Howard SJ (1995) Principles of clinical linguistics. In Perkins MR, Howard SJ (eds) Case Studies in Clinical Linguistics. London: Whurr, pp. 10–35.

Perkins MR, Varley R (1996) A Machine-Readable Corpus of Aphasic Discourse. University of Sheffield: Department of Human Communication Sciences/Institute for Language, Speech and Hearing (ILASH).

Chapter 33 extIPA Transcriptions of Consonants and Vowels Spoken by Dyspractic Children: Agreement and Validity

WILHELM H VIEREGGE and BEN MAASSEN

Introduction

The present study deals with agreement and validity of phonetic transcriptions of pathological speech made by using the extIPA system (= extended IPA system for the transcription of atypical speech; Duckworth et al., 1990). When discussing transcription evaluation two aspects appear to be relevant: agreement and validity (Vieregge, 1987; Cucchiarini, 1993). Agreement concerns the extent to which transcribers agree among themselves. From the literature on transcription two measures are known by which agreement can be objectively evaluated. The first one is 'percentage agreement', which is defined as follows (Amorosa et al., 1985; Pye et al., 1988; Shriberg and Lof, 1991; Otomo and Stoel-Gammon, 1992; Cucchiarini, 1993; Maassen et al., 1996):

$$\text{percentage agreement} = \frac{\text{agreements}}{\text{agreements} + \text{disagreements}} \times 100\%$$

Percentage agreement is a statistic which is obtained by an item-by-item comparison procedure. For a discussion of this measure see Cucchiarini (1993, p.68). The second measure is 'average distance' which is based on feature counting (Singh, 1976; Vieregge 1987; Cucchiarini 1993, 1996):

$$\text{average distance} = 1/N \sum_{i=1}^{N} di,$$

where N = number of consonant or vowel pairs, respectively, in a transcription corpus, d = phonetic-articulatory distance of such a pair, and i = running index. When, for a specific corpus, the average distance is high, the agreement will be low and vice versa. Both measures have advantages and disadvantages which cannot be discussed here (for a discussion, see Cucchiarini, 1996, p.150). Although percentage agreement and average distance measure quite different aspects of the two transcriptions to be evaluated, they are not independent of each other.

Validity can be captured by the following question: Does a given transcription measure what it purports to measure? Or, in other words, to what extent do transcriptions approximate what was actually spoken? In order to determine the validity of a given transcription it is necessary to have a correct representation of what was actually spoken. Since this is not available, we have to use an approximation of it. In general a consensus transcription is used (Shriberg et al., 1984). This is a transcription made by trained transcribers after they have reached agreement about each symbol. The authors mentioned above showed that by means of consensus errors are reduced drastically, which means that the actual realization can be approximated. In line with previous studies (Vieregge 1987; Vieregge and Broeders, 1995) validity is defined in this chapter as agreement between trained transcribers and an expert transcriber.

Although agreement and validity of transcriptions of normal speech have received some attention, very little is known about agreement and nothing about validity of transcriptions of pathological speech made by using the extIPA transcription system. Therefore in this chapter we will address validity and agreement of this kind of transcription by testing the following hypothesis (Maassen et al., 1996): compared with the transcription of running speech, the transcription of some selected tokens taken from running speech will show higher agreement and validity values.

Method

Subjects and speech material

A total number of 24 speech-language pathologists (SLPs) functioned as transcribers. The SLPs were following an academic study 'Speech and language pathology' at the University of Nijmegen. As part of this study, they took two transcription courses of 50 hours each: 'Transcription of normal speech', followed by 'Transcription of pathological speech'. Although these SLPs certainly cannot be considered expert transcribers, their transcription training can be considered above average as compared with SLPs working in a clinical setting. The 24 SLPs were divided into 12 pairs.

In turn these 12 pairs were divided into two groups: Group A (pairs 1–6) transcribed all vowels and the glides /l, R, w, j/ present in the speech material, whereas group B (pairs 7–12) transcribed the consonants in the speech material.

The speech material to be transcribed consisted of words produced in an imitation task by nine children with developmental apraxia of speech (DAS). This imitation task was carried out as part of a larger study (Thoonen et al., 1994; Maassen et al., 1996).

The material was proportionally divided into three samples, a, b and c, each of which consisted of speech produced by three of the nine children (about 90 words). Each of the 12 pairs transcribed one of these three samples. The material was assigned in such a way that in each of the two groups A and B, two pairs would transcribe the same material. The scheme below illustrates how the speech material was assigned to the various pairs:

pairs 1/4: sample a, vowels and glides
pairs 2/5: sample b, vowels and glides
pairs 3/6: sample c, vowels and glides

pairs 7/10: sample a, consonants
pairs 8/11: sample b, consonants
pairs 9/12: sample c, consonants

For determining validity, one-sixth of the material was quasi-randomly selected and transcribed by an expert transcriber (the first author). Validity was determined by computing agreement between the pairs of SLP transcribers and the expert transcriber.

Transcription analysis

For each utterance, three transcriptions were typed into LIPP (1991): those made by the two transcriber pairs and the one made by the expert transcriber. In our previous study (Maassen et al., 1996) we had extended the set of symbols, because the standard version of LIPP does not contain the complete extIPA. Percentage agreement was calculated between the two pairs of each combination of pairs in two conditions: (1) by taking into account all features and all diacritics (the +D condition) and (2) by ignoring diacritics (the -D condition).

Also, average distances between pairs were determined by counting all occurrences of distance 0 (perfect agreement between pairs), distance 1 with respect to place (e.g. bilabial versus alveolar), distance 2 with respect to place (e.g. bilabial versus palatal), distance 2 with respect to manner (e.g. plosive versus fricative), and so on, and calculating the weighted average per feature (place, manner, voice) and the overall weighted average. [Note that distance 1 with respect to manner does not occur due to the binary manner-features, e.g. plus or minus plosive, plus or minus fricative; see Cuchiarini (1993).] In exactly the same way validity measures were calculated. Thus, precentage agreement and average distances between each pair and the expert transcriber were calculated.

Results

In the following tables the main results of our study will be presented. The results will be interpreted in terms of trends.

Table 33.1. Percentage agreement in the +D condition

variable	speech sample a pairs 1/4	speech sample a pairs 7/10	speech sample b pairs 2/5	speech sample b pairs 8/11	speech sample c pairs 3/6	speech sample c pairs 9/12	averaged total
cons		33.3		13.6		75.0	40.4
glide	1.9		22.2		0.0		10.4
vowel	4.5		26.8		2.3		18.5
segments	**28.9**		**19.0**		**42.6**		**30.3**

Table 33.1 shows the percentage agreement between the various pairs of transcribers for consonants, glides, vowels and all segments in the +D condition. Some values are extremely low, like those for glides and vowels for pairs 3/6 and 1/4 and that for consonants for pairs 8/11. Other values reach a higher level, like that for consonants for 9/12. Furthermore, on the basis of these data it seems that transcribing consonants is less difficult than transcribing vowels and glides. This is confirmed by previous research (Vieregge and Cucchiarini 1988) and by impressions of people who learn to transcribe speech. Averaged over all pairs the total agreement of all segments is 30.3%.

In Table 33.2 the validity values in the +D condition are shown for consonants, glides, vowels and all segments. The values were computed for all pairs. The general trend of the data seems to be that agreement between the expert transcriber and the transcriber pairs (validity) is higher than agreement between the pairs of transcribers (compare Table 33.2 with Table 33.1); thus, the variability between pairs is larger than that between the various pairs and the expert transcriber. Here, too, poor and good pairs can be distinguished (pair 9 is the best and pairs 3 and 6 are the poorest). In addition, validity is higher for consonants than for vowels and glides, as was expected.

When diacritics are ignored, agreement between the pairs of transcribers improves considerably (see Table 33.3), as one would expect. The same holds for transcription of normal speech (Vieregge and Hettinga 1997). Again, consonants score much better than vowels and glides; place, manner and voice features are better than basic symbols, and manner and voice score better than place.

Table 33.2. Validity in the +D condition

variable	speech sample a				speech sample b				speech sample c				averaged total
	pair 1	pair 7	pair 4	pair 10	pair 2	pair 8	pair 5	pair 11	pair 3	pair 9	pair 6	pair 12	
cons		57.8		29.3		49.2		16.2		72.6		64.9	48.5
glide	28.6		16.7		16.7		16.7		0.0		0.0		12.2
vow	21.6		19.6		33.3		2.4		2.3		9.1		15.0
segments	43.3		41.6		41.7		25.2		11.5		41.3		34.3

Table 33.3. Percentage agreement in the -D condition

variable	speech sample a		speech sample b		speech sample c		averaged total
	pairs 1/4	pairs 7/10	pairs 2/5	pairs 8/11	pairs 3/6	pairs 9/12	
cons		81.0		75.8		80.9	79.4
glide	66.7		22.2		3.4		41.4
vowel	77.6		78.1		65.1		73.7
segments	78.9		72.4		71.3		**74.5**
place		82.8		84.0		84.8	83.8
manner		88.2		85.3		91.1	88.3
pla+man		88.2		81.3		86.1	85.4
voice		88.2		82.7		91.1	87.5

Also in this case, validity turns out to be higher than agreement between pairs. In addition, it is clear that when diacritics are ignored validity also improves drastically (compare Table 33.4 with Table 33.2). Furthermore, both agreements between pairs and validity are considerably higher for place, manner, and voice features than for the basic symbols (see Tables 33.3 and 33.4).

These findings are not surprising. As a matter of fact, ignoring diacritics and determining agreement for separate features have something in common: both processes reduce the degree of detail (number of categories) in the transcriptions, thus increasing the influence of chance agreement (see Cucchiarini, 1996: 142). Moreover, the fact that percentage agreement is very sensitive to the number of categories (see Cucchiarini, 1996: 143) explains why the degree of agreement increases so substantially from condition +D to condition -D.

So far we have presented results based on percentage agreement. In Table 33.5, on the other hand, the average distance is used as the dependent variable indicating transcription dissimilarity, for place, manner, and voice features. In comparing these results with those presented above it should be borne in mind that here the complement of agreement is indicated, i.e. disagreement. These values are obtained by feature counting (Singh, 1976). In order to get an idea of the order of magnitude of the average distance, it is instructive to point out that the value between [p] and [b] = 1 and that between [p] and [R] = 7. For normal speech with diacritics the average distance appeared to be about 0.9 for consonants and 1.0 for vowels in Cucchiarini (1993, p. 159) and about 0.7 in Vieregge and Hettinga (1997).

Considering the values given as reference above we may conclude that the picture emerging from Table 33.5 does not differ very much from that resulting from Table 33.4: in both cases the degree of agreement for place, manner and voice appears to be reasonable.

Table 33.4. Validity in the -D condition

variable	speech sample a				speech sample b				speech sample c				averaged total
	pair 1	pair 7	pair 4	pair 10	pair 2	pair 8	pair 5	pair 11	pair 3	pair 9	pair 6	pair 12	
cons		89		81		86		75		85		78	82.6
glide	86		67		67		33		62		250		56.1
vowel	65		61		83		64		82		59		68.6
segments	80		84		82		73		69		68		**76.1**
place		90		83		89		83		91		87	87.0
manner		93		86		92		86		96		90	90.6
p + m		93		86		92		85		93		87	89.3
voice		92		91		93		86		95		88	90.8

Table 33.5. Disagreement in terms of average distance for place, manner and voice for consonants; basic symbols without diacritics

pairs 7/10	pairs 8/11	pairs 9/12	averaged total
0.161	0.187	0.152	**0.170**

In Table 33.6 the degree of agreement between the various transcriber pairs and the expert transcriber (validity) is expressed in terms of average distance. Again we see that these values are higher than those in Table 33.5 and the degree of agreement is similar to that observed in Table 33.4 for place, manner and voice.

Table 33.6. Complement of validity in terms of average distance of place, manner and voice for consonants

pair 7	pair 8	pair 9	pair 10	pair 11	pair 12	averaged total
0.067	0.127	0.132	0.159	0.197	0.220	**0.150**

In order to test the hypothesis that higher agreement is achieved in transcribing selected tokens of speech rather than running speech, in Table 33.7 our new data are contrasted with older ones taken from Maassen et al. (1996). Before considering the results we would like to point out a possibly weak point in the experimental design of this investigation. We are aware of the fact that the design for 'the transcription of some selected tokens taken from running speech' such as formulated in our hypothesis is poorly operationalized, because in one session all consonants and in another session all vowels were transcribed. This is a situation which only approximates the one we would like to have, i.e. transcribing only few tokens within a selected speech corpus. At the moment it is not clear how this experimental setup may have influenced the results.

Table 33.7. Present data (new) compared with data from Maassen et al., 1996 (old)

	old		new	
	consonants	vowels	consonants	vowels
+D	48%	52%	40.4%	18.5%
–D	58%	68%	79.4%	73.7%

From Table 33.7 it appears that in the -D condition higher agreement is achieved in the new data, both for consonants and for vowels. In the +D condition the reverse applies, though. We think that this is due to the fact that more diacritics were used in the present study than in the Maassen et al. study. As mentioned above, using more diacritics makes it more difficult to achieve high agreement, because of the influence of chance agreement. The analyses to test this hypothesis are complicated and have not been carried out yet.

Furthermore, in line with the fact that consonants do have more clearly defined articulatory points of contact than vowels, in the present study consonants show higher agreements than vowels (consonants +D: 40.4 % versus vowels +D: 18.5%; consonants -D: 79.4% versus vowels -D: 73.7%). In the Maassen et al. study this was just the other way around: consonants +D: 48% versus vowels +D: 52%; consonants -D: 58% versus vowels -D: 68%.

A novelty in this investigation is the calculation of validity and average distance values, which have never been applied before to the use of the extIPA symbols. Validity was low for basic symbols with diacritics (34.3 %) and high for basic symbols only (segments: 76.1%; consonants: 82.6%; glides: 56.1%; vowels: 68.6%). Here, too, consonants are better than vowels and glides. As expected, validity values in terms of features are higher: place: 87%, manner: 90.6 % and voice: 90.8%.

Conclusion

From the present study and from Maassen et al. (1996) it appears that the use of diacritics in transcription leads to very low values of percentage agreement. However, this may be a consequence of the fact that in this measure agreement is treated in an all-or-none fashion (Cucchiarini, 1996: 143), which means that all differences between transcriptions count the same. This way of assessing agreement may inflate the differences observed between the two conditions +D and -D. Unfortunately, we were not able to determine the effect of diacritics on the average distance. So, the influence of diacritics upon this measure for pathological speech has still to be investigated. If we compare this situation with that of transcribing normal speech (Vieregge and Hettinga, 1998) we expect that the effect of diacritics upon the average distance will be much lower than upon percentage agreement.

Furthermore, under one condition, i.e. that the transcriptions be not too detailed, our data confirm the hypothesis we wanted to test. As a matter of fact, in the -D condition agreement appeared to be higher and of an acceptable level, for transcriptions of selected tokens taken from running speech.

Acknowledgement

The authors are indebted to Catia Cucchiarini for her critical comments on an earlier draft of this chapter. Thanks are due to the Speech and Language Pathology students who functioned as transcribers in this study.

Refererences

Amorosa HU, Benda von E, Wagner E, Keck A (1985) Transcribing phonetic detail in the speech of unintelligible children: a comparison of procedures. British Journal of Disorders of Communication 20, 281–7.

Cucchiarini C (1993) Phonetic Transcription: a Methodological and Empirical Study. Doctorate thesis, University of Nijmegen.

Cucchiarini C (1996) Assessing transcription agreement: methodological aspects. Clinical Linguistics and Phonetics, 10, 131–55.

Duckworth M, Hardcastle WJ, Ball MJ (1990) Extensions to the International Phonetic Alphabet for the Transcription of Atypical Speech. Clinical Linguistics and Phonetics, 4, 273–80.

LIPP (1991) Logical International Phonetics Program V 1:40. Miami, FL: Intelligent Hearing Systems.

Maassen B, Offeringa S, Vieregge WH,Thoonen G (1996) Transcription of pathological speech in children by means of extIPA: agreement and relevance. In Powel TW (ed.) Pathologies of Speech and Language: Contributions of Clinical Phonetics and Linguistics. New Orleans: International Clinical Phonetics Association.

Otomo K, Stoel-Gammon C (1992) The acquisition of unrounded vowels in English. Journal of Speech and Hearing Research, 35, 604–16.

Pye C, Wilcox KA, Siren KA (1988) Refining transcriptions: the significance of transcriber 'errors'. Journal of Child Language, 15, 17–37.

Shriberg LD, Lof L (1991) Reliability studies in broad and narrow phonetic transcription. Clinical Linguistics and Phonetics, 5, 225–79.

Singh S (1976) Distinctive Features, Theory and Validation. Baltimore, MD: University Park Press.

Thoonen G, Maassen B, Gabreëls F, Schreuder R (1994) Feature analysis of singleton consonant errors in developmental verbal dyspraxia (DVD). Journal of Speech and Hearing Research, 37, 1424–40.

Vieregge WH (1987) Basic aspects of phonetic segmental transcriptions. In Almeida A, Braun A (eds) Probleme der Phonetischen Transkription. Stuttgart: Franz Steiner Verlag.

Vieregge WH, Broeders APA (1995) Agreement in consensus transcriptions of trained and untrained transcribers. In Elenius K, Branderud P (eds) Proceedings of the XIIIth International Congress of Phonetic Sciences (ICPhS 95), 3, 174–7.

Vieregge WH, Cucchiarini C (1988) Evaluating the transcription process. In Ainsworth WA, Holmes JN (eds) Proceedings Speech '88, Edinburgh, pp. 73–80.

Vieregge WH, Hettinga P (1999) Effiziente Zuverlässigleisbestimmung phonetisch-segmentaler Transkriptionen. Zeitschrift für Dialektologie und Linguistik, 66, 31–47.

Chapter 34
Isochronicity in Speech Production and the Perception of Categorical Timing Relations

VICTOR BOUCHER

Introduction

Temporal aspects such as stop gap duration, voice onset time (VOT), and formant transitions are known to provide cues for phonological categorization. Generally, such temporal details have been measured or experimentally manipulated by reference to absolute (ms) values. A central example is VOT, which is defined by reference to the millisecond delays between a stop consonant release and the onset of F0. VOT has been used not only in investigating the acoustic correlates of phonological categories (Lisker and Abramson, 1970), but also in experiments bearing on infant and animal perception, in investigating the neurological substrates of feature detection, and in clinical protocols (e.g. Kuhl and Miller, 1978; Molfese and Hess, 1978; Sinex and Narayan, 1994; Stark and Tallal, 1988). However, a number of reports have indicated that the production and perception of temporal aspects such as VOT vary as a function of the timing properties of the utterance context. For instance, the ms values of VOT for stops vary with speaking rate and yet this does not affect voicing categorization since listeners apparently perceive such details relative to the timing of rhythmical units such as syllables in the utterance context (Summerfield 1981; see also Miller, 1981; Miller and Volaitis, 1989). With reference to these 'relative-timing' effects, this chapter presents a summary of preliminary results focusing on two exploratory questions: (1) Since listeners may perceive temporal details by reference to the timing of rhythmical units such as syllables, are listeners influenced by within-syllable timing relations or do they simply refer to the absolute durations of rhythmical units in the utterance context?; and (2) Is categorical perception of temporal details such as VOT across changes in speech rate directly supported in speech production by within-syllable timing ratios?

Experiment 1: Relative-timing effects on the perception of isochronic rhythms

The issue of perceived timing of spoken sequences has been investigated in terms of listeners' judgements of the locus of rhythmical units or *P-centre*. Experiments in this area essentially involve judgements of the isochronicity of rhythmic units in sequences where various details are manipulated. From previous work, essentially two perspectives have emerged. Marcus (1981, among others) suggests that *P-centre* location can be predicted by reference to ratios of C and VC components (specifically, *P-centre* = 0.65 C + 0.25 VC + constant), whereas others submit that the perceived locus follows the time course of dB rises corresponding to syllables or rhythmic groups (e.g. Pompino-Marschal, 1989). The first experiment attempted to determine whether listeners' judgements of isochronicity in speech are influenced by modifications of relative-timing aspects within CVC or by modifications of the (absolute) duration separating the dB rises of rhythmic units.

Method

Stimuli

Two series of stimuli were constructed from a spoken sequence /əˈtæpəˈtæpəˈtæpəˈtæp/ which was digitized at 10 kHz and manipulated using computer software. In the first series, splicing at zero-crossing (to within ± 2 ms) was applied to oscillographic waveforms while maintaining the original ratios of release, gap and vowel duration in CVC (these proportional reductions were applied alternatively to the fourth and sixth syllable of the sequence). In this series, then, the manipulations led to stable ratios of elements within CVC but to a reduction (in 20 ms steps) of the overall duration of the syllable, thereby also reducing the interval between the intensity rises of vowel onsets. The second series of stimuli involved manipulations where the interval separating the dB rises of vowel onsets was held constant while altering within-CVC timing relations. This was performed by splicing in 20 ms steps the duration of the vowel and adding an equivalent duration of silence to the following consonant gap (see Figure 34.1). The manipulations led to 'normal-sounding' sequences only when splices did not exceed 80 ms. The stimuli (containing two tokens of each of the manipulated sequences) were arranged in a quasi-random order on digital audio tape. The prediction was that, if listeners are primarily influenced by relative-timing properties rather than by the durations separating the dB rises of rhythmic units, then judgements of isochronicity would be more frequent for the first set of stimuli.

A. Original sequence with isochronic dB rises

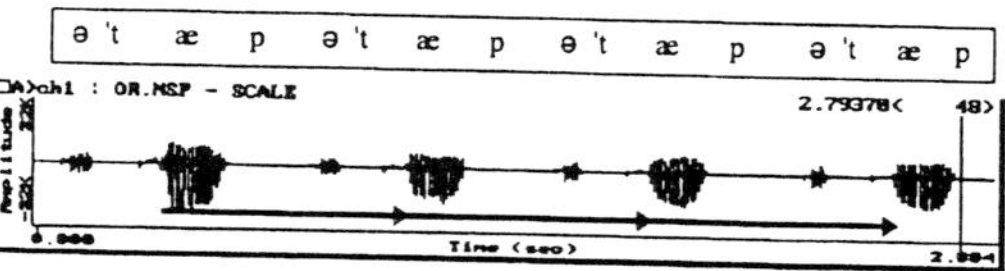

B. Spliced: maintains within-CVC ratios but alters the interval separating the dB rises (here by 40 ms)

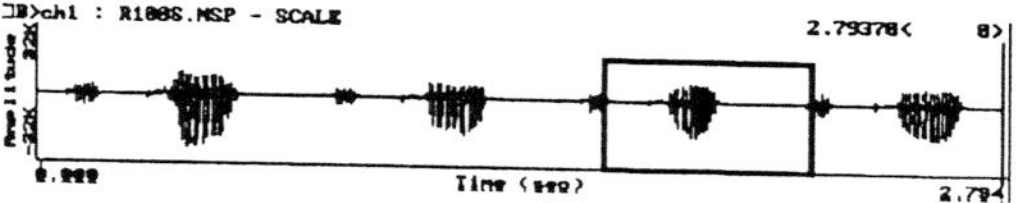

C. Splices: alters within-CVC ratios but maintains the interval separating the dB rises

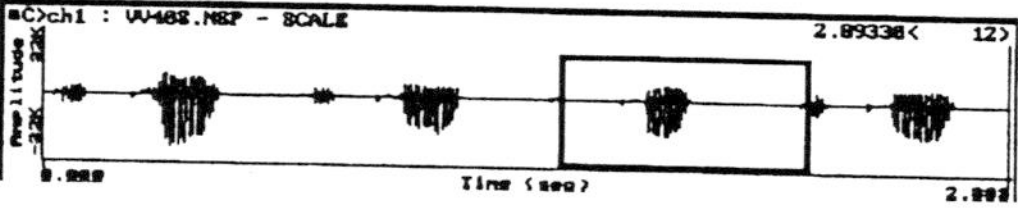

Figure 34.1. The stimuli include spliced waveforms as in B and C. In B within-CVC ratios are held constant but the interval separating dB rises (at vowel onsets) varies, here by 40 ms. In C, the interval between dB rises is held constant but ratios within CVC vary.

Participants and procedure

The task of judging the isochronicity of sequences requires some training (see also Pompino-Marschal, 1989). Twenty subjects participated in a training session and of these 15 were selected for the experiment. A hearing evaluation was performed according to the ASHA (1978) recommended guidelines and showed normal hearing from 250 to 8 kHz bilaterally for all participants. Subjects were instructed to listen with headphones and determine whether or not the heard sequence containing repetitions of the words *a tap* was equally timed throughout.

Results

Overall, reductions in subsyllabic ratios produced a greater proportion of judgements of anisochronicity than the reductions affecting the intervals separating the dB onsets, though both series of manipulations influenced listener judgements. Figure 34.2 shows that, when there is a 60 ms reduction of the time separating the dB rises of rhythmic groups but subsyllabic ratios are maintained, the unit is judged (in 75% of the trials) to be similar to neighbouring rhythms. On the other hand, when 60 ms reductions affect subsyllabic ratios (but not the interval between dB rises), the heard sequence was judged as anisochronic in 77% of the trials.

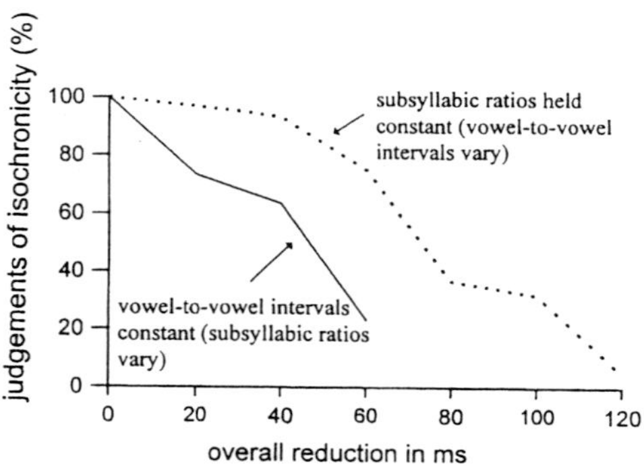

Figure 34.2. Results of the perception task in terms of the two series of stimuli.

Experiment 2: Categorical patterns of VOT in relative-time

Method

Seven monolingual speakers of English were asked to repeat several times over /əˈtæp . . ./ and /əˈdæp . . ./ at 10 different rates. These productions were recorded on digital audio tape and subsequently processed at a sampling rate of 20 kHz using a computer-based analysis system (Computerized Speech Lab, Kay Elemetrics). Measurements of VOT values were performed for /t/ and /d/ and ratios by reference to synchronized oscillograms and narrow-band spectrograms. Ratios were subsequently calculated by reference to CVC, CV, and VC extents. Negative VOTs and doubtful cases were eliminated leaving a total of 168 measures for /d/ and 192 measures for /t/.

Results

Figure 34.3 shows that the distribution of ms values of VOT for /t/ and /d/ tended to converge at faster rates so that one cannot infer from the distribution of scores an invariant boundary across changes in speaking rate. However, relative measures, whether these are calculated by reference to, CV, VC, or CVC syllables all presented clear categorical distributions across rate changes, as illustrated in Figure 34.4 in the case of the CV reference frame. From these patterns in the relative-timing values, one can infer an invariant boundary between voiced and voiceless VOTs across changes in speaking rates.

Discussion and conclusion

The previous findings suggest that, to a certain degree, listeners attend to temporal relations within rhythmic units such as syllables when asked

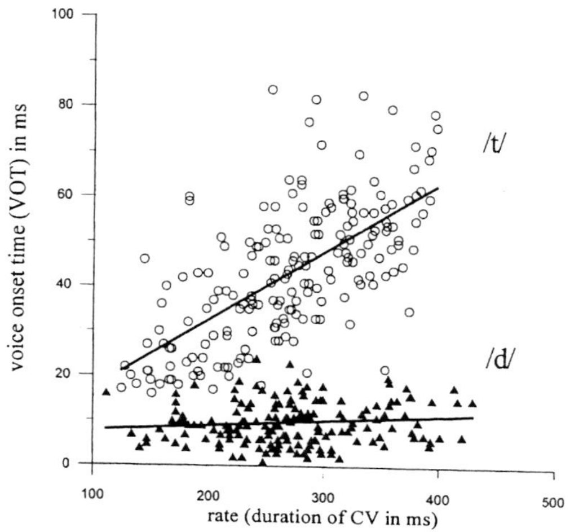

Figure 34.3. Absolute values of VOT for /t/ and /d/ across rate changes showing that VOT values for /t/ and /d/ tend to converge at faster rates. Compare this with the categorical patterns of the following figure.

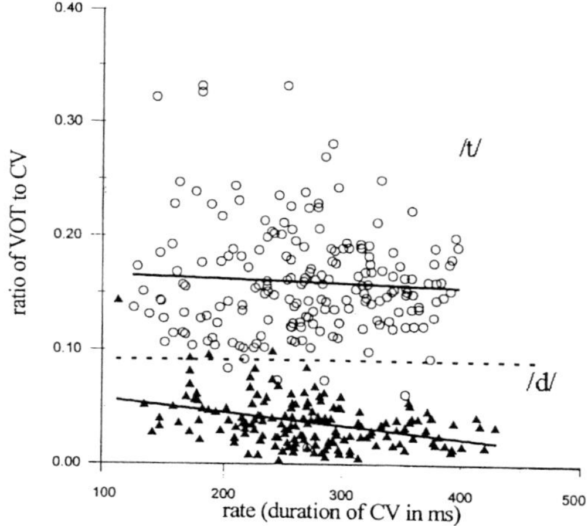

Figure 34.4. Relative-timing values of VOT within CV.

to judge the timing of an utterance context. To a certain extent, when rhythmical units in a sequence contain similar timing relations – even if the (absolute) durations of the units differ – they are judged to be equally timed. This conforms to previous findings on *P-centres*. One may also see a parallel with previous studies of timing details such as VOT: as noted, the timing of such subsyllabic aspects varies with speaking rate, yet listeners apparently categorize these by reference to the timing properties of the utterance. In both instances, and to some degree, timing appears to be perceived not so much in terms of the millisecond values of elements but in terms of temporal relations. It should be recognized, however, that the present study only provides indirect support for this perspective of the role of timing relations in perception. Moreover, the paradigm may be questioned in terms of the use of manipulated stimuli with artificial rhythms that may not reflect natural speech. For these reasons, a different paradigm is currently being exploited by the present author where stimuli for voicing categorization involve syllables segmented from speech produced at different rates. The results are forthcoming. Further investigation is warranted particularly in light of the present results showing categorical patterns in the relative-timing values of VOT which have both methodological and fundamental implications. That is, the findings suggest that one may not presuppose that VOT categorization rests on particular ms values. In fact, part of the inconsistency of the ms values of VOT cited in the literature may stem from the failure to recognize the perceptual effects of contextual changes such as those bearing on speech rate. In a more fundamental perspective, the above findings suggest that applying an absolute metric to spoken elements may have confounded possible solutions to the invariance issue. That is, in attempting to fathom how it is that invariant voicing categories can derive from variable ms values of VOT, the present results suggest that applying relative measures can reveal categorical distributions where one can infer invariant boundaries. The implication is that categorical patterns are present in speech production and may provide a physical support for categorical perception.

References

Kuhl P, Miller J (1978) Speech perception by the chinchilla: identification functions for synthetic VOT stimula. Journal of the Acoustical Society of America, 63, 905–17.

Lisker L, Abramson A (1970) The voicing dimension: Some experiments in comparative phonetics. In Proceedings of the Sixth International Congress of Phonetic Sciences. Prague: Academia.

Marcus S (1981) Acoustic determinants of perceptual center (*P-center*) location. Perception and Psychophysics, 30, 247–56.

Miller J (1981) Effects of speaking rate on segmental distinctions. In Eimas P, Miller J (eds) Perspectives on the Study of Speech. Hillsdale NJ: Erlbaum.

Miller J, Volaitis L (1989) Effect of speaking rate on the perceptual structure of a phonetic category. Perception and Psychophysics, 46, 505–12.

Molfese D, Hess T (1978) Hemispheric specialization for VOT perception in the preschool child. Journal of Experimental Child Psychology, 26, 71–84.

Pompino-Marshall B (1989) On the psychoacoustic nature of the *P-center* phenomenon. Journal of Phonetics, 17, 175–92.

Sinex D, Narayan S (1994) Auditory-nerve fiber representation of temporal cues to voicing in word-medial stop consonants. Journal of the Acoustical Society of America, 95, 897–903.

Stark R, Tallal P (1988) Language, Speech, and Reading Disorders in Children: Neuropsychological Studies. Boston, MA: College-Hill.

Summerfield A (1981). On articulatory rate and perceptual constancy in phonetic perception. Journal of Experimental Psychology: Human Perception and Performance, 7, 1074–95.

Chapter 35
Effects of Stricture-force Changes on the Coordination of Oral and Glottal Aperture Motions in Normal Speech

VICTOR BOUCHER

Introduction

When native speakers utter the same sequence of phonemes, the spatio-temporal aspects of their motor performance differ across languages. As an example, for ±*voice* stops, English speakers produce varying positive delays of voice onset time (VOT), whereas, in French, both positive and zero values are produced (Wajskop and Sweerts, 1973). There are also aspirated delays in English which are most often absent in French. These variations suggest differences in oral-laryngeal coordination (or in the *phase* of oral and glottal aperture motions). Some authors suggest that the timing differences are attributable to central processes. However, the view that speakers elaborate different programmes of coordination for such short-time aspects as VOT and aspiration appears questionable. The present chapter offers a different explanation.

Wyke's mechanoreceptors

Wyke (1963, 1974) observed afferent discharge into the vagus nerve in response to mechanical and air pressure stimulation of laryngeal muscles. This led to the claim that identified nerve endings coiled around muscle fibres, and corpuscles in the capsules of the cricorytenoid and cricothyroid joints behaved as mechanoreceptors. Considering these observations, one may infer that, in speech, vocal tract strictures of varying force which alter flow and pressure would create variable passive changes to laryngeal muscles and joints. Consequently, associated mechanoreceptors may serve to trigger phasic aperture motions of the glottis at stable intervals relative to the force and timing of oral strictures.

The result would be characteristic phase angles between oral and glottal aperture motions, which has been attested in previous work (Löfqvist and Yoshioka, 1981; Munhall et al., 1994). By reference to this principle, the general hypothesis tested in the present study is that normal variations in oral stricture force which impact on pressure and flow within the airways can shift the phase of oral and glottal aperture motions. It is submitted that the phase of these aperture motions, and the language-specific patterns which arise from a phase shift, can be explained by reference to pressure- and flow-sensitive mechanoreceptors so the patterns in question are not directly attributable to central programmes.

To illustrate the role of force-related changes on oral-laryngeal phase, one can refer to languages which show opposite tendencies with respect to the force of vocal tract strictures. Such contrastive tendencies are present in a 'syllable-timed' language such as French and a 'stress-timed' language like English (but see Dauer, 1986). In French, syllables tend to bear equal stress suggesting equivalent force for oral strictures. English uses alternating patterns of strong and weak strictures. The claim here is that this contrastive use of stricture force affects flow and pressure and therefore the timing of mechanoreceptor response which shifts the phase of oral and glottal aperture motions thereby creating a number of variants. This is illustrated in Figure 35.1. Note that the underlying phase shift leads to changes in (1) aspiration duration (see the interval between points 1 and 2 on the acoustic waveform), (2) relative vowel length (see between points 3 and 4), and (3) the relative timing of gaps and releases (relating to 'syllabification'; Boucher, 1988).

Method

Subjects

Participants included two groups of monolingual, adult males, one French (n = 7) and one English (n = 7).

Procedure and measurement strategy

Measurements were based on flow and pressure changes in the production of reiterated syllables using a clinical instrument, *Aerophone II* (Kay Elemetrics). This transducer-based instrument requires that the subject speak into a mask (with an intraoral catheter) mounted on a flowhead to which is attached an electret-type microphone. Signals were sampled at the given rate of 1 kHz and this digital information was processed with the *Aerophone* software running on a 486 processor PC. Subjects were instructed in their language to repeat the orally presented words a *pat* /('pat/ (for English speakers) or *patte* /'pat(/ (for French speakers who were asked to produce the final schwa). The resulting production reflected phonologically equivalent sequences across the two languages, that is /...(pat(pat../.

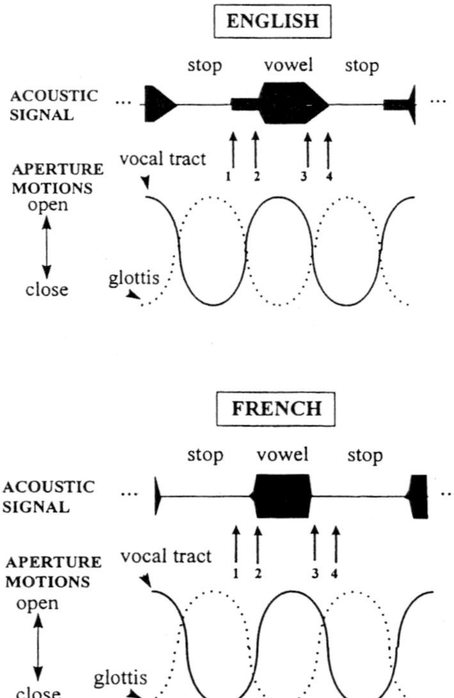

Figure 35.1. Hypothetical waveforms illustrating the acoustic correlates (top waveform of each panel) of an underlying phase shift in oral and glottal aperture motions.

Variables

The effects of variations in speaking rate and intensity were minimized given that all measures were relativized according to the following definitions.

Variable 1

Relative-timing or phase of glottal opening is the timing of a rise in intra-oral pressure for /p/ relative to the cycle of vocal tract opening motions for /pat/. The latter is measured by reference to the onsets of dB rises of 'releases' (a complete cycle being the release-to-release interval for /pat/; with this ratio, for instance, 0.5 = 180°). See Figure 35.2.

Variable 2

Change in peak flow bears on the difference between the peak flow (L/sec) at the release of /t/ and at the release of the following /p/ relative to the value for /t/. This delta change constitutes an indicator of relative

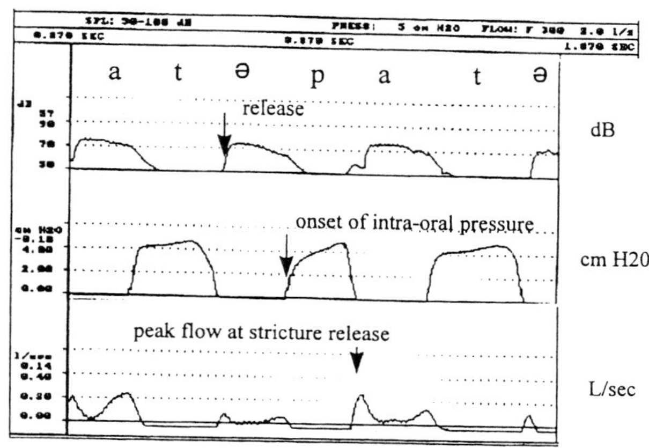

Figure 35.2. Output of *Aerophone* transducers illustrating various points of measurement.

change in stricture force (this assumes a linear relationship between force and flow in that an increase in stricture force leads to an increase in intraoral pressure and, consequently, a greater flow of air upon stricture release).

Variable 3

Relative duration of release is the time between the release burst of /p/ and the rise in periodic energy relative to the cycle of vocal tract opening (as in Variable 1).

Variable 4

Ratio of release duration to gap duration is the intervocalic interval which contains the gap and the release portions of /p/; ratios of these elements have been shown to constitute an independent correlate of distinctive syllabifications (Boucher, 1988).

Variable 5

Ratio of vowel to following gap duration is the ratio given by the duration of periodic energy of a 'vowel' and that of the quasi-silent gap associated with /p/.

Results and Discussion

The subjects produced a range of changes in peak flow with clear group differences suggesting that, whereas French speakers tend to maintain a stricture force, English speakers alternate between weak and strong closures. Moreover, as Figure 35.3 illustrates, the hypothesized impact of these force-related changes on oral-glottal coordination was confirmed to the extent that a non-linear function of flow change explains two-thirds of the variance in oral-laryngeal phase. The limit effects observed for values over (approximately) 40% change in peak flow suggest the presence of some unexamined factors perhaps relating to constraints on the kinematics of laryngeal abduction. Within these limits, however, changes in flow were highly correlated with the phase or relative-timing of glottal and vocal tract opening motions. The impact is such that increases in flow relating to a relative increase in stricture force lead to shorter delays between opening motions of the glottis and the vocal tract. This conforms to the general principle that, in speech, the phase of oral and glottal opening motions can be attributed to the workings of flow- and pressure-sensitive receptors at the periphery operating within certain constraints on glottal aperture motions.

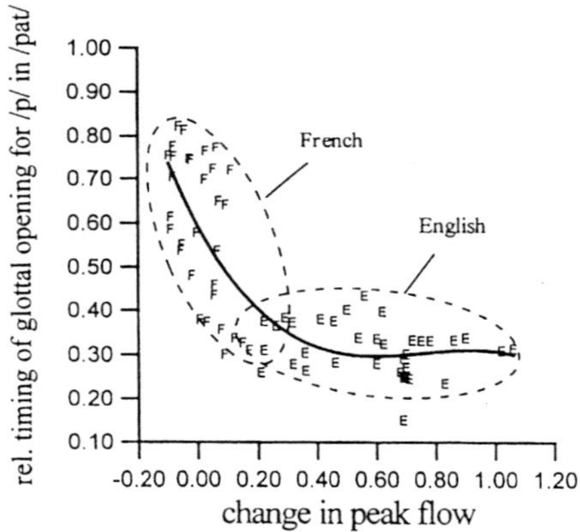

Figure 35.3. Effects of changes in peak flow (an indicator of variation in stricture force) on the relative timing of glottal opening (see Variable 1). A third degree equation approximates the trend. Note that English and French values tend towards opposite ends of a continuum of values. Values under approximately 40% change in peak flow present a linear relationship but there are clear limit effects above such changes.

Considering the variables relating to language-specific timing aspects (aspiration, syllabification and 'vowel lengthening' phenomena: see Variables 3, 4 and 5), within the limit effects noted above – i.e. bellow approximately 40% delta peak flow – both predictors of flow change and oral-glottal phase correlated to a high degree with the three specified variables, as indicated in Table 35.1.

The correlations suggest that, beyond certain limit effects (likely relating to constraints on the velocity of glottal motions), language-specific variations in release, gap and vowel durations are linked to the phase of oral and laryngeal aperture motions and to changes in peak flow.

Table 35.1. Correlation matrix for values under 40% change in peak flow (n = 44). All coefficients are significant at $p < 0.001$.

	relative timing of glottal opening	relative release duration	ratio of release duration within intervocalic interval	ratio of vowel duration to gap duration
Δpeak flow	–0.722	0.687	0.705	–0.715
relative timing of glottal opening	–	0.836	–0.794	0.726

Conclusion

The above results are compatible with the view that changes relating to stricture force can impact within a given range on the coordination of oral and glottal aperture motions. The impact is such that increases in flow relating to a relative increase in stricture force can lead to shorter delays between opening motions of the glottis and the vocal tract. This conforms to the general principle that, in speech, and within certain limits, the phase of oral and glottal opening motions may be attributed to the workings of peripheral mechanoreceptors. Moreover, stricture force (as observed indirectly by reference to flow changes at stricture release) and its effect on oral-laryngeal timing correlates, to a significant extent, with certain short-time language-specific variants of French and English so that, by reference to the possible role of the aforementioned mechanoreceptors, one need not postulate central programmes or linguistic devices for variations relating to such aspects as aspiration duration or vowel length effects (see Table 35.1). Though the present results provide no direct evidence linking specific mechanoreceptors to oral-laryngeal coordination, further work in this direction is warranted by the strong correlations observed between oral-glottal phase and force-related changes in flow. It should be noted that the preceding principle of oral-laryngeal coordination offers a means of systematizing observations across clinical populations: for instance, perceptual criteria such as 'imprecise consonants' used to characterize some dysarthrias and apraxia, and the irregular rhythmicities, abnormal VOTs and transitions observed in these populations may all basically attest to deficient control of stricture force and tonus with consequences on oral-glottal coordination. Also given the importance of volitional control in intervention, future enquiries should focus on subjects' capacity to control mechanoreceptor-based coordination by altering stricture-force.

References

Boucher V (1988) A parameter of syllabification for VstopV and relative-timing invariance. Journal of Phonetics, 16, 299–326.

Dauer R (1983) Stress-timing and syllable-timing reanalysed. Journal of Phonetics, 11, 51–62.

Löfqvist A, Yoshioka H (1981) Interarticulator programming in obstruent production. Phonetica, 38, 21–34.

Munhall K, Löfqvist A, Kelso J (1994) Lip-larynx coordination in speech: Effects of mechanical perturbations to the lower lip. Journal of the Acoustical Society of America, 95, 3605–16.

Wajskop M, Sweerts J (1973) Voicing cues in oral stop consonants. Journal of Phonetics, 1, 121–30.

Wyke B (1963) Reflexogenic contributions to vocal fold control systems. In Titze I, Scherer R (eds) Vocal Fold Physiology: Biomechanics, Acoustics and Phonatory Control. Denver, CO: Denver Centre for Performing Arts.

Wyke B (1974) Laryngeal myotatic reflexes and phonation. Folia Phoniatrica, 26, 249–64.

Chapter 36 Articulation Difficulties Following Maxillofacial Surgery: A Single Case Study

ALISON MAIN, STEVE KELLY and GRAHAM MANLEY

Introduction

Hypernasality and inaccurate tongue placement are common causes of poor speech intelligibility. The velum controls nasal coupling and hence resonance, and forms an essential seal, allowing the build up of intraoral pressure required for obstruent sounds. Velopharyngeal insufficiency (VPI), the inability to make adequate velopharyngeal closure, may result from either structural or neurological abnormalities (Albery and Russell, 1990).

The tongue is the most versatile of the articulators, being involved in the production of all vowels and the majority of consonants. By altering tongue position and shape, the size of the oral cavity, and hence its resonating characteristic, changes and different sounds are created. In order to speak, these complex movements must be coordinated with the controlled movement of the other articulators. Any errors in coordination, speed of movement, shape, or place of tongue contact will cause distortion, and speech intelligibility will be affected.

Objective measurement of these parameters can be difficult. Two new systems have been developed by the University of Kent Medical Electronics Research Team, Kent and Canterbury Hospital Speech and Language Therapy Department and Canterbury and Thanet Community Dental Department. SNORS (Super Nasal Oral Ratiometry System) measures both nasal and oral airflow during speech, allowing the very rapid movement of the velum to be inferred. Linguagraph is a clinical electropalatography system, which measures tongue–palate contact. A single case study is presented on a patient with whom both systems have been used.

Case history

TW was a 52-year-old male, diagnosed as having carcinoma of the right tonsil, extending to the anterior border of the soft palate and the tongue base, in June 1995. He was treated with chemo- and radiotherapy, but a year later this recurred. Surgical excision included the right tonsillar fossa, tongue base, soft palate to the uvula, a right partial pharyngectomy and right partial mandibulectomy. He also had a right selective neck dissection preserving the accessory nerve. The defect was reconstructed with a pectoralis major myocutaneous flap and he had a temporary tracheotomy.

Three months post surgery, TW was left with mild dysphagia, limited sensation on the right of his oral cavity, and a reduction in the intelligibility of his speech. He was very hypernasal; some palatal movement could be observed, but he did not seem able to sustain closure. Assessment using SNORS confirmed this.

SNORS

SNORS overcomes the limitations of nasal anemometry by using high-speed sensors to detect sudden changes in airflow caused by rapid movement of the velum. Also, the effect of speech intensity is overcome by measuring both the nasal and the oral airflow. This allows 'nasalance', the amount of nasal airflow as a percentage of total airflow, to be calculated (McLean et al., 1997). Therefore, using SNORS, coordination and duration of velopharyngeal closure can be inferred. Simultaneous sound recording allows this to be related to speech outcome.

Real-time visual feedback indicates nasal and oral components of airflow on a bar display, allowing the patient to visualize nasal escape. Maximum airflow and targets are provided. SNORS can also record and compare data taken at different times, to objectively measure change. A 'test' assessment uses 10 prompt words, chosen to show how effective velopharyngeal closure is (Ellis et al., 1978), and the resulting data can be analysed and displayed in graphical form.

The trial

The trial compared the use of conventional speech and language therapy with SNORS biofeedback. TW was given a six-week block of each. Conventional exercises included sucking and blowing, contrasting obstruents with nasals, and articulation exercises, to encourage opening of the mouth and more precise articulation. Therapy also focused on self-monitoring, to raise awareness of the sensation of palatal movement and auditory differences between oral and nasal resonance. TW found these easy to detect, as he is an ex-professional musician. All exercises were practised at home, with therapy once a week for motivation and encouragement.

SNORS biofeedback therapy, using the bar display, followed. Assessment had shown that TW could make velopharyngeal closure, but was unable to maintain this. The hypothesis was that enabling TW to visualize velopharyngeal closure would increase awareness of velar movement and accompanying sensation. TW could be helped to increase duration of closure. Work started on sustained vowels. Initially, the level of nasal airflow was comparable to oral airflow. TW was encouraged to increase the oral, indicated by an extension of the oral bar, while maintaining and/or reducing the nasal airflow. Small adjustments that TW tried could be seen either to work or not. As this task became easier, TW's target level of nasal airflow was reduced.

TW was repeatedly asked to explain what was happening, and what it felt and sounded like. He was asked to reproduce the sensations and the sounds, first with, and as he became more practised, without the visual image. Therapy progressed from sustained vowels to obstruent CV syllables. Initially TW was unable to make velopharyngeal closure and thus build up sufficient intraoral air pressure. Considerable progress was made in reducing nasal escape during the closed phase of the plosive, allowing an increase in oral air pressure and a stronger oral release. Obstruents in other word positions and in polysyllabic words were then attempted. Changes and improvements were recorded throughout this therapy, and a final assessment was carried out.

Trial results

Assessment was carried out, using SNORS, prior to and following conventional and SNORS therapy, and nasalance was calculated. TW was required to say 10 words. Because there is variability between repeated recordings made by individual subjects (Folkins, 1986), three recordings were made on each occasion and the average used. Examples of baseline and final recordings of the assessment word 'cheese' are shown in Figures 36.1 and 36.2.

The top trace shows the amplitude of the speech signal, detected by microphones. The middle trace shows nasal airflow and the lower trace oral airflow. Note that the scale for each trace is different. The maximum value on the y-axis is 100%, but a smaller range is used in each case, to show maximum detail. Although peaks may look the same amplitude, they are generally different. The x-axis represents time, in seconds, and is the same for all traces. A measurement cursor has been placed at the point of maximum oral airflow, and the nasalance at this point is indicated.

In Figure 36.1, the oral airflow initially shows a small peak, as TW makes alveolar closure for the affricate, /tʃ/. This is followed by the closure, shown as 0% oral airflow, and the release, shown as a peak. Oral airflow continues to the end of the word. This general pattern is

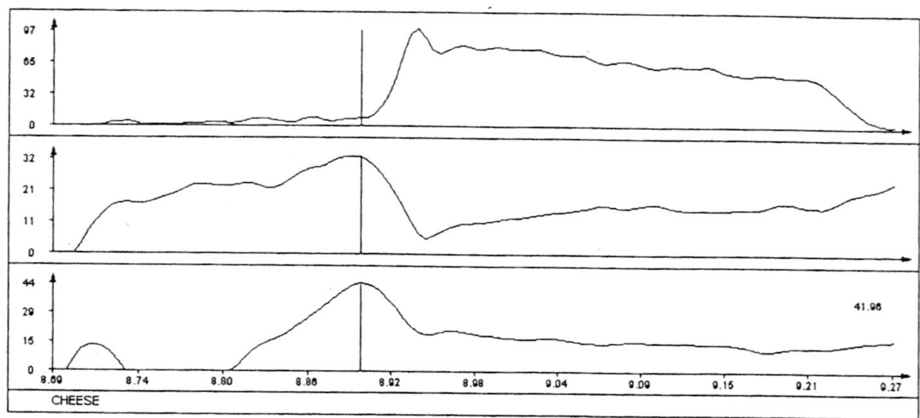

Figure 36.1. Baseline recording of TW 'cheese'. Top trace: speech envelope, middle trace: nasal airflow, bottom trace: oral airflow.

what would be expected in the normal production of this word. However, the nasal airflow shows an abnormal pattern, with nasal airflow continuing throughout the closure phase for the affricate. The fairly high levels may be due to attempts to increase intra-oral air pressure, and there is a peak of nasal airflow corresponding to the oral peak. There is an attempt at velopharyngeal closure following the affricate, where the trace dips, but closure is incomplete and fleeting. Nasal airflow rises during the vowel, /i/, and remains greater than oral during the final fricative, /z/. The rise in both airflows at the end of the word is caused by exhalation.

The consequential speech sound trace shows low level sound during the closure phase of the affricate, due to nasal emission. The sound level builds slightly during the affricate, and peaks with the onset of voicing, remaining high during the vowel, and decaying during the final fricative.

Following conventional therapy, nasal airflow was slightly reduced, suggesting a better approximation, though velopharyngeal closure was still not achieved. A final assessment was made following SNORS biofeedback therapy. This shows substantial improvement.

In Figure 36.2, the overall oral airflow pattern is the same. Nasal airflow is reduced and is virtually zero during most of the oral closure. The periodic small peaks here may indicate vibration of the velum, much as would happen during snoring, suggesting that the velum has reduced tone. Closure is not maintained during the plosive, but does occur immediately after it. Although absolute closure is brief, nasal airflow remains very low throughout the remainder of the word, indicating a close approximation to closure. Figure 36.3 shows the nasalance values for all 10 words at the three assessment points.

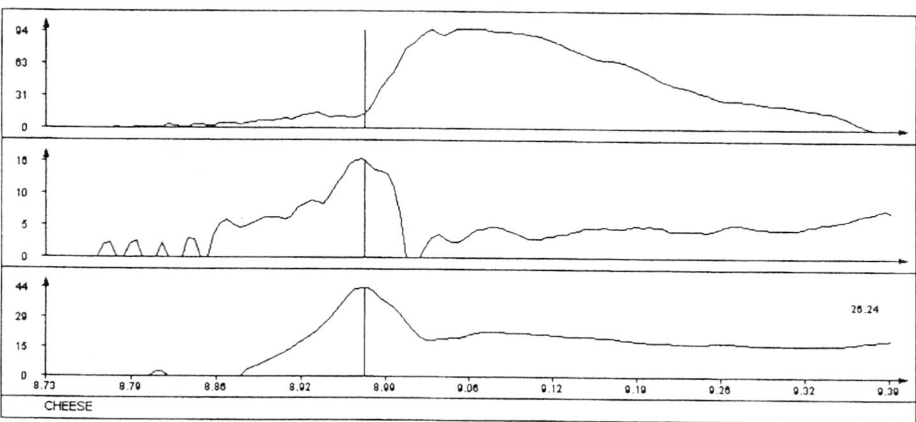

Figure 36.2. TW 'cheese' following SNORS biofeedback therapy. Top trace: speech envelope, middle trace: nasal airflow; bottom trace: oral airflow.

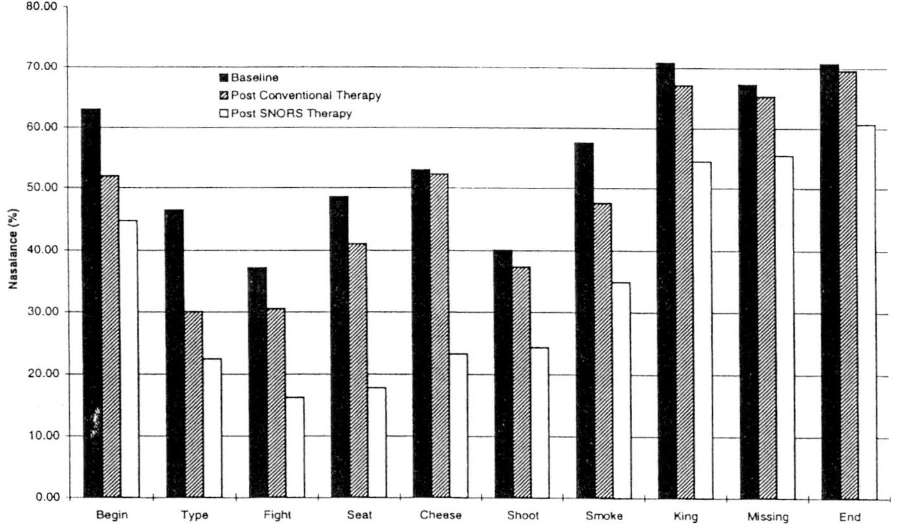

Figure 36.3. Nasalance summary for TW.

It can be clearly seen that for the majority of words, there is some reduction in nasalance following conventional therapy, but a much greater reduction after SNORS therapy. The significance of this greater improvement was assessed, using the Chi Squared test, and found to be highly significant ($p < 0.001$).

However, TW's speech remained somewhat hypernasal, with reduced intelligibility. TW had a very high hard palate and large oral cavity, so it was probably difficult to build up oral pressure. It was decided to try a built-up palate to decrease oral cavity size. This did not reduce hypernasality, but articulation nevertheless improved. Surgery may have affected tongue–palate contact, but the resulting articulation difficulties had been masked by TW's dominant hypernasality. Hence, TW was fitted with an electropalatography palate.

Linguagraph

Electropalatography is an instrumental technique for determining tongue–palate contact (Hardcastle et al., 1989; MorganBarry, 1989). The system used was the Kent Linguagraph (Kelly and Main, 1997; Main et al., 1997). This clinical system works with a PC and standard interface card. Features include a large, bright display (which can be single, two channel or full screen) and the facility to record and replay data. The system is easy to use for both therapy and assessment. Electropalatography gives the therapist an objective view of tongue–palate contact, and enables accurate diagnosis of the degree and manner of difficulty.

Linguagraph assessment

TW was making almost continual tongue–palate contact on the right, while using the left side of his tongue to compensate. Weakness and lack of sensation on the right of his oral cavity was the probable reason for this peculiar articulatory pattern. The effect on TW's articulation was slurring and imprecision of consonants. An illustration of TW's production of /s/ appears in Figure 36.4. The necessary groove is achieved on the left, and in a retracted position.

Multiparameter assessment

Simultaneous assessment using SNORS and Linguagraph would have enabled more accurate diagnosis of TW's speech difficulties, and better targeting of therapy. Initially this was not possible. However, during the course of TW's therapy period, further developments by the team enabled simultaneous recording and analysis. A SNORS/Linguagraph recording was made.

In Figure 36.4, showing the word 'smoke', the top trace is the envelope of the speech sound and the next two represent the nasal and oral airflows. The bottom three traces show the total lingua-palatal contact in each of the alveolar, palatal and velar regions (Jones and Hardcastle, 1995). To the right is a snapshot of the tongue contact pattern at the point indicated by the cursor.

Looking at the speech waveform, we see low-level sound at the start, representing the voiceless fricative /s/, followed by a small peak, as TW makes bilabial closure for the /m/. The sound level rises, during the /m/, and is sustained during the diphthong /əʊ/. Sound level drops, during the closure for the /k/, which is released silently. Although oral airflow

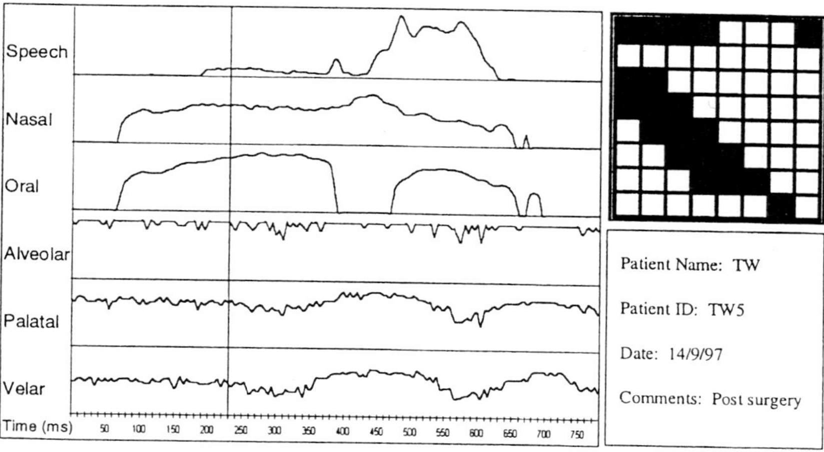

Figure 36.4. SNORS/Linguagraph recording of TW 'smoke'. Speech, airflow and tongue–palate contact trends on the left, as labelled; electropalatography snapshot and patient details to the right.

stops during the nasal /m/, the nasal airflow persists throughout the word, except for a brief closure just prior to the final plosive /k/. Tongue contact, in the alveolar region, is virtually 100% at all times. In the palatal and velar regions, it is also high, falling slightly for the fricative /s/ and the /ʊ/ part of the diphthong. Detail, such as the grooving for the /s/, can only be seen in a complete contact pattern snapshot. This is provided at the cursor position (maximum contact for /s/).

These results reflect TW's impaired velar and lingual function.

Summary and conclusion

Radical maxillofacial surgery can have a detrimental effect on speech production. The function of various articulators may be impaired and sensation reduced. In this case, both tongue and velum were affected. The use of SNORS proved invaluable, both as an assessment and therapy tool.

Objective analysis, using SNORS, provided clear graphical and numerical evidence of improvement in velopharyngeal function following conventional therapy, where it was barely detectable subjectively. SNORS biofeedback raised TW's awareness of remaining function, and enabled him to maximize this to improve velopharyngeal closure. The ability to monitor even small changes was motivating for TW and his therapist. The significant reduction in nasal airflow, following this biofeedback therapy, was accurately determined using SNORS.

The initially severe and dominant hypernasality masked TW's other articulatory difficulties. As these became more apparent, further assessment was carried out using Linguagraph, to determine their precise nature. This confirmed that TW had a unilateral weakness and demonstrated his peculiar articulatory patterns. It would not have been possible to predict such patterns from the resulting speech outcome. A course of Linguagraph therapy was planned. However, TW returned to full-time employment and has subsequently left his manual job to take up a managerial post. Since the completion of this therapy, TW has maintained the improvements made.

Despite his remaining articulation difficulties, TW is very pleased with his level of intelligibility, and reports that his speech rarely causes difficulties. So the outcome for him has been very good. However, if it had been possible to combine electropalatography with SNORS in initial assessment of TW's speech, targeting of therapy might have been different, and the improvements to intelligibility might have come sooner.

Acknowledgements

Thanks are due to Dr Hamid Mirlohi, Dr Calum McLean, M Jean Skoda, and Mr Tim Lewis, at the University of Kent, for their work in the development of SNORS and Linguagraph. Also Mr Chris Hendy, Consultant Maxillofacial Surgeon, for his helpful comments and Dr Rosemarie MorganBarry, Consultant Speech and Language Therapist, for encouragement and advice.

References

Albery E, Russell J (1990) Cleft palate and orofacial abnormalities. In Grunwell P (ed.) Developmental Speech Disorders. London: Whurr, pp. 63–82.

Ellis RE, Flack FC, Curle HJ, Selly WG (1978) A system for the assessment of nasal airflow during speech. British Journal of Disorders of Communication, 13(1), 31–40.

Folkins JW (1986) Issues in speech motor control and their relation to the speech of individuals with cleft palate. Cleft Palate Journal, 22, 106–22.

Hardcastle WJ, Jones W, Knight C, Trudgeon A, Calder G. (1989) New developments in electropalatography: a state of the art report. Clinical Linguistics and Phonetics, 3, 1–38.

Jones W, Hardcastle WJ (1995) New developments in EPG3 software. European Journal of Disorders of Communication, 30, 183–92.

Kelly SW, Main A (1997) SNORS and Linguagraph. Royal College of Speech and Language Therapists Bulletin, May, 7.

Main A, Kelly S, Manley G (1997) Teaching the tongue and looking at listening. Royal College of Speech and Language Therapists Bulletin, Nov 1997, 8–9.

McLean CC, Kelly SW, Manley MCG (1997) An instrument for the non-invasive objective assessment of velar function during speech. Medical Engineering and Physics, 19(1), 7–14.

MorganBarry RA (1989) EPG from square one: An overview of electropalatography as an aid to therapy. Clinical Linguistics and Phonetics, 3, 81–91.

Chapter 37 CLEFTNET Scotland: Applications of New Technology to the Investigation and Treatment of Speech Disorders Associated with Cleft Palate within a Scottish Context

MORAY J. NAIRN, WILLIAM J. HARDCASTLE, FIONA GIBBON, ROZ RAZZELL, LISA CRAMPIN, LIS HARVEY and BEVERLEY REYNOLDS

Introduction

It is estimated that, on entering school, approximately 12% of children have some form of speech disorder which requires the attention of a speech and language therapist (Enderby, 1989). The presence of a speech disorder not only affects the process of everyday communication, particularly if intelligibility is poor, but also has far-reaching secondary consequences for social, psychological and educational development (Watkins and Rice, 1994). Certain populations of children are particularly at risk from having a speech disorder, for example, those born with cleft lip and palate, hearing impairment or neurological abnormalities, although a significant number of speech disorders have no identifiable cause.

Children with intractable speech disorders pose a special problem for the speech and language therapy service, particularly if they live in remote areas. These children require therapy, but do not respond readily to conventional techniques. This makes management costly, since on-going therapy is needed, but the benefit from such therapy is small in terms of progress made. Specialist therapy is often required, but not available at a local level.

A new form of treatment, electropalatography (EPG), is proving an efficient and effective method for treating intractable speech disorders (Gibbon and Hardcastle, 1989; Hardcastle et al., 1991a; Dent et al., 1992; Gibbon et al., 1993; Dent et al., 1995) but is currently not widely available to speech therapists working in Scotland for a variety of reasons. Referring to EPG, Peterson-Falzone (1988) states that, 'such devices are beyond the reach of most clinicians, but have demonstrated what biofeedback can accomplish in eliminating inappropriate articulatory placement'.

EPG

EPG is a safe, non-invasive procedure which records clinically-relevant details of tongue activity during speech, namely the location and timing of tongue contacts with the hard palate and has been adopted as a research and clinical tool in many institutions around the world. The clinical usefulness of the technique has been demonstrated in a recent project (Dent et al., 1995; Gibbon et al., 1995) in which two primary functions of EPG were identified:

- Speech assessment. EPG records precise details of abnormal articulations often not detected by listening to the speech.
- Visual feedback. EPG enables subjects to monitor and change their own abnormal articulation patterns as part of a therapy programme. The real-time visual feedback function is used in all therapy sessions and has enabled subjects to master more normal articulation patterns, which they had not achieved by conventional therapeutic methods.

Rationale

Peterson-Falzone (1988) accepts the ability of biofeedback information, such as is provided by EPG, to improve articulatory accuracy, however implies that it is often not available. There are a number of factors contributing to the relative unavailability. First, there is often a financial constraint. The need for data acquisition hardware (which requires a PC) at the speech assessment stage makes the current EPG device relatively expensive and not particularly cost-effective for speech therapy clinics with limited caseloads of clients who would be expected to benefit from EPG therapy. However, EPG therapy may save considerable clinical time so may prove in the long term to be cost-effective despite the relatively high cost of the initial outlay of equipment and the cost of the artificial palate. Second, there may be a technical constraint.

Although EPG is a straightforward system to operate, interpretation of EPG data is a specialist technique requiring a level of support which in the past has not always been freely available to speech and language therapists. Lastly, there is a particular difficulty in administering continuing therapy to clients who live in geographically remote districts. Journeys to and from clinics for speech therapy can take several hours and, in some cases, can limit the amount of therapy which is reasonably available. These practical factors have prevented the widespread use of EPG, rather than the clinical effectiveness of the technique.

Summary of Aims

A number of aims were established at the outset of the project. This chapter reports on how the first two aims on the list were addressed.

1. To establish an innovative model of EPG therapy for individuals with cleft palate throughout Scotland.
2. To evaluate the effectiveness of this new form of service delivery over traditional methods for this group.
3. To design and construct a database of information which includes articulation (EPG) and acoustic data linked with relevant medical details to comprise the 'CLEFTNET database'.
4. To devise a strategy for delivering this form of EPG therapy to other client groups (e.g. subjects with speech disorders of unknown origin, disorders associated with hearing impairment and neurological disorders).

Methodology

Subjects

This project aims to investigate the feasibility of delivering EPG therapy in an innovative form to a group of subjects with intractable speech disorders. The group selected for the project have speech disorders associated with cleft palate. There are several research and methodological advantages in piloting the new form of service delivery with this group:

- These subjects can have intractable speech disorders, and previous research has shown that they respond positively to EPG therapy (Gibbon and Hardcastle, 1989; Dent et al., 1995).
- They are a readily identifiable group making subject selection straightforward, and some are likely to live in remote areas of Scotland.
- Cleft Palate Centres (CPCs) in Scotland already exist. There are five centres, located in Aberdeen, Ayr, Dundee, Edinburgh and Glasgow,

which already comprise a cross-centre audit group funded by the Scottish Office (Scottish Cleft Lip and Palate Association – SCALP).

- The CPCs see large numbers of clients with cleft palate and are in a position to select those who are likely to benefit from EPG therapy.
- The specialist speech and language therapists working in the centres support the aims of this project, and have undertaken to cooperate fully.

CLEFTNET (Scotland) addresses the difficulties listed above by implementing a totally new form of EPG service delivery. In order to combat the combined problems of financial resources and geographic remoteness, we have recently developed a cheap portable therapy unit (PTU) which provides EPG visual feedback only (Jones and Hardcastle, 1995). A combination of one centrally based EPG plus several PTUs potentially enables EPG therapy to be delivered in a cost-effective way. EPG assessment (using the full EPG system) of subjects takes place at specialist centres where large numbers of subjects are seen, with EPG therapy (using a PTU, on loan from the specialist centre) taking place at a local base.

The issue of technical support is addressed by establishing an IT network which links all of the specialist speech centres to the project headquarters at Queen Margaret College, Edinburgh.

CLEFNET IT Network

Each CPC is equipped with a full Reading EPG3 analysis and recording system and modems have also been installed on the host PCs. These modems provide the means of transferring data collected during EPG sessions to QMC for analysis. The remote access facilities provided at QMC ensure that only authorized users can carry out this process so the security of data is not compromised.

Custom software was written to control the process of data transfer from the remote centres to QMC. This software was designed to be as simple and intuitive as possible for busy clinicians. IT support for the centres is provided by use of 'remote control' software installed on machines at each site. This software allows manipulation of the computers from QMC and includes an interactive 'chat' facility that can be used to explain procedures or answer specific queries. This has proved invaluable for the project and is very popular with the clinicians.

Speech Therapy

Speech therapy is carried out either at the CPC using the full EPG3 system, or, where appropriate, using the PTU at a local base. All subjects undertake an initial recording which involves capturing acoustic and articulatory information using EPG. Following this assessment, the subjects are randomly divided into two equal-sized groups, the first group receiving four conventional therapy sessions followed by four EPG therapy sessions, whereas the second group receives four EPG therapy sessions followed by four conventional therapy sessions. There are further recorded assessments after each of the blocks of therapy.

Results – a case study

CG is a Scottish girl aged 9;10 at the start of CLEFTNET therapy. She had a submucous cleft of the soft palate which was repaired by pharyngoplasty at age 9;4. She displayed mild, intermittent hypernasality and cleft-type articulations. Figure 37.1 shows data summaries for CG across the three assessment sessions. These samples are for target words which begin with the phoneme /s/.

There is clearly some effect of therapy on the articulatory placement of the subject's /s/ productions. We have used a *centre of gravity* (COG) index (Hardcastle et al., 1991b) to summarize the shift in place of articulation, which appears to be from velar in the first recording to alveolar in the second and third recordings. The COG is an algorithm which computes a single figure from a frame or set of frames and represents the position along the front–back dimension of the greatest concentration of activated electrodes in the palate. If the subject is effecting a change in the place of articulation, particularly in terms of anteriority/posteriority, this will be revealed in a change in the COG figure. Larger numbers represent increased anterior articulatory contact. In Figure 37.1, the numbers below each frame show the centre of gravity (COG) calculation for that point in the utterance. The average COG is shown in the leftmost column for both subject and control speakers.

Figure 37.2 shows COG plots for the five target words recorded with /s/-initial contexts. All COG values at assessment 1, prior to therapy, are below 2.5 indicating posterior articulations. Following EPG therapy at assessment 2, all values have increased appreciably, which implies an improvement (fronting) of the place of articulation. Interestingly, following subsequent conventional therapy (assessment 3) the COG values have fallen slightly. This would seem to indicate that advances made by EPG therapy are not wholly sustained throughout later conventional therapy. These results have implications for the management of speech therapy programmes which involve EPG.

Conclusions

Preliminary results from the project indicate that this form of speech therapy service delivery is effective in bringing about improvements in articulatory patterns associated with cleft palate speech. EPG can also quantify changes in articulation using measures such as the COG.

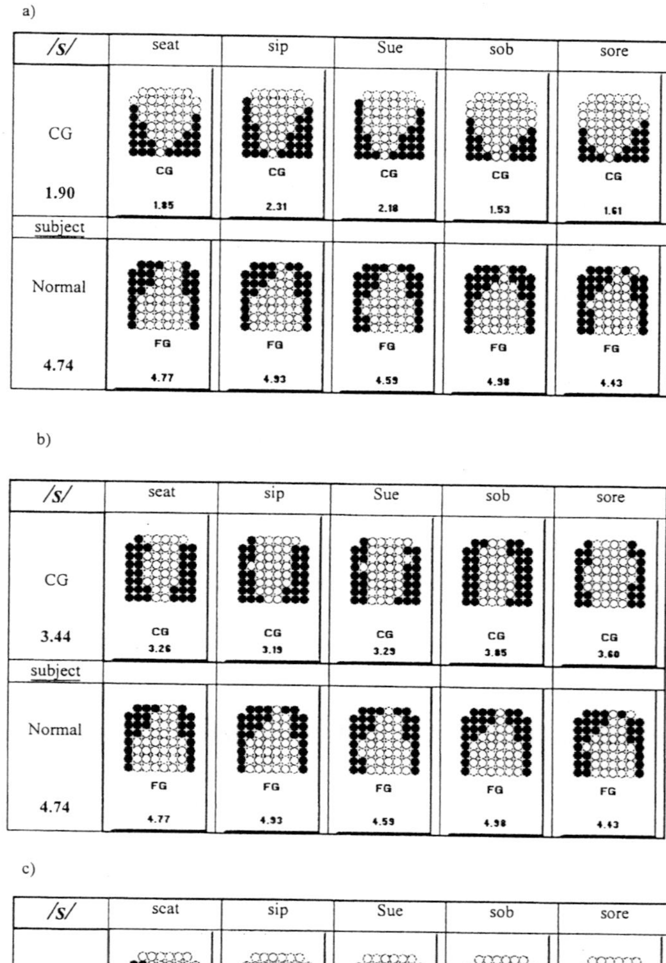

Figure 37.1. This figure has three parts: Figure 1 (a) shows the data recorded prior to any CLEFTNET therapy, Figure 1 (b) shows the data recorded following EPG therapy, Figure 1 (c) shows the data recorded following conventional therapy. The top row of each section shows the subject's EPG data for the EPG frame, which represents the temporal mid-point of the fricative. The lower row indicates the representative point in the utterance spoken by a normal control speaker.

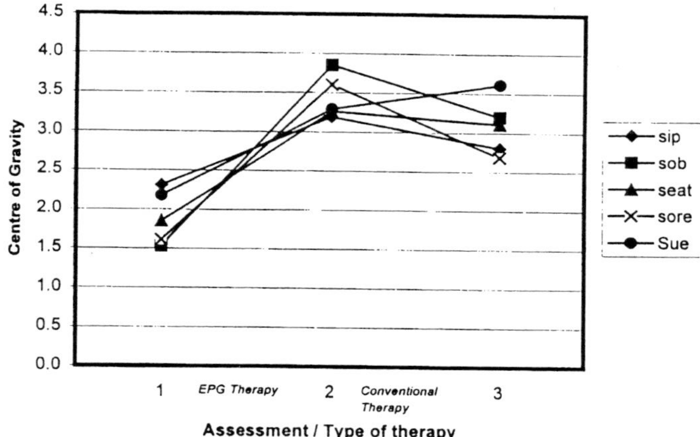

Figure 37.2. COG plots for the five target words recorded with /s/-initial contexts. The horizontal axis shows the assessments and therapy blocks. This subject received EPG therapy first and conventional therapy second.

The CLEFTNET project has demonstrated the value of the network structure in therapy management. Among the advantages are:

- the online exchange of EPG, acoustic and other electronic data;
- the provision of online technical support to facilitate operation of hardware and software;
- access to expertise and experience not available at local speech therapy clinics which allows EPG data analysis and can suggest guidelines for carrying out therapy.

Within the CLEFTNET paradigm, local speech and language therapists, specialist SLTs and experts in speech analysis and computer systems all work in their own field of expertise to successfully facilitate an improvement in delivery of speech therapy to clients who might otherwise be disadvantaged by financial, geographical and technical constraints.

Acknowledgements

The authors would like to express their gratitude to Jim Murphy for technical support and software programming and to the Scottish Office, Department of Health for project funding.

References

Dent H, Gibbon F, Hardcastle W (1992) Inhibiting an abnormal lingual pattern in a cleft palate child using electropalatography. In Leahy MM, Kallen JL (eds) Interdisciplinary Perspectives in Speech and Language Pathology. Dublin: School of Clinical Speech and Language Studies, pp. 211–21.

Dent H, Gibbon F, Hardcastle W (1995) The application of EPG to the remediation of speech disorders in school aged children and young adults. European Journal of Disorders of Communication, 30, 264–77.

Enderby P (1989) Communication disorders: planning a service to meet the needs. British Journal of Disorders of Communication, 24, 301–31.

Gibbon F, Hardcastle W (1989) Deviant articulation in a cleft palate child following late repair of the hard palate: a description and remediation procedure using electropalatography. Clinical Linguistics and Phonetics, 3, 93–110.

Gibbon F, Dent H, Hardcastle W (1993) Diagnosis and therapy of abnormal alveolar stops in a speech-disordered child using EPG. Clinical Linguistics and Phonetics, 7, 247–68.

Gibbon F, Hardcastle W, Dent H (1995) A study of obstruent sounds in school-age children with speech disorders using electropalatography. European Journal of Disorders of Communication, 30, 213–25

Hardcastle WJ, Gibbon FE, Jones W (1991a) Visual display of tongue-palate contact: electropalatography in the assessment and remediation of speech disorders. British Journal of Disorders of Communication, 26, 41–74.

Hardcastle W, Gibbon F, Nicolaidis K (1991b) EPG data reduction methods and their implications for studies of lingual coarticulation. Journal of Phonetics, 19, 251–66.

Jones W, Hardcastle W (1995) New developments in EPG3 software. European Journal of Disorders of Communication, 30, 183–92.

Peterson-Falzone S (1988) Speech disorders related to craniofacial structural defects: part 2. In Lass NJ, McReynolds LV, Northern JL, Yoder DE (eds) Handbook of Speech-Language Pathology and Audiology. Toronto: BC Decker Inc.

Watkins RV, Rice ML (1994) (eds) Specific Speech-Language Impairments in Children. Baltimore, MD: Paul Brookes Publishing Co.

Chapter 38 MoDiaS – A PC-based System for Routine Acoustic Analysis of Neurogenic Speech Disorders

MICHAEL MERK and WOLFRAM ZIEGLER

Introduction

Although the value of acoustic analysis methods in the assessment of dysarthric speech is generally accepted and several valuable PC-based systems have been developed during the past years (Read et al., 1990, 1992; Buder et al., 1996), most clinicians are still hesitant using these systems in their routine work. Many of the parameters proposed for diagnostic use depend on time-consuming segmentations of the speech signal (e.g. VOT, segment duration, etc.), others require suitable normalization in order to be meaningful (e.g. formant frequencies), and some parameters are characterized by a high between- or within-subject variability (e.g. F_0-Variation). Furthermore, few systems offer facilities for handling all aspects of a clinical examination based on acoustic measures, i.e. stimulus presentation, speech recording, signal analysis, detection and handling of artefacts, and presentation of results.

The prototype system presented here provides clinical users with a small but useful number of robust and clinically relevant speech parameters. It guides therapists through a complete assessment procedure, from patient examination to data evaluation, thereby trying to meet the needs of speech pathologists working in a clinical environment. Diagnostic parameters are based on acoustic measures obtained from the microphone signal. Acoustic variables are focused on *speech rate, fluency, consonant and vowel articulation* and *voice quality*.

System architecture

At present, the Modular Diagnostic System (MoDiaS) contains a total of four modules for the diagnosis of (1) rate, rhythm, and fluency;

(2) consonant articulation; (3) vowel articulation; and (4) sustained phonation. These modules are based on computations of the acoustic parameters that are considered most relevant for the description of disordered speech; in addition, they combine acoustic and auditory measures by including auditory judgement protocols. Each module comprises:

- a *recording component* (including the presentation of standard materials and the recording of a patient's utterances);
- an *evaluation component* (including a pre-selection of trials to be evaluated, exclusion of artefacts, and facilities to enter expert ratings based on auditory evaluation); and
- a *statistics and graphics component* for the presentation of results.

Signal analysis methods are optimized with regard to precision and stability rather than computational speed. No manual segmentation is required. Results can be checked for their plausibility and can be accepted or rejected/corrected, respectively, at different stages of the analysis process. Individual tasks can easily be repeated in cases of inconsistent or questionable results. The system further allows for an evaluation of auditory judgements of the acoustically analysed materials. Diagnostic data are presented graphically or in tabular form, either with reference to normative data or in a follow-up format. In addition, all results are stored in ASCII-interface files for further processing by standard statistics and graphics software.

The system is based on a PC with a commercial sound card and uses MATLAB as programming environment. The concept allows for rapid prototyping, fast code generation and a convenient fitting of algorithms according to the results obtained in clinical tests.

Module 1: Speech rate, rhythm and fluency

Altered speech rate is among the most prominent signs of neurogenic speech disorders. Both slowed and accelerated speech may occur, although slowness is by far more frequent (Ziegler et al., 1988, 1993; Ackermann and Ziegler, 1992). Several different features can account for slowness, i.e. prolongation of sounds or of transitions, frequent or prolonged pauses, iterations, repairs, etc. While simple time-by-count measures of speech rate (in terms of syllables per second) can easily be determined, a differentiation between distinctive types of slowed speech is mostly made on a qualitative basis, although quantitative measures of dysfluency types would be diagnostically most relevant. In particular, fluency measures of aphasic speech may contribute to the differential diagnosis of anterior and posterior aphasic syndromes (Gandour et al., 1994). Furthermore, measures of syllable repetition rate ('articulatory diadochokinesis') can be used as an index of the nature and severity of motor speech impairment (Ziegler and Wessel, 1996).

In the *sentence-production* component of Module 1, a standard set of 24 test sentences is presented to be spoken by the patient. The sentences are composed of a constant carrier phrase ('*Ute kann die . . . bekommen*', 'Ute can get the . . .') with embeddings of three types of target words: (1) two-syllabic words of a simple CVCV-structure, e.g. /ty:tə/ ('paper-bag'), two-syllabic words containing consonant clusters, e.g. /ʃtrYmpfə/ ('stockings'), and (3) three-syllabic words, e.g. /trɔmpe:tə/ ('trumpet'). Evaluation is based on a syllable-segmentation algorithm operating on loudness contours of the speech signal. These contours are computed by weighted summations over 24 bark bands, the weights being chosen appropriately to enhance the energy contained in the syllabic nuclei relative to the consonantal onsets. The construction of the carrier phrase guarantees high success rates of the automatic segmentation routine. The algorithm marks the nucleus and the boundaries of each of the detected syllables. The results of this procedure are inspected with the use of a segmentation editor (Figure 38.1). Syllables not pertaining to the target sentence must be marked appropriately, i.e. as *iterations, false starts*, etc. Likewise, syllable elision slots must eventually be indicated. Finally, each of the target syllables can be marked for the quality of its segmental make-up, i.e. as containing phonetic distortions or phonemic paraphasias (Figure 38.1).

Thus, for each sentence the metric grid of a patient's realization can be analysed in terms of syllable durations, pause durations, or 'intrusions' of additional syllables or sounds. Moreover, segmental errors can be assessed in relation to the temporal structure of an utterance, which

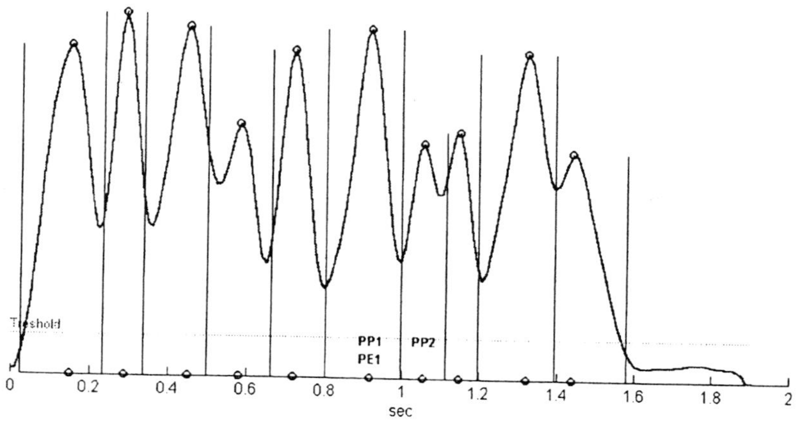

Figure 38.1. Segmentation editor for the sentence production task of Module 1. The top panel contains a loudness contour of one of the test sentences (three-syllabic target word), the oscillogram is plotted in the bottom panel. Three syllables are marked for segmental errors (PP = phonemic paraphasia, PE = phonetic distortion). Marking of syllables is performed via pull-down menus.

may be useful in the diagnosis of aphasic and apraxic disorders. In particular, the influence of syllabic length and segmental complexity of an embedded target word on the syllabic timing of a phrase can be determined by comparing the three subsets of test sentences mentioned above.

By the *diadochokinesis* component of Module 1, temporal aspects of a patient's performance on rapid syllable repetition tasks can be examined. Syllabic rate as well as the regularity of a syllable repetition chain can be analysed for different standard tasks ('dada . . .', 'daba . . .', 'data . . .'). For each trial a segmentation editor similar to the one seen in Figure 38.1 displays a loudness contour based on suitably weighted critical band summations. Automatic segmentation of syllables is performed and can be inspected and corrected interactively, using both visual and auditory information. Repetition chains can be evaluated for selected analysis windows. In order to reveal irregularities in duration and intensity, the duration and loudness of successive syllables can be displayed in a scatter plot. Major analysis parameters are average repetition rates and measures of period and intensity variation over time.

Module 2: Consonant articulation

Most dysarthric syndromes are characterized by imprecise consonant articulation (Darley et al., 1975) which may, in more severe cases, lead to intelligibility problems. Acoustic descriptions of impaired consonant articulation are rare and mostly restricted to the voice onset time of plosives. VOT measurements, however, are time-consuming and therefore not practical in clinical diagnostics. Instead, Module 2 is focused on the assessment of disturbances of fricative articulation and of the faculty of contrasting nasal and oral sounds.

The *sentence production* component of Module 2 includes presentation of two sets of five test sentences each. Each sentence contains only voiced segments, except for four target consonants. The target consonants of the first set are *voiceless fricatives* of different places of articulation, those of the second set are *nasal consonants*. Acoustic evaluation is based on short-term spectra of the speech signal with appropriate weightings of the energy proportions contained in different frequency bands (Ziegler et al., 1990). Weightings are empirically determined in such a way that the contrast between the voiced oral 'backgound' of the carrier phrase and the 'foreground' of the target segments is maximized. Two different sets of weights are used for the voiceless fricative and the nasal consonant subtests. For each sentence the resulting contour is presented in an editor window similar to the one seen in Figure 38.1. In normal productions, the target consonants are represented by sharp peaks. In cases of reduced friction energy of the voiceless fricatives or of a reduced nasal-oral contrast, respectively, the trajectories are flatter, showing less marked peaks for the target consonants. As in Module 1, the editor allows for the positioning of an analysis frame and computation of relative peak heights. Further, auditory ratings of the feature under consideration (fricative articulation, nasal-oral distinction) can be entered for each target consonant and evaluated statistically.

The *syllable repetition* component of Module 2 requires subjects to produce voiceless fricatives or nasal-oral contrasts in rapid succession (sasasa . . ., danadana . . .). Acoustic evaluation is based on the same parameters as in the sentence production component of this module. Here, the faculty of producing the required contrasts is measured in combination with the temporal information describing the patient's diadochokinetic performance.

Module 3: Vowel articulation

Articulation disorders in neurologic patients usually extend to vowel articulation. Conventionally, vowel articulation is analysed on the basis of formant frequencies. Important features of dysarthric speech such as vowel centralization or unrounding of rounded vowels can be detected by alterations in the frequencies of the first and second formant (Ziegler and von Cramon, 1983a,b). Measures like the area of the vowel triangle of /a/, /i/ and /u/ in the F1-F2-plane can also be used in longitudinal studies of spontaneous or therapeutically induced recovery of articulation (Ziegler and von Cramon, 1983a).

Module 3 of MoDiaS is based on a formant tracking algorithm for vowels spoken in isolation. Patients are required to sustain each of the four cardinal vowels /a/, /i/, /y/, and /u/ for approximately 2–3 s. The system selects the most stable 2 s portion of the signal to compute formant frequencies from LPC-spectra over 23 ms frames at 5 ms steps (LPC-order 14, root-solving algorithm). A specially-designed tracking algorithm allows for interactive modifications of the start value, in order to obtain stable trajectories even in cases of poor voice quality or other abnormalities. Each vowel is then characterized by the median values of the F1- and F2-trajectories. Parametric analysis is based on measures describing the range of an individual's vowel space, i.e. the formant triangle area (see Figure 38.2), the F2-distance between /i/ and /y/ (as a measure of lip rounding), the F2-distance between /y/ and /u/ (as a measure of front-back-contrastiveness), and the F1-distance between /a/ and the high vowels (as a measure of height).

Again, auditory judgements can be entered for each vowel and can be summarized to obtain auditory-based diagnostic data of vowel articulation in addition to the described acoustic measures.

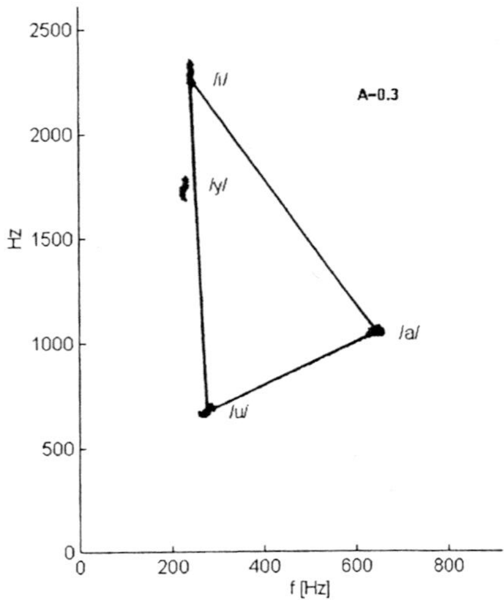

Figure 38.2. Example of a display of vowel formant tracking results in Module 3: Vowel triangle for German vowels /a/, /i/, /u/ spoken in isolation by a neurologically normal subject. The values of the formant trajectories scatter around the corners of the triangle.

Module 4: Sustained phonation

While Modules 1–3 deal with speech rate and articulation, Module 4 is focused on voice problems in patients with neurogenic speech disorders. It is primarily based on the sustained vowels of Module 3, but requires additional productions of sustained /a/ with the instruction to speak at a higher or lower pitch (two steps each). The cardinal vowels of Module 3 are used to determine a patient's normal pitch, voice quality and stability of phonation, while the vowels spoken at decreased or increased pitch levels may serve to detect limitations in the patient's ability to alter laryngeal configurations voluntarily. Parameters describing voice quality are mean F_0, vocal jitter and shimmer, and the ratio of the first two harmonics. Vocal stability is assessed by variation measures of these parameters over time. Fundamental periods of the speech signal are detected by an adaptive tracking algorithm which uses a cepstrum-based estimate of the mean F_0 as its start value. Jitter values are normalized for mean F_0. Variations over time include linear trend and slow oscillations around the linear trend (e.g. voice tremor). Like other modules, Module 4 permits users to add, item-by-item, auditory judgements of voice quality (rough/breathy/tense voice) and vocal stability (voice breaks, fluctuations of pitch or loudness, tremor etc.). Thus, a combined profile of acoustic and auditory parameters of disordered phonation is obtained.

References

Ackermann H, Ziegler W (1992) Articulatory deficits in Parkinsonian dysarthria: an acoustic analysis. Journal of Neurology, Neurosurgery and Psychiatry, 54, 1093–8.

Buder EH, Kent RD, Kent JF, Milenkovic P, Workinger M (1996) FORMOFFA: an automated formant, moment, fundamental frequency, amplitude analysis of normal and disordered speech. Clinical Linguistics and Phonetics, 10, 31–54.

Darley FL, Aronson A, Brown J (1975) Motor Speech Disorders. Philadelphia, PA: Saunders.

Gandour J, Dechongkit S, Ponglorpisit S, Khunadorn F (1994) Speech timing at the sentence level in Thai after unilateral brain damage. Brain and Language, 46, 419–38.

Read C, Buder EH, Kent RD (1990) Speech analysis systems: a survey. Journal of Speech and Hearing Research, 33, 363–74.

Read C, Buder EH, Kent RD (1992) Speech analysis systems: An evaluation. Journal of Speech and Hearing Research, 35, 314–32.

Ziegler W, Von Cramon D (1983a) Vowel distortion in traumatic dysarthria: a formant study. Phonetica, 40, 63–78.

Ziegler W, Von Cramon D (1983b) Vowel distortion in traumatic dysarthria: lip rounding versus tongue advancement. Phonetica, 40, 312–22.

Ziegler W, Hartmann E, Hoole P, von Cramon D (1990) Entwicklung von diagnostischen Standards und von Therapieleitlinien für zentrale Stimm-und Sprechstörungen (Dysarthrophonien). München: GSF.

Ziegler W, Hoole P, Hartmann E, von Cramon D (1988) Accelerated speech in dysarthria after acquired brain injury: Acoustic correlates. British Journal of Disorders of Communication, 23, 215–28.

Ziegler W, Wessel K (1996) Speech timing in ataxic disorders. Sentence production and rapid repetitive articulation. Neurology, 47, 208–14.

Chapter 39 A Comparison of Computerized Speech/Voice Analysis Programs

SHAHEEN N AWAN and SHELLEY SCARPINO

Introduction

Speech-language pathologists are responsible for diagnosing and treating a variety of speech and language disorders. Within the realm of speech disorders are those more specifically classified as voice disorders. A voice disorder is 'a problem in producing voice that is primarily caused by a disturbance or loss of normal laryngeal function' (Hillman et al., 1990). Because speech clinicians often cannot utilize instruments which allow direct observation of the condition and vibratory patterns of the vocal folds, they must rely on other means to arrive at a diagnosis and plan of treatment. Acoustic analysis provides an indirect and non-invasive method of assessing the functional capabilities of the phonatory mechanism. According to Colton and Casper (1990), there is an interdependence between anatomy, physiology, neurology and acoustics. Research has shown that a great deal can be inferred about the physiology of the vocal folds based on acoustic measures (Colton and Casper, 1990; Eskenazi et al., 1990).

The instrumentation used to provide objective acoustic measures of voice production are becoming more accessible and are used more frequently in clinical practice (Hillman et al., 1990). According to Orlikoff (1992), an accurate diagnosis using objective measures depends on the validity and reliability of the obtained data. Today's instruments are believed to be more reliable and more valid than in the past (Baken, 1987). In recent years, several commercial computer programs have become available for the acoustic analysis of voice. According to Read, Buder and Kent (1990), there are now at least 15 systems available commercially for this purpose. Computer analysis is appealing to clinicians because it is relatively easy to use, efficient, and is assumed to be accurate in its calculations. A number of studies have been published which have provided descriptive reviews of commercially available speech/voice analysis programs (Mann, 1987; Thomas-Stonell, 1987; Read et al., 1990, 1992; Ryalls and Baum, 1990). These reviews have focused primarily on describing the various features of each system including hardware requirements, user interface, types of displays and available analyses. Unfortunately, only a few studies have attempted to objectively examine the validity and reliability of commercially available software programs (Karnell et al., 1995; Bielamowicz et al., 1996).

While computer software for the analysis of voice would appear to be a useful addition to the tools of the speech and voice pathologist, questions still remain regarding the validity and accuracy of available software packages. It is imperative that computer analysis accurately measures voice characteristics in order that clinicians may confidently differentiate disordered voice characteristics from those within the range of normal productions. The purpose of this study was to assess the accuracy of four currently available software systems for speech and voice analysis:

- Computerized Speech Lab – CSL Model 4300 v. 4 (Kay Elemetrics, Pine Brook, NJ, USA)
- CSpeechSP (Milenkovic P and Read C, Madison, WI, USA)
- Dr Speech for Windows v.3.0 – Voice Assessment (Tiger Electronics, Inc, Seattle, WA, USA)
- EZVoice Voice Analysis Software v. 1.2 (VoiceTek Enterprises, Nescopeck, PA, USA)

These four computer programs were compared in terms of their accuracy in measuring various key parameters of vocal frequency commonly used in the clinical evaluation of voice. The inclusion of the Dr Speech and EZVoice programs presents the first assessment of the validity of PC-Windows based voice analysis programs. In addition, this study attempted to extend the results of the Bielamowicz et al. (1996) study by evaluating the possible effects of age and gender on the results of computerized analysis of voice parameters.

Method

Subjects

Voice types from a both genders and from various points within the aging continuum were included in this study. Ten male and 10 female subjects ranging in age from 18–30 years were recruited from the student population of Bloomsburg University, Bloomsburg, PA. In addition, 10 children (five males; five females), ranging in age from 5–9 years were recruited from the Campus Child Center of Bloomsburg

University. Subjects had no prior history of trauma or disease which may have affected their ability to produce normal voice, and all were non-smokers. Subjects were judged by a trained speech pathologist to have voice characteristics within normal limits for pitch, loudness and quality for their respective age and gender. All subjects passed a hearing screening at 25 dB HL at 0.5 , 1, 2 and 4 kHz.

Elicitation of voice samples

All subjects were asked to carry out two tasks: (a) sustain the vowel /a/ at a comfortable pitch and loudness for approximately 3 s; and (b) read 'The Rainbow Passage' (Fairbanks, 1960). The productions were recorded using an Optimus Digital Compact Cassette Tape Deck (Model DCT-2000) and Scotch (3M) Digital Compact Cassette tape at a sampling rate of 48 kHz. Signals were input to the digital tape recorder using a Realistic microphone (Model 33-1073A) and a Radio Shack preamplifier-mixer (Model 32-1200C). Recording levels on the tape recorder were set to peak at -3 VU during the sustained vowel production. Subjects were seated in front of the microphone at a zero degree angle of incidence and maintained an approximate mouth to microphone distance of 30 cm.

Data analysis procedures

The vowel and continuous speech productions were later redigitized at a sampling rate of 44 100 Hz with 16 bits of resolution using a Gateway Pentium-75 computer (Gateway 2000, North Sioux City, SD, USA) and a SoundBlaster 16 sound card (Creative Labs Inc, Milpitas, CA, USA). Control of the SoundBlaster 16 board was exercised through the Dr Speech software. Following recording, all files were saved to disk in .WAV format. This format is a standard format which could be accessed by all of the programs used in this study and eliminated any contaminating effects which may have presented due to the use of different A-to-D hardware with different software packages. The Dr Speech software was then used to edit and save (1) the middle one second from the sustained vowel production for each subject, and (2) the second sentence of 'The Rainbow Passage' to separate files.

The four commercial software programs (Dr Speech, CSL - Base Module, CSpeech, and EZVoice) were used to analyse the speech/voice samples on measures of mean fundamental frequency (F_0), F_0 Standard deviation and range. A hand-marking method (peak-picking) using a wave editor programmed by the first author was also employed to obtain the aforementioned measures. Program parameters for all of the commercial software programs were originally configured to the instructions provided in each program's respective user manual. In the event that instructions were not provided, the default values of the program were used. However, preliminary results (Awan and Scarpino, 1997) indicated that vocal frequency calculations were so poor (using default program values) in the case of the CSpeech program that allowances had to be made. Dr P. Milenkovic, the author of CSpeech, was contacted for specific instructions on how to improve CSpeech performance. It is unfortunate that the CSpeech author does not provide adequate information in the user manual on how to configure the CSpeech program for optimal performance. Studies which have used CSpeech and which do not provide specific description of how the frequency tracking algorithms were configured prior to analysis should be approached with caution regarding the validity of their results.

Information regarding the algorithms employed in the various computer programs included in this study is often absent or poorly detailed in their respective user manuals. The CSL and CSpeech programs reportedly use autocorrelation techniques for pitch tracking. The reader should refer to Bielamowicz et al. (1996) for a comprehensive description of the algorithms employed in the CSL and CSpeech packages. The Dr Speech user manual (Huang et al., 1995) does not provide any information regarding the basic frequency tracking algorithm employed in its Voice Assessment package. A real-time display of waveform analysis is provided which appears to show identification of zero-crossing points. EZVoice employs frequency tracking algorithms that are similar to those proposed in a pattern recognition process described by Kent and Read (1992). EZVoice uses a time-domain processing method which incorporates digital low-pass filtering, centre clipping, and peak detection techniques to identify the boundaries of each cycle of the periodic component of the voice signal under analysis (Awan, 1996). The EZVoice program also includes detailed post-processing error-correction routines to deal with any frequency tracking errors that may occur (Awan, 1996, 1997).

Hand-marking reliability

All primary statistical comparisons reported in this study are made in relation to the hand-marking results. It appears to be reasonable to use hand-marking as a standard by which the validity of the various programs could be assessed since (1) hand-marking employs easily understood and executed procedures which all speech clinicians and researchers have been exposed to, and (2) hand-marking associated with visual review of the waveform under analysis has consistently been used as the 'last resort' technique employed to assess the accuracy of computerized vocal frequency analysis and by which errors in computerized analysis are corrected.

It was expected that the computer analysis programs would always analyse data files in a similar fashion on subsequent analyses if algorithm parameters were held constant. However, since the hand-marking results were to be used as a comparative standard by which the results of the commercial software would be evaluated, it was felt that reliability assessment was important for the hand-marking aspects of this study. To assess hand-marking reliability, the sustained vowel samples from three subjects from each of the male, female, and children groups (total N = 9) were selected at random for reanalysis by (1) the second author (SS) and (2) a second judge familiar with the hand-marking methods employed in this study. Tables 39.1 and 39.2 present the inter- and intra-judge reliability results for measures of mean F_0 and F_0 standard deviation from both sustained vowel and continuous speech samples. Results indicate that hand-marking can be a highly reliable technique for identification of vocal frequency.

Table 39.1. Inter-judge reliability results for measures of vocal F_0 for sustained vowels and for continuous speech samples. All *T* values are non-significant.

Sample type	Measure	Judge 1	Judge 2	Mean difference	T	df	r
Sustained vowel	Mean F_0 (Hz)	189.46	189.46	0.00	0.00	16	1.0*
	F_0 standard deviation	1.71	1.75	0.04	0.12	16	0.99*
Continuous speech	Mean F_0 (Hz)	197.45	196.40	1.05	0.03	16	0.99*
	F_0 standard deviation	20.53	19.54	0.99	0.22	16	0.93*

*$p < 0.001$

Table 39.2. Intra-judge reliability results for measures of vocal F_0 for sustained vowels and for continuous speech samples. All *T* values are non-significant.

Sample type	Measure	Test	Retest	Mean difference	T	df	r
Sustained vowel	Mean F_0 (Hz)	188.45	188.45	0.00	0.43	8	1.0*
	F_0 standard deviation	1.59	1.62	0.03	1.08	8	0.99*
Continuous speech	Mean F_0 (Hz)	194.79	195.43	0.64	1.51	8	0.99*
	F_0 standard deviation	20.09	20.53	0.44	0.89	8	0.99*

*$p < 0.001$

Results

Sustained vowel analysis

A series of 1 Between (3 levels of group); 1-Within (5 levels of program) ANOVAs were computed to analyse inter-program differences in computing mean F_0 and F_0 standard deviation from sustained vowel samples. Results indicated no significant differences in the computation of mean F_0 and F_0 standard deviation amongst the four programs tested, as well as no difference between computer program calculations and hand-marking estimates. No significant effects of gender were observed.

Continuous speech analysis

A series of 1 Between (3 levels of group); 1-Within (5 levels of program) ANOVAs were computed to analyse inter-program differences in computing mean F_0, pitch sigma (F_0 standard deviation converted to semitones), and speaking range (in semitones). Results indicated that, as expected, inter-program comparisons of the analysis of vocal frequency from continuous speech samples are much more problematic than found in the sustained vowel analysis.

Mean F_0 estimation

Results of analysis of mean F_0 from continuous speech (see Figure 39.1) indicated a significant Group x Program interaction ($F = 3.53$; df 8, 108; $p = 0.001$). Post-hoc analyses using a Fisher Least Significant Difference (LSD) means comparison test (Critical Difference = 2.88 Hz) indicated the following:

1. The CSpeech program produces significantly lower estimates of mean F_0 than the three other programs or the hand-marking method when analysing adult male voices.
2. The Dr Speech, CSpeech, and CSL programs produce significantly lower estimates of mean F_0 than the hand-marking technique when analysing adult female voices. The CSL estimate was also significantly lower than that provided by the EZVoice program.
3. All four programs produced significantly lower estimates of mean F_0 than hand-marking when analysing child voices. The CSpeech program provided the lowest estimate of mean F_0, significantly different from all other techniques analysed.

Pitch sigma estimation

Analysis of computations of pitch sigma (see Figure 39.2) from continuous speech indicated a significant Group x Program interaction ($F = 2.32$; df 8, 108; $p = 0.02$). Post-hoc analyses (Fisher LSD : Critical Difference = 0.86 ST) indicated the following:

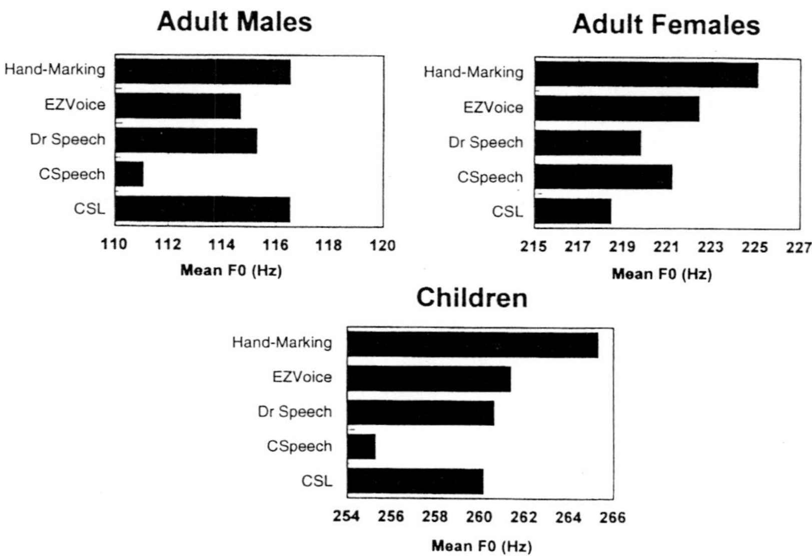

Figure 39.1. Mean F_0 estimations for the adult male, adult female, and child groups as derived using commercially available voice analysis software. Results from the hand-marking method are also provided.

1. Dr Speech, CSpeech, and CSL provide significantly greater estimates of pitch sigma than the EZVoice program or estimates from hand-marking when analysing adult male voices.
2. CSpeech and CSL provide significantly greater estimates of pitch sigma than the Dr. Speech and EZVoice programs, as well as in comparison to the hand-marking technique when analysing adult female voices.
3. In the child voices, CSpeech was observed to provide a significantly greater estimate of pitch sigma than the EZVoice program. All other comparisons were non-significant.

Speaking range in semitones

Results of analysis of speaking range in semitones from continuous speech (see Figure 39.3) indicated a significant main effect of Program ($F = 22.21$; df 4, 108; $p < 0.001$). Post-hoc analyses (Critical Difference = 1.89 ST) indicated the following:

1. The Dr Speech, CSpeech, and CSL programs all provide significantly greater estimates of speaking range (STs) than either the EZVoice program or the hand-marking.

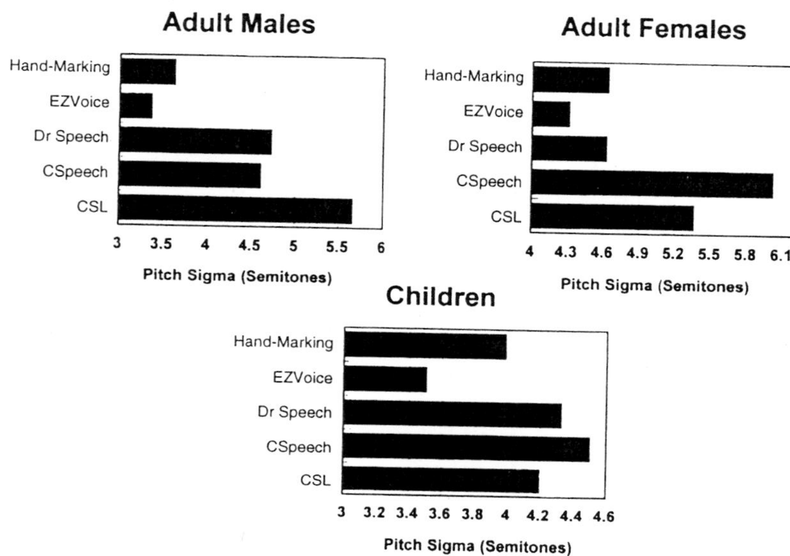

Figure 39.2. Estimations of F_0 standard deviation for the adult male, adult female and child groups as derived using commercially available voice analysis software. Results from the hand-marking method are also provided.

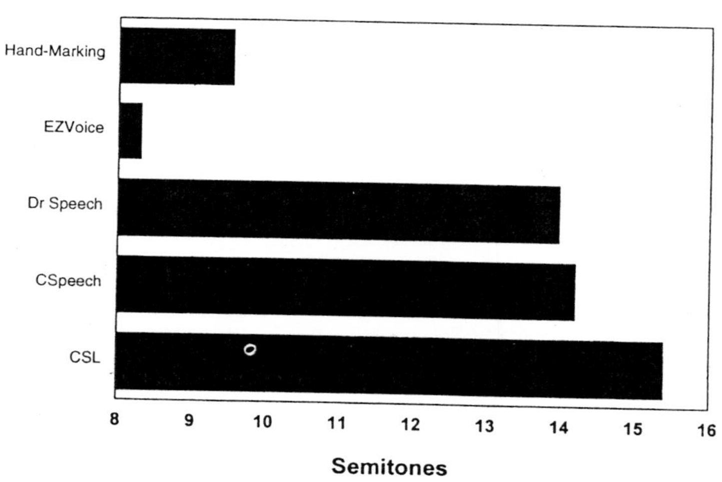

Figure 39.3. Mean estimations of speaking range in semitones as derived using commercially available voice analysis software. Results from the hand-marking method are also provided.

Discussion

While the voice/speech analysis programs analysed in this study were highly comparable in terms of their measures of mean F_0 and F_0 standard deviation from sustained vowels, it is evident that the variations in vocal F_0 that accompany the production of continuous speech present difficulties which may result in significant differences between computational results. Each program's ability to distinguish voiced/voiceless distinctions may also result in errors in F_0 tracking. Depending on the voice sample, error correction routines may need to be incorporated prior to the final estimation of signal frequency. There are many instances in which 'false' peaks/zeroes are mistaken as 'true' cycle boundary markers.

The general lack of agreement in estimation of pitch sigma and speaking range between the Dr Speech, CSpeech, and CSL programs with the hand-marking standard are primarily reflective of pitch-tracking errors. A review of the raw data from this study showed numerous instances in which *different* subjects had *identical estimations* of their low and high frequency. In addition, these identical estimations invariably were F_0 estimations that matched the low and high frequency limits of the respective F_0 analysis windows of each program. In contrast, the EZVoice program consistently showed much greater similarity to the hand-marking standard on all measures of vocal F_0. The EZVoice program was designed to include stringent error correction routines which will correct common errors in pitch estimation such as those attributable to period doubling, or to the isolated errors in pitch tracking that may accompany voiceless-to-voiced transitions in words. In addition, when analysing continuous speech samples, the EZVoice program implements a form of single exponential smoothing prior to computing final estimates of mean F_0, standard deviation, etc. This explains why EZVoice consistently produces F_0 estimates which slightly underestimated those produced by hand-marking.

The measures of vocal F_0 investigated in this study are commonly used to differentiate voice types. Pitch sigma and speaking range have both been described as measures of phonatory control which may be disrupted in the disordered voice. It is our opinion that it is essential for the developers of voice analysis programs to prevent obvious errors in F_0 estimation which may possibly lead to misclassification in voice type. This is particularly pertinent to the less experienced clinician who may not be aware of the limitations in computer estimation of vocal F_0 characteristics.

The results of this study indicate that the validity of commercially available programs for voice analysis should not be assumed. It is hoped that future studies will investigate the capabilities of these programs to accurately calculate other characteristics of the voice signal.

Summary

This study compared four commercially available speech/voice analysis software programs (CSL, CSpeech, Dr Speech, and EZVoice) on measures of mean F_0, pitch sigma (F_0 standard deviation concerted to semitones), and F_0 range (in semitones) from groups of adult males, adult females, and children with normal voice characteristics. Comparisons to a hand-marking standard were also included. Results indicate that the various analysis programs perform similarly in deriving estimations from sustained vowels. However, analysis of continuous speech may result in highly significant errors in F_0 estimation. The EZVoice program was consistently observed to show no significant differences from the hand-marking standard. The need for inclusion of stringent post-processing error correction routines into voice analysis algorithms is discussed.

Acknowledgements

We would like to express our appreciation to G. Gargiulo and L. Granato for their aid in the data analysis aspects of this paper.

References

Awan S (1997) Pattern-recognition frequency tracking using EZVoice. Presented at the 1997 American Speech-Language-Hearing Association Convention in Boston, MA.

Awan S (1996) EZVoice: Voice Analysis Software. Nescopeck, PA: VoiceTek Enterprises.

Awan S, Scarpino S (1997) A comparison of computerized speech/voice analysis programs. Presented at the Voice Foundations 26th Annual Symposium: Care of the Professional Voice, Philadelphia, PA.

Baken, RJ (1987) Clinical Measurement of Speech and Voice. Boston, MA: College Hill Press.

Bielamowicz S, Kreiman J, Gerratt B, Dauer M, Berke G (1996) Comparison of voice analysis systems for perturbation measurement. Journal of Speech and Hearing Research, 39, 126–34.

Colton R, Casper J (1990) Understanding Voice Problems: A Physiological Perspective for Diagnosis and Treatment. Baltimore, MD: Williams and Wilkins.

Eskenazi L, Childers D, Hicks D (1990) Acoustic correlates of vocal quality. Journal of Speech and Hearing Research, 33, 298–306.

Fairbanks G (1960) Voice and Articulation Drill Book. New York: Harper and Bros.

Hillman R, Gress, C Hargrave J, Walsh M, Bunting G (1990) The efficacy of speech-language pathology intervention: Voice Disorders. Seminars in Speech and Language, 11(4), 297–309.

Huang DZ, Lin S, O'Brien R (1995) Dr Speech for Windows Version 3: User's Guide. Seattle, WA: Tiger Electronics, Inc.

Karnell M, Hall K, Landahl K (1995) Comparison of fundamental frequency and perturbation measurements among three analysis systems. Journal of Voice, 9, 383–93.

Kent RD, Read C (1992) The Acoustic Analysis of Speech. San Diego, CA : Singular Publishing.

Mann V (1987) Review of DSPS Realtime Signal Lab. American Speech-Language-Hearing Association, 29, 64–5.

Orlikoff R (1992) The use of instrumental measures in the assessment and treatment of motor speech disorders. Seminars in Speech and Language, 13(1), 25–37.

Read C, Buder E, Kent R (1990) Speech analysis systems: A survey. Journal of Speech and Hearing Research, 33, 363–74.

Read C, Buder E, Kent R (1992) Speech analysis systems: An evaluation. Journal of Speech and Hearing Research, 35, 314–32.

Ryalls J, Baum S (1990) Review of three software systems for speech analysis: CSPEECHSP, BLISS, and CSRE. Journal of Speech-Language Pathology and Audiology,14, 49–52.

Thomas-Stonell N (1989) Review of Speech Viewer. Journal of Speech-Language Pathology and Audiology, 13, 59–60.

Chapter 40
Measures Of RMS Nasalance Using NasalView In Patients Undergoing Secondary Osteoplasty

S. AWAN, T. BRESSMAN, R. SADER and H. HORCH

Introduction

The measurement of nasalance has often been described as a useful measure in the assessment of hyperrhinophonia. Hyperrhinophonia commonly includes the speech characteristics of excessive nasal resonance (hypernasality), as well as the presence of nasal emission (particularly during the production of high-pressure consonants). Hyperrhinophonia is a common speech characteristic of patients with cleft palates, but is also associated with deaf speech and dysarthric speech. Nasalance has been defined as the ratio of nasal (*n*) to oral (*o*) sound pressure level, and is commonly derived via the following formula:

$$\frac{n}{n + o} \times 100$$

Studies by Dalston, Warren and Dalston (1991a,b), Hardin, Van Demark, Morris and Payne (1992), and Dalston, Neiman and Gonzalez-Landa (1993) have all indicated that measures of nasalance provide strong specificity, sensitivity and overall efficiency when used to identify subjects with and without more than mild hypernasality in their speech. Nasalance may be considered one of our stronger objective assessment methods of the nasal speech signal since it may be derived through non-invasive and fairly simple methods. The measurement of nasalance also lends itself well to both diagnostic and therapeutic situations.

The instrumentation necessary for the measurement of nasalance has been available since 1989 in the form of the Nasometer (Kay Elemetrics

Inc, Pinehurst, NJ, USA). The system devised by Kay comprises headgear (oral and nasal microphones and separation plate), hardware for the analog filtering of the acoustic signals (500 Hz centre frequency; 300 Hz bandwidth) and analog-to-digital conversion (sampling frequency = 120 Hz), and computer software for the display of nasalance (over time or as a summary statistic for a given speech sample). While the Nasometer has been observed to be clinically useful, the relatively high cost of the instrument coupled with limited capability to digitize and reproduce speech signals presents significant constraints to the effective clinical use of this instrument (Hardin et al., 1992; Awan,1997).

In an effort to address the limitations of the Nasometer, Awan (1996a, b 1997) has developed *NasalView*. *NasalView* (VoiceTek Enterprises, Nescopeck, PA , USA) is a new PC Windows-based speech analysis system designed for the detailed analysis of nasalance. This system provides for the recording and playback of high resolution speech signals using Windows-compatible sound cards (sampling at up to 44.1 kHz at 8 or 16 bits of resolution). Like the Nasometer , the *NasalView* system uses a headset with two microphones for separate recordings of the nasal and the oral speech signal (see Figures 40.1a and 40.1b).

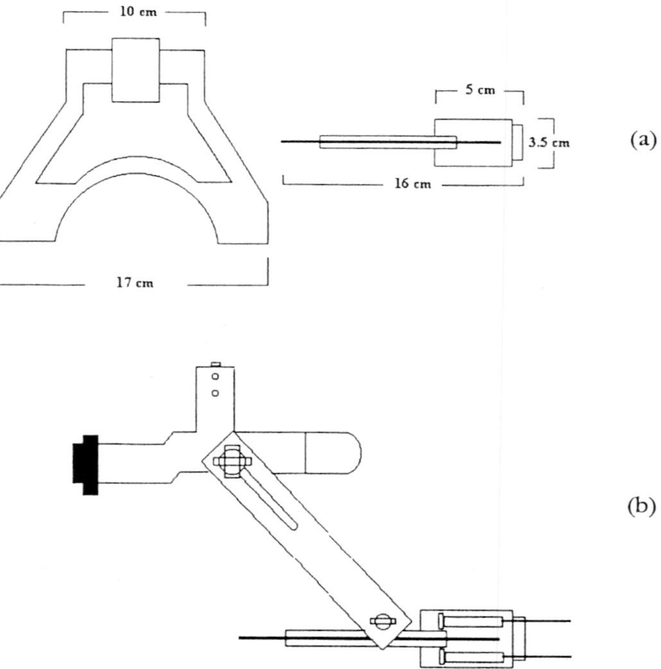

Figure 40.1. (a) Superior and (b) lateral views of the *NasalView* headgear. Position of the nasal and oral microphones within the headgear separator plate is also shown.

With a light weight styrene sound separator plate and the addition of acoustical barrier material, an effective signal separation of 23 dB can be achieved between the two microphones (Awan, 1996a). A custom-made preamplifier boosts the signals and passes them on to the stereo line-in input jack of a soundboard (e.g. SoundBlaster 16 by Creative Labs). At a sampling rate of 11, 22 or 44 kHz (8 or 16 bit), the signal is then A/ D converted. For analysis, signal data are compressed in steps of 0.01 s according to a root mean square (RMS) procedure. Nasalance is then calculated according to the nasalance formula. In contrast to the Nasometer, the signal is not bandlimited. Therefore, the entire frequency range (as defined by the selected sampling rate) is included in the data analysis. The signal or signal selections can be played back and edited. Oscillograms of the nasal and oral signal and a nasalance trace/curve are displayed together with summary statistics of the measured nasalance (see Figure 40.2). This is an important improvement in the computer analysis of nasalance since it allows the clinician to make accurate time-aligned measurements between the acoustic events and the derived nasalance trace. *NasalView* has been designed to be a low-cost system, which will aid clinicians and researchers in a variety of settings in the diagnosis and treatment of resonance disorders. (*NasalView* has recently been licensed to Tiger Electronics Inc, Seattle, WA, USA. The commercial release of this system is expected during 1998.)

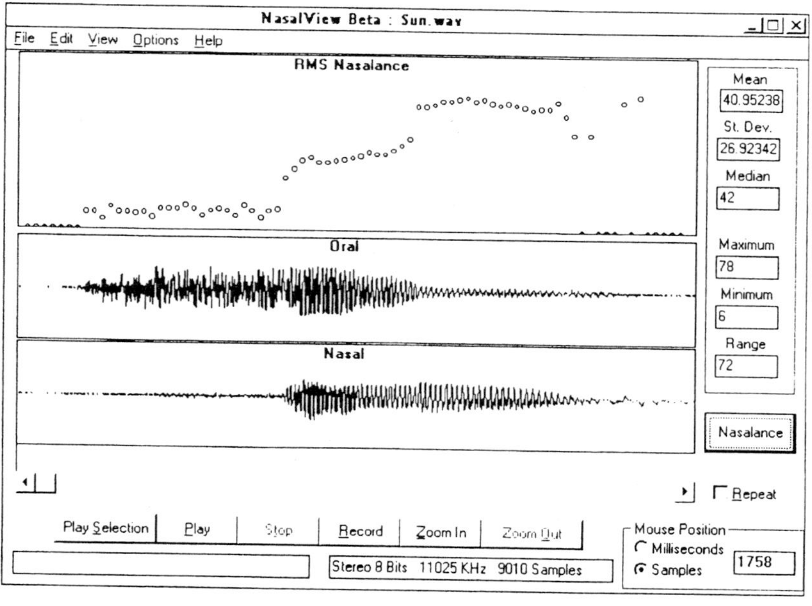

Figure 40.2. Screen shot of the *NasalView* program. Oral and nasal oscillograms and the nasalance trace are shown, as well as summary nasalance statistics for the utterance (the word 'sun').

A number of studies have presented results which indicated that the *NasalView* system is able to effectively separate varying degrees of nasal and non-nasal speech in normal subjects (Awan, 1996a, 1997). The present study aimed to assess the utility of the *NasalView* system in the assessment of a clinical population of patients who presented with varying degrees of hyperrhinophonia. Specifically, *NasalView* was used in a clinical context to differentiate hypernasal patients from patients with normal nasal resonance during the course of a medical follow-up of 156 patients who had undergone alveolar bone graft in the Department of Oral and Maxillofacial Surgery at the University of Technology, Munich, Germany.

Method

Subjects

A total of 155 patients were invited to a follow-up examination following closure of an alveolar cleft via secondary osteoplasty using autogenous spongiosa as the last primary operation according to our interdisciplinary treatment plan (Horch, 1991). The 155 patients comprised 103 males and 52 females. The mean age for the total group of patients was 18.8 years (SD = 7.23 years; range = 10–66 years).

Materials

Speech samples were collected using a slightly modified version of the Heidelberg Rhinophonia Assessment Form as developed by Heppt, Westrich, Strate and Möhring (1991) and Stellzig, Heppt and Komposch (1994). Test materials included long vowel productions, productions of words containing various pressure consonants in word-initial position, and both non-nasal sentences and sentences heavily weighted with nasal consonants. Patients were asked to repeat the test items after they were spoken by the examiner while wearing the *NasalView* headgear. Speech samples were recorded using a PC-compatible computer at 8-bits of resolution with a sampling rate of 22050 Hz and saved to disk in .WAV file format. These files would later be analysed for measures of RMS nasalance.

In addition to the nasalance measures, speech samples were also judged for presence and severity of hyper- and hyponasality. Based on perceptual analysis, 45 patients were found to have normal nasal resonance; 7 patients were classified as hyponasal; 4 patients were classified as having changing nasality (Rhinophonia alternans); and 98 patients were found to be hypernasal (38 mild; 33 moderate; 27 severe). Two patients could not be classified because of a lack of cooperation in providing adequate speech samples. Since clinically relevant hyponasality and alternating nasality were observed in less than 10% of the patient population, these patients were not included in further data analysis. Therefore, data analysis was completed using 140 patients with both normal and abnormal degrees of perceived hypernasality.

As a measure of intra-rater reliability, a second rating of all speech samples was conducted. Intra-rater reliability was deemed acceptable for the purposes of this study with 91.3% exact agreement achieved. The internal consistency of the rating was evaluated using Kendall's tau-b statistic. Results indicated a high degree of internal consistency between the nasality ratings conducted in this study (Kendall's tau-b = 0.866). Though subject reliability was not assessed in this study, previous work by Awan (1996b) indicates that measures of RMS nasalance using the *NasalView* system are generally found to be within 1–2% accuracy on test-retest measures.

Results

Receiver-Operator-Characteristics (ROC-curves) for each test item were computed using Mathworks MATLAB, Microsoft Excel and the Statistical Package for the Social Sciences (SPSS). On the basis of the Youden-index and distance, cut-offs were defined. At these cut-offs, each item of the test differentiated with optimum sensitivity (proportion of true positives who test positive) and specificity (proportion of true negative who test negative) between the normal and hypernasal subjects. Since the three last sentences of the Heidelberg form were heavily weighed with nasal consonants, cut-offs could not be effectively identified. Therefore, these sentences were not included in further analysis.

Initial analysis focused on 15 items from the Heidelberg Rhinophonia Assessment form. Three cut-off values for each item were defined in order to distinguish patients with normal nasal resonance from the following groups: (1) all hypernasal patients; (2) patients with moderate and severe hypernasality; (3) patients with severe hypernasality. Cut-off values for the 15 items are presented in Table 40.1.

Though the Heidelberg Rhinophonia Assessment is comprised of both single word and sentence-length stimuli, the use of single words may present limitations in the assessment of nasalance in patients presenting with hyperrhinophonia. Recent data by Watterson, Folly-Holman, and Lewis (1997) indicates that nasalance measured from two-syllable words may be significantly different from nasalance data collected from longer speech samples, and therefore, may not be a representative measure of the patient's nasality characteristics in continuous speech. Based on the Watterson et al. (1997) findings, we have decided to no longer include single word stimuli in our diagnostic analysis of nasalance. Therefore, the results of this study will focus on measures of RMS nasalance and associated sensitivity and specificity measures as derived from the non-nasal sentence-length stimuli. Use of

Table 40.1. Summary of the 15 stimuli items used from the Heidelberg Rhinophonia Assessment form and calculated RMS nasalance cut-off points separating normal from varying degrees of hypernasal patients

Test item	Controls versus mild-to-severe hypernasal patients (%)	Controls versus moderate-to-severe hypernasal patients (%)	Controls versus severe hypernasal patients (%)
/a:/	29	30	32
/i:/	37.5	39.7	44.7
/u:/	35	36.2	41
/y:/	35.5	39.1	40.4
Pappe, Pille, Polster	28.1	29.9	30.5
Tasche, Tulpe, Tiger	27.6	29.3	29.5
Koffer, Kerze, Karte	27.6	28.6	31
Feder, Foto, Feige	29.5	30.7	31.8
Schiefer, Schere, Schaukel	29.8	30.7	31.8
Ampel, Lampe	41.2	41.5	41.5
Peter spielt auf der Staße	27.3	28.5	30
Das Pferd steht auf der Weide	27.2	28.7	31.3
Die Schokolade ist sehr lecker	29.4	30.3	32.2
Der Vater liest das Buch	28.7	30	33
Fritz geht zur Schule	27.7	28.3	30

this type of stimuli also allows for improved comparison to previous nasometry studies which have generally focused on measures of nasalance derived from the commonly used non-nasal *Zoo Passage*.

A combined ROC-analysis was computed for the mean nasalance scores of the five sentences without nasal consonants. With a cut-off of 28.6% nasalance, normal and mildly to severely hypernasal patients could be differentiated with a sensitivity of 74.0% and a specificity of 73.0%. With the same cut-off of 28.6% nasalance, normal and moderately to severely hypernasal patients could be differentiated with a sensitivity of 89.9% and a specificity of 73.0%. With a cut-off of 32.0% nasalance, normal and severely hypernasal patients could be differentiated with sensitivity of 91.1% and a specificity of 88.5%. Table 40.2 summarizes the sensitivity and specificity results for the non-nasal sentences.

Discussion

The results of this study indicate that the *NasalView* system appears to effectively separate varying degrees of nasal speech in a wide range of disordered patients. The results of this study are comparable to those reported by Anglo-American and German research groups for the Nasometer. A relatively recent study by Dalston, Neiman, and Gonzalez-Landa (1993) observed sensitivity measures ranging from 0.77 to 0.90

Table 40.2. RMS nasalance cut-off points calculated using the five non-nasal sentences from the Heidelberg Rhinophonia Assessment form. Corresponding sensitivity and specificity results are also provided

	Nasalance cut-off (%)	Sensitivity (%)	Specificity (%)
Controls versus mild-to-severe hypernasal patients	28.6	74.0	73.0
Controls versus moderate-to-severe hypernasal patients	28.6	89.9	73.0
Controls versus severe hypernasal patients	32.0	91.1	88.5

and specificity measures ranging from 0.78 to 0.90 in nasometry data collected from four clinics. The specificity and sensitivity results of the present study coincide well with the Dalston et al. (1993) results, particularly in light of the obvious confounding effects of differences in speech task and the use of German-speaking patients in the present study. The cut-off value (28.6% RMS nasalance) which was found to most effectively separate patients with more than mild degrees of hypernasality is also consistent with previous data presented by Awan (1997), which reported a mean RMS nasalance of 24.67% (SD = 2.91%) for a group of 124 normal speaking subjects. From the Awan (1997) data, it can be seen that a z-score = +1.5 would result in a cut-off value of 29.035% RMS nasalance, remarkably similar to cut-off results derived via ROC analysis in the present study.

It is hoped that future modifications to the *NasalView* system may produce improvements to the results reported in the present study (particularly in the area of specificity). The commercial version of *NasalView* will incorporate a thicker separation plate (5 mm versus 3 mm) which should provide improved separation characteristics between oral and nasal signals. In addition, application of post-processing digital filtering and improved methods of scaling the relative amplitude of nasal versus oral signals may also improve the sensitivity and specificity of the *NasalView* system.

On the basis of the data presented, *NasalView* would appear to be a valid and valuable instrument for the analysis and classification of pathological nasal resonance. It appears that *NasalView* has the capability to be a highly effective tool for the assessment of nasalance at a substantially lower cost than other currently available systems. Systems such as *NasalView* would appear to be important contributions to the interdisciplinary treatment concept for patients with cleft lip and palate, which must closely monitor each individual patient's development. Accurate and objective diagnosis is important for the planning and implementation of varied therapeutic and/or operative steps. The interdisciplinary approach is especially important in the differentiation of functional incompetence from structural inadequacy, since operative treatment may not improve the speech status in many kinds of functional hyper-rhinophonias. Prior to velopharyngoplasty, three different aspects of the velopharyngeal closure mechanism have to be analysed: (1) the morphological status; (2) the functional status in speech and swallowing; and (3) the acoustic and perceptual consequences of a velopharyngeal insufficiency. Sader and colleagues (1994) emphasize the important role of high frequency videocineradiography for the detailed analysis of velopharyngeal closure and articulatory gestures. While the videocineradiographic examination can help to evaluate the morphology and function of the soft palate and the pharynx, this technique cannot objectively aid in the analysis of the acoustic and perceptual consequences of hyperrhinophonia. This is the area of analysis in which systems such as *NasalView* may play an important role. *NasalView* has already become an integrated part of our routine diagnostics. Together with the findings from other diagnostic procedures such as high frequency videocineradiography, endoscopy or acoustic analysis, *NasalView* gives us valuable information for operation planning and evaluation of operative success and thus helps us to further improve our treatment concept. Only optimum treatment concepts can grant our patients improved functional and aesthetical outcomes which will provide them with the benefit of unimpaired and unrestricted psychosocial and communicative development.

Summary

Results are presented of a clinical validation study for *NasalView*, a new instrument for the objective evaluation of hyperrhinophonia. The *NasalView* system was used to measure RMS nasalance in 156 patients with operated cleft lip and palate. A modified version of the Heidelberg Rhinophonia Assessment form was used for the speech task. Results indicate that *NasalView* differentiates between normal and moderate-to-severe hypernasal patients with a sensitivity of 89.9% and a specificity of 73.0%, and between normal and severely hypernasal patients with a sensitivity of 91.1% and a specificity of 88.5%. Results indicate that *NasalView* provides important information regarding operation planning and evaluation of operative success in cleft patients.

Acknowledgements

We would like to express our appreciation to Dr W. Ziegler for his help in arranging the collaboration between the various authors of this research study.

References

Awan SN (1997) Analysis of nasalance: *NasalView* (the Nasalance Acquisition System). In Ziegler W, Deger K (eds) Clinical Phonetics and Linguistics. London: Whurr Publishers.

Awan SN (1996a) Development of a low-cost Nasalance Acquisition System. In Powell T (ed.) Pathologies of Speech and Language: Contributions of Clinical Phonetics and Linguistics. New Orleans: ICPLA.

Awan SN (1996b) The Nasalance Acquisition System (NAS v.2.0). Presented at the 1996 American Speech-Language-Hearing Association Convention, Seattle, WA, USA.

Dalston R, Warren D, Dalston E (1991a) Use of nasometry as a diagnostic tool for identifying patients with velopharyngeal impairment. Cleft Palate Journal, 28, 185–8.

Dalston R, Warren D, Dalston E (1991b) A preliminary investigation concerning the use of nasometry in identifying patients with hyponasality and/or nasal airway impediment. Journal of Speech and Hearing Research, 34, 11–18.

Dalston R, Neiman G, Gonzalez-Landa G (1993) Nasometric sensitivity and specificity: A cross dialect and cross culture study. Cleft Palate Journal, 30, 285–91.

Hardin M, Van Denmark D, Morris H, Payne M (1992) Correspondence between nasalance scores and listener judgements of hypernasality and hyponasality. Cleft Palate Journal, 29, 346–51.

Heppt G, Westrich M, Strate B, Möhring L (1991) Nasalanz: Ein neuer Begriff in der objektiven Nasalitätsanalyse. Laryngorhinootologie, 70, 208–13.

Horch HH (1991) Lippen-Kiefer-Gaumenspalten. In Horch HH (ed.) Mund- Kiefer-Gesichtschirurgie II. München: Urban & Schwarzenberg.

Sader R, Horch H, Herzog M, Zeilhofer H, Hannig C, Hess U, Bünte E, Böhme G (1994) Hochfrequenz-Videokinematographia zur objektiven Darstellung des velopharyngealen Verschlußmechanismus bei Gaumenspaltpatienten. Fortschritte der Kieferorthopädie, 55, 169–75.

Stellzig A, Heppt W, Komposch G (1994) Das Nasometer: Ein Instrument zur Objektivierung der Hyperrhinophonie bei LKG-Patienten. Fortschritte der Kieferorthopädie, 55, 176–80.

Watterson T, Folly-Holman N, Lewis K (1997) Relationship between nasalance measures and stimulus length. Presented at the 1997 American Speech-Language-Hearing Association Convention, Boston, MA, USA.

Chapter 41
Does the Syllable Affiliation of Intervocalic Consonants Have an Articulatory Basis? Evidence from Electromagnetic Midsagittal Articulography[1]

NIELS O SCHILLER, PASCAL HHM VAN LIESHOUT, ANTJE S MEYER and WILLEM JM LEVELT

Introduction

In Levelt's (1989, Levelt et al., 1999) model of speech production syllables are conceived as articulatory units. Previous research has shown that the syllable can function as a processing unit in Dutch speech production (Levelt and Wheeldon, 1994; Wheeldon and Levelt, 1995; Schiller et al., 1996, 1997; Schiller, 1997; Levelt et al., 1998, 1999; Schiller, 1998). However, very little is known about the mechanisms that underlie the articulatory control of speech production, and Levelt's model does not offer a theory of articulatory execution. The model of *gestural phonology* is more explicit about the processes related to phonetic encoding and articulation (Browman and Goldstein, 1992). In this framework, the customary distinction between phonology and phonetics is given up. The activity of the articulatory motor system is described in terms of underlying *articulatory gestures*. These gestures are the basic units of phonological contrast, and at the same time they characterize articulatory events, i.e. movements in space and time. These articulatory events consist of formations and releases of the vocal tract.

[1]For original version of this chapter, see Schiller, 1997.

The dimensions of these constrictions, e.g. constriction location and constriction degree, are specified by *tract variables* (e.g. lip protrusion, tongue tip constriction location, etc.). The targets of the vocal tract variables are achieved by *model articulators* representing relatively independent articulatory subsystems of the vocal tract, e.g. lips, tongue tip, tongue body, jaw, velum, etc. The model articulators are located on different *articulatory tiers*. Within gestural phonology, a gestural *score* takes care of the coordination of the articulatory gestures, i.e. it specifies the phasing between individual gestures in time and space.

The present study investigated whether the articulatory timing of intervocalic consonants was affected by their syllable affiliation. The results of Browman and Goldstein (1988) and Byrd (1995) were inconclusive with respect to the effect of syllable affiliation on articulatory timing of segments. We tested the *syllable timing hypothesis*, which predicts that segments within a syllable are more stably timed relative to each other than segments that belong to different syllables. The rationale behind this hypothesis is that if syllables are articulatory motor units, the motor coordination of segments that belong to the same unit should be less variable than the coordination of segments from different units. Thus the articulatory timing of two consonants, e.g. /f/ and /k/, should be more stable for CVC items, e.g. *fak.tor*, since both segments are in the same syllable, than for CV items, e.g. *fa.kir*, because /f/ and /k/ belong to different syllables. For CV[C] items, such as *fa[kk]el*, in which the intervocalic consonant is ambisyllabic, the timing between /f/ and /k/ should be even more variable than for the CV items because it is not clear with which syllable /k/ is affiliated.

Experiment

Method

Speech materials

In previous research on the role of the syllable in Dutch speech production (see Schiller et al., 1997; Schiller, 1999) three categories of items were investigated, i.e., CVC words such as *faktor* /fɑk.tɔr/ ('factor') beginning with a CVC syllable, CV words like *fakir* /fa.kir/ ('fakir'), and CV[C] words such as *fakkel* /fɑ[k]əl/ ('torch'), which have an ambiguous syllable boundary. We created 10 item triplets that overlapped in the first three segments (disregarding vowel length) but differed with respect to syllable structure, as in the case of *faktor – fakir – fakkel*. All words were stressed on the first syllable. Dutch phonological structure does not allow for short vowels to occur in open syllables (Branching Rhyme Constraint (BRC), Lahiri and Koreman, 1988), hence the CV words had to include a long vowel, and the other words a short vowel.

Participants

Three female and one male speakers took part in the experiment. They were native speakers of Dutch. None of them reported any speech or hearing disorders.

Apparatus

Tongue, lip, and jaw movements were monitored using the AG100 EMMA system (Carstens Medizinelektronik, Göttingen, Germany; Schönle, 1988), which consists of three transmitter and five receiver coils (for details see Tuller et al., 1990; Perkell et al., 1992; Alfonso et al., 1993; van Lieshout et al., 1995; Schiller, 1997). Movement data were recorded at a sampling rate of 400 Hz. Simultaneously with the monitoring of the articulatory movements, acoustic recordings were made at a sampling rate of 16 kHz. Speech and movement data were digitized simultaneously and aligned by means of the AG100 system software (see Figure 41.1)

Procedure

Participants were seated in a chair, and the helmet necessary to monitor their articulatory movements was attached to a suspending device to improve the stability of its position on the participant's head and to compensate for a substantial portion of the helmet's weight (Alfonso et al., 1993; van Lieshout et al., 1995).

Before the recording session participants' occlusal planes were recorded. Participants were instructed to bite on a plate on to which two receiver coils were attached in the midline. The positions of the two coils were recorded and served as an individual anatomical reference plane to which the experimental data could be rotated in order to compare data across subjects. Immediately before and after data collection the static receiver coil positions were recorded for an informal check of the system's stability during the experiment.

On each test trial participants received one test item. Test items were presented visually on sheets of paper. Participants waited until the experimenter gave a *go*-signal, and then produced multiple repetitions of the test item for a period of 10 seconds. The speech rate was self-selected. Inter-trial intervals were approximately 20 seconds. The recording session lasted approximately 40 minutes. The entire experiment took about one and a half hours. Each participant produced all items. The order of items was randomized individually for each participant with the restriction that items belonging to the same triplet or to the same item category were separated by at least one other trial.

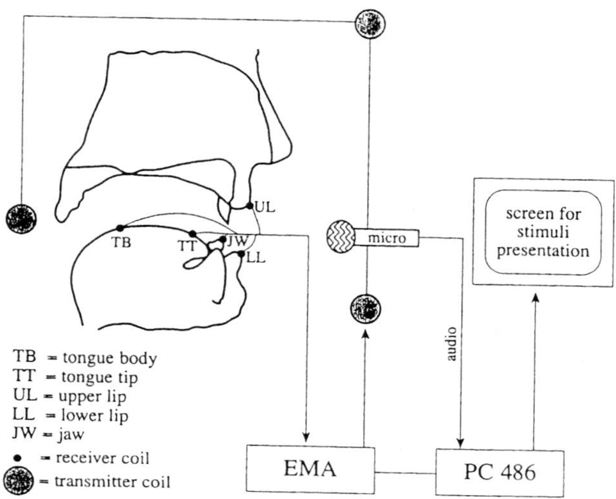

Figure 41.1. Overview of the experimental set-up indicating the location of the transmitter and receiver coils.

Data analysis

The computer routines for the analysis of the articulatory data were similar to the XHADES (Haskins Analysis/Display/Experiment System) software developed at Haskins Laboratories (New Haven, CT, USA) (see Rubin et al., 1991). The analysis routines were integrated into the waves/ESPS speech analysis package (Entropics Inc.), which allows the simultaneous display of the time-aligned acoustic and articulatory signals.

Analysis

After preprocessing the data, the articulatory analyses were based on the displacement data recorded by the coils, which were assumed to reflect most directly reflect the articulatory movement for the constriction gestures under investigation. Research by Gracco and Abbs (1986, 1988; Gracco, 1988) and Hoole et al. (1994) has shown that velocity profiles play an important role in articulatory control during vowel production. Here, we used the velocity characteristics of vertical tongue and lip movements to investigate the articulatory timing of intervocalic consonants.

For the analysis, the second to ninth tokens of each test item were considered. To determine the articulatory timing of the intervocalic consonants, two landmarks were kinematically determined in each test word. The first (anchor point C_1) corresponded to the moment when the articulator(s) forming the release for the onset consonant reached the maximum in the movement signal. The velocity was derived from the displacement signal using a standard differentiation algorithm. The second landmark (C_2) was defined as the articulatory target position of the intervocalic consonant. An articulatory target is generally conceived as a point of minimum velocity (e.g. Perkell et al., 1992). In this study, C_2 corresponded to the temporal midpoints of the consonantal centres (C-centres) of the corresponding consonantal gestures.

At low to moderate speech rates consonantal gestures often display a plateau-like shape, i.e. a quasi-steady state phase, rather than a peak. Hence, the point of zero crossing is not appropriate to determine the articulatory target position. To determine the C-centre of consonantal gestures we adapted a procedure used by Hoole et al. (1994) to define the displacement plateau of the intervocalic consonants. Intervals in the first derivative of the corresponding position signal were demarcated by points in time where for a given cycle both positive and negative velocities became lower than 20% of the peak velocity. Thus, the onset of the interval corresponded to the point in time when the velocity fell below 20% of the peak velocity of a given cycle, whereas the offset corresponded to the point in time when the velocity rose above 20% of the peak velocity. The C-centre was defined as the temporal midpoint of the interval between the two markers, in most cases corresponding to the peak displacement in the position signal.

To quantify stability of the temporal relation between C_1 and C_2 we measured the time interval between C_1 and C_2 for each token (see Figure 41.2), and computed the standard deviation (SD) of the length of this interval C_2-C_1 across the eight repetitions of each test item.

Results and Discussion

The SD of the interval C_2-C_1 across the eight repetitions was determined per item and participant to compare the stability of the articulatory timing within each item. The means of the SDs per participant and category are shown in Table 41.1. As can be seen, the SD was markedly smaller for the CVC items than for the remaining item types for only one participant. Analyses of variance were run per participant to compare the three item categories (CV, CVC, or CV[C]). The main effect of item category was not significant for any of the participants (participant 1: $F(2,27) = 2.28$, $F < 1$ for the other participants).

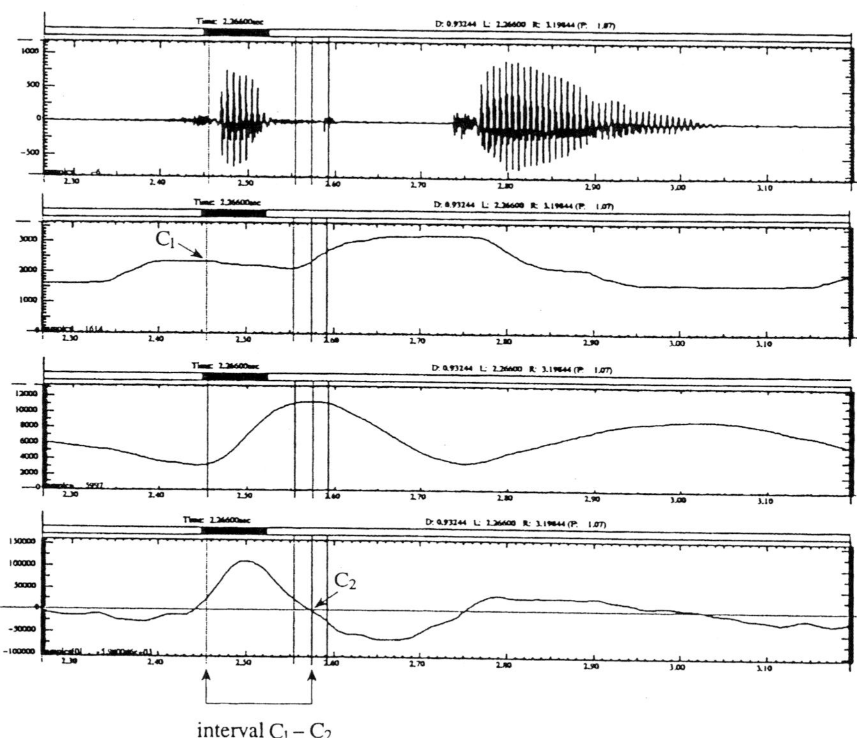

Figure 41.2. Display of the speech signal, the jaw and tongue body movement signal, and the velocity profile of the tongue body movement for one token of the experimental trial *faktor* produced by participant 3. The upmost panel displays the acoustic signal, the upper middle panel the jaw movement (recorded from coil JW), the lower middle panel the tongue body movement (recorded from coil TB), and the lowest panel the velocity profile of the tongue body movement. The anchor point C_1 and the C-Centre (C_2) as well as the interval C_2-C_1 are indicated in the figure.

Table 41.1. Mean SDs of the interval C_2-C_1 per participant and item category

	Mean SD of the interval C_2-C_1 (in ms)		
participant	CV items	CVC items	CV[C] items
1	28	15	29
2	55	47	56
3	31	36	31
4	38	38	35

The length of the first vowel significantly differed between the three item categories as was determined in the acoustic signal by sonagraphic analyses (means: CVC: 78 ms, CV[C]: 80 ms, and CV: 167; F (2 957) = 803.14, MS_e = 1022.33, $p < 0.001$). The mean length and the SD of the interval C_2-C_1 correlated significantly for three of the four participants (participant 1: r = 0.50, p = 0.01; participant 2: r = 0.42, p = 0.05; participant 3: r = 0.64, p < 0.001). Therefore, we ran analyses of covariance entering the mean length of the interval C_2-C_1 as a covariate in order to take into account the vowel length differences between the item categories. However, the differences of the SDs between the categories only reached significance for one participant (participant 3: F (2,26) = 5.88, p = 0.01).[2]

The results did not provide any evidence for the hypothesis that the syllable affiliation of an intervocalic consonant plays a role in articulatory timing. The variability of the articulatory timing in different item categories did not show a stable pattern across participants. The fact that the timing of consonants within a syllable was *not* more stable than the timing of onset consonants of successive syllables came as a surprise. This result clearly contradicts the syllable timing hypothesis according to which the variability of the articulatory timing should be highest for the CV items since C_1 and C_2 belong to different syllables. The fact that items including ambisyllabic consonants did not significantly differ from the other two item categories with respect to the articulatory timing of the intervocalic consonant was also unexpected.

Summary and conclusion

Syllables are seen as articulatory-motor units in Levelt's model of speech production. We investigated whether the phonological syllable affiliation of intervocalic consonants is reflected on the articulatory output level, i.e. at the stage of motor execution. The results revealed no significant differences between the timing of segments within a syllable and the timing of the same segments when a syllable boundary occurred between them. But since the difference in vowel length is problematic for comparisons between items, future research may focus on the articulatory timing of onset and coda consonants in monosyllables with short versus long vowels.

Nevertheless, this study has proved the usefulness of the EMMA method for the observation of articulatory movements during speaking in a non-clinical setting with real speech material.

---

[2]Analyses of variance using the quotient of the SD and the mean of the C_2-C_1 interval as a coefficient of variation revealed the same pattern of results (participant 1: F (2,27) = 1.47, MS_e <0.01, ns; participant 2: F (2,27) <1; participant 3: F (2,27) = 5.29, MS_e <0.01, p = 0.012; participant 4: F (2,27) <1).

References

Alfonso PJ, Neely JR, van Lieshout PHHM, Hulstijn W, Peters HFM (1993) Calibration, validation, and hardware-software modifications to the Carstens EMMA System. Haskins Laboratories Status Report on Speech Research, SR-114, 101–12.

Browman CP, Goldstein L (1988) Some notes on syllable structure in articulatory phonology. Phonetica, 45, 140–55.

Browman CP, Goldstein L (1992) Articulatory phonology: An overview. Phonetica, 49, 155–80.

Byrd D (1995) C-centers revisited. Phonetica, 52, 285–306.

Gracco VL (1988) Timing factors in the coordination of speech movements. The Journal of Neuroscience, 8, 4628–39.

Gracco VL, Abbs JH (1986) Variant and invariant characteristics of speech movement planning. Experimental Brain Research, 65, 156–66.

Gracco VL, Abbs JH (1988) Central patterning of speech movement timing. Experimental Brain Research, 71, 515–26.

Hoole P, Mooshammer C, Tillmann HG (1994) Kinematic analysis of vowel production in German. Proceedings of the Third International Conference on Spoken Language Processing, Yokohama, pp. 53–6.

Levelt WJM (1989) Speaking. From Intention to Articulation. Cambridge, MA: MIT Press.

Levelt WJM, Roelofs A, Meyer AS (1999) A theory of lexical access in speech production. Behavioral and Brain Sciences, in press.

Levelt WJM, Schiller NO (1998) Is the syllable frame stored? Commentary on the BBS target article 'The frame/content theory of evolution of speech production' by MacNeilage PF. Behavioral and Brain Sciences, 21, 520.

Levelt WJM, Wheeldon L (1994) Do speakers have a mental syllabary? Cognition, 50, 239–69.

Perkell JS, Cohen MH, Svirsky MA, Matthies ML, Garabieta I, Jackson MTT (1992) Electromagnetic midsagittal articulometer systems for transducing speech articulatory movements. Journal of the Acoustical Society of America, 92, 3078–96.

Rubin P, MacEachron M, Tiede M, Maverick V (1991) HADES - Haskins Analysis/Display/Experiment/System: Documentation. New Haven: Haskins Laboratories.

Schiller NO (1997) The role of the syllable in speech production. Evidence from lexical statistics, metalinguistics, masked priming, and electromagnetic midsagittal articulography. PhD dissertation, Nijmegen University.

Schiller NO (1998) The effect of visually masked syllable primes on the naming latencies of words and pictures. Journal of Memory and Language, 39, 484–507.

Schiller NO, Meyer AS, Baayen RH, Levelt WJM (1996) A comparison of lexeme and speech syllables in Dutch. Journal of Quantitative Linguistics, 3, 8–28.

Schiller NO, Meyer AS, Levelt WJM (1997) The syllabic structure of spoken words: Evidence from the syllabification of intervocalic consonants. Language and Speech, 40, 101–39.

Schönle PW (1988) Elektromagnetische Artikulographie. Ein neues Verfahren zur klinischen Untersuchung der Sprechmotorik. Berlin: Springer.

Tuller B, Shao S, Kelso JAS (1990) An Evaluation of an Alternating Magnetic Field Device for Monitoring Tongue Movements. Journal of the Acoustical Society of America, 88, 674–9.

van Lieshout PHHM, Alfonso PJ, Hulstijn W, Peters HFM (1995) Electromagnetic Midsagittal Articulography (EMMA). In Maarse FJ, Akkerman AE, Brand AN, Mulder LJM, van der Stelt MJ (eds) Computers in Psychology: Applications, Methods, and Instrumentation. Lisse: Swets & Zeitlinger, pp. 62–76.

Wheeldon L, Levelt WJM (1995) Monitoring the time course of phonological encoding. Journal of Memory and Language, 34, 311–34.

Chapter 42
Registration of Lip and Tongue Movement with a New Electromagnetic Articulography Instrument

HANSJÖRG HORN, THOMAS SCHOLL, HERRMANN ACKERMANN, INGO HERTRICH, RÜDIGER BERNDT and GERNOT GÖZ

Introduction

Malfunctions of orofacial movements during speaking and swallowing are of diagnostic and therapeutic relevance in orthodontics as well as neurology (Andrianopoulos and Hanson, 1987). Standard diagnostic measures to determine tongue malfunctions are based largely on clinical inspection, pressure measurements, palatography, sonography and radiographic methods (Horn et al., 1995). These methods do not admit a direct and reproducible representation of any path of movement over a period of time with defined measuring points, especially not at the tongue. Some of them are connected with radiation.

Maximal tension measurements of the pressure from lips and tongue showed under standardized measuring conditions in comparison with a simultaneously taken functional diagnosis that no conclusion is possible from the maximal tension measurement on functional changes. Furthermore, measurements are to be preferred which were conducted under functional conditions (Engelke and Schönle, 1991; Horn et al., 1995).

So far simultaneous lip and tongue movements can only be recorded by using radiographic methods (X-ray-microbeam method). Next to exposure to radiation, these methods involve high investing and operating costs. Furthermore, tooth fillings interfere with kinematic measurements. An alternative is electromagnetic articulography (EMA), which is not as expensive and non-invasive (Engelke and Schönle,

1991). It offers the possibility of calculating the trajectories of small receiver coils attached to relevant orofacial structures with the aid of magnetic alternating fields. The development of an electromagnetic articulograph was carried out at the University of Tübingen, department of orthodontics in cooperation with the neurological clinic. The new system tries to optimize the following points: reciprocal influence of transmitter coils, improved utilization of the analog-digital converter, additional measurement of the torsion of coils as well as extension to unlimited recording capability. Moreover, a light-weight measuring helmet and ease of operation were desired.

Method

The system works according to the principle of measuring distances via electromagnetic induction (Figure 42.1). For indicating the position of receiver coils, three cylindrical coils attached to a helmet transmit inhomogeneous magnetic alternating fields. For the acquisition of coil torsion, a pair of Helmholtz coils is used which produces another homogeneous magnetic alternating field.

In order to avoid a reciprocal influence of magnetic fields, the alternating fields are activated by pulse-time multiplex in the new construction. Thus, the reciprocal influence of the transmitting signals can be

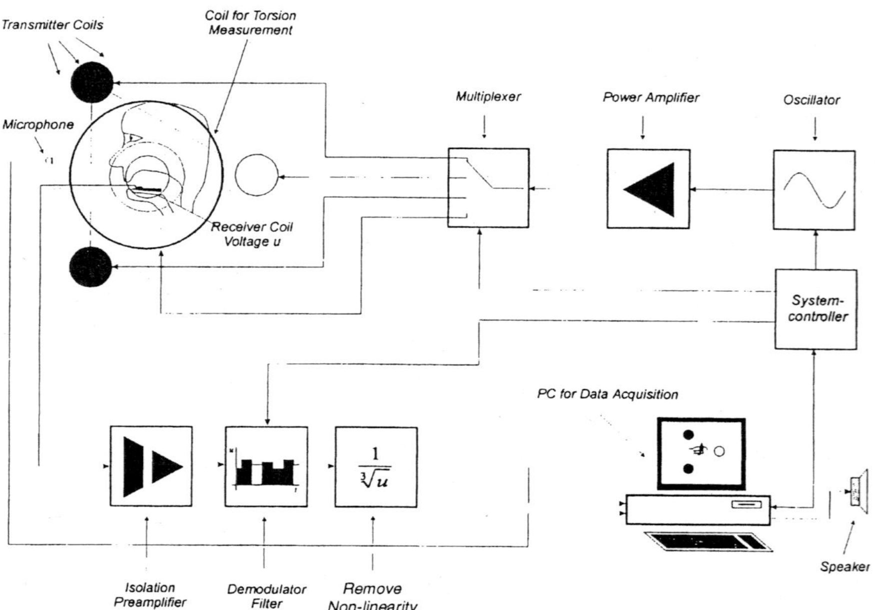

Figure 42.1. Block diagram presenting the functioning of the articulograph.

eliminated. Therefore, the definition of position is obtained from four time sequences in which three distances and one angle are measured.

The received signals from the coils attached at the lip and tongue are now linearized in the analoguous part of the measuring device. This leads to a linear dependency of the measured variables with regard to the sensor position and the transformation area of the analog-digital converter can be utilized better during digitalization. As a result the position-dependent quantization noise is reduced. The extensive computational effort compared with linearization solely done by software is also reduced. The processing of the signals is done with a personal computer, whereby the data can be saved continuously (Figure 42.1).

Results

The new system is capable of recording the movement of the receiver coils in the sagittal plane as well as torsions with a measuring rate up to 1 kHz for each of the 10 measuring channels. The mean, absolute measuring accuracy in the clinical relevant centre of the helmet (diameter of the measuring area = 80 mm) is 10^{-4} m. The maximal available measuring area has a diameter of about 120 mm. Lateral deviations from the sagittal plane can be determined by the amount of movement. For the first time torsion and measuring errors resulting from the turning of the sensor coils can be recorded and corrected automatically by separate measurement of the rotation angle. At the same time acoustic signals can be recorded simultaneously on two channels with a sampling frequency up to 44 kHz and 16 bit.

The helmet is built in the shape of a equilateral triangle, each side being 0.4 m, and is a lightweight construction of carbon fibre rods in combination with a shell made out of high-resistance foam. The transmitting coils for evaluation of the position are attached to each of the corners of the triangle. The pair of Helmholtz coils is integrated in the carbon fibre construction. The entire weight is 1300 g. A nose saddle serves to stabilize the helmet and to avoid sliding movements. The dimensions of the receiver coils are 1 mm x 1.5 mm x 3 mm. The calibration of the measuring system is carried out on a stand with an especially built-in calibration plate.

Conclusion

With the aid of the newly designed instrument it is possible to record torsion and lateral deviation of the receiving coils in the magnetic field and for the first time to apply it for improved definition of position. Because of the continuously saved data and comfort this measuring device provides new possibilities for investigation of lip and tongue malfunctions especially in children.

References

Andrianopoulos MV, Hanson ML (1987) Tongue-thrust and the stability of overjet correction. Angle Orthodontics, 57(2), 121–35.

Engelke W, Schönle PW (1991) Elektromagnetische Artikulographie: Eine neue Methode zur Untersuchung von Bewegungsfunktionen des Gaumensegels. Folio Phoniatrica, 43, 147–52.

Horn H, Göz G, Bacher M, Koch J, Axmann-Krcmar D (1995) Maximalkraftmessungen des Lippen- und Zungendruckes und ihre Bedeutung für die klinische Diagnostik orofazialer Dyskinesien. Fortschritte Kieferorthopädie, 56(4), 187–93.

Chapter 43 Variability of Tongue Movement During Speaking Sequences in Diagnosis of Tongue-thrust

HANSJÖRG HORN, GERNOT GÖZ, MARGIT BACHER, JOHANNES LUTHER and DETLEF AXMANN-KRCMAR

Introduction

Major aetiologic significance for the development of speech disorders and malocclusions is attributed to malfunctions of the tongue. So far it has been unclear to what extent malfunctions in the orofacial area result in a pathological shaping of anatomic structures or malfunctions can be caused by developmental disorders (Andrianopoulos and Hanson, 1987; Horn et al., 1995).

While sonography was a limited technique to measure selective soft tissue points during temporal movement, the electromagnetic articuolography (EMA) allows us to examine the tongue's function at certain points over a period of time and to record its movement in the midsagittal plane. Thereby, the distances between receiver coils and three transmitting coils are measured (Horn et al., 1997).

Material and method

Thirty-one subjects (14 male, 17 female) aged 14.3–37.3 years with an average age of 26.5 ± 4.1 years were examined. The German syllables /asa/, /ascha/, /ata/, /ala/, /ana/, /aka/, which are vowel-consonant-vowel sequences (VCV-sequences), were repeated five times. The registration of the tongue movement was conducted with an 'Articulograph AG 100®' of the Carstens Medizinelektronik company. Three transmitting coils, positioned in a measuring helmet in the area of the forehead, chin and neck, radiate a magnetic field inducing tension in small receiver coils attached to the soft tissues to be recorded. In this study three receiver coils aligned parallel to the transmitting coils were attached at the tongue surface with the physiological glue 'Histoacryl® blau'. The first coil was placed at the tip of the tongue, the other two 10 mm and 20 mm further dorsal.

The path of motion of all three tongue coils was evaluated. Additionally, the registration of the palate and the masticatory plane served as reference contours. For speaking following distances (D) and courses of time (T) between the measuring points first vowel, palate contact point, palate separation point and second vowel were defined respectively:

- D1/T1 = first vowel – palate contact point
- D2/T2 = palate contact point – palate separation point
- D3/T3 = palate separation point – second vowel
- D4/T4 = first vowel – second vowel

Furthermore, the following angles were defined:

- Alpha1 = angle between D1 and reference plane
- Alpha2 = angle between D3 and reference plane

The single functional movements in combination with the coil positions were expressed as: /asa/ at coil 1 = /asa/1.

In case of sufficient reproducibility the variability of data in one subject is small compared to the variability between all subjects. For evaluation of the statistic relations the intra-class-correlation coefficient (ICC) was calculated reflecting the portion of variance between the subjects in relation to the overall variability. Therefore, an ICC > 0.5 reflects a greater variance between the subjects than within them.

The clinical diagnosis as well as a functional status were prerequisites for evaluation and differentiation of orofacial malfunctions. In consideration of the clinical results, the study population was divided into two subgroups with normal swallowing and tongue-thrust syndrome. In order to establish the group of functional conspicuous subjects the following criteria were applied:

a) language apparition (sigmatism) *or*
b) a combination of criteria:
    - perceptible variance of lip position and/or lip appearance e. g. incompetent lip closure; *as well as*
    - hyperactivity of the orofacial muscles during swallowing e.g. needlepoint tracing because of hyperactivity of the mentalis; *and*
    - conspicuous palatographic diagnosis, e. g. smear print on the palate

From the according to functional points of view mixed study population the subjects showing tongue malfunctions were removed. The remaining group of 22 subjects was highly probably considered to be the only normal swallowing group. By comparing the ICC values of the remaining group with those of the entire study population, it should have been possible to see the influence of tongue malfunction on the variability of speaking motion. For measuring purposes of significant differences between the groups it was established that the confidence intervals connected to the ICC values had to be disjunct, which means that they should not touch each other.

Results and discussion

As a minimum requirement for a definable difference between the two groups the ICC differences were established at ≥ 0.1 provided that there were no disjunct confidence intervals. It was shown that the separate variables of distances, angles and courses of time intervals behaved very differently (Table 43.1). Concerning the distances and angles, there was an increase as well as a decrease of the recorded ICC values in the normal swallowing subgroup in comparison with the entire study population. Therefore, only the significant deviations of tongue malfunctions are supposed to be demonstrated.

Influence on the controlled path of movement

Here only the variable D2 corresponding to the distance between palate contact point and palate separation point showed a significant reduction from 0.74 in the entire group to 0.22 in the subgroup when speaking /asa/.

Influence on the angle

In the variable alpha1 a reduction of 0.16 and 0.39 occurred during /asa/2 and /asa/3, while /ascha/1 increased significantly in spite of the small difference of 0.07. In the area of the first tongue coil the ICC value

Table 43.1. ICC values of the complete and mixed study population (ICC complete) and the normal swallowing subgroup (ICC normal swallowing) in regard to distances (D) and angles (alpha) during VCV-sequences.

variable	function	coil	ICC complete	ICC normal swallowing
D2	asa	1	0.74	0.22
alpha1	asa	2	0.93	0.77
alpha1	asa	3	0.60	0.21
alpha1	ascha	1	0.91	0.98
alpha1	ana	1	0.32	0.75
alpha2	ala	2	0.34	0.83
alpha2	ata	3	0.42	0.81

increased from 0.32 to 0.75 during the syllable /ana/. The variable alpha2 showed a considerable increase of 0.49 or 0.39 during the syllables /ala/2 and /ata/3 respectively.

Influence on the time

While significant differences in distances as well as in angles were recorded between the two groups, no significant differences were noted in the time variables according to the above-mentioned criteria. It was noticeable that the ICC differences ≥ 0.1 occurred solely in connection with a decrease in the ICC values of the subgroup in comparison with the entire study population. This means that the normal swallowing rest group showed a smaller reproducibility with regard to the time variables when compared with the entire study population.

The results can be summarized as follows:

1. Significant changes in the ICC values occurred solely in geometric parameters. It can be deducted that subjects with altered functional ways of movement during swallowing show a distinctly different variability of certain sections in the path of movement in comparison with normal swallowing subjects. This is dependent on the choice of VCV sequences, the coil position and the choice of angle or sections of distances.
2. The variability of these parameters can be higher or lower in normal swallowers compared with tongue-thrust. An explanation of these results has still to be found.
3. Significant ICC changes occurred mostly in the examined angle alpha 1. This means that they occurred in the direction of upward movement in relation to the masticatory plane after the first vowel. Therefore, this variable is especially affected by influences of tongue-thrust on the paths of movement.
4. The time parameters with allowed ICC differences ≥ 0.1 only showed an increase in the variability of the path of movement in normal swallowing subjects in comparison with tongue-thrust. The criteria for the presence of significant differences were disjunct confidence intervals. The question is raised that maybe because of these strict criteria clinical relevant differences might possibly be overlooked, since in the remaining variables such a clear tendency did not occur. For clarification purposes a more accurate examination of the paths of movement should be conducted.

Conclusions

The analysis of geometric parameters and time intervals of articulatory movements by use of electromagnetic articulography records offers a new possibility for assessment of tongue-thrust and objective diagnosis of tongue malfunction. This is especially true for changes of tongue movements during myofunctional or orthodontic therapy.

References

Andrianopoulos MV, Hanson ML (1987) Tongue-thrust and the stability of overjet correction. Angle Orthodontics, 57 (2), 121–35.

Horn H, Göz G ,Bacher M, Koch J, Axmann-Krcmar D (1995) Maximalkraftmessungen des Lippen- und Zungendruckes und ihre Bedeutung für die klinische Diagnostik orofazialer Dyskinesien. Fortschritte der Kieferorthopädie, 56(4), 187–93.

Horn H, Göz G, Bacher M, Müllauer M, Kretschmer I, Axmann-Krcmar D (1997) Reliability of electromagnetic articulography recording during speaking sequences. European Journal of Orthodontics, 19(6), 647–55.

Chapter 44
Variability of Tongue Movement During Normal Swallowing and Tongue-thrust

HANSJÖRG HORN, GERNOT GÖZ, MARGIT BACHER, JOHANNES LUTHER and DETLEF AXMANN-KRCMAR

Introduction

For clarification of the aetiologic significance of orofacial malfunctions for the beginning and establishment of developmental and articulation disorders, it is necessary to examine tongue movement more closely with objectifiable methods. Next to pressure measuring and radiological procedures, sonography and palatography serve as possibilities for examining malfunctions within the oral cavity (Horn et al., 1995).

In contrast to sonography as an image system, the electromagnetic articulography (EMA) offers the possibility of examining tongue function at certain points and time sequences and of recording data of movement in the median sagittal plane with the aid of artificially generated magnetic fields (Engelke and Schönle, 1991; Horn et al., 1997).

Material and method

Thirty-one subjects (14 male, 17 female) aged 14.3–37.3 years (mean 26.5 ± 4.1 years), who were students of our department, were monitored during five repetitions of swallowing sequences of either natural deglutition or swallowing 20 ml of water. Additionally, the palate contour was recorded as reference contour. The registration of tongue movements was conducted with an 'Articulograph AG 100®' of the Carstens Medizinelektronik company. The system works according to the principle of inductive distance sensing. Three transmitting coils radiating a magnetic field are positioned in a measuring helmet in the area of the forehead, chin and neck. Three receiver coils aligned parallel to the transmitting coils were attached at the tongue surface in the area of the sulcus medianus with the physiological glue 'Histoacryl® blau'.

The first coil was placed at the tip of the tongue, the other two 10 mm and 20 mm further dorsal.

The path of motion of all three tongue coils was evaluated. For swallowing following distances (D) and courses of time (T) between the measuring points start of swallowing, palate contact point, palate separation and end of swallowing were defined respectively.

- D1/T1 = start of swallowing – palate contact point
- D2/T2 = palate contact point – palate separation point
- D3/T3 = maximal distance of palate contact
- D4/T4 = palate separation point – end of swallowing
- D5/T5 = start of swallowing – end of swallowing

The variability of data between the subjects is high compared to the overall variability of all observations in the case of well reproducible observations. For statistical evaluation purposes the so-called intra-class-correlation coefficient (ICC) was calculated reflecting the portion of variance between the subjects in relation to the overall variability. The higher this value, the more reproducible are the paths of motion.

Additionally, the clinical diagnosis as well as the functional status were recorded to register orofacial malfunctions. Based on those data the entire study population was divided into a normal swallowing and a subgroup experiencing tongue-thrust. The following criteria were applied in order to define the group with the functional conspicuous subjects

- language apparition (sigmatism) *or*
- a combination of criteria:
  - perceptible variance of lip position and/or lip appearance e.g. incompetent lip closure *as well as*
  - hyperactivity of the orofacial muscles during swallowing e.g. needlepoint tracing because of hyperactivity of the mentalis *and*
  - conspicuous palatographic diagnosis e.g. smear print on the palate

From the – according to functional points of view – mixed study population, the subjects experiencing tongue malfunctions were removed. The remaining group of 22 subjects was regarded as highly probably as the solely normal swallowing group. The comparison of the calculated ICC values of the remaining group with those of the entire study population, therefore, allows a conclusion as to whether malfunctions influence the variability of the swallowing process.

Results and discussion

It was noticeable that the ICC differences ≥ 0.1 occurred solely in connection with an increase of the ICC values in the remaining group in comparison with the entire study population e.g. the somatic swallowing rest group showed an increased reproducibility in comparison to the entire study population (Table 44.1). Therefore, only the significant deviations of tongue malfunctions are supposed to be demonstrated in the following:

Table 44.1. ICC values of the complete and mixed study population (ICC complete) and the normal swallowing subgroup (ICC normal swallowing) for distances (D) and time intervals (T) during the functions of swallowing of water (W) and natural deglutition (D)

variable	function	coil	ICC complete	ICC normal swallowing
D3	W	1	0.42	0.89
D4	W	2	0.66	0.76
T2	W	2	0.55	0.68
T2	W	3	0.56	0.66
T3	W	1	0.26	0.54
T3	W	2	0.18	0.89
T3	W	3	0.32	0.51
T4	W	1	0.32	0.76
T4	W	2	0.34	0.76
T4	W	3	0.36	0.68
T4	D	1	0.55	0.77
T4	D	2	0.55	0.86
T4	D	3	0.52	0.77
T5	W	2	0.53	0.66

Influence of tongue-thrust on the distance

When swallowing water a significant increase in the ICC values was noted in the area of the coil on the tip of the tongue for the maximal distance of palate contact (D3), namely from 0.42 in the entire study population to 0.89 in the remaining study population. This means normal swallowers showed a higher reproducibility of the path of movement. For the caudal movement of the tongue (D4) an increase of the ICC values of at least 0.1 could be registered at the middle coil.

Influence of tongue-thrust on the time

During the time interval between palate contact and palate separation (T2) the middle and back coil showed an increase on the ICC values varying from 0.10 to 0.13 when swallowing water.

For the maximal distance of palate contact viewed from sagittal, the interval T3 showed a considerable increase of the ICC value at all three coils during the swallowing of water. At the middle coil this was significant with an increase from 0.18 tò 0.89. The time interval T4 characterized as the time between the last palate contact to the end of swallowing was noticeable because of a significant increase in the ICC values in the area comprising all coils during the swallowing of water. During natural deglutition all coils showed an increase as well, but only in the area of the middle coil – same as in T3 – was the increase significant.

For the entire time period of the swallowing motion T5 the middle coil attracted attention again during the swallowing of water; this time, however, because of the insignificant increase of 0.13. Therefore, the results are interpreted as follows.

1. Since changes in the ICC value according to above-mentioned criteria always led to an increase of the ICC values in the remaining group of normal swallowers in comparison with all subjects, it may be concluded that subjects with functional conspicuous movements during swallowing show increased variability and subsequently smaller reproducibility.
2. This increased variability occurred mostly during the swallowing of water and hardly during natural deglutition. The swallowing of water is more variable in contrast to natural deglutition in the tongue-thrust subgroup than in normal swallowers, which means it is less stable.
3. Significant ICC-increases occurred most often in the examined time intervals. The time component is therefore influenced especially by variable movements in the tongue-thrust subgroup.
4. The most significant differences occurred in the area of the middle coil positioned about 1 cm after the tip of the tongue. The pattern of movement of this part of the tongue is thus especially variable in tongue-thrust swallowers in comparison with normally functioning subjects.
5. The path of movement between palate separation point and end of swallowing was noticeable by showing the most significant differences and is thus the most variable part during the swallowing motion in tongue-thrust swallowers.

Conclusions

Considering the results of the electromagnetic articulography, the differentiation between normal swallowers and tongue-thrust syndrome is now possible; furthermore it gives us the possibility to objectify and control function improving measures.

References

Engelke W, Schönle PW (1991) Elektromagnetische Artikulographie: Eine neue Methode zur Untersuchung von Bewegungsfunktionen des Gaumensegels. Folio Phoniatrica, 43, 147–52.

Horn H, Göz G, Bacher M, Koch J, Axmann-Krcmar D (1995) Maximalkraftmessungen des Lippen- und Zungendruckes und ihre Bedeutung für die klinische Diagnostik orofazialer Dyskinesien. Fortschritte der Kieferorthopädie, 56(4), 187–93.

Horn H, Göz G, Bacher M, Müllauer M,Kretschmer I, Axmann-Krcmar D (1997) Reliability of electromagnetic articulography recording during speaking sequences. European Journal of Orthodontics, 19(6), 647–55.

Index